Doidge's Auction
West Street,
BLACKPOOL

20,000 Volumes of New Standard Books.

Just imported direct from America, **£1,000** worth
Ladies' and Gent.'s

Waltham Lever Watches,

High-Class Pottery, and thousands of
Articles adapted for

**WEDDING, BIRTHDAY, and COMPLIMENTARY
PRESENTATION.**

SALES DURING THE SEASON—
MORNINGS, 10.30; EVENINGS, 6.30.
Private Sales from 2.30 to 5 p.m. daily.

N.B.—Special attention paid to orders sent by post.
Orders amounting to £1 and upwards sent
carriage paid to any part of Great Britain.

Doidge's Great Sale of Household Furniture
commences each year in **February** and continues
to the **end of March.**

MRS. BEETON'S COOKERY BOOK.

MRS. BEETON'S
COOKERY BOOK

A HOUSEHOLD GUIDE

ALL ABOUT

COOKERY, HOUSEHOLD WORK, MARKETING,
PRICES, PROVISIONS, TRUSSING,
SERVING, CARVING, MENUS,

ETC., ETC.

WITH NEW COLOURED AND OTHER ILLUSTRATIONS.

NEW EDITION.

J. S. DOIDGE,
WEST STREET, BLACKPOOL.

National Library of Australia
Cataloguing-in-Publication entry

Beeton, I. (Isabella), 1836–1865
Mrs Beeton's cookery book.

Facsim. of: new ed. London: Ward, Lock, 1902.
Includes index.
ISBN 0 7270 1420 x.

1. Cookery, English. 2. Home economics. I. Title.

641.5942

RIGBY PUBLISHERS LIMITED • ADELAIDE
SYDNEY • MELBOURNE • BRISBANE
NEW YORK • LONDON
This edition first published 1981
Printed in Hong Kong

PREFACE

In Mrs. Beeton's preface to the first edition of her Shilling Cookery Book she expresses a hope that "mistress and maid will find the information serviceable." Her wish has been granted in full measure, for among all low-priced works on cookery, Mrs. Beeton's has been without a rival since its first publication; and in fact the editors venture to assert that there are few households in England where a copy of it would not be found. For many, the large edition of Mrs. Beeton's Household Management is too costly, for many others the shilling one is all that is needed, and by a still greater number of persons it is kept especially for handy and everyday reference; therefore if it is to be the one oracle in the kitchen, it should contain all needful information that can possibly be condensed into a book of this size. Hence the present enlarged edition. From this nothing has been taken away, but much added that is calculated to make the work a complete guide on cookery and household matters.

Other reasons for publishing a new edition may be found in the fact that great changes have been made in the style of our English cookery and the way of serving our dinners and other meals. It is now thought well for all to know a little about the foods themselves and the science of cookery. Our insular prejudices have to a great extent disappeared, and we are ready to welcome new dishes and new styles that we have before despised as un-English. So much for the reasons for the enlargement and improvement of the Shilling Cookery Book. Now for what has been done.

In the chapter on housekeeping, it has been the endeavour to give practical hints with regard to the duties of the mistress of a small household; and later in the book will be found instructions for all kinds of ordinary housework, which should be useful both to mistress and maid.

The price list of provisions, a great feature in this new edition, has

been prepared at considerable trouble and expense, and will be found
thoroughly trustworthy, and a striking indication of the changes in the
cost of all provisions and foodstuffs that the passing years have
brought about. In its columns the good housewife can see at a glance
not only when provisions are in season, but when they are at their
cheapest and best. " THE COOK'S TIME TABLE " will also be found of
constant value, showing, as it does, the time to allow for the cooking
of all kinds of food by all methods. The entirely new directions for, and
photographs of, trussing of all kinds of poultry and game, should prove
a great boon, the art being an extremely difficult one to acquire from
descriptions alone, and a most valuable one when properly mastered.
Amongst the new recipes will be found many from America, Australia,
France, and all parts of the world. These will prove interesting as well
as useful to those who like novelty. Vegetarian dishes, for which we
give a good many tried recipes, will also serve to vary the daily fare.

The recipes for preparing tinned and preserved meats, fish, soups,
fruits, and provisions of all kinds, will be found most valuable both as
an aid to economy and as a safe and ready resource to the housekeeper
whose larder might otherwise fail to meet the demands of unexpected
guests.

Some considerable space has been devoted to the consideration of
meals and their serving, the laying of the cloth, the decoration of the
table and the folding of the serviettes; while the menus in all seasons
for breakfast, luncheon, dinners—these also in French, after the fashion
of the times—tea and supper are as complete and well chosen as in a
larger and more costly book. They include, in addition to those for
ordinary dinner and other parties, meals of all kinds for the family,
economically considered, and should be found of great use to young
housekeepers by giving variety in the daily fare. Space does not
permit further enlargement upon the additions and improvements, but
the following list gives a brief summary of what subjects have been
treated of :—

Practical advice to young housekeepers.

Cookery as a necessity, reasons for and science of various foods.

Cookery for invalids.

Fresh provisions, their price and season, when best and cheapest. A
guide to young housekeepers in the art of marketing.

The cook's time table, a ready reckoner for the kitchen showing what
time to allow in cooking.

Tinned foods, new recipes for preparing.

Confectionary and ices, home-made.

Savouries useful for dinner, &c.

Bread, buns, and tea-cakes, new recipes for.

Beverages of all kinds, cups, summer drinks, home-made wine and liqueurs.

The trussing and preparing of all kinds of game and poultry, illustrated by photographs from the actual objects.

Breakfast, laying the cloth for, serving, menus for guests, wedding and family breakfasts.

Luncheon, laying and serving of; menus for guests, picnic and family luncheons, and recipes for luncheon dishes.

Dinner, setting the table, table decorations, serviettes, menus for parties of various sizes, at different seasons; vegetarian and family dinners.

Tea, menus for At-home, high and family teas for various seasons.

Supper: menus for guest and family suppers in summer and winter.

Household work and servants' duties.

The coloured and other illustrations introduced in the new edition of Shilling Cookery form one of the special attractions of the book, and will be seen to be artistic reproductions of the various dishes and other articles which they represent, and should materially add to the value of a book that may not unworthily be called a worthy descendant of "Mrs. Beeton's Household Management." These illustrations, in fact, are accurate reproductions of actual dishes and articles, and the kind assistance rendered by Messrs. W. Hill & Son, the well-known confectioners and caterers, of Bishopsgate Street Within, London, E.C., who prepared many of the dishes, has to be acknowledged. Hundreds of pounds have been spent in producing the illustrations in this new edition, and to make these of general utility has been the constant aim. For instance, the picture of the "Mayonnaise of Salmon" shows more plainly how to dress that dish for the table than any number of words could show.

In presenting this new, enlarged, and revised edition of a work of which millions of copies of the earlier issues have been sold it is confidently hoped that the public will pronounce the new "Beeton's Shilling Cookery" to be as far in advance of the old editions as those were in front of all would-be competitors.

PREFACE TO THE FIRST EDITION

———◇———

To help both mistress and servant to a knowledge of some of their duties, and to assist them in the important task of dressing and serving daily food, I have printed the following Recipes, along with some directions and hints as to the Arrangement and Economy of the Kitchen. The recipes are taken from my book on "Household Management," and I hope both mistress and maid will find some of the information serviceable. I have sought to make all the directions plain and practical, eschewing everything that was not likely to be useful and was not to the point.

I. B.

Good Cooking at Home.

Fine dishes at little cost can be prepared by using "Lemco" in the kitchen. Good cooking is not dear cooking. "Lemco" enables the cook to use up all ingredients and to prepare many new savoury dishes.

LEMCO
MEANS
Liebig
COMPANY'S EXTRACT.

GENERAL CONTENTS

———◆◇◆———

LIST OF COLOURED ILLUSTRATIONS

LIST OF ILLUSTRATIONS

MRS. BEETON'S COOKERY BOOK

THE HOUSEKEEPER

IMPORTANCE OF HER DUTIES.

IT is not given to us all to become famous, but in this busy world there are few who, metaphorically speaking, need "waste their sweetness on the desert air," or, in less poetical language, lead a useless life. Specially does this apply to women, for they can always find a vocation.

Far from the humblest or the least dignified one is that of a housewife, in whom, if she faithfully fulfil her duties, will centre all the home interests and cares; while to her principally is given the power of making her house, however humble, the embodiment of our ideal, "Home, sweet Home."

The young housekeeper should never deem any of her duties ignoble ones. "The daily round, the common task," call for the exercise of virtues that would hold but a poor place in pleasure or gaiety. Unselfishness, industry, patience, perseverance, and thoughtful care for others are most needful qualities for the good housekeeper to possess, for with her rest many responsibilities.

Take a very homely illustration that may serve to show what we mean.

It falls to the lot of the housewife to prepare the dinner. Does she, grudging the time and disliking the task, get this over in the quickest possible manner, caring but little *how* the food is cooked or whether it is likely to please those for whom it is intended, the result is in nine cases out of ten an unsatisfactory meal. Now, an unsatisfactory meal is not only a meal wasted, but it may be one that has done harm to some one. An infinitesimal injury, it may be said; but, as bricks go one by one to build a house, and by their good or bad qualities determine its stability or instability, so do the meals of a life-time, one by one, according to their suitability and nourishment, help to build up a sound constitution or the reverse. We shall have to introduce this subject again in our remarks on the science of cookery; so to return to the housekeeper and her duties. One of the first we should think of is early rising, to which, in many households, sufficient importance is not attached. It is allowed to be necessary where there are no servants or only one, and where the first duties and the first meal of the day depend upon one pair of hands, but where there are several servants it is thought a small matter for the mistress of the house to be late in the morning. Yet this should not be except in cases of illness or infirmity

EARLY RISING.

To begin with, few query the truth of "Poor Richard's" maxim, "Early to bed and early to rise makes a man healthy and wealthy and wise," or at any rate will allow that the practice reversed is an injurious one to health; but there are other things to be considered. We are all creatures of example, servants and children being no exception to the rule, and it seldom happens that a late mistress does not make a late household.

There is no work like morning work, particularly household tasks, and those we take up early in the day, when fresh from a night's rest and a good breakfast, are "trifles light as air" in comparison with the same dragged or hurried through later when there is not time for their proper performance.

17

Further on, we detail the ordinary routine of domestic work in a small household, which can only be accomplished satisfactorily when early rising and method are the order of the day.

MANAGEMENT OF SERVANTS.

Where there is a large staff of servants or a number proportionate to the work that is to be done in the house, there should be no need for the mistress to give any assistance; her duty should be only to supervise or see that each domestic thoroughly does his or her own work. We cannot approve of the system of continually watching servants. Those who need their mistress at their elbows to see that they do their work are not worth keeping. Let them know exactly what they have to do, and the way and order in which it is to be done, being quite sure that they have *time* for the performance of their daily duties, show them anything they have to learn, then exact the strict carrying out of each day's programme. Do not gloss over faults or carelessness, and never allow one day's work to be left for the next. Be firm, strict, yet kind and thoughtful for your servants, and they should respect you and carry out your wishes. If they will not do so after a fair trial it is better to part with them rather than have any discomfort in the household. A far less easy task is it to manage where there is but one servant to do all the work. We say all the work, but a general servant cannot thoroughly do *all* that is to be done, unless it be in a very small house. The question of how to help in these cases is rather a vexed one. Some say the mistress should do all the cooking, but this we think a mistake, for should she be unavoidably prevented from going into the kitchen the servant may not be able to take her place.

If the servant is inexperienced, her mistress should be able to show her how to do all that is necessary in plain cooking, and let her do that part of it every day, reserving for herself the task of making pastry or any other troublesome or fanciful dish that a general servant would not have time to undertake.

There are many ways in which a mistress can help without being much in the kitchen. Say in the turning out of a room. The hard work may be the sweeping and scrubbing, but the time absorbed is in the preparation of the room for sweeping and the dusting and arranging afterwards. Leaving the harder part to the servant, the mistress might well do the other; also she might lay the cloth and do very many other little tasks that vary in every household, only remembering that her servant should know how to do all that she herself undertakes, in case she may on occasion be prevented from rendering assistance.

TASTE.

Independent of *necessary* household duties, such as keeping a house clean and tidy and having the food properly cooked and served, there are others that no good housekeeper should neglect. In every household these vary, but there is one rule that may be equally applied to all, that of making the home as attractive and pretty as possible.

One need not be rich to have pretty surroundings, particularly in these times, when there are so many ways of adding to the decoration of our rooms at a small cost. With determination to have her house as elegant as it should be clean, the young housewife will find that, with her heart in her work, a little labour and a very small outlay of money will achieve wonderful results.

As a good heart and sweet disposition will shine out of and glorify the plainest, homeliest face, so will a few artistic touches, a little labour given to improve and beautify even a humble home, give to it that charm that is found in " beauty less seen than felt."

HOUSEHOLD WORK.

METHOD.

Whether cottage or mansion, whether there are many servants or only one or none, there need be but little difference in the way household duties are performed.

Cleanliness, neatness, and regularity should be the ruling qualities of the good housekeeper and her subordinates, and there may be as much comfort and order in homes where but little labour can be hired as in those where there is a full staff of servants.

A great deal, of course, hinges upon the management; and if this is good there is always time for everything.

We have spoken of the help that the housekeeper can give to the servants, also we have lightly touched upon her duties, which must vary in every home; yet, before giving a little advice to servants, we may be allowed to say a few words to those who do not actually do the work themselves.

Let us take anything in hand for the first time and do it thoroughly, and in nine cases out of ten it occupies more time than we thought it would.

Servants are no quicker than we are, and we should know for ourselves exactly how long it takes to do every household task, so that we need not allow laziness, or expect too much from those we employ.

Knowing then the time it takes to scrub a floor, sweep a room, &c., let the mistress reckon up the weekly work of the house and divide it as well as she can, so that all can be got through without hurry or fuss. Should it be found in this reckoning of time against labour that they will not balance, and there is more than her help or helpers can accomplish unaided, let her assign to herself certain duties, and carefully and *regularly* perform them, thus setting a good example. In every day's work, allow a margin of time for delay caused by interruptions or accidents, and remember that servants need, and should have, a little time to call their own.

RESPONSIBILITIES OF SERVANTS.

According to their duties and position in a household so are the responsibilities of servants, but in every situation there *are* responsibilities. A cook has to a great extent the health of the family in her hands. Ill-cooked food is not only wasteful and distasteful, it is positively injurious; pots and pans not properly cleaned have often caused illness, if not death. Want of cleanliness in a kitchen is not only bad for the cook herself, but for those who have to share the room.

A housemaid has a great deal to do with the comfort, if not health, of the household. Fresh, cleanly rooms, well-made beds, dust conspicuous by its absence, are healthful and pleasant.

A nurse has the highest responsibilities of all servants, generally having the care of those who are helpless; and in no part of the house is cleanliness more necessary than in the nursery, for it is absolutely essential to the health of children.

ADVICE TO COOKS AND KITCHENMAIDS.

Cleanliness is the most essential ingredient in the art of cooking; a dirty kitchen being a disgrace both to mistress and maid.

Be clean in your person, paying particular attention to the hands, which should always be clean.

Constant washing of the hands and thorough drying not only keeps them softer and whiter, but prevents them chapping in cold weather.

Do not go about slipshod. Provide yourself with good, well-fitting boots. You will find them less fatiguing in a warm kitchen than loose, untidy slippers.

Provide yourself with at least a dozen good-sized, serviceable cooking-aprons, made with bibs. These will save your gowns, and keep you neat and clean. Have them made large enough round so as to nearly meet behind.

Never waste or throw away anything that can be turned to account. In warm weather any gravies or soups that are left from the preceding day should be just boiled up, and poured into clean pans. This is particularly necessary where vegetables have been added to the preparation, as it then so soon turns sour. In cooler weather, every other day will be often enough to warm up these things.

Every morning, visit your larder, change dishes and plates when necessary, empty and wipe out the bread-pan, and have all in neatness by the time your mistress comes down to order the dinner. Twice a week the larder should be scrubbed out.

In hot weather keep fish and meat covered with wire screens or muslin to keep off flies. A large porous flower-pot wrapped in a wet cloth and turned over the butter, or some fresh cabbage leaves wrapped round it, will keep it firm.

If you have a spare kitchen cupboard, keep your baked pastry in it: it preserves it crisp, and prevents it from becoming wet and heavy, which it is liable to do in the larder.

In cooking, clear as you go; that is to say, do not allow a host of basins, plates, spoons, and other utensils to accumulate on the dressers and tables whilst you are engaged in preparing the dinner. By a little management and forethought, much confusion may be saved in this way. It is as easy to put a thing in its right place when it is done with, as it is to keep continually moving it, to find room for fresh requisites. For instance, after making a pudding, the flour-tub, rolling-pin, and the pasteboard, should be put away, and any basins, spoons, &c., taken to the scullery, neatly packed up near the sink, to be washed when the proper time arrives. Neatness, order, and method should be observed.

Much time is saved by putting all pots and pans away clean and ready for further usage, and all meat and other food should be placed on clean dishes or plates before they are consigned to the lardor.

Never let your stock of spices, salt, seasonings, herbs, &c., dwindle down so low that, some day, in the midst of preparing a large dinner, you find yourself minus a very important ingredient, thereby causing much confusion and annoyance. Think of all you require, and acquaint your mistress in the morning, when she is with you, so that she can give out any necessary stores.

If you live in the country, have your vegetables gathered from the garden at an early hour, so that there is ample time to make your search for caterpillars, &c. These disagreeable additions need never make their appearance on table in cauliflowers or cabbages, if the vegetable in its raw state is allowed to soak in salt and water for an hour or so. Of course, if the vegetables are not brought in till the last moment this precaution cannot be taken.

Be very particular in cleansing all vegetables free from grit. Nothing is so unpleasant, and nothing so easily avoided, if but common care be exercised.

When you have done peeling onions, wash the knife at once, and put it away to be cleaned, and do not use it for anything else until it has been cleaned. Nothing is nastier, or more indicative of a slovenly and untidy cook, than to use an oniony knife in the preparation of any dish where the flavour of the onion is a disagreeable surprise.

Thrusting the knife once or twice into the earth will take away the smell.

After you have washed your saucepans, fish-kettle, &c., stand them before the fire for a few minutes, to get thoroughly dry inside, before putting them away. They should then be kept in a dry place, in order that they may escape the deteriorating influence of rust, and thereby be quickly destroyed. Never leave saucepans dirty from one day's use to be cleaned the next; it is slovenly and untidy. Be careful that the lids are kept clean, a dirty cover will often spoil the flavour of a dish.

Empty soups or gravies into a basin as soon as they are ready ; never allow them to remain all night in the stockpot.

In copper utensils, if the tin has worn off, have it immediately replaced.

Pudding-cloths and jelly-bags should have your immediate attention after being used : the former should be well washed, scalded, and hung up to dry. Let them be perfectly aired before being folded up and put in the drawer, or they will have a disagreeable smell when next wanted.

After washing up your dishes, wash your dish-tubs with a little soap and water and soda, and scrub them often. Wring the dishcloth, after washing this also, and wipe the tubs out. Stand them up to dry after this operation. The sink-brush and sink must not be neglected. Do not throw anything but water down the sink, as the pipe is liable to get choked, thereby causing expense and annoyance to your mistress.

Do not be afraid of hot water in washing up dishes and dirty cooking utensils. As these are essentially greasy, lukewarm water cannot possibly have the effect of cleansing them effectually. Do not be chary also of changing and renewing the water occasionally. You will thus save yourself much time and labour in the long run.

Clean your coppers with turpentine and fine brick-dust, rubbed on with flannel, and polish them with a leather and a little dry brick-dust.

Clean your tins with soap and whiting, rubbed on with a flannel, wipe them with a clean, dry, soft cloth, and polish with a dry leather and powdered whiting. Mind that neither the cloth nor leather is greasy.

Do not scrub the inside of your frying-pans, unless they be of enamelled iron, as, after this operation, any preparation fried is liable to catch or burn to the pan. If the pan has become black inside, rub it with a hard crust of bread, and wash in hot water, mixed with a little soda. It is a good plan to have one regular day in the week upon which every culinary utensil should have a thorough cleaning, those that can be polished being cleaned as directed.

Punctuality is a quality indispensable in a cook; therefore, if the kitchen be not provided with a clock, beg your mistress to purchase one. There can then be no excuse for dinner being half an hour behind time.

If you have a large dinner to prepare, much may be got ready the day before, and many dishes are a great deal better for being thus made early. To soups and gravies this remark is particularly applicable. Ask your mistress for the bill of fare the day before, and see immediately what you can commence upon.

A general servant has of necessity some of the responsibilities and the work of housemaid, parlour-maids, and cook piled upon her shoulders; but it does not always follow that her work is harder than that of any of the other three. Change of work is said to be, to a certain extent, a rest, and we know many good general servants who say they absolutely could not settle to only one branch of domestic work.

ORDER OF WORK.

We give the following routine of the work of an imaginary small house, where there would be one or two servants only to wait upon and serve a family of four or six persons.

Monday.—The home washing.

Tuesday.—Sweeping and cleaning of servants' bedroom or one or two other rooms, and stairs cleaned down to lower floor.

Wednesday. — The sweeping and cleaning of best bedroom, and windows.

Thursday.—Cleaning and turning out of cupboards, and cleaning of passages and remaining stairs.

Friday.—Sweeping and cleaning of drawing-room, and cleaning of silver.

Saturday.—Sweeping and cleaning of dining-room and kitchen, tins, coppers, &c.

Besides these daily tasks mentioned, must be reckoned the bed-making, the dusting, the cooking and washing-up, and all the hundred and one things that have to be accomplished in the

smallest of households, these generally coming in the following order: the shutters and windows must first be opened, then the kitchen range must be brushed and cleaned, the fire lighted and the kettle put on. Next comes the sitting-room in daily use to be got ready for breakfast; the rug must be rolled up, the table cover shaken and folded, the room swept (using tealeaves), the grate cleaned (if in winter) and the fire lighted, then the room must be dusted and the cloth laid for breakfast. Next in order comes the hall; which must be swept, the doorsteps cleaned, and the brass handles of the door polished. Boots and knives must also be cleaned before the breakfast is cooked. Directly the servants' breakfast is over, beds should be stripped and bedroom windows opened. Then will come the clearing away of the breakfast things and the washingup; then the slops should be taken from the bedrooms, the jugs filled, the beds made and the rooms tidied and dusted; and between the time that this work is finished and the midday meal time, the cooking (if any) can be done, and the cleaning of whatever rooms arranged for on that day accomplished. Where there are two servants, one of whom is a housemaid, she will have to be dressed by the midday meal; but where there is only a general servant she is not expected to change her gown till after she has washed up and tidied her kitchen.

Then comes the getting of the tea or dinner, the clearing away and washingup of this, the emptying of any slops in the bedroom, and the taking up of hot water for the night.

Thus, very roughly sketched, the day's work has to be done in the ordinary small household. Further on we give some useful recipes for housework.

KITCHEN MAXIMS.

" There is no work like early work."

" A good manager looks ahead."

" Clear as you go: muddle makes more muddle."

" Not to wash plates and dishes soon after using makes work."

" Spare neither soda nor hot water in washing up greasy articles."

" Dirty saucepans filled with hot water begin to clean themselves."

"Wash well a saucepan, but clean a frying-pan with a piece of bread."

"Never put the handles of knives into hot water."

"Thrust an oniony knife into the earth to take away the smell."

"Search for the insects in greens *before* putting them in soak."

"Green vegetables should be boiled fast with the lid off."

"Bread or vegetables left in stock turns it sour."

"Baked meat should start in a hot oven."

"When pastry comes out of the oven, meat may go in."

"Fish, boiled, should be done slowly, with a little vinegar in the water."

"A spoonful of vinegar will set a poached egg."

"Water boils when it gallops, oil when it is still."

"A stew boiled is a stew spoiled."

"Take away nearly all fat before making a stew."

"Save all pieces of fat to try down for frying or pastry."

"Only dry frying can be done without plenty of fat."

"Pour boiling water over frying fat to clarify it, and set it aside for using again."

"Fat used for frying fish must only again be used for that purpose."

"Melt a teaspoonful of fat in a frying-pan before putting in bacon."

"Put spare crusts in the oven to grate for breadcrumbs."

"Make mint sauce two hours before serving it."

"For making fish sauce use some of the water in which the fish has been boiled."

"Pare potatoes as thinly as possible."

"Never put salt in salad."

"Salt or cold water makes scum rise."

"Scum as it rises in boiling should be taken off."

"No more water than is needed for gravy should be put in the pan."

"Salt brings out other flavours:"

"When using ketchup be sparing with salt."

"A handful of salt will clear the fire for broiling."

"Salt meat should go into cold water and be brought slowly to the boil."

"Always save the liquor in which a joint of meat has boiled."

"One egg well beaten is worth two not beaten."

"Boiled puddings should fill the basin."

"Put fresh water in the kettle to boil for tea or coffee."

"Make the tea directly the water boils."

"Pour nothing but water down the sink."

"When washing-up is over for the day, wash the tea-cloth; it saves the cloths and cleanses the hands."

WASHING AT HOME.

As in so many households it is necessary that a portion, if not all, the family washing should be done at home, any suggestions and help that can be offered here will no doubt be welcome to our readers.

It is so customary to quote the reasons *against* home washing that we often lose sight of its real advantage, particularly to those who have to study economy.

Perhaps the greatest saving that is effected by doing this branch of domestic labour ourselves is not that of the laundress's bill, but that of the wear and tear of clothes.

Where there are children, who should never be stinted in their supply of clean underclothing, it is easily proved that the little garments carefully washed at home will last twice the time that they would if sent to a laundry, where certainly in nine cases out of ten, chemicals are used to make the linen a good colour and save labour at the expense of the clothing.

Few ordinary laundresses wash flannels as they should be washed, so that when clean and dry they retain their original softness and clearness, while if nothing more destructive than soda be used in washing white articles, too much of this generally finds its way into the laundry tubs, and if baby clothing be put in soda-water the effect is fatal to the delicate infant skin.

In olden days it was not thought derogatory to the dignity of mistress or daughters of the house to assist with as well as superintend the home washing, and now, in households where only one or two servants are kept, it is most essential that the housekeeper should consider whether they have really time to do the washing properly if no aid is given, also if they really understand *how* it should be done, for both knowledge and patience are absolutely essential to make washing at home a satisfactory process.

The hardships of washing should belong to the past, with our many labour-saving machines and cleansing soaps of the present day, but opinions vary considerably about their advantages.

Many argue that machines destroy the linen and drag off the buttons, but it depends more upon the washer than the machine whether the former does damage or saves labour.

Where there is not room in kitchen or scullery for a washing machine, or where it is preferred to do the washing by hand, then a small wringer and mangler will be found invaluable. This can be fixed to tub, shelf, or table, and it is wonderful how much time and labour it saves, particularly in the case of heavy articles such as blankets and quilts. We give recipes for the washing of various articles, but a word of advice as to the management of the wash may perhaps be useful.

Washing day should be one on which there is no large amount of household work to be done. If there are several hands to do the work, the boiling, wringing-out, &c., may be done on the same day, but if one pair of hands have to accomplish the task, then it is a good plan to get through with the actual washing on the first day and have the copper lighted early on the following one, so that the linen may be put out to dry betimes, thus leaving the washer free to attend solely to the blueing, rinsing, hanging-out, and bringing-in of the clothes; for if this is steadily attended to much time is saved, as the linen is brought in just when it is ready for folding, and no damping is needed except in the case of starched things. Try to arrange that some simple cookery should be all that need be done, or better still, have a stew or soup prepared the day before, or cold meat and salad, according to the season, so that the work is not delayed; and in no case let it extend to the evening, when it is bound to cause inconvenience to some member of the family.

RECIPES FOR WASHING CLOTHES.

WASHING OF WHITE ARTICLES.

The day before these are washed sort them as follows :—Put the fine things, such as cuffs, collars, &c., into a small pan, the ordinary body linen into another, and the rougher and dirtier kind into a third, then soak them thus : Fill the pans with lukewarm water, and rub over the dirty parts with Sunlight soap, and leave the articles in " soak " till the following day.

Let all small pieces of soap be put in the copper, and having first rinsed out, then washed the clothes, put them in in their order, putting such small things as collars and handkerchiefs into a bag or old pillow case. About twenty minutes' boiling should suffice, when the next panful should be ready to go into the copper, this being replenished with hot water. As the clothes are boiled have ready some cold water, ready blued, in which rinse out the clothes in their order.

The water for washing white clothes should be about 100° Fahr., and for dirty clothes a small quantity of soda should be put into it.

WASHING OF COLOURED AND WOOLLEN ARTICLES.

To wash these make a soap jelly by dissolving and boiling in hot water all small pieces of soap, or some sliced up, this when cold forming a firm jelly, and put enough of this into hot water to make it of a creamy consistency. In this wash the coloured things as quickly as possible, and hang them out directly they are rinsed.

The more quickly coloured things are washed and dried the less likely are the colours to run.

In washing flannels and blankets make the water thicker with the soap jelly, and having rubbed or scrubbed them well, rinse in several waters and hang out at once.

Blankets and white flannels should not be wrung much, but allowed to drip, and they should not hang in a strong sun as it makes them yellow.

Recipes for Starch and " to Glaze Linen " will be found amongst " Recipes for Housework."

RECIPES FOR HOUSEWORK.

BRASS, TO CLEAN.

Mode.—Mix pulverised rottenstone to a liquid state with turpentine, rub on with a piece of washleather, leave it for a few minutes, then wipe off with a soft cloth. Now and again a little stronger treatment may be necessary, when oxalic acid may be used in the proportion of one ounce to a pint of soft water. This should be rubbed on the brass with a piece of flannel, and polished with another dry piece.

The bottle should be well shaken before the liquid is used, and it should be labelled "poison."

CARPETS, TO CLEAN.

INGREDIENTS.—½ *lb. of washing soda,* 1 *lb. of yellow soap,* 1 *oz. of nitric acid,* 1 *gallon of water.*

Mode.—Melt the soap and soda in the oven; then mix with the water and add the acid; with a clean scrubbing-brush wash the carpet from seam to seam with this, doing only a small piece at a time, and rinsing and drying it as quickly as possible.

CARPETS, TO SCOUR.

INGREDIENTS.—1 *pint of ox-gall,* 3 *gallons of soft warm water.*

Mode.—After the carpets have been well beaten and freed from dust and grit, lay and nail them and scour them quickly with the mixture, which should both extract the grease and refresh the colours. It is best to mix but a small quantity and wash a small piece at a time, then as the water gets cold and dirty it can be thrown away.

FLOORCLOTH, TO CLEAN.

INGREDIENTS.—½ *oz. of beeswax, turpentine.*

Mode.—Shred the beeswax into a saucer, pour over enough turpentine to cover it, and set in the oven till melted. Wash the floorcloth in the ordinary way, wait till dry, and rub lightly over with the wax and turpentine, then with a dry cloth.

Another way in which linoleum or floorcloth may be cleaned is by rubbing it over with milk when dried after washing.

FURNITURE, POLISHED, TO CLEAN.

INGREDIENTS.—1 *oz. of white wax,* 3 *oz. of beeswax,* 1 *oz. of curd soap,* 1 *pint of turpentine,* 1 *pint of water boiled and allowed to get cold again.*

Mode.—Mix all the ingredients together, bottle, shake often, and do not use for two days. Dust the furniture well, rub the mixture on with a flannel, then polish with a duster and afterwards with an old silk handkerchief. A good furniture cream bought ready for use may be found to save trouble.

LOOKING-GLASS, TO CLEAN.

First take off fly stains or any other soils with a sponge damped with spirits of wine, or any other spirit, then dust over the glass with fine sifted powder blue and polish with an old silk handkerchief or very soft dry cloth.

MARBLE, TO CLEAN.

INGREDIENTS.—½ *lb. of soda,* 4 *oz. of chalk,* 4 *oz. of finely powdered pumice-stone, water.*

Mode.—Powder the soda, add to it the pumicestone and chalk, and sift through a fine sieve. Mix to a paste with water, which, by rubbing over the marble, should remove all stains; then wash with soap and water.

PAINT, TO CLEAN.

Dirty paint should have the dust removed first with the bellows, afterwards with a brush; it should never be wiped with a cloth, and the great secrets in cleaning paint are not to use much water and to dry quickly. The water used should have a little soda or pearlash dissolved in it; and after dipping the flannel used in this, it should be wrung almost dry before being applied to the paint. Directly this is done (a small piece only being done at a time, unless two are at work, and one can rinse as the other washes) it must be rinsed with clean water and dried with a clean cloth.

There are several widely advertised brands of soap especially intended for paint cleaning.

PLATE, TO CLEAN.

Few things add more to the neat and comfortable appearance of a dinner table than well-polished plate; indeed, the state of the plate is a certain indication of a well-managed or ill-managed household. Nothing is easier than to keep plate in good order, though many servants make it the greatest trouble of all things under their care. It should be remembered that it is utterly impossible to make greasy silver take a polish; and that as spoons and forks in daily use are continually in contact with grease, they must require good washing in soap-and-water, or with washing powder, to remove it. Silver should be washed with a soapy flannel in one water, rinsed in another, and then wiped dry with a clean cloth. Once a week all the silver should receive a thorough cleaning with plate powder.

PLATE-POWDER.—Many of the ordinary plate-powders sold in boxes contain more or less quicksilver, and this, in course of time, is sure to make the plate brittle. A thoroughly effective article may be made by well mixing ⅓ lb. of jeweller's rouge with ¾ lb. of prepared chalk or burnt hartshorn. When all the grease has been removed from the plate as directed above, mix as much of the powder as will be required into a thick paste with cold water; smear this lightly over the plate with a piece of soft rag, and leave it for some little time to dry. When perfectly dry brush it off quite clean with a soft plate brush, and polish the plate with a dry leather. If the plate be much tarnished, spirits of wine will be found to answer better than water for mixing the paste. Silversmith's soap is excellent for brightening as well as cleansing plate, and there are several well advertised brands of polishing paste.

STARCH, COLD-WATER.

INGREDIENTS.—*A teacupful of starch, a dessertspoonful of borax, a teaspoonful of turpentine, water.*

Mode.—Mix the starch to a cream with cold water, then add the borax dissolved in a little boiling water, next add the turpentine, and rub all well together.

STARCH, HOT-WATER.

INGREDIENTS.—2 *tablespoonfuls of starch, ½ pint of cold water, a quart of boiling water.*

Mode.—Mix the starch in a good-sized basin with the cold water till smooth, stirring it with a wooden spoon, and, putting the basin close to the fire, pour over the boiling water, stirring all the time. Put in

a little borax or stir with a wax candle, then cover the basin, and when the starch is cool enough for the hand to be put in, use it. A few drops of turpentine and a tiny piece of spermaceti are sometimes used to prevent the starch from sticking when ironing.

TINS AND COPPERS, TO CLEAN.

If whiting is used for this purpose it is simply made into a paste with water (to which, if the tins are very dirty, a little spirit should be added), is applied with a rag and rubbed off again with a leather. The handles of covers or any chased part require a brush.

A less dusty way of cleaning tins and coppers is to use one of the good polishing pastes sold for this purpose.

TO GLAZE LINEN.

The gloss upon shirt fronts, collars, &c., which so improves their appearance, is produced mainly by the friction of a warm iron. The linen to be glazed should first receive as much strong starch as it is possible to charge it with and then be dried. In making the starch a piece of sperm or white wax about the size of a walnut should be added to each pound. When ready for ironing the linen should be laid upon the table, slightly moistened with a clean wet cloth, and first ironed in the usual way with a flat-iron, or box-iron. After this is done a different kind of iron rounded at the bottom, very heavy and very bright, is used for the glossing process, which consists merely of rubbing with force just in the same way as one would polish any other surface.

WALL PAPER, TO CLEAN.

If not very dirty tie a soft clean cloth over a long soft broom and brush the walls with it in straight lines; if, however, the paper be very much soiled, stale bread should be used to cleanse it. Cut a stale quartern loaf in thick slices and rub the paper very lightly with it, going always in one direction and discarding the bread when dirty. Dough may be used instead of bread; and in either case it is best first to take off all the dust from the paper with a broom, in the way described above.

ARRANGEMENT AND ECONOMY OF THE KITCHEN

THE importance of a good kitchen can hardly be exaggerated—it is the great laboratory of the household, and it ought to be remembered that not only the comfort but the health of the family also is greatly dependent upon the manner in which food is prepared. A kitchen should be proportioned to the size of the house, reasonably large, with a good height of ceiling, well lighted and properly ventilated. It should also be easy of access without passing through the house, and sufficiently remote from the principal apartments, so that neither the members, visitors, nor guests of the family may hear the noise or detect the odours of culinary operations. The scullery, pantry, store-room and coal-cellar should be so arranged as to offer the least possible trouble in reaching them. Unfortunately these considerations are too often insufficiently attended to in the erection of even first-class houses; in smaller residences they are frequently altogether neglected, and it remains only to make the best use of such accommodation as architects and builders have thought proper to afford.

Kitchens abroad are in many countries prettier and more dainty than our own, partly due to the fact of their being kept in such perfect order, with the many pots and pans so brightly polished and burnished that they are really ornamental, forming a brilliant contrast to our (too often) black and dingy looking saucepans and utensils. In the majority of kitchens of moderate size, however, we have not the same facilities for keeping our cooking utensils bright and clean, by reason of our stoves and ranges. On some of these it is next to impossible to cook without dirt caused by smoke and bad coal, while their stoves (particularly those in which charcoal is burned) can be kept in order with so little trouble. Fortunate is the housekeeper who can choose the range she prefers, one that she has seen tried and tested; but there have been very great improvements made in these most important features of the kitchen, and in the majority of cases we may find a good and suitable stove even in the smallest house.

Where we find a stove or range faulty, it is more than likely it is the way in which it is "set." However good and perfect a range may be supplied by the manufacturers, it is often made unfit for use by reason of its being fixed by incompetent workmen. We later on describe the ranges with which we need run no risk of this kind.

A gas stove as a supplement to a fuel-burning grate is invariably a great advantage, particularly in summer-time, and the slot system applied to them in payment for the gas is an excellent one, though perhaps somewhat expensive. There are very different opinions as to the merits of gas stoves *versus* those burning fuel, many still urging that they are extravagant and cost more than an ordinary range or kitchener, but we contend that properly understood and used they cost less for cooking than the fuel ones. Their great merit lies in the fact that no gas whatever need be wasted. The oven retains its heat for a long time, and if well heated before the article to be cooked goes in, the gas can be quickly lowered and the temperature will remain the same, while in many cases the cooking can be completed with the gas turned quite out.

A saucepan once boiling can be kept so with a very tiny glimmer of gas, and the very moment the cooking is over we can put it out as we cannot a fire, which in hot weather often burns to waste.

Another great merit a gas stove has, is its *certainty*. We can be *sure* of the temperature of the oven remaining the same once it is regulated to the required heat, and there is no fear of its burning the meat or pastry, or losing its heat so that the cooking is retarded.

The best gas stoves are those with white enamelled lining to the oven, as these are so very easily kept clean, and are non-absorbent, so that no disagreeable odour remains after cooking.

Many of the little oil cooking stoves will be found very useful as supplementors of the range or kitchener, but unless they are used with more care than they would be by many ordinary servants, objection will be taken to the smell of the oil. Our neighbours across "the silver streak" have simpler, and in many respects, superior stoves to those employed here, and it seems a pity that we do not introduce their charcoal stoves, which are neat in appearance, easily set up, and cost but little for fuel.

KITCHEN RANGES

The chief considerations in choosing a range are that its qualifications should be—economy with regard to fuel; that it will serve for every mode of cooking; that it should be labour-saving by not causing dust and dirt by smoke.

One that combines these advantages should be acquired. A range supplied with iron flues carefully regulated and suitable for every size made, does away with the evil we have spoken of with regard to the setting of brick ovens.

In many cases a fire in the kitchen is not only needed for cooking, but for warming the room, and some ranges are very easily converted from a close to an open fire. Another very great advantage that a stove should possess is that it should be possible to increase or diminish the size of the fire at will. In some stoves, when the front of the fire, and that a large one, is not required for roasting, by raising a grating the fire is brought close to the top of the grate; where a very small one is sufficient to keep the oven hot and saucepans boiling.

The baking of pastry is often a trial to the cook or housekeeper, for the reason that the heat does not circulate in the ordinary oven as it does in those of the bakers; but in many patent ranges the heat is equalised, or as required; we may have the top or bottom of the oven hotter or cooler, and the flues conduct the heat entirely round the oven, so that much trouble caused by having to open the doors and turn the tins or dishes is obviated. Ovens can be fitted with transparent doors, through which we can watch the progress of baking, and save endless trouble by not having to open the oven continually to see that the food is not scorching or burning.

There are many most useful and suitable ranges for ordinary use in "medium" sized kitchens advertised. One of these 3 feet in width has a large oven, a saddle-back boiler, which supplies house and bath-room with hot water, a rack for warming plates, and a door to close up the fire when cooking.

These ranges, when kept well cleaned and in order, will do all the cooking needed in a household of moderate size, and will burn cheap coal that can be mixed with coke.

Stoves with a setting of fancy tiles are very ornamental.

SELF-SETTING RANGES.

These, as their name implies, are not fixtures, and where a house is rented the tenant who purchases them has the right to remove them. They are fitted as other ranges with good ovens, and as desired, with or without boilers. They have the recommendation of being of moderate price, and cost nothing for bricklayers' or masons' labour to set them up. On the whole they are useful and serviceable ranges, and a close or open fire can be had at will. There are so many good makes advertised that it is impossible to single out any for special recommendation. The boilers should be loose and they can then easily be replaced, should they be injured or wear out.

GAS COOKERS.

The easiest and surest methods of cooking are by gas. A good stove, well kept, in the hands of a person who thoroughly understands it, is the most economical stove of all, but it *must* be a good stove and *must* be kept clean. There is a good deal of risk in taking an old stove with a house, for it may have been imperfectly cleaned, and the food cooked in it will, in that case, acquire a nasty smell that by those who do not understand the stoves, is often put down to the gas itself. Gas companies are always willing to supply new stoves on the hire or slot system, so one can always have a stove with all the newest improvements. By the slot system we may also have gas fittings supplied throughout the house free of charge, and though we pay more for the gas supplied in this manner, it is an excellent plan.

A bill for a quarter's supply of gas is practically an unknown quantity, and there are but few housewives who do not often exclaim at the amount of their liabilities when the gas account comes in, thinking so much as calculated could not have been consumed. Now with the slot arrangement not only do we avoid all gas bills, but the fact of paying ready money for light and fire makes us more economical. We know what a pennyworth of gas will do, and get our full value for our money.

For a small family of three or four persons a small gas kitchener costing from 28s. to 36s. will be found sufficient for an ordinary amount of cooking. These have handy little ovens with two slides, grill, and boiling appliance above.

A treble-cased indestructible gas cooking range, with new patent removable lining can be bought for five guineas. These are made in eight different sizes, and are adapted for roasting, baking,

and all modes of cooking. Boilers can be fitted to these stoves, and are heated by the waste gas from the ovens.

To supplement a kitchen range there is a very useful stove with an oven and griller advertised. On this a kettle can be boiled in five minutes, and two rounds of toast made in two minutes, while the oven cooks well and consumes but little gas. These cost about £1, and are excellent breakfast stoves.

OIL-BURNING STOVES.

In small houses, and in places where gas is unobtainable, oil stoves are invaluable, particularly in summer when fires are not needed.

With careful usage these stoves are very economical ones, for as with gas stoves there need be no waste. The objection made to them by some persons that they have a disagreeable odour of the oil, can only be urged when there is carelessness or neglect on the part of the person whose duty it is to trim the wicks, for a good stove, properly looked after, emits no disagreeable smell whatever.

The cost of these stoves is less than that of gas ones. A most handy little one, with meat tray, grid, kettle, stewpan, steamer, and frying-pan, can be had complete for from 13s. 6d. For a very small family or for two or three persons living in apartments, where, maybe, the cooking has to be done in a living room instead of a kitchen, a stove of this kind is a boon.

Larger stoves to burn oil, suitable for the cooking for a family, fitted with the utensils we have before mentioned, can be bought from 29s. These are fitted with patent dampers and extinguishers. A stove which will bake bread, cakes, meat, &c., and has ornamental cast iron top and feet, and two 6 in. burners, is an excellent family one, and costs only 44s., or fitted with kettle, boiler, stewpan, and frying-pan, 49s. A very superior one fitted with patent central draught flat wick burners, 275 candlepower, costs only 75s, and is suitable for the cooking for a large family. A gallon kettle, a gallon stewpan, a steamer, a frying-pan with cover, and a toast hanger for this, cost about 10s.

KITCHEN UTENSILS, REQUISITES, AND FURNITURE.

KITCHEN UTENSILS.

To supply lists of these to meet the requirements of everybody would be almost impossible. There are so many things to be taken into consideration in furnishing a kitchen.

To begin with our own personal requirements for cookery, which will depend upon the way in which we live, whether plainly or the reverse, the number there are to be cooked for, the number of hands to do the cooking and to keep the utensils clean and in order, and the size and scope of the kitchen itself.

All these things should be remembered ere we start buying, and all the articles that are absolutely *necessary* should be bought first. As other needs make themselves felt, we may endeavour to supply them, but it is no use crowding into a kitchen a host of things that *may* be required, however useful they may appear to be. There are two golden rules, however, in buying culinary articles that should not be forgotten, namely, that they should be of good quality, and that there should be sufficient to prevent it being necessary to use any for purposes for which they were not intended. The truest economy is studied by observing these rules, for by so doing our *batterie de cuisine* will be long before it needs renewing. Those furnishing cannot do better than pay a visit to Messrs. Benetfink of Cheapside, London, who supply every requisite for the home at prices lower than most stores.

We give later a list of the articles that would probably be needed in the kitchen of a house of moderate size, where good but not elaborate cooking was the order of the day; and here we may particularise a few utensils and requisites that are indispensable to the cook. One of the first needed and most important is a good set of scales and weights, for though an experienced cook soon learns to guess pretty accurately at quantities there are many things that *must* be weighed, and the meat as it comes from the butcher should always be put in the scale.

Measures, too, should be at hand, at any rate pint and half-pint ones, with three spoons or small measures that can be relied upon for accuracy, to mete out severally a tea, dessert, and tablespoonful.

UTENSILS FOR BOILING AND STEWING.

A stock-pot should be found in every kitchen, for by its use every scrap of bone, gristle, or trimming that in its absence would probably be thrown away, will be made to yield stock or gravy, and obviate any necessity for soup meat.

The pot should be boiled up very slowly, cold water being put with the bones and trimmings, it may then simmer the day through; when the stock is cold it should be skimmed free of fat.

In hot weather the stock should be boiled up every day, and unless there is a chance of its being used very quickly it is better to omit the vegetables. Very greasy bones, such as those from salt pork, are better boiled separately to serve for pea, lentil, or other vegetable soups.

Draw off the stock at the end of the day, and when the pot has been washed and dried put back only such scraps of bone, &c., as those from which the virtue has not been sufficiently extracted.

A good boiling-pot of sufficient size to boil a ham or leg of mutton is a most useful utensil in a household where there are many to cook for, as it can be not only used for the purposes named, but for boiling large puddings or making soup.

A fish kettle should be considered a necessary utensil, for without it and a strainer, by which the fish may be lifted out and drained when ready, none can be properly boiled.

A porridge pot will be found very useful, and it can be used with advantage for custard.

A braising pan is rather an expensive article, and is one not absolutely indispensable, but is superior to a stewpan for extracting the finest gravy from the meat, which cooked by it is most delicious. The lid of it is hollow, to allow of its being filled with hot cinders.

A stewpan is always required for steak, haricot, &c., as it is almost impossible to make such dishes properly in a saucepan.

A good supply of saucepans of various sizes saves much time in cooking a large dinner, and there should be always two fitted with steamers to save room upon the stove, steaming being one of the best, easiest, and most approved processes of cooking.

It is well to have one or two moulds for boiled puddings, and a copper pan if jam be made at home

UTENSILS FOR ROASTING AND BAKING.

Perhaps the best method for roasting meat is to use a bottle-jack and screen, and hang the meat from the former in front of the fire; but this is but seldom found in any but very large kitchens, most persons baking or roasting their meat in the oven, by which much saving of fuel or gas is effected. Baking tins should therefore be provided, and two square ones of different sizes and one oval one will be, as a rule, sufficient.

A double dripping-pan with well is excellent for baking, and meat cooked in it does not smell so strongly during the baking.

For baking puddings and pies, besides several white earthenware dishes it is well to have one or two enamel tin ones, particularly for use in nursery and kitchen.

For baking cakes the ordinary cake tins should be provided, but it is easier to turn one out from a cake ring such as bakers and confectioners use. This is placed on a plain baking sheet covered with buttered paper, and the mixture poured in. For an open tart a tin one with fluted edge, such as that shown in illustration, is best, and for tartlets a sheet with hollows for the tartlets or patties obviates the perpetual shifting that small separate patty-tins require. Some small pans, however, as shown, should find a place, also a few small fancy tins for baking little puddings and cakes.

An open mould in which the crust for a game or other raised pie can be moulded is very useful.

UTENSILS FOR GRILLING, BOILING, OR FRYING.

A revolving gridiron is a very convenient one, for as the part on which the meat rests turns round, the necessity of frequently moving it is obviated. It has fluted bars lined with enamel, and the gravy from the meat flows from them into a small receptacle in the centre. The ordinary gridiron is made in all sizes, and one is usually provided with gas stoves.

For broiling an excellent thing is a hanging broiler; the fish or meat to be thus cooked being fixed between the double wires; but the ordinary Dutch oven answers well for broiling small birds and is quite the best thing for making a Welsh rarebit. For dry frying, by which such things as eggs, bacon, sausages, &c., are cooked, a frying-pan of iron or enamelled tin will be needed, but this should not be used for omelettes or pancakes, these requiring a small enamelled pan.

For frying those things which should be immersed in fat, a frying kettle with wire drainer is most convenient, or a deep pan may be used when a frying basket is a necessity. This is a very simple, inexpensive little article, and should always be used for such things as rissoles or croquettes, and without it it is impossible to cook whitebait properly.

The above-named utensils are those most needed in an ordinary kitchen, but there are a great many adjuncts required if we want our cookery to be successful. These will be mentioned in the list given, but a few may be illustrated here.

To prevent the juices of the steak from being lost by pricking the meat with a fork in turning it about on the gridiron, steak-tongs are brought into requisition for handling the steaks during the grilling process. By making use of these, the gravy is kept in the meat.

MEAT CHOPPER.

Used for chopping and disjointing bones. In cases where a little gravy is to be made for a hash, the bones of the joint should always be chopped in a few places to get as much goodness out of them as possible.

SUET-CHOPPER, OR MINCING-KNIFE.

A tool like this is convenient for chopping suet, and any ingredient that requires to be finely minced. Being made with a firm wooden handle, the hand does not get so fatigued as by using an ordinary knife, and the business of mincing is accomplished in a much shorter time. These utensils should be kept nice and sharp, and should be ground occasionally.

COPPER PRESERVING-PAN.

Jams, jellies, marmalades, and preserves are made in these utensils, which should be kept scrupulously clean, and well examined before being used.

BREAD-GRATER.

Nicely grated bread crumbs rank as one of the most important ingredients in many puddings, seasonings, stuffings, forcemeats, &c., and add much to the appearance of nicely fried fish. For the purpose of crumbling the bread smoothly and evenly, the bread-grater is used, which is perforated on both sides with holes.

Pestles and mortars are made in iron, brass, marble, and Wedgewood ware. The two latter kinds are decidedly to be preferred, as they can be so easily kept clean. This utensil is used for pounding sugar, spices, &c., required in many preparations of the culinary art.

VEGETABLE CUTTER.

Vegetables are cut out in fanciful shapes, by means of these little cutters. Stewed steaks, and suchlike dishes, where the vegetables form an important addition, are much improved in appearance by having them shaped.

CUCUMBER-SLICE.

For shredding cucumbers into the thinnest possible slices, this little machine is used. It is made of wood, with a steel knife running across the centre. After the cucumber is pared and levelled, it should be held upright, and worked backwards and forwards on the knife, bearing sufficiently hard to make an impression on the cucumber.

PASTE-BOARD AND ROLLING-PIN.

This is so familiar a piece of kitchen furniture that very little description will be required of it. The best kinds of paste-boards are made in hard wood, and require to be very nicely kept. They should not hang in a damp place, as then they are liable to get mildewed, which will very seldom scrub out. The best rolling-pin is one made of glass.

PASTE-JAGGER.

Used for trimming and cutting pastry. The little wheel at the end is made to revolve, and is useful for marking pastry which has to be divided after it is baked.

WIRE DISH-COVER.

This is an article belonging strictly to the larder, and is intended for covering over meat, pastry, &c., to protect it from flies and dust. It is a most necessary addition to the larder, especially in summer time.

KNIFE-BASKET.

This is made of wicker outside, lined with tin, and is a very clean and neat-looking knife-basket. It is very easily washed and kept in proper order, which is not always the case with the wooden boxes. Cheaper kinds are lined with baize.

COFFEE AND TEA CANISTERS.

Japanned tin is the metal of which these canisters are composed. The flavour of the tea and the aroma of the coffee are much preserved by keeping them in tin canisters like that illustrated.

HOT-WATER DISH.

In cold weather such joints as venison, a haunch, saddle, or leg of mutton should always be served on a hot-water dish, as they are so liable to chill. This dish is arranged with a double bottom, which is filled with very hot water just before the joint is sent to table, so keeping that and the gravy deliciously hot. Although an article of this description can scarcely be ranked as a kitchen utensil, still the utility of it is obvious.

The following lists, drawn from the catalogues of the principal London Stores will show at a glance the articles required for the kitchens of families ranging from those for whom a small cottage affords sufficient accommodation, to those sufficiently rich to occupy a large house where accommodation could be found for a large stock of kitchen utensils.

KITCHEN REQUIREMENTS.

Furniture—Utensils—Crockery —Linen.

FURNITURE.

Chairs (Windsor), oiled, 2s. 6d. to 3s. 6d. each.

Chairs (Windsor), polished, 2s. 9d. to 4s. 9d. each.

Chairs (Windsor), arm, 5s. 11d., 6s. 11d. each.

Clocks (kitchen), from 2s. 6d. to 10s. 6d.

Coal-scuttles, 1s. 9d. to 3s. 6d.

Fenders (iron), from 3s. to 10s. 6d.

Fire-irons, per set, from 2s. 6d. to 4s. 6d.

Hearthrugs, suitable for kitchens, from 2s. 6d. to 6s.

Linoleum (printed), from 1s. 11d. per square yard.

Linoleum (plain), from 1s. 9d. per square yard.

Mats (cocoa), from 1s. 7d. to 3s. 3d.

Tables with drawers—
    4 ft. by 2 ft. 9 in., 15s. 6d.; better quality, £1.
    5 ft. by 3 ft., £1 2s. 6d.; better quality, £1 7s. 6d.

KITCHEN UTENSILS.

TIN, IRON, AND COPPER WARE.

Bacon dishes, 10 in., 1s. 9d.; 12 in., 2s. 3d. Hot-water: 8s. 9d. to 18s. 6d.

Bain Marie (copper), with utensils, £3 3s.

Baking sheets (tin), from 6d. each.

Basting ladles, 1s. and 1s. 3d.

Boiling pot, from 2s. 3d.

„   „   (wrought iron), 7s. 6d. to 15s. 6d.

Braising pan (steel), 28s. to 31s.

„   „   (copper), 48s. to 58s. 6d.

Brass bottle-jacks, 4s. 6d., 6s. 3d., 7s. 3d.

Bread graters, 5d., 7d.

Bread pan (jap. steel), from 5s. 6d.

Broilers, from 2s. to 3s. 6d.

Cake tins, 3½d. to 1s.

Candlesticks (tin), 6½d. to 1s. 3d.

Cinder shovels, 1s. to 2s.

Coal hammers (iron), 6½d.

„   „   (steel), 1s. 4½d.

„ scuttles, 2s. to 4s.

„ shovels, 9½d., 1s. 4½d., 2s.

Coffee mills, 3s., 3s. 6d.

„ pot (tin), 1s. to 2s. 6d.

Colanders, 7d., 1s. 6d., 2s. 9d.

Cook's forks, 1s. to 1s. 9d.

„   „   (for beef), 1s. 6d.

„ knives, from 1s. 6d. to 2s. 6d.

Corkscrew, 6d. to 1s.

Dish covers (tin), set of 3—10 in., 14 in., 18 in., 14s.

Dish covers (block tin, plated handles), £1 1s.

Dish covers (wire), from 9d. each.

Dripping-pan and stand, from 4s. 6d.

Dustpan, 6d. to 1s. 6d.

Egg beaters, 1s. 3d. each.

„ poachers, 3¾d. to 7¾d.

„ slices, 6d. and 9d.

Egg whisks, 4½d. to 1s.

Fish fryer and drainer, from 6s.

„ kettle (tin), 2s. 10d. to 6s.

„ slicers, 9d. and 1s.

Flat irons, from 5d. to 1s. 3d. each.

„ iron stands, 3d. each.

Flour bins, 2s. 6d. to 5s. 6d.

„ dredger, 5½d. to 1s.

Forks (nickel silver), from 7d. each.

Freezing machines (Marshall's), 15s.

Frying baskets, from 10½d. to 1s. 6d.

„ pans, from 6½d.

Funnels, 2d. and 4d. each.

Game skewers, 5½d. the set.

Gravy strainers, 9d. to 1s. 5d.

Gridiron (double, hanging), 1s. to 2s. 6d.

Gridiron (fluted), from 1s.

„ (revolving), 1s. 6½d., 1s. 11½d., 2s. 6d. the set.

Hand bowls, from 1s.

Hot-water cans, 1s. 6d., 2s. 6d.

„ dishes, from 2s. 9d.

House pails, 1s., 1s. 3d.

Ice cream freezers, from 10s. 6d.

Kettles (tin), from 1s. to 3s.

„ (wrought iron), from 2s. 8d.

Knife cleaners, from 12s. 9d.

„ trays, from 1s. 6d.

Knives (kitchen), from 6s. dozen.

Larding needles, 1s. 6d. the set.

Mackerel saucepan, 2s. to 3s. 6d.

Meat chopper, from 1s. 2d.

„ graters, 9d.

„ screen (block tin), from 11s. 9d.

„   „   (wooden, lined), 49s.

„ saw, from 1s. 6½d.

Mincing knives, 10½d., 1s.

„ machines, 4s. 6d. to 21s.

Moulds (copper), from 4s. 6d. to 8s. each.

„ (tin), from 10d. to 1s. 9d.

Nutmeg graters, 1d. and 2d. each.

Omelette pans (steel), 1s. 2d., 1s. 9d.

„   „   (copper), from 3s. 9d.

Oyster knives, from 6d.

Paste cutters, 1s. 6d. the set.

„ jaggers, 9d. the set.

Pastry slabs (marble), 6s. to 10s. 6d.

Patty pans, per doz., 4d. to 1s.

Pepper box (tin), 3½d. to 6d.

Pestle and mortars, marble, from 5s. 6d. „ to 3s. 3d. „ compo, from 1s. 4d.

Plates (hot-water), from 1s. 3½d.

Preserving pans (copper), from 13s.

Pudding moulds, 2s., 2s. 6d. each.

Refrigerators, from 43s. 6d.

Root knives, 1s. each.

Salamanders (iron), from 3s. 6d.

Salt cellars, 1s. 2d. each.

Saucepans (enamelled), from 1s. 4d.

„ (iron), from 1s. 3d. to 6s.

„ with steamers, from 3s. 6d.

„ (wrought iron), 3s. 6d. to 9s.

KITCHEN UTENSILS.

A Bottle Roasting Jack—*B* Mincing Knife, or Suet Chopper.—*C* Meat Chopper—*D* Frying Pans—*E* Wire Meat Cover—*F* Pestle and Mortar—*G H* Mincing or Sausage Machine, with Table Clamp Screw—*I* Double Baking Pan, with Meat Stand—*J* Drip Pan, with Basting Ladle—*K* Bottle Jack Roasting Screen.

KITCHEN UTENSILS.

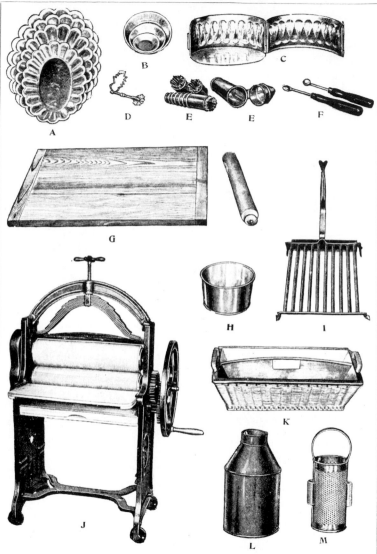

A Tart Pans—B Patty Pans—C Raised Pie Mould—D Paste Jagger—E Fancy
Vegetable Cutters and Case—F Vegetable Scoops—G Paste Board and Pin—
H Plain Charlotte Pudding Mould—I Gridiron—J Mangle or Wringer—K Tin-
lined wicker Knife Basket—L Coffee Canister—M Bread Grater.

Saucepans (wrought iron), with steamers, 7s. and 9s. 9d.
   " (porridge), 3s. 6d. to 6s. 6d.
   " sanitary, seamless, steel,
   " (patent), from 2s. 2d. to 10s
Sauté-pans (steel), from 2s. 4d.
Stewpans (copper), from 5s. 3d.
   " (iron), from 1s. 3d.
   " enamelled, from 1s.
Skewers, 8½d. and 10d. per set.
Slop-pails (galvanized), 3s. 3d.; (japanned), 3s. 6d., 4s.
Spice boxes, from 2s.
Spoons (iron), from 3d. to 9d. each.
   " (nickel-silver), table, 10d. each.
   " ' " . dessert, 7½d. each.
   " " " tea, 4d. each
Steak beaters, from 8d.
   " tongs, 1s. 6½d.
Stock-pots (copper), from 20s.; (wrought iron), 13s. 3d.
Sugar canisters, from 8d.
   " dredger, 9d.
   " nippers, 1s. 3d.
Tart tins, from 1½d.
Tea canisters, 10d., 1s.
Teapots (tin), 1s. 6d.
   " (metal), 2s. 6d
Tea trays, from 1s.
Tin openers, 9d. to 1s. each.
Toasting forks (wire), 5½d.
Turbot kettle (block tin), from 3s. 6d. to 10s. 9d.
Vegetable cutters, 1s. 6d. the set.
   " scoops, 1s. each.
Washing-up pans (zinc), 1s. 6d. to 5s.
Water cans, 2s. 6d. to 4s.
Weighing machines, with weights, from 7s. 6d.
Spring balance family scales to weigh 14 lbs., from 5s. 9d.
Yorkshire pudding tins, 5½d. to 1s.

TURNERY, &c.

Butter pats, 3d. to 10d. per pair.
   " prints, 3d. to 1s.
Bellows, 9d. to 5s.
Bowls, 3d. to 3s.
Chopping boards, 1s. to 3s.
Cinder sifters, 1s. 6d., 5s. 6d.
Clothes horses, 1s. to 5s.
Knife boards (India rubber), 6d. to 1s.
   " " (leather), 2s. 3d. to 6s.
Lemon squeezers, 5d. to 1s.
Pails, 10½d. to 2s. 6d.
Pastry boards, 1s. 9d. to 3s. 6d.
Potato mashers, 4d.
Pegs (clothes), 9d. per gross.
Rolling pins, from 3d. to 8d.
Sieves, from 4½d. to 2s.
Spoons (wooden), from 1d. to 4½d.
Steps (house), 2s. 6d. to 8s. 6d.
Tubs (flour), 1s. to 4s.

Towel rollers, 8d. to 1s.
Washleathers, from 5d. to 1s. 6d.

BROOMS AND BRUSHES.

BROOMS.

Bass brooms, 9½d. to 1s. 6½d.
Soft hair sweeping brooms, 1s. 6d. to 5s. 11d.
Stiff hair sweeping brooms, 2s. 6d. to 4s. 6d.

BRUSHES.

Banister brush, 1s 0½d. to 3s.
   " " (double), 2s. 6d. to 5s. 6d.
Blacklead brushes, 2d. and 6d.
Plate brushes, 5d. to 1s. 6d.
Saucepan brushes, 4d.
Scrubbing brushes (cocoa), 7½d., 9½d.
   " " (hair), 1s., 2s. 6d.
Sink brushes, 4d., 6d.
Stove brushes (bent), 7½d. to 2s.
   " " (double winged) 10½d., 2s. 3d.
   " " (sets), 2s., 4s. 6d.
Sweep's brushes, 4½d. to 1s.

CROCKERY AND GLASS.

Butter dishes, from 4½d. to 1s. 6d.
Dishes (fireproof), 6d. to 2s.
   " (kitchen) 6d. to 1s. 6d. each.
Egg poachers (fireproof), 4d. to 8d.
Jelly moulds, 1s. to 2s.
Jugs for kitchen use, from 1s., set of 3.
   " (milk), from 4½d. to 1s.
Kitchen plates, from 2s. to 5s. doz.
Milk bowls, with spouts, 3d. to 1s.
   " saucepans (fireproof), 6d. to 1s.
Pastry bowls, 4d. to 1s. 3d.
Pie dishes, 2d. to 10d.
Pudding basins, from 2d. to 1s.
Ramakin cases (fireproof), 4d. and 6d.
Salt cellars, from 1d. each.
Shells for scallops (fireproof), 4d. and 6d.
Soufflé dishes (fireproof), 11d. to 1s. 6d.
Sugar basins, 6d. to 1s.
Tumblers for kitchen use, from 2s. doz.

It is worth remembering that breakages of earthenware will occur in all households; and that to buy sets of tableware that cannot be matched, is to run unnecessary risk of vexation and expense. Unless economy is no object, those should be purchased that can be matched without much trouble. A breakage is then of less consequence as the articles can be replaced.

KITCHEN CLOTHS, &c.

Cooks' cloths (shambro), 7½d., 10½d.
Dish cloths (knitted, white) 3s. 6d. doz.
   " (knitted, brown) 4s. 6d. doz.

Dresser cloths, from 9d. per yard.

Dusters, blue and white checked, 1s. 6d. to 10s. per doz.

Dusters, twill, 2s. 11d. to 10s. per doz.

Glass cloths (checked), 3¾d. to 10¾d.

„ (plain), 3¾d. to 10¾d.

Hearth cloths, from 6¾d. per yard.

House cloths, 32 in. wide, 4¾d., 8¾d.

„ flannel, 3¾d. to 8¾d. per yard.

Kitchen cloths, 27 in. wide, 5¾d.; 36 in. wide, 8¾d.

Knife cloths, 2s. 6d. to 4s. 6d. per doz.

Pudding cloths, 3¾d. to 8¾d. per yard.

Roller towels (Barnsley), 16 in., 3¾d., 7¾d. per yard; 20 in., 4¾d., 8¾d. per yard.

Roller towels (crash) 2¾d. to 6d. per yard.

Table cloths (bleached), 1½ yards square, 1s. 6d. to 4s. 3d.; 1¾ yards square, 2s. 6d. to 4s. 11d.

Table cloths (unbleached), 1½ yards square, 1s. 6d. to 2s. 6d.; 1¾ yards square, 2s. to 3s. 6d.

Tea cloths (Barnsley) 4¾d. to 1s. 0½d. per yard.

Tea cloths (linen), 3¾d. to 10¾d. per yard.

The following price list includes all that would be needed by persons of small incomes starting housekeeping.

FURNITURE FOR SMALL KITCHEN.

	s.	d.
3 chairs (Windsor), 2s. 6d. each	7	6
1 clock	2	6
1 coal-scuttle	2	6
Fender	2	6
Set fireirons	2	0
Hearthrug	2	6
Linoleum at 1s. 6d. square yard, about 9 yards	14	6
Table with drawer	15	0
	£2 9	0

KITCHEN UTENSILS.

	s.	d.
2 baking tins for cakes, 4½d., 6½d.	0	11
2 baking tins for meat, 5½d. each	0	11
2 baking tins for tarts, 3½d., 5½d.	0	9
1 baking sheet	0	6
1 bread grater	0	5
1 broiler	2	0
Butter dish (glass)	0	6
Chopping board	1	0
Coffee mill	3	0
„ pot	1	0
Colander	0	11

	s.	d.
Cook's knife and fork	2	0
Corkscrew	0	6
1 dish (fireproof)	0	9
Dish tub	1	0
3 dishes for kitchen use	2	0
Dutch oven	0	9
Egg whisk	0	6
„ poacher	0	3
„ slice	0	6
Fish kettle	3	6
„ slice	0	9
Flour dredger	0	5½
„ tub	2	0
3 forks for kitchen use	1	6
Frying basket	0	10½
„ pan	0	10½
Funnel	0	2
Gravy strainer	0	9
Gridiron (wire)	0	9
3 jugs for kitchen use	1	0
1 jug for milk	0	6
1 kettle (iron)	3	0
1 kettle (small, tin)	0	9
Knife board	0	9
„ sharpener	0	9
„ tray	1	6
3 knives for kitchen use	1	6
Lemon squeezer	0	5
Meat chopper	1	2
„ saw	1	6½
Mincer	3	6
2 moulds for puddings or jellies	1	0
Mustard pot (glass)	0	3
Nutmeg grater	0	1
Omelette pan	1	2
Oyster knife	0	3
Paste jagger	0	6
Pastry board	1	9
2 pastry bowls, 6d. and 1s. ..	1	6
6 patty pans	0	6
Pepper pot	0	2
3 pie dishes, 4d., 6d., 8d. ..	1	6
Pint and half-pint measures (glasses)	1	0
Plate basket	1	9
6 plates for kitchen use	2	0
Potato masher	0	4
3 pudding basins	0	10
Rolling pin	0	6
Salt cellar	0	2
3 saucepans (iron), 1s. 3d., 1s. 9d., 2s. 3d.	5	3
1 saucepan (enamel)	2	0
Set of skewers	0	6
Two sieves, 4½d., 7½d.	1	0
2 spoons (dessert)	1	0
2 „ (table)	1	3
2 „ (tea)	0	9
2 „ (metal)	0	9
2 „ (wooden), 1d., 2d. ..	0	3
Steak tongs —	1	3
1 stewpan	3	0

	s.	d.
Steamer to fit saucepan	2	0
Stock-pot	10	0
Sugar basin (glass)	0	6
„ dredger	0	6
Teapot (earthenware)	0	9
Tin opener	0	6
Toasting fork (wire)	0	3
2 tumblers	0	4
2 wash-up pans (zinc) 1s. and 2s.	3	0
Weights and scales	7	0
	£5 5	1

BROOMS, BRUSHES, &c.

	s.	d.
Broom (bass)	0	9½
„ hair, soft	2	6
„ hair, stiff	3	0
Brushes	1	0½
1 cook's brush	0	6
1 dusting brush	0	9
1 plate brush	0	9
1 stair brush (double, soft and hard)	2	6
1 scrubbing brush (cocoa) ..	0	9
1 sink brush	0	4
2 stove brushes	1	6
1 stove brush for black lead ..	0	3

	s.	d.
Clothes horse	1	0
1 slop-pail	3	0
2 pails for house	2	0
2 washleathers	1	3
	£1 1	11

KITCHEN CLOTHS, &c.

	s.	d.
2 dish cloths, 3½ each	0	7
2 dresser cloths, 1s. each ..	2	0
4 dusters, 2d. each	0	8
6 glass cloths	2	0
2 hearth cloths	0	7
2 house flannels	0	8
6 kitchen cloths	3	0
2 knife cloths	0	6
2 pudding cloths	0	6
2 roller towels	1	6
2 table cloths, 1½ yards square	3	0
6 tea cloths	1	9
	16	9

	£	s.	d.
Furniture	2	9	0
Kitchen utensils	5	5	1
Brooms, brushes, &c. ..	1	1	11
Kitchen cloths, &c.	0	16	9
	£9	12	9

MARKETING

A THRIFTY housekeeper will find it advantageous to do the marketing for the household herself, instead of simply ordering the butcher's meat and other provisions. By carefully observing the state of the market and judiciously selecting what is wanted, she will secure three advantages, *variety*, *excellence*, and *economy*. It is not sufficient to bear in mind what is in season, as the market is not necessarily fully stocked with every description of seasonable food, and it will thus frequently happen that an order sent to the tradesman, irrespective of the temporary abundance or scarcity of particular joints, &c., will result, either in disappointment from their inferior quality, or vexation at the enhanced price. We are, indeed, sorry to say that there are too many tradesmen who have two scales of prices, one for persons who do their own marketing, and another, perceptibly higher, for those who " order." The first class, if they are careful buyers, may always secure the benefit of a fall in the market price, the other must not expect to receive any advantage from temporary fluctuations. Those who live in or near London will find that a big saving can be effected by buying from one of the wholesale and retail butchers in Farringdon Market. Messrs. Gunton Bros., of 334, Farringdon Road, are one of the best known firms there.

If not possible to do daily marketing for fish, flesh, and vegetable foods, most housekeepers could find time to go about once a week to the tradesfolk, when, if the day chosen be a Saturday, the time for the visits should be early.

The importance of *variety* should always be borne in mind in providing for a household; it is essential alike to health and comfort. Variety in the methods of preparation may be secured by attention to the recipes supplied in the following pages. Variety in the selection of the articles of diet must be the care of the housekeeper. When marketing, she should endeavour to provide a succession of different kinds of food, both animal and vegetable. We do not know any point on which, generally speaking, English management has hitherto been more at fault than this, nor one in which reform is more imperatively required. Unfortunately, it is often imagined that variety involves expense, whereas the very opposite is true, as the wider the range of a housekeeper's ideas in marketing, the greater the opportunity of purchasing to advantage.

In addition to the special directions given below, it may be useful to observe that moderately fat meat is the best in every respect. If it is very lean, the animal has been underfed, and the meat will probably be tough and tasteless; if there is an excess of fat, it renders the joint costly, when purchased at current rates. Lean meat is dear at any price.

BEEF.

Beef should have an open grain, smooth and juicy; should be soft to the touch, and of a rich carnation colour, the fat of a fine cream colour. When the animal has been fed upon oil-cake, the fat will be of a deeper colour. The bone should be small and the flesh full.

HIND-QUARTER.

Contains:

Leg of beef (for stewing); round (prime boiling piece); aitch-bone (boiling or roasting); rump (finest part for steaks); thick flank (prime boiling piece); thin flank (boiling); sirloin (roasting).

FORE-QUARTER.

Fore-rib (prime roasting piece); middle-ribs (economical joint for roasting); brisket (for salting and boiling); chuck and leg-of-mutton piece (used for second quality steaks); clod and sticking (used for soups; gravies, stocks, pies, and trimmings for sausages); shin; cheek.

The following is a classification of the qualities of meat, according to the several joints of beef, when cut up in the London manner:—

First-class—includes the sirloin, with the kidney suet, the rump-steak piece, the fore-rib.

Second-class—the buttock, the thick flank, the middle-rib.

Third-class the aitch-bone, the thin flank, the chuck, the leg-of-mutton piece, the brisket.

Fourth-class—the neck, clod, and sticking-piece.

Fifth-class—the hock, the shin.

MUTTON.

Mutton should be of a rich red colour, close in the grain, and juicy; whitish in the fat, but not slimy and tallowy. The flesh should pinch tender, and rise again when dented with the finger. The

HIND-QUARTER.

is divided into the leg; the loin—the two loins, when cut in one piece, being called the saddle. The

FORE-QUARTER.

is divided into the shoulder; the neck, the upper part being called, for distinction, the scrag, which is generally afterwards separated from the lower and better joint; the breast. The haunch of mutton, so often served at public dinners and special entertainments, comprises all the leg and so much of the loin, short of the ribs or lap, as is shown in the engraving.

LAMB.

In lamb the flesh should be of a faintish white in colour, smooth and firm to the touch; the fat white and light in appearance. It is cut up into rib, breast, shoulder, loin, leg, forequarter.

PORK.

In the best pork the meat is fine and close grained, without a superabundance of fat. The fat itself is firm, solid, and of a pinkish white.

In a sucking pig the tongue should be clean, the flesh pinkish in hue, and the skin clear and fresh.

Small pork to cut for table in joints is cut up, in most places throughout the kingdom, as represented in the engraving.

The side is divided with nine ribs to the fore-quarter; and the following is an enumeration of the joints in the two respective quarters:—

HIND-QUARTER.

Hind-loin, leg, belly or spring.

FORE-QUARTER.

Hand, fore-loin.

HAM AND BACON.

It is difficult to give special directions for the selection of ham and bacon. As a general rule, moderate sized hams are best; when small they are frequently lean, tough, and salt; when very large they are commonly too fat. The ordinary method of testing the sweetness of a ham is to run a sharp knife or skewer into it close to the bone, and if when withdrawn they have an agreeable odour, the ham is good; if the blade has a greasy appearance and an offensive smell, the ham is bad. In small families it is sometimes convenient to purchase half a ham instead of a whole one; when thus divided it is easy to judge of the quality. The lean should be firm and bright, the fat white, and the smell agreeable. As the upper half of a divided ham will of course contain the most fat and the least bone, and the knuckle end less fat and more bone, the purchaser will select the one or the other according to taste.

Large bacon is almost always coarse, and lean bacon is seldom good. When it is intended to be eaten with lean meat it can scarcely be too fat; when boiled as a separate dish, a fair amount of lean is required. As in ham, the fat should be white, the lean bright red and firm, but not hard.

VEAL.

Veal must be fresh killed to be good. The lean should be white, smooth, and juicy; the fat, white, firm, and abundant. Stale veal is moist and clammy, the joints are flabby, and there is a faint musty smell.

HIND-QUARTER.

Hind knuckle or hock, fillet, loin, chump end, do., best end.

FORE-QUARTER.

Breast, neck, shoulder, fore-knuckle.

VENISON.

In venison the fat should be clear, bright, and thick, and the cleft of the haunch smooth and close.

GAME AND POULTRY.

In selecting a TURKEY see that the legs are smooth and black, its spurs short, breast full, and neck long. The eyes should be bright and full, and the feet supple. If the eyes are sunk and the feet dry the bird is stale.

In a young FOWL the spurs are short and the legs smooth. When fresh the vent is close and dark. White-legged fowls are generally preferred—for no special reason, however, except that the flesh is whiter.

A young GOOSE has a yellowish bill and pliable feet, with few hairs on either. If the bill and feet are reddish, with many hairs, the bird is old, and if the feet are dry it is stale,

DUCKS also (wild and tame) should have pliable feet, the breast should be full and hard, and the skin clear.

PIGEONS. The vent should be close and hard, and the feet pliable.

In selecting GAME pluck a few feathers from the under part of the leg; if the skin is not discoloured the bird is fresh. M. Soyer says, " The age may be known by placing the thumb into the beak, and holding the bird up with the jaw part; if it breaks it is young; if not, it is old, and requires keeping longer before cooking to be eatable."

A HARE when fresh killed is stiff and whitish; when stale, the body is supple and the flesh in many parts black. If the hare be old the ears will be tough and dry, and will tear readily. RABBITS may be judged in the same manner. In both the claws should be smooth and sharp. In a young hare the cleft in the lip is narrow, and the claws are readily cracked if turned sideways.

FISH.

In every kind of fish the flesh should be thick and firm, the gills red and the eyes bright. If, on pressing the fingers on the flesh, the impression remains, the fish is stale. Freshness is best indicated by the smell. Medium-sized fish are generally preferable to those which are very large or very small.

VEGETABLES

should be procured as fresh as possible. In this respect the inhabitants of the metropolis suffer some disadvantage. Cabbages, cauliflowers, broccoli, spinach, peas, beans, lettuces, cucumbers, &c., &c., sold in London and other big cities have always lost some of their flavour by being packed and brought to market. If in addition they are allowed to get stale by lengthened exposure, they are scarcely worth eating.

Carrots, turnips, and parsnips are not so quickly spoiled, but are best when fresh. Carrots and parsnips are preserved by being " pitted " in sand.

Potatoes, when properly stored, do not lose much of their flavour by keeping. There are a great many varieties sold, but the confusion of names, and the deterioration of the best qualities when grown in unsuitable soils, render it impossible to recommend any particular kind. Medium-sized potatoes are generally the best.

EGGS, BUTTER, AND MILK.

In choosing EGGS, apply the tongue to the large end of the egg, and, if it feels warm, it may be relied on as fresh. Another mode of ascertaining the freshness of eggs is to hold them before a lighted candle or to the light, and if the egg looks clear, it will be tolerably good; if thick, it is stale; and if there is a black spot attached to the shell, it is worthless. No egg should be used for culinary purposes with the slightest taint in it, as it will render perfectly useless those with which it has been mixed. Eggs may, however, be preserved for a considerable time without any further special precaution than that of keeping them in a cool place. A very effective method of preserving eggs for winter use is to rub a little melted lard over each to close the pores, and then to pack the eggs in bran or sawdust, not allowing them to touch each other. Or they may be packed in a vessel, and covered with a mixture of freshly slaked lime in water mixed to the consistency of cream. Eggs so preserved will keep for months, but the process renders the shells very brittle.

BUTTER AND MILK are the despair of housekeepers who live in large towns; for, although Parliamentary enactments have done much to protect the public from imposition, both articles are still frequently adulterated.

Butter, with regard to its properties, as food, may be regarded nearly in the light of vegetable oils and animal fats; but it becomes sooner rancid than most other fat oils. When fresh, it is very wholesome; but it should be quite free from rancidity. If slightly salted when it is fresh, its wholesomeness is probably not at all impaired, but should it begin to turn rancid, salting will not correct the rankness. When salt butter is put into casks, the upper part next the air is very apt to become rank, and this rancidity is also liable to affect the whole cask.

Fresh butter comes to London from Buckinghamshire, Suffolk, Oxfordshire, Yorkshire, Devonshire, &c. *Cambridge butter* is esteemed next to fresh; *Devonshire butter* is nearly similar in quality to the latter; *Irish butter* sold in London is all salted, but is generally good. Our best salt butter is *Dorset*.

Danish butter is excellent. *Dutch butter* is in good repute all over Europe, America, and even India; and no country in the world is more successful in the manufacture of this article. Large quantities of butter are now imported to this country from the United States.

At certain seasons of the year *Australian butter* which is good and pure will be found in the market, and is sold at a lower rate than our own. *Brittany butter* is invariably good and of pleasant flavour, and may be bought at the same price as English butter.

The adulteration of *milk* is usually limited to the addition of water, but as it is more or less injured by being conveyed long distances, it is seldom to be obtained in London of equal quality to that procured in the country. Where a supply of really pure and fresh milk is not available, the *condensed milk*, sold in tins, is invaluable, and under most circumstances it is worth while to keep a can or two in the house to meet any sudden requirements. One canful mixed with warm water is equivalent to nearly *two* quarts of ordinary milk. The *condensed milk* is made by evaporating nearly the whole of the water of the milk from which it is prepared, and adding sugar.

TIMES WHEN THINGS ARE IN SEASON

JANUARY.

Fish.—Bloaters, brill, cod, cray-fish, dorys, eels, flounders, haddock, hake, halibut, herrings, lobsters, mussels, oysters, plaice, prawns, scallops, skate, smelts, soles, sprats, turbot, whiting.

Meat.—Beef, house lamb, mutton, pork, veal. —

Poultry. — Capons, fowls, geese, pigeons, rabbits, turkeys.

Game.—Hares, partridges, pheasants, snipe, wild fowl, woodcock.

Vegetables.—Artichokes (Jerusalem), beetroot, broccoli, cabbages (green and red), carrots, celery, endive, leeks, lettuces, onions, sprouts (Brussels), parsnips, potatoes, seakale, savoys, spinach, watercress.

Fruit. — Apples, bananas, grapes (foreign), nuts, oranges, pears, dried fruits.

FEBRUARY.

Fish.—Bloaters, brill, cod, crayfish, dorys, eels, flounders, hake, halibut, herrings, lobsters, mussels, oysters, plaice, prawns, shrimps, skate, smelts, soles, sprats, turbot, whitebait, whiting.

Meat.—Beef, mutton, house lamb, veal.

Poultry.—Capons, chickens, ducks, fowls, geese, pigeons, rabbits, turkeys.

Game.—Hares, partridges, pheasants, plovers, snipe, woodcock.

Vegetables.—Beetroot, broccoli, Brussels sprouts, cabbages, carrots, celery, cresses, endive, lettuces, parsnips, potatoes, savoys, seakale, spinach, turnips.

Fruit.—Apples, grapes (foreign), nuts, oranges, pears, rhubarb, dried fruits.

MARCH.

Fish.—Bloaters, brill, crabs, crayfish, eels, flounders, hake, halibut, herrings, lobsters, mullet, mussels, oysters, plaice, prawns, salmon, scallops, skate, smelts, soles, sturgeon, turbot, whitebait, whiting.

Meat.—Beef, house lamb, mutton, pork, veal.

Poultry.—Capons, chickens, ducklings, rabbits.

Game.—Snipe, woodcock.

Vegetables. — Asparagus, beetroot, broccoli, cabbage, carrots, celery, endive, lettuces, onions, parsnips, potatoes, savoys, seakale, spinach, sprouts, watercress.

Fruit.—Apples, grapes (foreign), nuts, oranges, pears, rhubarb, dried fruits.

APRIL.

Fish.—Brill, crabs, dorys, flounders, lobsters, mackerel, mullet (red and grey), mussels, oysters, prawns, salmon, shad, smelts, shrimps, skate, trout, turbot, whitebait, whiting.

Meat.—Beef, lamb, mutton, veal.

Poultry.—Capons, chickens, ducklings, fowls, guinea fowls, pigeons, rabbits.

Vegetables.—Asparagus, broccoli, cabbages, carrots, lettuces, onions (spring), parsnips, potatoes, seakale, sprouts, spinach, watercress.

Fruit.—Apples, nuts, pears, rhubarb.

MAY.

Fish.—Crabs, crayfish, dory, lobsters, mackerel, mullet (red and grey), plaice, prawns, salmon, shad, smelts, soles, trout, turbot, whitebait, whiting.

Meat.—Beef, lamb, mutton, veal.

Poultry.—Chickens, ducklings, fowls, green geese, guinea fowls, pigeons, rabbits.

Vegetables.—Asparagus, broccoli, cabbage, carrots (new), cauliflower, cucumbers, lettuces, onions (spring), potatoes (new), radishes, spinach.

Fruit.—Apples, gooseberries (green), rhubarb.

JUNE.

Fish.—Crayfish, eels, halibut, herrings, lobsters, mackerel, mullet, plaice, prawns, salmon, sturgeon, soles, trout, turbot, whitebait, whiting.

Meat.—Beef, lamb, mutton, veal, buck venison.

Poultry.—Chickens, ducklings, fowls, green geese, pigeons, rabbits.

Vegetables.—Artichokes, asparagus, broccoli, cabbage, carrots (new), cauliflower, cucumbers, lettuces, onions, peas, potatoes (new), radishes, spinach, tomatoes.

Fruit.—Apples, apricots, cherries, currants, gooseberries, melons, rhubarb, strawberries.

JULY.

Fish.—Crabs, crayfish, dory, flounders, hake, halibut, herrings, lobsters, mackerel, mullet (red and grey), prawns, salmon, soles, sturgeon, trout, turbot, whitebait, whiting.

Meat.—Beef, lamb, mutton, veal, buck venison.

Poultry.—Chickens; ducklings, fowls, green geese, guinea fowl, pigeons, rabbits.

Vegetables.—Artichokes, asparagus, beans (broad and French), broccoli, cauliflower, carrots (new), cabbages, cucumbers, lettuces, onions, peas, potatoes, tomatoes, vegetable marrows.

Fruit.—Apricots, cherries, currants gooseberries, melons, strawberries.

AUGUST.

Fish.— Brill, crayfish, cod, crabs, dorys, eels, flounders, hake, halibut, lobsters, mullet, prawns, salmon, soles, sturgeon, trout, turbot, whitebait, whiting.

Meat.—Beef, lamb, mutton, veal, buck venison.

Poultry.— Chickens, ducks, fowls, green geese, pigeons, rabbits.

Game.—Grouse, leverets, snipe, woodcock.

Vegetables.—Artichokes, beans (broad and French), cabbages, carrots, cauliflowers, cucumbers, lettuces, onions, peas, potatoes, radishes, spinach, tomatoes, vegetable marrow.

Fruit.—Apricots, currants, gooseberries, greengages, plums, strawberries.

SEPTEMBER.

Fish.—Brill, cod, crabs, dorys, eels, flounders, hake, halibut, lobsters, mullet, mussels, oysters, plaice, prawns, salmon, soles, turbot, whiting.

Meat.—Beef, mutton, pork, veal, buck venison.

Poultry.—Chickens, ducks, fowls, geese, larks, pigeons, rabbits.

Game. — Blackcock, grouse, hares, partridges, ptarmigan, snipe, woodcock.

Vegetables.—Beans (French), beetroot, Brussels sprouts, cabbages, carrots, cauliflowers, cucumbers, lettuces, onions, potatoes, spinach, tomatoes, vegetable marrow.

Fruit.—Apricots, damsons, grapes,

greengages, melons, nectarines, peaches, plums, quinces.

OCTOBER.

Fish.—Brill, cod, crabs, eels, flounders, haddocks, hake, halibut, herrings, lobsters, mullet, mussels, oysters, plaice, prawns, skate, smelts, soles, turbot, whiting.

Meat.—Beef, mutton, pork, veal, doe venison.

Poultry.—Ducks, fowls, geese, larks, pigeons, rabbits, turkeys.

Game.—Black game, grouse, hares, partridges, pheasants, plovers, ptarmigan, snipe, wild duck, woodcock.

Vegetables.—Beetroot, broccoli, Brussels sprouts, cabbages, carrots, celery, lettuces, onions, parsnips, potatoes, savoys, spinach, tomatoes, vegetable marrow.

Fruit.—Apples, bullaces, damsons, grapes, medlars, melons, nectarines, peaches, pears, pines, plums, quinces.

NOVEMBER.

Fish.—Brill, cod, crabs, eels, flounders, haddocks, hake, halibut, herrings, lobsters, mussels, oysters, soles, sprats, smelts, turbot, whiting.

Meat.—Beef, mutton, pork, doe venison.

Poultry.—Ducks, fowls, geese, larks, pigeons, rabbits, turkeys.

Game.—Black game, grouse, hares, partridges, pheasants, plovers, ptarmigan, snipe, wild duck, woodcock.

Vegetables.—Artichokes (Jerusalem), beetroot, broccoli, Brussels sprouts, cabbages, carrots, celery, onions, parsnips, potatoes, savoys, spinach, tomatoes.

Fruit.—Apples, grapes (foreign), medlars, melons, oranges, pears.

DECEMBER.

Fish.—Brill, bloaters, cod, eels, haddocks, hake, halibut, herrings, lobsters, oysters, plaice, prawns, skate, smelts, soles, sprats, turbot, whiting.

Meat.—Beef, mutton, pork, doe venison.

Poultry.—Ducks, fowls, geese, larks, pigeons, rabbits, turkeys.

Game.—Black game, hares, partridges, pheasants, plovers, snipe, wild duck, woodcock.

Vegetables. — Beetroot, Brussels sprouts, cabbages, carrots, celery, endive, onions, parsnips, potatoes, savoys, spinach, tomatoes.

Fruit.—Apples, grapes (foreign), medlars, oranges, pears, dried fruits.

HINTS TO PREVENT WASTE.

When fuel and food have been procured, the next consideration is, how the latter may be best preserved, with a view to its being suitably dressed. Much waste is often occasioned by the want of judgment or of necessary care in this particular. In the absence of proper places for keeping provisions a hanging safe, suspended in an airy situation, is the best substitute.

A well-ventilated larder, dry and shady, is better for meat and poultry which require to be kept for some time; and the utmost skill in the culinary art will not compensate for the want of proper attention to this particular.

In favourable weather (that is, when the atmosphere is cool, clear, and dry) BEEF may be kept to advantage from two to four days; MUTTON, under the same circumstances, may, with care, be kept still longer, and will hang for some time without deterioration. When the atmosphere is at all thick and moist, meat will soon turn. It should then be wiped every day with a cloth.

VEAL, LAMB, and PORK ought not to be kept more than a day or two.

Though it is advisable that animal food should be hung up in the open air till its fibres have lost some degree of their toughness, yet, if it is kept till it loses its natural sweetness, its flavour has become deteriorated. As soon, therefore, as the slightest trace of putrescence is detected, it has reached its highest degree of tenderness, and should be dressed immediately. During the sultry summer months it is difficult to procure meat that is not either tough or tainted. It should, therefore, be well examined when it comes in, and if flies have touched it, the part must be cut off, and the remainder well washed.

GAME may be hung for two or three weeks, but this is a question of individual taste. When the feathers come out very easily they are considered by some persons just fit for cooking, while others prefer them almost as fresh as a chicken or fowl should be. Birds with the feathers on, or fowls, will keep for a week; turkeys for a fortnight; geese not more than

eight or nine days. Hares should be paunched before they are hung.

FISH, with the exception of salmon and turbot, should be cooked as fresh as possible. Salmon and turbot will be improved if kept for a day or so. Flat fish generally do not spoil so soon as most other kinds.

In very cold weather, meat and vegetables touched by the frost should be brought into the kitchen early in the morning, and soaked in cold water. In loins of meat, the long pipe that runs by the bone should be taken out, as it is apt to taint. Rumps and aitchbones of beef, when bruised, should not be purchased.

All these things ought to enter into the consideration of every household manager; and great care should be taken that nothing is thrown away or suffered to be wasted in the kitchen which might, by proper management, be turned to a good account. The shank-bones of mutton, so little esteemed in general, give richness to soups or gravies, if well soaked and crushed before they are added to the boiling. They are also particularly nourishing for sick persons. Roast-beef bones, or shank-bones of ham, make excellent stock for pea-soup. When the whites of eggs are used for jelly, confectionery, or other purposes, a pudding or a custard should be made, that the yolks may be used.

All things likely to be wanted should be in readiness: sugars of different sorts; currants washed, picked, and perfectly dry; spices pounded and kept in very small bottles closely corked, or in canisters. Much waste is always prevented by keeping every article in the place best suited to it.

Vegetables keep best on a stone-floor, if the air be excluded; meat in a cold, dry place; as also salt, sugar, sweetmeats, candles, dried meats, and hams. Rice, and all sorts of cereals for puddings, should be closely covered, to preserve them from insects; but even this will not prevent them from being affected by these destroyers, if they are long and carelessly kept. Pears and grapes should be strung, and hung up in a cold, dry place. Apples should be laid on straw, after being carefully wiped, and should not touch each other.

COOKERY

NECESSITY FOR COOKING.

In all ages and in all countries the pleasures of the table have been appreciated and cultivated. They are those that we taste the oftenest, and the first and last that we enjoy. In spite of all that is said in favour of our being content without luxuries and taking only what is absolutely necessary in the way of food and drink, the majority of us are quite ready to accept the fact that the good things of this earth were sent for our *use* (not abuse); and the more carefully and pleasantly these good things are prepared for our delectation the better.

It is a great mistake to think that our great men do not appreciate good cooking as well as dainty fare. *Apropos* of them, we recall the saying of Descartes, the French philosopher. One of the French noblesse, whose rank was superior to his brains, seeing the philosopher engaged upon an epicurean repast, exclaimed: "What! do you philosophers eat dainties?" and received the rebuff from Descartes, "Do you think that God made all the good things for fools?"

Dr. Johnson used to hold in contempt those who did not, or pretended not to care for good eating and drinking, and used to consider the consumption of good food a pleasurable part, but still a part of his work.

He was perfectly right, for it may be said the stomach is the mainspring of our system, and unless sufficient nourishment is given to it in the shape of good and digestible food, it cannot support either nerves or circulation.

To quote a great man of this present day, Ruskin says: "Cookery means much tasting and no wasting; it means English thoroughness, French art, and Arabian hospitality; it means the knowledge of all the fruits and herbs and balms and spices, it means carefulness, inventiveness, and watchfulness; the economy of our great-grandmothers and the science of modern chemistry."

Animal and intellectual organs are more nearly connected than many would believe. A well nourished person is not only capable of better work, either mental or bodily, but is less liable to temptations of drink or excess of any kind than one who is badly fed. French people are proverbially light-hearted and temperate, and this we think might well be attributed to the fact that, no matter to what rank they belong, they eat heartily at few meals of *well-cooked* food.

Quantities and even qualities are secondary considerations compared with the cooking of our food. It is possible to eat a large meal of well prepared food and digest it perfectly, whereas a much smaller quantity, indifferently cooked, would disagree with us; and while a meal of the lightest description may afford nourishment for hours, a heavy one may be as equally unsatisfactory.

No better motto could be found for a cook than to "make the best of everything," and that is where the science of cookery comes in, teaching us, as it does, the constituents and properties of foods, looking upon them in the light of medicines and blending them accordingly, so that out of the minimum of material we may get the maximum of good.

THE SCIENCE OF COOKERY.

Till lately, chemistry has not been in active growth, but day by day it is now adding to our physiological knowledge, and is fast becoming a more popular science. With it and by its aid, advances the science of cookery.

A dietary cure is now as common, if not more so, than a medicinal one for even the greatest disorders, particularly in cases of mental aberration; and to this reason may be partly owing the giant strides that cookery has taken during the last few years.

It is argued by some who object to the term "science of cookery" that people lived as long before such a thing was heard of. So they did, just as they lived before they knew the laws of gravitation or elementary mathematics, before the days of wonderful machinery or steam. But as we are ready to acknowledge the fact that these discoveries have done much good, specially that science applied to agriculture enables us to support a larger population in greater comfort, why should we not be ready to say whether science in cookery will not aid us in the feeding of our starving millions, inasmuch as its very backbone is economy—economy in the use of the digestive organs as well as in the preparation of the food itself.

We venture to assert that gradually but surely our methods of cooking and our combinations of foods will be based upon the most carefully tested scientific discoveries, and that from laboratory to kitchen, through, it may be, treatise or lecture, the information will be handed down.

It stands to reason that we should study and learn for ourselves the properties of the foods we consume every day of our lives, even before we know those of the medicines we occasionally take, and not test them at the expense of our bodily health, as we may do, not knowing of what they are composed.

REASONS FOR COOKERY.

We may say there are five good reasons for cooking: to make it pleasant to taste, to render mastication easy, to facilitate digestion, to combine foods, and to economise them by eating them warm.

To take the first reason. No one can enjoy and many cannot even be healthily nourished by a monotonous diet. Tasteless food is not simply unpleasant; it is not healthful; and the same food taken day after day, although it may contain all the necessary constituents, looking at it from the point of view of chemical analysis, does not give the requisite sustaining power.

It has been actually pointed out how a great improvement has been effected in the inmates of large public institutions by a change in the dietary.

We cannot give too much importance to this reason for good cooking, which is never monotonous, for it affects so materially the *health* as well as the comfort of us all.

The second reason, that of making mastication easier, is apparent without much consideration. The act may be said to be that of dividing and subdividing the food so that it exposes a greater surface to the action of the digestive juices with which it afterwards comes in contact; and it can easily be seen how the sufficient cooking of food facilitates this. Some of our greatest and strongest animals, chiefly carnivorous ones, can swallow their food raw and without mastication, but their digestion is very different from our human one, and we should require to devote a great deal longer time to our meals had we to accomplish all the grinding and subdividing by our teeth alone.

By cooking, fibre is softened, starch hydrated, dough vesiculated, albumen coagulated, and a very large portion of indigestible matter, or matter difficult of mastication, removed; so half our work is done for us in the kitchen.

To the action of heat upon food may be ascribed the most important results of cookery. Cooking may not alter the chemical constitution of food, but it may utterly change its value, turning it from indigestible to digestible matter as well as rendering it pleasant to the taste. Some of the changes wrought by heat are easily explained: whether fibre is shrivelled or swelled; whether gelatine is brittle or dissolved, we do not require science to discover, but science tells us why these things are, and so enables us to more easily bring our food into the conditions we require it.

The fourth reason we have for cooking is the combination of foods, which should be carefully done in the right proportions, so that by supplying deficiencies and counteracting superabundant qualities in various foods, we may materially help digestion and supply the body with *all* its needs.

In many cases this has been done from an early period in cookery by natural instinct. Such as that which prompts us to serve peas with bacon, egg sauce with salt fish, or butter and milk with rice; but this has probably been done long before we could give the reasons, not knowing the constituents of the foods—that peas contain the starch, or floury matter, necessary to combine with fat bacon, or that egg sauce would supply the lack of nourishment in salt fish. Daily, cooks learn these things, but there is still a wide field for their discoveries.

The fifth reason for cooking is the economising of our food by heating it. Part of what we eat is heat-giving food to keep the heat of our bodies at a certain point. So long as we are in health we should be always 98° on a Fahrenheit thermometer—warm but not hot: a higher or lower temperature shows that something is amiss.

A simple illustration may serve to show why warm food is more nourishing than cold. When we put fresh coals on the fire the temperature of the room is lowered at once, because some of the heat from the live coals is absorbed into the fresh coals. This is just the case with the cold food, for some of the heat of our bodies must be employed to heat it.

There are gas burners that give a brilliant light and are yet economical, because the spare heat of the flame is used to heat the gas that will be presently burnt, and we warm our food on the same principle, the coals saving the heat of our bodies. It should be a known fact that whereas hot food is not wholesome, warm food is not only more nourishing than cold, but it goes farther, and is, therefore, as we have said, more economical.

Cookery now in England is one of the most popular arts of the day, and where we had one, we have now twenty writers on the subject. We owe a debt of gratitude to many Continental authorities for the information we have been able to gain from their works upon Cookery, and as we give many recipes for French, German, American and Indian dishes, we may well devote a page or two to the consideration of—

FOREIGN COOKERY.

FRENCH COOKERY.

The cooking of the French people ranks deservedly higher than that of any other nation; and not only is a French *chef* considered the best cook in the world, but the peasantry and lower ranks in the country are remarkable for their talent in the culinary art. Early cultivation is the secret of the fact that so many French women can cook well; even the little children have toy kitchens in which to commence their studies, and cookery has always been a part of the education of the young French girls as it is now amongst English ones.

One decided advantage the French have over us is that they know how to make the *most* of everything in the way of food. Any good plain cook in England can send up an excellent leg of mutton with plain vegetables, and, may be, a Yorkshire pudding cooked to perfection; but a French woman would make a comparatively elaborate dinner out of the same material, or less.

It is said by many English people (who may have not had the happiness of enjoying good cooking) in disparagement of the French, that they think so much of their eating. But why not? They have but two to our three or four meals a day, and they like to have plenty of variety at these two meals— to have vegetables cooked in many different ways, appetising yet not extravagant soups, and dainty dishes from half the meat that we use for our plain dinners.

The French rise early and come to their *déjeuner* with hearty appetite, and this meal takes the place of what used to be in England, in olden times, an early dinner, just as their late dinners do for the old-fashioned supper. Almost every provision is to be had in France in abundance, and we want no stronger proof of this than the quantity imported here. Condensed milk, butter, cheese, eggs and poultry we have from France in very great quantities, and we also depend upon her for a large supply of fruit and vegetables. Fruit is, in fact, so plentiful in France, that the pigs are often fed upon melons and pomegranates in the South. There is a good supply of fish, too, and on the Western Coast the catching and preserving of sardines finds employment for a great many people. Besides sardines, we are indebted to France for other luxuries in the shape of truffles, olives, wines and pâtes, among the latter the celebrated "*foie gras.*"

Fish, eggs, vegetables and sweets are some of the best of the good dishes in France, perhaps from the fact that these must form the only fare on one, if not two days a week; and looking at the question of this prescribed diet from a healthful and not a religious point of view, it almost seems a pity we cannot observe the same custom here, and not think meat an absolutely essential element in our daily food. French bread, as well as most other cookery, is known well in England, and in this, like all the other branches of the art, there is much more variety than we can boast.

GERMAN COOKERY.

In these days it is so easy to travel that many of us have had opportunities of trying foreign dishes and testing the merits of foreign cookery; but, unless they have been a good deal abroad, English people are too apt to find fault with the dishes placed before them, merely from the fact that the food is prepared in a way totally different from the form in which they are accustomed to see it.

This is a mistake, for one may thus often lose a dainty dish from the fear of not liking it or from prejudice, the recipe for which we might have found a valuable addition to our cookery books.

Germans *should* be good cooks, for in no other country is it so much a part of the education of the girls as there. It is considered absolutely necessary for the German *hausfrau* in the middle and upper middle class, besides those in a lower station in life, to thoroughly understand the cooking of their country. In many cases where the income would not warrant the keeping of a good cook the German housewife will take the head of the kitchen herself; and in establishments where a cook, as well as other servants, is kept, it is no unusual thing for a mistress to spend her mornings in personal supervision of the chief meal of the day.

Germans rise earlier than we do, and therefore are accustomed to take an earlier breakfast, which with them is a very informal meal. The cloth is laid without either plates or knives; and the breakfast itself consists only of hot rolls and coffee. If, as it sometimes happens, this breakfast is served between 6 and 7, about 10 there is a sort of snatch luncheon consisting only of fruit and cakes; for not later than one o'clock arrives the chief meal of the day, the early dinner.

At this is ordinarily served soup, bouilli, with sauces and pickles, a roast, two vegetables and a sweet. After

this meal comes the 4 o'clock coffee, with its accompanying substantial cakes. It must be remembered that, rising so early, the work in a German household is almost or quite done before the principal repast; and therefore, they are more in a position to enjoy it than we should be so early in the day.

At between 7 and 8 comes supper, which is either hot or cold according to the season of the year, and in summer this sometimes consists of an extremely nice dish called "thick milk." The milk is taken fresh and put into large stone jars in a cold cellar, and after three or four days comes out quite solid. The cream is first taken off and made quite smooth with a wooden spoon in a tureen, then the milk is broken up and added, spoonful by spoonful, until the whole mass is perfectly smooth. It is then served with grated bread-crumbs, powdered sugar and cinnamon. In winter hot soups are commonly served, and after that the inevitable "sausage" in some form or other. Late dinners are not a common thing in Germany, and in place of these, guests are more bidden to suppers, which are sometimes quite elaborate meals, equivalent to late dinners and served on tables decorated as our own.

One of the branches of German cookery most esteemed by the English is the making of cakes and sweets, in which we must confess ourselves most behind-hand. Here it is only in comparatively few households that we find people capable of making the more elaborate kinds of fancy cakes or pastry; and should we desire such, it is too often the fact that we *buy* them. But in Germany every household can supply its own sweets, be they rich or plain; although, strange to say, it is not a common thing to find the making and baking of bread done at home.

One of the greatest contrasts between German cookery and our own is in the seasoning of the meats and vegetables. What we are accustomed to enjoy in a plain form, such as a well roasted joint and plainly boiled vegetables, they would consider only half prepared for table. True it is that our meat is superior to that of most foreign countries and does not so much need the seasoning of herbs, &c., used in Germany; but we must acknowledge we might, with advantage, make our cooked vegetables more savoury. These are most daintily prepared and serve for dishes in themselves, instead of being merely belongings of the joint with no more individuality than its gravy.

The greatest lesson we can learn from cookery in Germany as in France, is, however, *economy*. When butter is at its cheapest, it is bought in quantities, clarified and stored; eggs when most plentiful are rubbed over with salad oil, to form a supply for winter's use; apple parings are made into jelly and the fruit used for tarts, and so on *ad infinitum*.

Two great institutions in German cookery are *nudeln* (a sort of macaroni), and sausages; while the pickled fish of the country are deservedly esteemed. We give a recipe for *nudeln*, so we need only say that it is used in a very large number of dishes of all kinds—soup, meat and sweets. The sausages of Germany are now so well known in England; suffice it to say that they are of infinite variety and size; and their patés, brawns and galantines are extremely good.

AMERICAN COOKERY.

Now that we receive American provisions in such good condition, it is as well we should know something about American cookery. We give, therefore, some recipes for the cooking of those provisions with which we are already familiar, together with some for purely American dishes that as yet we have not had an opportunity of trying here, feeling sure that ere long means will be found to bring the required ingredients within our reach.

Amongst the plentiful supply of fresh provisions in America, fish takes a prominent place, and forms a larger diet than here. The immense extent of the American coasts, Atlantic and Pacific, supplemented by the large lakes and rivers, yield an ample supply of not only those fish familiar to us, but many others as yet unknown, amongst which are those named from their colour, such as the blue and the white fish, and the celebrated clam, while oysters are extremely plentiful and far too cheap to be considered a luxury. Game (although not preserved as here), poultry vegetables and fruit are all found in abundance in America.

One lesson we might learn from the Americans, and that is to make a greater variety in our bread and breakfast and tea-cakes. There is a terrible sameness in this branch of bakery in England, and we seldom rise above white or brown bread, tea-cakes, muffins or hot rolls; while at American breakfast - tables breads of various flours (often blended), dainty biscuits, crackers, and many other nice substitutes for these will be found to vary the monotony of these necessary adjuncts of the meals.

American drinks, candies, and ice creams we scarcely need speak of here, for they have come to us and been appreciated by most English people. We ought to be grateful to Americans for having introduced us to the fluid beef, and other preparations of meat that form such good substitutes for alcoholic drinks in the cold weather, putting strength as well as life into our bodies when at all overcome by cold or fatigue. The iced drinks for summer we think are far less valuable, for, though very refreshing for the time, they have, when partaken of very freely, an injurious effect.

INDIAN COOKERY.

The English housekeeper in India cannot undertake the personal supervision of the kitchen, which, in many cases, may be some distance away from the house or bungalow, but she will soon learn that it is impossible to treat or to trust Indian servants as we can our English ones. The cook, having the marketing to do, will in all probability try to make out of it some profit for himself; it is, therefore, necessary that the mistress of the household should make herself acquainted with the regular prices for all provisions, as also the value of the various coins, so as to have to some extent a check upon undue expenditure. A sensible relief to an English housekeeper going to India is the fact that she has only to provide for herself and family, and not for the large number of servants required for the daily duties, whose wages are always given to include their board.

Meat in India, having to be eaten so soon after it is killed, is never very good, the beef especially being very coarse and tasteless ; but in an Indian cook's hands it is made to form very tasty dishes. These cooks are generally very clever, and will turn out a good dinner from materials that would not serve for the plainest one in ordinary houses. Poultry is good and plentiful, and game is the latter, but rather wanting flavour. Chickens, fowls and rabbits are quite staple foods, and snipe, teal and quail (particularly the last named bird) are excellent in India. In such a thirsty climate drink is often a serious item in housekeeping, and English people are too apt to give way to what is after all more of a habit than of necessity, and take more liquid than can do them good

The water, unfortunately, is generally very bad, so filled with animalculæ that it has to be boiled and filtered, and so rendered more flat and unpalatable as a beverage. To take its place there are some most refreshing drinks made from the juice of the lime and other fruits, and iced tea is another pleasant one, but unfortunately the predilection is in favour of alcoholic drinks, and these are very expensive. Amongst them bottled beer, soda and brandy have the largest consumption.

The quantity and variety of the fruit in India is well known, but to many English persons the lack of the *quality* of our fruit at home prevents their due appreciation of them. Amongst the best of Indian fruits are generally considered mangoes, bananas, dates, melons, and cocoa-nuts. Vegetables are not so plentiful as fruit, and the cooks make too often a substitute for them of rice; but with proper care English vegetables will grow, and Indian cooks soon learn to prepare them in the form most preferred.

INVALID COOKERY.

There is no form of cookery that requires more thought and care than that intended for the diet of the sick.

The choice of the food alone is a difficult question—to select what will nourish each particular individual in each particular case, for what is good for one person is not necessarily good for another, even if they be suffering from the same complaint.

It would be well for those who nurse the sick, whether amateur or professional, to know for themselves the value and the constituents of the food they have to administer.

A sick person's diet is as important as his physic, in fact, in many cases it is his physic—in the dietary cures of which we have before spoken. It should, therefore, be prepared as carefully as medicine would be mixed, and administered with the greatest consideration and punctuality.

A sick-room diet, particularly in the case of long and serious illness, should be one that will give the least possible work to that part of the digestive canal that is least able to bear it; to compensate for the waste and drain upon the system. To ensure this, the doctor will prescribe the diet as well as the medicine, and his instructions should be faithfully carried out. It is cruel kindness to give whatever a sick person craves for, in defiance of doctors' opinions. For example, after a fever a person may develop an abnormal appetite which it would be dangerous to gratify.

LITTLE AND OFTEN.

A much more common difficulty in dealing with the sick is to get them to take enough food; but this is sometimes the fault of the nurse. With the kindest intentions, she will bring a plateful of jelly or a basin of beef-tea to her patient, and he will reject it with disgust, because, in his weak state, the sight of so much food is most distasteful to him; whereas, did she but bring a few spoonfuls at a time, he might rouse himself to make the slight exertion that the swallowing of a small quantity would entail.

Give little food and often. What is taken willingly and with relish, if even a very little, does more good than double the amount swallowed with disgust.

PUNCTUALITY.

In some cases it is absolutely essential that to get the patient to take any food at all, it must be only given exactly when he chooses to take it, but as a rule there are times and hours dictated. In these cases, punctuality is of the utmost importance. Never let the patient wait for a meal or even a spoonful beyond the appointed time, unless asleep and it is undesirable to wake him. Most essential is this in the small hours of the morning, when the patient's strength is at its lowest ebb. This is the most trying time for the amateur nurse, but, feeling as she will probably feel then, weak and worn out, she must remember that so will her patient be, and be careful that both food and medicine be punctually given. If kept waiting, most patients lose their desire to eat, and will reject the food when brought. When there is no

KITCHEN UTENSILS.

Household Weighing Machine.

Oval Boiling Pot.

Turbot Kettle.

Copper Preserving Pan.

Fish Kettle.

Bain Marie Pans.

Iron Stockpot, with tap.

Saucepan and Steamer.

Steak Tongs.

Fish Slice.

appetite, give such food as affords the most nourishment with the least amount of exertion either to teeth or digestion. Put the greatest amount of nourishment into the smallest space, and let the food, if solid, be divided.

LEAVING FOOD IN THE ROOM.

Never leave food in a sick-room. If the patient cannot eat it, take it away out of the room, and bring it again after a due interval.

Miss Nightingale says, " To leave the patient's untasted food by his side from meal to meal, in hopes that he will take it in the interval, is simply to prevent him taking food at all. I have known patients literally incapacitated from taking any one article of food after another from this piece of ignorance. Let the food come at the right time, and be taken away, eaten or uneaten, at the right time; but never let a patient have ' something always standing by him,' if you don't wish to disgust him with everything."

IN CASES OF INFECTION.

When disease is infectious, no one should take any of the food that comes from the sick-room ; anything that remains should be burnt. In acute diseases the diet is generally limited to liquids, such as milk and beef-tea. The former is the best food of any in such cases, and it is a most fortunate thing if the patient is able to take it. If he cannot digest it as it is, he may possibly be able to do so if it be boiled and given warm, or if it be mixed with lime-water or soda-water.

When every preparation of fresh milk has been used in vain, whey is sometimes found useful, also koumiss, or fermented milk may be tried. In many illnesses the patient suffers from sickness and nausea, when all food should be given iced or as cold as possible. Milk may be stood on ice for a long time, and if no ice is at hand it is a good plan to wrap a wet cloth round the jug containing it and stand it outside window or door in a draught; it can also be made cooler by setting the jug in a pan of salt and water.

KEEPING FOOD HOT.

There is often a difficulty in keeping food hot in a sick-room. The best thing we knew to do this is a Norwegian cooking apparatus, a box thickly padded with a non-conducting material containing a double tin receptacle, the outer for the hot water and the inner for the food that has to be kept hot. In this, beef-tea or other preparations may be kept hot for some hours.

BEEF TEA.

A word about beef-tea may not be out of place. It is the most common of all invalid food, but it is really not a very nourishing one, for there is not more than half an ounce of solid in a whole pint of beef-tea ; yet it is something of a stimulant and is very generally prescribed by medical men. If it can be varied, and given alternately with other food, it is better. We give recipes for beef-tea, but we may remark here that it should never be made in an iron saucepan ; nor should milk be heated in one. The best beef-tea is that made in the oven. For patients suffering from acute disease it is better to omit the salt or other flavouring, for if the tea be made as strong as possible it will, in all probability, when the organs of taste are in an extremely sensitive condition, taste too salt from the presence of the saline matter in the meat. A nourishing food can be made of raw beef, scraped free from fibre, seasoned with a little pepper and salt, and served as sandwiches between thin bread and butter, or, if for very young children, it may have a little sugar or jam instead of the savoury flavouring. A quickly prepared beef-tea can be made by rubbing raw beef through a sieve and warming it in a little of one of the advertised extracts.

It is generally considered right to skim off every particle of fat from beef-tea, but if the patient does not object to a little being left, it aids in the digestion of the food.

IN CONVALESCENCE.

In convalescence, invalid diet is comparatively easy to manage, though it may take longer to prepare the food from the fact that it should be as *varied* as possible.

Never make a large quantity of anything at one time, thinking that what the invalid has liked he may continue to like, for in nine cases out of ten his appetite will be very capricious. Never let him get tired of any food.

In convalescence eggs are valuable, and are easily digested if beaten to a froth with a little sugar, if liked, and a spoonful of brandy, if desirable. If they are cooked, they should be done very lightly. Sago, tapioca, and bread puddings are generally acceptable to the invalid after a long course of beef-tea, broth, arrowroot, and jelly. The next step is generally to fish, of which the first should be whiting, as it is of all fish the easiest of digestion. It is condemned by many as tasteless, but this can be remedied if a nice sauce be served with it, the foundation of which may be melted butter.

Mutton is generally the first meat an invalid is allowed to take; but, if in season, lamb is more delicate. Whichever meat it is, it should not be fat, nor should it be fried for the first meat meal. The most digestible way of cooking it is by stewing. We give a very nice recipe for an invalid's cutlet in our recipes for invalid cookery. In everything prepared for a sick-room the greatest attention must be paid to cleanliness. If the kitchen utensils are not scrupulously clean, some disagreeable flavour may be imparted to the preparation. A flavour, it may be, imperceptible to the healthy palate, but perfectly obvious to the sick person. It is safer to use china or earthenware than metal for very delicate cookery.

GENERAL REMARKS.

A good nurse will always serve a patient's food in the most dainty and tempting way possible, and will see that everything the invalid uses is exquisitely clean. Glass will be bright, silver burnished, napkin unsoiled, saucers free from slops. Although the sick person may not be able to comment upon the way his food is served, he will most likely notice every detail; and, in a weak state, there is actual pain or pleasure in them to him. Let the food itself be made to look as tempting as possible—garnished as prettily as taste may devise. In health we like to see our food nicely and daintily served, but in sickness it is absolutely necessary that it should be so, and while we do not grudge the trouble of cooking the food, we need not mind that of arranging it as carefully as possible to suit the tastes of our invalids.

One or two little things in connection with serving invalid's food we must not forget to mention. In the first place see that his position is as comfortable as it can be made to partake of the meal or draught; take care that there be nothing spilt in a saucer from which he has to lift a cup, so that sheet or dress may not be soiled, also be careful that no crumbs are left in the bed.

VARIOUS FOODS.

The most abundant and the cheapest are the starch and floury foods. Bread, potatoes, rice, barley, and other floury foods contain a large proportion of starch, while cornflour, arrowroot, sago, and tapioca contain but very little else.

There is starch in beans and peas, but they also contain a large amount of casein, and are, therefore, usually spoken of as albuminoids, or flesh-forming foods.

There is no starch in milk, but it is, nevertheless, as a single food, the most perfect, and said to sustain life alone longer than any other.

Sugar is a good food and replaces starch, but it is apt to produce acidity if used too freely.

Fats, starches and sugars are called heat-givers because they are oxydised in the body to keep it up to its proper temperature. From the starch and sugars fat is deposited, if more is consumed than is required to burn, therefore those who wish to get thin should eat little or none of these, or take sufficient exercise to burn them up.

Fat is a very necessary element in food, and should be eaten in some form or other by every one. By fat we mean not only the fat of meat, but butter, cream, oil, or dripping. Of these the most easily digested are cream and oil; hence the ordering of these for delicate or consumptive persons who have often a very great dislike to, or who cannot digest the fat of fresh meat or bacon.

Fat and starch, to a certain extent, replace one another. Carbonate and salts include besides common salt, potash, phosphates of lime and iron.

Iron is generally looked upon as a medicine rather than a food, but all others are necessary foods. Lime is wanted to make bone, and should be found in milk for the young. When it has been absent we often see weak and rickety limbs and broken and decayed teeth. Potash salt is found in all fresh vegetables and fruits; and a common defect in diet is the lack of these. Common salt, being used for dried fish and flesh, finds too large a place in the diet of the poorer classes.

Albuminoids, or flesh formers, are supplied by lean meat, poultry, game, fish, cheese, eggs, gelatine, gluten in flour, fibrine in oats and in beans, peas, and lentils. Albumen, which exists most largely in eggs, is also found in meat, the blood of animals containing it also. It may be discovered in vegetable juices as well as in seeds and nuts.

Flesh formers being as a rule more expensive than the starchy foods, the poor often suffer from the want of them.

It is reckoned that a good diet for a healthy man, doing a moderate amount of work, should consist of 22½ oz. in the following proportions by avoirdupois.

Albuminoids 3
Fats, starch, sugar, &c... 14
Salts 1
Water.. .. .. 4½
                    22½

For a woman the ration should be about 3 oz. smaller, but the proportions the same. The various constituents of a healthy diet being yielded alike by both the animal and the vegetable world, it is clear that we can draw our supplies from either; and those who prefer what is termed a vegetarian diet need not find it less nourishing than another in which animal food enters.

FRESH PROVISIONS AND THEIR COST.

Under the head of "Times when things are in Season," we give a list of all the fresh provisions to be obtained in each month; but as to many of us a more important question is the cost of the article, we give the following price list in addition.

TABLE OF SEASONS AND PRICES OF FRESH PROVISIONS.

MEAT.

(Meat, with the exception of early lamb, varies but little in price the year round.)

SEASONS AND PRICES OF BEEF, DIFFERENT JOINTS AND PARTS.

PART.	IN SEASON.	BEST.	AVERAGE PRICE.
Aitch-bone	All the year ..	During Winter ..	7d. per lb.
Brisket	,, ..	,, ..	7d. ,,
Buttock	,, ..	,, ..	9d. ,,
,, (in Steaks) ..	,, ..	,, ..	1s. ,,
Fillet	,, ..	,, ..	1s. 2d. ,,
Neck	,, ..	,, ..	6d. ,,
Rump	,, ..	,, ..	9d. ,,
,, (in Steaks) ..	,, ..	,, ..	1s. 1d. ,,
Silverside	,, ..	,, ..	9d. ,,
Sirloin	,, ..	,, ..	11d. ,,
Ox-cheek	,, ..	,, ..	5d. ,,
Heart	,, ..	,, ..	2s. each
Kidney	,, ..	,, ..	10d. per lb.
Tail..	,, ..	,, ..	From 2s. 6d. each
Tongue	,, ..	,, ..	From 3s. 6d. each

SEASONS AND PRICES OF VEAL, DIFFERENT JOINTS AND PARTS.

PART.	IN SEASON.	BEST.	AVERAGE PRICE.
Breast	Feb. to Nov. ..	Summer	8d. per lb.
Cutlet	,, ..	,, ...	1s. 2d. per lb.
Fillet	,, ..	,, ...	1s. per lb.
Knuckle..	,, ..	,, ...	7d. per lb.
Loin	,, ..	,, ...	10d. per lb.
Shoulder	,, ..	,, ...	8½d. per lb.
Head (half)	,, ..	,, ...	3s. 6d. each
Heart	,, ..	,, ...	8d. to 1s. each
Sweetbread	,, ..	,, ...	From 3s.

SEASONS AND PRICES OF MUTTON, DIFFERENT JOINTS AND PARTS.

PART.	IN SEASON.	BEST.	AVERAGE PRICE.
Breast	All the year ..	Sept. to April ..	5d. per lb.
Leg	,, ..	,, ..	10d. ,,
Loin	,, ..	,, ..	9½d. ,,
Neck (Best End)	,, ..	,, ..	9½d. ,,
,, (Scrag).. ..	,, ..	,, ..	7d. ,,
Saddle	,, ..	,, ..	10d. ,,
Shoulder	,, ..	,, ..	9d. ,,
Head	,, ..	,, ..	1s. each
Heart	,, ..	,, ..	4d. to 5d. each
Kidneys	,, ..	,, ..	3d. each
Chops	,, ..	,, ..	10d. per lb.

SEASONS AND PRICES OF LAMB, DIFFERENT JOINTS AND PARTS.

PART.	IN SEASON.	BEST.	AVERAGE PRICE.
Breast	March to Sept...	May to July ..	9d. per lb.
Fore-quarters	,, ..	,, ..	10d. per lb.
Hind-quarters	,, ..	,, ..	1s. per lb.
Leg	,, ..	,, ..	1s. per lb.
Loin	,, ..	,, ..	1s. per lb.
Neck (Best End)	,, ..	,, ..	11d. per lb.
,, (Scrag)	,, ..	,, ..	8d. per lb.
Shoulder	,, ..	,, ..	10d. per lb.
Fry	,, ..	,, ..	About 8d. per lb.

SEASONS AND PRICES OF PORK, DIFFERENT JOINTS AND PARTS.

PART.	IN SEASON.	BEST.	AVERAGE PRICE.
Hand	Sept. to April ..	Nov. to March ..	7½d. per lb.
Fore-loin	,, ..	,, ..	9d. ,,
Hind-loin	,, ..	,, ..	9d. ,,
Leg	,, ..	,, ..	8½d. ,,
Spare rib	,, ..	,, ..	8d. ,,
Spring	,, ..	,, ..	8d. ,,
,, (salted)	,, ..	,, ..	8d. ,,

FISH.
SEASONS AND PRICES OF FISH OF VARIOUS KINDS.

NAME OF FISH.	IN SEASON.	BEST AND CHEAPEST.	AVERAGE PRICE.
Bloaters..	Sept. to April ..	In Winter	1s. to 2s. per doz.
Bream	All the year ..	Autumn	8d. each
Brill	Aug. to May ..	In Winter	1s. to 5s. each
Carp	Nov. to March ..	Jan. & Feb. ..	4d. to 1s. per lb.
Cockles	All the year ..	Summer	2d. to 4d. per quart
Cod	Aug. to April ..	Nov. to Jan. ..	4d. to 1s. per lb.
Chub	June to Dec. ..	Summer	4d. to 6d. per lb.
Crabs	April to Oct. ..	,, ...	1s. to 3s. each
Crayfish..	All the year ..	,, ...	1s. to 3s. per doz.
Dory	,, ..	Winter	1s. to 5s. each
Eels	June to March ..	Sept. to Nov. ..	9d. to 1s. 2d. per lb.
Flounders	All the year ..	Aug. to Nov. ..	1d. to 8d. each
Haddocks	Aug. to Feb. ..	Winter	4d. to 1s. each
Hake	June to March ..	,, ..	6d. to 8d. per lb.
Halibut	Aug. to March ..	,, ...	4d. to 1s. per lb.
Herrings	May to Jan. ..	June to Sept. ..	6d. to 1s. per doz.
Ling	Aug. to March ..	Autumn	4d. to 6d. per lb.
Lobsters..	All the year ..	Summer	9d. to 4s. each
Mackerel	March to Sept...	April to July ..	4d. to 6d. each
Mullet (Grey)	Nearly all the yr.	Winter	4d. to 1s. each
,, (Red)..	,,	April to Oct. ..	10d. to 1s. 6d. each
Mussels	Sept. to April ..	Winter	1d. to 3d. per quart
Oysters	Aug. to April ..	,, ...	1s. to 4s. per doz.
Plaice	All the year ..	May to Nov. ..	6d. to 1s. per lb.
Prawns	,, ..	May to Dec. ..	6d. to 1s. per doz.
Salmon	Feb. to Sept. ..	Spring, Summer	1s. to 4s. per lb.
Shad	,, ..	May to Aug. ..	6d. to 9d. per lb.
Shrimps..	All the year ..	April to Nov. ..	3d. to 4d. per pint
Skate	Sept. to April ..	Oct. to March ..	4d. to 1s. per lb.
Scallops	Spring ..	Jan. to June ..	6d. to 1s. per doz.
Smelts	Oct. to May ..	Winter	6d. to 2s. per doz.
Soles	All the year ..	April to July ..	1s. to 2s. per lb.
Sprats	Nov. to Feb. ..	Nov. & Dec. ..	1d. to 3d. per lb.
Sturgeon	April to Sept. ..	Summer	9d. to 1s. 1d. per lb.
Trout	,, ..	April to July ..	1s. to 2s. per lb.
Turbot	All the year ..	Spring, Summer	3s. to 15s. each
Whitebait	Jan. to Sept. ..	Feb. to May ..	1s. 6d. to 2s. 6d. pint
Whiting..	All the year ..	Spring, Summer	3d. to 9d. each

POULTRY.
SEASONS AND PRICES OF POULTRY OF VARIOUS KINDS.

POULTRY.	IN SEASON.	BEST AND CHEAPEST.	AVERAGE PRICE.
Chickens	Feb. to Oct. ..	June to Sept. ..	2s. to 3s. 6d. each
Ducklings	March to Aug...	May to July ..	2s. 6d. to 3s. 6d. each
Ducks	Aug. to Feb. ..	Sept. & Oct. ..	2s. 6d. to 3s. 6d. each
Fowls	All the year ..	June to Oct. ..	2s. 6d. to 3s. 6d. each
Geese	Sept. to Feb. ..	Sept. to Nov. ..	6s. to 10s. each
,, (green)	May to Aug. ..	June	6s. to 9s. each
Guinea Fowl	Feb. to Aug. ..	Summer	3s. to 4s. each
Larks	Sept. to Dec. ..	November	2s. to 3s. per doz.
Pigeons	Aug. to April ..	Winter	9d. to 1s. each
,, (Bordeaux) ..	All the year ..	,, ...	1s. to 1s. 4d. each
Rabbits	,, ..	Oct. to Feb. ..	1s. to 1s. 6d. each
,, (Ostend) ..	,, ..	,, ..	7d. & 8d. per lb.
Turkeys	Oct. to March ..	Nov. to Jan. ..	10s. to 21s. each

GAME.

SEASONS AND PRICES OF GAME OF VARIOUS KINDS.

GAME.	IN SEASON.	BEST AND CHEAPEST.	AVERAGE PRICE.
Blackcock	Aug. to Nov. ..	Sept. & Oct. ..	3s. to 4s. brace
Ducks (wild)	Oct. to Dec. ..	Nov. & Dec. ..	3s. to 4s. brace
Grouse	Aug. to Nov. ..	September ..	3s. 6d. to 5s. brace
Hares	Sept. to March..	October	3s. 6d. to 5s. each
Leverets	Aug. to Sept. ..	August	3s. to 4s. each
Partridges	Sept. to Feb. ..	Oct. & Nov. ..	3s. to 5s. brace
Pheasants	Oct. to Feb. ..	Winter	5s. to 7s. brace
Plovers	,, ..	,, ...	1s. to 1s. 6d. each
Ptarmigan	Sept. to April ..	September.. ..	1s. to 1s. 6d. each
Quail	Sept. to Feb. ..	Sept. & Oct. ..	1s. to 1s. 6d. each
Snipe	Aug. to Feb. ..	Oct. & Nov. ..	2s. 6d. to 3s. 6d. brace
Teal	,, ..	Winter	1s. to 1s. 6d. each
Venison (Buck) ..	June to Sept. ..	July & Aug. ..	1s. to 2s. per lb.
,, (Doe)	Oct. to Dec. ..	November.. ..	1s. to 2s. per lb.
Widgeon	Oct. to Feb. ..	Sept. & Oct. ..	1s. to 1s. 6d. each
Woodcock	,, ..	,, ..	3s. 6d. to 5s. brace

VEGETABLES.

SEASONS AND PRICES OF VEGETABLES OF VARIOUS KINDS.

VEGETABLES.	IN SEASON.	BEST AND CHEAPEST.	AVERAGE PRICE.
Artichokes (Globe) ..	June to Oct. ..	August	3d. to 6d. each
,, (Jerusalem)	Nov. to Feb. ..	December	1½d. to 2d per lb.
Asparagus	March to July ..	April & May ..	1s. 6d. to 4s. 6d. bundle
Beans (French)	May to Nov. ..	Sept. & Oct. ..	2d. to 4d. per lb.
,, (Broad)	June to Aug. ..	August	6d. to 8d. per peck
,, (Runner)	July to Oct. ..	Aug. & Sept. ..	2d. to 4d. per lb.
Beetroot	All the year ..	Autumn	1d. to 3d. each
Broccoli,different kinds	..	,, ...	2d. to 3d. each.
Sprouts	Jan. to May ..	April	1d. to 2d. per lb.
,, (Brussels) ..	Sept. to Feb. ..	Oct. to Dec. ..	2d. to 4d. per lb.
Cabbages	All the year ..	Spring, Summer	1d. to 2d. each
,, (red)	Oct. to Feb. ..	Nov. & Dec. ..	4d. to 6d. each
Carrots	All the year ..	Autumn	4d. to 6d. per bunch
Cauliflower	May to Aug. ..	July	2d. to 6d. each
Celery	Oct. to March ..	Oct. to Dec. ..	1d. to 6d. per stick
Cucumbers	May to Oct. ..	Summer	2d. to 1s. 4d. each
Endive	Sept to March ..	Oct. & Nov. ..	1d. to 6d. each
Horseradish	All the year ..	Winter	1d. to 2d. per stick
Leeks	Oct. to May ..	Oct. & Nov. ..	4d. to 6d. per bunch
Lettuces	May to Nov. ..	July & Aug. ..	1d. to 2d. each
,, (French)	Dec. to May ..	Winter	2d. to 4d. each
Onions	All the year ..	Sum. & Aut. ..	1d. to 2d. per lb.
,, (Spring)	March to June ..	April & May ..	1d. & 2d. per bunch
Parsnips	Oct. to April ..	Winter	1d. & 2d. each
Peas	June to Sept. ..	July & Aug. ..	6d. to 2s. per peck
Potatoes	All the year ..	Autumn	9d. to 1s. per peck
,, (new)	May to Sept. ..	June & July ..	3d. to 8d. per lb.
Radishes	,, ..	June to Aug. ..	1d. per bunch
Savoys	Oct. to March ..	Nov. to Jan. ..	1d. to 4d. each
Sea Kale	Jan. to May ..	Feb. & March ..	1s. to 2s. 6d. per basket
Spinach	All the year ..	Summer	2d. to 4d. per lb.
Tomatoes	June to Dec. ..	Sept. & Oct. ..	4d. to 8d. per lb.
Vegetable Marrow ..	June to Oct. ..	Aug. & Sept. ..	1d. to 6d. each
Watercress	All the year ..	Summer	1d. per bunch

FRUIT.
SEASONS AND PRICES OF FRUIT OF VARIOUS KINDS.

FRUIT.	IN SEASON.	BEST AND CHEAPEST.	AVERAGE PRICE.
Apples	All the year ..	Oct. to Dec. ..	2d. to 6d. per lb.
Apricots	June to Sept. ..	August	1s. 6d. to 3s. 6d. dos.
Bullaces	Autumn	October ..	1d. to 3d. per lb.
Cherries	June to Aug. ..	July	4d. to 8d. per lb.
Currants	July to Sept. ..	August	3d. to 8d. per lb.
Damsons	Sept. to Oct. ..	October ..	1d. to 4d. per lb.
Figs	July to Sept. ..	August	1d. to 3d. each.
Gooseberries	July to Sept. ..	August	4d. to 8d. per quart
,, (Green) ..	May to July ..	June	3d. to 6d. per quart
Grapes (Foreign) ..	All the year ..	Autumn ..	4d. to 8d. per lb.
,, (Hothouse) ..	Sept. to Dec. ..	October ..	2s. per lb. & upwards
Greengages	July to Sept. ..	August ..	3d. to 6d. per lb.
Medlars	Oct. to Jan. ..	Oct. & Nov ..	4d. to 8d. per lb.
Melons	June to Nov. ..	October ..	1s. to 3s. each
Nectarines	Sept. & Oct. ..	,, ..	3s. to 4s. per doz.
Oranges	All the year ..	Winter ..	From 4d. per doz.
Peaches	Sept. & Oct. ..	October ..	4s. to 8s. per doz.
Pears	Oct. to March ..	Oct. & Nov. ..	1d. to 6d. each
Pines	Sept. to Dec. ..	October ..	5s. to 15s. each
,, (Foreign) ..	June to Nov. ..	September ..	1s. to 3s. each
Plums	Aug. to Oct. ..	Sept. & Oct. ..	2d. to 6d. per lb.
Quinces	Sept. & Oct. ..	October ..	2s. to 3s. per doz.
Rhubarb	Jan. to July ..	April & May ..	4d. to 8d. per bunch
Strawberries	June to Sept. ..	July	4d. to 1s. per lb.

DAIRY PRODUCE, ETC.
BUTTER, CHEESE, BACON, &c.

ARTICLE.	AVERAGE PRICE.	ARTICLE.	AVERAGE PRICE.
Butter, Fresh ..	1s. to 1s. 3d. per lb.	Eggs, Geese's ..	3s. to 4s. per doz.
,, English ..	1s. 2d. to 1s. 4d. per lb.	,, Guinea fowls' ..	1s. to 2s. per doz.
,, Foreign ..	1s. 3d. to 1s. 6d. per lb.	,, Plovers' ..	4s. to 5s. per doz.
,, Dorset ..	1s. 2d. to 1s. 4d. per lb.	,, Turkeys' ..	3s. to 4s. per doz.
,, Salt	10d. to 1s. per lb.	Milk, New	3d. & 4d. per quart
,, Margarine	6d. to 8d. per lb.	,, Separated ..	1½d. to 2d. per quart
Cheese, American	7d. to 9d. per lb.	Cream	2s. to 3s. per pint
,, Cheddar ..	10d. per lb.	Whey	2d. per pint
,, Cheshire ..	10d. per lb.	Bacon, best parts	10d. and 11d. per lb.
,, Cream ..	6d. each	,, Rolled ..	7d. per lb.
,, Dutch ..	7d. per lb.	Ham, English ..	11d. & 1s. per lb.
,, Gorgonzola	10d. & 1s. per lb.	,, American	6d. to 8d. per lb.
,, Grugere ..	10d. & 1s. per lb.	Lard	6d. to 8d. per lb.
,, Stilton ..	1s. per lb.	Pork, Pickled ..	8d. per lb.
Eggs, Hens'	1s. to 2s. 6d. per doz.	Sausages	9d. to 1s. per lb.
,, Ducks' ..	1s. to 3s. per doz.		

These prices are the ordinary ones charged at good shops in London and other large towns for the best provisions. Cheaper and inferior ones are to be purchased, as, for example, American meat, and that and poultry, which is imported in a frozen state; also French eggs; but the articles named in our lists, with the exception of some of the cheeses, are fresh home produce. In our Chapter on "Marketing" will be found instructions for choosing all sorts of fresh provisions, how to judge of their quality and freshness, and other hints for getting the best value for our money.

THE VARIOUS MODES OF COOKING AND PREPARING FOOD

Roasting—Baking—Boiling—Stewing—Frying—Braising—Broiling—Grilling—Sautéing—Steaming—Larding—Barding—Browning.

ROASTING.

OF the various methods of preparing meat this is the most generally appreciated in this country, but it is not the most economical or advantageous, and is not to be recommended for small joints. It is effected by hanging the meat before the fire, and keeping it in motion to prevent the scorching of any particular part. When meat is properly roasted the outer layer of its albumen is coagulated, and thus the natural juices are prevented from escaping. In roasting meat the heat must be strongest at first, and it should then be much reduced. To have a good juicy roast, therefore, the fire must be red and vigorous at the very commencement of the operation. In the most careful roasting some of the juice is squeezed out of the meat, and evaporating on its surface, gives it a dark brown colour, a rich lustre, and a strong aromatic taste. Besides these effects on the albumen and the expelled juice, roasting melts the fat out of the fat cells.

Constant basting is necessary when roasting meat.

Very good roasts can be made in gas ovens.

In stirring the fire, or putting fresh coals on it, the dripping-pan should always be drawn back, so that there may be no danger of the coal, cinders, or ashes falling down into it.

Under each particular recipe there is stated the time required for roasting each joint; but, as a general rule, it may be here noted that for every pound of meat, beef or mutton, in ordinary-sized joints, a quarter of an hour should be allowed.

White meats, and the meat of young animals, require to be very well roasted, both to be pleasant to the palate and easy of digestion. Thus veal, pork, and lamb should be thoroughly done to the centre, and require more time than red meats.

Mutton and beef, on the other hand, do not, generally speaking, require to be so thoroughly done, and they should be dressed to the point that, in carving them, the gravy should just run, but not too freely. Of course, in this, as in most other dishes, the tastes of individuals vary; and there are many who cannot partake, with satisfaction, of any joint unless it is what others would call overdressed.

BAKING.

The principal difference between roasting meat and baking it is that, in baking, the fumes caused by the operation are not carried off in the same way as in roasting. Much, however, of this disadvantage is obviated by the improved construction of modern ovens, and especially those in connection with the best kitcheners and gas-cooking stoves, in which meat, as before stated, can be *roasted* in the oven. With meat baked in the generality of ovens there is undoubtedly a peculiar taste, which does not at all equal the flavour developed by roasting meat.

Should the oven be very brisk, it will be advisable to cover the joint with a piece of white paper, to prevent the meat from being scorched outside before the heat can penetrate into the inside. This paper should be removed half an hour before the time of serving

THE VARIOUS MODES OF COOKING AND PREPARING FOOD 57

dinner, so that the joint may take a good colour.

By means of a jar many dishes may be economically prepared in the oven. The principal of these are soups, gravies, jugged hare, beef tea; and this mode of cooking may be advantageously adopted with a ham, previously covered with a common crust of flour and water. There are some dishes which are at least equally well cooked in the oven as by roasting; thus, a shoulder of mutton and baked potatoes, a fillet or breast of veal, a sucking-pig, a hare well basted, will be received by connoisseurs as well when baked as if they had been roasted. Indeed, the baker's oven, or the family oven, may often, as we have said, be substituted with greater economy and convenience.

BOILING.

Boiling, though one of the easiest processes in cookery, requires careful management. Boiled meat should be tender, savoury, and full of its own juice, or natural gravy; but, through carelessness, it is too often sent to table hard, tasteless, and innutritious. To ensure a successful result the heat of the fire must be judiciously regulated, the proper quantity of water kept up in the pot, and the scum which rises to the surface carefully removed. Only sufficient water to cover the meat should be used in boiling unless the flesh is boiled for the purpose of soup-making.

Many writers on cookery assert that the meat to be boiled should be put into *cold water*, and that the pot should be heated gradually; but Liebig, the highest authority on all matters connected with the chemistry of food, has shown that meat so treated loses some of its most nutritious constituents. "If the flesh," says the great chemist, "be introduced into the boiler when the water is in a state of brisk ebullition, and if the boiling be kept up for a few minutes, and the pot then placed in a warm place, so that the temperature of the water is kept at 158° to 165°, we have the united conditions for giving to the flesh the qualities which best fit it for being eaten." When a piece of meat is plunged into boiling water, the albumen which is near the surface immediately coagulates, forming an envelope, which prevents the escape of the internal juice, and most effectually excludes the

water, which, by mixing with this juice, would render the meat insipid. Meat treated thus is juicy and well-flavoured when cooked, as it retains most of its savoury constituents. On the other hand, if the piece of meat be set on the fire with cold water, and this slowly heated to boiling, the flesh undergoes a loss of soluble and nutritious substances; while, as a matter of course, the soup becomes richer in these matters. The albumen is gradually dissolved from the surface to the centre; the fibre loses, more or less, its quality of shortness or tenderness, and becomes hard and tough: the thinner the piece of meat is the greater is its loss of savoury constituents. This does not, however, apply to salted meat, which is best cooked by putting in cold water, and being brought very slowly to the boil.

In order to obtain well-flavoured and eatable meat, we must relinquish the idea of making good soup from it, as that mode of boiling which yields the best soup gives the driest, toughest, and most vapid meat. Slow boiling whitens the meat; and we suspect that it is on this account that it is in such favour with the cooks. The wholesomeness of food is, however, a matter of much greater moment than the appearance it presents on the table. It should be borne in mind that the whiteness of meat that has been boiled slowly is produced by the loss of some important alimentary properties.

The objections raised to the practice of putting meat on the fire in cold water, apply with equal force to the practice of soaking meat before cooking it, which is so strongly recommended by some cooks. Fresh meat ought never to be soaked, as all its most nutritive constituents are soluble in water. Salted and dried meats, however, require to be soaked for some time in water before they are cooked if they are over salted and hard.

For boiling meat, the softer the water is the better. When spring water is boiled the chalk, which gives to it the quality of hardness, is precipitated. This chalk stains the meat, and communicates to it an unpleasant earthy taste. When nothing but hard water can be procured it should be softened by boiling it for an hour or two before it is used for culinary purposes.

The fire must be watched with great attention during the operation of boiling, so that its heat may be properly regulated. As a rule the pot should be kept in a simmering state, and this cannot be done without vigilance.

The temperature at which water boils, under usual circumstances, is 212° Fahr. Water does not become hotter after it has begun to boil, however long or with whatever violence the boiling is continued. This fact is of great importance in cookery, and attention to it will save much fuel. Water made to boil in a gentle way by the application of a moderate heat is just as hot as when it is made to boil on a strong fire with the greatest possible violence. When once water has been brought to the boiling point the fire may be considerably reduced, as a very gentle heat will suffice to keep the water at its highest temperature.

The scum which rises to the surface of the pot during the operation of boiling must be carefully removed, or it will attach itself to the meat, and thereby spoil its appearance. The cook must not neglect to skim during the whole process, though by far the greater part of the scum rises at first. The practice of wrapping meat in a cloth may be dispensed with if the skimming be skilfully managed. If the scum be removed as fast as it rises, the meat will be cooked clean and pure, and come out of the vessel in which it was boiled, much more delicate and firm than when cooked in a cloth.

When taken from the pot the meat may be wiped if necessary with a clean cloth, or a sponge previously dipped in water and wrung dry. The meat should not be allowed to stand a moment longer than necessary, as boiled meat cannot be eaten too hot.

The time allowed for boiling must be regulated according to the size and quality of the meat. As a general rule, a quarter of an hour or twenty minutes, reckoning from the moment when the boiling commences, may be allowed for every pound of beef or mutton. Veal requires from 20 to 25 minutes per lb., and pork 25 to 30 minutes.

A few observations on the nutritive value of salted meat may be properly introduced in this place. Every housewife knows that dry salt in contact with fresh meat gradually becomes fluid brine. The application of salt causes the fibres of meat to contract, and the juice to flow out from its pores. Now, as this juice is pure

extract of meat, containing albumen, osmazome, and other valuable principles, it follows that meat which has been preserved by the action of salt can never have the nutritive properties of fresh meat.

Fish, to be boiled, should as a rule be put into cold water, and the white-fleshed ones take less time to cook than the red.

Salmon should be put into boiling water.

Poultry should be put into warm water, and be simmered very slowly. The skimming must not be neglected, or the flesh will lose its whiteness.

The vessels used for boiling should be made of cast iron, well tinned within, and provided with closely fitting lids. They must be kept scrupulously clean, otherwise they will render the meat cooked in them unsightly and unwholesome. Copper pans, if used at all, should be reserved for operations that are performed with rapidity ; as, by long contact with copper, food may become dangerously contaminated. The kettle in which a joint is dressed should be large enough to allow room for a good supply of water ; if the meat be cramped and be surrounded with but little water, it will be stewed, not boiled.

STEWING.

In stewing it is not requisite to have so great a heat as in boiling. A gentle simmering in a small quantity of water, so that the meat is stewed almost in its own juices, is all that is necessary. The great merit that this process of cooking possesses is that it will render palatable and nutritious parts of meat that could not be eaten if cooked by any other mode, and it is one of the most (if not *the* most), economical ways of cooking.

It has been said of a frying-pan and a stewpan, that the former is "the poor man's enemy," the latter "his friend."

Too often stewing is confounded with boiling, but they are actually different modes. *A stew should never boil*, as the meat will harden. Cook slowly and long. A large fire is not needed, and there is no process of cooking so easy as stewing. With a gentle heat under the pan we may leave a stew, as one cannot a roast or boil, to take care of itself. According to the quality of the meat, so must the heat of the water used for stewing be regulated. For hard, gristly parts, or for an old fowl, cold water to start with is best, but it may be brought to boiling point before a prime steak or other good piece of meat be put in.

FRYING.

This very favourite mode of cooking may be accurately described as boiling in fat or oil. Substances dressed in this way are generally well received, for they introduce an agreeable variety, possessing, as they do, a peculiar flavour. By means of frying, cooks can soon satisfy many requisitions made on them, it being a very expeditious mode of preparing dishes for the table, and one which can be employed when the fire is not sufficiently large for the purposes of roasting and boiling. The great point to be borne in mind in frying is that the liquid must be hot enough to act instantaneously, as all the merit of this culinary operation lies in the invasion of the boiling liquid, which carbonises or burns, at the very instant of the immersion of the body placed into it. It may be ascertained if the fat is heated to the proper degree by cutting a piece of bread and dipping it in the frying-pan for five or six seconds; and if it be firm and of a dark brown when taken out, put in immediately what you wish to prepare; if it is not, let the fat be heated until of the right temperature. This having been effected, moderate the fire, so that the action may not be too hurried, and that by a continuous heat the juices of the substance may be preserved and its flavour enhanced. A frying basket or kettle must be used for fish and other things that do not supply any fat in themselves. They should be *immersed* in the fat used for frying them, and such things as rissoles and croquettes cannot be properly cooked by dry frying. The oil, butter, or lard used need not be wasted, but can be strained and put away for another frying. All dishes fried in fat should be placed before the fire on a piece of blotting-paper or sieve reversed, and there left for a few minutes, so that any superfluous greasy moisture may be removed.

BRAISING.

One of the most delicious ways of cooking meat, &c., is this. Heat given below by means of the stove on which the braising-pan is placed, and heat above with the hot cinders with which the upper part of the vessel is filled, produces the effect that is obtained by first browning, then stewing.

The meat to be cooked is placed in the pan with sufficient water just to cover it, and vegetables, seasoning, herbs, and spice to thoroughly well flavour it, then the lid is set on, and the whole may be left, as a stewpan, almost to take care of itself. The vegetables, &c., are to help form and flavour the gravy, and when dry meats are cooked in this way they may be larded with advantage, the larded side being uppermost; crispness to the lardoons will be given by the heat above.

The gravy obtained by this method of cookery should be strained, a little browning, thickening, and seasoning added if necessary, and served poured over the meat.

The nearest approach to a braise may be made by first browning chops or steak with some onions and a little butter in a stewpan, then adding some few cut-up vegetables, seasoning, a bouquet of herbs and enough water to cover, and simmering till the meat is tender, when it should be lifted out upon a hot dish, a little thickening of cornflour or ordinary flour added to the gravy, this boiled for two minutes then strained over the meat

BROILING.

This may be done over the fire, but the orthodox way is to enclose the article to be cooked in a broiler, which is hung in front of the fire. This should be heated and the wires greased before using. An old-fashioned Dutch oven may be used for this mode of cooking.

GRILLING.

When by such a simple process as this a chop or steak may be so perfectly cooked, it seems strange that any one should destroy both flavour and quality by *frying* such things.

To grill successfully much depends upon the fire, which should be clear and hot. A little coke put with the coal makes the red, bright heat so essential for the grill, and it is better to cook in any other way than to attempt grilling over a dull or smoky fire. Well hung, juicy meat is served to perfection by grilling.

The grid should first be well heat 1,

then rubbed over with perfectly sweet suet, and meat laid upon this, exposed at once to a fierce heat, will retain its flavour and juices. Beef and mutton are generally preferred with some little red gravy left in, but veal cutlets or pork chops, after the first exposure to the red heat, should be lifted higher from the fire, as they need cooking through. The meat should be turned often upon the grid so as to avoid burning, but not with a fork: if steak tongs are not at hand sugar tongs will suffice.

SAUTÉING.

This mode of cooking is a sort of combination of frying and stewing. The pan used is a very shallow kind of stewpan, in which a little butter or very well clarified fat is melted, then the chop, kidney, or whatever is to be cooked is put into this, and when nearly done the fat is drained off and the article finished in sauce or stock.

This mode of cooking makes a savoury dish of mutton or lamb cutlets or olives.

STEAMING.

The great importance and usefulness of this mode of cooking has till of late been overlooked, but now we begin to realise that steaming is one of the most economical ones known — economical in more than one sense. Not only is a saving of fuel effected by putting, say a steamer full of potatoes over a boiling cabbage, thus using only one space on a stove for two vegetables, but the saving in the actual bulk and worth of articles steamed is great. It is such an easy, simple mode of cooking that it should be a popular one. Take, for example, a pudding, say a batter one. This is placed in the steamer over a boiling saucepan containing something not too strong in flavour to impart smell or taste to the steam given out, and there can be no anxiety on the part of the cook as to the result of the cooking of the pudding, no fear of its being watery or heavy as it may be if boiled, provided it be taken out directly it is done.

For some months of the year before new potatoes are within the reach of the majority, the old ones are almost invariably best when cooked by steam. Meat cooked by steam is delicate in flavour, but unlike vegetables it must be put in a tin of a smaller size than the bottom of the steamer, as it is necessary to preserve the gravy. Slow cooking of this gives more gravy than could be obtained from the water in which a joint is boiled. Double and treble steamers are sometimes used, but for ordinary family cooking two fitted saucepans would be found sufficient.

The rules for steaming are simple enough: To keep the pot underneath that supplies the steam boiling, and to only cook such viands by means of the combination as are not likely to affect one another by smell or taste. Steaming is most useful for re-heating cooked vegetables or other foods.

LARDING.

Dry meats and poultry are far better if larded, and with very little practice larding will not be difficult.

Bacon sold specially for the purpose must be sliced thinly, not more than a quarter of an inch thick, and this must be again cut in strips about three to the inch for a large surface or narrower for a small bird or pieces of meat. The lardoons must then be put into the split end of the needle and drawn through the flesh as we should draw an ordinary cotton through, leaving equal quantities projecting where the needle enters and is drawn out.

The usual length for lardoons is from $1\frac{1}{2}$ to 2 inches, but long strips may be used run in and out again several times as we use cotton, but this is more difficult, particularly in hot weather when the bacon is apt to get soft and break. It should be always kept in a cool place to render it hard and firm, and if it can be laid on ice for a time so much the better. A guinea fowl should always be larded, and the breast of a turkey is better for being so treated; veal also gains much in flavour by larding.

When the larding is completed if the pieces look at all uneven or ragged, they may be snipped into equality with a sharp pair of scissors.

A much simpler method is called

BARDING,

this consisting of placing thin slices of larding bacon with little incisions in them completely to cover that which should be otherwise larded. The bacon may be left on baked or roast articles when the bird or meat is sent to table, when if a little glaze is at hand it should be brushed over with it.

but it should be removed from boiled foods. A string should be used to tie these sheets of bacon upon the article barded, and this way of treating poultry and game saves a great deal of time in the basting that must otherwise be done.

BROWNING.

Namely, to give a bright brown colour to the upper part of many baked dishes, must be done with a salamander or, failing this, a hot shovel. Either one or the other is made red hot and held for a few moments over the dish till a bright brown colouring is given.

Such things as scalloped oysters and macaroni cheese are often quite cooked without being brown on the top, and if they are allowed to remain in the oven till the required colour is reached, they will become too dry.

Gas ovens are fitted so that no salamander is needed, but articles cooked in a kitchener or range oven very often require one to make them look inviting in appearance.

THE COOK'S TIME TABLE.

Times to Allow for Cooking.

When consulting these tables the following facts must be borne in mind :—

In every instance the times allowed for Cooking have been estimated by good average fires, properly kept up and suitable for each particular thing.

That during roasting or baking the joints, &c., have been carefully basted and looked after.

That in boiling the times stated have been after the water boils, and that the skimming has not been neglected.

From these tables it should be found easy to reckon the times to allow for cooking joints of different weights to those given, by adding or deducting in proportion to that stated. Thus, if a joint of ribs of beef weighing 8 lbs. takes 2 hours to roast, and one of 10, 2½ hours, the time allowed will be found 15 minutes to the lb. between those weights, therefore a joint of 9 lbs. should take 2¼ hours if cooked in the same manner.

TIMES TO ALLOW FOR COOKING BEEF BY VARIOUS MODES.

JOINT.	HOW COOKED.	WEIGHT.	TIME.	WEIGHT.	TIME.	WEIGHT.	TIME.
		lbs.	h. m.	lbs.	h. m.	lbs.	h. m.
Aitch-bone	Boiled	8 ..	2 0	10 ..	2 30	12 ..	2 45
Brisket	Boiled	7 ..	2 0	8 ..	2 15	10 ..	2 30
Ribs	Roasted	8 ..	2 0	10 ..	2 30	12 ..	2 45
„ (Boned)	Roasted	7 ..	2 0	9 ..	2 30	11 ..	2 50
Round..	Roasted	6 ..	1 30	9 ..	2 10	12 ..	2 45
Rump-steak	Grilled	1 ..	0 5	2 ..	0 8.	3 ..	0 12
Rump-steak	Fried	1 ..	0 8	2 ..	0 10	3 ..	0 14
Shin	Stewed	6 ..	3 30	8 ..	4 0	10 ..	4 15
Silverside (Salt)	Boiled	7 ..	2 0	10 ..	2 30	14 ..	3 15
Sirloin	Roasted	10 ..	2 35	13 ..	3 15	16 ..	4 0
Heart	Baked	4 ..	1 45	5 ..	1 30	— ..	—
Tail	Stewed	1½ ..	1 30	2 ..	1 50	— ..	—
Tongue	Boiled	6 ..	3 15	— ..	—	— ..	—

TIMES TO ALLOW FOR COOKING VEAL BY VARIOUS MODES.

JOINT.	How Cooked.	Weight.	Time.	Weight.	Time.	Weight.	Time.
		lbs.	h. m.	lbs.	h. m.	lbs.	h. m.
Breast..	Stewed	6 ..	2 15	8 ..	2 30	10 ..	3 0
Cutlet..	Fried	1 ..	0 12	2 ..	0 15	3 ..	0 18
Fillet	Roasted	9 ..	3 45	12 ..	4 15	14 ..	4 30
Knuckle	Stewed	3 ..	2 30	5 ..	2 45	6 ..	3 0
Loin	Roasted	10 ..	2 50	12 ..	3 10	16 ..	3 20
Shoulder	Roasted	8 ..	3 15	10 ..	3 30	12 ..	4 0
Shoulder	Stewed	8 ..	3 80	10 ..	3 50	12 ..	4 10
Head	Boiled	12 ..	2 30	13 ..	2 45	14 ..	3 0
Head	Stewed	12 ..	4 40	13 ..	4 50	14 ..	5 0
Heart	Roasted	1 ..	0 40	1½..	0 50	— ..	—
Sweetbread	Stewed	1 ..	0 25	1½..	0 30	— ..	—

TIMES TO ALLOW FOR COOKING MUTTON BY VARIOUS MODES.

JOINT.	How Cooked.	Weight.	Time.	Weight.	Time.	Weight.	Time.
		lbs.	h. m.	lbs.	h. m.	lbs.	h. m.
Breast..	Boiled	3 ..	1 30	4 ..	1 45	5 ..	2 0
Haunch	Roasted	10 ..	3 20	12 ..	4 0	16 ..	4 30
Leg	Boiled	7 ..	2 0	10 ..	2 30	12 ..	3 0
Leg	Roasted	7 ..	2 0	10 ..	2 30	12 ..	2 45
Loin	Roasted	6 ..	1 40	7 ..	1 50	8 ..	2 10
Neck (Best End)	Roasted	3 ..	0 50	4 ..	1 5	5 ..	1 20
„ (Scrag)	Stewed	1 ..	1 45	1½..	2 0	2 ..	2 10
Saddle	Roasted	12 ..	3 0	14 ..	3 15	16 ..	3 35
Shoulder	Roasted	6 ..	1 30	8 ..	1 45	9 ..	2 0
Head	Boiled	5 ..	1 30	6 ..	1 45	7 ..	2 0
Heart	Roasted	0½..	0 30	— ..	—	— ..	—
Kidney	Grilled	1 ..	0 6	— ..	—	— ..	—

TIMES TO ALLOW FOR COOKING LAMB BY VARIOUS MODES.

JOINT.	How Cooked.	Weight.	Time.	Weight.	Time.	Weight.	Time.
		lbs.	h. m.	lbs.	h. m.	lbs.	h. m.
Breast..	Stewed	1 ..	1 10	2 ..	1 20	3 ..	1 30
Fore-quarter	Roasted	6 ..	1 20	7 ..	1 35	8 ..	1 45
Hind-quarter	Roasted	7 ..	1 35	8 ..	1 45	9 ..	1 50
Leg	Roasted	3 ..	1 20	4 ..	1 30	6 ..	1 40
Loin	Roasted	3 ..	0 50	4 ..	1 5	5 ..	1 15
Neck (Best End)	Baked	2 ..	0 40	3 ..	0 50	4 ..	1 0
Shoulder	Roasted	3 ..	0 50	4 ..	1 0	5 ..	1 10

TIMES TO ALLOW FOR COOKING PORK BY VARIOUS MODES.

PART.	How Cooked.	Weight.	Time.	Weight.	Time.	Weight.	Time.
		lbs.	h. m.	lbs.	h. m.	lbs.	h. m.
Ham (Smoked)..	Baked	8 ..	3 45	10 ..	4 0	12 ..	4 20
Ham	Boiled	8 ..	3 50	10 ..	4 15	12 ..	4 30
Hand	Boiled	3 ..	2 0	4 ..	2 15	5 ..	3 25
Fore-loin	Roasted	6 ..	2 15	8 ..	2 40	10 ..	3 0
Hind-loin	Roasted	6 ..	2 15	8 ..	2 40	12 ..	3 0
Leg	Boiled	6 ..	3 0.	8 ..	3 30	10 ..	4 0
Leg	Roasted	6 ..	2 15	8 ..	3 10	10 ..	3´30
Bacon..	Boiled	2 ..	1 30	4 ..	2 0	6 ..	2 20
Face (half)..	Boiled	2 ..	1 30	3 ..	1 40	4 ..	1 50

TIMES TO ALLOW FOR COOKING FISH BY VARIOUS MODES.

NAME.	How COOKED.	SIZE OR QUANTITY.	TIME.	NAME.	How COOKED.	SIZE OR QUANTITY.	TIME.
			h. m.				h. m.
Bloaters ..	Grilled	Medium.. 0 5		Plaice ..	Broiled	Small .. 0 5	
Brill	Boiled	Medium.. 0 20		„ (Fillets)	Fried	Large .. 0 5	
Cod (Head)	Boiled	Medium.. 0 30		Salmon ..	Boiled	8 lbs. .. 1 0	
„ (Middle)	Boiled	3 lbs. .. 0 30		„ (Head}	Boiled	3 lbs. .. 0 24	
„ Steaks	Fried	Thick .. —		Sho'ld'rs) }			
John Dory	Boiled	Medium.. 0 25		„(Middle)	Boiled	3 lbs. .. 0 30	
Eels	Souché	2 lbs. .. 0 35		„ (Tail)	Boiled	3 lbs. .. 0 28	
Eels	Stewed	2 lbs. .. 0 45		„ Cutlets	Fried	Thick .. 0 7	
Flounders	Fried	Small .. 0 5		Shad ..	Boiled	Medium 0 40	
Haddocks	Baked	Large .. 0 45		Smelts ..	Fried	1 doz. .. 0 5	
„ Dried	Broiled	Medium.. 0 5		Soles ..	Boiled	Large .. 0 9	
Herrings..	Baked	Medium.. 0 30		Soles ..	Fried	Medium 0 7	
Lobster ..	Boiled	Large .. 0 40		Sprats ..	Fried	Medium 0 3	
Lobster ..	Boiled	Small .. 0 30.		Trout ..	Baked	Medium 0 30	
Mackerel ..	Boiled	Large .. 0 13		Trout ..	Stewed	Medium 0 40	
Mackerel ..	Broiled	Small .. 0 10		Turbot ..	Boiled	Large .. 0 30	
Mullet (Red)	Baked	Medium.. 0 25		„ (Cut)..	Boiled	2 lbs. .. 0 15	
„ (Grey)	Baked	Medium.. 0 30		„ (Fillet'd)	Fried	Medium 0 10	
Oysters ..	Scallop'd	Small tin 0 15		Whitebait	Fried	1 quart .. 0 1½	
Plaice ..	Fried	Medium.. 0 5		Whiting..	Fried	Small .. 0 6	

TIMES TO ALLOW FOR COOKING POULTRY AND GAME BY VARIOUS MODES.

NAME.	How COOKED.	SIZE OR QUANTITY.	TIME.	NAME.	How COOKED.	SIZE OR QUANTITY.	TIME.
			h. m.				h. m.
Ducklings	Roasted	Medium.. 0 35		Guinea Fowl	Roasted	Medium 1 0	
Ducks ..	Roasted	Large .. 1 0		Larks ..	Baked	1 doz. .. 0 15	
Fowl.. ..	Boiled	Large .. 1 0		Pigeon ..	Grilled	Medium 0 15	
Fowl.. ..	Boiled	Medium.. 0 45		Pigeon ..	Stewed	Medium 0 30	
Fowl.. ..	Roasted	Medium.. 0 50		Rabbit ..	Boiled	Medium 0 40	
Goose ..	Roasted	Large .. 1 50		Rabbit ..	Roasted	Large .. 0 50	
Goose ..	Roasted	Small .. 1 25		Turkey ..	Boiled	Medium 1 45	
Blackcock	Roasted	Large .. 0 50		Turkey ..	Roasted	Large .. 2 40	
Duck (Wild)	Roasted	Medium.. 0 25		Plover ..	Roasted	Medium 0 12	
Grouse ..	Roasted	Medium.. 0 30		Ptarmigan	Roasted	Medium 0 35	
Hare.. ..	Jugged	Medium.. 3 30		Quail ..	Roasted	Medium 0 25	
Hare.. ..	Roasted	Large .. 1 55		Snipe ..	Roasted	Medium 0 20	
Leveret ..	Roasted	Medium.. 0 45		Teal ..	Roasted	Medium 0 12	
Partridge..	Roasted	Medium.. 0 30		Venison,)	Roasted	Large .. 4 30	
Pheasant..	Roasted	Large .. 0 50		Haunch }	Roasted	Small .. 3 0	
Green Goose	Roasted	Medium.. 0 50		Woodcock	Roasted	Medium 0 25	

RECIPES

—◆◆—

*It will be seen by reference to the following Recipes that
an entirely original and most intelligible system has been
pursued in explaining the preparation of each dish. We
would recommend the young housekeeper, cook, or whoever
may be engaged in the important task of "getting ready"
the dinner, or other meal, to practically follow precisely the
order in which each Recipe is given. Thus, let them first
place on their table all the* INGREDIENTS *necessary; then the*
MODE *of preparation will be easily managed. By a careful
reading, too, of the Recipes, there will not be the slightest
difficulty in arranging a repast for any number of persons,
and an accurate notion will be gained of the* TIME *the cooking
of each dish will occupy, of the periods at which it is*
SEASONABLE, *as also of its* AVERAGE COST.

SPEAKING specially of the recipes for soups, it may be added
that when stock is used, according to its quality so will the
quality and cost of the soups be proportionately increased or
lessened.

A similar remark may be made with respect to many of
the recipes for other dishes which, when economy is an
object, may be prepared somewhat more frugally than they
are indicated in the book. The ingredients enumerated are
required for producing each dish in the best manner; but it
must be obvious that considerable latitude must be allowed
to meet diversities of tastes and circumstances.

SOUPS

GENERAL DIRECTIONS FOR MAKING SOUPS.

Lean, juicy beef, mutton, and veal form the basis of all good soups; therefore it is advisable to procure those pieces which afford the richest succulence, and such as are fresh-killed. Stale meat renders soups bad, and fat is not well adapted for making them. The principal art in composing good rich soup is so to proportion the several ingredients that the flavour of one shall not predominate over another, and that all the articles of which it is composed shall form an agreeable whole. Care must be taken that the roots and herbs are perfectly well cleaned, and that the water is proportioned to the quantity of meat and other ingredients, allowing a quart of water to a pound of meat for soups, and half that quantity for gravies. In making soups or gravies, gentle stewing or simmering is absolutely necessary. It may be remarked, moreover, that a really good soup can never be made but in a well-closed vessel, although, perhaps, greater wholesomeness is obtained by an occasional exposure to the air. Soups will, in general, take from four to six hours doing, and *are much better prepared the day before they are wanted.* When the soup is cold, the fat may be easily and completely removed; and in pouring it off, care must be taken not to disturb the settlings at the bottom of the vessel, which are so fine that they will escape through a sieve. A very fine hair sieve or cloth is the best strainer, and if the soup is strained while it is hot, let the tamis or cloth be previously soaked in cold water. Clear soups must be perfectly transparent, and thickened soups about the consistency of cream. To obtain a really clear and transparent soup, it is requisite to continue skimming the liquor until there is not a particle of scum remaining, this being commenced immediately after the water is added to the meat. To thicken and give body to soups and gravies, potato-mucilage, arrowroot, bread - raspings, isinglass, flour and butter, barley, rice, or oatmeal, are used. A piece of boiled beef pounded to a pulp, with a bit of butter and flour, and rubbed through a sieve, and gradually incorporated with the soup, will be found an excellent addition. When soups and gravies are kept from day to day in hot weather, they should be warmed up every day, put into fresh-scalded pans or tureens, and placed in a cool larder. In temperate weather, every other day may be sufficient. Stock made from meat only keeps good longer than that boiled with vegetables, the latter being liable to turn the mixture sour, particularly in very warm weather.

STOCKS FOR SOUPS.

In England too little importance is given to soup as a food, though it is really an economical and valuable article of diet, but one too rarely seen on the tables of the middle class. Perhaps the reason is that an old-fashioned idea still remains amongst many English cooks that a stock requiring in its making a good deal of meat is necessary in the preparation of soup.

We readily admit that a first-class stock is needed for some of the best soups, but for those for daily fare the cost of stock may be an item of small consideration.

If more housekeepers who have to be very careful in their household expenditure could realise how much could be saved by turning to account all bones, trimmings, &c., to form good stock by the use of the stock-pot, they would esteem it one of the most useful of kitchen utensils. In a large household there should be very seldom necessity for the making of stock, for the stock-pot should be at hand to supply it for soups, sauces, and gravies, and even in small households, by wasting nothing, there may always be a foundation for soup, &c., in a stock-pot, properly treated.

We say advisedly "properly treated," for many persons fall into the error of day by day adding to its contents and emptying it but seldom, whereas in reality a stock-pot should have its stock drawn off every day, should be washed out, dried out of doors if possible, if not before the fire.

Should a good deal of stock remain from previous days, drain it off and put in the fresh bones, &c., and when these have had a fair stewing, the stock drawn off may be added.

To start the pot going, boil some plain water in it, drain this off and put in all the bones, gristle, and trimmings at hand with a little salt and a few vegetables (none in summer) and cover with cold water. Let the contents come slowly to the boil. Just before boiling-point is reached, strain well. A little salt and a spoonful of cold water will bring the scum up quickly. A day is not too long to let the stock boil, filling up with water as it boils away, and in this manner a good stock is gained at an almost nominal cost, and with but very little trouble.

The liquor in which a joint or poultry has been boiled is excellent as stock for pea, lentil, and plain vegetable soups, but if it is from pork or other fat meat it should be allowed to cool before it is used that the fat may be removed. Should this stock by long simmering of the meat be fairly strong and good, the lentils, peas, &c., may be boiled till tender in plain water with onions or any vegetable needed, then simmered in the soup; this being a very good plan when the liquor is from salt beef or pork, liable to be salt. Excellent stock can be made from the bones of fresh meat, bought at a very small price from the butchers, these requiring very long stewing to extract the gelatine.

STOCKS FOR ALL KINDS OF SOUPS.

RICH STRONG STOCK.

INGREDIENTS.—3 *lbs. shin of beef*, 3 *lbs. knuckle of veal, ¼ lb. lean ham, any* poultry trimmings, 2 *oz. butter*, 3 *onions*, 3 *carrots*, 2 *turnips* (*the latter should be omitted in summer, lest they ferment*), 1 *head of celery, a few chopped mushrooms when obtainable*, 1 *tomato, a bunch of savoury herbs, not forgetting parsley;* 1½ *oz. salt*, 3 *lumps sugar*, 12 *white peppercorns*, 6 *cloves*, 3 *small blades mace*, 4 *quarts water.*

Mode.—Melt the butter in a delicately clean stewpan, put in the ham cut in thin broad slices, trimming off all its rusty fat; cut the beef and veal in pieces about 3 inches square, and lay them on the ham; set it on the stove, and stir frequently. When the meat is browned, put in the beef and veal bones, the poultry trimmings, and pour in the cold water. *Skim well*, and occasionally add a little cold water, to stop its boiling, until it becomes quite clear; then put in the other ingredients, and simmer slowly for 5 hours. Strain through a very fine hair-sieve or cloth, and the stock will be fit for use next day.

Time, 5 hours. *Average cost*, 1s. 4d. per quart.

MEDIUM STOCK.

INGREDIENTS.—3 *lbs. shin of beef, or* 3 *lbs. knuckle of veal, or* 2 *lbs. of each ; any bones, trimmings of poultry or fresh meat ; ¼ lb. lean bacon or ham*, 2 *oz. butter*, 2 *large onions, each stuck with* 3 *cloves ;* 1 *turnip*, 3 *carrots, ½ a leek*, 1 *head celery*, 2 *oz. salt*, 3 *lumps sugar, ½ a teaspoonful whole pepper*, 1 *large blade of mace*, 1 *small bunch savoury herbs*, 4 *quarts and ½ a pint of cold water.*

Mode.—Cut up the meat into pieces about 3 inches square; rub the butter on the bottom of the stewpan; put in ½ pint of water and the meat, cover the stewpan, and place it on a sharp fire, occasionally stirring its contents. When the bottom of the pan becomes covered with a pale firm gravy, add the 4 quarts of cold water, with the other ingredients, and simmer for 5 hours. Remove every particle of scum whilst it is doing, and, before putting it away, strain it through a fine hair-sieve.

This stock is the basis of many of the soups afterwards mentioned.

Time, 5 hours. *Average cost*, 10d. per quart.

ECONOMICAL STOCK.

INGREDIENTS.—*The liquor in which a joint of meat has been boiled, say* 4 *quarts ; trimmings of fresh meat or* poultry, shank-bones, &c., roast beef bones, any pieces the larder may furnish; vegetables, spices, and seasoning as in the foregoing recipe.

Mode.—Let all the ingredients simmer for 5 hours, taking care to skim carefully at first. Strain and put it by for use.

Time, 5 hours. *Average cost*, 3d. per quart.

WHITE STOCK (to be used in the Preparation of White Soups).

INGREDIENTS.—4 lbs. knuckle of veal, any poultry trimmings, 4 slices lean ham, 1 carrot, 2 onions, 1 head celery, 12 white peppercorns, 1 oz. salt, 1 blade mace, 1 oz. butter, 4 quarts water.

Mode.—Cut up the veal, and put it with the bones and trimmings of poultry, and the ham, into the stewpan, which has been rubbed with the butter. Moisten with ½ a pint of water, and simmer till the gravy begins to flow. Then add 4 quarts of water with the remainder of the ingredients, and simmer for 5 hours. Skim and strain carefully through a very fine hair-sieve.

Time, 5½ hours. *Average cost*, 10d. per quart.

Note.—When stronger stock is desired double the quantity of veal, or put in an old fowl. The liquor in which a young turkey has been boiled is an excellent addition to all white stocks or soups.

FISH STOCK.

INGREDIENTS.—*The bones and trimmings of fish, or the liquor in which fish has been boiled, to which, if not strong enough, some cheap white fish may be added, and to each quart 1 onion, 1 carrot, and a few herbs.*

Mode.—Cut up the fish and put with the vegetables, prepared in the usual way, in the stock or water, and simmer for 2 hours, carefully skimming the while, then strain.

Time, 2 hours. *Average cost* (if made with fish), 3d. per quart. *Seasonable* at any time.

BROWNING FOR STOCK.

INGREDIENTS.—2 oz. powdered sugar, and ½ a pint of water.

Mode.—Place the sugar in a stewpan over a slow fire until it begins to melt, keeping it stirred with a wooden spoon until it becomes black, when add the water, and let it dissolve. Cork closely, and use a few drops when required.

Burnt onions may also be used to give colour to soup, or a piece of bread toasted a dark colour, but not burnt, can be put into the cold stock, heated in it, and taken out when sufficient colour is imparted. It must not be put into boiling stock, as in that it would crumble.

THICKENING FOR SOUPS.

FLOUR (BROWNED).

INGREDIENTS.—½ lb. flour.

Mode. — Put the flour through a sieve, then spread it on a tin and place in a cool oven. Turn it over occasionally till it is all a nice dark brown; again sieve it, and when cold store it in bottles.

ROUX (BROWN).

INGREDIENTS.—¼ lb. fine flour, ¼ lb. butter.

Mode. — Oil the butter in an enamelled pan, and after skimming it lightly pour it off into another pan, leaving any sediment behind. Shake in the flour slowly, stirring all the while, and when boiling and beginning to take colour, stir more quickly, and occasionally take the pan off the fire if it boils too fast. One or two slices of onion may be added if the flavour be liked. These should be thrown in when the mixture is boiling, then take the pan off the fire, stirring, however, till the bubbling ceases.

Pour off the thick liquid, and when cold put in small jars. *Average cost*, 4d.

ROUX (WHITE).

INGREDIENTS.—½ lb. flour, ¼ lb. butter.

Mode.—Make this in precisely the same manner as the brown rouse, but cook a little more slowly, and remove the pan from the fire before the mixture takes colour. *Average cost*, 4d.

These two preparations are excellent thickenings for brown and white soups respectively, and a large teaspoonful to a pint of soup is an average allowance.

TO CLARIFY STOCK.

INGREDIENTS.—2 quarts of stock, 4 eggs, ½ lb. lean raw beef.

Mode.—Let the stock be cold, when very carefully remove every speck of fat, and pour it off through a strainer, leaving any sediment behind. Chop the meat finely, and put it, with the whites of the eggs whisked, and their shells crushed, into the stock, adding a little flavouring if needed. Whisk the stock over the fire until the scum rises, when leave it to simmer *very* gently for an hour with the lid half off the pan.

Strain very carefully through a tammy cloth laid over the edges of a deep pan, and when the liquid has run through lift the cloth lightly away without squeezing it. It may be necessary to strain the stock a second time, but once should be sufficient if these directions are followed.

RECIPES FOR SOUPS GIVEN HERE.

ARTICHOKE SOUP (JERUSALEM)
(Palestine Soup).

INGREDIENTS.—*3 slices lean bacon or ham, ½ head celery, 1 turnip, 1 onion, 3 oz. butter, 4 lbs. artichokes, 1 pint boiling milk or ½ pint boiling cream; salt and cayenne to taste, 2 lumps sugar, 2½ quarts white stock.*

Mode.—Cut the vegetables into thin slices, put them with the bacon and the butter into a stewpan and braise for ¼ hour, keeping them well stirred. Wash and pare the artichokes, cut them into thin slices, and add with a pint of stock to the other ingredients. Stew gently to a smooth pulp and add the remainder of the stock. Stir; add the seasoning; simmer for 5 minutes and pass it through a strainer. Pour back into the stewpan, simmer for 5 minutes, skim well, and stir in the boiling milk or cream. Serve with small sippets of bread fried in butter.

Time, 1 hour. *Average cost*, 1s. 2d. per quart. *Seasonable*, June to October. *Sufficient* for 10 persons.

ASPARAGUS SOUP.

INGREDIENTS. — *A bundle of asparagus (about 50 to 100 heads, according to size), a pint of milk, 2 tablespoonfuls each of cream, flour, and butter, 1 pint medium stock, seasoning of white pepper and salt.*

Mode.—Cut off the tips of the asparagus and put them in cold water. Slice the remainder, all but the hard ends, and boil in water till tender, then press through a sieve. Put in the butter melted, the milk thickened with flour, and the cream; stir till boiling, then add the asparagus tips, the stock and seasoning, and simmer for about 10 minutes, till the tips are cooked, but not broken.

Serve with or without fried croûtons, according to taste.

Time, ½ hour. *Average cost,* 2s. *Sufficient* for 6 persons. *Seasonable* in spring.

BARLEY SOUP.

INGREDIENTS.—2 *lbs. shin of beef,* ¼ *lb. pearl barley,* 4 *onions,* 4 *good-sized potatoes, a bunch of parsley, pepper and salt,* 4 *quarts water.*

Mode.—Cut up the beef and break the bones; put it with the vegetables, prepared in the usual way, the barley, parsley, and seasoning in the water, and simmer for 3½ hours. Take out the bones, and serve with fried croûtons.

Time, 3½ hours. *Average cost,* 4d. per quart. *Seasonable* in winter. *Sufficient* for 8 persons.

BEEF SOUP.

INGREDIENTS.—5 *lbs. leg or shin beef,* 2 *heads celery,* 5 *carrots,* 3 *onions,* 4 *turnips,* 2 *tomatoes, bunch of sweet herbs,* 1 *gallon water, teaspoonful salt.*

Mode.—Cut the beef into two or three pieces, lay them in the stewpan with the water and salt, simmer gently and remove the scum as it rises. Stew for about 4 hours; then add the celery, turnips, carrots (cut small), tomatoes, the onions sliced and fried, and the sweet herbs tied up in muslin. Whatever meat is required for table should be taken out a couple of hours before dinner. Strain the soup through a hair-sieve.

Time, 4½ hours. *Average cost,* 3s. *Sufficient* for 12 persons.

BOUILLE BAISE.

INGREDIENTS.—3 *lbs. of fish of any kind, such as plaice, whiting, haddock, or mackerel, according to the season, a bouquet of herbs, a clove of garlic, a pinch of saffron, a dessertspoonful of olive oil, half a lemon,* 2 *tomatoes or a little tomato sauce,* 3 *pints of water or weak stock, a glass of sherry, seasoning of salt and cayenne, a little parsley.*

Mode.—Cleanse the fish and cut it up in small pieces and put it in a pan. Add a few slices of lemon, the oil, the sauce, the herbs tied in a piece of muslin, the garlic, the saffron, the wine, and the seasoning, and cover with the stock or water. Boil till the fish is done, well skimming frequently, and when ready to serve throw in a tablespoonful of finely chopped parsley.

Time, 10 to 15 minutes. *Average cost,* 1s 9d. *Sufficient* for 6 persons. *Seasonable* at any time.

CARROT SOUP.

INGREDIENTS.—4 *quarts of liquor in which some mutton or beef has been boiled, a few beef bones,* 6 *large carrots,* 2 *large onions,* 1 *turnip, salt and pepper to taste,* 3 *lumps of sugar, cayenne.*

Mode.—Put the liquor, bones, onions, turnip, pepper and salt into a stewpan, and simmer 3 hours. Scrape and cut the carrots thin, strain the soup on them, and stew them till soft enough to pulp through a hair-sieve or coarse cloth; then boil the pulp with the soup, which should be of the consistency of pea soup. Add cayenne. Make this soup the day before it is wanted.

Time, 4½ hours. *Average cost,* 1½d. per quart. *Seasonable* from October to March. *Sufficient* for 12 persons.

CELERY SOUP.

INGREDIENTS.—9 *heads celery,* 1 *teaspoonful salt, nutmeg to taste,* 1 *lump sugar,* ½ *pint strong stock, a pint cream, or* ½ *pint each milk and cream,* 2 *quarts of boiling water.*

Mode.—Cut the celery into small pieces; throw into the water, seasoned with the nutmeg, salt, and sugar. Boil till tender; pass it through a sieve, add the stock, and simmer for half an hour; put in the cream and milk, bring it to the boiling-point, and serve.

Time, 1 hour. *Average cost,* 9d. per quart. *Seasonable* in winter. *Sufficient* for 10 persons.

CEREAL SOUP.

INGREDIENTS.—2 *oz. French semolina,* 2 *oz. potato flour,* 1½ *pints of milk, the same of vegetable stock, a blade of mace, a little nutmeg,* 3 *eggs, pepper and salt.*

Mode.—Bring the stock to the boil, and with one hand sprinkle in the semolina crushed), while stirring with the other, as in making porridge. When the soup gets clear add the seasoning; thicken the milk with the potato flour, and beat up the yolks of the eggs. Boil the milk and slowly add the eggs; when thickened put into the tureen, and add the soup boiling.

Time, about 20 minutes. *Average cost,* 10d. *Sufficient* for 8 persons *Seasonable* at any time.

CLEAR SOUP.

This is made from good rich stock, clarified (see recipe "To Clarify Stock"), and is very commonly served with tiny

dice of savoury custard, as below, and
a few brightly coloured vegetables, cut
as peas, boiled in plain water and
added to the soup at the time of
serving.

CUSTARD (SAVOURY) FOR SOUP.

INGREDIENTS.—2 eggs, a teacupful of
water, a small spoonful of Lemco.

Mode.—Beat the eggs and mix with
the Lemco dissolved in water; put into
a small basin and steam for about 15 to
20 minutes. It should be well set. When
cold cut it in thin slices and stamp out
tiny fancy shapes with a cutter, or, to
be more economical, cut it in diamonds,
when none will be wasted.

Time, 15 minutes. Average cost, 3d.
Sufficient for a tureen of soup.

COCK-A-LEEKIE.

INGREDIENTS.—A large old fowl,
trussed for boiling, 2 or 3 bunches of
leeks, 5 quarts stock, pepper and salt.

Mode.—Well wash the leeks (if old,
scald them), taking off the roots and
part of the heads, and cut them into
lengths of about an inch. Put the fowl
into the stock with, at first, one half
the leeks, and simmer gently. In half
an hour add the remaining leeks, and
simmer for 3 or 4 hours longer.
Skim carefully and season to taste.
In serving take out the fowl and carve
it neatly, placing the pieces in a tureen
and pouring over them the soup, which
should be very thick of leeks.

Time, 4 hours. Average cost, 1s. per
quart. Seasonable in winter. Sufficient
for 12 persons.

Note.—Without the fowl the above,
which would then be called a leek soup,
is very good and economical.

COTTAGE SOUP.

INGREDIENTS.—1 lb. meat, 2 onions,
2 carrots, 2 oz. rice, a pint of whole peas,
pepper and salt, gallon of water.

Mode.—Slice the meat and lay one or
two slices at the bottom of an earthenware jar or pan, lay on it the onions
sliced, then meat again, then the carrots
sliced, and the peas previously soaked
all night, add the gallon of water. Tie
down the jar and put it into a hot oven
for 3 or 4 hours.

Time, 3½ hours. Cost, about 9d.
Sufficient for 8 or 10 persons.

COWHEEL SOUP.

INGREDIENTS.—2 heels, 2 onions, 1
carrot, 1 turnip, a bunch of herbs,
pepper and salt.

Mode.—Very carefully cleanse the
heels. Cut them in four and put them in
cold water with a little salt, then bring
them slowly to the boil, skimming well.
Next add the vegetables and the herbs
tied in muslin, and simmer till the meat
drops from the bones. When vegetables
and meat are done strain the soup, bring
it again to boiling-point, and thicken
with cornflour, sago, or rice, and season
to taste. Some of the meat from the
heels may be cut in neat pieces and
returned to the soup. The remainder,
with a little of the soup and ½ oz.
gelatine, makes an excellent dish of
brawn.

Time, 4 to 5 hours. Average cost,
10d. Sufficient for 8 or 10 persons.
Seasonable at any time.

CRAYFISH SOUP.

INGREDIENTS.—2 doz. freshly boiled
crayfish, a French roll, 2 oz. butter, an
onion, cloves, a bayleaf, cayenne, salt,
a glass of sherry.

Mode.—Having removed the shells
of the fish and cleaned the latter, break
them up in a mortar, pound them as
smooth as possible (with a shell of a
lobster if at hand), and put them on
with the butter, the crumb of the roll
grated, the onion stuck with 3 or 4
cloves, and a seasoning of cayenne and
a little salt, in 1½ pints of water or
weak stock, and boil gently for 2 hours.
Set aside the tails of the fish, pound
the remainder, and heat well in the
soup, then rub through a sieve. Put
the soup back in the pan to get
thoroughly hot, then add the tails and
wine, and in 5 minutes serve with
fried croûtons.

Time, 2 hours. Average cost without the fish, which vary in price, 7d.
Sufficient for 6 persons. Seasonable at
any time.

FAMILY SOUP.

INGREDIENTS.—Remains of a cold
tongue, 2 lbs. shin of beef, any cold
pieces of meat or beef-bones, 2 turnips,
2 carrots, 2 onions, 1 parsnip, 1 head
celery, 4 quarts water, ½ teacupful rice,
salt and pepper to taste.

Mode.—Put the ingredients in a
stewpan, and simmer for 4 hours, or
until the goodness is drawn from the
meat. Strain off the soup, and let it
stand to get cold. When the soup is
wanted, skim off the fat, put in the
kernels and soft parts of the tongue,

slice in a small quantity of fresh carrot, turnip, and onion; stew till the vegetables are tender, and serve with toasted bread.

Time, 5 hours. *Average cost*, 6d. per quart. *Seasonable* at any time. *Sufficient* for 10 persons.

GAME SOUP.

INGREDIENTS.—*The remains of any cold game, 2 carrots, 2 onions, a bunch of sweet herbs, 2 eggs, a little milk, 1 quart of stock, pepper and salt.*

Mode.—Take the meat from the bones, put them with the trimmings into the stock with the vegetables. When the latter are tender rub them through a sieve and add to them the meat taken from the bones, first minced, then pounded in a mortar with a little stock. Strain the soup and add the pounded meat and vegetables, and when slightly cool add the eggs beaten with a little milk and the seasoning. Heat again, but do not let the soup boil.

Time, 1 hour. *Average cost* (exclusive of the cold game), 1s. 6d. *Seasonable* in autumn and winter. *Sufficient* for 4 or 5 persons.

GRAVY SOUP.

INGREDIENTS.—*4 lbs. shin of beef, 3 lbs. knuckle of veal, a few pieces of trimmings of meat or poultry, 3 slices lean ham, 2 oz. butter, 2 onions, 4 carrots, 1 turnip, nearly a head of celery, 1 blade mace, 6 cloves, a bunch savoury herbs, salt and pepper to taste, 3 lumps sugar, 5 quarts of boiling soft water. Flavour with ketchup, Leamington sauce* (see SAUCES) *and a little soy.*

Mode.—Brown the meat and ham in the butter, but do not let them burn; pour to it the water, put in the salt, and as the scum rises take it off; add then the other ingredients, and simmer slowly by the fire for 6 hours without stirring it any more from the bottom; take it off, and pass it through a sieve. When cold, all the fat should be removed, leaving the sediment untouched, which serves very nicely for thick gravies, hashes, &c. Flavour when the soup is heated for table.

Time, 7 hours. *Average cost*, 1s. per quart. *Sufficient* for 12 persons.

GREEN-CORN SOUP (American Recipe).

INGREDIENTS.—*A fowl (one that is too tough for boiling or roasting will do), 12 ears of green corn, 4 oz. of rice, a bunch of herbs, 2 quarts of water, pepper and salt.*

Mode.—Cut the fowl into joints, put them in a stewpan with the water, and boil 1½ hours. Cut the corn from the cob, add it to the soup, and stew for another hour. Take out the joints of fowl when perfectly tender, cut the meat from the bones, then into dice, and add it with the parsley chopped, and the rice and seasoning, and boil 20 minutes. This should make a very thick soup, and it may be necessary to add more water.

Time, 3 hours. *Average cost*, 3s. 6d. *Sufficient* for 8 persons. *Seasonable* from July to September.

HARE SOUP.

INGREDIENTS.—*A hare fresh-killed, 1 lb. lean gravy-beef, a slice of ham, 1 carrot, 2 onions, a faggot of savoury herbs, ¼ oz. whole black pepper, a little browned flour, ¼ pint port wine, the crumb of 2 French rolls, salt and cayenne to taste, 3 quarts of water.*

Mode.—Skin and paunch the hare, saving the liver and as much blood as possible. Cut it in pieces, and put it in a stewpan with the ingredients, and simmer gently for 5 or 6 hours. When the prime joints of the hare are sufficiently cooked take them out. This soup should be made the day before it is wanted. Strain through a sieve, put the best parts of the hare in the soup, and serve.

Time, 5 or 6 hours. *Average cost*, 1s. 9d. per quart. *Seasonable* from September to February. *Sufficient* for 8 persons.

HODGE-PODGE.

INGREDIENTS.—*2 lbs. shin of beef, 3 quarts water, 1 pint table-beer, 2 onions, 2 carrots, 2 turnips, 1 head celery, pepper and salt, thickening of butter and flour.*

Mode.—Put the meat, beer, and water in a stewpan; simmer for a few minutes, and skim. Add the vegetables and seasoning; stew gently till the meat is tender. Thicken with butter and flour, and serve with turnips and carrots, or spinach and celery.

Time, 3 hours, or rather more. *Average cost*, 6d. per quart. *Sufficient* for 10 persons.

JULIENNE.

INGREDIENTS.—*2 quarts good clear*

stock, 2 carrots, 1 turnip, 1 leek, or some small spring onions.

Mode.—Cut the vegetables into narrow fine strips about 1½ inches long, or cut them in thin slices and stamp them out with a cutter. Stew till tender in plain water, then strain and add them to the soup already heated, adding a glass of sherry if liked.

Time, 1½ hours. *Average cost*, 1s. per quart. *Seasonable* all the year. *Sufficient* for 8 persons.

Note.—When fresh vegetables are scarce Chollet's Julienne is an excellent substitute for them, containing all the vegetables needed, together with herbs and seasoning, mixed according to Soyer's recipe.

KALE BROSE.

INGREDIENTS.—*Half an ox-head, or a cowheel, teacupful toasted oatmeal, salt to taste, 2 handfuls sprouts, 3 quarts water.*

Mode.—Make a broth of the ox-head or cowheel, and boil it until oil floats on the top of the liquor, then boil the sprouts, shred, in it. Put the oatmeal, with a little salt, into a basin, and mix with it a teacupful of the fat broth; it should not run into one doughy mass, but form knots. Stir it into the whole, give it one boil and serve very hot.

Time, 4 hours. *Average cost*, 6d. per quart. *Seasonable* in winter. *Sufficient* for 10 persons.

LENTIL SOUP (German Recipe).

INGREDIENTS.—*1 pint of green German lentils, 1 quart of liquor in which a piece of pickled pork has been boiled, 2 oz. of butter, 2 or 3 cloves of garlic, pepper and salt.*

Mode.—Put the lentils in a lined saucepan and boil them in water for ¼ of an hour; then pour off the water, add a little fresh, with the butter and seasoning, and simmer till the lentils are perfectly soft. Stir in the liquor and the garlic (for which a few fried onions may be substituted if preferred), and serve hot, with or without fried bread.

Time, 4 hours. *Average cost*, 5d. per quart. *Sufficient* for 4 or 5 persons. *Seasonable* in winter.

LOBSTER SOUP.

INGREDIENTS.—*2 large lobsters, crumb of a French roll, 2 anchovies, 1 onion, 1 small bunch of sweet herbs, 1 strip lemon peel, 2 oz. butter, a little nut-*meg, 1 teaspoonful flour, 1 pint cream, 1 pint milk, forcemeat balls, mace, salt and pepper to taste, breadcrumbs, 1 egg, 2 quarts water.

Mode.—Pick the meat from the lobsters and beat the fins, chine, and small claws in a mortar, previously taking away the brown fin, and the bag in the head. Put it in a stewpan with the crumb of the roll, anchovies, herbs, lemon-peel, and the water; simmer until the goodness is extracted, and strain off. Pound the spawn in a mortar with the butter, nutmeg, and flour, and mix with it the cream and milk. Give a boil up, at the same time adding the flesh from the tails cut in pieces. Make the forcemeat balls with the remainder of the lobster, seasoned with mace, pepper, and salt, adding a little flour and a few breadcrumbs; moisten them with the egg, heat them in the soup, and serve.

Time, 2 hours, or rather more. *Average cost*, 2s. 6d. per quart. *Seasonable*, April to October. *Sufficient* for 10 persons.

MACARONI SOUP.

INGREDIENTS.—*3 oz. of macaroni, a piece of butter the size of a walnut, salt to taste, 2 quarts clear stock.*

Mode.—Throw the macaroni and butter into boiling water, with a pinch of salt, and simmer for ½ an hour. When tender, drain and cut into thin rings or lengths, and drop it into the boiling stock. Stew gently for 5 minutes, and serve grated Parmesan cheese with it.

Time, ¾ hour. *Average cost*, 10d. per quart. *Sufficient* for 7 or 8 persons.

MAIGRE SOUP (without meat).

INGREDIENTS.—*4 oz. butter, 6 onions sliced, 4 heads celery, 2 lettuces, a small bunch parsley, 2 handfuls spinach, 3 pieces bread crust, 2 blades mace, salt and pepper to taste, the yolks of 2 eggs, 3 teaspoonfuls vinegar, 2 quarts water.*

Mode.—Melt the butter in a stewpan, and put in the onions, to stew gently for 3 or 4 minutes; then add the celery, spinach, lettuces, and parsley cut small. Stir well for 10 minutes. Now put in the water, bread, seasoning, and mace. Boil gently for 1½ hours, and at the moment of serving beat in the yolks of the eggs, but do not let it boil or the eggs will curdle.

Time, 2 hours. *Average cost*, 8d. per quart. *Sufficient* for 8 persons.

MOCK TURTLE.

I.

INGREDIENTS.—½ *a calf's head, ¼ lb. butter, ¼ lb. lean ham, 2 tablespoonfuls of minced parsley, a little minced lemon thyme, sweet marjoram, basil, 2 onions, a few chopped mushrooms (when obtainable), 2 shallots, 2 tablespoonfuls of flour, 2 glasses madeira or sherry, forcemeat balls, cayenne, salt and mace, juice of 1 lemon and 1 Seville orange, 1 dessertspoonful of pounded sugar, 3 quarts of good strong stock.*

Mode.—Scald the head with the skin on, remove the brain, tie the head up in a cloth, and boil for 1 hour. Then take the meat from the bones, cut it into small square pieces, and throw them into cold water. Now take the meat, put it into a stewpan, and cover with stock; let it boil gently for an hour, or until quite tender, and set it on one side. Melt the butter in another stewpan, and add the ham, cut small, with the herbs, parsley, onions, shallots, mushrooms, and nearly a pint of stock; simmer slowly for 2 hours, and then dredge in as much flour as will dry up the butter. Fill up with the remainder of the stock, add the wine, stew gently for 10 minutes, rub it through a sieve, and put it to the calf's head; season with cayenne, and, if required, a little salt; add the juice of the orange and lemon; and when liked, ¼ teaspoonful of pounded mace, and the sugar. Put in the forcemeat balls, simmer 5 minutes, and serve very hot.

Time, 4½ hours. *Average cost*, 2s. 6d. per quart, or 2s. without wine or forcemeat balls. *Seasonable* in winter. *Sufficient* for 10 or 12 persons.

Note.—The bones of the head should be well stewed in the liquor it was first boiled in, and will make good white stock, flavoured with vegetables, &c.

II.

(*More Economical.*)

INGREDIENTS.—*5 or 6 lbs. knuckle of veal, 2 cowheels, 2 large onions stuck with cloves, 1 bunch sweet herbs, 3 blades mace, salt, 12 peppercorns, 1 glass sherry, 24 forcemeat balls, a little lemon-juice, 4 quarts water.*

Mode.—Put all the ingredients, except the forcemeat balls, lemon-juice, and wine, in an earthen jar, and stew for 6 hours. Do not open it till cold. When wanted, skim off all the fat,

strain; place the liquor on the fire, cut up the meat into inch-and-a-half squares, put it, with the forcemeat balls, lemon-juice, and wine, into the soup, and when it has simmered for 5 minutes, serve. Flavour with tablespoonful of Worcester sauce.

Time, 6 hours. *Average cost*, 1s 2d. per quart. *Seasonable* in winter. *Sufficient* for 10 persons.

MULLAGATAWNY SOUP.

INGREDIENTS.—*2 tablespoonfuls curry powder, 6 onions, 1 clove garlic, 1 oz. pounded almonds or grated cocoanut, lemon-pickle, or mango-juice, to taste; 1 fowl or rabbit, 4 slices lean bacon, 3 quarts stock.*

Mode.—Slice and fry the onions; line the stewpan with the bacon; cut rabbit or fowl into small joints, and slightly brown them; put in the fried onions, the garlic, and stock; simmer till the meat is tender; skim carefully, and when the meat is done, rub the curry-powder to a smooth batter with a little stock; add it to the soup with the almonds (pounded), or the cocoanut, with a little of the stock. Season and serve with boiled rice.

Time, 2 hours. *Average cost*, 1s. 10d. per quart. *Seasonable* in winter. *Sufficient* for 8 persons.

Note.—This soup can be made with breast of veal or calf's head. Vegetable mullagatawny is made with veal stock, by boiling and pulping chopped vegetable-marrow, cucumbers, onions, and tomatoes, and seasoning with curry-powder and cayenne. Nice pieces of meat, good curry-powder, and strong stock are necessary to make this soup good.

MUTTON BROTH (SCOTCH).

INGREDIENTS.—*5 quarts water, ½ lb. barley, 1 small turnip, 2 carrots, a little parsley, 1 onion, 4 lbs. scrag of mutton, ½ peck green peas when in season, 1 teaspoonful of salt, 1 teaspoonful of pepper.*

Mode.—Put the meat into the pot and take off the scum as it rises; then add the vegetables (the turnip, carrot, and onion, cut into small pieces) and simmer altogether for 3 hours.

Time, 3 hours. *Average cost*, about 8d. per quart.

OX-CHEEK SOUP.

INGREDIENTS.—*An ox-cheek, 2 oz. butter, 3 or 4 slices lean ham or bacon, 1 parsnip, 3 carrots, 2 onions, 4 heads celery, 2 blades mace, 4 cloves, a faggot savoury herbs, 1 bayleaf, a teaspoonful* salt, half that of pepper, browning, the crust of a French roll, 5 quarts water.

Mode.—Lay the ham in the bottom of the stewpan, with the butter; break the bones of the cheek, wash it clean, and put it on the ham. Cut the vegetables small, add them, with the exception of one head of celery, and set the whole over a slow fire for ¼ of an hour. Now put in the water, and simmer till it is reduced to 4 quarts; take out the fleshy part of the cheek, and strain the soup into a stewpan; thicken with flour, put in a head of sliced celery, and simmer till tender. Cut the meat into small square pieces, pour the soup over, and serve with the crust of a French roll. A glass of sherry much improves this soup.

Time, 3 to 4 hours. *Average cost*, 7d. per quart. *Seasonable* in winter. *Sufficient* for 12 persons.

OX-TAIL SOUP.

INGREDIENTS.—2 *ox-tails*, 2 *slices ham*, 1 *oz. butter*, 3 *carrots*, 2 *turnips*, 3 *onions*, 1 *leek*, 1 *head celery*, 1 *bunch savoury herbs*, 1 *bayleaf*, 12 *whole peppercorns*, 4 *cloves*, *a tablespoonful salt*, 3 *small lumps sugar*, 2 *tablespoonfuls ketchup*, ½ *glass port wine*, 3 *quarts water*.

Mode.—Cut the tails into joints; wash and put into a stewpan, with the butter. Put in ½ pint of water, and stir them over a sharp fire till the juices are drawn. Fill up the stewpan with the water; when boiling, add the salt. Skim; cut the vegetables in slices, add them, with the peppercorns and herbs, and simmer gently for 4 hours, or until the tails are tender. Take them out, skim and strain the soup, thicken with flour, and flavour with ketchup and wine. Put back the tails, simmer for 5 minutes, and serve.

Time, 4½ hours. *Average cost*, 1s. 3d. per quart. *Seasonable* in winter. *Sufficient* for 8 or 9 persons.

OYSTER SOUP.

INGREDIENTS. — 1 *dozen blue-point oysters*, 1 *tin oysters*, ¾ *pint of milk*, *a teaspoonful anchovy sauce*, ¾ *pint plain white stock*, *thickening of white roux*, *a little white pepper*.

Mode.—Open the oysters and put the liquor in a small pan, add that from the tin, and heat. In this plump the fresh oysters, but do not let them boil, or they will get hard; then take them out. Cut up the tinned ones and rub them through a sieve, then add them

to the liquor with the stock; next add the milk boiling to this. Boil up altogether, put in the flavouring of anchovy and a little pepper, and thicken with the roux. Lastly, add the oysters, let them just get hot through, and serve.

Time, about 20 minutes. *Average cost*, 2s. *Seasonable*, September to April. *Sufficient* for 4 persons.

PEA SOUP (Green).

INGREDIENTS.—3 *pints green peas*, ¼ *lb. butter*, 2 *or* 3 *thin slices ham*, 4 *onions sliced*, 4 *shredded lettuces*, *the crumb of* 2 *French rolls*, 2 *handfuls spinach*, 1 *lump sugar*, 2 *quarts medium stock*.

Mode.—Put the butter, ham, 1 quart of the peas, onions, and lettuces to a pint of stock, and simmer for an hour; then add the remainder of stock, with the crumb of the rolls, and boil for another hour. Now boil the spinach, squeeze it dry, and rub it, *with the soup*, through a sieve, to give the preparation a good colour. Have ready a pint of *young* peas boiled; add them to the soup, put in the sugar, give one boil, and serve. If necessary, add salt.

Time, 2½ hours. *Average cost*, 1s. 6d. per quart. *Seasonable*, June to the end of August. *Sufficient* for 8 persons.

PEA SOUP (Yellow).

INGREDIENTS.—1 *quart split peas*, 2 *lbs. shin beef*, *trimmings of meat or poultry*, *slice of bacon*, 2 *large carrots*, 2 *turnips*, 5 *large onions*, 1 *head celery*, *seasoning to taste*, 2 *quarts soft water*, *bones left from roast meat*, 2 *quarts common stock*, *or liquor in which meat has been boiled*.

Mode.—Put the peas to soak over night in soft water, and float off such as rise to the top. Boil till tender; add the ingredients mentioned above, simmer for 2 hours, stirring the soup occasionally. Press through a sieve, skim, season, and serve with fried bread, cut in dice, and dried mint.

Time, 4 hours. *Average cost*, 8d. per quart. Most suitable for cold weather. *Sufficient* for 10 persons.

A quicker and equally good way of preparing this soup is to use Symington's pea-flour in place of the split peas, in the proportion of 2 oz. to every quart of liquor.

PEA SOUP (Inexpensive).

INGREDIENTS.—¼ *lb. onions*, ¼ *lb. carrots*, 1 *head celery*, 1 *quart split peas*, *a little mint shred fine*, 1 *tablespoonful coarse brown sugar*, *salt and pepper*, 4 quarts water, or liquor in which a joint of meat has been boiled.

Mode.—Cut the vegetables into small pieces and fry for 10 minutes in a little butter or dripping; pour the water on them, and when boiling, add the peas (soaked over night, as in the preceding recipe). Simmer for nearly 3 hours, or until the peas are thoroughly done. Add the sugar, seasoning, and mint; boil for ¼ of an hour.

Time, 3½ hours. *Average cost*, 1¼d. per quart. *Seasonable* in winter. *Sufficient* for 10 persons.

POT AU FEU.

INGREDIENTS.—1½ lbs. beef, 3 quarts of water, 2 carrots, 2 turnips, 2 leeks, 1 head of celery, pepper and salt.

Mode.—Take the bones out of the beef, break them up and put them in a stewpan. Tie the meat into a neat shape and lay it on them, adding salt and the water. When it has boiled till the scum rises take it off and add a little cold water; repeat this twice, then add the vegetables cut in large pieces, and after boiling up again, gradually lessen the heat and simmer very gently. Take out all vegetables and pour in a tureen. The meat and vegetables should form a second course.

Time, 3 hours to simmer. *Average cost*, 1s. 3d. *Seasonable* at any time. *Sufficient* for 6 persons.

POTATO SOUP.

INGREDIENTS.—4 lbs. mealy potatoes boiled or steamed very dry, pepper and salt, 2 quarts of medium stock.

Mode.—Mash boiled potatoes smoothly with a fork, and gradually put them to the boiling stock; pass it through a sieve, season, and simmer for 5 minutes. Skim well, and serve with fried bread.

Time, ½ hour. *Average cost*, 10d. per quart. *Seasonable* from September to March. *Sufficient* for 8 persons.

POTAGE À LA CONDÈ (French Recipe).

INGREDIENTS.—1 quart of red haricot beans, 2 quarts of common stock, 2 onions, a little chervil, pepper and salt, 2 oz. of butter.

Mode.—Soak the beans over night, putting them in cold water with a little salt. Boil them till perfectly tender in a little water; then add the stock, butter, onions, sliced, and the seasoning, and simmer for 2 hours. Pass through a sieve, then pour boiling over some fried croûtons.

Time, 4 hours. *Average cost*, 10d. a quart. *Sufficient* for 10 persons. *Seasonable* in winter.

RABBIT SOUP.

INGREDIENTS.—1 rabbit, a Spanish onion, a stick of celery, a turnip, some white stock, a bunch of herbs, thickening of cornflour, a little cream if at hand, pepper, salt.

Mode.—Skin and wash the rabbit, and set aside the head, liver, and kidney for gravy. Boil the rabbit in water, then strain it off and add the vegetables and herbs, &c. Cook in the stock till the meat drops off the bones. Take it out, cut the meat into small, neat pieces, putting back the bones and odds and ends into the soup. Boil for another hour, then strain and thicken to a cream-like consistency with the cornflour. One rabbit should make nearly 2 quarts of soup, and milk will answer in it as well as stock; more of whichever is used can be added to make up the required quantity after the soup is strained. When thickened add the pieces of rabbit to the soup to heat through.

Time, about 3 hours. *Average cost*, 1s. 6d. *Sufficient* for 6 persons. *Seasonable* in winter.

RICE SOUP.

INGREDIENTS.—4 oz. rice, salt, cayenne, and pounded mace to taste, 2 quarts white stock.

Mode.—Throw the rice into boiling water, let it remain 5 minutes; then pour it into a sieve, and allow it to drain. Now add it to the stock boiling, and allow it to stew till tender; season to taste.

Time, 1 hour. *Average cost*, 10d. per quart. *Seasonable* all the year. *Sufficient* for 8 persons.

SHEEP'S HEAD SOUP, OR BROTH.

INGREDIENTS.—A sheep's head, ¼ lb. pearl barley, 2 oz. rice, 2 oz. each carrots, turnips, and onions, a leek, a bunch of herbs, pepper and salt, and a little ketchup if liked.

Mode.—Thoroughly cleanse the head by soaking and washing, take out the brains, and put on the fire in a pan of cold water. Skim till it reaches boiling point, when add the vegetables and other ingredients. (Other vegetables, such as green peas or cabbage, may be added if at hand.) Stew the head till perfectly done, the meat readily leaving the bones, then take it out and cut the best parts into neat, small pieces. Remove the tongue and put back the scraps of meat into the soup. Thicken with a little roux or flour, and flavour with a little ketchup or sauce. Boil up, then add the small pieces of meat to heat through. The brains and tongue will form another dish, that may be served separately, as with the soup.

Wash and blanch the brains and boil them till perfectly tender in milk. Chop them with the sheep's tongue, previously skinned, add a cupful of fine breadcrumbs, seasoning of pepper and salt, and a dessertspoonful of chopped parsley. Moisten with beaten egg and make into little flat cakes. Dredge these with flour, dip them in beaten egg, then into breadcrumbs, and fry a bright golden brown in hot fat.

Time, 2 hours. *Average cost* of soup, 1s. 6d., with brain cakes, 2s. *Sufficient* for 6 persons. *Seasonable* in winter.

SKATE SOUP.

INGREDIENTS.—1 *large skate*, 2 *onions, parsley*, 2 *oz. butter, salt and pepper to taste, dessertspoonful ketchup*, 1 *wineglassful sherry*, 2 *quarts water*.

Mode.—Clean the skate thoroughly, let it hang a day (two days in cold weather), skin, cut the thick part in fillets, about 2 inches square. Boil the head and trimmings with the onion and parsley, and reduce until only 1 quart is left; skim, strain, brown the butter and colour the soup with it. Put in the fillets and boil for ¼ hour, adding seasoning and ketchup.

Time, 2 hours. *Average cost*, 1s. 8d. per quart. *Sufficient* for 4 persons. *Seasonable*, August to April.

SORREL SOUP (French Recipe).

INGREDIENTS.—1 *pint of sorrel leaves*, 4 *oz. of butter, yolks of* 4 *eggs*, 2 *quarts of common or medium stock, salt and pepper*.

Mode.—Blanch the leaves and chop them fine, then put them in a stewpan with the butter, seasoning, and stock. As soon as the soup boils, put in the yolks of the eggs, beaten up, with a little milk. Slice a French roll into a tureen, and pour the soup, when boiling, over.

Time, ½ hour. *Average cost*, 1s. 3d. a quart. *Sufficient* for 8 persons. *Seasonable* from May to December.

SPRING SOUP.

INGREDIENTS.—½ *a pint green peas, a little chervil*, 2 *shredded lettuces*, 2 *onions, a very small bunch of parsley*, 2 *oz. butter, the yolks of* 3 *eggs*, 1 *pint water, seasoning to taste*, 2 *quarts medium or clear stock*.

Mode.—Put in a clean stewpan the chervil, lettuces, onions, parsley, and butter, to 1 pint water, and simmer till tender. Season with salt and pepper. Strain the vegetables and put two-thirds of the liquor they were boiled in to the stock. Beat up the yolks of the eggs with the other third, give it a toss over the fire, and add, with the vegetables which have been strained off, to the soup. If a clear soup is to be made prepare the vegetables as for "Julienne," and add none of the liquor in which they have been boiled to the stock, a little of which can be used in beating the eggs.

Time, ¾ of an hour. *Average cost*, 1s. per quart. *Seasonable* from May to September. *Sufficient* for 6 or 8 persons.

TAPIOCA, SAGO, or SEMOLINA SOUP.

INGREDIENTS.—5 *oz. tapioca*, 2 *quarts of medium stock*.

Mode.—Put the tapioca into cold stock, bring it gradually to the boil. Simmer till tender, and serve.

Time, rather more than 1 hour. *Average cost*, 10d. per quart. *Seasonable* all the year. *Sufficient* for 8 persons.

Sago and Semolina soups are made in the same manner as the above.

TOMATO SOUP (German Recipe).

INGREDIENTS.—3 *large tomatoes*, 2 *French rolls*, 1 *onion*, 3 *oz. of butter*, 1 *quart of common or medium stock, salt and pepper*.

Mode.—Peel, stir, and fry the onion in the butter; cut the tomatoes in four and the rolls in slices, and add, with the seasoning and a quart of water, and boil for 1½ hours. Strain through a tammy and add the stock, boiling.

Time, 1½ hours. *Average cost*, 1s. *Sufficient* for 6 persons. *Seasonable* in autumn.

TURKEY SOUP (a Seasonable Dish at Christmas).

INGREDIENTS. — 2 *quarts medium stock, the remains of a cold roast turkey*, 2 *oz. rice-flour or arrowroot*, salt and pepper, 1 tablespoonful sauce, and the same of ketchup.

Mode. — Cut the turkey in small pieces, and put it in the stock; simmer slowly until the bones are quite clean. Take the bones out, work the soup through a sieve; when cool, skim well. Mix the rice-flour or arrowroot to a batter with a little of the soup; add it, with the seasoning and sauce, or ketchup; give one boil, and serve.

Time, 4 hours. *Average cost*, 1s. 2d. per quart. *Seasonable* at Christmas. *Sufficient* for 8 persons.

Note.—Instead of thickening this soup, vermicelli or macaroni may be served in it.

USEFUL SOUP FOR BENEVOLENT PURPOSES.

INGREDIENTS. — *An ox-cheek, any pieces of trimmings of beef (say 4 lbs.), a few bones, any pot-liquor the larder may furnish, 1 peck onions, 6 leeks, a large bunch herbs, 3 heads of celery (the outside pieces, or green tops do very well), 6 carrots, 6 turnips, ½ lb. coarse brown sugar, ½ a pint of beer, 4 lbs. common rice or pearl barley, ½ lb. salt, 1 oz. black pepper, a few bread-raspings, 9 gallons of water.*

Mode.—Cut the meat in small pieces, break the bones, put them in a copper, with the 9 gallons of water, and stew for ½ an hour. Cut up the vegetables, put them in with the sugar and beer, and boil for 4 hours. Two hours before the soup is wanted, add the rice and raspings, and keep stirring till it is well mixed in the soup, which simmer gently. If the liquor reduces too much, fill up with water.

Time, 6½ hours. *Average cost*, 1½d. or 2d. per quart

VEGETABLE SOUP.

INGREDIENTS.—6 *potatoes*, 2 *carrots*, 2 *onions*, 4 *turnips, a head of celery, a few mushrooms (if obtainable), a large slice of bread, 2 teaspoonfuls sauce, salt, pepper, 4 quarts of water.*

Mode.—Peel and prepare the vegetables, cutting them up small, toast the bread brown, and simmer with the water and seasoning till they are reduced to a pulp, then pass through a sieve. Warm up again and add the sauce.

Time, 3½ hours. *Average cost*, 8d. *Seasonable* at any time. *Sufficient* for 12 persons.

VENETIAN SOUP (Italian Recipe).

INGREDIENTS.—6 *eggs*, ½ *a lemon*, 1 *French roll, pepper and salt*, 2 *quarts of medium stock.*

Mode.—Beat up the yolks of the eggs in a saucepan with a little lemon-juice, and a seasoning of salt and pepper. Stir in the cold stock slowly, then place over a slow fire and continue stirring till thick without letting the soup boil. Slice the roll in a tureen and pour over it the soup.

Time, 20 minutes. *Average cost*, 2s. 0d. *Sufficient* for 8 persons *Seasonable* at any time.

VERMICELLI SOUP.

INGREDIENTS.—¼ *lb. vermicelli*, 2 *quarts clear medium stock.*

Mode.—Put the vermicelli in the boiling soup; simmer gently for ¼ hour, and stir frequently.

Time, ¼ *hour. Average cost*, 10d. per quart. *Seasonable* all the year. *Sufficient* for 8 persons.

WHITE SOUP.

INGREDIENTS.—¼ *lb. sweet almonds*, ¼ *lb. cold veal or poultry, a thick slice of stale bread, a piece of fresh lemon-peel*, 1 *blade mace pounded*, ¾ *pint cream, the yolks of* 2 *hard-boiled eggs*, 2 *quarts of white stock.*

Mode.—Reduce the almonds in a mortar to a paste, with a spoonful of water, and add to the meat, which should be previously pounded with the bread. Beat altogether, add the chopped lemon-peel and the mace. Pour the boiling stock, and simmer for an hour. Rub the eggs in the cream, put in the soup, bring it to the boiling-point, and serve.

Time, 1½ *hours. Average cost*, 1s. 8d. per quart. *Sufficient* for 8 persons.

Note.—A more economical white soup may be made by using common veal stock, and thickening with roux or flour, and milk. Vermicelli should be served with it. *Average cost*, 5d. per quart.

FISH

CLASSIFICATION OF FISH.

THERE are three classes of fish—white fish, red fish, and shell-fish.

The first named, the principal kinds of which are cod, soles, turbot, brill soles, whiting, plaice, &c., considered the most digestible of this class of food, are lacking in fat, but have plenty of nitrogenous matter. Of these whiting and soles rank first as the lightest diet for invalids; cod, plaice, and turbot are more satisfying and more substantial, but not so easily digested as the two first named.

The richer fishes are salmon, mackerel, herrings, and eels, the latter having a large proportion of fat. These are all solid, nourishing fish, that might more often than they do take the place of meat, but many delicate persons cannot digest them.

Amongst shell-fish comes the most digestible of all, the oyster, one of the most valuable of articles of diet when uncooked, and it may be here remarked that it is often abused in the cooking and hardened by being allowed to boil, or baked too long when scalloped. Other shell-fish, such as crabs and lobsters, are generally considered very palatable and enjoyable foods, and can be eaten with impunity by the majority; but the small shell-fish, such as prawns, cockles, and periwinkles, may be partaken of by the few without risk, mussels being sometimes a dangerous food, as they are often collected from the iron upon ships, and when so are poisonous.

No hard and fast rule, however, can be laid down as to what fish should be eaten, because it so entirely depends upon the individual digestive powers of each person what may be partaken of with safety.

TO CHOOSE FISH.

The general rules for choosing fish are these: The eyes should be full and bright, the flesh elastic to the touch, when pressed with the finger it should rise again and not remain indented, the scales should not be rubbed off, the gills should be red. Fish to be wholesome *must* be perfectly fresh, and the young or inexperienced housekeeper must beware of that offered, as it sometimes very temptingly is at a much lower price than it generally obtains.

The head and shoulders of *cod* should be thick, the flesh very white, and the skin a light clear silver.

On *plaice* the spots should be of a bright colour, and a thick fish is better than a thin one.

Eels are so generally sold alive that there is but little fear in choosing them fresh.

Smelts when fresh have always a faint perfume like cucumber, and, like whitebait, they must be *perfectly* fresh, glittering like silver. They will not keep.

Salmon and *turbot*, on the contrary, are better for keeping a day or two. In the former the head and tail should be small, the scales very light and bright, and the flesh a deep pink.

The flesh of *soles* should be a cream colour.

Lobsters and *crabs* should be heavy when weighted in the hand, and the tails of the former when pulled out should spring sharply back.

TO KEEP FISH.

Cleanse the fish, thoroughly dry it, lay it on a dish, and put over a little salt and a few drops of vinegar. Keep it in a cool place.

Perfect cleanliness and careful drying are essential for fish, particularly if they are to be kept.

TO PREPARE FISH FOR COOKING.

Where the skin is not removed in

some cases the scales should be rubbed off, and this should be done with an ivory paper-knife, as with a steel one one is liable to cut the flesh. Where it is very difficult to scrape off the scales they may be more easily removed if the fish is dipped for a moment in boiling water. Fish should be scaled and skinned at a sink where the tap can be running over them.

To skin a sole or other flat fish, make a slit across just above the tail, and run the finger round to loosen the skin, then, holding it with a cloth, drag off the skin from tail to head. Next trim fins and tail. Reverse this process with a whiting, and pull the skin from head to tail.

To fillet a plaice, sole, or other flat fish, first remove the head, then make an incision down the backbone, and another each side just at the fins. A sharp knife is necessary, and with this kept firmly and flat against the bone, cut off the fillet on the left side, then turn round the fish and take off the other. Treat the other side the same way. In rolling them up put the skin side inwards.

If fish is to be fried be very careful that it is *perfectly* dry, and after flouring it may be kept in a warm place for a little time before cooking.

To egg and crumb fish, dip them first in the well-beaten egg (the whole of which may be used, but if economy is not an object the yolk alone is better), then, having put your breadcrumbs into a large sheet of paper, and laying the fish one by one in this, shake the paper from side to side till a good coating of crumbs is obtained. White-bait should be shaken in a cloth with flour.

RECIPES FOR FISH GIVEN HERE.

BLOATERS.

INGREDIENTS. — *Bloaters, a little butter.*

Mode.—Make incisions in the skin across the flesh, or split them open; lay them over a greased gridiron, and cook over a clear fire. Rub over with a little piece of butter before serving. If very dry soak for an hour and dry before grilling. The hard roe, which is seldom liked plain, may be taken out and pounded with a little anchovy and cayenne, heated and spread upon toast.

Time, about 5 minutes. *Average cost,* 1d. each. *Seasonable* at any time.

Note.—Red herrings require soaking for a night to suit most tastes, and may then be cooked in hot water.

BRILL.

INGREDIENTS.—$\frac{1}{4}$ *lb. salt to each gallon of water; a little vinegar.*

Mode.—Clean the brill, cut off the fins, and rub it over with a little lemon-juice, to preserve its whiteness. Set the fish in sufficient cold water to cover it; throw in the salt and a little vinegar, and bring it gradually to boil; simmer gently till the fish is done—in about 10 minutes, according to its size. Serve on a hot napkin, and garnish with cut lemon, parsley, horseradish, and a little lobster coral sprinkled over the fish. Send lobster or shrimp sauce or plain melted butter to table with it.

Time, after the water boils, a small brill, 10 minutes; a large brill, 15 to 20 minutes. *Average cost,* from 3s. upwards. *Seasonable* from August to April.

TO CHOOSE BRILL.—The flesh of this fish should be of a yellowish tint, and should be chosen on account of its thickness. If it has a bluish tint it is not good.

CARP (BAKED).

INGREDIENTS. — 1 *carp, forcemeat, breadcrumbs,* 1$\frac{1}{2}$ *oz. butter,* $\frac{1}{2}$ *pint stock,* $\frac{1}{2}$ *pint port wine,* 6 *anchovies,* 2 *onions sliced,* 1 *bayleaf, faggot of sweet herbs, flour to thicken, juice of* 1 *lemon, cayenne and salt to taste,* $\frac{1}{2}$ *teaspoonful pounded sugar.*

Mode.—Stuff the carp with delicate forcemeat, after thoroughly cleansing it, and sew it up to prevent the stuffing from falling out. Rub it over with an egg, and sprinkle with breadcrumbs; lay it in a deep earthen dish, and drop the butter oiled over the breadcrumbs. Add the stock, onions, bayleaf, herbs, wine, and anchovies, and bake for an hour. Put 1 oz. butter into a stewpan, melt it, dredge in sufficient flour to dry it up, put in the strained liquor from the carp, stir frequently, and when it has boiled add the lemon-juice and seasoning. Serve the carp on a dish garnished with parsley and cut lemon, and the sauce in a boat.

Time, 1$\frac{1}{4}$ hours. *Seasonable,* June to October.

CARP (STEWED).

INGREDIENTS.—1 *carp, salt stock,* 2 *onions,* 6 *cloves,* 12 *peppercorns,* 1 *blade mace,* $\frac{1}{4}$ *pint port wine, juice of* $\frac{1}{2}$ *lemon, cayenne and salt to taste, faggot of savoury herbs.*

Mode. — Scale the fish, clean carefully, and if very large divide it; lay it in the stewpan, after having rubbed a little salt on it, and put in sufficient stock to cover; and the herbs, onions, and spices, and stew gently for an hour or more. Dish up the fish with great care; strain the liquor, add the port wine, lemon-juice, and cayenne, give one boil, pour it over the fish, and serve.

Time, 1$\frac{1}{4}$ hours. *Seasonable,* June to October. *Sufficient* for 1 or 2 persons.

Note.—This fish may be boiled plain and served with parsley and butter. CHUB and CHAR, DACE and ROACH may be cooked in the same manner.

CLAM CHOWDER (American Recipe).

INGREDIENTS. — 1 *doz. clams,* 3 *oz. salt pork or bacon,* 3 *onions,* 1$\frac{1}{2}$ *pints milk, pepper, salt.*

Mode.—Cut the bacon or pork into small pieces, and frizzle for a minute or two in a stewpan, then add the onions sliced very thinly, the liquor from the fish, and $\frac{1}{2}$ pint of milk. When the pork and onions are quite done, add the pint of milk, seasoning, and the clams. Bring to boiling-point, but do not boil or the clams, like oysters, will harden. Cook for about 15 minutes and serve hot. Clams may also be scalloped as oysters, or fried.

Time, $\frac{3}{4}$ hour. *Average cost,* seldom bought in England. *Sufficient* for 3 persons.

COD (CURRIED).

INGREDIENTS.—2 *slices large cod, or the remains of any cold fish,* 3 *oz. butter,*

FISH AND VEGETABLES.

Red Mullet.

Asparagus.

Chicory and Toast.

Mayonnaise of Lobster.

French Beans.

Sea Kale.

Salmon.

OYSTER PATTIES.

WHITING.

TURBOT.

WHITEBAIT.

MACKEREL.

MAYONNAISE SALMON.

LOBSTER.

CRAB.

1 *onion sliced, a teacupful white stock, thickening of butter and flour,* 1 *tablespoonful curry-powder,* ¼ *pint milk, salt and cayenne to taste.*

Mode.—Flake the fish, and fry of a nice brown colour with the butter and onions; put this in a stewpan, add the stock and thickening, and simmer for 10 minutes. Stir the curry-powder into the milk; put it, with the seasoning, to the other ingredients; give one boil, and serve with boiled rice.

Time, ¾ hour. *Average cost,* with fresh fish, 2s. *Seasonable* from November to March. *Sufficient* for 4 persons.

COD DRESSED IN THE NEAPOLITAN FASHION (Italian Recipe).

INGREDIENTS.—4 *lbs. of cod,* 3 *oz. of butter, some mushroom buttons preserved in oil, a bunch of sweet herbs,* 2 *glasses of Marsala, a teacupful of Neapolitan sauce, a teacupful of cream.*

Mode.—Having cleansed the fish, cut it in slices and put it in a stewpan with the butter, herbs, mushrooms, and wine. Simmer till the same is reduced, then pour in the Neapolitan sauce. When the cod is done take it out and arrange it on a dish, with a garnish or border of macaroni stewed in stock. Stir the cream with the reduced stock and, when quite smooth, pour over the fish.

Time, ½ to ¾ hour. *Average cost,* 3s. *Sufficient* for 8 to 10 persons. *Seasonable* from November to March.

COD PIE (Economical).

I.

INGREDIENTS.—*Any remains of cold cod,* 12 *oysters or half a tin, sufficient melted butter to moisten it; mashed potatoes enough to fill up the dish.*

Mode.—Flake the fish from the bone, and take away the skin. Lay it in a pie-dish, season with pepper and salt, pour over the melted butter and oysters (or oyster sauce, if there is any at hand), and cover with mashed potatoes. Bake for ½ an hour.

Time, ½ hour. *Seasonable* from November to March.

II.

INGREDIENTS.—2 *slices cod, pepper and salt,* ½ *teaspoonful grated nutmeg,* 1 *large blade pounded mace,* 2 *oz. butter.* ½ *pint of medium stock, a paste crust* (see PASTRY). *For sauce,* 1 *tablespoonful of stock,* ¼ *pint of milk, thickening of flour and butter, chopped lemon-peel to taste,* 12 *oysters or* ½ *a tin.*

Mode.—Lay the cod in salt for 4 hours; then wash it and place it in a dish; season, and add the butter and stock: cover with the crust, and bake for 1 hour, or rather more. Now make the sauce, with ingredients as above; give it one boil, and pour it into the pie by a hole at the top of the crust, which can be covered by a piece of pastry cut and baked in any shape—such as a leaf or otherwise.

Time, 1½ hours. *Average cost,* with fresh fish, 2s. 6d. *Seasonable* from November to March. *Sufficient* for 6 persons.

Note.—The remains of cold fish may be used for this pie.

COD (SALTED), COMMONLY CALLED "SALT-FISH."

INGREDIENTS.—3 *lbs. fish, sufficient water to cover the fish.*

Mode.—Wash the fish, and lay it all night in water, with ¼ pint of vinegar. See that it is perfectly clean, and put it in the fish-kettle with sufficient cold water to cover it. Heat it gradually, and do not let it boil fast, or the fish will be hard. Skim, and when done, drain the fish and put it on a napkin, with hard-boiled eggs cut in rings.

Time, about 1 hour. *Average cost,* 6d. per lb. *Seasonable* in the spring. *Sufficient* for 8 persons.

Note.—Serve with egg sauce and parsnips. This is an especial dish on Ash Wednesday.

COD SOUNDS.

These, which are considered a great delicacy, may be either broiled, fried, or boiled. They should be well soaked for ½ hour in salt and water, and well scraped before dressing, and if they are boiled, a little milk should be mixed with the water. Serve on a napkin with egg sauce. To broil or fry, first give them a gentle boil, then dry and flour them, sprinkle with a little salt and pepper. They will then be ready for the frying-pan or gridiron. Serve with any sauce that may be preferred.

Time, ½ hour. *Average cost,* 6d. per lb. *Seasonable* from November to March.

COD STEAKS (BROILED).

INGREDIENTS.—3 *slices cut from the middle of the fish,* 2 *eggs, a few capers, oil, vinegar, pepper and salt.*

Mode.—Clean and dry the fish, warm

then grease, a gridiron, and broil the steaks upon it till thoroughly done. Break the yolks of the eggs into a basin, adding oil enough to make a thick cream. When these are well blended, add a little vinegar, the capers chopped, a seasoning of pepper and salt, stir well, and pour this sauce over the fish. Serve garnished with lemon and parsley.

Time, 15 minutes to grill the steaks. *Average cost*, 1s. 8d. *Sufficient* for 6 persons.

COD'S HEAD AND SHOULDERS.

INGREDIENTS. — *Sufficient water to cover the fish; 5 oz. salt to each gallon of water.*

Mode.—Cleanse the fish, rub a little salt over the thick part and inside of the fish, 1 or 2 hours before dressing it, as this very much improves the flavour. Lay it in the fish-kettle, with sufficient hot water to cover it. Keep it just simmering. If the water should boil away, add a little by pouring it in *at the side of the kettle*, and not on the fish. Add the salt, and bring gradually to a boil. Skim carefully, and draw it to the side of the fire, and let it simmer till done. Serve on a hot napkin, and garnish with cut lemon, horseradish, and the liver.

Time, according to size, $\frac{1}{2}$ an hour, more or less. *Average cost*, from 4d. to 8d. per lb. *Sufficient* for 6 or 8 persons. *Seasonable* from November to March.

Note.—Oyster sauce or plain melted butter should be served with this.

To CHOOSE COD.—Cod should be plump and round near the tail, the hollow behind the head deep, and the sides undulated as if they were ribbed. The glutinous parts about the head lose their delicate flavour after the fish has been twenty-four hours out of the water. Although the flesh of the cod is not firm when it is alive, its quality may be arrived at by pressing the finger into the flesh. If this rises immediately the fish is good; if not, it is stale. Another sign of its goodness is, if the fish, when it is cut, exhibits a bronze appearance, like the silver side of a round of beef.

COD'S ROE.

INGREDIENTS.—1 *roe, lard for frying, 1 egg, flour, milk, a little vinegar, salt.*

Mode.—Boil the roe in water with a little vinegar for 10 minutes, take it out, drain and dry. Make a thin batter with the egg, flour, and milk, and a little salt. Cut the roe in slices, dip in the batter, and fry a bright brown.

Time to boil and fry about 20 minutes. *Average cost*, 1s. 3d. *Sufficient* for a good breakfast dish.

CRAB (DRESSED).

INGREDIENTS.—1 *good-sized crab, 2 tablespoonfuls vinegar, 2 ditto oil, $\frac{1}{2}$ teaspoonful made mustard; salt, white pepper, and cayenne to taste, a large cup of breadcrumbs.*

Mode.—Empty the shells, mix the meat with the above ingredients, and put it in the large shell. Garnish with lobster coral and parsley.

Average cost, from 10d. to 2s. *Seasonable* all the year, but not so good in May, June, and July. *Sufficient* for 6 persons.

To CHOOSE CRAB.—The middle-sized crab is the best; and the crab, like the lobster, should be judged by its weight; for if light, it is watery.

CRAB (HOT).

INGREDIENTS.—1 *crab; nutmeg, salt, and pepper to taste; 3 oz. butter, $\frac{1}{4}$ lb. breadcrumbs, 3 tablespoonfuls vinegar.*

Mode.—Boil the crab, pick the meat out from the shells, and mix with it the nutmeg and seasoning. Cut up the butter in small pieces, and add the breadcrumbs and vinegar. Mix, put the whole in the large shell, and brown before the fire, or with a salamander.

Time, 1 hour. *Average cost*, from 10d. to 2s. *Seasonable* all the year, but not so good in May, June, and July. *Sufficient* for 3 or 4 persons

DABS, OR SLIPS (FRIED).

INGREDIENTS.—1 *doz. fish flour, some clarified dripping.*

Mode.—Cleanse the fish, and take off the heads, dry, and flour well. Melt some dripping in a pan, and when quite hot put in the fish and fry a bright brown. Serve with melted butter and lemon.

Time, about 5 minutes, according to size. *Average cost*, 6d. to 1s. doz. *Seasonable* all the year. *Sufficient* for 3 persons.

EEL PIE.

INGREDIENTS. — 1 *lb. eels, a little chopped parsley, 1 shallot, grated nutmeg, pepper and salt to taste, the juice of $\frac{1}{2}$ a lemon, small quantity forcemeat, $\frac{1}{4}$ pint good gravy, puff-paste.*

Mode.—Skin and wash the eels, cut into pieces 2 inches long, and line the bottom of the pie-dish with forcemeat.

Put in the eels, and sprinkle with the parsley, shallot, nutmeg, seasoning, and lemon-juice, and cover with puff-paste. Bake for 1 hour, or rather more; make the gravy hot, pour into the pie, and serve.

Time, 1 hour. *Average cost*, 1s. 6d. *Seasonable* from June to March.

EELS (BOILED).

INGREDIENTS.—2 *lbs. eels, sufficient water to cover them, a large bunch of parsley.*

Mode.—Put the eels in a stewpan with the parsley, and sufficient boiling water to cover; simmer till tender. Take them out, pour a little parsley and butter over them, and serve some in a tureen.

Time, ½ hour. *Average cost*, 10d. per lb. *Seasonable* from June to March. *Sufficient* for 4 persons.

EELS (FRIED).

INGREDIENTS.—1 *lb. eels*, 1 *egg, a few breadcrumbs, hot lard.*

Mode.—Wash the eels, cut them into pieces 3 inches long, trim, and wipe them dry; dredge with flour, rub them over with egg, and cover with bread crumbs; fry to a nice brown in hot lard. If the eels are small, curl them round, instead of cutting them up. Garnish with fried parsley.

Time, 20 minutes, or rather less. *Average cost*, 10d. per lb. *Seasonable* from June to March.

EELS (STEWED).

INGREDIENTS.—2 *lbs. middling-sized eels*, 1 *pint medium stock*, ¼ *pint port wine ; salt, cayenne, and mace ;* 1 *teaspoonful essence of anchovy, the juice of* ½ *a lemon.*

Mode.—Skin, wash, and clean the eels; cut them into pieces 3 inches long, and put them into strong salt and water for 1 hour; dry them well with a cloth, and fry brown. Put the stock on with the heads and tails of the eels, and simmer for ½ hour; strain it, and add the other ingredients. Put in the eels, stew gently for nearly ½ hour.

Time, including the hour for soaking, 2 hours. *Average cost*, 2s. 6d. *Seasonable* from June to March.

FISH CAKE.

INGREDIENTS.—*The remains of any cold fish*, 1 *onion*, 1 *faggot sweet herbs, salt and pepper*, 1 *pint water, equal quantities of breadcrumbs and cold potatoes*, ⅓ *teaspoonful parsley*, 1 *egg, breadcrumbs.*

Mode.—Pick the meat from the bones of the fish, and the latter put, with the head and fins, into a stewpan with the water ; add pepper and salt, the onion and herbs, and stew slowly for gravy about 2 hours ; chop the fish fine, mix it well with breadcrumbs and cold potatoes, parsley and seasoning ; make the whole into a cake with the white of an egg, brush it over with egg, cover with breadcrumbs, and fry of a light brown ; strain the gravy, pour it over, and stew gently for ¼ hour, stirring it once or twice. Serve hot, and garnish with slices of lemon and parsley.

Time, ½ hour after the gravy is made. *Average cost*, 4d., without fish.

FISH AND OYSTER PIE.

INGREDIENTS.—*Any remains of cold fish, such as cod or haddock, dozen oysters, or* ½ *tin, pepper and salt, sufficient breadcrumbs*, ½ *teaspoonful grated nutmeg*, 1 *teaspoonful finely chopped parsley, some made melted butter.*

Mode.—Clear the fish from the bones, and put a layer of it in a pie-dish, sprinkle with pepper and salt; then a layer of breadcrumbs, oysters, nutmeg, and chopped parsley. Repeat this till the dish is full. Cover either with browned breadcrumbs or puff-paste ; the latter should be cut into strips, and laid in cross-bars over the fish, with a line of paste first laid round the edge. Before putting on the top, pour in some made melted butter, or a little thin white sauce, and the oyster-liquor, and bake.

Time, if made of cooked fish, ¼ to ½ hour ; if made of fresh fish and puff-paste, ¾ hour. *Seasonable* from September to April.

Note.—A nice little dish may be made by flaking any odd fish, adding a few oysters, seasoning with pepper and salt, and covering with mashed potatoes; ¼ to ½ hour will bake it.

FISH PUDDING.

INGREDIENTS.—1 *lb. of the flesh of any white fish, or cold boiled fish*, ½ *lb. breadcrumbs, a little anchovy sauce, cayenne*, 2 *eggs*, ¼ *lb. suet, a little of the liquor in which the fish was boiled, or milk.*

Mode.—Take the flesh from the bones of fresh fish, and pound it, or flake the cold. Put it with the breadcrumbs and the suet, finely chopped, into a basin adding anchovy and cayenne. Mix with the liquids, put in a buttered dish, and steam for an hour.

Time, 1 hour. *Average cost*, 1s. *Sufficient* for 3 persons. *Seasonable* at any time.

FLOUNDERS (FRIED).

INGREDIENTS.—*Flounders, egg, and breadcrumbs; boiling lard.*

Mode.—Cleanse the fish, and, 2 hours before they are wanted, rub them inside and out with salt, wash and wipe them dry, dip them into egg, sprinkle over with breadcrumbs; fry in boiling lard, dish on a hot napkin, and garnish with crisped parsley.

Time, from 5 to 10 minutes, according to size. *Average cost*, from 1d. each. *Seasonable* from August to November. *Sufficient*, 1 or 2 for each person.

HADDOCK (BAKED).

INGREDIENTS.—*A nice forcemeat* (see FORCEMEAT), *butter to taste, egg, and breadcrumbs.*

Mode.—Scale and clean the fish, without cutting it open much ; put in a nice delicate forcemeat, and sew up the slit. Brush it over with egg, sprinkle over breadcrumbs, and baste frequently with butter. Garnish with parsley and cut lemon, and serve with a brown gravy, plain melted butter, or anchovy sauce.

Time, large haddock, ¾ hour ; moderate size, ¼ to ½ hour. *Seasonable* from August to February. *Average cost*, from 6d. upwards.

HADDOCK (BOILED).

INGREDIENTS. — *Sufficient water to cover the fish ; ¼ lb. of salt to each gallon of water.*

Mode.—Scrape the fish, take out the inside, wash it, and lay it in a kettle, with enough water to cover, adding salt as above. Simmer gently from 15 to 20 minutes, or more. For small haddocks, fasten the tails in their mouths, and put them into boiling water. Serve with plain melted butter or anchovy sauce.

Time, large haddock, ½ hour ; small, ¼ hour, or rather less. *Average cost*, from 6d. upwards. *Seasonable* from August to February.

HADDOCK (DRIED).

INGREDIENTS. — 1 *haddock, water, butter.*

Mode.—Trim the haddock, and lay it

in a frying-pan of boiling water. Cook for about 3 minutes, take it out, drain, and rub over with a little butter.

Time, 3 minutes. *Average cost*, from 4d. each. *Seasonable*, best in winter. *Sufficient* for—allow 1 good-sized haddock for 2 persons.

HADDOCK (DRIED)

(*Another mode.*)

INGREDIENTS.—1 *large thick haddock,* 2 *bay-leaves,* 1 *small bunch of savoury herbs, not forgetting parsley, a little butter and pepper ; boiling water.*

Mode.—Cut the haddock into small pieces. Lay the fish in a hot basin, with the bay-leaves and herbs ; cover with boiling water ; put a plate over to keep in the steam, and let it remain for 10 minutes. Take out the slices, rub over with butter and pepper, and serve on a hot dish.

Time, 10 minutes. *Seasonable* at any time, but best in winter.

HAKE (BAKED).

INGREDIENTS.—*Hake, veal stuffing, egg, and breadcrumbs.*

Mode.—Clean the fish and stuff it with veal stuffing, sew it up with a needle and fine pack-thread. Brush it over with egg, sprinkle with breadcrumbs ; and bake in a hot oven.

Time, according to size. *Seasonable* from November to March.

HALIBUT STEAKS.

INGREDIENTS.—3 *or* 4 *slices of a fish,* 2 *eggs, crackers* (*here we should substitute breadcrumbs*), *lard or dripping for frying, salt, flour.*

Mode.—Wash and dry the steaks, roll out the crackers into powder, and beat the eggs. Dredge the steaks with flour, shake over a little salt, then dip them first in the egg and then in the powdered crackers, and fry in plenty of hot fat. They can also be broiled upon a greased gridiron (seasoning them first) in the same manner as cod or salmon steaks.

Time, 10 to 15 minutes. *Seasonable* at any time.

HERRINGS, FRESH (BAKED).

INGREDIENTS.—12 *herrings,* 4 *bay-leaves,* 12 *cloves,* 12 *allspice,* 2 *small blades of mace, cayenne pepper and salt, sufficient vinegar to fill up the dish.*

Mode.—Cut off the heads of the

herrings and gut them ; put them in a pie-dish, heads and tails alternately, and, between each layer, sprinkle over some of the above ingredients. Cover with the vinegar, and bake for ½ hour, but do not use it till quite cold. The herrings may be cut down the front, the backbone taken out, and closed again. Sprats done in this way are very delicious.

Time, ½ an hour. *Average cost,* from 4d. per doz. *Seasonable* from July to March.

To CHOOSE THE HERRING.—The more scales this fish has, the surer its freshness. If red about the head, it has been dead for some time.

HERRINGS, FRESH (FRIED).

Mode.—Clean, scale, and dry the fish ; fry to a bright colour with a little butter; garnish with crisp parsley.

Time, about 8 minutes. *Average cost,* from 4d. per doz.

HERRINGS, FRESH (BOILED).

INGREDIENTS. — *Herrings, scraped horseradish, vinegar and salt.*

Mode.—Clean, wash, and dry the fish in the usual manner. Rub over a little vinegar and salt, and lay them on a strainer in a stewpan of boiling water, and simmer for 20 minutes. Serve with parsley and butter sauce, and garnish with scraped horseradish.

Time, 20 minutes.

JOHN DORY.

INGREDIENTS.—¼ *lb. salt to each gallon of water.*

Mode.—This fish, which is esteemed as a delicacy, is dressed as a turbot. Cleanse it ; cut off the fins ; lay it in a fish-kettle, cover it with cold water, and add the salt. Bring it gradually to a boil, simmer gently for ¼ hour, or longer. Serve on a hot napkin, and garnish with cut lemon and parsley. Lobster, anchovy, or shrimp sauce, plain melted butter, should be sent to table with it.

Time, after the water boils, ¼ to ½ hour, according to size. *Average cost,* from 2s. to 3s. *Seasonable* all the year, but best from September to January.

Note.—Small John Dories are very good baked.

KIPPERS.

INGREDIENTS.—*Kippers, water, butter.*
Mode.—Trim the kippers and plunge

them into boiling water, then take them out, drain, and rub over with a little butter. Kippers may also be fried or grilled, but are then somewhat hard and dry.

Time, 3 minutes. *Average cost,* 2d. per pair. *Seasonable,* best in winter. *Sufficient* for—allow a pair for each person.

LING.

INGREDIENTS. — *Ling, breadcrumbs, herbs, butter, pepper and salt.*

Mode.—Wash the fish and cut it in slices. Butter a shallow dish, put over some breadcrumbs, lay over the slices of fish. Season well with herbs, pepper, and salt, and add a little vinegar and water. Cover with a layer of crumbs, put small pieces of butter over the top, and bake in a slow oven from ¾ to 1 hour.

Time, ¾ to 1 hour.

LOBSTER (POTTED).

INGREDIENTS.—2 *lobsters ; seasoning of nutmeg, pounded mace, white pepper, and salt ;* ¼ *lb. butter, or 4 bay-leaves.*

Mode.—Take out the meat from the shell, but do not cut it up. Put some butter at the bottom of a dish, lay in the lobster as evenly as possible, with the bay-leaves and seasoning between ; cover with butter, and bake for ¾ hour in a gentle oven. Drain the whole on a sieve, and lay the pieces in potting-jars, with the seasoning about them. When cold, pour over it clarified butter, and, if highly seasoned, it will keep some time.

Time, ¾ hour. *Average cost* for this quantity, 4s. 4d.

LOBSTER SALAD.

INGREDIENTS.—1 *hen lobster, lettuces, endive, small salad (whatever is in season), a little chopped beetroot,* 2 *hard-boiled eggs, a few slices of cucumber. For dressing, see salad dressing.*

Mode.—Wash the salad, and dry it by shaking it in a cloth. Cut up the lettuces and endive, pour the dressing on them, and lightly throw in the small salad. Mix all well together with the pickings from the body of the lobster; pick the meat from the shell, cut it up, into nice square pieces ; put half in the salad, the other half reserve for garnishing. Separate the yolks from the whites of 2 hard-boiled eggs; chop the whites fine, rub the yolks through a sieve, and afterwards the coral from the inside. Put the salad lightly on a glass dish, and garnish, first with a row of sliced cucumber, next with the pieces of lobster, then the yolks and whites of the eggs, coral, and beetroot placed alternately.

Average cost, 3s. 6d. *Sufficient* for 5 or 6 persons. *Seasonable* from April to October; may be had all the year; but salad is scarce and expensive in winter.

Note.—A few crayfish make a pretty garnishing to lobster salad.

LOBSTER (to boil and dress).

INGREDIENTS. — *A lobster, boiling water, salad oil.*

Mode.—Put the lobster head downwards into fast boiling water. When it is boiled, rub it over with a little salad-oil, which wipe off again; separate the body from the tail, break off the great claws, and crack them at the joints, without injuring the meat; split the tail, head, and body in halves, and arrange all neatly in a dish, with the body upright in the middle, and garnish with parsley.

MACKEREL (BAKED).

INGREDIENTS.—4 *middling-sized mackerel, a delicate forcemeat* (see FORCE-MEAT), 3 *oz. butter; pepper and salt.*

Mode.—Clean the fish, take out the roes, fill up with forcemeat, and sew up the slit. Flour, and put them in a dish, heads and tails alternately, with the roes; between each layer put some little pieces of butter, and pepper and salt. Bake for ½ an hour, and serve with plain melted butter or a *maître d'hôtel.*

Time, ½ hour. *Average cost* for this quantity, 2s. *Seasonable* from April to July. *Sufficient* for 8 persons.

Note.—Baked mackerel may be dressed in the same way as baked herrings, and may also be stewed in wine.

MACKEREL (BOILED).

INGREDIENTS.—¼ *lb. of salt to each gallon of water.*

Mode.—Cleanse the inside of the fish, and lay them in the kettle with sufficient water to cover; add salt as above; bring them gradually to boil, skim, and simmer gently till done; dish them on a hot napkin, heads and tails alternately, and garnish with fennel. Serve with plain melted butter; caper or anchovy sauce is sometimes preferred.

Time, after the water boils, 10 minutes; for large mackerel, allow more time. *Average cost,* 4d. each. *Seasonable* from April to July.

Note.—When variety is desired, fillet the mackerel, boil it, and pour over parsley and butter; send some of this to table in a tureen.

TO CHOOSE MACKEREL.—If it have a transparent, silvery hue, the flesh is good; but if it be red about the head, it is stale.

MACKEREL (BROILED).

INGREDIENTS — *Pepper and salt to taste; a small quantity of oil.*

Mode.—Mackerel should never be washed when intended to be broiled, but merely wiped clean and dry, after taking out the gills and insides. Open the back, and put in a little pepper, salt, and oil; broil it over a clear fire, turn it over on both sides, and also on the back. When sufficiently cooked the flesh can be detached from the bone. Chop a little parsley, work it up in the butter, with pepper and salt, and a squeeze of lemon-juice, and put it in the back. Serve before the butter is quite melted, with a *maître d'hôtel* sauce in a tureen.

Time, small mackerel 10 minutes. *Average cost,* 4d. each. *Seasonable* from April to July.

MACKEREL (PICKLED).

INGREDIENTS.— 12 *peppercorns, 2 bay-leaves,* ½ *pint of vinegar, 4 mackerel.*

Mode.—Boil the mackerel as in the recipe given, and lay them in a dish; to half the liquor they were boiled in add as much vinegar, and the above proportion of peppercorns and bay-leaves; boil for 10 minutes, and when cold pour it over the fish.

Time, ½ hour. *Average cost,* 1s. 6d.

MULLET (GREY).

INGREDIENTS.—¼ *lb. salt to each gallon of water.*

Mode.—If the fish be large it should be laid in cold water, and gradually brought to a boil; if small put it into boiling water. Serve with anchovy sauce and melted butter.

Time, according to size, ¼ to ¾ hour. *Average cost,* 1s. each. *Seasonable* from July to October.

MULLET (RED).

INGREDIENTS.—*Oiled paper, thickening of butter and flour, ½ teaspoonful of anchovy sauce, 1 glass sherry; cayenne and salt to taste.*

Mode.—Clean the fish and take out the gills, but leave the inside; fold in oiled paper, and bake them gently. When done take the liquor that flows from the fish, add a thickening of butter kneaded with flour, put in the other ingredients, and boil for 2 minutes. Serve the sauce in a tureen, and the fish either with or without the paper cases.

Time.—About 25 minutes. *Average cost*, 1s., often much dearer. *Seasonable* at any time.

Note.—Red mullet may be broiled folded in oiled paper as above, and seasoned with pepper and salt. Serve with melted butter, Italian or anchovy sauce.

OYSTER PATTIES.

INGREDIENTS.—*2 doz. oysters, ¼ pint thick white sauce, ¼ pint cream, seasoning of nutmeg, cayenne, lemon-peel, and anchovy sauce. Puff paste.*

Mode.—Put the oyster liquor with the beards into an enamelled pan with a piece of lemon-peel and flavouring of cayenne, sauce and nutmeg. Boil for about 10 minutes, then strain and mix with the cream and sauce, boiling, adding a little more seasoning if necessary. Cut each oyster in four pieces and steam by putting them in a small strainer over boiling water for about a minute. If the patties are to be served hot the cases should be ready at the same time as the filling. Make them in the following manner:—Stamp out some rounds of paste rolled very thin, with a fluted cutter about 3 in. in diameter, and the same number from the paste ½-in. thick. Stamp the thicker ones again with a plain and rather smaller cutter, so as just to leave a ring. Lay the rings over the rounds, joining them with a little white of egg, fill the cavities with bread and put the small rounds on the top of each. When the cases are baked take out the bread, fill with the mixture to which the steamed oysters have been added, replace the rounds on the top and return for a minute to the oven.

Time, 25 minutes. *Average cost*, 3s. 6d. *Seasonable* from September to April. *Sufficient* for 12 patties.

OYSTERS (SCALLOPED).

INGREDIENTS.—*2 doz. oysters, 1 oz. butter, flour, 2 tablespoonfuls of white stock, 2 tablespoonfuls cream or milk; pepper and salt to taste; breadcrumbs, oiled butter.*

Mode.—Scald the oysters in their own liquor; take them out, beard them, and strain the liquor free from grit. Put 1 oz. of butter into a stewpan; when melted, dredge in sufficient flour to dry it up; add the stock, cream or milk, and strained liquor, and give one boil. Put in the oysters and seasoning; let them gradually heat through, *but do not allow them to boil*. Have ready the scallop shells buttered; lay in the oysters, and as much of the liquid as they will hold; cover them with breadcrumbs, over which drop a little oiled butter. Brown them in the oven, or before the fire, and serve quickly and very hot.

Time, altogether, ¼ hour. *Average cost*, 3s. *Sufficient* for 5 or 6 persons.

OYSTERS (SCALLOPED).

(*Another mode.*)

Prepare the oysters as in the preceding recipe, put them in a scallop shell or saucer, and between each layer sprinkle over a few breadcrumbs, pepper, salt, and grated nutmeg. Put sufficient breadcrumbs on the top to make a smooth surface, as the oysters should not be seen, and put small pieces of butter over. Bake in a Dutch oven.

Time, about ¼ hour. *Seasonable* from September to April.

OYSTERS (STEWED).

INGREDIENTS.—*2 doz. oysters, 1 oz. butter, flour, ¼ pint milk, cayenne and salt to taste, 1 blade pounded mace.*

Mode.—Scald the oysters in their own liquor; take them out, beard them, and strain; put the butter into a stewpan, dredge in sufficient flour to dry it up, add the oyster liquor and mace, and stir it over a sharp fire with a wooden spoon; when it comes to a boil, add the milk, oysters, and seasoning. Simmer for 1 or 2 minutes, but not longer, or the oysters would harden. Serve on a hot dish, and garnish with croûtons or toasted sippets of bread. A small piece of lemon-peel boiled with the oyster-liquor, and taken out before the milk is added, will be found an improvement.

Time, altogether 15 minutes. *Seasonable* from September to April. *Sufficient* for 6 persons.

OYSTERS (TO KEEP).

Put them in a tub, and cover them with salt and water. Let them remain for 12 hours, when they are to be taken out, and allowed to stand for another 12 hours without water. If left without water every alternate 12 hours, they will be much better than if constantly kept in it. Never put the same water twice to them

PIKE (BAKED).

INGREDIENTS.—1 *or* 2 *pike, a nice delicate stuffing,* 1 *egg, breadcrumbs* ¼ *lb. butter*

Mode.—Scale and clean the fish, take out the gills, wash and wipe it thoroughly dry, stuff it with forcemeat, sew it up, and fasten the tail in the mouth by means of a skewer; brush it over with egg, sprinkle with breadcrumbs, and baste with butter before putting it into the oven, which should be well heated. As soon as the fish is of a nice brown colour cover it with buttered paper, as the outside would otherwise become too dry. Serve anchovy or Dutch sauce and plain melted butter with it.

Time, according to size, 1 hour or more. *Seasonable* from September to March.

PIKE (BOILED).

INGREDIENTS.—¼ *lb. of salt to each gallon of water : a little vinegar.*

Mode.—Scale and clean the pike, and fasten the tail in its mouth by means of a skewer. Lay it in a saucepan of water, put it on the fire, and when it simmers throw in the salt and vinegar. A middling size pike will take about ½ hour. If the water is allowed to pass beyond the most gentle simmer possible the fish will be spoiled. Serve with Dutch or anchovy sauce and melted butter.

Time, according to size, from ½ hour to 1 hour. *Seasonable* from September to March.

PIKE (FRIED).

INGREDIENTS. — *Egg, breadcrumbs, olive oil.*

Mode.—Scale the fish carefully, remove the entrails, rub salt well within and without, take out the backbone, and divide the fish into fillets. Place them separately under a dish or any flat surface with a weight thereon, leave them a night, then rinse them in fresh water, glaze thinly with white of egg, strew them with breadcrumbs, and fry in boiling olive oil. Many of the most *recherché* dishes made from eels may be closely simulated with slips of the belly part of pike, which will be found not to possess the rich and oily flavour of the former fish, so objectionable to some persons. With the coarser portion of the pike—the back—excellent rissoles may be made.

Seasonable from September to March.

Note.—The above is given on the authority of Mr. G. Fennell, as a Jewish recipe. As that gentleman very properly remarks, the quality of a pike depends greatly upon where it has been fed and what it has eaten. If taken out of stagnant and foul water it should be kept for a couple of days in a large tub of pure water.

PLAICE, FILLETED (BOILED).

INGREDIENTS.—2 *good sized fish, vinegar, salt.*

Mode.—Fillet the fish, making 4 or 8 fillets of each fish according to size. Wash them in salt and water, roll them up inside out, and skewer. Have ready a kettle with sufficient water to cover the fish, salted in the proportion of a tablespoonful to a quart of water, with a dessertspoonful of vinegar, and boil for about 10 minutes. Serve with melted butter flavoured with anchovy.

Time, about 10 minutes. *Average cost* from 6d. to 1s. each. *Seasonable* from May to November. *Sufficient* for 4 persons.

PLAICE (FRIED).

INGREDIENTS.—*Hot lard or clarified dripping, egg, and breadcrumbs.*

Mode.—Wash and wipe the fish dry, and let them remain in a cloth until it is time to dress them. Brush them over with egg, and cover with breadcrumbs mixed with a little flour. Fry of a nice brown in hot dripping or lard, and garnish with parsley and cut lemon. Serve with plain melted butter or anchovy sauce.

Time, about 5 minutes. *Average cost* from 4d. lb. *Seasonable* from May to November. *Sufficient*, 4 plaice for 6 persons

Note.—Plaice may be boiled plain, and served with melted butter. Garnish with parsley and cut lemon.

SALMON (BOILED).

INGREDIENTS.—6 *oz. salt to each gallon of water; sufficient water to cover the fish.*

Mode.—Scale and clean the fish, and be particular that no blood is left inside; lay it in the fish-kettle with sufficient boiling water to cover, adding salt as above. Bring it quickly to a boil, take off the scum, and let it simmer till the fish is done, which will be when the meat separates easily from the bone Drain it, and if not wanted for a few minutes, keep it warm by means of warm cloths laid over it. Serve on hot napkin, garnish with cut lemon and parsley, and send Tartare or Dutch sauce, or plain melted butter to table with it. A dish of dressed cucumber usually accompanies this fish.

Time, 8 minutes to each lb. for large, thick salmon ; 6 minutes for thin fish. *Average cost*, in full season, 1s. to 3s. 6d. per lb. *Seasonable* from April to August. *Sufficient*, ½ lb., or rather less, for each person.

To CHOOSE SALMON.—The belly should be firm and thick, which may readily be ascertained by feeling it with the thumb and finger. The circumstance of this fish having *red* gills is not at all to be relied on, as this quality can be easily given them by art.

SALMON CUTLETS.

INGREDIENTS.—2 *slices of salmon, butter.*

Mode.—Cut the slices 1 inch thick, season with pepper and salt ; butter a sheet of white paper, lay each slice on a separate piece, with the ends twisted ; broil gently over a clear fire, and serve with anchovy, caper, or any piquant sauce.

Time, 5 to 10 minutes. *Average cost*, 2s. 6d. *Seasonable* in summer. *Sufficient* for 4 persons.

SALMON (FRICANDEAU OF).

(French Recipe.)

INGREDIENTS.—2½ *lbs. of the middle cut of a salmon*, 2 *onions*, 2 *carrots*, sliced fine, some lardoons, 2 bay-leaves, 1 pint of stock, some white pepper, salt and grated nutmeg.

Mode.—Scale and thoroughly wash and dry the salmon. Lard it carefully, and put it in a stewpan with the other ingredients, and allow it to simmer very gently for 2 hours. Strain the sauce, skim off the fat, reduce it to a glaze and glaze the fricandeau. Dilute what remains of the glaze with a little stock, and serve poured round the salmon.

Time, 2¼ hours. *Average cost*, 5s. *Sufficient* for 6 to 8 persons. *Seasonable* in summer.

SALMON (MAYONNAISE OF).

INGREDIENTS.—2 *lbs. cold boiled salmon*, 2 *lettuces, some small salad, a little beetroot, a very little oil and vinegar, rather less than ½ pint mayonnaise sauce, hard-boiled eggs.*

Mode.—Clean and dry the lettuces and take the outer leaves dipped in oil and vinegar to lay on the dish as a foundation. On this lay a ring of cutlets cut from the salmon and well masked with the sauce. Round these and in the centre put the salad, cut up and arranged nicely, then pour over the remainder of the sauce and garnish with the eggs cut-up, beetroot, or any other pretty garnish.

Average cost, 3s. 6d. *Seasonable* in spring and summer. *Sufficient* for 8 persons.

SALMON (PICKLED).

INGREDIENTS.—*Salmon*, ½ *oz. whole pepper*, ½ *oz. whole allspice*, 1 *teaspoonful salt*, 2 *bay-leaves, equal quantities of vinegar and the liquor in which the fish was boiled.*

Mode.—After the fish comes from table, lay it in a dish, take away the bone, and cover so as to exclude the air ; boil the liquor and vinegar with the other ingredients for 10 minutes, and let it stand to get cold ; pour it over the salmon, and in 12 hours it will be fit for the table.

Time, 10 minutes, to boil the liquor and vinegar.

SCALLOPS (FRIED).

INGREDIENTS. — *Scallops, egg, and breadcrumbs ; pepper and salt, sprig* of minced parsley, flour, spoonful of lemon pickle.

Mode.—Take out the scallops, trim them and divide each into 4 pieces, cover with egg and crumbs, season with pepper, salt, and parsley, and fry. Pour a little water into the pan to make gravy, thicken with the flour, and season with pepper and salt, adding the lemon pickle. Pour this over the scallops and serve.

Time, ½ an hour. *Average cost* from 6d. to 1s. dozen.

SCALLOPS (SCALLOPED).

INGREDIENTS.—½ *dozen scallops, breadcrumbs, butter,* ½ *pint milk, seasoning of cayenne and salt.*

Mode.—After trimming the scallops stew them in the milk for 10 minutes. Take them out, cut them in small pieces, clean and butter the shells (the deeper ones). Put in each a layer of breadcrumbs, then fill with the fish, adding seasoning and sufficient of the milk to moisten them. Cover with crumbs, put some oiled butter over, and bake brown in a quick oven.

Time, about 15 minutes to bake. *Average cost,* 9d. *Sufficient* for 4 persons.

SKATE (CRIMPED).

INGREDIENTS.—½ *lb. salt to each gallon of water.*

Mode.—Clean, skin, and cut the fish into slices, which roll and tie round; put the fish into highly salted water and boil till it is done. Drain well, remove the string, dish on a hot napkin, and serve with melted butter, caper, or anchovy sauce; or dished without a napkin, and the sauce poured over.

Time, about 20 minutes. *Average cost,* 6d. per lb. *Seasonable* from August to April.

TO CHOOSE SKATE.—This fish should be chosen for its firmness, breadth, and thickness, and should have a creamy appearance. When crimped, it should not be kept longer than a day or two, as all kinds of crimped fish soon become sour. Skate should never be eaten out of season.

SMELTS (BAKED).

INGREDIENTS. — 12 *smelts, breadcrumbs,* ¼ *lb. fresh butter,* 2 *blades*

pounded mace; salt and cayenne to taste.

Mode. — Wash and dry the fish thoroughly in a cloth, and arrange in a flat baking-dish. Cover with fine breadcrumbs, and place little pieces of butter all over them. Season and bake for 15 minutes. Before serving, add a squeeze of lemon-juice, and garnish with fried parsley and cut lemon.

Time, ½ hour. *Average cost,* 6d. to 1s. per dozen. *Seasonable* from October to May. *Sufficient* for 6 persons.

TO CHOOSE SMELTS.—When good this fish is of a fine silvery appearance, and when alive their backs are of a dark brown shade, which, after death, fades to a light fawn. They ought to have a refreshing fragrance, resembling that of a cucumber.

SMELTS (FRIED).

INGREDIENTS. — *Egg and breadcrumbs, a little flour, boiling lard.*

Mode.—Smelts should be very fresh, and not washed more than is necessary to clean them. Dry them in a cloth, lightly flour, dip them in egg, sprinkle with very fine breadcrumbs. Fry of a nice pale brown in boiling lard, and be careful not to take off the light roughness of the crumbs. Dry before the fire on a drainer, and serve with plain melted butter. This fish is often used as a garnish.

Time, 5 minutes. *Average cost,* 6d. to 1s. per dozen. *Seasonable* from October to May.

SOLE A LA NORMANDE.

INGREDIENTS.—1 *large sole, about a* ¼ *pint cider,* 1 *dozen oysters,* ¼ *pint white sauce,* 1 *onion, a little thyme and parsley, cayenne, salt, butter.*

Mode.—Cleanse and skin the sole. Finely mince the onion and parsley, and scatter them with the thyme over the bottom of a well-buttered shallow pie-dish, dust over a little seasoning, and lay in the sole. Cover with cider and bake gently till the fish is well done. Beard the oysters and cook them by steaming, then lay them over the sole. Put the oyster liquor, and a little from the sole with the sauce, and return it over the fire till it is very thick, then coat the fish and return to the oven for a few minutes to get thoroughly hot. It is best to send the sole to table in the dish in which it is cooked, if it be a presentable one.

Time, 15 minutes. *Average cost*, 3s. *Seasonable* at any time. *Sufficient* for 4 persons.

SOLE AU GRATIN.

INGREDIENTS. — *A pair of medium-sized soles, 1 onion, 6 to 12 mushrooms according to size, a few sprigs of parsley, a glass of white wine, salt, cayenne, breadcrumbs, butter.*

Mode.—Mince the onion and cook it in a little butter for about 6 minutes, then add to it the mushrooms and parsley also minced, and cook for another few minutes, adding the seasoning. Put this mixture at the bottom of a fireproof dish and lay over it the soles filleted. Dust over a little cayenne and salt, pour in the wine, and cover with grated breadcrumbs, dotted over with small pieces of butter. Bake for about 15 minutes, and if the crumbs are not browned use a salamander or hot shovel; serve in the dish.

Time, 15 minutes to bake. *Average cost*, 3s. *Seasonable* at any time. *Sufficient* for 4 or 5 persons.

SOLES (BOILED).

INGREDIENTS.—*Soles, ¼ lb. salt to each gallon of water.*

Mode.—Cleanse and wash the fish, but do not skin it, and place in a stew-pan or kettle with enough hot water to cover them. Bring slowly to the boil and keep simmering till done. Drain the fish, dish it on a napkin heated on the dish, garnish with cut lemon and parsley, and send to table with shrimp, parsley, or anchovy sauce.

Time, about 6 to 10 minutes after the water boils. *Average cost*, from 1s. lb. *Sufficient*—allow 1 large sole for 3 persons. *Seasonable* at any time.

SOLES (FRIED).

INGREDIENTS.—*2 middling-sized soles, hot lard or clarified dripping, egg, and breadcrumbs.*

Mode.—Skin and carefully wash the soles; cut off the fins; wipe very dry, and let them remain in the cloth until it is time to dress them. Dredge the soles with a little flour, brush them

over with beaten egg, and cover with breadcrumbs. Put them in a deep pan, with plenty of clarified dripping or lard or oil, heated, so that it may neither scorch the fish nor make them sodden. When sufficiently cooked on one side, turn them carefully, and brown them on the other; they may be considered ready when a thick smoke rises. Lift them out carefully, and lay them before the fire on a reversed sieve and soft paper, to absorb the fat, as nothing is more disagreeable than greasy fish. Dish the soles on a hot napkin, garnish with cut lemon and fried parsley, and send to table with plain melted butter or sharp sauce.

Time, 10 minutes for large soles, less time for small ones. *Average cost*, from 1s. lb. *Seasonable* at any time. *Sufficient* for 4 or 5 persons.

SPRATS.

Sprats should be cooked very fresh, which can be ascertained by their bright and sparkling eyes and silvery appearance. Wipe them dry; fasten them in rows by a skewer run through the eyes; dredge with flour, and broil them on a gridiron over a nice clear fire. The gridiron should be rubbed with suet. Serve very hot.

Time, 3 or 4 minutes. *Average cost*, 1d. to 1½d. per lb. *Seasonable* from November to March.

SPRATS (Fried in Batter).

INGREDIENTS.—*Eggs, flour, milk, breadcrumbs; seasoning of salt and pepper.*

Mode.—Wipe the sprats, dip them in a batter made of above ingredients. Fry of a nice brown, serve very hot, and garnish with fried parsley. Sprats may be baked like herrings.

TROUT (FRIED).

INGREDIENTS.—*A large trout, a few breadcrumbs, a little butter, a few truffles and mushrooms (if obtainable), a teaspoonful of thyme, parsley and chervil, minced finely. For the stock— a pint of white wine vinegar, a quart of water, a small head of celery, 2 bay-leaves, 1 oz. butter, a bouquet of herbs, some white wine.*

Mode.—Slice the vegetables for the

stock and put them in a stewpan with the other ingredients over a strong fire. The stock should be reduced in this manner and as it diminishes add 2 glasses of wine ½ glass at a time, then strain and set aside to cool. Stuff the trout with the herbs, truffles, and mushrooms, chopped and made into a forcemeat with the breadcrumbs and butter, tie up the head, and simmer in the stock for 15 minutes. Take out the fish, drain it, roll in egg and bread-crumbs, fry a nice brown, and serve with tomato sauce or some of the stock.

Time, ½ hour. *Sufficient* for 4 persons. *Seasonable* from May to September.

TROUT (STEWED).

INGREDIENTS. — 2 *middling - sized trout,* ½ *onion sliced, a little parsley,* 2 *cloves,* 1 *blade of mace,* 2 *bay-leaves, a little thyme, salt and pepper to taste,* 1 *pint medium stock,* 1 *glass port wine, thickening of butter and flour.*

Mode.—Wash the fish clean, and wipe it dry. Lay it in a stewpan with all the ingredients except the butter and flour; simmer for ½ hour or more. Take it out, strain the gravy, add the thickening, and stir it over a sharp fire for 5 minutes; pour it over the trout, and serve.

Time, according to size, ½ hour or more. *Seasonable* from June to September, best at the end of August. *Sufficient* for 4 to 6 persons.

TURBOT (BOILED).

INGREDIENTS.—6 *oz. of salt to each gallon of water.*

Mode.—Choose a middling-sized tur-bot; if very large, the meat will be tough and thready. Three or four hours before dressing, soak the fish in salt and water to take off the slime; then thoroughly cleanse it, and with a knife make an incision down the middle of the back, to prevent the skin of the belly from cracking. Rub it over with lemon, and be particular not to cut off the fins. Lay the fish in a very clean turbot-kettle, with cold water to cover it, and salt in the above proportion. Let it gradually come to a boil, and skim carefully ; keep it gently sim-mering, and on no account let it boil fast. When the meat separates easily

from the bone, it is done ; then take it out, let it drain well, and dish it on a hot napkin. Rub a little lobster spawn through a sieve, sprinkle it over the fish, and garnish with tufts of parsley and cut lemon. Lobster, oyster, or shrimp sauce should be sent to table with it.

Time, after the water boils, about ½ hour for a large turbot; middling size, about 20 minutes. *Average cost,* 1s. lb. *Seasonable* at any time. *Sufficient,* 1 middling-sized turbot for 8 persons.

TURBOT (Italian Fashion).
(Italian Recipe.)

INGREDIENTS.—*A turbot of medium size,* 1 *trout,* 2 *carp's roes, button mush-rooms, a few truffles and prawns,* 2 *oz. of butter, wine, sauce.*

Mode.—Cleanse and prepare the fish as usual and simmer it in white wine for 2 hours. Drain and put on a dish, with a garnish of the trout and carp's roe, fried in small pieces, and the mush-rooms glazed. Stick in some orna-mental skewers, decorated with truffles and prawns, and serve with a good sauce.

Time, 2 hours. *Average cost,* 12s. *Sufficient* for 8 persons. *Seasonable* from May to September.

WHITEBAIT.

INGREDIENTS. — *Whitebait, flour, a little salt, lard for frying.*

Mode.—Drain the fish in a sieve and pick them over. Shake them well in a floured cloth till they are coated, put them a few at a time in a frying basket and immerse them in boiling lard. Take them out directly they are done and lay them on an inverted sieve covered with blotting paper before the fire to thoroughly dry. When all are cooked sprinkle over a little salt, dish them on a very hot dish and serve with cut lemon, and thin brown bread-and-butter.

If the fish has to be kept at all after it is bought, it should be laid in very cold water.

Time, about 2 minutes to cook. *Average cost,* 1s. per pint. *Seasonable* from April to August. *Sufficient*—allow 1 pint for 3 persons.

WHITING (BOILED).

INGREDIENTS.—¼ *lb. salt to each gallon of water.*

Mode.—Cleanse the fish, but do not

skin them; lay them in a fish-kettle, with cold water to cover, and salt as above. Bring gradually to a boil, simmer gently for about 5 minutes, or rather more should the fish be very large. Dish on a hot napkin, and garnish with tufts of parsley. Serve with anchovy sauce or plain melted butter.

Time, after the water boils, 5 minutes. *Average cost* for small whiting, from 2d. each. *Seasonable* all the year; best from October to March. *Sufficient*, 1 small whiting for each person.

To CHOOSE WHITING.—Choose for the firmness of its flesh and its silvery hue.

WHITING (BROILED).

INGREDIENTS.—*Salt and water, flour.*

Mode.—Wash the whiting in salt and water; wipe them thoroughly. Flour them well and broil them over a very clear fire. Serve with *maître d'hôtel* sauce or plain melted butter. (*See* SAUCES.) Be careful to preserve the

liver, as by some it is considered very delicate.

Time, 5 minutes for small whiting. *Average cost*, from 2d. each. *Seasonable* all the year, but best from October to March. *Sufficient*, 1 small whiting for each person

WHITING (FRIED).

INGREDIENTS. — *Egg and bread-crumbs, a little flour, hot lard or clarified dripping.*

Mode.—Take off the skin, clean and thoroughly wipe the fish free from all moisture, that the egg and bread-crumbs may properly adhere. Fasten the tail in the mouth with a small skewer, brush over with egg, dredge with a little flour, and cover with bread crumbs. Fry in hot lard or dripping, of a nice colour, and serve on a napkin, garnished with fried parsley. Send to table with plain melted butter.

Time, about 6 minutes. *Average cost*, 2d. each. *Seasonable* all the year; best from October to March. *Sufficient*, 1 small whiting for each person.

FORCEMEATS, GRAVIES, AND SAUCES

FORCEMEAT AND STUFFING.

Forcemeat and stuffing to be pleasant additions to the dishes they are intended for should be very carefully made. The suet should be finely chopped, the bread-crumbs equally finely grated, the eggs well beaten, &c., &c., and the whole thoroughly blended with judicious seasoning. Forcemeat balls should be *well* flavoured as they lose a little in process of cooking, and should be firm enough to fry without fear of breaking.

CHESTNUT FORCEMEAT (for Turkey, &c.).

INGREDIENTS.—*2 doz. chestnuts, a slice of ham or a pork sausage, 1 or 2 eggs according to size, a cupful of bread-crumbs, half an onion, 1 oz. butter, the liver of the fowl or turkey, a strip of lemon-peel, pepper and salt.*

Mode.—Peel the chestnuts and boil them with the onion and the liver in water or a little stock. Chop the ham finely, also the onion, or turn the sausage out of its skin. Pound chestnuts and liver to a paste with a little moistening of the stock, then add the other ingredients (the lemon-peel grated), and work together thoroughly. When well mixed add the egg and form into a paste, adding more stock if necessary.

Time, 15 minutes to boil the chestnuts. *Average cost*, 8d. *Sufficient* for large fowl or small turkey. *Seasonable* in winter.

FORCEMEAT FOR FISH.

INGREDIENTS. — *A cupful of breadcrumbs, ½ doz oysters, or 18 tinned ones, a teaspoonful minced herbs, 2 oz. of suet, pounded mace and pepper to taste, a dessertspoonful of anchovy sauce, a little milk, 1 large egg.*

Mode.—Mince the oysters and chop the suet finely, then thoroughly mix all the ingredients, seasoning to taste, and blending with the egg beaten and a little milk. Put the forcemeat thus made in a small stewpan, stir till it thickens, when it is ready for use.

Veal forcemeat is often used for fish such as fresh haddock and others.

Time, 5 minutes to stir over the fire. *Average cost*, 10d. *Sufficient* for good sized fish. *Seasonable* at any time.

FORCEMEAT FOR GAME PIES, &c.

INGREDIENTS.—*A teacupful of breadcrumbs, 2 oz. each of cooked calf's liver and bacon, ½ doz. mushrooms (if obtainable), a teaspoonful of minced parsley and other herbs, ¼ teaspoonful grated lemon-rind, seasoning of pepper and salt, an egg.*

Mode.—Mince very finely the liver and bacon, then pound together. Add the breadcrumbs, the mushrooms chopped, and the seasoning, and blend all with the egg, beaten.

Time, 15 minutes to cook the liver. *Average cost*, 8d. *Sufficient* for a pie. *Seasonable* for game pies in autumn or winter.

FORCEMEAT FOR VEAL, TURKEYS, FOWLS, HARE, &c.

INGREDIENTS. — *2 oz. ham or lean bacon, ¼ lb. suet, the rind of ½ a lemon, 1 teaspoonful minced parsley, 1 teaspoonful minced sweet herbs; salt, cayenne, and pounded mace to taste; 6 oz. bread crumbs, 2 eggs.*

Mode.—Shred the ham or bacon, chop the suet, lemon-peel, and herbs, taking care that all be very finely minced; season with salt, cayenne, and mace, and blend all thoroughly together with

the breadcrumbs before wetting. Now beat and strain the eggs; work these up with the other ingredients, and the forcemeat will be ready. When made into balls, fry of a nice brown in boiling lard, or put them on a tin and bake for half hour in a moderate oven. No one flavour should predominate greatly, and the forcemeat should be of sufficient body to cut with a knife, and yet not dry and heavy. For ve *j* delicate forcemeat, pound the ingredients together before binding with the egg; but, for ordinary cooking, mincing very finely answers the purpose.

Average cost, 7d. *Sufficient* for a turkey, a moderate-sized fillet of veal, or a hare.

LIVER FORCEMEAT.

INGREDIENTS.—*¼ lb. each veal and calf's liver, 2 oz. bacon or ham, 2 eggs, a dessertspoonful butter, a tablespoonful of chopped truffle (if obtainable), parsley, bay-leaf, and lemon thyme (a dessertspoonful altogether when minced), pepper and salt.*

Mode.—Boil the liver, bacon, and veal, the latter mixed with the onion, then pound and rub through a sieve. Add the herbs, the truffles, butter, and seasoning, and blend with the eggs, well beaten. Chicken or any white meat will serve in place of the veal. This forcemeat should be very similar in flavour to *Foie Gras*.

Time, 15 minutes to boil the bacon, &c. *Average cost*, 1s. 6d. with truffles. *Sufficient* for an *entrée*. *Seasonable* at any time.

PANADA.

INGREDIENTS.—*4 oz. of stale crumb of bread, 1 egg, 1 oz. butter.*

Mode.—Scald the bread with boiling water, then squeeze it as dry as possible in a cloth. Break it up in a small saucepan, adding the butter, then stir in the egg till the mixture leaves the sides of the saucepan, when it is ready for use.

Time, about 10 minutes. *Average cost*, 3d.

SAGE AND ONION STUFFING FOR GEESE, DUCKS, AND PORK.

INGREDIENTS. — *4 large onions, 10 sage leaves, ¼ lb. breadcrumbs, 1 oz. butter, salt and pepper.*

Mode.—Peel the onions, put them into boiling water, simmer for 5 minutes, or rather longer, and put in the sage leaves for a minute or two to take off their rawness. Chop both very fine, add the bread, seasoning, and butter, and work the whole together with a little of the liquor in which the onions were boiled, when the stuffing will be ready for use. It should be rather highly seasoned, and the sage leaves finely chopped. Many cooks do not parboil the onions, but use them raw. The stuffing then is not so mild. When made for a goose, a portion of the liver of the bird, simmered for a few minutes and very finely minced, is frequently added.

Time, rather more than 5 minutes to simmer the onions. *Average cost*, for this quantity, 3d. *Sufficient* for 1 goose, or a pair of ducks.

GRAVIES.

In the hands of a good cook a joint (with the exception of one of veal) will always yield enough gravy to serve with it, but for game, poultry, and other dishes, it must be made. Any of the stocks for which recipes are given in this book will serve as a basis for the gravies, with the addition (if necessary) of store sauces and thickening. The goodness and strength of spices, wines, flavourings, &c., evaporate, and lose a great deal of their fragrance, if added a long time before they are wanted. If this point be attended to, a saving of one half the quantity of these ingredients will be effected, as, with long boiling, the flavour almost entirely passes away. The shank-bones of mutton, previously well soaked, will be found a great assistance in enriching gravies; a kidney or melt, beef skirt, trimmings of meat, &c., answer very well when only a small quantity is wanted. A good gravy need not be very expensive, for economically prepared dishes are oftentimes found as savoury and wholesome as dearer ones. The cook should also remember that the fragrance of gravies should not be overpowered by too much spice, or any strong essences, and that they should always be warmed in a *bain marie* after they are flavoured, or else in a jar or jug placed in a saucepan of boiling water. The remains of roast-meat gravy should always be saved, as, when no meat is at hand a very nice

gravy in haste may be made from it, which, when added to hashes, ragouts, &c., is a great improvement. Gravies, like soups, are always much nicer if made, with the exception of the flavourings, the day before they are wanted.

BROWNING AND THICKENING FOR GRAVIES.

The browning for soups (*which see*) answers equally well for sauces and gravies; but where they can be made to look brown by using ketchup, wine, browned flower, tomatoes, or any colour sauce, it is far preferable. When no browning is at hand, and the colour of the gravy is to be heightened, dissolve a lump of sugar in an iron spoon over a sharp fire, and drop it into the sauce or gravy quite hot. Care must be taken not to put in too much, as it would impart a very disagreeable flavour.

Thickening for gravies may be of plain flour, but roux (*see* " Recipes for Soups ") is far better.

BEEF GRAVY.

INGREDIENTS.—$\frac{1}{2}$ *lb. lean beef*, 1 *pint cold water*, 1 *shallot or small onion*, $\frac{1}{2}$ *a teaspoonful salt, a little pepper*, 1 *tablespoonful sauce, or mushroom ketchup*, $\frac{1}{4}$ *a teaspoonful arrowroot*.

Mode.—Cut the beef up into small pieces, and put it, with the water, into a stewpan. Add the shallot and seasoning, and simmer gently for 3 hours. A short time before it is required mix the arrowroot with a little cold water, and pour it into the gravy, which keep stirring, adding the sauce, and just letting it boil. Strain off the gravy in a tureen, and serve.

Time, 3 hours. *Average cost*, 6d. per pint.

BROWN GRAVY.

INGREDIENTS.—2 *oz. butter*, 2 *large onions*, 2 *lbs. shin of beef*, 2 *small slices lean bacon (if at hand), salt and whole pepper to taste*, 3 *cloves*, 2 *quarts water. For thickening*, 2 *oz. butter*, 3 *oz. flour*.

Mode.—Put the butter into a stewpan; set this on the fire, throw in the onions, cut in rings, and fry them a light brown; add the beef and bacon, cut into small square pieces; season, and pour in a teacupful of water; let it boil for about 10 minutes, or until of a nice brown colour, occasionally stirring. Fill up with water in the above pro-

ROAST LOIN OF PORK.

ROAST HAUNCH OF MUTTON.

ROAST AITCHBONE OF BEEF.

ROUND OF BEEF.

LEG OF MUTTON

CALF'S HEAD

HAM.

SIRLOIN OF BEEF.

SHOULDER OF MUTTON.

SADDLE OF MUTTON.

portion; let it boil up, when draw it to the side of the fire to simmer gently for 1½ hours; strain, and when cold, take off the fat. In thickening this gravy, melt 8 oz. of butter in a stewpan, add 2 oz. of flour, and stir till of a light-brown colour; when cold, add it to the strained gravy, and boil up quickly. This thickening may be made in larger quantities, and kept in a stone jar for use when wanted.

Time, altogether 2 hours. *Average cost* for this quantity, 1s. 6d.

BROWN GRAVY WITHOUT MEAT.

INGREDIENTS.—2 *large onions*, 1 *large carrot*, 2 *oz. butter*, 3 *pints boiling water*, 1 *bunch savoury herbs, a wine-glassful of good beer; salt and pepper.*

Mode.—Slice, flour, and fry the onions and carrots in the butter until of a nice light-brown colour; add the boiling water and remaining ingredients; let the whole stew gently for about an hour; strain, and when cold skim off the fat. Thicken it as in preceding recipe, and, if necessary, add a few drops of colouring.

Time, 1 hour. *Average cost*, 2d. per pint.

Note.—A small quantity of ketchup or sauce very much improves the flavour.

GRAVY (CHEAP) FOR HASHES, &c.

INGREDIENTS.—*Bones and trimmings of the cooked joint intended for hashing, ¼ teaspoonful of salt, ¼ teaspoonful whole pepper, ¼ teaspoonful whole allspice, a small faggot savoury herbs, ½ head celery, 1 carrot, 1 onion, 1 oz. butter, thickening, sufficient boiling water to cover the bones.*

Mode.—Chop the bones in small pieces and put them in a stewpan, with the trimmings, salt, pepper, spice, herbs, and vegetables. Cover with boiling water, and let the whole simmer gently for 1½ or 2 hours. Slice and fry the onion in the butter till of a pale brown, and mix it gradually with the gravy made from the bones: boil for ¼ hour, and strain into a basin; now put it back into the stewpan; flavour with walnut pickle or ketchup, pickled-onion liquor, or other sauce. Thicken with a little butter and flour kneaded together on a plate. After the thickening is added the gravy should just boil, to take off the rawness of the flour.

Time, 2 hours or rather more. *Average cost*, 3d., exclusive of bones &c.

GRAVY (CHEAP) FOR MINCED VEAL.

INGREDIENTS.—*Bones and trimmings of cold roast or boiled veal, 1½ pints water, 1 onion, ¼ teaspoonful minced lemon-peel, ¼ teaspoonful salt, 1 blade pounded mace, the juice of ¼ lemon; thickening of butter and flour.*

Mode.—Put all the ingredients into a stewpan, except the thickening and lemon-juice, and simmer very gently for rather more than 1 hour, or until the liquor is reduced to a pint, when strain through a hair-sieve. Add a thickening of butter and flour, and the lemon-juice, and let it just boil up. It may be flavoured with a little tomato sauce, and, where a rather dark-coloured gravy is not objected to, ketchup, or sauce, may be added.

Time, rather more than 1 hour. *Average cost*, 2d

GRAVY FOR FISH.

INGREDIENTS.—*A cupful of fish stock (if at hand), or water, a teaspoonful or rather more of white or brown roux, a dessertspoonful each vinegar and ketchup, salt and pepper.*

Mode.—If for baked fish, when the fish is done, take it out of the tin and make the gravy in it in the usual way, adding the ingredients named to the gravy that has run from the fish, then boiling it up over the fire and straining it into the dish. If for boiled fish use the same ingredients, with sufficient liquor in which the fish was boiled.

Time, 3 minutes to boil. *Average cost*, 2d. *Sufficient* for medium-sized dish.

GRAVY (QUICKLY MADE).

INGREDIENTS.—½ *lb. shin of beef, ½ onion, ¼ carrot, 2 or 3 sprigs parsley and savoury herbs, butter about the size of a walnut; cayenne and mace; ¾ pint water.*

Mode.—Cut the meat into very small pieces; slice the onion and carrot, and put them into a small saucepan with the butter. Keep stirring over a sharp fire until they have taken a little colour, when add the water and the remaining ingredients. Simmer for ½ hour, skim well, strain, and flavour.

Time, ½ hour. *Average cost*, for this quantity, 4d.

SAUCES.

There is no more important branch of the culinary art than the making of sauces, not only to render them pleasant in flavour, but pleasant to regard. In many cases the sauce governs the dish. A simple serving of fish, for example, will take its various names, and be subservient to, the sauces with which it is accompanied to table, and the same may be said of many *entrées* of fish and game. In other cases the sauce has to be, not a contrast, but in harmony with whatever it be served. In both cases, however, the same care and art is needed, and every sauce should have a character of its own.

All sauces intended for masking such things as cutlets and fish should be made of sufficient consistency, this applying particularly to such as mayonnaise. Where eggs are used in hot sauces they must not be allowed to boil. Hot sauces cannot be served too hot, nor cold ones too cold.

Where many sauces have to be made, proper utensils for their making *must* find a place. Copper, enamelled iron, and fireproof china pans are constantly needed, and tammy cloths are indispensable, while a *bain marie* is of the greatest service.

ANCHOVY SAUCE.

INGREDIENTS.—4 *anchovies*, 1 *oz. butter,* ½ *pint melted butter, cayenne to taste.*

Mode.—Bone the anchovies and pound them to a paste with 1 oz. butter. Make the melted butter hot, stir in the pounded anchovies and cayenne, simmer for 3 or 4 minutes, and add a squeeze of lemon-juice. A more general and expeditious way is to stir in 1½ tablespoonfuls of anchovy essence to ½ pint melted butter, and season to taste. Boil the whole up for 1 minute and serve hot.

Time, 5 minutes. *Average cost,* 5d. for ½ pint. *Sufficient,* this quantity, for a brill, small turbot, 3 or 4 soles, &c.

APPLE SAUCE FOR GEESE, PORK, &c.

INGREDIENTS.—6 *good-sized apples, sifted sugar to taste, a piece of butter the size of a walnut, water.*

Mode.—Pare, core, and quarter the apples; throw them into cold water to preserve their whiteness. Put them in a saucepan with sufficient water to moisten, and boil till soft enough to pulp. Beat them up, adding sugar and a small piece of butter.

Time, about ¾ hour. *Average cost,* 4d. *Sufficient,* this quantity, for a goose or couple of ducks. *Seasonable* from August to March.

ARROWROOT SAUCE FOR PUDDINGS.

INGREDIENTS.—2 *small teaspoonfuls arrowroot,* 4 *dessertspoonfuls pounded sugar, the juice of* 1 *lemon,* ¼ *teaspoonful grated nutmeg,* ½ *pint water.*

Mode.—Mix the arrowroot smoothly with the water; put this into a stewpan; add the sugar, strained lemon-juice and grated nutmeg, and stir these ingredients over the fire until they boil. A small quantity of wine, or any liqueur, improves the flavour; it is usually served with bread, rice, custard, or any dry pudding that is not very rich.

Time, altogether, 15 minutes. *Average cost,* 4d. *Sufficient* for 6 or 7 persons.

BÉCHAMEL SAUCE.

INGREDIENTS. — *A cupful of good white stock, a few drops of lemon-juice, a grate of nutmeg, a little white roux or cornflour, pepper and salt.*

Mode.—Put the stock into a small enamelled pan, with a small grate of nutmeg, a seasoning of pepper and salt (if needed), thicken it and boil up, when add a few drops of lemon-juice.

Time, about 5 minutes. *Average cost,* 2d. or 3d., according to the stock.

Note.—The above sauce is made much richer and nicer by the addition of a cupful of cream, and it may be made *maigre* by using vegetarian white stock, milk, &c.

BREAD SAUCE (to serve with Roast Turkey, Fowl, Game, &c.).

INGREDIENTS.—1 *pint milk,* ¾ *lb. the crumb of a stale loaf,* 1 *onion; pounded mace, cayenne, and salt to taste;* 1 *oz. of butter.*

Mode.—Peel and quarter the onion, simmer in the milk till perfectly tender. Break the bread into small pieces, picking out any hard outside pieces; put it in a clean saucepan, strain the milk over it, cover it up, and let it remain for an hour to soak. Beat it up with a fork very smoothly, add a seasoning of pounded mace, cayenne, and salt, with 1 oz. butter; give the whole one boil.

Time, altogether, 1¾ hours. *Average*

cost for this quantity, 4d. *Sufficient* to serve with a turkey, pair of fowls, or brace of partridges.

CAPER SAUCE FOR BOILED MUTTON, &c.

INGREDIENTS.—$\frac{1}{2}$ pint melted butter, 3 tablespoonfuls capers, 1 tablespoonful of their liquor.

Mode.—Chop the capers twice or thrice, and add them, with their liquor, to $\frac{1}{2}$ pint of melted butter; keep stirring well; let the sauce simmer, and serve in a tureen. Pickled nasturtium pods may be used as a substitute for capers.

Time, after the melted butter is made, 2 minutes to simmer. *Average cost* for this quantity, 6d. *Sufficient* to serve with a leg of mutton.

CELERY SAUCE.

INGREDIENTS.—2 heads of celery, $\frac{1}{4}$ pint of melted butter, made with milk, a blade of mace, pepper and salt.

Mode.—Having washed the celery, boil it in salted water till tender, then cut it in small pieces and add it to the melted butter with the pounded mace and the seasoning, and simmer for a few minutes.

Time, $\frac{1}{2}$ hour. *Average cost,* 5d. *Sufficient* for a fowl.

CRANBERRY SAUCE (American Recipe).

INGREDIENTS.—A quart of cranberries, $\frac{1}{2}$ pint of water, white sugar to taste.

Mode.—Having washed and pickled the cranberries carefully, put them in a lined saucepan with the sugar and enough water to cover them. Let them stew very slowly for an hour or more, till reduced to a pulp, stirring them often. Take them off the fire and put in a wetted mould or small jars to cool. Serve in a small glass dish with roast turkey, ducks, or game, as we serve currant jelly with hare or mutton.

Time, about an hour. *Seasonable* from October to March.

DUTCH SAUCE.

INGREDIENTS.—2 oz. butter, 2 tablespoonfuls vinegar, 4 of water, yolks of 2 eggs, juice of $\frac{1}{2}$ a lemon, a little flour.

Mode.—Put all the ingredients except the lemon-juice into a small stewpan, and stir over the fire till the sauce is sufficiently thick. It must not boil or it will curdle.

Time, about 10 minutes. *Average cost,* 5d.

EGG SAUCE FOR SALT FISH.

INGREDIENTS.—4 eggs, $\frac{1}{2}$ pint melted butter; when liked a very little lemon-juice.

Mode — Boil the eggs about 20 minutes, and put them into cold water for $\frac{1}{2}$ hour. Strip off the shells, chop the eggs into small pieces, not, however, too fine. Make the melted butter and, when boiling, stir in the eggs; and serve very hot. Lemon-juice may be added at pleasure.

Time, 20 minutes to boil the eggs. *Average cost,* 6d. *Sufficient* for 3 or 4 lbs. of fish.

Note.—When a thicker sauce is required, use one or two more eggs.

FENNEL SAUCE FOR MACKEREL.

INGREDIENTS.—$\frac{1}{2}$ pint melted butter, rather more than a tablespoonful of chopped fennel.

Mode.—Make the melted butter by recipe, and chop the fennel rather small, carefully cleansing it from grit or dirt, and put it to the butter when on the point of boiling. Simmer for a minute or two, and serve in a tureen.

Time, 2 minutes. *Average cost,* 3d. *Sufficient* to serve with 5 or 6 mackerel.

GENEVÉSE SAUCE.

INGREDIENTS.—1 onion, 1 carrot, a bunch of sweet herbs, a bay-leaf, a blade of mace, a few mushrooms (if obtainable), 2 oz. butter, a glass of sherry, 1$\frac{1}{2}$ pints white stock, a little flour, $\frac{1}{2}$ a lemon.

Mode.—Slice the onion and carrot and put them in a stewpan with the herbs, mushrooms, bay-leaf, and mace. Add the butter, and simmer very slowly over a slow fire till the onion is tender. Add the sherry and stock, and stew gently for an hour, then strain into another saucepan. Put in a thickening of butter and flour, and stir into the sauce, let it boil, then stir till it is quite smooth, and then add the juice of the $\frac{1}{2}$ lemon.

Time, about 2 hours. *Average cost,* 1s. 3d. *Seasonable* at any time.

HOLLANDAISE SAUCE.

INGREDIENTS.—A small cupful of béchamel, the juice of $\frac{1}{2}$ lemon, colouring of parsley-green, salt, cayenne.

Mode.—Bring the béchamel to the

boil, and let it just simmer. Add the seasoning and colouring, and the moment before serving, the lemon-juice.

Average cost, 3d.

Note. — The colouring is procured by pounding parsley till the juice is extracted.

HORSERADISH SAUCE (to serve with Roast Beef).

INGREDIENTS. — 4 *tablespoonfuls grated horseradish*, 1 *teaspoonful pounded sugar*, 1 *teaspoonful salt*, ½ *teaspoonful pepper*, 2 *teaspoonfuls made mustard*, *vinegar*.

Mode. — Grate the horseradish, and mix it well with the sugar, salt, pepper, and mustard. Moisten with sufficient vinegar to give it the consistency of cream, and serve in a tureen ; 3 or 4 tablespoonfuls of cream will much improve the sauce. Heat it in a *bain marie*, or a jar, which place in a saucepan of boiling water. It will curdle if allowed to boil.

Average cost (without cream), 3d.

HORSERADISH SAUCE (COLD), FOR FISH.

INGREDIENTS. — 2 *tablespoonfuls horseradish, finely grated*, 1 *of vinegar*, ½ *pint cream, a dessertspoonful castor sugar, a saltspoonful each salt and made mustard.*

Mode. — Whisk the cream stiff, add the horseradish, then the other ingredients, and mix well together.

Average cost, 10d.

LEMON SAUCE FOR SWEET PUDDINGS.

INGREDIENTS. — *The rind and juice of* 1 *lemon*, 1 *tablespoonful flour*, 1 *oz. butter*, 1 *large wineglassful sherry*, 1 *wineglassful water, sugar to taste, the yolks of* 4 *eggs.*

Mode. — Rub the rind of the lemon on to some lumps of sugar ; squeeze out the juice, and strain it ; put the butter and flour into a saucepan ; stir them over the fire, and when of a pale brown, add the wine, water, and strained lemon-juice. Crush the lumps of sugar that were rubbed on the lemon ; stir these into the sauce, which should be very sweet. When well mixed and the sugar melted, put in the beaten yolks of 4 eggs ; keep stirring the sauce until it thickens, when serve. Do not allow it to boil, or it will be entirely spoiled.

Time, altogether 15 minutes. *Average cost*, 9d. *Sufficient* for 7 or 8 persons.

LOBSTER SAUCE, to serve with Turbot, Salmon, Brill, &c. (Very Good.)

INGREDIENTS. — 1 *middling-sized hen lobster*, 1 *pint melted butter*, 1 *tablespoonful anchovy sauce*, ½ *oz. butter, salt and cayenne, a little pounded mace when liked*, 2 *or* 3 *tablespoonfuls of cream.*

Mode. — Pick the meat from the shell of a hen lobster, and cut it into small square pieces ; put the spawn, which will be found under the tail, into a mortar with ½ oz. of butter, and pound it quite smooth ; rub it through a hair-sieve, and cover up till wanted. Make 1 pint of melted butter by recipe given, put in all the ingredients except the lobster-meat, and well mix the sauce before the lobster is added to it. Put in the meat, let it get thoroughly hot, but do not allow it to boil, as the colour, which should be bright red, would be spoiled. If served with turbot or brill, a little of the spawn (dried and rubbed through a sieve without butter) should be saved for garnish for the fish.

Time, 1 minute to simmer after the lobster has become *thoroughly hot through*. *Average cost*, for this quantity, 2s. *Seasonable* at any time. *Sufficient* to serve with a small turbot, a brill, or salmon for 6 persons.

Note. — Melted butter made with milk will be found to answer very well for lobster sauce. Less quantity may be made by using a very small lobster, to which add only ½ a pint of melted butter, and season as above. The cream may be dispensed with, and a lobster left from table may be converted into a very good sauce, if used before the fish is allowed to become stale. Tinned lobster, if well drained, answers very well for this sauce.

MAIGRE SAUCE, made without Meat (Hot).

INGREDIENTS. — ½ *pint of melted butter, a heaped tablespoonful chopped parsley, salt and pepper to taste, the juice of* ½ *large lemon*, 2 *minced shallots.*

Mode. — Make the melted butter by recipe given, stir in the above ingredients, and let them just boil.

Time, 1 minute to simmer. *Average cost*, 4d.

MAÎTRE D'HÔTEL SAUCE (Hot), to serve with Calf's Head.

INGREDIENTS. — 1 *slice minced ham, a few poultry trimmings or a little veal*, 2 *shallots*, 1 *clove garlic*, 1 *bay-leaf*, ¾ *pint water*, 2 *oz. butter*, 1 *dessertspoonful flour*, 1 *heaped tablespoonful chopped parsley, salt, pepper, and cayenne to taste, the juice of ½ large lemon, ¼ teaspoonful pounded sugar.*

Mode.—Put at the bottom of a stewpan the minced ham, and over it the poultry trimmings or veal, with the shallots, garlic, and bay-leaf. Pour in the water, and simmer gently for 1 hour (or until the liquor is reduced to ½ pint). Strain this gravy, put it in another saucepan, make a thickening of the butter and flour, and stir it to the gravy over a clear fire, care being taken that the butter does not float on the surface. Skim well, add the remaining ingredients, let the sauce gradually heat, but not boil. If intended for an *entrée*, make it of sufficient thickness to adhere to what it is intended to cover.

Time, 1½ hours. *Average cost,* 1s. per pint. *Sufficient* for rewarming the remains of ½ calf's head, or a small dish of cold flaked turbot, cod, &c.

MAYONNAISE SAUCE (for Cold Chicken, Salmon, &c.).

INGREDIENTS.—*The yolks of 2 eggs, 6 tablespoonfuls of salad oil, 2 tablespoonfuls vinegar, salt and white pepper to taste, 3 tablespoonfuls cream.*

Mode.—Put the yolks of the eggs into a basin with seasoning of pepper and salt; have ready the above quantities of oil and vinegar in separate vessels; add them very gradually to the eggs; continue stirring and rubbing the mixture with a wooden spoon. It cannot be stirred too frequently, and it should be made in a very cool place, or if ice is at hand, it should be mixed over it. When the vinegar and oil are well incorporated with the eggs, add the cream, stirring all the time, and it will be ready for use.

For a fish mayonnaise, this sauce may be coloured with lobster spawn pounded, and for poultry or meat, a little parsley juice may be used. Cucumber, tarragon, or any other flavoured vinegar may be substituted for plain.

The cost for this quantity, 9d. *Sufficient* for a small salad.

Note.—In mixing the oil and vinegar with the eggs, put in first a few drops of oil; then a few drops of vinegar, never adding much at one time. Patience and practice are required to make this sauce good.

MELTED BUTTER.

INGREDIENTS.—*2 oz. butter, 1 dessertspoonful flour, salt to taste, ½ pint water.*

Mode.—*Mix the flour and water to a smooth batter,* which put into a saucepan. Add the butter and a seasoning of salt; keep stirring *one way* till the ingredients are perfectly smooth; let the whole boil for a minute or two, and serve.

Time, 2 minutes to simmer. *Average cost* for this quantity, 2d.

MELTED BUTTER MADE WITH MILK.

INGREDIENTS.—1 *teaspoonful flour, 2 oz. butter, ½ pint milk, a few grains of salt.*

Mode. — Mix the butter and flour smoothly together on a plate; put it into a lined saucepan, and pour in the milk. Keep stirring it *one way* over a sharp fire; let it boil quickly for a minute or two, and it is ready to serve. This is a very good foundation for onion, lobster, or oyster sauce; using milk instead of water makes the preparation look more delicate.

Time, altogether, 10 minutes. *Average cost* for this quantity, 3d.

Note.—The French, in fact the real "melted butter," is simply butter melted and flavoured with lemon-juice.

MINT SAUCE (to serve with Roast Lamb).

INGREDIENTS. — 4 *dessertspoonfuls chopped mint, 2 dessertspoonfuls pounded white sugar, ¼ pint vinegar.*

Mode.—Wash the mint, which should be young and fresh-gathered, free from grit; pick the leaves from the stalks, mince them very fine, and put into a tureen; add the sugar and vinegar, and stir till the former is dissolved. This sauce is better by being made 2 or 3 hours before wanted for table. By many persons, the above proportion of sugar would not be considered sufficient.

Average cost, 3d. *Sufficient* to serve with a middling-sized joint of lamb.

Note.—Where green mint is not obtainable, mint vinegar may be substituted for it, or dried mint may be used.

MUSHROOM SAUCE (BROWN).

INGREDIENTS.—½ *pint button mushrooms, or large mushrooms cut into pieces, ½ pint good beef gravy, tablespoonful ketchup, thickening of butter and flour.*

Mode.—Put the gravy into a saucepan, thicken it, and stir over the fire until it boils. Wipe the mushrooms clean, cutting off the stalks; put them

into the gravy, simmer gently for about
10 minutes, then add the ketchup and
serve.

Time, rather more than 10 minutes.
Seasonable from August to October.

MUSHROOM SAUCE (WHITE).

INGREDIENTS.—½ *pint melted butter,
made with milk*, ¾ *pint button mushrooms*, 1 *dessertspoonful mushroom ketchup, cayenne and salt.*

Mode.—Make the melted butter by
recipe given, and add the mushrooms,
nicely cleaned, free from grit, and the
stalks cut off.   Simmer gently until
tender (about 10 minutes).   Put in the
seasoning and ketchup, and let it just
boil.

Time, rather more than 10 minutes.
Average cost, 8d.   *Seasonable* from
August to October.

MUSTARD SAUCE.

INGREDIENTS.—2 *oz. butter, a dessertspoonful brown roux, the same of mustard, about ½ wineglassful vinegar, salt.*

Mode.—Put the flour, mustard, and
butter together, adding a pinch of salt
in a saucepan with a wineglass of
boiling water, simmer for a few
minutes, then add the vinegar.

Time, 6 minutes.   *Average cost*, 3d.

NEAPOLITAN SAUCE (Italian Recipe).

INGREDIENTS.—½ *pint of white stock,*
1 *pint of Spanish sauce,* 1 *pint of
tomato sauce,* ½ *lb. of ham,* ½ *pint of
marsala, a few mushrooms,* 2 *or* 3
cloves, 2 *bay-leaves,* 1 *onion, whole
pepper, butter.*

Mode.—Chop the ham and onion and
fry in butter, add the wine, the stock,
mushrooms and seasoning; cover this
and allow to simmer until the quantity
is reduced to half.   Into another saucepan put the Spanish and tomato sauce ;
let these reduce a little, then pour
together, boil for one minute and strain
through a tammy.

Time, about ¼ hour.   *Average cost*,
2s. 6d.

ONION SAUCE.

INGREDIENTS.—9 *large onions, or* 12
middle-sized ones, 1 *pint melted butter,*
½ *teaspoonful salt, or rather more.*

Mode.—Peel the onions and put them
into water, to which a little salt has
been added, to preserve their whiteness,
and let them remain for ¼ hour.   Then
put them in a stewpan, cover with

water, and let them boil until tender;
and, if the onions are strong, change
the water after they have been boiling
for ¼ hour.   Drain thoroughly, chop,
and rub them through a sieve.   Make
1 pint melted butter, by recipe, and
when that boils, put in the onions with
the salt ; stir it till it simmers.

Time, from ½ to 1 hour, to boil the
onions.   *Average cost*, 6d. per pint.
Sufficient to serve with roast shoulder
of mutton or boiled rabbit.   *Seasonable*
from August to March.

Note.—To make this very mild and
delicate, use Spanish onions, which can
be procured from the beginning of September to Christmas.   2 or 3 tablespoonfuls of cream added, just before
serving, will be found to improve its
appearance.   Small onions, when very
young, may be cooked whole, and served
in melted butter.   A sieve or tammy
should be kept expressly for onions, as it
is liable to retain the flavour and smell.

OYSTER SAUCE (to serve with Fish, Boiled Poultry, &c.).

INGREDIENTS.—2 *dozen oysters,* ½ *pint
melted butter, made with milk.*

Mode.—Open the oysters carefully,
and save the liquor ; strain into a clean
saucepan (a lined one is best) ; put in
the oysters, and let them just come to
the boiling-point.   Take them off the
fire immediately, and put the whole
into a basin.   Strain off the liquor, mix
with it sufficient milk to make ½ pint
altogether, and follow the directions
for making melted butter.   When the
melted butter is ready and very smooth,
put in the oysters, previously bearded,
if you wish the sauce to be really nice.
Set it by the side of the fire to get
thoroughly hot, *but do not allow it to
boil*, or the oysters will immediately
harden.   Using cream instead of milk
makes this sauce extremely delicious.

Average cost, 2s. 3d.   *Sufficient* for
6 persons.   *Seasonable* from September
to April.   Tinned oysters may be used
for this sauce.

PARSLEY AND BUTTER (to serve with Calf's Head, Boiled Fowls, &c.).

INGREDIENTS. — 2 *tablespoonfuls
minced parsley,* ½ *pint melted butter.*

Mode.—Put into a saucepan a small
quantity of water, slightly salted, and
when it boils throw in a good bunch of
parsley previously washed and tied in
a bunch ; boil for 5 minutes, drain,
mince the leaves *very fine*, and put the
above quantity in a tureen ; pour over
it ½ pint of smoothly made melted

butter; stir once, that the ingredients may be thoroughly mixed and serve.

Time, 5 minutes to boil the parsley. *Average cost*, 3d. *Sufficient* for 1 large fowl; allow rather more for a pair.

Note.—When parsley leaves are not to be had, tie up a little parsley seed in a small piece of muslin, and boil it for 10 minutes in a small quantity of water; use this water to make the melted butter with, and throw into it a little boiled spinach, minced rather fine, which will have an appearance similar to that of parsley.

PIQUANTE SAUCE.

INGREDIENTS.—½ *small Spanish onion, a spoonful of capers, a tablespoonful of vinegar, a few drops of tarragon, ½ pint brown (meat) gravy.*

Mode.—Mince the onion and cut the capers in halves and simmer them in the vinegar till it is nearly evaporated, then add the gravy, with salt if necessary, and serve very hot.

Average cost, 6d.

RAVIGOTE SAUCE.

INGREDIENTS.—1½ *oz. butter, 2 oz. flour, a tablespoonful each tarragon and plain vinegar, and anchovy sauce, a little chopped parsley, ½ a lemon, a cupful of milk, cayenne.*

Mode.—Rub the flour into the butter, add to it the parsley, the lemon-juice and a little pepper and salt, then put into a saucepan with the milk and simmer till on the point of boiling. In another pan heat the sauce and vinegar, and when the milk, butter, &c., are slightly cool, mix the contents of the two pans.

Time, about 15 minutes. *Average cost* 5d. together.

SALAD DRESSING (Excellent).

INGREDIENTS.—1 *teaspoonful mixed mustard,* 1 *teaspoonful pounded sugar,* 2 *tablespoonfuls salad oil,* 4 *tablespoonfuls milk,* 2 *tablespoonfuls vinegar, cayenne and salt to taste.*

Mode.—Put the mixed mustard into a salad-bowl with the sugar, add the oil drop by drop, and carefully mix them well together. Proceed in this manner with the milk and vinegar, which must be added very *gradually,* or the sauce will curdle. Put in the seasoning. This dressing will be found very delicious with crab, or cold fried fish (the latter cut into dice), as well as with salads. In mixing salad dressings, the ingredients cannot be added *too gradually,* or *stirred too much.*

Average cost, for this quantity, 4d. *Sufficient* for a small salad.

This recipe can be confidently recommended. It was supplied by a lady noted for her salads.

SALAD DRESSING.

INGREDIENTS.—4 *eggs,* 1 *teaspoonful mixed mustard,* ¼ *teaspoonful white pepper, half that quantity cayenne, salt to taste,* 4 *tablespoonfuls cream, equal quantity oil and vinegar.*

Mode.—Boil the eggs hard, which will be in about ¼ hour or 20 minutes; put them into cold water, take off the shells, and pound the yolks in a mortar to a smooth paste. Add the other ingredients, except the vinegar, stir until the whole is thoroughly incorporated, and pour in sufficient vinegar to make it of the consistency of cream, taking care to add but little at a time.

Average cost, for this quantity, 10d. *Sufficient* for a large salad.

Note.—The white of the eggs cut into rings, will serve very well as a garnish.

Note.—In making salads, the vegetables, &c., should never be added to the sauce long before they are wanted; the dressing, however, may be prepared some hours before required. It is a good plan to bottle off sufficient dressing for a few days' consumption; if kept in a cool place, it will remain good for 4 or 5 days.

SHRIMP SAUCE (for various kinds of fish).

INGREDIENTS.—½ *pint melted butter,* ¼ *pint pickled shrimps, cayenne to taste.*

Mode.—Make the melted butter very smoothly by recipe; shell the shrimps (sufficient to make ¼ pint when picked), and put them into the butter; season with cayenne, and let the sauce just simmer. A teaspoonful of anchovy sauce may be added.

Time, 1 minute to simmer. *Average cost,* 6d. *Sufficient* for small dish of fish.

SUPRÉME SAUCE.

INGREDIENTS.—1½ *pints very good stock,* ½ *pint each milk and cream, a little salt and cayenne.*

Mode.—Reduce the stock by boiling to a third of its quantity, boil the cream and milk together with a pinch of salt, and a very small seasoning of cayenne and add to the stock.

Average cost, 2s.

SWEET SAUCE FOR PUDDINGS.

INGREDIENTS.—½ pint melted butter made with milk, 3 heaped teaspoonfuls pounded sugar, flavouring of grated lemon-rind, or nutmeg, or cinnamon.

Mode.—Make ½ pint of melted butter by recipe, omitting the salt; stir in the sugar, add a little grated lemon-rind, nutmeg, or powdered cinnamon, and serve. The milk can be flavoured with bitter almonds, by infusing about half a dozen of them in it for about ½ hour; the milk should then be strained before it is added to the other ingredients. This simple sauce may be served for children with rice, batter, or bread puddings.

Time, altogether 15 minutes. Average cost, 4d. Sufficient for 6 or 7 persons.

TARTARE SAUCE.

INGREDIENTS.—½ pint of thick mayonnaise sauce, a dessertspoonful of capers, a teaspoonful of chopped parsley.

Mode.—Make the mayonnaise sauce by the recipe and add the capers minced and the parsley, and if liked a dash of cayenne or nepaul pepper. This is one of the best sauces to serve with salmon cutlets or cold salmon.

Average cost, 9d.

WHITE SAUCE (Good).

INGREDIENTS.—¼ pint white stock, ¼ pint cream, ¼ pint milk, 1 dessertspoonful flour, salt to taste.

Mode.—Put the stock, which should be well flavoured with vegetables, and rather savoury, into a delicately-clean saucepan; mix the flour smoothly with the cream, add to the stock, season with a little salt, and boil very gently for about 10 minutes, keeping them well stirred, as this sauce is very liable to burn.

Time, 10 minutes. Average cost, 9d. Sufficient for a pair of fowls.

WHITE SAUCE (made without meat).

INGREDIENTS.—2 oz. butter, 2 small onions, 1 carrot, ½ small teacupful flour, 1 pint new milk, salt and cayenne to taste.

Mode.—Cut the onions and carrot very small, and put them into a stewpan with the butter; simmer till the butter is nearly dried up; stir in the flour and add the milk; boil the whole gently until it thickens, strain it and season with salt and cayenne.

Time, ¼ hour. Average cost, 5d. Sufficient for a pair of fowls.

WHITE SAUCE (a very Simple and Inexpensive Method).

INGREDIENTS.—1½ pints milk, 1½ oz. rice, 1 strip lemon-peel, 1 small blade pounded mace, salt and cayenne to taste.

Mode.—Boil the milk with the lemon-peel and rice until the latter is perfectly tender; then take out the lemon-peel, and pound the milk and rice together; put it back into the stewpan, add the mace and seasoning, give it one boil, and serve. This sauce should be of the consistency of thick cream.

Time, about ½ hour to boil the rice. Average cost, 4d. Sufficient for a pair of fowls.

WINE SAUCE FOR PUDDINGS.

INGREDIENTS.—½ pint sherry, ¼ pint water, the yolks of 5 eggs, 2 oz. pounded sugar, ½ teaspoonful minced lemon-peel, a few pieces candied citron, cut thin.

Mode.—Separate the yolks from the whites of 5 eggs; beat them, and put them into a very clean saucepan (a lined one is best); add the other ingredients, place them over a sharp fire, and keep stirring until the sauce begins to thicken; then take it off and serve. If it is allowed to boil, it will curdle and be spoiled.

Time—to be stirred over the fire 3 or 4 minutes; but it must not boil. Average cost, 1s. 3d. Sufficient for a large pudding; half the quantity for a moderate-sized one.

WINE OR BRANDY SAUCE FOR PUDDINGS.

INGREDIENTS.—½ pint melted butter, 3 heaped teaspoonfuls pounded sugar, 1 large wineglassful port or sherry, or ¾ of a small glassful brandy.

Mode.—Make ½ pint melted butter by recipe, omitting the salt; then stir in the sugar and wine or spirit, and bring the sauce to the point of boiling. Serve in a boat or tureen separately, and pour a little of it over the pudding. To convert this into punch sauce, add to the sherry and brandy a small wineglassful of rum and the juice and grated rind of ½ lemon. Liqueurs, such as curaçoa, may be substituted for the brandy.

Time, altogether 15 minutes. Average cost, 9d. Sufficient for 6 or 7 persons.

BEEF

BEEF BAKED, ROAST, AND BOILED

BEEF, AITCH-BONE OF (TO BOIL).

INGREDIENTS.—*Beef, water.*

Mode.—After this joint has been in salt 5 or 6 days it will be ready for use. Wash the meat, and, if too salt, soak it for a few hours, changing the water once or twice. Put it into a saucepan with sufficient cold water to cover the meat; set it over the fire, and when it boils draw the pot to the side of the fire, and let it remain until the water is sufficiently cooled that the finger may be borne in it. Then draw the pot nearer the fire, and keep the water *gently simmering* until the meat is done; it will be hard and tough if *rapidly* boiled. Carefully remove the scum, and continue doing this for a few minutes after it first boils. Carrots and turnips and suet dumplings may be boiled with the beef. Garnish with a few of the carrots and turnips, and serve the remainder in a vegetable dish. Brisket of beef is cooked in the same way.

Time, an aitch-bone of 10 lbs., 2½ hours after the water boils; one of 20 lbs., 4 hours. *Average cost,* 6d. to 7d. per lb. *Sufficient,* 10 lbs. for 10 persons. *Seasonable* all the year round, but best from September to March. It is more convenient to carve if the bones are removed before boiling.

Note.—The liquor in which the meat has been boiled may be easily converted into a very excellent pea-soup. It will require but few vegetables, as it will be flavoured by those boiled with the meat.

BEEF DRIPPING (to Clarify).

Good, fresh dripping answers very well for basting everything except game and poultry, and, when well clarified, serves for frying nearly as well as lard; it should be kept in a cool place, and will remain good some time. To clarify it, put the dripping into a basin, pour over it boiling water, and keep stirring the whole to wash away the impurities. Let it stand to cool, when the water and dirty sediment will settle at the bottom of the basin. Remove the dripping, and put it away in jars or basins for use.

Another way.

Put the dripping into a clean saucepan, and let it boil for a few minutes over a slow fire, and skim it well. Let stand to cool a little, then strain it through a piece of muslin into jars for use. Beef dripping is preferable to any other for cooking, as with mutton dripping there is liable to be a tallowy taste and smell.

BEEF, FILLET OF (LARDED).

INGREDIENTS. — *About 4 lbs. inside fillet of the sirloin,* 1 *onion, a small bunch parsley, salt and pepper to taste, sufficient vinegar to cover the meat, glaze, Spanish sauce.*

Mode.—Lard the beef with bacon, and put into the pan with sufficient vinegar to cover it, with an onion sliced, parsley and seasoning, and let it remain in this pickle 12 hours. Roast it before a clear fire 1¼ hours, and when done glaze it. Pour some Spanish sauce round the beef, and the remainder serve in a tureen. It may be garnished with Spanish onions boiled and glazed.

Time, 1¼ hours. *Average cost,* exclusive of sauce, 5s. *Sufficient* for 8 persons.

BEEF KIDNEY.

INGREDIENTS.—1 *lb. kidney.*

Cut the kidney into thin slices, flour them, and fry to a nice brown. When done, make a gravy in the pan by pouring away the fat, putting in a small piece of butter, ¼ pint boiling water, pepper and salt, and a tablespoonful mushroom ketchup. Let the gravy just boil up, pour over the kidney, and serve.

Time, 10 to 15 minutes. *Average cost,* 10d. per lb.

BEEF, RIBS OF (BAKED OR ROASTED).

INGREDIENTS.—*Beef, a little salt.*

Mode.—The fore-rib is the primest roasting piece, but the middle rib is the most economical. Let the meat be well hung; cut off the thin ends of the bones, which should be salted for a few days, and boiled. Put the meat down to a clear fire, or in a good oven, with some clean dripping and a little water in the pan; dredge the joint with a little flour, and keep basting the whole time it is cooking. Sprinkle fine salt over it (this must never be done until the joint is dished, as it draws the juices from the meat); pour the dripping from the pan, put in a little boiling water slightly salted, and *strain* the gravy over the meat. Garnish with tufts of scraped horseradish, and send horseradish sauce to table with it. A Yorkshire pudding will be found a very agreeable addition.

Time, 10 lbs. of beef, 2½ hours; 14 to 16 lbs., from 3½ to 4 hours. *Average cost,* 10d. per lb. *Sufficient,* a joint of 10 lbs. for 8 to 10 persons.

RIBS OF BEEF (Boned and Rolled).

INGREDIENTS.—1 *or* 2 *ribs of beef.*

Mode.—Choose a fine rib of beef, according to the weight required, either wide or narrow. Bone and roll the meat round, secure it with wooden skewers, and, if necessary, bind it round with a piece of tape; put the joint on the hook, and place it *near* a nice clear fire, or in an oven, as directed in preceding recipe. When the outside of the meat is set, draw it to a distance, and keep basting until the meat is done, which can be ascertained by the steam from it drawing towards the fire. As this joint is solid, rather more than ¼ hour must be allowed for each pound. Remove the skewers, put in a plated or silver one, and send the joint to table with gravy in the dish, and garnish with tufts of horseradish. Horseradish sauce is a great improvement.

Time, for 10 lbs. of the rolled ribs, 3 hours (as the joint is very solid, we have allowed an extra ¼ hour); for 6 lbs., 1½ hours. *Average cost,* 10d. per lb. *Sufficient,* a joint of 10 lbs. for 10 or 12 persons.

Note.—When the weight exceeds 10 lbs., we would not advise the above method of boning and rolling. The bones should be put on with a few vegetables and herbs and made into stock.

BEEF, ROUND OF (BOILED).

INGREDIENTS.—*Beef, water.*

Mode.—As a whole round of beef is very seldom required, we give the recipe for dressing a portion of the silver-side. Take from 8 to 10 lbs., after it has been in salt about 10 days; just wash off the salt, skewer it up in a nice round-looking form, and bind it with tape to keep the skewers in their places. Put it in a saucepan of cold water, as in recipe for aitch-bone, set it upon a good fire, and when it begins to boil remove all scum, as, if this is not attended to, it sinks on to the meat, and presents a very unsightly appearance. When it is well skimmed, draw the pot to the corner of the fire, and let it simmer gently until done. Remove the tape and skewers, which should be replaced by a silver one; pour over a little of the pot-liquor, and garnish with carrots.

Time, ½ hour per lb. *Average cost,* 9d. lb. *Sufficient* for 8 to 10 persons *Seasonable* at any time.

BEEF, SIRLOIN OF (ROAST).

INGREDIENTS.—*Beef, a little salt.*

Mode.—See that the fire is well made up about ¾ hour before it is required, so that when the joint is put down it is clear and bright. Choose a nice sirloin, not exceeding 16 lbs., or the outside will be too much done, whilst the inside will not be done enough. Hook it on to the jack firmly, dredge slightly with flour, and place it near the fire at first, as directed in the preceding recipe. Then draw it to a distance, and keep basting until the meat is done. Sprinkle a small quantity of salt over it, empty the dripping-pan of all the dripping, pour in some boiling water slightly salted, stir it about, and *strain* over the meat. Garnish with tufts of horseradish, and send horseradish sauce and Yorkshire pudding to table with it.

Time, a sirloin of 10 lbs. 2½ hours; 14 to 16 lbs., about 4 or 4½ hours. *Average cost,* 10d. per lb. *Sufficient,* a joint of 10 lbs. for 10 or 12 persons.

The rump, round, and other pieces of beef are roasted in the same manner, allowing for solid joints ¼ hour to every lb. This joint may be baked in a good oven.

BEEF, SPICED (to serve cold).

INGREDIENTS.—14 *lbs. thick flank or rump beef,* ½ *lb. coarse sugar,* 1 *oz. of pounded saltpetre,* ¼ *lb. pounded allspice,* 1 *lb. common salt.*

Mode.—Rub the sugar well into the beef and let it lie for 12 hours, then rub the saltpetre and allspice over the meat, let it remain for another 12 hours, and then rub in the salt. Turn daily in the liquor for a fortnight, soak for a few hours in water, dry with a cloth, cover with a coarse paste, put a little water at the bottom of the pan, and bake in a moderate oven for 4 hours. If it is not covered with a paste, be careful to put the beef into a deep vessel, and cover with a plate, or it will be too crisp. While the meat is in the oven it should be turned once or twice.

Time, 4 hours. *Average cost,* 7d. per lb.

BEEF, OR RUMP-STEAK AND KIDNEY PIE

INGREDIENTS.—2 *lbs. beef, or rump-steak,* 4 *sheep's kidneys, or* ½ *lb. bullock's kidney, pepper, salt, flour, a little nutmeg, a dessertspoonful Worcester sauce, pastry either short or puff.*

Mode.—Take off any superfluous fat from the steak and put it with the kidneys in a saucepan, with just enough cold water to cover them, and a little salt. Let them come to the boil, then simmer gently for ¾ hour. Take them out and set aside, then thicken the liquor with flour or brown roux. Cut the steak and kidney into neat pieces, adding pepper and salt and a grate of nutmeg. As you fill up the pie-dish, then add the sauce to the made gravy, with a little more water if needed, and pour into the pie-dish. Cover with paste, first putting a rim round the edge, decorate the top, and brush over with yolk of egg. Bake till the paste is done in a good oven.

Time altogether, 1½ hours. *Average cost,* 3s. *Sufficient* for 6 persons. *Seasonable* at any time.

BEEF OR RUMP-STEAK AND KIDNEY PUDDING.

INGREDIENTS.—2 *lbs. rump-steak*, 2 *kidneys, seasoning to taste of salt and black pepper, suet crust made with milk, in the proportion of 6 oz. suet to each 1 lb. of flour.*

Mode.—Divide the steak into pieces about an inch square, and cut each kidney into 8 pieces. Line the basin with crust made with suet and flour in the above proportion, leaving a small piece to overlap the edge. Cover the bottom with a portion of the steak and a few pieces of kidney; season with salt and pepper (some add a little flour to thicken the gravy), and then add another layer of steak, kidney, and seasoning. When the dish is full, pour in sufficient water to come within 2 inches of the top. Moisten the edges of the crust, cover the pudding over, press the two crusts together, that the gravy may not escape, and turn up the overhanging paste. Wring out a cloth in hot water, flour it, and tie up the pudding; put it into boiling water, and let it boil *for at least* 4 hours. If the water diminishes, replenish with some, hot, in a jug, as the pudding should be kept covered and not allowed to stop boiling. When the cloth is removed, cut out a round piece in the top of the crust, to prevent the pudding bursting, and send it to table *in the basin*, either in an ornamental dish or with a napkin pinned round it. Serve quickly.

Time, for a pudding with 2 lbs of steak and 2 kidneys allow 4 hours. *Average cost*, 3s. *Sufficient* for 6 persons. *Seasonable* all the year, but more suitable in winter.

Note.—Beef-steak pudding may be very much enriched by adding a few oysters or mushrooms. The above recipe was contributed by a Sussex lady, in which county the inhabitants are noted for their savoury puddings.

BRAZILIAN STEW.

INGREDIENTS.—2 *lbs. leg of beef, lean*, 1 *carrot*, 1 *turnip*, 2 *onions*, 6 *peppercorns, vinegar*, 1 *dessertspoonful Worcester sauce, salt, a little nutmeg, and lemon-juice.*

Mode.—Cut the meat in thick, small pieces, dip each of these in vinegar, and put them in a stewpan with the vegetables sliced rather thinly. Let the meat and vegetables heat very slowly as no water should be used, then add salt, the sauce, the lemon-juice, the peppercorns, and a grate of

nutmeg. Put the lid on, and do not take it off for 3 hours, during which simmer the contents of the pan, giving it an occasional shake.

Time, 3½ hours. *Average cost*, 1s. 4d. *Sufficient* for 4 or 5 persons. *Seasonable* at any time, but most suitable for a winter dish.

BULLOCK'S HEART (BAKED).

INGREDIENTS.—1 *heart, stuffing of veal forcemeat.*

Mode.—Put the heart into warm water to soak for 2 hours; then wipe it well with a cloth, and, after cutting off the lobes, stuff the inside with a highly seasoned forcemeat. Fasten it in by means of a needle and coarse thread; tie the heart up in paper, and set it in a good oven, and keep it well basted, or it will be dry. Two or three minutes before serving, remove the paper, baste well, let it brown, and serve with good gravy and red-currant jelly or melted butter. If the heart is very large it will require 2 hours, and, covered with a caul, may be baked as well as roasted.

Time, large heart, 2 hours. *Average cost*, 2s. 8d. *Sufficient* for 6 or 8 persons. *Seasonable* all the year.

Note.—This is an excellent family dish, and very savoury.

MARROW-BONES.

INGREDIENTS.—*Marrow-bones, paste of flour and water, toast.*

Mode.—Saw the bones into equal lengths, cover the ends with the paste, tie them up in cloths, put into boiling water, and boil for 2 hours. Take them out, remove cloths and paste, and send them to table quickly, with napkins pinned round them, and a dish of hot toast.

Time, 2 hours. *Sufficient*—allow one bone to each person. *Seasonable* in winter

OX-CHEEK (STEWED).

INGREDIENTS.—1 *cheek, salt and water*, 4 *or 5 onions, butter and flour*, 6 *cloves*, 3 *turnips*, 2 *carrots*, 1 *bay-leaf*, 1 *head celery*, 1 *bunch savoury herbs, cayenne, black pepper and salt to taste*, 1 *oz. butter*, 2 *dessertspoonfuls flour*, 2 *tablespoonfuls chili vinegar*, 2 *tablespoonfuls port wine*, 2 *tablespoonfuls sauce.*

Mode.—Have the cheek boned, clean, and put it to soak all night in salt and water. The next day wipe it dry and clean and put it into a stewpan. Just cover it with water, skim well when it boils, and let it simmer till the meat is nearly tender. Slice and fry 3 onions in a little butter and flour, and put them into the gravy; add 2 whole onions, each stuck with 3 cloves, 3 turnips quartered, 2 carrots sliced, a bay-leaf, 1 head of celery, a bunch of herbs, and seasoning to taste of cayenne, black pepper, and salt. Let these stew till perfectly tender ; then take out the cheek, divide into pieces fit to help at table, skim and strain the gravy, and thicken 1½ pints of it with butter and flour in the above proportions. Add the vinegar, ketchup, and port wine ; put in the pieces of cheek ; let the whole boil up, and serve quite hot in a ragout dish.

Time, 4 hours. *Average cost*, 2s. 6d. *Sufficient* for 8 persons.

OX-TAIL (STEWED).

INGREDIENTS.—2 *ox-tails*, 1 *onion*, 3 *cloves*, 1 *blade mace*, ¼ *teaspoonful whole black pepper*, ¼ *teaspoonful allspice*, ½ *teaspoonful salt, a small bunch savoury herbs, thickening of butter and flour*, 1 *tablespoonful lemon-juice*, 1 *teaspoonful mushroom ketchup*.

Mode.—Divide the tails at the joints, wash, and put them into a stewpan with sufficient water to cover, and set them on the fire ; when the water boils, remove the scum, and add the onion cut into rings, the spice, seasoning, and herbs. Cover the stewpan closely, and simmer gently until tender, which will be in about 2½ hours. Take the tails out, make a thickening of butter and flour, add it to the gravy, and let it boil for ¼ hour. Strain it through a sieve into a saucepan, put back the tails, add the lemon-juice and ketchup; let the whole just boil up, and serve. Garnish with croûtons or sippets of toasted bread.

Time, 2½ hours to stew the tails. *Average cost*, from 1s. to 2s., according to the season. *Sufficient* for 8 persons.

OX-TONGUE (BOILED).

INGREDIENTS.—1 *tongue, a bunch of savoury herbs, water.*

Mode.—In choosing a tongue, select one with a smooth skin, which denotes its being young and tender. If dried and rather hard, soak it for 12 hours; if it is fresh from the pickle, 2 or 3 hours will be sufficient. Put the tongue into a stewpan with plenty of cold water and a bunch of savoury herbs; let it

gradually come to a boil ; skim and simmer gently until tender. Peel off the skin, and garnish with tufts of cauliflowers or Brussels sprouts. Boiled tongue is frequently sent to table with boiled poultry, instead of ham. If to serve cold, peel it, fasten it down to a piece of board by sticking a fork through the root, and another through the tip, to straighten it. When cold, glaze it, put a paper ruche round the root, and garnish with parsley.

Time, a large smoked tongue, 4 to 4½ hours ; a small one, 2½ to 3 hours. A large unsmoked tongue, 3 to 3½ hours ; a small one, 2 to 2½ hours. *Average cost*, for a moderate-sized tongue, 3s. 6d.

RUMP-STEAKS AND OYSTER SAUCE.

INGREDIENTS.—3 *dozen oysters, ingredients for oyster sauce* (see Recipe), 2 *lbs. rump-steaks, seasoning to taste of pepper and salt.*

Mode.—Make the oyster sauce by recipe, and put it by the side of the fire, but do not let it keep boiling. Broil the steaks, put them on a very hot dish, smother with the oyster sauce, and the remainder send to table in a tureen. Serve quickly.

Time, about 8 to 10 minutes, according to the thickness of the steak. *Average cost*, 1s. 2d. lb. *Sufficient* for 4 persons. *Seasonable* from September to April

RUMP-STEAK (BROILED).

INGREDIENTS.—*Steaks, a piece of butter the size of a walnut, salt to taste*, 1 *tablespoonful good ketchup or sauce.*

Mode.—The success of a good broil depends on the state of the fire, which should be bright and clear, and perfectly free from smoke ; do not add any fresh fuel *just before the gridiron is to be used.* Sprinkle a little salt over the fire ; put in the ketchup, and, when liked, a little minced shallot; dish up the steaks, rub them over with butter, and season with pepper and salt. The exact time for broiling must be determined by taste, whether they are liked underdone or well-done : more than from 8 to 10 minutes for a steak ¾ inch in thickness, we think, would spoil and dry up the juices of the meat. To have broiled steaks in perfection, they should not be cooked till everything else prepared for the meal has been dished up. They may be garnished with scraped horseradish. Oyster, tomato, onion, and many other sauces are usual accompaniments to rump-steak.

Time, 8 to 10 minutes. *Average cost.* 1s. 2d. per lb. *Sufficient*—allow ½ lb. to each person. *Seasonable* all the year, but not so good in the height of summer, as the meat cannot hang long enough to be tender.

RUMP-STEAK (FRIED).

INGREDIENTS.—*Steaks, butter or clarified dripping.*

Mode.—The steaks should be cut rather thinner than for broiling, and with a small quantity of fat to each. Put some butter or clarified dripping into a frying-pan; let it get quite hot, then lay in the steaks. Turn them frequently until done, which will be in about 8 minutes, or rather more. Serve on a very hot dish, in which put a small piece of butter and a tablespoonful of ketchup, and season with pepper and salt. They should be sent to table quickly.

Time, 8 minutes for a medium-sized steak; rather longer for a very thick one. *Average cost*, 1s. 2d. per lb. *Seasonable* all the year, but not good in summer, as the meat cannot hang to get tender.

Note.—Where much gravy is liked, make it in the following manner:—As soon as the steaks are done, dish them, pour a little boiling water into the frying-pan, add a seasoning of pepper and salt, a small piece of butter, and a tablespoonful of sauce or ketchup. Hold the pan over the fire for a minute or two, just let the gravy simmer, then pour on the steak, and serve.

ENTRÉES AND MADE DISHES FROM BEEF.

BEEF À LA MODE.

INGREDIENTS.—*A thick slice of beef, about 3 lbs. without fat, ½ lb. fat bacon, ½ lemon, a glass of claret, 1 carrot, 2 onions, brown roux, pepper, nutmeg salt, a bunch of herbs, stock or water.*

Mode.—With a wooden rolling-pin beat the steak well, then lard it with the bacon, first rolled in the seasoning. Cut up the vegetables very small, and tie the herbs in a piece of muslin, and put them with the meat and the wine in a stewpan. Squeeze over the juice of the half lemon, and enough stock to barely cover the meat. Cook for about 2 hours in the pan well covered, then

take out the meat and keep in a hot place. Boil up the gravy, and thicken with the roux; add seasoning to taste, then strain, and when re-heated, pour it round the meat.

Time, 2 hours. *Average cost*, 3s. 9d. *Sufficient* for 6 or 7 persons. *Seasonable* in winter.

BEEF (BAKED).

(Cold Meat Cookery.)

INGREDIENTS.—*About 2 lbs. cold roast beef, 2 small onions, 1 large carrot or 2 small ones, 1 turnip, small bunch savoury herbs, salt and pepper to taste, 12 tablespoonfuls gravy, 3 tablespoonfuls ale, crust or mashed potatoes.*

Mode.—Cut the beef in slices, allowing a little fat to each slice; place a layer in the bottom of a pie-dish, with a portion of the onions, carrots, and turnips, sliced; mince the herbs, strew them over the meat, and season with pepper and salt. Then put another layer of meat, vegetables, and seasoning; and proceed until all the ingredients are used. Pour in the gravy and ale (water may be substituted for the gravy), cover with a crust or mashed potatoes, and bake for ½ hour, or rather longer.

Time, rather more than ½ hour. *Average cost*, exclusive of the meat, 6d. *Sufficient* for 5 or 6 persons.

Note.—It is as well to parboil the carrots and turnips before adding them to the meat, and to use some of the liquor in which they were boiled when there is no gravy at hand. Cut the onions into very *thin* slices.

BEEF (BAKED).

(*Another way.*)

INGREDIENTS.—*Slices cold roast beef, salt and pepper to taste, 1 sliced onion, 1 teaspoonful minced savoury herbs, about 12 tablespoonfuls gravy or sauce of any kind, mashed potatoes.*

Mode.—Butter the sides of a deep dish, and spread mashed potatoes over the bottom; on this place layers of beef sliced thin or minced, well seasoned with pepper and salt, and a very little onion and herbs, previously fried of a nice brown; then another layer of mashed potatoes, beef, &c., as before; pour in the gravy or sauce, cover with another layer of potatoes, and bake for ½ hour. This may be served in the dish, or turned out.

Time, ½ hour. *Average cost*, exclusive of the cold beef, 4d. *Sufficient*, a large pie-dish full for 5 or 6 persons.

BEEF (BRAISED).

INGREDIENTS.—6 lbs rump of beef, ½ pint of sherry or other white wine, 3 each carrots, turnips, and onions, a few peppercorns and allspice, stock, salt and pepper, a little nutmeg.

Mode.—Take the bones from the meat, and tie it in a neat round shape, put it in a stewpan, with some cheap stock or water, and cook gently for 2 hours. Prepare the vegetables, and cut them up and place them in a braising-pan with the spice, peppercorns, and seasoning. Lay in the beef, and pour over about ½ pint of good stock and the wine. Stew gently for an hour, basting with the stock and wine, and adding more of the former if needed. When cooked drain off the gravy, and if a braising-pan is used, put some fresh hot cinders on the top to brown the meat. If only a stewpan is at hand, use a salamander, or, with care, some cinders may be put on the lid. Boil up the gravy in a small saucepan, and thicken it, adding more seasoning if necessary. Some of this pour round the meat, the rest serve separately. For a garnish a few prettily cut vegetables, cooked separately, should be used, or some bright green Brussels sprouts. The stock in which the meat was first cooked and the vegetables left in the pan will serve for an excellent soup.

Time, 3 hours. Average cost, about 7s. Sufficient for 12 persons. Seasonable at any time, but best in winter.

BEEF (BROILED) AND MUSHROOM SAUCE (Cold Meat Cookery).

INGREDIENTS.—2 or 3 dozen small button mushrooms, 1 oz. butter, salt and cayenne to taste, 1 tablespoonful mushroom ketchup, mashed potatoes, slices of cold roast beef.

Mode.—Wipe the mushrooms free from grit with a piece of flannel, and salt; put them in a stewpan with the butter, seasoning, and ketchup; shake the pan over the fire until the mushrooms are done, when pour them in the middle of mashed potatoes, browned. Place round the potatoes slices of cold roast beef, broiled, over a clear fire. In making the sauce, the ketchup may be dispensed with, if there is sufficient gravy.

Time, ¼ hour. Average cost, exclusive of the meat, 8d. Seasonable from August to October.

BEEF (BROILED) AND OYSTER SAUCE (Cold Meat Cookery).

INGREDIENTS.—2 dozen oysters, 3 cloves, 1 blade mace, 2 oz. butter, ½ teaspoonful flour, cayenne and salt to taste, mashed potatoes, a few slices cold roast beef.

Mode.—Put the oysters in a stewpan with their liquor strained; add the cloves, mace, butter, flour, and seasoning, and let them simmer for 3 minutes. Have ready in the centre of a dish round walls of mashed potatoes, browned; into the middle pour the oyster sauce, and round the potatoes place, in layers, slices of the beef, previously broiled.

Time, 5 minutes. Average cost, exclusive of the meat, 2s. 6d. Sufficient for 4 or 5 persons. Seasonable from September to April.

BEEF (BROILED) SLICED (Cold Meat Cookery).

INGREDIENTS.—A few slices cold roast beef, 4 or 5 potatoes, a thin batter, pepper and salt to taste.

Mode.—Peel and pare the potatoes; fry the parings in a thin batter seasoned with salt and pepper, until they are of a light brown, and place them on a dish over slices of beef, nicely seasoned and broiled. The potatoes should be pared round and round as an apple is, so that the parings are in rings and twists.

Time, 5 minutes to broil the meat.

BEEF COLLOPS.

INGREDIENTS.—2 lbs. lean beef-steak, about 8 potatoes, some stock or gravy, ½ oz. butter, pepper and salt, sauce.

Mode.—Mince the meat and gently stew it in a little weak stock till done. Boil and mash the potatoes and make a wall of them on a dish. Add to the minced meat a little good gravy, a dessertspoonful of sauce, and a seasoning of salt and pepper, then pour into the centre of the potatoes. Garnish with bright-coloured pickles cut in slices and laid on the wall of potato. Should no gravy be at hand fry an onion in a little butter, and with hot water and thickening make a gravy in the pan.

Time, about ¾ hour. Average cost, 2s. Sufficient for 4 or 5 persons. Seasonable at any time.

BEEF (CURRIED).
(Cold Meat Cookery.)

INGREDIENTS.—*A few slices tolerably lean cold roast or boiled beef*, 3 *oz. butter*, 2 *onions*, 1 *wineglassful beer*, 1 *dessertspoonful curry-powder.*

Mode.—Cut the beef into pieces about 1 inch square; put the butter into a stewpan with the onions sliced, and fry them of a light brown colour. Add the other ingredients, and stir gently over a brisk fire for about 10 minutes. More beer, or a spoonful or two of gravy or water, may be added; but a good curry should not be very thin. Place it in a deep dish, and serve with a dish of boiled rice.

Time, 10 minutes. *Average cost*, exclusive of the meat, 5d. *Seasonable* in winter.

BEEF FRICANDEAU.

INGREDIENTS.—*A fillet of beef* (*about* 2 *lbs.*), *a glass of sherry, stock*, 2 *carrots*, 1 *turnip*, 2 *onions, a bunch of herbs, cloves, mace, pepper and salt, bacon for larding.*

Mode.—Prepare the vegetables and cut them small, with the exception of 1 onion, which stick with cloves, and put these at the bottom of a stewpan with a bunch of herbs. Lard the upper side of the meat, sprinkle it with pepper, salt, and powdered mace, and lay it in the pan, pouring over the wine and about a teacupful of stock. Cook till the wine and stock are absorbed, then transfer the meat to a pan in the oven with ¾ pint of stock and simmer gently for 1½ hours. Let the top of the meat brown in the oven, then lay it on a dish with nicely cut cooked vegetables, or a border of spinach round. Strain the gravy and serve separately.

Time, about 2 hours. *Average cost*, 3s. 6d. *Sufficient* for 4 persons. *Seasonable* at any time.

BEEF (FRIED).
(Cold Meat Cookery.)

INGREDIENTS.—*A few slices cold salt beef, pepper to taste, dripping, mashed potatoes.*

Mode.—Cut any part of cold salt beef into thin slices, fry them gently in dripping, and season with a little pepper. Have ready some very hot mashed potatoes, lay the slices of beef on them, and garnish with 3 or 4 pickled gherkins. Cold salt beef, warmed in a little liquor from mixed pickle, drained, and served as above, will be found good.

Time, about 5 minutes. *Average cost*, exclusive of the meat, 3d.

BEEF FRITTERS (Cold Meat Cookery).

INGREDIENTS.—*The remains of cold roast beef, pepper and salt to taste,* ¾ *lb. flour,* ½ *pint water,* 2 *oz. butter, the whites of* 2 *eggs.*

Mode.—Mix the flour very smoothly with the above proportion of water; stir in 2 oz. of butter, melted, but not oiled; just before it is to be used, add the whites of two well-whisked eggs. Should the batter be too thick, more water must be added. Pare the beef into thin shreds, pepper and salt, and mix with the batter. Drop a small quantity at a time into a pan of boiling lard, and fry from 7 to 10 minutes. When done on one side, turn and brown on the other. Dry a minute or two before the fire, and serve on a folded napkin. A small quantity of finely minced onions may be mixed with the batter.

Time, from 7 to 10 minutes. *Average cost*, exclusive of the meat, 4d.

BEEF (HASHED).
(Cold Meat Cookery.)

INGREDIENTS.—*Gravy saved from the meat,* 2 *teaspoonfuls tomato sauce,* 1 *teaspoonful good mushroom ketchup,* ½ *wineglass port wine or strong ale, pepper and salt to taste, a little flour to thicken,* 1 *onion finely minced, a few slices cold roast beef.*

Mode.—Put all the ingredients but the beef into a stewpan with the gravy; simmer for 10 minutes, then take the stewpan off the fire; *let the gravy cool*, and skim off the fat. Cut the beef into thin slices, dredge them with flour, and lay them in the gravy; simmer gently for 3 minutes. Serve very hot, and garnish with sippets of toasted bread. If there is no gravy left from the roast joint, a little must be made from the bones, as in the following recipe.

Time, 20 minutes. *Average cost*, exclusive of the cold meat, 4d.

BEEF (HASHED).
(Cold Meat Cookery.)
Another way.

INGREDIENTS.—*The remains of ribs or sirloin of beef,* 2 *onions,* 1 *carrot,* 1 *bunch savoury herbs, pepper and salt to taste,* ½ *blade pounded mace, thicken-*

ing of flour, rather more than 1 pint water.

Mode.—Take off all the meat from the bones of ribs or sirloin of beef; remove the outside brown and gristle; place the meat on one side, and well stew the bones and pieces, with the above ingredients, for about 2 hours, till it becomes a strong gravy, and is reduced to rather more than ½ pint; strain this, thicken with a teaspoonful of flour, and let the gravy cool; skim off the fat; lay in the meat, let it get hot through, but do not allow it to boil, and garnish with sippets of toasted bread. The gravy may be flavoured as in the preceding recipe.

Time, rather more than 2 hours. *Average cost,* exclusive of the cold meat, 3d.

Note.—Either of the above recipes may be served in walls of mashed potatoes, browned, omitting the sippets. Hashed meat must not boil, or it will be tough.

BEEF (MINCED).
(Cold Meat Cookery.)

INGREDIENTS.—1 *oz. butter,* 1 *small onion, about* 12 *tablespoonfuls gravy left from the meat,* ½ *teaspoonful flour, salt and pepper to taste, a few slices lean roast beef.*

Mode.—Put into a stewpan the butter with an onion chopped fine; add the gravy, and ½ a teaspoonful of flour; season with pepper and salt, and stir over the fire until the onion is a rich brown. Cut the meat *very fine,* or put through a mincer, add it to the gravy, stir till quite hot and serve. Garnish with sippets of toasted bread.

Time, about ½ hour. *Average cost,* exclusive of the meat, 2d.

BEEF OLIVES.

INGREDIENTS.—2 *lbs. rump-steak,* 1 *egg,* 1 *tablespoonful minced savoury herbs, pepper and salt to taste,* 1 *pint stock, a few very thin slices bacon,* 2 *tablespoonfuls of any store sauce, a slight thickening of butter and flour.*

Mode.—Have the steaks cut rather thin, cut them into 6 or 7 pieces, brush over with egg, and sprinkle with herbs finely minced; season with pepper and salt, put in each a very thin slice of bacon, roll up the pieces tightly, and fasten with a small skewer. Put the stock in a stewpan that will exactly hold them, and lay in the rolls of meat.

Stew very gently for 2 hours or more. Take them out, remove the skewers, thicken the gravy with butter and flour, and flavour with sauce. Give one boil, pour over the meat, and serve.

Time, 2 hours. *Average cost,* 3s. *Sufficient* for 6 persons.

BEEF RAGOUT (Cold Meat Cookery).

INGREDIENTS.—*About* 2 *lbs. cold roast beef,* 6 *onions, pepper, salt, and mixed spices to taste,* ½ *pint boiling water,* 3 *tablespoonfuls gravy.*

Mode.—Cut the beef into rather large pieces, and put them into a stewpan with the onions sliced. Season well with pepper, salt, and mixed spices, and pour over about ½ pint of boiling water, and gravy in the above proportion (gravy saved from the meat answers the purpose); let the whole stew very gently for about 2 hours, and serve with pickled walnuts, gherkins, or capers just warmed in the gravy.

Time, 2 hours. *Average cost,* exclusive of the meat, 3d.

BEEF RISSOLES (Cold Meat Cookery).

INGREDIENTS.—*The remains of cold roast beef; to each pound of meat allow* ¾ *lb. breadcrumbs, salt and pepper to taste, a few chopped savoury herbs,* ½ *a teaspoonful minced lemon-peel,* 1 *or* 2 *eggs, according to the quantity of meat.*

Mode.—Mince the beef, which should be rather lean, very fine, and mix with this breadcrumbs, herbs, seasoning, and lemon-peel, in the above proportion. Make all into a thick paste with 1 or 2 eggs; divide into balls or cones, and fry a rich brown. Garnish with fried parsley, and send to table some good brown gravy in a tureen. Instead of garnishing with fried parsley, gravy may be poured in the dish: in this case it will not be necessary to send any in a tureen.

Time, from 5 to 10 minutes, according to size. *Average cost,* exclusive of the meat, 5d. *Sufficient* for about 12 rissoles.

BEEF ROLLS (Cold Meat Cookery).

INGREDIENTS.—*The remains of cold roast or boiled beef, seasoning to taste of salt, pepper, and minced herbs, puff paste.*

Mode.—Mince the beef tolerably fine

with a little of its own fat; add pepper, salt, and chopped herbs; put the whole into a roll of puff paste, and bake for ½ hour, or rather longer, should the roll be very large. Beef patties may be made of cold meat, by mincing and seasoning beef as above, and baking in a rich puff paste in patty-tins.

Time, ½ hour.

BEEF STEWED WITH CELERY (Cold Meat Cookery).

INGREDIENTS.—2 *heads of celery*, 1 *pint gravy*, 2 *onions sliced*, 2 *lbs. cold roast or boiled beef*.

Mode.—Cut the celery into 2-inch pieces, put them in a stewpan, with the gravy and onions, simmer until the celery is tender, let the gravy cool, then add the beef cut into rather thick pieces; let it just boil up, and serve with fried potatoes.

Time, from 20 to 25 minutes to stew the celery. *Average cost*, exclusive of the meat, 6d. *Seasonable* from September to January.

BEEF STEWED WITH OYSTERS (Cold Meat Cookery).

INGREDIENTS.—*A few thick steaks of cold ribs or sirloin of beef*, 2 *oz. butter*, 1 *onion sliced, pepper and salt to taste*, ½ *glass port wine, a little flour to thicken*, 1 *or* 2 *dozen oysters, rather more than* ½ *pint of water*.

Mode.—Cut the steaks rather thick, from cold sirloin or ribs of beef; brown lightly in a stewpan, with the butter and a little water; add ½ pint of water, the onion, pepper, and salt; cover the stewpan closely, and simmer gently for ½ hour; then mix about a teaspoonful of flour smoothly with a little of the liquor; add the port wine and oysters, their liquor having been previously strained and put into the stewpan; stir till the oysters plump, and serve. It should not boil after the oysters are added.

Time, ½ hour. *Average cost*, exclusive of the meat, 2s. 6d. *Seasonable* from September to April.

BEEF STEWED WITH VEGETABLES.

INGREDIENTS.—*About* 2 *lbs. beef or rump-steak*, 3 *onions*, 2 *turnips*, 3 *carrots*, 2 *oz. butter*, ½ *pint water*, 1 *teaspoonful salt*, ½ *do. pepper*, 1

tablespoonful ketchup, 1 *tablespoonful flour*.

Mode.—Have the steaks cut tolerably thick, and rather lean; divide into convenient-sized pieces, and fry in the butter a nice brown on both sides. Cleanse and pare the vegetables, cut the onions and carrots into thin slices, and the turnips into dice, and fry these in the fat the steaks were done in. Put all into a saucepan, add ½ pint of water, or rather more, and simmer gently for 2½ or 3 hours; when nearly done, skim well, add salt, pepper, and ketchup, and thicken with a tablespoonful of flour mixed with 2 of cold water. Boil up for a minute or two after the thickening is added, and serve. When a vegetable-scoop is at hand, use it to cut the vegetables into fanciful shapes. Tomato, ordinary sauce, or walnut-liquor may be used to flavour the gravy. If stewed the previous day, the fat may be taken off when cold; and when wanted for table it will merely require warming through.

Time, 3 hours. *Average cost*, 2s. 2d. *Sufficient* for 6 persons.

BUBBLE-AND-SQUEAK (Cold Meat Cookery).

INGREDIENTS.—*A few thin slices cold boiled beef, butter or dripping, cabbage*, 1 *sliced onion, pepper and salt to taste*.

Mode.—Fry the slices of beef gently in a little butter or dripping, taking care not to dry them up. Lay them on a flat dish, and cover with fried cabbage sprouts or green savoys. These should be boiled till tender, well drained, minced, and placed, till quite hot, in a frying-pan, with butter, a sliced onion, and seasoning.

TOAD-IN-THE-HOLE (a Homely but Savoury Dish).

INGREDIENTS.—1½ *lbs. rump-steak*, 1 *sheep's kidney, pepper and salt to taste. For the batter*, 2 *eggs*, 1 *pint milk, tablespoonful flour*, ½ *saltspoonful of salt*.

Mode.—Cut the steak and kidney into convenient-sized pieces, and put into a buttered pie-dish, with a good seasoning of salt and pepper; mix the flour with a small quantity of milk, to prevent its being lumpy; add the remainder and the 2 eggs, well beaten; put in the salt, stir for about 5 minutes, and pour it over the steak. Place it in a tolerably brisk oven, and bake for 1½ hours.

Time, 1½ hours. *Average cost*, 2s. 4d. *Sufficient* for 4 or 5 persons.

Note.—The remains of under-done cold beef may be substituted for the steak, and the smallest possible quantity of minced onion or shallot added.

TRIPE.

INGREDIENTS.—*Tripe, onion sauce, milk and water.*

Mode.—Have the tripe cleaned and dressed, cut away the coarsest fat, and boil it in equal proportions of milk and water for ¾ of an hour. Should the tripe be entirely undressed, more than double that time should be allowed. Have ready onion sauce; dish the tripe, smother it with the sauce, and the remainder send to table in a tureen.

Time, ¾ hour; for undressed tripe, 2½ to 3 hours. *Average cost*, 7d. per pound.

Note.—Tripe may be cut in pieces and fried in batter, stewed in gravy with mushrooms, or cut into collops, sprinkled with minced onions and savoury herbs, and fried a nice brown in clarified butter.

MUTTON AND LAMB

MUTTON, BREAST OF (STEWED).

INGREDIENTS.—*Breast of mutton*, 2 *onions, salt and pepper to taste, flour, a bunch savoury herbs, green peas.*

Mode.—Cut the mutton (which should be tolerably lean) into pieces about 2 inches square, put it into a stewpan, with a little fat or butter, and fry it a nice brown; dredge in a little flour, slice the onions, and put them with the herbs in a stewpan; pour in sufficient water *just* to cover the meat, and simmer until tender. Take out the meat, strain, skim the fat, and put the meat and gravy back into the stewpan; add a quart of green peas, and boil gently until done. 2 or 3 slices of bacon stewed with the mutton give an additional flavour; to insure the peas being a beautiful green colour, *they may be boiled in water separately*, and added to the stew when served.

Time, 2½ hours. *Average cost*, 7d. per lb. *Sufficient* for 4 or 5 persons. *Seasonable* from June to August.

MUTTON CHOPS.

INGREDIENTS.—*Loin of mutton, pepper and salt, a small piece of butter.*

Mode.—Cut the chops from a tender loin, remove a portion of the fat, trim into a nice shape; slightly beat and level them; place the gridiron over a bright fire, rub the bars with a little fat, and lay on the chops. Whilst broiling, frequently turn them, and in about 8 minutes they will be done. Season with pepper and salt, dish them on a very hot dish, and rub a small piece of butter on each chop.

Time, about 8 minutes. *Average cost*, 1s. per lb. *Sufficient*—allow 1 chop to each person.

MUTTON CHOPS (SAVOURY).

INGREDIENTS.—2 *lbs. best end of neck of mutton*, 2 *onions*, 1½ *oz. butter*, 2 *sprigs of parsley, a little lemon thyme, a grate of lemon-peel, pepper and salt, breadcrumbs.*

Mode.—Finely shred and chop the onion, melt the butter in a pan, put in the onion, the parsley chopped, the thyme and the seasoning. Cook this a little time, say 5 minutes, then trim the chops neatly, removing the ends and superfluous fat, dip each one into the butter mixture, then into crumbs, and fry a bright brown, or grill on a well greased gridiron. Make a little gravy in the pan and pour over.

Time, 6 to 8 minutes. *Average cost*, 1s. 9d. *Sufficient* for 3 persons.

MUTTON (HARICOT).

INGREDIENTS.—4 *lbs. of the middle or best end of the neck of mutton*, 3 *carrots*, 3 *turnips*, 3 *onions*, *pepper and salt to taste*, 1 *tablespoonful of ketchup or sauce.*

Mode.—Trim off some of the fat, cut the mutton into rather thin chops, and put them into a frying-pan with the fat trimmings. Fry a pale brown, but do not cook them enough for eating. Cut the carrots and turnips into dice, and the onions into slices, and slightly fry them in the fat that the mutton was browned in, but do not allow them to take any colour. Now lay the mutton at the bottom of a stewpan, then the vegetables, and pour over them just sufficient water to cover. Give one boil, skim well, and set the pan on the side of the fire to simmer until the meat is tender. Skim off every particle of fat, add a seasoning of pepper and salt, and a little ketchup, and serve in rather a deep dish.

Time, 2½ hours to simmer gently. *Average cost*, for this quantity, 3s. 8d. *Sufficient* for 8 persons.

MUTTON (HARICOT).

(*Another mode.*)

INGREDIENTS. — *Breast or scrag of mutton, flour, pepper and salt to taste,* 1 *large onion*, 3 *cloves, a bunch savoury herbs*, 1 *blade mace, carrots and turnips, sugar.*

Mode.—Cut the mutton into square pieces, and fry a nice colour; then dredge over them a little flour and a seasoning of pepper and salt. Put all into a stew-pan, and moisten with boiling water, adding the onion, stuck with 6 cloves, the mace, and herbs. Simmer gently till the meat is nearly done, skim off all the fat, and add the carrots and turnips, previously cut in dice and fried with a little sugar to colour them. Let the whole simmer again for 10 minutes; take out the onion and bunch of herbs, and serve.

Time, about 3 hours to simmer. *Average cost*, 7d. per lb. *Sufficient* for 4 or 5 persons.

MUTTON, HAUNCH OF (ROAST).

INGREDIENTS.—*Haunch of mutton, a little salt, flour.*

Mode.—Let this joint hang as long as possible without becoming tainted, and while hanging dust flour over it, which keeps off the flies, and prevents the air from getting to it. If not well hung, the joint will not be tender. Wash the outside well, then flour it and put it down to a nice brisk fire, at some distance, that it may gradually warm through. Keep basting, and about ½ hour before it is served, draw it nearer to the fire to get nicely brown. Sprinkle a little fine salt over the meat, pour off the dripping, add a little boiling water slightly salted, and strain this over the joint. Place a paper ruche on the bone, and send red currant jelly and gravy in a tureen to table with it.

Time, from 2½ to 3½ hours. *Average cost*, 1s. per lb. *Sufficient* for 10 to 12 persons. *Seasonable*, in best season from September to March.

MUTTON HOT-POT.

INGREDIENTS.—2 *lbs. scrag of mutton*, 6 *onions*, 12 *potatoes* (*more if small*), *dripping, pepper and salt.*

Mode.—Parboil both onions and potatoes and slice them. Well grease a deep baking-dish and line with the potatoes, put over a layer of onions, then the meat cut in small pieces with good seasoning of salt and pepper, another layer of onions, and fill up with potatoes. Pour in ½ a pint of gravy or stock to which a little sauce may be added, then cover with a tin or old dish and bake for 2 hours. Next take off the

118

MUTTON AND LAMB

tin, put some dripping over the potatoes, and put the dish back in the oven to brown.

Time, 2 hours to bake. *Average cost,* 1s. 6d. *Sufficient* for 6 persons. *Seasonable* in winter.

MUTTON, LEG OF (BOILED).

INGREDIENTS.—*Mutton, water, salt.*

Mode.—A leg of mutton for boiling should not hang too long, as it will not look a good colour when dressed. Cut off the shank-bone, trim the knuckle, and wash and wipe it very clean; plunge it into sufficient boiling water to cover it; let it boil up, then draw the saucepan to the side of the fire, where it should remain till the finger can be borne in the water. Then place it sufficiently near the fire that the water may gently simmer, and be very careful that it does not boil fast, or the meat will be hard. Skim well, add a little salt, and in about 2¼ hours, a moderate-sized leg of mutton will be done. Serve with carrots and mashed turnips, which may be boiled with the meat, and send caper sauce to table with it in a tureen.

Time, a moderate-sized leg of mutton of 9 lbs., 3 hours after the water boils; one of 12 lbs., 3¾ hours. *Average cost,* 10d. per lb. *Sufficient,* a moderate-sized leg of mutton for 8 or 10 persons. *Seasonable* nearly all the year, but not so good in June, July, and August.

Note.— When the meat is liked very *thoroughly* cooked, allow more time than stated above. The liquor should be converted into soup.

MUTTON, LEG OF (STUFFED).

INGREDIENTS.— *Small leg mutton (6 or 7 lbs.), veal forcemeat,* 2 *shallots finely minced.*

Mode.—Bone the leg of mutton without spoiling the skin, and cut off some of the fat. Fill the hole with forcemeat, adding 2 shallots finely minced, and sew it up underneath. Bind and tie up compactly and roast or bake for rather over 2½ hours.

Time, 2½ hours or more. *Sufficient* for 6 or 7 persons.

MUTTON, LEG OF (ROAST OR BAKED).

INGREDIENTS.—*Leg of mutton, a little salt.*

Mode. — As mutton, when freshly killed, is never tender, flour it, and put it in a cool, airy place for a few days, if the weather will permit. Wash off the flour, wipe it very dry, and cut off the

shank-bone; put it down to a brisk, clear fire, or into a good oven, dredge with flour, and keep continually basting. About 20 minutes before serving draw it near the fire to get nicely brown; sprinkle over it a little salt, dish the meat, pour off the dripping, add some boiling water slightly salted, strain it over the joint, and serve. If the joint is baked let the oven be very hot at first, then a little cooler. Keep the meat well basted.

Time, a leg of mutton weighing 10 lbs., about 3 hours; one of 7 lbs., about 2½ hours, or rather less. *Average cost,* 10d. per lb. *Sufficient,* a moderate-sized leg of mutton for 8 to 10 persons. *Seasonable* at any time, but not so good in June, July, and August.

MUTTON, LOIN OF (BAKED).

INGREDIENTS.—*Loin of mutton, salt.*

Mode.—See that it is properly jointed and trim off all superfluous fat. Put it into a good hot oven, in a tin with a little water in it salted; after a short time slacken the heat of the oven a little and dredge the joint with flour. Baste and turn the joint while it is cooking, and when done pour off the dripping and make some gravy in the pan.

Time, 15 to 20 minutes per lb. *Average cost,* 9d. lb. *Sufficient* for 8 persons. *Seasonable* all the year.

MUTTON, LOIN OF (BONED AND ROLLED)

INGREDIENTS.—*About 6 lbs. loin mutton,* ½ *teaspoonful pepper,* ¼ *teaspoonful pounded allspice,* ¼ *teaspoonful mace,* ¼ *teaspoonful nutmeg,* 6 *cloves, forcemeat,* 1 *glass port wine,* 2 *tablespoonfuls mushroom ketchup.*

Mode.—Hang the mutton until it is tender, bone it and sprinkle over the spices as above, all pounded very fine. Let it remain for a day, then cover the meat with veal forcemeat, and roll and bind it up firmly. Half bake in a slow oven, let it grow cold, take off the fat, and put the gravy into a stewpan, flour the meat, put it into the gravy and stew it perfectly tender. Take out the meat, unbind it, add the wine and gravy to the ketchup, give it a boil, and pour over the meat. Serve with red currant jelly; a few mushrooms may be stewed for a few minutes in the gravy.

Time, 1½ hour to bake the meat, 1½ hour to stew gently. *Average cost,* 9d. lb. *Sufficient* for 6 or 8 persons.

MUTTON, NECK OF (BOILED).

INGREDIENTS.—4 *lbs. of the middle or best end of the neck of mutton; a little salt.*

Mode.—Trim off a portion of the fat, and if it is to look particularly nice, the chine-bone should be sawn down, the ribs stripped halfway down, and the ends of the bones chopped off. Put the meat into sufficient *boiling* water to cover it; when it boils add a little salt, and remove all the scum. Draw the saucepan to the side of the fire, and let the water get so cool that the finger may be borne in it; then simmer very *slowly* and gently until the meat is done, which will be in about 1½ hour, or rather more. Serve with turnips and caper sauce, and pour a little of it over the meat. The turnips should be boiled with the mutton; and a few carrots will, cut into long, thinnish pieces, also be found an improvement. Garnish the dish with carrots and turnips placed alternately round the mutton.

Time, 4 lbs. of the neck of mutton, about 1½ hour. *Average cost*, 8d. or 9d. per lb. *Sufficient* for 6 or 7 persons.

MUTTON PUDDING.

INGREDIENTS.—*About* 2 *lbs. chump end of the loin of mutton, weighed after being boned; pepper and salt to taste, suet crust made with milk, in the proportion of 6 oz. suet to each pound of flour; very small quantity of minced onion (this may be omitted when the flavour is not liked).*

Mode.—Cut the meat into rather thin slices, and season with pepper and salt; line the pudding with crust; lay in the meat, and nearly, but do not quite, fill it up with water; when the flavour is liked add a small quantity of minced onion; cover with crust, and proceed as directed in recipe for steak pudding.

Time, about 3 hours. *Average cost*, 2s. 6d. *Sufficient* for 6 persons. *Seasonable* all the year, but more suitable for a winter dish.

MUTTON, SADDLE OF (ROAST).

INGREDIENTS.—*Saddle of mutton; a little salt.*

Mode.— This joint should be hung for 10 days or a fortnight if the weather permits. Cut off the tail and flaps, &c., and have the skin taken off and skewered on again. Put it down to a bright, clear fire, and, when the joint has been

cooking for an hour, remove the skin and dredge it with flour. It should not be placed too near the fire, as the fat should not be in the slightest degree burnt. Keep constantly basting, both before and after the skin is removed. Sprinkle some salt over the joint, make a little gravy in the dripping-pan, and pour it over the meat, which send to table with a tureen of made gravy and red-currant jelly.

Time, a saddle of mutton weighing 10 lbs., 2½ hours; 14 lbs., 3¼ hours. *Average cost*, 10d. per lb. *Sufficient*, a moderate-sized saddle of 10 lbs. for 8 to 10 persons. *Seasonable* all the year; not so good when lamb is in full season.

MUTTON, SHOULDER OF (ROAST OR BAKED).

INGREDIENTS.—*Shoulder of mutton a little salt.*

Mode.—Put the joint down to a bright, clear fire; flour it well, and keep continually basting. About ¼ hour before serving draw it near the fire, that the outside may acquire a nice brown colour. Sprinkle a little fine salt over the meat, empty the dripping-pan, pour in a little boiling water slightly salted, and strain over the joint. Onion sauce, or stewed Spanish onions, are usually sent to table with this dish, and sometimes baked potatoes.

Time, a shoulder of mutton weighing 6 or 7 lbs., 1¼ hours. *Average cost*, 9d. per lb. *Sufficient* for 6 to 8 persons.

Note.—This joint may be dressed in a variety of ways—boiled, and served with onion sauce; boned, and stuffed with a good veal forcemeat; or baked, with potatoes, in the dripping-pan. This last-named way is often considered the best.

SHEEP'S HAGGIS.

INGREDIENTS. — *The large stomach bag of a sheep, 1 of the smaller bags known as the king's hood, sheep's pluck (lights, liver, and heart), ½ lb. beef suet, 2 small teacupfuls oatmeal, pepper and salt.*

Mode.—Wash the bags thoroughly in cold water, then plunge them into boiling water and scrape, taking especial care not to injure the larger bag, which must also be allowed to soak in cold water, with a handful of salt, all night. Wash the pluck and boil. Do not remove the windpipe, but let the end of it hang over the edge of the pot, that the impurities may pass out. The smaller bag should be boiled in the same pot, and both will be done in about 1½ hours. When cold, cut away the windpipe and trim off any pieces of skin or gristle. Grate *one quarter* of the liver only, mince the heart, lights, and small bag very small with half a pound of beef suet. Mix these and the grated liver with the oatmeal, previously dried before the fire; add half a pint of beef gravy, or same quantity of the liquor in which the pluck was boiled, black pepper and salt; stir all together. Now take the large bag (thoroughly cleaned), and put the mince into it. Let it be little more than half filled. Sew up the bag with needle and thread; put it into a pot of boiling water, with a plate placed beneath to prevent its sticking. Prick the bag occasionally as it swells, to allow the air to escape. If the bag appears thin tie a cloth outside. Serve in a napkin on a dish, without garnish or gravy.

Time, 1½ hours to boil the pluck and smaller bag, 3 hours for the haggis. *Average cost*, 3s. *Seasonable* in winter.

SHEEP'S HEAD.

INGREDIENTS.—1 *sheep's head, sufficient water to cover it, 3 carrots, 3 turnips, 2 or 3 parsnips, 3 onions, a small bunch parsley, 1 teaspoonful pepper, 3 teaspoonfuls salt, ¼ lb. Scotch oatmeal.*

Mode.—Clean the head well, and let it soak in warm water for 2 hours, to get rid of the blood; put into a saucepan, with sufficient cold water to cover it, and when it boils, add the vegetables, peeled and sliced, and the remaining ingredients; before adding the oatmeal mix it to a smooth batter with a little of the liquor. Keep stirring till it boils up; then shut the saucepan closely, and let it stew gently for 1½ or 2 hours. It may be thickened with rice or barley instead of oatmeal.

Time, 1½ or 2 hours. *Average cost*, 1s. each. *Sufficient* for 3 or 4 persons.

LAMB, BREAST OF (STEWED).

INGREDIENTS.—1 *breast lamb, pepper and salt to taste, sufficient stock to cover it, 1 glass sherry, thickening of butter and flour.*

Mode.—Skin the lamb, cut it into pieces, and season with pepper and salt, lay these in a stewpan, pour in sufficient stock or gravy to cover them, and stew very gently until tender (about 1½ hours). Before serving,

thicken the sauce with butter and flour; add the sherry, give one boil, and pour it over the meat. Green peas, or stewed mushrooms, may be strewed over the meat.

Time, 1½ hours. *Average cost*, 9d. per lb. *Sufficient* for 3 persons. *Seasonable*, grass lamb, from Easter to Michaelmas.

LAMB, FORE-QUARTERS OF (ROAST).

INGREDIENTS.—*Lamb; a little salt.*

Mode.—To obtain the flavour of lamb in perfection it should not be long kept; time to cool is all that it requires. Place the joint before a clear, brisk fire at a sufficient distance to prevent the fat from burning, and baste constantly till the moment of serving. Lamb should be *thoroughly* done, without being dried up, and not the slightest appearance of red gravy should be visible. This rule is applicable to all young white meats. Serve with gravy made in the dripping-pan, and send to table with it a tureen of mint sauce. Lamb may also be baked as directed in recipes for mutton.

Time, fore-quarter of lamb weighing 10 lbs., 2 to 2½ hours. *Average cost*, 1s. per lb. *Sufficient* for 8 persons. *Seasonable*, grass lamb. from Easter to Michaelmas.

LAMB, LEG OF (BOILED).

INGREDIENTS.—*Leg of lamb; white sauce.*

Mode. — Choose a joint weighing about 5 lbs. Plunge it into a saucepan of boiling water, and when it boils up again, draw it to the side of the fire, and let the water cool a little. Then stew very gently for about 1½ hours. Make some white sauce by recipe, dish the lamb, pour the sauce over it, and garnish with tufts of boiled cauliflower or carrots. Melted butter may be substituted for the white sauce, but it is not nearly so nice. Send to table with it some of the sauce in a tureen, and boiled cauliflowers or spinach, with whichever vegetable the dish is garnished.

Time, 1¼ hours after the water simmers. *Average cost*, 1s. per lb. *Sufficient* for 5 or 6 persons. *Seasonable* from Easter to Michaelmas.

LAMB, LEG OF (ROAST).

INGREDIENTS.—*Lamb; a little salt.*
Mode.—Place the joint at a good dis-

BEEF.

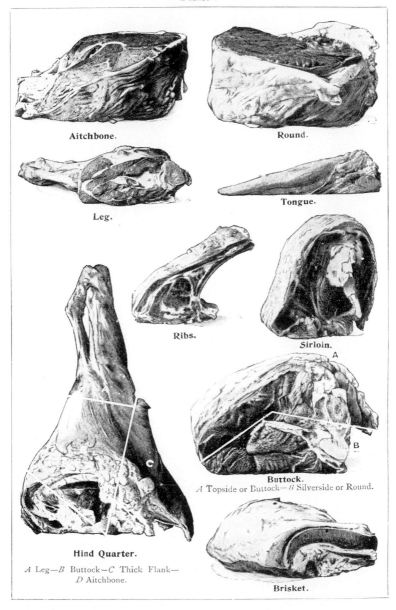

Aitchbone.

Round.

Leg.

Tongue.

Ribs.

Sirloin.

Buttock.
A Topside or Buttock—*B* Silverside or Round.

Hind Quarter.

A Leg—*B* Buttock—*C* Thick Flank—
D Aitchbone.

Brisket.

PORK AND VEAL.

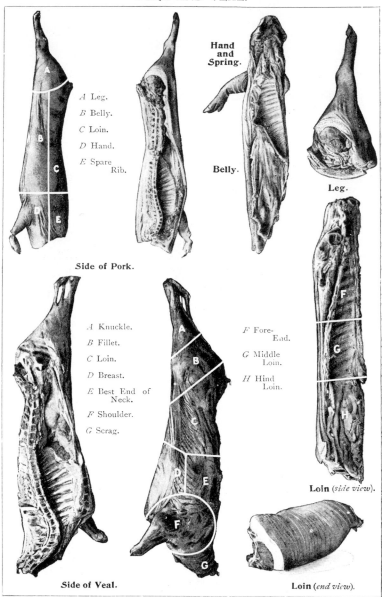

A Leg.
B Belly.
C Loin.
D Hand.
E Spare Rib.

Hand and Spring.

Belly.

Leg.

Side of Pork.

A Knuckle.
B Fillet.
C Loin.
D Breast.
E Best End of Neck.
F Shoulder.
G Scrag.

F Fore-End.
G Middle Loin.
H Hind Loin.

Loin (*side view*).

Side of Veal.

Loin (*end view*).

MUTTON.

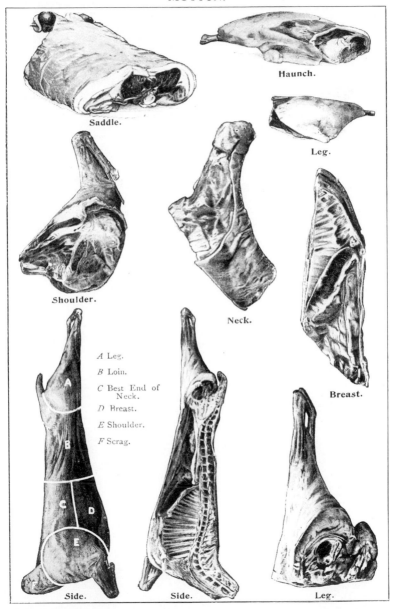

Saddle.

Haunch.

Leg.

Shoulder.

Neck.

Breast.

A Leg.
B Loin.
C Best End of
   Neck.
D Breast.
E Shoulder.
F Scrag.

Side.

Side.

Leg.

tance from the fire at first, and baste well the whole time it is cooking. When nearly done, draw it near to the fire to brown. Sprinkle a little fine salt over the meat; empty the dripping-pan; pour in a little boiling water, and strain over the meat. Serve with mint sauce, and send peas, spinach, or cauliflowers to table with it.

Time, a leg of lamb weighing 5 lbs., 1½ hours. *Average cost*, 1s. per lb. *Sufficient* for 5 or 6 persons. *Seasonable* from Easter to Michaelmas.

Note.—A shoulder of lamb requires rather more than 1 hour to roast. A small saddle, about 2 hours; a larger saddle, 2½ hours, or longer. Loin of lamb, 1¼ to 1½ hours. Ribs of lamb, from 1 to 1¼ hours.

ENTREES AND MADE DISHES.

BAKED MINCED MUTTON (Cold Meat Cookery).

INGREDIENTS.—*The remains of any joint of cold roast mutton, 1 or 2 onions, 1 bunch savoury herbs, pepper and salt to taste, 2 blades pounded mace or nutmeg, 2 tablespoonfuls gravy, mashed potatoes.*

Mode.—Mince an onion rather fine and fry it a light brown; add the herbs and mutton, finely minced and well mixed; season with pepper and salt, and a little pounded mace or nutmeg, and moisten with the gravy. Put a layer of mashed potatoes at the bottom of a dish, then the mutton and another layer of potatoes, and bake for ½ hour. *Time*, ½ hour. *Average cost*, exclusive of the meat, 3d.

BROILED MUTTON AND TOMATO SAUCE (Cold Meat Cookery).

INGREDIENTS.—*A few slices of cold mutton; tomato sauce.*

Mode.—Cut some nice slices from a cold leg or shoulder of mutton; season with pepper and salt, and broil over a clear fire. Pour tomato sauce over the mutton, and serve very hot.

Time, about 5 minutes to broil the mutton. *Seasonable* in September and October.

COLLOPS (MUTTON).

INGREDIENTS.—*A few slices of a cold leg or loin of mutton, salt and pepper to taste, 1 blade pounded mace, 1 small bunch savoury herbs minced very fine,*

2 *or* 3 *shallots*, 2 *or* 3 *oz. butter*, 1 *dessertspoonful flour*, ½ *pint gravy*, 1 *tablespoonful lemon-juice.*

Mode.—Cut some very thin slices from a leg or the chump end of a loin of mutton; sprinkle with pepper, salt, pounded mace, minced savoury herbs and minced shallot; fry them in butter, stir in a dessertspoonful of flour, add the gravy and lemon-juice, simmer gently about 5 or 7 minutes, and serve immediately.

Time, 5 to 7 minutes. *Average cost*, exclusive of the meat, 5d.

CURRIED MUTTON (Cold Meat Cookery).

INGREDIENTS.—*The remains of any joint of cold mutton, 2 onions, 2 oz. butter, 1 dessertspoonful curry-powder, 1 dessertspoonful flour, salt to taste, ¼ pint stock or water.*

Mode.—Slice the onions in thin rings, put them in a stewpan with the butter, and fry a light brown; stir in the curry-powder, flour, and salt, and mix well together. Cut the meat into nice thin slices (or it may be minced) and add it to the other ingredients; when browned, add the stock or gravy, and stew gently for about ½ hour. Serve with rice.

Time, ½ hour. *Average cost*, exclusive of the meat, 9d. *Seasonable* in winter.

HARICOT MUTTON (Cold Meat Cookery).

INGREDIENTS.—*The remains of cold neck or loin of mutton, 2 oz. butter or dripping, 3 onions, 1 dessertspoonful flour, ½ pint good gravy, pepper and salt to taste, 2 tablespoonfuls port wine, 1 tablespoonful ketchup, 2 carrots, 2 turnips, 1 head celery.*

Mode. — Cut the cold mutton into chops, and take off the fat; slice the onions, and fry with the chops, in a little butter or dripping, a nice brown colour; stir in the flour, add the gravy, and let it stew gently nearly an hour. In the meantime boil the vegetables until *nearly* tender, slice them, and add them to the mutton about ¼ hour before it is to be served. Season with pepper and salt, add the ketchup and port wine, give one boil, and serve.

Time, 1 hour. *Average cost*, exclusive of the cold meat, 1s.

HASHED MUTTON.

INGREDIENTS.—*The remains of cold roast shoulder or leg of mutton, 6 whole peppers, 6 whole allspice, a faggot savoury herbs, ½ head celery, 1 onion, 2 oz. butter, flour.*

Mode.—Cut the meat in even slices, trimming off all superfluous fat and gristle; chop the bones and fragments of the joint; put them into a stewpan with the pepper, spice, herbs, and celery; cover with water, and simmer for 1 hour. Slice and fry the onion a pale-brown colour in the butter; dredge in a little flour to make it thick, and add this to the bones, &c. Stew for ¼ hour, strain the gravy, and let it cool; then skim off every particle of fat, and put it, with the meat, into a stewpan. Flavour with ketchup, tomato sauce, or any other flavouring, and let the meat gradually warm through. To hash meat properly, it should be laid in cold gravy, and only left on the fire just long enough to warm through.

Time, 1½ hours to simmer the gravy. *Average cost,* exclusive of the meat, 3d.

HODGE-PODGE (Cold Meat Cookery).

INGREDIENTS.—*About 1 lb. of under-done cold mutton, 2 lettuces, 1 pint green peas, 5 or 6 green onions, 2 oz. butter, pepper and salt to taste, 1 tea-cupful water.*

Mode.—Mince the mutton, and cut up the lettuces and onions in slices. Put these in a stewpan with all the ingredients except the peas, and let these simmer gently for ¾ hour, keeping them well stirred. Boil the peas separately, mix these with the mutton, and serve very hot.

Time, ¾ hour. *Sufficient* for 3 or 4 persons. *Seasonable* from the end of May to August. *Average cost,* exclusive of the meat, 1s.

IRISH STEW.

INGREDIENTS.—*3 lbs. loin or neck of mutton, 5 lbs. potatoes, 5 large onions, pepper and salt to taste, rather more than 1 pint water.*

Mode.—Trim off some of the fat, and cut the meat into chops of moderate thickness. Pare and halve the potatoes, and cut the onions into thick slices. Put a layer of potatoes at the bottom of a stewpan, then a layer of mutton and onions, and season with pepper and salt; proceed in this manner until the stewpan is full, taking care to have plenty of vegetables at the top. Pour in the water, and let it stew gently for 2½ hours, keeping the lid of the stewpan

closely shut, and occasionally shaking the pan to prevent it burning.

Time, 2½ hours. *Average cost for this quantity,* 2s. 6d. *Sufficient* for 5 or 6 persons. *Seasonable,* most suitable for a winter dish.

KEBOBBS.

INGREDIENTS.—*Remains of cold roast mutton, about ½ lb. after mincing, a mixture for seasoning of a small tea-spoonful of curry paste, a grate of nut-meg, salt and finely chopped herbs, 2 eggs, fat for frying, breadcrumbs.*

Mode.—Mince the mutton freed from fat in a mincer (there should be about ½ lb.), add the seasoning, which may be varied according to taste, and make into little flat cakes with beaten egg, dip these into egg and crumbs, and fry a bright golden brown. Send cut lemon to table with them.

Time, about 5 minutes to fry the kebobbs. *Average cost,* exclusive of the meat, 6d. *Sufficient* for 2 or 3 persons. *Seasonable* in winter.

KIDNEY TOAST.

INGREDIENTS.—*3 sheep's kidneys, 1 oz. of butter, a little lemon, cayenne and salt, 3 slices of hot buttered toast.*

Mode.—Gently stew the kidneys in a very little water till perfectly tender, when remove all skin and gristle and pound them in a mortar with the butter till they form a smooth paste. Squeeze a little lemon into them and season highly with the cayenne and salt; spread the paste upon the toast and put the slices in the oven for a few minutes, that they may be perfectly hot when served.

A more economical dish may be made by substituting bullock's kidney (about ½ lb.) for the sheep's.

Average cost (with sheep's kidneys), 11d. *Sufficient* for 3 persons. *Seasonable* in winter.

KIDNEYS (BROILED).

INGREDIENTS.—*Sheep's kidneys, pepper and salt to taste.*

Mode.—Cut the kidneys open very evenly, lengthwise, down to the root, but do not separate them; skin them, and pass a skewer under the white part of each half to keep them flat, and broil over a clear fire, placing the inside downwards; turn them when done enough on one side, and cook them on the other. Remove the skewers, place the kidneys on a very hot dish, season with pepper and salt, and put a tiny piece of butter in the middle of each. Serve very hot and quickly, and send very hot plates to table.

Time, 6 to 8 minutes. *Average cost,* 3d. each. *Sufficient*—allow one for each person.

Note.—The kidneys may be served each on a piece of buttered toast cut in any fanciful shape, with the addition of a little lemon-juice.

KIDNEYS (FRIED).

INGREDIENTS.—*Kidneys, butter, pepper and salt to taste.*

Mode.—Cut the kidneys open without quite dividing them, remove the skin, and put a small piece of butter in the frying-pan. When the butter is melted, lay in the kidneys the flat side downwards, and fry for 7 or 8 minutes, turning them when they are half-done. Serve on a piece of dry toast, season with pepper and salt, and put a small piece of butter in each kidney; pour the gravy from the pan over them, and serve very hot.

Time, 7 or 8 minutes. *Average cost,* 3d. each. *Sufficient*— allow one kidney to each person.

KIDNEYS (STEWED).

INGREDIENTS. — 4 *kidneys, fat for frying, some good brown gravy, a glass of sherry.*

Mode.—Divide the kidneys, take out the core and skin them, and fry them lightly in butter or good dripping, then stew them gently for about 20 minutes in the gravy and sherry. They must not boil or they will harden, but they must be perfectly tender.

Time, 20 minutes. *Average cost,* for this quantity, 1s. 9d. *Sufficient* for 4 persons.

MUTTON CUTLETS AND TOMATOES.

INGREDIENTS.—*Neck of mutton, best end, sufficient for* 8 *cutlets, ½ tin tomatoes, some brown gravy, ½ a lemon,* 1 *carrot,* 1 *onion, butter for frying.*

Mode.—Cut the mutton into cutlets and trim them very neatly, taking off the ends (but leaving a small piece of bone on each) and most of the fat. Fry them brown in a little butter but do not cook them. Cut the vegetables in thin slices and put them with the cutlets and a seasoning of pepper and salt, the gravy and a glass of sherry if liked. Stew till the cutlets are tender,

then take them out and put them on a hot dish. Heat the tomato and put it over the cutlets, add a little lemon-juice to the gravy and pour round.

Time, about ½ hour. *Average cost,* 2s. 6d. *Sufficient* for 4 persons. *Seasonable* at any time.

MUTTON CUTLETS WITH MASHED POTATOES.

INGREDIENTS. — *About* 3 *lbs. of the best end of the neck of mutton, salt and pepper to taste, mashed potatoes.*

Mode.—Procure a well-hung neck of mutton, saw off about 3 inches of the top of the bones, and cut the cutlets of a moderate thickness. Shape them by chopping off the thick part of the chine-bone; beat them flat with a cutlet-chopper, and scrape quite clean a portion of the top of the bone. Broil them over a nice clear fire for about 7 or 8 minutes, and turn frequently. When the cutlets are done, season with pepper and salt; arrange them with the thick end of the cutlets downwards round mashed potatoes, and serve very hot and quickly.

Time, 7 or 8 minutes. *Average cost,* for this quantity with potatoes, 2s. 6d. *Sufficient* for 6 or 8 persons.

Note.—Cutlets may be served in various ways; with peas, tomatoes, onions, sauce piquante, &c.

MUTTON PATTIES (Cold Meat Cookery).

INGREDIENTS.—*Some cold roast mutton, the more underdone the better,* 1 *onion, pepper, salt, puff paste,* 1 *egg.*

Mode.—Cut the meat into slices, then mince it finely, also the onion, and season well with the pepper and salt, and use any gravy at hand to moisten the mixture. Roll out the paste thin, line some patty pans with it and stamp out some rounds to cover them. Fill them full of the mince, wet the edges and put on the tops, then brush over with beaten yolk of egg and bake in a quick oven.

Time, about 20 minutes to bake the patties. *Average cost,* 1½d. each. *Sufficient*—allow 9 for 6 persons. *Seasonable* at any time.

MUTTON PIE (Cold Meat Cookery).

INGREDIENTS.—*The remains of a cold leg, loin, or neck of mutton, pepper and salt to taste,* 2 *blades pounded mace,* 1 *dessertspoonful chopped parsley,* 1 *teaspoonful minced savoury herbs, when liked, a little minced onion or shallot;*

3 *or* 4 *potatoes,* 1 *teacupful gravy,*
crust.

Mode.—Cold mutton may be made
into very good pies if well seasoned
and mixed with a few herbs; if the
leg is used, cut it into very thin slices;
if the loin or neck, into thin cutlets.
Place some at the bottom of the dish;
season well with pepper, salt, mace,
parsley, and herbs; then put a layer
of potatoes sliced, then more mutton,
and so on till the dish is full; add the
gravy, cover with a crust, and bake for
1 hour.

Time, 1 hour. *Average cost,* without
meat, 8d.

Note.—The remains of an underdone
leg of mutton may be converted into a
very good family pudding.

MUTTON RAGOUT (Cold Meat Cookery).

INGREDIENTS.—*The remains of cold
neck or loin of mutton,* 2 *oz. butter, a
little flour,* 2 *onions sliced,* ½ *pint water,*
2 *small carrots,* 2 *turnips, pepper and
salt to taste.*

Mode.—Cut the mutton into small
chops, and trim off the greater portion
of the fat; put the butter into a stewpan, dredge in a little flour, add the
sliced onions, and keep stirring till
brown; then put in the meat. When
this is quite brown, add the water, and
the carrots and turnips, cut into very
thin slices; season and stew till quite
tender (about ¾ hour). Green peas may
be substituted for the carrots and turnips; they should be piled in the centre
of the dish, and the chops laid round.

Time, ¾ hour. *Average cost,* exclusive
of meat, 4d. *Seasonable,* with peas,
from June to August.

SHEEP'S BRAINS.

Mode.—Detach the brains from the
head without breaking them, and put
them into a basin of hot water; let
them remain for an hour. Remove
the skin, tie up in a small cloth, put
into boiling water, and simmer for ten
minutes. Season with pepper and salt,
and serve hot, with or without melted
butter.

Time, 10 minutes. *Average cost,* 3d.

Note.—Bullocks' brains require rather
more boiling. Calves' about the same
time as sheep's.

SHEEP'S HEARTS.

INGREDIENTS.—3 *sheep's hearts, veal
stuffing, a little dripping or butter.*

Mode.—Make a nice savoury stuff-

ing, cleanse the hearts and stuff them,
tying them round or skewering them
so that the stuffing does not fall out.
Put them in a baking-pan with a little
dripping, and bake for about ¾ hour,
turning and basting when needed.

Time, ¾ hour. *Average cost,* 1s.
Sufficient for 3 persons. *Seasonable*
at any time.

SHEEP'S TROTTERS (Soyer's Recipe).

INGREDIENTS.—12 *feet,* ¼ *lb. beef or
mutton suet,* 2 *onions,* 1 *carrot,* 2 *bay-
leaves,* 2 *sprigs thyme,* 1 *oz. salt,* ½ *oz.
pepper,* 2 *tablespoonfuls flour,* 2½ *quarts
water,* ¼ *lb. fresh butter,* 1 *teaspoonful
salt,* 1 *teaspoonful flour,* ¼ *teaspoonful
pepper, a little grated nutmeg, the juice*
1 *lemon,* 1 *gill milk, yolks of* 2 *eggs.*

Mode.—Have the feet cleaned, and
the long bone extracted. Put the suet
into a stewpan, with the onions and
carrot sliced, the bay-leaves, thyme,
salt and pepper, and simmer 5 minutes.
Add 2 tablespoonfuls flour and the
water, and keep stirring till it boils;
then put in the feet. Let these simmer
for 3 hours, or until tender, then take
them out. Mix together, on a plate,
butter, salt, flour (1 tablespoonful),
pepper, nutmeg, and lemon-juice as
above. Put the feet, with a gill of
milk, into a stewpan and when very
hot add the butter, &c., and stir till
melted. Now mix the yolks of 2 eggs
with 5 tablespoonfuls of milk; stir this
to the other ingredients, keep moving
the pan over the fire for a minute or
two, but do not allow it to boil after
the eggs are added. Serve in a hot
dish, and garnish with croûtons, or
sippets of toasted bread.

Time, 3 hours. *Average cost,* 3s. 10d.
Sufficient for 6 or 8 persons.

TOAD-IN-THE-HOLE (Cold Meat Cookery).

INGREDIENTS.—6 *oz. flour,* 1 *pint
milk,* 3 *eggs, butter, a few slices cold
mutton, pepper and salt,* 2 *kidneys.*

Mode.—Make a smooth batter of
flour, milk, and eggs in the above
proportion; butter a baking-dish, and
pour in the batter. Into this place a
few slices of cold mutton, previously
well seasoned, and the kidneys cut
into rather small pieces; bake about
1 hour, or rather longer, and send it
to table in the dish it was baked in.
Mushrooms may be substituted for the
kidneys.

Time, rather more than 1 hour.

Average cost, exclusive of the cold meat, 1s.

LAMB CUTLETS, à la Constance (French Recipe).

INGREDIENTS.—8 *cutlets*, 2 *oz. of butter, the livers and cock's combs of 2 fowls, a few mushroom buttons, pepper and salt.*

Mode.—Clean the combs, put them for a moment in boiling water, then rub off the outer skin, and let them lie in water for 3 hours. Take them out, and, having wiped them, cut them with the livers and mushrooms into small pieces, and stew them with a little butter, stock, and seasoning till all are well done. Mix this stew with some béchamel sauce if at hand, or with a little butter made into a paste with flour. Shape and trim the cutlets neatly, fry them on both sides in a little butter, adding pepper and salt. When done, drain and glaze the cutlets, arrange them in a ring on a very hot dish, and pour the stew in the centre.

Time, 10 minutes to fry the cutlets. *Average cost*, 2s. 6d. *Sufficient* for 5 or 6 persons. *Seasonable* from Easter to Michaelmas.

LAMB CHOPS.

INGREDIENTS.—*Loin of lamb; pepper and salt to taste.*

Mode.—Trim off the flap from the loin, and cut it into chops about ¾ inch in thickness. Lay the chops on a gridiron, and broil them over a bright, clear fire of a nice pale brown. Season with pepper and salt, and garnish with crisped parsley, or place them on mashed potatoes. Asparagus, spinach, or peas are favourite accompaniments.

Time, about 8 or 10 minutes. *Average cost*, 1s. per lb. *Sufficient*—allow 2 chops to each person. *Seasonable* from Easter to Michaelmas.

LAMB DARIOLES.

INGREDIENTS.—¾ *lb. cold lamb free from fat, 4 eggs, a little red tongue, and white of 1 boiled egg, some brown gravy, a little butter, a dessertspoonful sauce (tomato or Worcester), salt.*

Mode.—Put the mutton twice through a mincer, add to it the eggs beaten, the sauce, seasoning, and a tablespoonful of gravy. Butter some dariole moulds thickly, lay in the tops of each a star or other devise of the tongue with half moons of white of egg round, and fill with the mixture. Steam for half an hour, and serve turned out on a hot dish with a pile of green peas in the centre. Heat the gravy and pour round.

Time, ½ hour. *Average cost*, exclusive of the meat, 1s. *Sufficient* for 6 darioles. *Seasonable* in spring.

LAMB (HASHED) AND BROILED BLADE-BONE.

INGREDIENTS.—*The remains of a cold shoulder of lamb, pepper and salt to taste, 2 oz. butter, about ½ pint stock or gravy, 1 tablespoonful shallot vinegar, 3 or 4 pickled gherkins.*

Mode. — Cut the meat neatly into collops, season the blade-bone with pepper and salt, pour a little oiled butter over it, and warm through in the oven. Put the stock into a stew-pan, add ketchup and shallot vinegar, and lay in the pieces of lamb. Let these heat gradually through, but do not allow them to boil. Take the blade-bone out of the oven, and place it on a gridiron over a sharp fire to brown. Slice the gherkins, put them into the hash, and dish it with the blade-bone in the centre. Garnish with croûtons or sippets of toasted bread.

Time, altogether ½ hour. *Average cost*, exclusive of meat, 4d. *Seasonable*—house lamb, Christmas to March; grass lamb, Easter to Michaelmas.

LAMB'S SWEETBREADS.

INGREDIENTS.'— *Sweetbreads, 1 egg, breadcrumbs, fat for frying.*

Mode.—Parboil the sweetbreads, take them out and let them get thoroughly cold in cold water. Dry and flour them, then dip them in beaten egg and crumbs, and fry a golden brown.

Time, about 5 minutes to boil and the same to fry. *Seasonable* in spring

PORK

BACON (TO BOIL).

INGREDIENTS.—*Bacon ; water.*

Mode.—Soak the bacon if very salt in warm water for an hour or two ; then pare off the rusty parts, and scrape the underside and rind clean. Put it into a saucepan of cold water, let it come gradually to a boil, and as the scum rises to the surface, remove it. Let it simmer very gently until *thoroughly* done ; take it up, strip off the skin, sprinkle over a few bread raspings ; garnish with tufts of cauliflower or Brussels sprouts. When served alone, broad beans or green peas are the usual accompaniments.

Time, 1 lb. of bacon, ¾ hour ; 2 lbs. 1½ hours. *Average cost*, 10d. to 1s. per lb. for the primest parts. *Sufficient*, 2 lbs. for 8 persons, when served with poultry or veal.

BOLOGNA SAUSAGES.

INGREDIENTS.—*3 lbs. lean beef, 3 lbs. lean pork, 2 lbs. fat bacon, 1½ lbs. beef suet ; pepper, salt, 1 sprig thyme, and ground mace.*

Mode—Put the meat and suet into a stewpan of hot water, stew for half an hour, and then mince each sort by itself. Season with pepper, thyme chopped fine, and ground mace ; fill ox skins with it, tie them in lengths, and put them in a beef brine for ten days ; then smoke them the same as ham or tongue. Rub ground ginger or pepper over the outside after they are smoked, and keep them in a cool, dry place.

Average cost, for this quantity, 7s.

FRANKFORT SAUSAGES.

INGREDIENTS.—*2 lbs. of tender, lean pork, 1 lb. of fat, mace, coriander seeds, sauce, claret, sausage skins.*

Mode.—Chop both lean and fat very fine, add the other ingredients to taste, mix to the consistency of sausage meat with the claret, and fill the skins. Boil the sausages gently in mild beer or water, enough to cover them, for ¾ of an hour, then fry for 15 minutes in butter. In Germany they are often served with well-sweetened apple-sauce, flavoured with cinnamon.

Time, 1 hour. *Average cost*, 2s. 9d. *Seasonable* from September to March.

HAM (TO BAKE).

INGREDIENTS. — *Ham ; a common crust.*

Mode.—Let the ham be soaked in

water for at least 12 hours. Wipe it dry, trim away any rusty places, and cover it with a common crust of sufficient thickness to keep the gravy in. Place it in a moderately heated oven, and bake for nearly 4 hours. Take off the crust and skin, cover with raspings, as a boiled ham, and garnish the knuckle with a paper frill. This method of cooking a ham is, by many persons, considered far superior to boiling it, as it cuts fuller of gravy and has a finer flavour, besides keeping a much longer time good.

Time, a medium-sized ham, 4 hours. *Average cost*, 10d. per lb. for an English ham, 6½d. for an American one. *Seasonable* all the year.

HAM (TO BOIL).

INGREDIENTS.—*Ham, water, glaze or rasping.*

Mode.—To ascertain that the ham is perfectly sweet, run a knife into it, close to the bone; if, when the knife is withdrawn, it has an agreeable smell, the ham is good; if the blade has a greasy appearance and offensive smell, the ham is bad. If it is very dry and salt, let it soak for 24 hours, changing the water frequently. This is only necessary in the case of its being very hard; from 8 to 12 hours would be sufficient for a Yorkshire or Westmorland ham. Wash it thoroughly clean, and trim away all the rusty and smoked parts. Put it into a boiling-pot, with sufficient cold water to cover it; bring it gradually to boil, and as the scum rises, carefully remove it. Keep it simmering gently until tender, and be careful that it does not stop boiling. When done, take it out, strip off the skin, and sprinkle over it a few fine bread-raspings, put a frill of cut paper round the knuckle, and serve. If to be eaten cold, let the ham remain in the water until nearly cold, by this method the juices are kept in, and it will be found greatly superior to one taken out of the hot water. The ham must *not*, however, remain in the saucepan *all* night. When the skin is removed, sprinkle over bread-raspings, or glaze it. Place a frill round the knuckle, and garnish with parsley or cut vegetable flowers.

Time, a ham weighing 10 lbs., 4 hours to *simmer gently ;* 15 lbs., 5 hours; a very large one, about 6 hours. *Average cost*, 10d. per lb. for an English ham, 6½d. for an American one. *Seasonable* all the year.

HAM (TO PICKLE).

INGREDIENTS.—*To a ham from* 10 *to* 12 *lbs. allow* 1 *lb. coarse sugar,* ¾ *lb. salt,* 1 *oz. saltpetre,* ½ *teacupful vinegar.*

Mode.—Rub the hams well with common salt, and leave them for a day or two to drain; then rub well in the above proportion of sugar, salt, saltpetre, and vinegar, and turn the hams every other day. Keep them in pickle 1 month, drain, and send to be smoked over a wood fire for 3 or 4 weeks.

Time, to remain in the pickle, 1 month; to be smoked 3 weeks or 1 month. *Sufficient*, the above proportion of pickle to 1 ham. *Seasonable*—hams should be pickled from October to March.

HAMS (TO SALT).

INGREDIENTS.—2 *lbs. treacle,* ½ *lb. saltpetre,* 1 *lb. bay salt,* 2 *lbs. common salt.*

Mode.—Two days before they are put into pickle rub the hams well with salt, to draw away all slime and blood, which throw away, and then rub them with treacle, saltpetre, and salt. Lay them in a deep pan, and let them remain 1 day ; boil the above proportion of treacle, saltpetre, bay salt, and common salt for ¼ hour, and pour this pickle boiling hot over the hams; there should be sufficient of it to cover them. For a day or two rub them well with it; afterwards they will only require turning. They ought to remain in this pickle for 3 weeks or a month, and then be sent to be smoked. An ox-tongue pickled in this way is most excellent, to be eaten either green or smoked.

Time, to remain in the pickle, three weeks or a month ; to be smoked about a month. *Seasonable* from October to March.

LARD (TO MAKE).

Mode.—Melt the inner fat of the pig by putting it in a stone jar, and placing this in a saucepan of boiling water, previously stripping off the skin. Let it simmer gently, and as it melts, pour it carefully from the sediment. Put it into small jars or bladders, and keep it in a cool place. The flead or inside fat of the pig, before it is melted, makes exceedingly light crust, and is particularly wholesome. It may be preserved a length of time by salting it well, and occasionally changing the brine. When wanted, wash and wipe it, and it will answer for making into paste as well as fresh lard.

Average cost, 6d. per lb

PIG'S FRY (a Savoury Dish).

INGREDIENTS. — 1½ *lb. pig's fry*, 2 *onions, a few sage-leaves*, 3 *lbs. potatoes, pepper and salt to taste.*

Mode.—Put the lean fry at the bottom of a pie-dish, sprinkle over it minced sage and onion, with pepper and salt; put a layer of sliced potatoes on the seasoning, then the fat fry, then more seasoning, and a layer of potatoes at the top. Fill the dish with boiling water, and bake for 2 hours, or rather longer.

Time, rather more than 2 hours. *Average cost*, 7d. per. lb. *Sufficient* for 3 or 4 persons. *Seasonable* from October to March.

PIG'S HEAD.

INGREDIENTS. — ½ *oz. sage*, 1 *tablespoonful salt*, 1 *dessertspoonful pepper.*

Mode.—Boil the head until it is easy to remove the bones. Then rub it over with a mixture of salt, pepper, and finely-powdered sage. Put it in a good oven and baste well. Pour over some good gravy, and serve with apple sauce.

Time, 1½ hour or more. *Average cost*, 2s. 6d.

Note.—Pig's head is frequently salted and boiled, and served with turnips and greens.

PIG'S LIVER (a Savoury and Economical Dish).

INGREDIENTS.—*The liver and lights of a pig*, 6 *or* 7 *slices bacon, potatoes*, 1 *large bunch parsley*, 2 *onions*, 2 *sage-leaves, pepper and salt to taste, a little broth or water.*

Mode.—Slice the liver and lights, and wash clean; parboil the potatoes; mince the parsley and sage, and chop the onions rather small. Put the meat, potatoes, and bacon into a deep tin dish, in alternate layers, with a sprinkling of the herbs, and seasoning of pepper and salt between each; pour on a little water or broth, and bake in a moderately heated oven for 2 hours.

Time, 2 hours. *Average cost*, 2s. *Sufficient* for 6 or 7 persons. *Seasonable* from September to March.

PIG'S PETTITOES.

INGREDIENTS.—*A thin slice of bacon, feet, heart, and liver of a pig*, 1 *onion,*

1 *blade mace*, 6 *peppercorns*, 3 *or* 4 *sprigs of thyme*, 1 *pint gravy, pepper and salt to taste, thickening of butter and flour.*

Mode.—Put the liver, heart, and feet into a stewpan, with all the other ingredients except the pepper and salt and thickening. Simmer gently for ¼ hour; then take out the heart and liver, and mince very fine. Stew the feet until tender (20 minutes to ½ hour); then put back the minced heart and liver; thicken with butter and flour, season with pepper and salt, and simmer for 5 minutes longer (stirring the while). Dish the mince; split the feet, and arrange them round alternately with sippets of toasted bread, and pour the gravy in the middle.

Time, altogether 40 minutes. *Average cost*, 1s. 6d. *Sufficient* for 4 persons. *Seasonable*, September to March.

PORK CHINE ROASTED.

INGREDIENTS.—½ *pint pork stuffing*, ½ *pint apple sauce.*

Mode.—Score the skin deeply, stuff the chine with pork-stuffing, and roast it gently by a clear fire, or bake in a moderate oven.

Time, about 20 minutes to every lb.

PORK CHOPS.

INGREDIENTS.—*Loin of pork ; pepper and salt to taste.*

Mode.—Cut the cutlets from a delicate loin of pork, bone and trim them, taking away the greater portion of the fat. Season with pepper; when the gridiron is quite hot lay on the chops and broil for ¼ hour, turning them 3 or 4 times; and be particular that they are *thoroughly* done, but not dry. Dish them, sprinkle over a little salt, and serve plain, or with tomato sauce, sauce piquante, or pickled gherkins, a few of which should be laid round the dish as a garnish.

Time, about ¼ hour. *Average cost*, 10d. to 1s. per lb. for chops. *Sufficient* —allow 6 for 4 persons. *Seasonable* from October to March.

PORK CUTLETS.

INGREDIENTS.—*Loin, or fore-loin of pork, egg and breadcrumbs, salt and pepper to taste ; to every tablespoonful breadcrumbs allow ½ teaspoonful minced sage ; clarified butter.*

Mode.—Cut the cutlets from a loin, or

tore-loin of pork, trim as mutton cutlets, and scrape the top part of the bone. Brush over with egg, sprinkle with breadcrumbs, mixed with minced sage and seasoning of pepper and salt; drop a little clarified butter on them and press the crumbs well down Put the frying-pan on the fire with some lard in it; when hot, lay in the cutlets, and fry them a light brown on both sides. Take them out, put them before the fire to dry, and dish on mashed potatoes. Serve with any sauce that may be preferred; such as tomato sauce, sauce piquante, sauce Robert, or pickled gherkins.

Time, from 15 to 20 minutes. *Average cost*, 10d. to 1s. per lb. for chops. *Sufficient*—allow 6 cutlets for 4 persons. *Seasonable* from October to March.

Note.—The remains of roast loin of pork may be dressed in the same manner

PORK CUTLETS (Cold Meat Cookery).

INGREDIENTS. — *Cold roast loin of pork*, 1 oz. butter, 2 onions, 1 dessertspoonful flour, ½ pint gravy, pepper and salt to taste, 1 teaspoonful vinegar and mustard.

Mode.—Cut the pork into nice-sized cutlets, trim off most of the fat, and chop the onions. Put the butter into a stewpan, lay in the cutlets and chopped onions, and fry a light brown; add remaining ingredients, simmer gently for 5 or 7 minutes, and serve.

Time, 5 to 7 minutes. *Average cost*, exclusive of the meat, 4d. *Seasonable* from October to March.

PORK, GRISKIN (ROAST).

INGREDIENTS.—*Pork; a little powdered sage.*

Mode.—Particular care should be taken that this joint is well basted. Put it down to a bright fire, and flour it. Roast in the usual manner; about 10 minutes before taking it up sprinkle over some powdered sage; make a little gravy in the dripping-pan, strain it over the meat, and serve with a tureen of apple sauce. This joint will be done in far less time when the skin is left on.

Time, griskin of pork weighing 6 lbs., 1½ hours. *Average cost*, 7d. per lb. *Sufficient* for 5 or 6 persons. *Seasonable* from October to March.

Note.—A spare-rib of pork is roasted in the same manner as above, and would take at least 1½ hours for one weighing about 6 lbs.

PORK, HASHED.

INGREDIENTS.—*The remains of cold roast pork*, 2 onions, 1 teaspoonful flour, 2 blades pounded mace, 2 cloves, 1 tablespoonful vinegar, ½ pint gravy, pepper and salt to taste.

Mode.—Chop the onions and fry them a nice brown, cut the pork into thin slices, season with pepper and salt, and add these to the remaining ingredients. Stew gently for about ½ hour, garnish with sippets of toasted bread.

Time, ½ hour. *Average cost*, exclusive of the meat, 3d. *Seasonable* from October to March.

PORK, LEG OF (BOILED).

INGREDIENTS.—*Leg of pork; salt.*

Mode.—Choose a small, compact, well-filled leg, and rub it well with salt; let it remain in pickle for a week or ten days, turning and rubbing it every day. Put it into cold water for an hour before dressing it, to improve the colour. If the pork has been long in pickle, it should be soaked more. Put it into a boiling-pot, with cold water to cover; let it gradually come to a boil, and remove the scum as it rises. Simmer gently until tender, and do not allow it to boil fast. Carrots, turnips, or parsnips may be boiled with the pork, and some laid round the dish as a garnish; and a well-made pease-pudding is indispensable.

Time, a leg of pork weighing 8 lbs., 3 hours after the water boils, and to be simmered very gently. *Average cost*, 9d. per lb. *Sufficient* for 7 or 8 persons. *Seasonable* from September to March.

Note.—The liquor makes excellent pea-soup.

PORK, LEG OF (ROAST OR BAKED).

INGREDIENTS.—*Leg of pork; a little oil.* (*For stuffing* see *recipe for sage and onion stuffing.*)

Mode.—Score the skin across in narrow strips, about ¼ inch apart. Cut a slit in the knuckle, loosen the skin, and fill it with a sage-and-onion -stuffing. Brush the joint over with a little salad-oil (this makes the crackling crisper, and a better colour), and put it down to a clear fire, not near enough to cause the skin to blister, or put it in a good, brisk oven. Baste well, and serve with gravy made in the dripping-pan. Send to table a tureen of well-made apple sauce.

Time, a leg of pork weighing 8 lbs.,

about 3 hours. *Average cost*, 9d. per lb. *Sufficient* for 7 or 8 persons. *Seasonable* from September to March.

PORK, LOIN OF (BAKED).

INGREDIENTS.—*Pork; a little salt.*

Mode.—Score the skin in strips rather more than ¼ inch apart, and place the joint in a good oven, but not too hot a one on account of the crackling, which would harden before the meat would be heated through. If very lean, it should be rubbed over with a little salad-oil, and kept well basted. Pork should be thoroughly cooked, but not dry. Serve with apple sauce, and a little gravy made in the dripping-pan; and a stuffing of sage and onion, which may be made separately, and baked in a flat dish.

Time, a loin of pork weighing 5 lbs., about 2 hours; allow more time should it be very fat. *Average cost*, 9d. or 10d. per lb *Sufficient* for 5 or 6 persons. *Seasonable* from September to March.

PORK, PICKLED (TO BOIL).

INGREDIENTS.—*Pork; water.*

Mode.—If very salt, let the pork remain in water about 2 hours before it is dressed; put it into a saucepan with sufficient cold water to cover it, let it gradually come to a boil, then simmer until tender. Nothing is more disagreeable than underdone pork, and when boiled fast, the meat becomes hard. May be served with boiled poultry and roast veal, or with pease-pudding.

Time, a piece of pickled pork, weighing 2 lbs., 1¼ hour; 4 lbs., rather more than 2 hours. *Average cost*, 8d. per lb. for the primest parts.

PORK STEAKS AND APPLES (American Recipe).

INGREDIENTS.—*Some nice steaks cut from a loin of pork, pepper and salt hot lard, apples.*

Mode.—Cut away the greater portion of the fat from the steaks and trim them neatly; put the gridiron over the fire, and when quite hot, slightly grease it and lay on the steaks, well seasoned with pepper and salt. Broil them until thoroughly done but not dry, turning them several times. Peel, core, and slice the apples, fry like onions in the

hot lard, and send to table round the steaks.

Time, about 15 minutes. *Seasonable* from October to March.

PORK (TO PICKLE).

INGREDIENTS.—*Pork; ¼ lb. saltpetre; salt.*

Mode.—Cut the pork into pieces of a suitable size as soon as the pig is cold. Rub them well with salt, and put them into a pan with a sprinkling of it between each piece: as it melts on the top, strew on more. Lay a cloth over the pan, a board over that, and a weight on the board, to keep the pork down in the brine. If excluded from the air, it will continue good for nearly 2 years.

Seasonable, the best time for pickling meat is late in the autumn.

PORK SAUSAGES (TO FRY).

INGREDIENTS. — *Sausages; a small piece of butter.*

Mode.—Prick the sausages with a fork (this prevents them from bursting), and put them into a frying-pan with a small piece of butter. Keep moving the pan about, and turn the sausages 3 or 4 times. In from 10 to 12 minutes they will be sufficiently cooked, unless they are *very large*, when a little more time should be allowed for them. Dish them with or without a piece of toast under them, and serve very hot. In some counties sausages are boiled and served on toast. They should be plunged into boiling water, and simmered for about 10 to 12 minutes.

Time, 10 or 12 minutes. *Average cost*, 9d. to 10d. per lb. *Seasonable*—good from September to March.

Note.—To prevent sausages from turning sour in warm weather, put them in the oven for a few minutes with a small piece of butter to keep them moist.

PORK SAUSAGES (TO MAKE).

(*Oxford Recipe.*)

INGREDIENTS.—*1 lb. pork, fat and lean, without skin or gristle ; 1 lb. lean veal, 1 lb. beef suet, ½ lb. breadcrumbs, the rind of half lemon, 1 small nutmeg, 6 sage-leaves, 1 teaspoonful pepper, 2 teaspoonfuls salt, ½ teaspoonful savoury herbs, ½ teaspoonful marjoram.*

Mode.—Chop the pork, veal, and suet finely together; add the breadcrumbs, the lemon-peel (well minced), and a small nutmeg grated. Wash and chop the sage-leaves very fine; add these with the remaining ingredients to the sausage-meat, and when thoroughly mixed, either put the meat into skins, or form it into little cakes, which should be floured and fried.

Average cost for this quantity, 2s. 8d. *Sufficient* for about 30 moderate-sized sausages. *Seasonable* from October to March.

(*Cambridge Recipe.*)

INGREDIENTS.—¼ *lb. beef*, ¼ *lb. veal,* ½ *lb. pork*, ½ *lb. bacon*, ⅛ *lb. suet; pepper and salt, a few sage-leaves, sweet herbs.*

Mode.—As in preceding recipe. *Average cost*, 1s. 7d.

SAVELOYS.

INGREDIENTS.—6 *lbs. pork*, 1 *lb. common salt*, 1 *oz. saltpetre*, 3 *teaspoonfuls pepper*, 12 *sage-leaves*, 1 *lb. breadcrumbs.*

Mode.—Salt the pork, after removing the skin and bone, using both the common salt and saltpetre, and let it remain in the pickle for three days, then mince it up very fine, and season it with pepper, and 12 sage-leaves, chopped as small as possible; add the grated bread, and mix all well together, fill the skins, and bake in a slow oven for ½ hour.

Average cost, 4s. 6d.

SUCKING-PIG (ROAST).

INGREDIENTS. — *Pig, 6 oz. breadcrumbs, 16 sage-leaves, pepper and salt to taste, a piece of butter the size of an egg, salad-oil or butter to baste with, about ½ pint gravy, 1 tablespoonful lemon-juice.*

Mode.—A sucking-pig should not be more than three weeks old, and should be dressed the day it is killed. After preparing the pig for cooking, stuff it with finely grated breadcrumbs, minced sage, pepper, salt, and a piece of butter the size of an egg, all well mixed to-

gether, and put into the body of the pig. Sew up the slit, and truss the legs back, to allow the inside to be roasted, and the under-part to be crisp. Put the pig down to a bright, clear fire, not too near, and let it lie till thoroughly dry; then rub the pig in every part with a piece of butter tied up in a piece of thin cloth, new. Keep it well rubbed the whole of the time it is roasting, and do not allow the crackling to become blistered or burnt. When half-done, hang a pig-iron before the middle part (if this is not obtainable, use a flat iron), to prevent its being scorched and dried up before the ends are done. Before it is taken from the fire, cut off the head, and part that and the body down the middle. Chop the brains and mix them with the stuffing; add ½ pint of good gravy, a tablespoonful of lemon-juice, and the gravy that flowed from the pig; put a little of this on the dish with the pig, and send the remainder to table in a tureen. Place the pig back to back in the dish, with one-half of the head on each side, and one of the ears at each end, and send it to table as hot as possible. Instead of butter, many cooks take salad-oil for basting, which makes the crackling *crisp.* The brains and stuffing may be stirred into a tureen of melted butter instead of gravy. Apple sauce should be served with sucking-pig.

Time, 1½ to 2 hours for a small pig. *Average cost*, 6s. and upwards. *Sufficient* for 9 or 10 persons. *Seasonable* from September to February.

SUCKING-PIG (BAKED).

INGREDIENTS.—*Sucking-pig.*

Mode.—Prepare the pig as for roasting, rub it with butter, and flour it all over. Well butter the dish in which you intend to bake it, and put it into the oven. When sufficiently done, take it out and dish as in preceding recipe.

Time, 1½ or 2 hours. *Average cost*, 6s. and upwards.

VEAL

CALF'S FEET AND PARSLEY AND BUTTER.

INGREDIENTS.—*2 calf's feet, 2 slices oacon, 1 oz. butter, 2 tablespoonfuls lemon-juice, salt and whole pepper to taste, 1 onion, a bunch savoury herbs, 4 cloves, 1 blade mace, water, parsley-and-butter sauce.*

Mode.—Procure 2 white calf's feet; bone them as far as the first joint, and soak in warm water 2 hours. Then put the bacon, butter, lemon-juice, onion, herbs, spices, and seasoning into a stew-pan; lay in the feet, and pour in just sufficient water to cover. Stew gently for about 3 hours; take out the feet, dish, and cover with parsley-and-butter sauce. The liquor should be strained and put by for use as an addition to gravies, &c.

Time, rather more than 3 hours. *Average cost*, in full season, 7d. each. *Sufficient* for 4 persons. *Seasonable* from March to October.

CALF'S HEAD (BOILED).

INGREDIENTS.—*Calf's head, water, a little salt, 4 tablespoonfuls melted butter, 1 tablespoonful minced parsley, pepper and salt to taste, 1 tablespoonful lemon-juice.*

Mode.—Clean the head, remove the brains, and soak it in warm water to blanch it. Soak the brains also in warm water for about an hour. Put the head into a stewpan, with sufficient cold water to cover it, and when it boils, add a little salt; take off the scum as it rises, and boil the head until perfectly tender. Boil the brains, chop them, and mix with melted butter, minced parsley, pepper, salt, and lemon-juice in the above proportion. Take up the head, skin the tongue, and put it on a small dish with the brains round it. Smother the head with parsley-and-butter, and send some also to table in a tureen. Bacon, ham, pickled pork, or a pig's cheek, is indispensable with calf's head. The brains are sometimes chopped with hard-boiled eggs, and mixed with a little Béchamel or white sauce.

Time, from 1½ to 2¼ hours. *Average cost*, according to the season, from 4s. 6d. to 7s. 6d. *Sufficient* for 6 or 7 persons. *Seasonable* from March to October.

Note.—The liquor should be saved for soup, gravies, &c. Half a calf's head is cooked in the same manner, and served with the same sauces, as in the preceding recipe.

CALF'S LIVER AND BACON.

INGREDIENTS.—2 or 3 lbs. *liver, bacon, pepper and salt to taste, a small piece of butter, flour,* 2 *tablespoonfuls of lemon-juice,* ½ *pint of water.*

Mode.—Divide the liver into thin slices, and cut nearly as many slices of bacon as there are of liver; fry the bacon and put that on a hot dish before the fire. Fry the liver in the fat which comes from the bacon, after seasoning it with pepper and salt and dredging over it a very little flour. Turn the liver occasionally to prevent its burning, and when done, lay it round the dish with a piece of bacon between each. Pour away the bacon fat, put in a small piece of butter, dredge in a little flour, add the lemon-juice and water, give one boil, and pour in the *middle* of the dish. Garnish with slices of cut lemon or forcemeat balls.

Time, according to the thickness of the slices, from 5 to 10 minutes. *Average cost*, 8d. per lb. *Sufficient* for 6 or 8 persons.

GALANTINE OF VEAL.

INGREDIENTS.—*Small breast of veal,* 1½ *lbs. of sausage-meat,* ½ *lb. of cooked tongue or ham, a few truffles, gherkins and pistachio-nuts.*

Mode.—Take the bones out of the meat and flatten it out on a board; lay over it a thick layer of sausage-meat, and if this is not already well flavoured with herbs, add some, finely minced. Over the sausage-meat lay small dice cut from the tongue, the nuts chopped, some slices of gherkin and the truffles cut in small pieces; then over these put another layer of sausage-meat. Roll up the meat in a cloth as a jam-pudding and boil for 6 hours. When cool tie up tight with broad tape and press with a heavy weight upon the top. Glaze a nice dark brown when cold and serve garnished with parsley and aspic jelly. It is better to cut off the first slice before sending to table, that the

pretty marbled appearance given by the truffles, tongue, &c., may be shown. The jelly may be made from the stock in which the veal was boiled, and can be either cut in lozenges or roughed with a fork for garnish.

Time, 6 hours to boil the meat. *Average cost*, 5s. 6d. *Sufficient* for supper or luncheon dish. *Seasonable* in summer.

VEAL AND HAM PIE.

INGREDIENTS.—2 lbs. *veal cutlets,* ½ *lb boiled ham,* 2 *tablespoonfuls minced savoury herbs,* ¼ *teaspoonful grated nutmeg,* 2 *blades pounded mace, pepper and salt to taste, a strip lemon-peel finely minced,* 8 *hard-boiled eggs,* ½ *pint water, nearly* ½ *pint good strong gravy, puff-crust.*

Mode.—Cut the veal into nice square pieces, and put a layer of them at the bottom of a pie-dish; sprinkle over a portion of the herbs, spices, seasoning, lemon-peel, and the eggs cut in slices; cut the ham very thin, and put a layer of this in. Proceed until the dish is full, so arranging it that the ham comes to the top. Lay a puff-paste on the edge of the dish, and pour in about ½ pint of water; cover with crust, ornament it with leaves, brush over the yolk of an egg, and bake in a well-heated oven for 1 or 1½ hours, or longer should the pie be very large. When it is taken out of the oven, pour in at the top, through a funnel, nearly ½ a pint of *strong* gravy. This pie may be very much enriched by adding a few mushrooms, oysters, or sweetbreads.

Time, 1½ hours, or longer should the pie be very large. *Average cost*, 4s. *Sufficient* for 5 or 6 persons. *Seasonable* from March to October.

VEAL, BREAST OF (ROAST).

INGREDIENTS.—*Veal; a little flour.*

Mode.—Wash the veal, well wipe and dredge it with flour; put it down to a bright fire, but not too near; or it may be put in a fairly quick oven and baked. Baste it plentifully until done; dish it, pour over the meat some melted butter, and send to table with it a piece of boiled bacon and a cut lemon.

Time, from 1½ to 2 hours. *Average cost*, 8d. per lb. *Sufficient* for 5 or 6 persons. *Seasonable* from March to October.

VEAL, BREAST OF, AND PEAS.

INGREDIENTS.—*Breast of veal,* 1 *oz.*

butter, a bunch savoury herbs, including parsley; 2 blades pounded mace, 2 cloves, 5 or 6 young onions, 1 strip lemon-peel, ½ teaspoonful pepper, 1 teaspoonful salt, thickening of butter and flour, 1 tablespoonful lemon-juice, 2 tablespoonfuls mushroom ketchup, green peas.

Mode.—Remove the bone underneath, cut the breast in half, and divide into convenient-sized pieces. Put the butter into a frying-pan, lay in the pieces of veal, and fry a nice brown. Place these in a stewpan with the herbs mace, cloves, onions, lemon-peel, allspice, and seasoning; pour over just sufficient boiling water to cover the meat, well close the lid, and simmer gently about 2 hours. Strain off as much gravy as is required, thicken with butter and flour, add the remaining ingredients, skim well, let it simmer about 10 minutes, then pour over the meat. Boil some green peas separately; sprinkle these over the veal, and serve. Garnish with forcemeat balls, or rashers of bacon curled and fried. Many persons prefer the meat dressed whole; in that case it should be half-roasted before the water, &c., are put to it.

Time, 2¼ hours. *Average cost*, 8d. per lb. *Sufficient* for 5 or 6 persons. *Seasonable* from March to October.

VEAL, FILLET OF (ROAST).

INGREDIENTS. — *Veal, forcemeat, melted butter.*

Mode.—Take out the bone, and after raising the skin from the meat, put under the flap a nice veal forcemeat. Prepare sufficient of this, as there should be some left to eat cold, and to season and flavour a mince if required. Skewer and bind the veal up in a round form; dredge well with flour, put it down at some distance from the fire at first, or bake in an oven hot at first but slackened afterwards, and baste continually. About ½ hour before serving, draw it nearer the fire, that the outside may acquire a rich brown colour. Dish it, replace the skewers by a silver one; pour over some melted butter, and serve with boiled ham, bacon, or pickled pork. Never omit to send a cut lemon and some good gravy to table with roast veal.

Time, a fillet of veal weighing 12 lbs., about 4 hours. *Average cost*, 1s. per lb. *Sufficient* for 9 or 10 persons. *Seasonable* from March to October.

VEAL, FILLET OF (TO RE-HEAT).

INGREDIENTS.—*A small fillet of veal, 1 pint of good gravy, a few breadcrumbs, clarified butter.*

Mode.—A fillet of veal roasted the preceding day may be dressed as follows:—Take the middle out rather deep, leaving a good margin round, from which to cut nice slices, and should there be any cracks, fill them up with forcemeat. Mince finely the meat taken out, mixing with it a little of the forcemeat, and stir to it sufficient gravy to make it of a proper consistency. Warm the veal in the oven for about an hour, taking care to baste it well; put the mince in the place where the meat was taken out, sprinkle a few breadcrumbs over, and drop a little clarified butter on the breadcrumbs; put it into the oven for ½ hour to brown, and pour gravy round the sides of the dish.

Time, altogether, 1½ hours. *Seasonable* from March to October.

VEAL, KNUCKLE OF (STEWED).

INGREDIENTS.—*Knuckle of veal, 1 onion, 2 blades mace, 1 teaspoonful salt, ½ lb. rice.*

Mode.—Choose a knuckle just large enough to be eaten the day it is dressed, as cold boiled veal is not a tempting dish. Break the shank-bone, wash it clean, and put the meat into a stewpan with sufficient water to cover it. Let it gradually come to a boil, put in the salt; remove the scum as it rises. When it has simmered for about ¾ hour, add remaining ingredients, and stew gently for 2¼ hours. Put the meat into a deep dish, pour over it the rice, &c., and send boiled bacon and a tureen of parsley-and-butter to table with it.

Time, a knuckle of veal weighing 6 lbs., 3 hours' gentle stewing. *Average cost*, 8d. per lb. *Sufficient* for 5 or 6 persons. *Seasonable* from March to October.

Note.—Macaroni, instead of rice, will be found good; or the rice and macaroni may be omitted, and the veal sent to table smothered in parsley-and-butter.

VEAL (ROAST LOIN).

INGREDIENTS.—*Veal; melted butter.*

Mode.—Paper the kidney fat; roll in and skewer the flap, which makes the joint a good shape; dredge well with flour, and put it down to a bright fire. Should the loin be very large, skewer the kidney back for a time to roast thoroughly. Keep it well basted, and before serving remove the paper from the kidney, and allow it to acquire a nice brown colour. Put some melted butter into the dripping-pan after it is emptied, pour it over the veal, and serve. Garnish with slices of lemon and forcemeat balls, and send to table with it boiled bacon, ham, pickled pork, or pig's cheek.

Time, a large loin, 3 hours. *Average cost*, 10d. per lb. *Sufficient* for 7 or 8 persons. *Seasonable* from March to October.

VEAL OLIVE PIE (Cold Meat Cookery).

INGREDIENTS.—*A few thin slices of cold fillet of veal, a few thin slices bacon, forcemeat, a cupful of gravy, 4 tablespoonfuls cream, puff-crust.*

Mode.—Place the slices of veal on thin slices of bacon, and over them a layer of forcemeat, with an additional seasoning of shallot and cayenne; roll them tightly, and fill up a pie-dish with them; add the gravy and cream, cover with a puff-crust, and bake for 1 to 1½ hours: should the pie be very large, allow 2 hours. The pieces of rolled veal should be about 3 inches in length, and about 3 inches round.

Time, moderate-sized pie, 1 to 1½ hours. *Seasonable* from March to October.

VEAL SAUSAGES.

INGREDIENTS.—*Equal quantities fat bacon and lean veal; to every pound meat allow 1 teaspoonful minced sage; salt and pepper to taste.*

Mode.—Chop the meat fine, and mix with the minced sage; add seasoning of pepper and salt. Make into flat cakes, and fry.

Average cost, 10d. per lb. *Seasonable*, March to October.

VEAL, SHOULDER OF (BAKED).

Mode.—Remove the knuckle for boiling, and bake what remains in the same manner as the fillet, with or without veal stuffing. If not stuffed, serve with oyster or mushroom sauce. Garnish with sliced lemon.

Average cost, 8d. per. lb.

CALF'S HEAD (HASHED).

INGREDIENTS.—*The remains of cold boiled calf's head, 1 quart of the liquor in which it was boiled, a faggot of savoury herbs, 1 onion, 1 carrot, strip of lemon-peel, 2 blades pounded mace, salt and white pepper, a little cayenne,*

rather more than 2 tablespoonfuls of sherry, 1 of lemon-juice, 1 of mushroom ketchup, forcemeat balls.

Mode.—Cut the meat into neat slices; put the bones and trimmings into a stewpan with the above proportion of liquor that the head was boiled in. Add a bunch of savoury herbs, 1 onion, 1 carrot, a strip of lemon-peel, and 2 blades of pounded mace; let these boil for 1 hour, or until the gravy is reduced nearly half. Strain into a clean stewpan, thicken with butter and flour, and add a flavouring of sherry, lemon-juice, and ketchup as above; season with pepper, salt, and cayenne; put in the meat, let it *gradually* warm through, but not boil more than *two* or *three* minutes. Garnish the dish with forcemeat balls and pieces of bacon rolled and toasted, placed alternately, and send it to table very hot.

Time, altogether, 1½ hours. *Average cost*, exclusive of the remains of the head, 9d. *Seasonable* from March to October.

CURRIED VEAL (Cold Meat Cookery).

INGREDIENTS.—*Cold roast veal, 4 onions, 2 apples sliced, 1 tablespoonful curry-powder, 1 dessertspoonful flour, ½ pint broth or water, 1 tablespoonful lemon-juice.*

Mode.—Slice the onions and apples, and fry in a little butter; take then out, cut the meat into neat cutlets, and fry these of a pale brown; add the curry-powder and flour, put in the onion, apples, and a little broth or water, and stew gently till tender; add the lemon-juice, and serve with a dish of boiled rice. The curry may be ornamented with pickles, capsicums, and gherkins arranged prettily on the top.

Time, ¾ hour. *Average cost*, exclusive of the meat, 4d. *Seasonable* from March to October.

FRIED PATTIES (Cold Meat Cookery).

INGREDIENTS.—*Cold roast veal, a few slices cold ham, 1 egg boiled hard, pounded mace, pepper and salt to taste, gravy, cream, 1 teaspoonful minced lemon-peel, good puff-paste.*

Mode.—Mince a little cold veal and ham—one-third ham to two-thirds veal; add an egg boiled hard and chopped, and a seasoning of pounded mace, salt, pepper, and lemon-peel; moisten with a little gravy and cream. Make a good puff-paste; roll it very thin, and cut it into round or square pieces; put the mince between two of them, pinch the edges, and fry a light brown. They may be also baked in patty-pans: in that case, they should be brushed over with the yolk of an egg before they are put in the oven. Oysters may be substituted for the ham.

Time, 15 minutes to bake. *Average cost*, exclusive of the veal, 1s.

LIVER DUMPLINGS (German Recipe).

INGREDIENTS.—*A calf's liver, 2 oz. of bacon, 4 eggs, 7 oz. of bread, grated nutmeg, suet, onions, flour, pepper and salt.*

Mode.—Skin the liver and rub it through a sieve; put it in a basin, with the bacon finely chopped, the bread cut into dice and fried in butter and suet, the eggs, the onions minced, and seasoning to taste. Mix well with a little cold water, and enough flour to bind the dumplings. Test the mixture by throwing a small piece into boiling water; it should hold together, but be very light; if it break, add a little more flour. Make the dumplings about the size of an ordinary apple and boil them in salt and water for 15 minutes. Serve them with fried breadcrumbs and a sauce of melted butter thickened with grated potatoes.

Time, ¼ hour. *Average cost*, 3s. *Sufficient* for 8 persons. *Seasonable* in summer.

MINCED VEAL.

INGREDIENTS.—*The remains of cold roast fillet or loin of veal, rather more than 1 pint water, 1 onion, ½ teaspoonful minced lemon-peel, salt and white pepper to taste, 1 blade pounded mace, 2 or 3 young carrots, a faggot of sweet herbs, thickening of butter and flour; 1 tablespoonful lemon-juice, 3 tablespoonfuls cream or milk.*

Mode.—Take about 1 lb. of veal, and should there be any bones, dredge them with flour, and put them into a stewpan with the brown outside, and a few meat trimmings; add rather more than a pint of water, the onion cut in slices, lemon-peel, seasoning, mace, carrots, and herbs; simmer for rather more than 1 hour, and strain the liquor. Rub a little flour into some butter; add to the gravy, set it on the fire, and, when it boils, skim well. Mince the veal finely by *cutting*, and not chopping it; put it in the gravy; let it get

warmed through gradually; add the lemon-juice and cream, and serve. Garnish with sippets of toasted bread and slices of bacon rolled and toasted. Forcemeat balls may be added. If more lemon-peel is liked, put a little very finely minced to the veal after it is warmed in the gravy.

Time, 1 hour to make the gravy. *Average cost*, exclusive of cold meat, 6d. *Seasonable* from March to October.

MINCED VEAL AND MACARONI.

INGREDIENTS.—¾ *lbs. of minced cold roast veal, 3 oz. ham, 3 or 4 tablespoonfuls gravy, pepper and salt to taste, ½ teaspoonful grated nutmeg, ¼ lb. breadcrumbs, ¼ lb. macaroni, 1 or 2 eggs to bind, a small piece of butter.*

Mode.—Cut some nice slices from a cold fillet of veal, trim off the brown outside, and mince the meat finely with the above proportion of ham: should the meat be very dry, add 3 or 4 spoonfuls of good gravy. Season with pepper and salt, add the grated nutmeg and breadcrumbs, and mix these ingredients with 1 or 2 eggs well beaten, which should bind the mixture and make it like forcemeat. Boil the macaroni in salt and water, and drain it; butter a mould, and line it with the macaroni at the bottom and sides; mix the remainder with the forcemeat, fill the mould up to the top, put a plate or small dish on it, and steam for ½ hour. Turn it out, and serve with good gravy poured round, but not over, the meat.

Time, ½ hour. *Average cost*, exclusive of the cold meat, 8d. *Seasonable* from March to October.

Note.—To make a variety, boil some carrots and turnips separately in a little salt and water; when done, cut them into pieces about ½ inch in thickness; butter an oval mould, and place these in it, in white and red stripes alternately, at the bottom and sides. Proceed as above, and be careful in turning the preparation out of the mould.

MOULDED MINCED VEAL (Cold Meat Cookery).

INGREDIENTS.—¾ *lb. of cold roast veal, a small slice of bacon, ½ teaspoonful of minced lemon-peel, ½ onion chopped fine, salt, pepper, and pounded mace to taste, a slice of toast soaked in milk, 1 egg.*

Mode.—Mince the meat very fine, after removing the skin and outside pieces, and chop the bacon; mix these well together, adding the lemon-peel, onion, seasoning, mace, and toast, and bind the mixture with an egg beaten up. Butter a shape, put in the meat, and bake for ¾ hour; turn it out of the mould carefully, and pour round it a good brown gravy. A sheep's head dressed in this manner is an economical and savoury dish.

Time, ¾ hour. *Average cost*, exclusive of the meat, 3d. *Seasonable* from March to October.

RAGOUT OF COLD VEAL (Cold Meat Cookery).

INGREDIENTS.—*The remains of cold veal, 1 oz. butter, ½ pint gravy, thickening of butter and flour, pepper and salt to taste, 1 blade pounded mace, 1 tablespoonful mushroom ketchup, 1 tablespoonful sherry, 1 dessertspoonful lemon-juice, forcemeat balls.*

Mode.—Cut the meat (any part of veal) into nice-looking pieces, put them in a stewpan with 1 oz. of butter, and fry a light brown; add the gravy (hot water may be substituted for this), thicken with a little butter and flour, and stew gently about ¼ hour; season with pepper, salt, and pounded mace; add the ketchup, sherry, and lemon-juice; give one boil, and serve. Garnish with forcemeat balls and fried rashers of bacon.

Time, altogether, ½ hour. *Average cost*, exclusive of the cold meat, 1s. *Seasonable* from March to October.

Note.—The above recipe may be varied, by adding vegetables, such as peas, cucumbers, lettuces, green onions cut in slices, a dozen or two of green gooseberries (not seedy), all of which should be fried a little with the meat, and then stewed with the gravy.

SAVOURY DISH OF VEAL.

INGREDIENTS.—3 *or* 4 *lbs. the loin or neck of veal, 15 young carrots, a few green onions, 1 pint green peas, 12 new potatoes, a bunch savoury herbs, pepper and salt to taste, 1 tablespoonful lemon-juice, 2 tablespoonfuls tomato sauce, 2 tablespoonfuls mushroom ketchup.*

Mode.—Dredge the meat with flour, and roast or bake it for about ¾ hour. Put the meat into a stewpan with the carrots, onions, potatoes, herbs, pepper and salt; pour over it sufficient boiling water to cover it, and stew gently for 2 hours. Take out the meat and herbs, put the former into a deep dish, skim off all the fat from the gravy, and flavour it with lemon-juice, tomato

sauce, and mushroom ketchup in the above proportion. Put a pint of green peas, boiled *separately*, with the meat, pour over it the gravy, and serve. Garnish with a few forcemeat balls. The meat may be cut into chops, and floured and fried, instead of being roasted.

Time, 3 hours. *Average cost*, 10d. per lb. *Sufficient* for 6 or 7 persons. *Seasonable*, with peas, from June to August.

SCOTCH COLLOPS (Cold Meat Cookery).

INGREDIENTS.—*Cold roast veal, a little butter, flour, ½ pint water, 1 onion, 1 blade pounded mace, 1 tablespoonful lemon-juice, ½ teaspoonful finely minced lemon-peel, 2 tablespoonfuls sherry, 1 tablespoonful ketchup.*

Mode.—Cut the veal the same thickness as for cutlets, rather larger than a crown-piece; flour the meat well, and fry a light brown in butter; dredge again with flour, and add ½ pint of water by degrees; set it on the fire, and when it boils, add the onion and mace, simmer very gently about ¾ hour; flavour with lemon-juice, peel, wine, and ketchup, as above; give one boil, and serve.

Time, ¾ hour. *Average cost*, exclusive of the meat, 6d. *Seasonable* from March to October.

SCOTCH COLLOPS, WHITE (Cold Meat Cookery).

INGREDIENTS.—*Cold roast veal, ½ teaspoonful grated nutmeg, 2 blades pounded mace, cayenne and salt, a little butter, 1 dessertspoonful flour, ¼ pint water, 1 teaspoonful anchovy sauce, 1 tablespoonful lemon-juice, ¼ teaspoonful lemon-peel, 1 tablespoonful mushroom ketchup, 3 of milk, 1 sherry.*

Mode.—Cut the veal into thin slices about 3 inches in width; score them with a knife; grate on the nutmeg, mace, cayenne, and salt, and fry them in a little butter. Dish, and make a gravy in the pan by putting in the remaining ingredients; give one boil, and pour it over the collops. Garnish with lemon and slices of toasted bacon, rolled. Forcemeat balls may be added.

Time, about 5 or 7 minutes. *Seasonable* from March to October.

SWEETBREADS À LA MAÎTRE D'HÔTEL.

INGREDIENTS.—3 *sweetbreads, egg, and breadcrumbs, ¼ lb. butter; salt and pepper to taste, rather more than ½ pint of maître d'hôtel sauce.*

Mode.—Soak the sweetbreads in warm water for an hour; boil them 10 minutes; cut in slices, egg-and-bread-crumb them, season with pepper and salt, and put them into a frying-pan with the butter. Keep turning them until done (about 10 minutes); dish and pour over them a maître d'hôtel sauce (*see* recipe " Sauces "). Garnish with slices of cut lemon.

Time, to soak 1 hour, to be boiled 10 minutes, to be fried about 10 minutes. *Average cost*, 3s. 6d. to 5s., according to the season. *Sufficient* for an *entrée*. *Seasonable* from May to August.

Note.—The egg and breadcrumbs may be omitted, and the slices of sweetbread dredged with a little flour instead, and a good gravy may be substituted for the maître d'hôtel sauce.

SWEETBREADS (BAKED).

INGREDIENTS.—3 *sweetbreads, egg, and breadcrumbs, oiled butter, 3 slices toast, brown gravy.*

Mode.—Put the sweetbreads into warm water; let them remain rather more than 1 hour; then put them into boiling water, and simmer for about 10 minutes, which renders them firm. Take them up, drain, brush over the egg, sprinkle with breadcrumbs; dip them in egg again, and then into more breadcrumbs. Drop on them a little oiled butter, and put the sweetbreads into a moderate oven, and bake for nearly ¾ hour. Place the sweetbreads on toast, and pour round, but not over them, a good brown gravy.

Time, to soak 1 hour, to be boiled 10 minutes, baked 40 minutes. *Average cost*, 3s. 6d. to 5s. *Sufficient* for an *entrée*. *Seasonable* from May to August.

SWEETBREADS IN CASES (French Recipe).

INGREDIENTS.—3 *sweetbreads, 1 oz. of bacon-fat, 1 oz. of butter, a teaspoonful of olive oil, a few chopped mushrooms, a lesser quantity of shallots, a little chopped parsley, salt, pepper, nutmeg, and breadcrumbs.*

Mode.—Soak the sweetbreads in water for an hour, boil them 10 minutes, put them in cold water for another 10 minutes, then cut them into small neat pieces. Chop the bacon-fat fine, and make a forcemeat with that, the butter, shallots, mushrooms, oil, and

breadcrumbs. Hold this in a small pan over the fire for 5 minutes, then add the parsley and seasoning, and hold for two or three minutes more, and set aside to cool. Butter some small paper cases, put a little of the forcemeat in each, then some pieces of the sweetbread, with a little seasoning, then cover with more forcemeat and breadcrumbs. Boil very gently for 15 minutes, and brown with a salamander or before the fire.

Time, ¼ hour. *Sufficient* for an *entrée*. *Seasonable* from May to August.

SWEETBREADS (STEWED).

INGREDIENTS.—3 *swee breads, 1 pint good white stock, thickening of butter and flour, 6 tablespoonfuls cream, 1 tablespoonful lemon-juice, 1 blade pounded mace, white pepper and salt to taste.*

Mode.—Soak the sweetbreads in warm water for 1 hour, and boil them for 10 minutes; put them into cold water for a few minutes; lay them in a stewpan with the stock, and simmer gently for rather more than ½ hour. Dish them; thicken the gravy with a little butter and flour; let it boil up, add the remaining ingredients, allow the sauce to get quite *hot*, but not *boil*, and pour it over the sweetbreads.

Time, to soak 1 hour, to be boiled 10 minutes, stewed rather more than ½ hour. *Average cost*, from 3s. 6d. to 5s. according to the season. *Sufficient* for an *entrée*. *Seasonable* from May to August.

Note.—A few mushrooms stewed with the sweetbreads improve the dish.

VEAL À LA BOURGEOISE (Excellent).

INGREDIENTS.—2 *or 3 lbs. loin or neck of veal, 10 or 12 young carrots, a bunch green onions, 2 slices lean bacon, 2 blades pounded mace, 1 bunch savoury herbs, pepper and salt to taste, a few new potatoes, 1 pint green peas.*

Mode.—Cut the veal into cutlets, trim them, and put the trimmings into a stewpan with a little butter; lay in the cutlets and fry them a nice brown colour on both sides. Add the bacon, carrots, onions, spice, herbs, and season-ing; pour in about a pint of boiling water, and stew gently for 2 hours on a slow fire. When done, skim off the fat, take out the herbs, and flavour the gravy with a little tomato sauce and ketchup. Boil the peas and potatoes *separately;* put them with the veal, and serve.

Time, 2 hours. *Average cost*, 4s. *Sufficient* for 5 or 6 persons. *Seasonable* from June to August with peas; rather earlier when these are omitted.

VEAL (BAKED).
(Cold Meat Cookery.)

INGREDIENTS.—½ lb. cold roast veal, 2 slices bacon, 1 pint breadcrumbs, ½ pint good veal gravy, ½ teaspoonful minced lemon-peel, 1 blade pounded mace, cayenne and salt to taste, 3 eggs.

Mode.—Mince finely the veal and bacon; add the breadcrumbs, gravy, and seasoning, and stir these ingredients well together. Beat up the eggs; add these, mix the whole well together, put into a dish, and bake from ¾ to 1 hour. A little good gravy may be served in a tureen as an accompaniment.

Time, from ¾ to 1 hour. *Average cost*, exclusive of the cold meat, 9d. *Sufficient* for 3 or 4 persons. *Seasonable* from March to October.

VEAL CAKE (a Convenient dish for a Picnic).

INGREDIENTS.—A few slices cold roast veal, a few slices cold ham, 2 hardboiled eggs, 2 tablespoonfuls minced parsley, pepper, good gravy.

Mode.—Cut off all the brown from the veal; cut the eggs into slices, lay veal, ham, eggs, and parsley in layers, with a little pepper and salt between each, in a mould, and when the mould is full, get some *strong* stock, and fill up the shape. Bake for ½ hour, and when cold, turn it out.

Time, ½ hour. *Average cost*, exclusive of the meat, 6d. *Sufficient* for 4 or 5 persons. *Seasonable* at any time.

VEAL CUTLETS.

INGREDIENTS.—About 3 lbs. of the prime part of the leg of veal, 1 lb. bacon, egg and breadcrumbs, 3 tablespoonfuls minced savoury herbs, salt and pepper to taste, a small piece butter.

Mode.—Have the veal cut into slices about ¾ of an inch in thickness, and level the meat with a cutlet-bat or rolling-pin. Shape and trim the cutlets, and brush them over with egg. Sprinkle with breadcrumbs, mixed with minced herbs and a seasoning of pepper and salt, and press the crumbs down. Fry of a delicate brown in fresh lard or clarified dripping. They should be very thoroughly done, but not dry. If the cutlets be thick, keep the pan covered for a few minutes at a good distance from the fire, after they have acquired a good colour. Lay the cutlets in a dish with the bacon cut in slices and curled round, and make a gravy in the pan as follows:—Dredge in a little flour, add a piece of butter the size of a walnut, brown it, then pour as much boiling water as is required over it, season with pepper and salt, add a little lemon-juice, give one boil, and pour it over the cutlets.

Time, for cutlets of a moderate thickness, about 12 minutes; if very thick allow more time. *Average cost*, 1s. per lb. *Sufficient* for 6 persons. *Seasonable* from March to October.

Note.—Veal cutlets may be merely floured and fried of a nice brown; the gravy and bacon as in the preceding recipe. They may also be cut from the loin or neck.

VEAL RISSOLES (Cold Meat Cookery).

INGREDIENTS.—A few slices cold roast veal, a few slices ham or bacon, 1 tablespoonful minced parsley, 1 tablespoonful minced savoury herbs, 1 blade pounded mace, a very little grated nutmeg, cayenne and salt to taste, 2 eggs well beaten, breadcrumbs.

Mode.—Mince the veal fine with a little ham or bacon; add the parsley, herbs, spices, and seasoning; mix into a paste with an egg; form into balls or cones; brush these over with egg, sprinkle with breadcrumbs, and fry a rich brown. Serve with brown gravy, and garnish with fried parsley.

Time, about 10 minutes to fry the rissoles. *Seasonable* from March to October.

VEAL ROLLS (Cold Meat Cookery).

INGREDIENTS.—The remains of a cold fillet of veal, egg and breadcrumbs, a few slices of fat bacon, veal forcemeat.

Mode.—Cut a few slices from a cold fillet of veal ½ inch thick; rub them over with egg; lay a thin slice of fat bacon over each piece of veal; brush these with the egg, and over this spread the forcemeat, thin; roll up each piece tightly, egg-and-breadcrumb them, and fry them a rich brown. Serve with mushroom sauce or brown gravy.

Time, 10 to 15 minutes to fry the rolls. *Average cost*, exclusive of the meat, 8d. *Seasonable* from March to October.

VEAL SCALLOPS (American Recipe).

INGREDIENTS.—*The remains of cold roast veal, crackers, 2 eggs, a little butter, milk, lemon-juice, pepper and salt.*

Mode.—Mince the veal very fine, and season it. Butter a pudding-dish, and put a layer of the mince next a layer of crackers crumbled, then put over a few bits of butter, and wet with a little milk. Proceed in this way till the dish is full. If there be any gravy left from the veal, dilute this with warm water, and add the lemon-juice. If there be no gravy, use warm water and a little sauce, and fill up the dish. Put a layer of crumbs at the top, and over these small pieces of butter.

Time, about ½ an hour to bake the scallop. *Average cost*, exclusive of the meat, 6d. *Seasonable* from May to October.

POULTRY

PREPARATION AND TRUSSING.

THIS may be said to be one branch of the art of cookery about which too little is known. It is so usual in London and other large towns to have the game and poultry sent in ready for cooking, that ordinary cooks in such places do not take the trouble to learn what they believe they need never practise.

A really good cook, however, one who took an interest in her work, would think differently, and would not rest content till she had mastered the difficulties of this part as well as of all other parts of her work.

To teach to draw, truss, and prepare different birds and animals for various modes of cooking by written instructions have been found so difficult that we have had a series of photographs taken by the courtesy of W. Bellamy, Esq., head of the well-known firm of West End poulterers (Messrs. Bellamy Brothers, of 118, Jermyn Street, London, W.C.), showing the various stages, and these will be found of great service to those wishing to learn the art. Mr. Bellamy is one of the judges at the Annual Poultry Show, and probably the best authority on trussing.

TO PLUCK AND SINGE POULTRY.

To pluck a bird hold it up by the left hand by the wing and commence to pluck from underneath the wing; do the same the other side, removing all feathers except the down. To singe the bird, hold it by the neck and pass a lighted paper quickly over it. Be careful to thoroughly singe those parts that will be hidden when the bird is trussed; for when this has been done, it is usual to give a second singeing. Not only is singeing to be carefully done, the bird must be well looked over to see that no feathers, left in after careless plucking, remain.

TO BONE A TURKEY OR FOWL.
(Miss Acton's Recipe.)

Cut through the skin down the centre of the back and raise the flesh carefully on either side, with the point of a sharp knife, until the sockets of the wings and thighs are reached. Till a little practice has been gained it will perhaps be best to bone these joints before proceeding further; but after they are once detached from it, the whole of the body may easily be separated from the flesh, and taken out entire; only the neck bones and merrythought will then remain to be removed. The bird thus prepared may either be restored to its original form, by filling the legs and wings with forcemeat and the body with the livers of 2 or 3 fowls mixed with alternate layers of parboiled tongue freed from the rind; fine sausage-meat or veal forcemeat, or thin slices of nice bacon, or anything else that is liked which will give a marbled appearance to the bird when it is carved, may be added; and then be sewn up and trussed as usual; or the legs and wings may be drawn inside the body, and the bird, first flattened on a table, may be covered with sausage-meat, and the various other ingredients we have named, so placed that it shall be of equal thickness in every part, then tightly rolled, bound firmly together with broad tape, wrapped in a thin pudding-cloth, closely tied at both ends, and dressed.

TO DRAW A FOWL

Lay the fowl back downwards upon the table, and cut off the ends of the pinions. Then turn the bird breast downwards, and cut a slit in the skin of the neck about two inches from the shoulders in the manner shown in illustration (Fig. 1), pass the knife under the skin, and cut through the neck at its junction with the body, taking care not to cut through the under skin of the neck in this motion. Then cut through the skin of the back of the neck at the place where the first incision was made and through the underneath skin about three inches from the breast, leaving the two flaps of neck skin to fold over the jagged opening (see Figs. 2 and 3), and draw out the neck. Then take out the crop, and well loosen the entrails by placing the forefinger inside the body, and working it round from left to right (see Fig. 4). Put the fowl on the table tail upwards and make a deep cut straight across the body between the tail and the vent. The vent can then be easily cut out, and the opening will be found sufficiently large to enable the fingers to be put inside the bird to take hold of the gizzard, &c. (see Fig. 5), and if the loosening at the other end has been properly performed, the whole of the inside of the fowl can be easily drawn away in one mass. Care should be taken not to draw away the fat on gizzard. This can be felt with the fingers and may be easily left inside the bird.

Be very careful not to break the gall-bladder, for this accident may ruin the bird by imparting a very bitter taste to the flesh. Now wipe out the inside with a clean cloth, and should any part of the inside have been broken in drawing, wash out the bird and dry it, not forgetting the flap of the neck; dip the legs of the bird in boiling water, scrape them, and cut off the claws.

TO TRUSS A FOWL FOR ROASTING.

To truss a fowl in the best and easiest way a trussing-needle (perfectly straight and about nine inches long) and a piece of strong string are required. Place the fowl upon the table as shown in illustration, and pass the needle and string through the centre of the fowl, just above the thigh-bone, exactly in the centre of the two joints (see Fig. 6), leaving the end of the string protruding from the place where the needle enters the bird. Turn the fowl over on to its breast, and carrying the twine on, pass it in a slanting direction between the two centre bones of the wing, catching the underneath part of the pinion (see Fig. 7), and then over the bird through the pinion and then the wing of the other side, and the string will come out

near the point where it first entered the fowl; then tie the two ends together, but not too tightly or the bird will not lay flat on the dish (Fig. 8). Next take the fowl in the left hand, breast downwards, and pass the needle and twine through the back, close to the end of the thigh-bones (Fig. 9); put the legs into position shown, turn the fowl on its back, and carry the string over the leg and then through the breast, catching up a small portion of the bone as the needle passes through. Take the string on over the other leg and tie the ends together, and the bird will be ready for roasting (see Fig. 10).

Now again singe the bird, going over it very carefully, so that no feathers remain; then, after cleaning and washing the gizzard and liver, put one in each of the pinions. A duck is trussed in the same manner, but the feet are left on, and placed under the bird.

TO TRUSS A FOWL FOR BOILING.

Draw the fowl as directed. Then loosen the skin of the leg by placing the two first fingers of the hand inside the body, and working round the leg as shown (Fig. 1, Plate 2). Make a cut in the drumstick of the fowl, about half an inch from the hock (Fig. 2), to prevent the bone from breaking under the next operation. Turn the shank inward on to the back of the fowl (Fig. 3), and draw the skin of the leg over the hock, tucking the joint into the body (as in Fig. 4). Next cut off the shank about half an inch above the foot, e.g., cutting off all the leg and foot that shows in Fig. 4. Sew with needle and string as for roasted fowl (see Fig 5).

TO TRUSS A GOOSE.

Having well plucked and singed the bird, cut off the feet at the joint, the pinions at the first joint, and the neck close to the back as directed for fowls, leaving enough skin to turn over the back. Next loosen the inside at the throat end. Cut the bird open between the vent and the rump and draw; then wipe out the bird and very carefully flatten the breastbone with a rolling-pin, taking care not to break the bone into splinters. Put a skewer through the under part of one wing and bring it through the other, as shown in Fig. 7. Skewer the legs by passing the skewer through the first joint and carrying it through the body so as to secure the other. Always remove the merry-thought from a duck or a goose.

Cut off the end of the vent and make a hole large enough for the passage of the rump, in order to keep in the seasoning, then stuff and fasten up as Fig. 8.

TO TRUSS A PIGEON.

Having plucked and drawn the bird, wash and wipe it perfectly dry.

Cut off the neck and head and the toes at the first joint. With the trussing-needle run a piece of twine through the breast, fasten the pinions as directed for fowl, and having placed the legs in position shown, tie the string on the back of the bird (see Fig. 11).

For stewing, twist the legs up on each side as in illustration and fasten up in the same way (see Fig. 12).

TO TRUSS A TURKEY.

First pluck and singe the bird, next draw the sinews. To do this break the leg bones close to the feet, run them on a hook placed in the wall (above you, so that weight as well as strength can be brought to bear), and draw out the sinews as shown in Fig. 9. This is sometimes rather a hard task, but it must be done or the legs would be uneatable.

Next cut off the neck close to the back, leaving enough skin to turn over it, and loosen the liver and the rest of the inside at the throat end. Cut off the vent, take out the gut and draw the bird with a hook sold for this purpose.

Great care is needed to do this not to break the gut joining the gizzard, for fear of grit, or the gall bladder, which, if broken, would make the flesh bitter.

Next dry the inside thoroughly. Cut the breastbone through at each side close to the back, beat it flat with a wooden rolling-pin, then place the pinions as shown in illustration (Fig. 10), and skewer.

Press the legs close to the body and skewer at first and second joints, and the turkey will now be ready for stuffing.

Having filled the bird with the forcemeat (the fuller the better and neater it will look), skewer over the flap of skin, also that at the neck.

Turn the bird back uppermost and put a string across and across as shown; except in the case of a very small turkey, when it will not be required.

As a fowl, a boned turkey has sometimes the legs put inside so that less stuffing is needed; and the aim is not to preserve its form, but to make it present a broad smooth surface that is easy to carve.

COOKING POULTRY

CAPON (BAKED OR ROASTED).

INGREDIENTS.—*A capon, stuffing of veal or chestnut forcemeat, oiled paper, gravy, watercress.*

Mode.—Truss as a fowl for roasting, and fasten some oiled paper over the breast. Put in a good forcemeat, sufficient to fill the bird, one of those named or an oyster forcemeat. Place in a good oven or before a bright fire and cook from an hour to an hour and a half according to size. Baste well, and serve with good gravy and a garnish of watercress.

Time, 1 to 1½ hours. *Average cost,* 4s. 6d. to 6s. *Sufficient* for 6 persons. *Seasonable* at any time.

CHICKENS (GERMAN FASHION)
(German Recipe.)

INGREDIENTS.—*A pair of chickens, lardoons, French rolls, breadcrumbs, 3 oz of butter, milk, 1 onion, 1 egg, parsley, thyme, grated lemon-peel, 2 tablespoonfuls of cream.*

Mode.—Stuff the birds with a forcemeat made of the rolls, the onion minced fine, the parsley, thyme, and grated lemon-peel, with a little butter and the egg. Stuff the chickens with this and lard them, put some breadcrumbs over and then a piece of fat on the breasts, that they may not become too brown. Place the chickens in a stewpan with 1 oz. of butter, and leave uncovered for a short time, then bake for 1½ hours. Half an hour before serving, baste with a little milk over a hotter fire.

Time, 1½ hours. *Average cost,* 5s. *Sufficient* for 8 persons. *Seasonable* at any time

DUCKS (BAKED OR ROASTED).

INGREDIENTS.—*A couple of ducks, sage-and-onion stuffing, a little flour.*

Mode.—Never dress the ducks the day they are killed; and if the weather permits, let them hang a day or two. Put them down to a brisk, clear fire, and keep them well basted. Before serving, dredge them lightly with flour, to make them froth and look plump, and when the steam draws towards the fire, send them to table hot and quickly, with a good brown gravy poured *round,* but not *over* the ducks, and a little of the same in a tureen. When in season green peas should invariably accompany the dish. Ducks may be equally well cooked in a good oven.

Time, full-grown ducks from ¾ to 1 hour; ducklings, from 25 to 35 minutes. *Average cost,* from 2s. 6d. to 3s. 6d. each. *Sufficient*—a couple of ducklings for 6 or 7 persons. *Seasonable*—ducklings from April to August; ducks from November to February.

Note.—Ducklings are trussed, cooked, and served in the same manner. When in season, apple sauce must not be omitted.

DUMPOKE (Indian Recipe).

INGREDIENTS.—*1 chicken, good veal forcemeat, mixed with double the quantity of boiled rice.*

Mode.—Bone the chicken, and stuff it with the forcemeat, and either roast or boil it. If roasted and served cold,

it should be glazed. It is cut through in slices, and makes a nice and convenient supper dish.

Time, ¾ hour to boil or roast the fowl. *Average cost,* 3s. *Seasonable* at any time.

FOWLS (BOILED).

INGREDIENTS.—*A pair of fowls; water.*

Mode.—Pick, draw, singe, wash, and truss the fowls. When trussed, put them into a stewpan with plenty of hot water; bring it to the boil, and remove all the scum as it rises. *Simmer very gently* until the fowl is tender; the slower it boils the plumper and whiter will the fowl be. Many cooks wrap them in a floured cloth to preserve the colour, and to prevent the scum from clinging to them; in this case a few slices of lemon should be placed on the breast, over these a sheet of buttered paper, and then the cloth: cooking them in this manner renders the flesh very white. Boiled ham, bacon, tongue, or pickled pork, are the usual accompaniments to boiled fowls, and they may be served with Béchamel, white sauce, parsley-and-butter, oyster, lemon, liver, celery, or mushroom sauce. A little should be poured over the fowls, and the remainder sent in a tureen to table.

Time, large fowl, 1 hour; moderate-sized one, ¾ hour; chicken, from 20 minutes to ½ hour. *Average cost,* in full season, 5s. the pair. *Sufficient* for 7 or 8 persons. *Seasonable* all the year, but scarce in early spring.

FOWLS (BOILED) WITH OYSTERS.

INGREDIENTS.—*1 young fowl, 1 doz. oysters, the yolks of 2 eggs, ½ pint cream, breadcrumbs.*

Mode.—Truss as for boiling; fill the inside with oysters bearded and washed in their own liquor; breadcrumbs and seasoning; secure the ends of the fowl, put it into a jar, and plunge the jar into a saucepan of boiling water. Boil for 1½ hours, or rather longer; then take the gravy that has flowed from the oysters and fowl, stir in the cream and yolks of eggs, add a few oysters scalded in their liquor; let the sauce get quite *hot,* but do not allow it to *boil;* pour some of it over the fowl, and the remainder send to table in a tureen. A blade of pounded mace added to the sauce will be found an improvement.

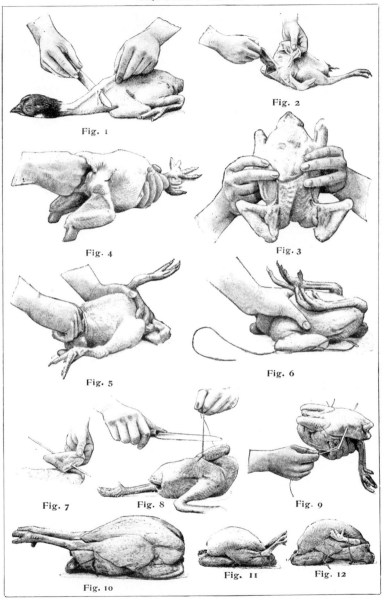

Fig. 1

Fig. 2

Fig. 4

Fig. 3

Fig. 5

Fig. 6

Fig. 7

Fig. 8

Fig. 9

Fig. 10

Fig. 11

Fig. 12

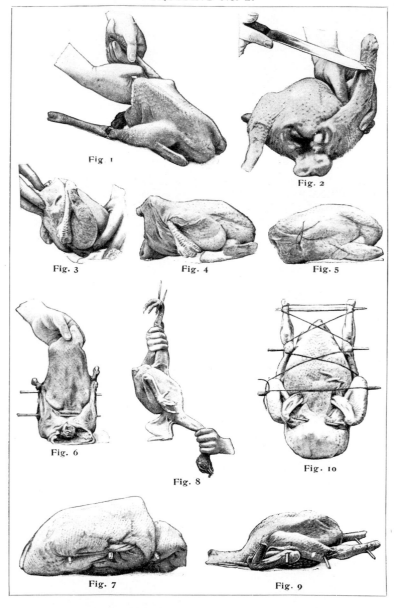

Fig. 1

Fig. 2

Fig. 3

Fig. 4

Fig. 5

Fig. 6

Fig. 8

Fig. 10

Fig. 7

Fig. 9

Time, 1½ hours. *Average cost*, 4s. 6d. *Sufficient* for 3 or 4 persons. *Seasonable* from September to April.

FOWL (BRAISED).

INGREDIENTS.—*A fowl, ½ tin tomatoes, thick white sauce, some tongue, a glass of light white wine, roux, ½ lemon, some peppercorns, a little cochineal, a pinch of ginger, cayenne, salt, 3 tablespoonfuls cream, a clove of garlic.*

Mode.—Truss the chicken or fowl in manner directed for " Fowl for Boiling " and put a buttered paper over the breast. Rub a stewpan well with the garlic, then lay in the fowl with a few strips of lemon-peel, the ginger, cayenne, peppercorns, a little salt, and the wine. Put over the fire and give an occasional shake till the liquor is absorbed, then add a little stock or water and cook the fowl till done. Next thicken the liquor in the pan with white roux, add the tomatoes, and boil up. Take out the fowl and keep it hot. Strain the gravy, add to it the cream hot, more seasoning if needed, and colour a pretty pink with cochineal. Cut some thin slices of cooked tongue and heat them in a little stock or water. Coat the fowl with the white sauce, lay the slices of tongue round it, and send the sauce made in cooking to table in a tureen. A little of it may be put round the fowl if liked.

Time, from 1 hour to 1½ hours to cook the fowl. *Average cost*, 4s. 6d. *Sufficient* for 4 or 5 persons. *Seasonable* at any time.

FOWLS (ROAST).

INGREDIENTS.—*A pair of fowls, a little flour.*

Mode.—Put the fowls down to a clear fire, paper the breasts with a sheet of buttered paper, and keep well basted. Roast for ¾ hour, more or less, according to size, and, 10 minutes before serving, remove the paper, dredge with a little fine flour, put a piece of butter into the basting-ladle, and as it melts baste the fowls with it; when nicely frothed and of a rich colour, serve with good brown gravy, a little of which should be poured over the fowls, and a tureen of well-made bread sauce. Mushroom or oyster sauce are suitable accompaniments to roast fowl. Chicken is roasted in the same manner. Should the fowl be a very large one it is a good plan to steam it for about ¾ hour, then transfer it to a good quick oven for another ½ hour.

Time, a very large fowl, quite 1 hour;

medium-sized one, ¾ hour; chicken, ½ hour, or rather longer. *Average cost*, in full season, 5s. the pair. *Sufficient* for 8 persons. *Seasonable* all the year, but scarce in early spring.

GIBLET PIE.

INGREDIENTS.—*A set of duck or goose giblets, 1 lb. of rump-steak, 1 onion, ½ teaspoonful whole black pepper, a bunch of savoury herbs, plain crust.*

Mode.—Clean and put the giblets into a stewpan, with an onion, whole pepper, and a bunch of savoury herbs; add rather more than a pint of water, and simmer for about 1½ hours. Take them out, let them cool, and cut them into pieces; line the bottom of a pie-dish with a few pieces of rump-steak; add a layer of giblets and a few more pieces of steak; season with pepper and salt, and pour in the gravy (strained) that the giblets were stewed in; cover with a plain crust, and bake for rather more than 1½ hours in a brisk oven. Cover a piece of paper over the pie, to prevent the crust taking too much colour.

Time, 1½ hours to stew the giblets, about 1 hour to bake the pie. *Average cost*, exclusive of the giblets, 1s. 8d. *Sufficient* for 5 or 6 persons.

GOOSE (ROAST).

INGREDIENTS.—*Goose, 4 large onions, 10 sage-leaves, ¼ lb. breadcrumbs, 1½ oz. butter, salt and pepper to taste, 1 egg.*

Mode.—Make a sage-and-onion stuffing of the above ingredients; put it into the body of the goose, and secure it firmly at both ends, by passing the rump through the hole made in the skin, and the other end by tying the skin of the neck to the back. Put it down to a brisk fire, keep it well basted, and roast from 1½ to 2 hours. Remove the skewers, and serve with a tureen of good gravy, and one of apple sauce. Should a very highly flavoured seasoning be preferred, the onions should not be parboiled, but minced raw. A ragout, or pie, should be made of the giblets, or they may be stewed down to make gravy. Only a small quantity of gravy should be poured round the goose, and the remainder sent in a tureen. A goose may be baked in a good oven, but must be basted as in roasting.

Time, a large goose, 1¾ hours; a moderate-sized one, 1¼ to 1½ hours. *Average cost*, from 5s. upwards each. *Sufficient* for 8 or 9 persons. *Season-*

able from September to March; but in perfection from Michaelmas to Christmas.

PIGEON PIE (Epsom Grand-Stand Recipe).

INGREDIENTS.—1½ *lbs. rump-steak*, 2 *or* 3 *pigeons*, 3 *slices ham, pepper and salt to taste*, 2 *oz. butter*, 4 *eggs, puff-crust.*

Mode.—Cut the steak into pieces about 3 inches square, and with it line the bottom of a pie-dish, seasoning it well with pepper and salt. Clean the pigeons, rub them with pepper and salt inside and out, and put into the body of each rather more than ½ oz. of butter; lay them on the steak, and a piece of ham on each pigeon. Add the eggs, boiled and sliced, and half fill the dish with stock; place a border of puff-paste round the edge of the dish, put on the cover, and ornament it in any way that may be preferred. Clean three of the feet, and place them in a hole made in the crust at the top. Glaze the crust—that is to say, brush it over with the yolk of an egg—and bake it in a well-heated oven for about 1¼ hours. A seasoning of pounded mace may be added.

Time, 1½ hours, or rather less. *Sufficient* for 5 or 6 persons.

PIGEON (GRILLED).

INGREDIENTS. — 2 *pigeons, butter, pepper, salt.*

Mode.—Cut the pigeons evenly in half lengthways, heat and grease a gridiron, lay them on it breast downwards, and as they cook occasionally add a tiny piece of butter, and a seasoning of pepper and salt.

Time, about 8 minutes. *Average cost*, 1s. 6d. *Sufficient* for 2 persons. *Seasonable* from April to September.

PIGEONS (ROAST).

INGREDIENTS.—2 *birds, pepper, salt, butter.*

Mode.—Wipe the birds very dry, season inside with pepper and salt, and put about ¾ oz. butter into the body of each. Put them down to a bright fire, and baste them well the whole of the time they are cooking (they will be done enough in from 20 to 30 minutes); garnish with fried parsley, and serve with a tureen of parsley and butter. Bread sauce and gravy, as for roast fowl, are usual accompaniments to roast pigeons.

Time, from 20 minutes to ½ hour. *Average cost*, 9d. to 1s. each. *Seasonable* from April till September; but in the greatest perfection from Midsummer to Michaelmas.

PIGEONS (STEWED).

INGREDIENTS.—2 *pigeons*, 2 *or* 3 *small onions, a few mushrooms (if obtainable)*, ½ *pint of stock, thickening of brown roux, a bunch of herbs, a teaspoonful grated lemon-peel, a tablespoonful of sherry, a little butter, pepper and salt.*

Mode.—Pare and slice the onions and after cleansing, cut the pigeons in neat pieces, then fry in a stewpan with a little butter. Add the stock, herbs, mushrooms, and lemon, and stew gently till the pigeons are done. When stewed keep the birds hot, thicken the gravy, add the seasoning and sherry, and serve very hot with the pigeons.

Time, about ½ hour to stew. *Average cost*, 9d. to 1s. each. *Sufficient* for 3 persons. *Seasonable* from April to September.

TURKEY (BAKED).
(Italian Recipe.)

INGREDIENTS.—*A turkey*, ¼ *lb. of sausage meat*, 8 *prunes*, 4 *pears, a glass of white wine*, ½ *pint of peeled and boiled chestnuts, a few slices of bacon.*

Mode.—Blanch and stone the prunes, peel and quarter the pears, then fry with the chestnuts in a little butter. Mince the liver of the turkey fine, mix with it the sausage, add to the other ingredients to make a forcemeat for the turkey, with which stuff it, first slightly salting it inside. Bake in a tin in a slow oven, with the butter and a little salt, basting occasionally. Serve with the gravy in a tin.

Time, about 2 hours. *Average cost*, 8s. *Sufficient* for 10 persons. *Seasonable* nearly all the year.

TURKEY (BOILED.)

INGREDIENTS.—*Turkey ; forcemeat.*

Mode.—Having drawn and trussed the turkey, fill it with forcemeat (chestnut or veal), and put it into sufficient *hot* water to cover it; let it come to a boil, and then carefully remove all the scum; if this is attended to, there is no occasion to boil the bird in a floured cloth; but it should be well covered with the water. Let it simmer very gently for about 1½ hours to 1¾ hours, according to the size, and serve with either white, celery, oyster, or mushroom sauce, or parsley-and-butter, a little of which should be poured over the turkey. Boiled ham, bacon, tongue, or pickled pork should accompany this dish; and when oyster sauce is served, the turkey should be stuffed with oyster force-meat.

Time, a small turkey, 1½ hours; a large one, 1¾ hours. *Average cost*, 7s. upwards each, but more expensive at Christmas on account of the great demand. *Sufficient* for 7 or 8 persons. *Seasonable* from December to February.

TURKEY (BRAISED).

INGREDIENTS.—*A turkey, ½ lb. fat bacon, 2 onions, 1 carrot, 1 turnip, a bouquet of herbs, a few cloves and peppercorns, stock or water, seasoning.*

Mode.—Prepare the bird as for boiling, and pare and slice the vegetables. Put a few slices of fat bacon at the bottom of a stewpan, over these put the vegetables, lay in the turkey with the giblets, ½ pint stock, the herbs tied in a piece of muslin, the peppercorns and the cloves, and a little salt. Keep the pan over the fire for ½ hour, shaking it now and then; next put in the pan enough stock to nearly cover the bird, and cook from 3 to 4 hours according to the size and age of the turkey. Place the turkey on a dish, if the breast be not brown enough use a salamander or put it in a quick oven; strain off nearly all the gravy and keep hot; reduce the remainder to a glaze, with which cover the bird. Serve with the bacon round the turkey and the sauce in a tureen. For this dish the turkey may be stuffed with chestnut or veal forcemeat.

Time, about 4 hours. *Average cost*, 7s. and upwards. *Sufficient* for 8 persons. *Seasonable* in winter.

TURKEY (ROAST).

INGREDIENTS.—*Turkey; veal or chestnut forcemeat, or sausage-meat.*

Mode.—Choose cock turkeys by their *short* spurs and *black* legs; if the spurs are long, and the legs pale and rough, they are old. If the bird has been long killed, the eyes will be sunk and the feet very dry; if fresh, the contrary will be the case. Middle-sized, fleshy turkeys are superior to those of an immense growth. They should never be dressed the day they are killed, but, in cold weather, should hang at least 8 days; if the weather is mild 4 or 5 days. Stuff with sausage-meat, or veal or chestnut forcemeat. Fasten a sheet

of buttered paper on to the breast of the bird, put it down to a bright fire, at some little distance *at first* (afterwards drawing it nearer), and keeping it well basted the whole of the time. About ½ hour before serving, remove the paper, dredge lightly with flour, and put a piece of butter into the basting ladle; as the butter melts, baste the bird with it. When of a nice brown and well frothed, serve with a tureen of good brown gravy and one of bread sauce. If the turkey is not stuffed with sausage-meat, fried sausages should be put round it when served, or a ham or bacon should be sent to table with it.

Time, from 1½ to 3 hours according to size. *Average cost*, from 7s. upwards. *Sufficient* for 8 to 12 persons. *Seasonable* in winter.

ENTRÉES AND MADE DISHES.

CHICKEN CREAM.

INGREDIENTS.—*½ lb. the white meat of a raw chicken, thick white sauce, 3 oz. panada, 4 eggs, a little red tongue, a scrap of truffle if obtainable, white pepper, salt.*

Mode. — Scrape and pound the chicken, add the panada and the eggs well beaten and a few spoonfuls of white sauce; season and mix all thoroughly and smoothly. Butter a mould, decorate the top with tongue and truffle, put in the mixture and steam for ½ hour. Turn the cream out of the mould, and serve with white sauce poured round. Game cream can be made in the same way, but brown instead of white sauce should be used, with a little sherry.

Time, ½ hour. *Average cost*, 3s. *Sufficient* for 4 persons. *Seasonable* at any time.

CHICKEN CUTLETS.

INGREDIENTS.—*The remains of cold roast or boiled fowl, fried bread, clarified butter, the yolk of 1 egg, breadcrumbs, ½ teaspoonful finely minced lemon-peel; salt, cayenne, and mace to taste. For sauce—1 oz. of butter, 2 minced shallots, a few slices carrot, a small bunch of savoury herbs, including parsley, 1 blade pounded mace, 6 peppercorns, ½ pint gravy.*

Mode.—Cut the fowls into cutlets; take a corresponding number of sippets all cut one shape; fry them a pale brown, put them before the fire, then dip the cutlets into clarified butter, mixed with the yolk of an egg, covered with breadcrumbs seasoned in the above proportion, with lemon-peel, mace, salt, and cayenne; fry them for about 5 minutes, put each piece on one of the sippets, pile them in the dish, and serve with the following sauce :— Put the butter into a stewpan, add the shallots, carrots, herbs, mace, and peppercorns; fry for 10 minutes or rather longer; pour in ½ pint of good gravy, made of the chicken bones, stew gently for 20 minutes, and strain.

Time, 5 minutes to fry the cutlets; 35 minutes to make the gravy. *Average cost*, exclusive of the chicken, 9d. *Seasonable* from April to July

CHICKEN OR FOWL SALAD.

INGREDIENTS.—*The remains of cold roast or boiled chicken*, 2 *lettuces, a little endive*, 1 *cucumber, a few slices boiled beetroot, salad-dressing*, 2 *eggs.*

Mode.—Trim neatly the remains of the chicken; wash, dry, and slice the lettuces, and place in the middle of a dish; put the pieces of fowl on the top, and pour the salad-dressing over them. Garnish the edge with hard-boiled eggs cut in rings, sliced cucumber, and boiled beetroot or tomato cut in slices; or the yolks of the eggs may be rubbed through a hair sieve, and the whites chopped very fine, and arranged on the salad in small bunches, yellow and white alternately. This salad should not be made long before it is wanted for table.

Average cost, exclusive of the cold chicken, 8d. *Sufficient* for 4 or 5 persons.

FOWL OR CHICKEN (CURRIED).
(Cold Poultry Cookery.)

INGREDIENTS.—*Remains of cold roast fowl*, 2 *large onions*, 1 *apple or a stick of rhubarb*, 2 *oz. butter*, 1 *dessertspoonful curry-powder*, 1 *teaspoonful flour*, ½ *pint gravy*, 1 *tablespoonful lemon-juice.*

Mode.—Slice the onions, peel, core, and chop the apple, cut the fowl into neat joints and fry in the butter a nice brown; then add the curry-powder, flour, and gravy, and stew for about 20 minutes. Put in the lemon-juice, and serve with boiled rice, placed in a ridge round the dish, or separately. Two or three shallots or a little garlic may be added.

Time, altogether, ½ hour. *Average cost*, exclusive of the cold fowl, 4d. *Seasonable* in winter.

FOWL (CURRIED).

INGREDIENTS.—1 *fowl*, 2 *oz. butter*, 3 *onions sliced*, 1 *pint white veal gravy*, 1 *tablespoonful curry-powder*, 1 *tablespoonful flour*, 1 *apple or a stick of rhubarb*, 4 *tablespoonfuls cream*, 1 *tablespoonful lemon-juice.*

Mode.—Put the butter into the stewpan, with the onions sliced, the fowl cut into small joints, and the apple peeled, cored, and minced. Fry of a pale brown, add the stock, and stew gently for 20 minutes; rub down the curry-powder and flour with a little of the gravy, and stir this to the other ingredients; simmer for rather more than ½ hour, and just before serving, add the hot cream and lemon-juice. Serve with boiled rice, heaped lightly on a dish by itself, or put round the curry as a border.

Time, 50 minutes. *Average cost*, 3s. *Sufficient* for 3 or 4 persons. *Seasonable* in winter.

DUCK (HASHED).

INGREDIENTS.—*The remains of cold roast duck, rather more than* 1 *pint weak stock or water*, 1 *onion*, 1 *oz. butter, thickening of butter and flour, salt and cayenne to taste*, ½ *teaspoonful minced lemon-peel*, 1 *dessertspoonful lemon-juice*, ½ *glass port wine.*

Mode.—Cut the duck into nice joints; and put the trimmings into a stewpan; slice and fry the onion in a little butter, add these to the trimmings, pour in the weak stock or water, and stew gently for 1 hour. Strain the liquor, thicken it with butter and flour, season with salt and cayenne, and add the remaining ingredients; boil it up and skim well; lay in the pieces of duck, and let them get thoroughly hot, but do not allow them to boil; they should soak in the gravy for about ½ hour. Garnish with sippets of toasted bread. A little spice or pounded mace may be added.

Time, 1½ hours. *Average cost*, exclusive of the cold duck, 5d. *Seasonable* from November to February; ducklings from May to August.

DUCK (STEWED), with peas.

INGREDIENTS.—*The remains of cold roast duck*, 2 *oz. butter*, 3 *or* 4 *slices of lean ham or bacon*, 1 *tablespoonful flour*, 2 *pints thin gravy*, 1 *large onion, or a small bunch green onions*, 3 *sprigs parsley,* 3 *cloves,* 1 *pint young green peas, cayenne and salt to taste,* 1 *teaspoonful pounded sugar.*

Mode.—Put the butter into a stewpan ; cut up the ducks into joints ; lay them in with the slices of lean ham or bacon ; make it brown ; then dredge in a tablespoonful of flour, and stir this well in before adding the gravy. Put in the onion, parsley, cloves, and gravy, and when it has simmered for ¼ hour, add a pint of young green peas, and stew gently for about ½ hour. Season with cayenne, salt, and sugar ; take out the duck, place it round the dish, and the peas in the middle.

Time, ¾ hour. *Average cost,* exclusive of the cold duck, 1s. *Seasonable* from June to August.

DUCK (STEWED), with turnips.

INGREDIENTS.—*The remains of cold roast duck,* ½ *pint good gravy,* 4 *shallots, a few slices carrot, a small bunch savoury herbs,* 1 *blade pounded mace,* 1 *lb. turnips, weighed after being peeled,* 2 *oz. butter, pepper and salt to taste.*

Mode.—Cut the ducks into joints, fry the shallots, carrots, and herbs, and put them, with the duck, into the gravy ; add the pounded mace, and stew gently for 20 minutes or ½ hour. Cut about 1 lb. of turnips, weighed after being peeled, into ½ inch squares, put the butter into a stewpan, and stew about ½ hour or rather more ; season with pepper and salt, and serve in the centre of the dish, with the duck, &c., laid round.

Time, rather more than ½ hour to stew the turnips. *Average cost,* exclusive of the cold duck, 9d. *Seasonable* from November to February.

FOWLS (FRIED).
(Cold Poultry Cookery.)

INGREDIENTS.—*The remains of cold roast fowls, vinegar, salt, and cayenne to taste,* 3 *or* 4 *minced shallots. For the batter,* ½ *lb. flour,* ½ *pint hot water,* 2 *oz. butter, the whites of* 2 *eggs.*

Mode.—Cut the fowls into nice joints ; steep them for an hour in a little vinegar, with salt, cayenne, and minced shallots. Make the batter by mixing the flour and water smoothly together ; melt in it the butter, and add the whites of eggs beaten to a froth ; take out the pieces of fowl, dip them in the batter, and fry, in boiling lard, a nice brown. Pile them in the dish, and garnish with fried parsley or rolled bacon. A sauce or gravy may be served with them.

Time, 10 minutes to fry the fowl. *Average cost,* exclusive of the cold fowl, 6d.

FOWL (FRICASSEED).
(Cold Poultry Cookery.)

INGREDIENTS.—*Remains of cold roast fowl,* 1 *strip lemon-peel,* 1 *blade pounded mace,* 1 *bunch savoury herbs,* 1 *onion, pepper and salt to taste,* 1 *pint water,* 1 *teaspoonful flour,* ¼ *pint milk, yolks of* 2 *eggs.*

Mode.—Carve the fowls into nice joints ; make gravy of the trimmings and legs, by stewing them with the lemon-peel, mace, herbs, onion, seasoning, and water, until reduced to ½ pint ; then strain, and put in the fowl. Warm it through, and thicken with a teaspoonful of flour ; stir the yolks of the eggs into the cream ; add these to the sauce, let it get thoroughly hot, but do not allow it to boil, or it will curdle.

Time, 1 hour to make the gravy, ½ hour to warm the fowl. *Average cost,* exclusive of cold chicken, 5d.

FOWL (HASHED).
(Cold Poultry Cookery.)

INGREDIENTS.—*The remains of cold roast fowl,* 1 *pint water,* 1 *onion,* 2 *or* 3 *small carrots,* 1 *blade pounded mace, pepper and salt to taste,* 1 *small bunch savoury herbs, thickening of butter and flour,* 1½ *tablespoonfuls ketchup.*

Mode.—Cut off the best joints, and make the remainder into gravy, by adding to the bones and trimmings a pint of water, an onion sliced and fried brown, the carrots, mace, seasoning, and herbs. Let these stew for 1½ hours ; strain the liquor, and thicken with a little flour and butter. Lay in the fowl, thoroughly warm it through, add the ketchup, and garnish with sippets of toasted bread.

Time, altogether, 1¾ hours. *Average cost,* exclusive of the cold fowl, 5d.

FOWL (HASHED).
(Indian Recipe.)

INGREDIENTS.—*The remains of cold roast fowl,* 3 *or* 4 *sliced onions,* 1 *apple,* 2 *oz. butter, pounded mace, pepper and salt to taste,* 1 *tablespoonful curry-powder,* 2 *tablespoonfuls vinegar,* 1 *tablespoonful flour,* 1 *teaspoonful pounded sugar,* 1 *pint gravy.*

Mode.—Cut the onions into slices, mince the apple, and fry these in the butter ; add the pounded mace, pepper, salt, curry-powder, vinegar, flour, and sugar; when the onion is brown, put in the gravy, previously made from the bones and trimmings of the fowl, and stew for ¾ hour; add the fowl, cut into nice-sized joints, let it warm through, and serve. Garnish with an edging of boiled rice.

Time, 1 hour. *Average cost,* exclusive of the fowl, 6d.

FOWL (MINCED).

INGREDIENTS.—*The remains of cold roast fowl,* 2 *hard-boiled eggs, salt cayenne, and pounded mace,* 1 *onion,* 1 *faggot savoury herbs,* 6 *tablespoonfuls cream,* 1 *oz. butter,* 2 *teaspoonfuls flour,* ½ *teaspoonful finely-minced lemon peel,* 1 *tablespoonful of lemon-juice.*

Mode.—Cut out all the white meat, and mince it fine; put the bones, skin, and trimmings into a stewpan with an onion, a bunch of savoury herbs, a blade of mace, and nearly a pint of water; stew for an hour, then strain the liquor. Chop the eggs small; mix them with the fowl; add salt, cayenne, and pounded mace; put in the gravy and remaining ingredients; let the whole just boil, and serve with sippets of toasted bread.

Time, rather more than 1 hour. *Average cost,* exclusive of the fowl, 1s.

FOWL RAGOUT.

INGREDIENTS.—*The remains of cold roast fowl,* 3 *shallots,* 2 *blades mace, a faggot savoury herbs,* 2 *or* 3 *slices lean ham,* 1 *pint stock or water, pepper and salt to taste,* 1 *onion,* 1 *dessertspoonful flour,* 1 *tablespoonful lemon-juice,* ½ *teaspoonful pounded sugar,* 1 *oz. butter.*

Mode.—Cut the fowl into neat pieces, as for a fricassee; put the trimmings into a stewpan with the shallots, mace, herbs, ham, onion, and stock (or water). Boil slowly for 1 hour, strain the liquor, and put a small piece of butter into a stewpan; when melted, dredge in sufficient flour to dry up the butter, and stir it over the fire. Put in the strained liquor, boil for a few minutes, and strain it again over the pieces of fowl. Squeeze in the lemon-juice, add the sugar, pepper, and salt, make it hot; lay the fowl on the dish, and garnish with croûtons.

Time, altogether, 1½ hours. *Average cost,* exclusive of the cold fowl, 9d.

FOWL SAUTÉ WITH PEAS (an Entrée).

INGREDIENTS.—*The remains of cold roast fowl,* 2 *oz. butter, pepper, salt,* and pounded mace to taste, 1 *dessertspoonful flour,* ½ *pint weak stock,* 1 *pint green peas,* 1 *teaspoonful pounded sugar.*

Mode.—Cut the fowl into nice pieces; put the butter into a stewpan; sauté or fry the fowl a nice brown, previously sprinkling it with pepper, salt, and pounded mace. Dredge in the flour, shake the ingredients well round, then add the stock and peas, and stew till the latter are tender (about 20 minutes); put in the pounded sugar, and serve, placing the chicken round, and the peas in the middle of the dish. Mushrooms may be substituted for the peas.

Time, altogether, 40 minutes. *Average cost,* exclusive of the fowl, with peas, 10d. *Seasonable* from June to August.

GOOSE (HASHED).

INGREDIENTS.—*The remains of cold roast goose,* 2 *onions,* 2 *oz. butter,* 1 *pint boiling water,* 1 *dessertspoonful flour, pepper and salt to taste,* 1 *tablespoonful port wine,* 2 *tablespoonfuls ketchup.*

Mode.—Cut up the goose into pieces; the inferior joints, trimmings, &c., put into a stewpan to make the gravy; slice and fry the onions in the butter to a very pale brown; add these to the trimmings, and pour over about a pint of boiling water; stew these gently for ¾ hour, then skim and strain the liquor. Thicken it with flour, and flavour with port wine and ketchup; add pepper and salt, and put in the pieces of goose; let them get thoroughly hot through, and serve with sippets of toasted bread.

Time, altogether, rather more than 1 hour. *Average cost,* exclusive of the cold goose, 5d. *Seasonable* from September to March.

PILAU (Indian Recipe).

INGREDIENTS.—1 *chicken,* 6 *large onions,* 2 *mangoes,* 6 *oz. of butter, rice, seasoning.*

Mode.—Peel and chop the onions, and slice the mangoes, and put them in a stewpan with 4 oz. of the butter and the seasoning. Cut the chicken into joints, and fry in the other 2 oz. of butter, then put it in the stewpan, and let the whole stew for an hour. Boil some rice, as for curry, lay it on a hot-water dish over this the joints of fowl, and again over this pour the sauce. Instead of preparing the rice in the ordinary way, it may be dressed as follows :— Wash ¾ lb. of rice and boil it gently for

¼ hour in a pint of stock, then pour off
the gravy, add 3 oz. of butter, and stir
over a bright fire until the rice is nicely
coloured; then moisten with a little
stock, and season with a pinch of
minced herbs and nutmeg and the
finely grated rind of ½ a lemon. Simmer
again until the rice is quite tender
without being broken, and add a little
thick cream. Spread half the rice on a
hot dish, lay the joints of chicken on it,
squeeze over a little lemon juice, put
over the remainder of the rice, and
garnish with hard-boiled eggs. This
is a most excellent way of preparing
rice for other dishes besides pilau.

Time, 1 hour. *Average cost*, 3s. 6d.
Sufficient for 4 persons

POOLOOT (Indian Recipe).

INGREDIENTS.—*A fowl, 1 lb. of rice,
1 quart of stock, 8 onions, 1 tablespoonful of ground ginger, 6 hard-boiled
eggs, a few thin rashers of bacon, 1
lemon, butter for frying, peppercorns,
cardamoms, salt.*

Mode.—Truss the fowl as for boiling,
and boil the rice for 5 minutes, and
drain. Put both with the stock into a
stewpan over a slow fire. Bruise 4 of
the onions, and squeeze out the juice,
and add with the ginger tied in a piece
of muslin, and the lemon-juice. When
the fowl is sufficiently done, take it out
and keep hot while the rice is drying
before the fire. Slice and fry the rest
of the onions, then cut up the fowl and
fry it in the same butter. Pile the rice
in the centre of a dish with the joints
of fowl on the top, and over these the
onions. Strew the peppercorns and
cardamoms over the rice, and garnish
with the bacon, fried, and the eggs cut
in slices.

Time, to boil the fowl, ¾ hour. *Average
cost*, 4s. *Seasonable* at any time.

TURKEY CROQUETTES.

INGREDIENTS.—*The remains of cold
turkey; to every ½ lb. of meat allow 2
oz. of ham or bacon, 1 shallot, 1 oz.
butter, 1 teaspoonful flour, the yolks
of 2 eggs, egg and breadcrumbs.*

Mode.—The smaller pieces, that will
not do for a fricassee or hash, answer
very well for this dish. Mince the
meat finely with the ham or bacon;
make a gravy of the bones and trimmings, well seasoning it; mince the
shallots, put them into a stewpan with
the butter, add the flour; mix well,
then put in the mince, and add about ½
pint of gravy made from the bones.

When just boiled, add the yolks of 2
eggs; put the mixture out to cool, and
then shape it in a wineglass. Cover
the croquettes with egg and breadcrumbs, and fry them a delicate brown,
and serve with rolled bacon cut very
thin.

Time, 8 minutes to fry the croquettes.
Seasonable from December to February.

TURKEY (FRICASSEED).

INGREDIENTS.—*The remains of cold
roast or boiled turkey, a strip lemon-
peel, a bunch savoury herbs, 1 onion,
pepper and salt to taste, 1 pint water,
4 tablespoonfuls cream, the yolk of an
egg.*

Mode.—Cut some nice slices from the
remains of a cold turkey, and put the
bones and trimmings into a stewpan
with the lemon-peel, herbs, onion,
pepper, salt, and the water; stew for
an hour, strain the gravy, and lay in
the pieces of turkey. When warm
through, add the cream and the yolk of
an egg; stir it well round, and, when
getting thick, take out the pieces, lay
them on a hot dish, and pour the sauce
over. Garnish the fricassee with sippets of toasted bread. Celery (boiled)
or cucumbers, cut into small pieces,
may be put into the sauce.

Time, 1 hour to make the gravy.
Average cost, exclusive of the cold
turkey, 6d. *Seasonable* from December
to February.

TURKEY (HASHED).

INGREDIENTS.—*The remains of cold
roast turkey, 1 onion, pepper and salt to
taste, rather more than 1 pint water, 1
carrot, 1 turnip, 1 blade mace, a bunch
savoury herbs, 1 tablespoonful mushroom ketchup, 1 tablespoonful port
wine, thickening of butter and flour.*

Mode.—Cut the turkey into neat
joints; the best pieces reserve for the
hash, the inferior joints and trimmings
put into a stewpan with an onion cut
in slices, pepper and salt, a carrot, turnip, mace, herbs, and water in the above
proportion; simmer for an hour, then
strain the gravy, thicken it with butter
and flour, flavour with ketchup and port
wine, and lay in the pieces of turkey to
warm through; if there is any stuffing
left, put that in also. When it boils,
serve and garnish with sippets of
toasted bread.

Time, 1 hour to make the gravy.
Seasonable from December to February.

GAME

TO SKIN AND TRUSS A HARE.

CUT the hare open lengthwise and the fore legs at the first joint. Raise the skin of the back and draw it over the hind legs, leaving the tail whole; then draw it over the back and slip out the fore legs, easing it over the neck and head with a knife, if necessary, and being very careful not to injure the ears This is the most difficult part of skinning a hare, but when it is roasted it is considered spoilt if the ears are torn or damaged. It is far more convenient to hang the hare to be drawn on a hook, when both hands are free to ease off the skin, but the hind legs must first be drawn out. Next, cut open the hare and paunch it, clean the vent, and wash and wipe the inside thoroughly; after this has been done, if the hare is an old one, it is better to wash it in vinegar and water.

Having cut the sinews of the legs, bring them forward, pressing well against the body; then with 2 skewers fix firmly the two fore and the two hind legs.

Put the head well back between the shoulders and skewer it there, putting the skewer through the shoulders, and making sure that it is firm. Next butter two pieces of white paper and pin carefully over the ears.

TO TRUSS A RABBIT FOR ROASTING.

Empty, skin, and wash the rabbit thoroughly, then take out the eyes, put in some stuffing (if liked) and sew it up.

Cut off the fore joints of the shoulders and legs, and, after bringing them close to the body, skewer firmly. Lastly, raise the head, put it well back between the shoulders, and skewer it there like that of a hare.

TO TRUSS A RABBIT FOR BOILING.

Empty, skin, and wash the rabbit well. Take out the eyes and cut off the fore joints of both shoulders and legs. Draw the legs forward, lay them close to the body, bring the head round to the side and skewer through all.

TO TRUSS A SNIPE.

Pluck the birds and wipe them with a cloth, remove the gizzard, but do not draw them; twist the legs as shown, then put them close to the body.

Skin the neck and head and bring the beak round under the wing, as in illustration.

Plovers and woodcock are treated in the same way and cooked upon toast to preserve the trail.

Quails are trussed in the same manner as pigeons, except that they should be drawn from the side and not the vent.

TO TRUSS GROUSE.

The skin of this bird is tender, therefore it is better to leave the breast feathers on as a protection whilst trussing.

Having plucked the rest of the bird, cut off the head, leaving enough skin to skewer back; loosen the inside of the bird, then wipe it out. Bring the legs close to the breast between it and the side bones, and pass the needle and thread through the pinions and the thick part of the thighs; then remove the breast feathers by the aid of a knife to avoid breaking the skin.

Partridges and pheasants are dressed in the same manner, but the latter are large enough to be drawn like a fowl.

COOKING GAME.

BLACKCOCK (ROAST).

INGREDIENTS. — Blackcock, butter, toast.

Mode.—Let these birds hang for a few days, or they will be tough and tasteless. Pluck and draw them, and wipe the insides and outsides with a damp cloth, as washing spoils the flavour. Cut off the heads and truss them, as a roast fowl, cutting off the toes, and scalding and peeling the feet. Put them down to a brisk fire, well baste them with butter, and serve with a piece of toast under, and a good gravy and bread sauce. After trussing, some cooks cover the breast with vine-leaves and slices of bacon, and then roast them.

Time, 45 to 50 minutes. Average cost, from 5s. to 6s. the brace; but seldom bought. Sufficient, 2 or 3 for a dish. Seasonable from the middle of August to the end of December.

GROUSE (ROAST).

INGREDIENTS.—Grouse, butter, a thick slice of toasted bread.

Mode.—Let the birds hang as long as possible; pluck and draw them; wipe, but do not wash them, inside and out, and truss them without the head, as for a roast fowl. Put them down to a sharp, clear fire; keep them well basted the whole time they are cooking, and serve on a buttered toast, soaked in the dripping-pan, with a little melted butter poured over them, or with bread sauce and gravy.

Time, ½ hour, or 35 minutes. Average cost, 5s. to 7s. 6d. the brace; but seldom bought. Sufficient, 2 for a dish. Seasonable from the 12th of August to the beginning of December.

GUINEA FOWL (LARDED).

INGREDIENTS.—A guinea fowl, some fat bacon, flour, a larding-needle.

Mode.—Truss the bird as a pheasant, cut some thin narrow strips of bacon-fat about 1½ inches long and draw them through the skin of the breast of the bird at equal distances apart, making them look as even as possible. Bake in a good oven, basting well, and shortly before it is done flour it and let it froth before serving. A good gravy must be sent to table with it.

Time, about 1¼ hours. Average cost, 3s. 6d. Sufficient for 3 or 4 persons. Seasonable in winter.

HARE (ROAST).

INGREDIENTS. — Hare, forcemeat, a little milk, butter.

Mode.—Choose a young hare; which may be known by its smooth and sharp claws, and by the cleft in the lip not being much spread. To be eaten in perfection, it must hang for some time; and, if properly taken care of, it may be kept for several days. It is better to hang without being paunched; but should it be previously emptied, wipe the inside every day, and sprinkle over it a little pepper and ginger, to prevent a musty taste. When ready for cooking wipe the inside well out, fill with the forcemeat. The hare should be kept at a distance from the fire when it is first laid down. Baste it well with milk for a short time, and afterwards with butter; particular attention must be paid to the basting. When it is almost roasted enough, flour and baste well with butter. When nicely frothed dish it, remove the skewers, and send it to table with a little gravy in the dish, and a tureen of the same. Red-currant jelly is an indispensable accompaniment to roast hare. Good beef dripping may be substituted for the milk and butter to baste with; but the basting must be continued without intermission. If the liver is good, it may be parboiled, minced, and mixed with the stuffing; but it should not be used unless quite fresh.

Time, a middling-sized hare, 1½ hours; a large hare, 1½ to 2 hours. *Average cost*, from 4s. upward. *Sufficient* for 5 or 6 persons. *Seasonable* from September to the end of February.

LARKS (BAKED).

INGREDIENTS.—1 *dozen larks, butter, toast.*

Mode.—Pluck, cleanse, and draw the larks, cut off the feet, and run the birds on a skewer. Put them in a tin in the oven with a little butter and baste them well with it. They should be done in about 12 minutes in a good oven, when they should be served on slices of hot buttered toast with a little gravy made in the tin.

Time, 12 minutes. *Average cost*, 2s. doz. *Sufficient* for 3 persons. *Seasonable* in autumn.

LEVERET (ROAST).

INGREDIENTS. — *A leveret, butter, flour.*

Mode.—Leverets should be trussed in the same manner as hare, but do not require stuffing. Roast before a clear fire, and keep them well basted. A few minutes before serving, dredge lightly with flour, and froth them nicely. Serve with plain gravy in the dish, and send red-currant jelly to table.

Time, ½ to ¾ hour. *Average cost*, in full season, from 3s. each. *Sufficient* for 5 or 6 persons. *Seasonable*, May to August.

ORTOLANS.

INGREDIENTS. — 6 *ortolans, 6 slices toast, vine-leaves, ½ lb. butter.*

Mode. — Keep them until tender; pluck, truss, and wipe carefully, but do not draw them. Wrap each bird in a freshly-gathered vine-leaf, and tie them ın a bird-spit; roast or bake for 25 minutes, or less if very small. Place the slices of toast in the dripping-pan to catch the trail; as soon as the butter melts, begin to baste, and never leave the birds until they are done. Dish up

the toast, and serve very hot with orange gravy, made of white stock, flavoured with the juice of a Seville orange, or a lemon and a glass of port wine.

Time, 25 minutes to roast. *Seasonable* from November to February.

PARTRIDGE (ROAST).

INGREDIENTS.—*Partridges; butter.*

Mode. — Choose young birds with dark-coloured bills and yellowish legs, and let them hang a few days. The time they should be kept entirely depends on the taste of those for whom they are intended, as some persons would consider delicious what would be to others disgusting and offensive. When trussed, roast them before a nice bright fire, or bake in a hot oven; keep them well basted, and a few minutes before serving flour and froth them well. Serve with gravy and bread sauce, and send to table hot. A little of the gravy should be poured over the birds.

Time, 25 to 35 minutes. *Average cost*, 3s. 6d. upwards a brace. *Sufficient*, 2 for a dish. *Seasonable* from the 1st of September to the beginning of February.

PARTRIDGES (STEWED).
(Italian Recipe.)

INGREDIENTS.—2 *partridges, 1 lemon, 2 slices of fat bacon, 2 carrots, 3 onions, cloves, thyme, parsley, 2 bay-leaves, 1 glass of white wine, ½ pint of stock, butter, pepper and salt.*

Mode.—Draw the birds, cut off the heads. Truss them; putting a piece of butter inside, and skewering the skin of the neck over this. Cut some slices of the lemon and lay on the breasts, covering with a slice of the bacon. Put the birds into a stewpan with the carrots and two of the onions sliced, the other stuck with cloves, the stock, wine and seasoning, and simmer for 1 hour, and skim off the fat. Strain the gravy and thicken with a little butter and flour. Just before serving, remove the lemon. A few stewed mushrooms or a *purée* of green peas are a nice accompaniment to this dish.

Time, 1 hour. *Average cost*, 4s. *Sufficient* for 4 persons. *Seasonable*, September to March.

PHEASANT (ROASTED).

INGREDIENTS. — *Pheasant; flour, butter.*

Mode.—Old pheasants may be known

by the length and sharpness of their spurs; in young ones they are short and blunt. The cock bird is the best. They should hang some time before they are dressed, as if cooked fresh the flesh will be dry and tasteless. After the bird is plucked and drawn, wipe the inside with a damp cloth, and truss it as directed. If the head is left on, bring it round under the wing, and fix it on to the point of the skewer. Roast before a brisk fire, keep it well basted, and flour and froth it nicely. Serve with brown gravy (a little of which should be poured round the bird), and a tureen of bread sauce. Two or 3 of the pheasant's best tail-feathers are sometimes stuck in the tail as an ornament. Potatoes fried in ribbons are usually put round the dish, and a garnish of watercress.

Time, ½ to 1 hour, according to the size. *Average cost*, 3s. 6d. upwards each. *Sufficient*, a brace for a dish. *Seasonable* from the 1st of October to the beginning of February.

PLOVERS (ROAST).

INGREDIENTS.—*3 plovers, butter, flour, toasted bread.*

Choosing and Trussing. — Choose those that feel hard at the vent, as that shows their fatness. There are 3 sorts —the grey, green, and bastard plover, or lapwing. They will keep good for some time, but if stale, the feet will be very dry. Plovers are scarcely fit for anything but roasting, though they are sometimes stewed, or made into ragout.

Mode.—Pluck off the feathers, wipe the outside of the birds with a damp cloth, and do not draw them; truss with the head under the wing, put them down to a clear fire, and lay slices of moistened toast in the dripping-pan to catch the trail. Keep them *well basted*, dredge lightly with flour a few minutes before they are done, and let them be nicely frothed. Dish them on the toasts, over which the trail should be equally spread. Pour round the toast a little good gravy, and send some to the table in a tureen.

Time, 10 minutes to ¼ hour. *Average cost*, from 1s. 6d. the brace, if plentiful. *Sufficient* for 2 persons. *Seasonable*, in perfection from the beginning of September to the end of February

PTARMIGAN (ROAST).

INGREDIENTS.—*2 or 3 birds, butter, flour, fried breadcrumbs.*

Mode. — The ptarmigan, or white grouse, when young and tender, are exceedingly fine eating, and should be kept as long as possible, to be good. Pluck, draw, and truss them in the same manner as grouse, and roast them before a brisk fire. Flour and froth them nicely, and serve on buttered toast, with a tureen of brown gravy. Bread sauce, when liked, may be sent to table with them, and fried bread-crumbs substituted for the toasted bread.

Time, about ½ hour. *Average cost*, 1s. 6d. to 2s. each. *Sufficient*, 2 for a dish. *Seasonable* from the beginning of February to the end of April.

QUAILS (ROAST).

INGREDIENTS.—*Quails, butter, toast.*

Mode.—These birds keep good several days, and may be roasted without drawing. Truss them in the same manner as pigeons. Roast them before a clear fire, keep them well basted, and serve on toast.

Time, about 20 minutes. *Average cost*, 1s. to 2s. each. *Sufficient*, 2 for a dish. *Seasonable* from October to December.

RABBIT (BOILED).

INGREDIENTS.—*Rabbit ; water.*

Mode.—For boiling, choose rabbits with smooth and sharp claws; should these be blunt and rugged, and the ears dry and tough, the animal is old. After emptying and skinning it, wash it well in cold water, and let it soak for about ¼ hour in warm water, to draw out the blood. Bring the head round to the side, and fasten it there by a skewer run through that and the body. Put the rabbit into sufficient hot water to cover it, let it boil gently until tender (from ½ to ¾ hour, according to size and age). Dish it, and smother it with onion, mushroom, or liver sauce, or parsley-and-butter; the former is generally preferred. When liver sauce is preferred, the liver should be boiled for a few minutes, and minced very fine, or rubbed through a sieve.

Time, a very young rabbit, ½ hour; a large one, ¾ hour; an old one, 1 hour or longer. *Average cost*, from 1s. to 1s. 9d. each. *Sufficient* for 4 persons. *Seasonable* from September to February.

RABBIT (ROAST).

INGREDIENTS.—*Rabbit, ¼ lb. butter, 4 dessertspoonfuls milk, 1 tablespoonful* flour, yolks of 2 eggs, brown gravy, the peel of ½ lemon grated, pepper, salt, nutmeg.

Mode.—Truss the rabbit in the same manner as a hare, fill the paunch with veal stuffing, and roast it before a clear fire, basting it well with butter. Before serving mix a spoonful of flour with 4 of milk, stir into it the yolks of 2 well-beaten eggs, and season with a little grated nutmeg, pepper, and salt; baste the rabbit thickly with this, to form a light coating over it. When dry, baste it with butter to froth it up, place it on a dish, and pour round it some brown gravy boiled up with the liver minced, and a little grated nutmeg. Serve with gravy in a tureen, and red-currant jelly.

Time, ¾ hour; if baked, the same time in a good oven should be allowed. *Average cost,* 2s. 8d.

ROOK PIE.

INGREDIENTS.—*4 rooks, ½ lb. puff-paste, ¼ lb. rump-steak, 2 oz. butter, 3 eggs hard boiled.*

Mode.—Pick and clean the birds well, remove the heads and feet, and cut out the backbone of each. Lay the rump-steak in the pie-dish, lay the birds on the meat, breasts upwards, well season; lay the butter in knobs, and add the eggs hard boiled. Bake as pigeon pie.

Time, 1 hour.

SNIPE (ROAST).

INGREDIENTS.—*Snipe, butter, flour, toast.*

Mode.—These, like woodcocks, should be dressed without being drawn. Pluck, and wipe them outside and truss as directed; place four on a skewer, tie them on to the jack or spit, and roast before a clear fire for about ¼ hour. Put some pieces of buttered toast into the dripping-pan to catch the trails, flour and froth the birds nicely, dish the pieces of toast with the snipes on them, and pour round, but not over them, a little good brown gravy. They should be sent to table very hot, or they will not be worth eating.

Time, about ¼ hour. *Average cost,* 1s. 6d. to 2s. 6d. the brace. *Sufficient,* 4 for a dish. *Seasonable* from November to February.

TEAL (ROAST).

INGREDIENTS.—*Teal, butter, a little flour.*

Mode.—Choose flat, plump birds,

after the frost has set in, as they are generally better flavoured; truss them in the same manner as wild duck, roast before a brisk fire, and keep well basted. Serve with brown or orange gravy, watercresses, and a cut lemon. The remains of teal make excellent hash.

Time, from 9 to 15 minutes. *Average cost,* 1s. 6d. each, but seldom bought. *Sufficient,* 2 for a dish. *Seasonable* from October to February.

VENISON, HAUNCH (ROAST).

INGREDIENTS.—*Venison, coarse flour-and-water paste, a little flour.*

Mode.—Keep this joint perfectly dry, by wiping it with clean cloths till not the least damp remains, and sprinkle over with powdered ginger or pepper, as a preventative against the fly. With care it will keep a fortnight, except in very mild weather. When required for use, wash it with warm water, and dry it well with a cloth; butter a sheet of white paper, put it over the fat, lay a coarse paste about ½ inch in thickness over this, and then a sheet or two of strong paper. Tie the whole firmly on to the haunch with twine, and put down the joint to a strong close fire; baste immediately, and continue to do so the whole time of cooking. About twenty minutes before it is done, carefully remove the paste and paper, dredge the joint with flour, and baste well with butter until nicely frothed and of a pale brown colour. Garnish the knuckle bone with a frill of white paper, and serve with good, unflavoured gravy in a tureen, and red-currant jelly, or melt the jelly with a little port wine, and serve that also in a tureen. The above is the best mode of preparing the haunch for roasting, but the paste may be dispensed with and a double paper used instead; it will not then require so long cooking. Hot-water plates should be used at table.

Time, a large haunch of buck venison with the paste, 4 or 5 hours; doe venison, 3¼ to 3¾ hours; less time without the paste. *Sufficient* for 18 persons. *Seasonable,* buck venison, June to Michaelmas; doe venison, November to end of January.

Note.—Neck and shoulder are roasted in the same manner.

WILD DUCK (ROAST).

INGREDIENTS.—*Wild duck, flour, butter.*

Mode.—Carefully pluck, draw, and

truss them. Roast before a quick fire, and when first put down, let them remain for 5 minutes without basting (this will keep the gravy in); afterwards baste plentifully with butter; a few minutes before serving dredge lightly with flour, baste well, and send them to table nicely frothed. If overdone, the flavour is lost. Serve with a good gravy in the dish, and send to table a cut lemon. To take off the fishy taste which wild fowl sometimes have, baste for a few minutes with hot water, to which has been added an onion and a little salt; then take away the pan, and baste with butter. Lemonjuice, port, and cayenne mixed in a spoon and poured over slashes cut in breast improve the flavour.

Time, when liked underdressed, 20 to 25 minutes; well done, 25 to 35 minutes. *Average cost*, 6s. 6d. the couple upwards. *Sufficient*, 2 for a dish. *Seasonable* from November to February.

WOODCOCK (ROAST).

INGREDIENTS.—*Woodcocks*, *butter flour, toast.*

Mode.—Woodcocks should not be drawn, as the trails are considered a great delicacy. Pluck, and wipe them well outside; truss with the legs close to the body, and the feet pressing upon the thighs; skin the neck and head, and bring the beak round under the wing. Place slices of toast in the dripping-pan to catch the trails, allowing a piece of toast for each bird. Roast before a clear fire from 15 to 25 minutes; keep them well basted, and flour and froth them nicely. When done, dish the pieces of toast with the birds upon them, pour round a very little gravy, and send some more to table in a tureen. These are most delicious birds when well cooked, but they should not be kept too long: when the feathers drop, or easily come out, they are fit for table.

Time, when liked underdone, 15 to 20 minutes; if liked well done, allow an extra 5 minutes. Seldom bought. *Sufficient*, 2 for a dish. *Seasonable* from November to February

---

ENTREES AND MADE DISHES FROM GAME.

GAME (HASHED).
(Cold Meat Cookery.)

INGREDIENTS.—*The remains of cold game*, 1 *onion stuck with* 3 *cloves, a few whole peppers, a strip lemon-peel; salt to taste, thickening of butter and flour,* 1 *glass port wine,* 1 *tablespoonful lemon-juice,* 1 *tablespoonful ketchup,* 1 *pint water or weak stock.*

Mode.—Cut the remains into joints, reserve the best pieces, and put the inferior ones and trimmings into a stewpan with the onion, pepper, lemonpeel, salt, and water or weak stock; stew for about an hour, and strain the gravy, thicken with butter and flour; add the wine, lemon-juice, and ketchup; lay in the pieces of game, and let them gradually warm through by the side of the fire. When on the point of simmering, serve. Garnish with sippets of toasted bread.

Time, altogether 1¼ hour. *Seasonable* from August to March.

Note.—Any kind of game may be hashed by the above recipe.

GAME PIE.

INGREDIENTS.—1 *pheasant,* 1 *partridge,* 3 *slices cooked ham, forcemeat, allspice, pepper, salt, gravy, raised pie crust* (see " PASTRY ").

Mode.—Having prepared the birds, cut them up and take away as much bone as possible. Line the pie-mould, which should be one that opens, with the crust rolled out about ½ inch in thickness, and be sure there are no cracks by which the gravy may escape. Put in the pieces of game, with the forcemeat and seasoning and the ham cut up very small, and a *very* little gravy, put on the top of the pie, ornament it, brush it over with yolk of egg, and bake in a moderate oven for 4 hours. Make a good strong gravy with the bones of the birds, and when the pie comes out of the oven pour it into the pie (using a funnel) from a hole at the top, which the centre ornament should hide. The remains of cold game and cooked steak may be used for this pie, when not more than 2 hours baking would be needed.

Time, 4 hours. *Average cost*, 6s. *Seasonable* in autumn and winter.

GAME RISSOLES.

INGREDIENTS.—*Any scraps of cold game,* ½ *the quantity of breadcrumbs, some finely minced herbs and lemonpeel, seasoning, eggs to bind, some plain pastry, lard for frying.*

Mode.—Finely mince the scraps of game, add to them the breadcrumbs, seasoning, &c., and bind with one or more eggs, according to the quantity. Roll out the paste as thin as possible and stamp it in rounds or cut it in squares. Into each of these put as much of the game mixture as they will hold, wet and fasten the edges, brush over with egg, and fry in plenty of hot fat a nice brown. The rissoles may be made and fried without the pastry, when the paste should be formed into balls or rolls, dipped in egg, and rolled in crushed vermicelli.

Time, about 5 minutes to fry the rissoles. *Seasonable* in autumn and winter

GROUSE PIE.

INGREDIENTS. — *Grouse; cayenne, salt, and pepper to taste; 1 lb. rump-steak, ½ pint well-seasoned broth, puff-paste.*

Mode.—Line the bottom of a pie-dish with the rump-steak cut into neat pieces, and should the grouse be large, cut them into joints; but, if small, they may be laid in the pie whole; season highly with salt, cayenne, and black pepper; pour in the broth, and cover with puff-paste; brush the crust over with the yolk of an egg, and bake from ¾ to 1 hour. If the grouse is cut into joints, the backbones and trimmings will make the gravy by stewing them with an onion, a little sherry, a bunch of herbs, and a blade of mace; this should be poured in after the pie is baked.

Time, ¾ to 1 hour. *Average cost*, exclusive of the grouse, 1s. 9d. *Seasonable* from the 12th of August to the beginning of December.

HARE (HASHED).

INGREDIENTS.—*The remains of cold roast hare, 1 blade pounded mace, 2 or 3 allspice, pepper and salt to taste, 1 onion, a bunch savoury herbs, 3 tablespoonfuls port wine, thickening of butter and flour, 2 tablespoonfuls ketchup.*

Mode.—Cut the cold hare into neat slices, and put the head, bones, and trimmings into a stewpan with ¾ pint of water; add the mace, allspice, seasoning, onion, and herbs, stew for nearly an hour, and strain the gravy; thicken it with butter and flour, add the wine and ketchup, and lay in the pieces of hare, with any stuffing that may be left. Let the whole gradually heat by the side of the fire, and when it has simmered for about 5 minutes, serve, and garnish the dish with sippets

of toasted bread. Send red-currant jelly to table with it.

Time, rather more than 1 hour. *Average cost*, exclusive of the cold hare, 8d. *Seasonable* from September to the end of February.

HARE (JUGGED).

I.

INGREDIENTS.—*1 hare, 1½ lbs. gravy beef, ½ lb. butter, 1 onion, 1 lemon, 6 cloves; pepper, cayenne, and salt to taste, ½ pint port wine.*

Mode.—Skin, paunch, and wash the hare, cut it into pieces, dredge them with flour, and fry in boiling butter. Have ready 1½ pints of gravy, made from the above proportion of beef, and thickened with a little flour. Put this into a jar; add the fried pieces of hare, an onion stuck with 6 cloves, a lemon peeled and cut in half, and a good seasoning of pepper, cayenne, and salt; cover the jar down tightly, put it up to the neck into a stewpan of boiling water, and let it stew until the hare is quite tender. When nearly done, pour in the wine, and add a few forcemeat balls, fried or baked in the oven for a few minutes before they are put to the gravy. Serve with red-currant jelly.

Time, 3½ to 4 hours. If the hare is very old, allow 4½ hours. *Average cost*, 7s. 6d. *Sufficient* for 7 or 8 persons. *Seasonable* from September to the end of February.

II.

A Quicker and more Economical Way.

INGREDIENTS.—*1 hare, a bunch sweet herbs, 2 onions, each stuck with 3 cloves, 6 whole allspice, ½ teaspoonful black pepper, a strip lemon-peel, thickening of butter and flour, 2 tablespoonfuls ketchup, ¼ pint port wine.*

Mode.—Wash the hare nicely, cut it up into joints (not too large), and flour and brown them as in preceding recipe; then put them into a stewpan with the herbs, onions, cloves, allspice, pepper, and lemon-peel; cover with hot water, and when it boils, carefully remove all the scum, and let it simmer till tender (1¾ hours, or longer, should the hare be very old). Take out the pieces of hare, thicken the gravy with flour and butter, add the ketchup and port wine, let it boil for about 10 minutes, strain it through a sieve over the hare, and serve. A few fried forcemeat balls should be added at the moment of serving, or instead of frying them they may be stewed in the gravy about 10 minutes before the hare is wanted for table. Do not omit to serve red-currant jelly with it.

Time, altogether 2 hours. *Average cost*, 6s. *Sufficient* for 7 or 8 persons. *Seasonable* from September to the end of February.

Note—Should there be any left, re-warm it the next day by putting the hare, &c., into a covered jar, and placing this jar in a saucepan of boiling water.

LARKS IN ONIONS (Italian Recipe).

INGREDIENTS.—1 *doz. larks*, 12 *Spanish onions*, 1 *pint of stock*, 3 *or* 4 *slices of bacon*, 2 *fowls' livers*, 1 *bunch of herbs*, ½ *lb. of veal forcemeat*, *salt and pepper*.

Mode.—Clean and bone the larks and stuff them with the liver and herbs, finely chopped. Put the bacon at the bottom of a stewpan, lay the larks on it and cover with stock, simmer for about 15 minutes. Peel and blanch the onions; let them cool, wipe them dry, then take out enough of the inside to make room for the larks; put a little forcemeat in each, then a lark, salt the onions slightly, then wrap them in buttered paper and bake in the oven. Take them out carefully, glaze, and serve with Spanish sauce.

Time, ½ an hour. *Average cost*, 4s. *Sufficient* for 12 persons. *Seasonable* in autumn.

LARK PUDDING.

INGREDIENTS.—1½ *doz. larks*, 1½ *doz. oysters*, 1 *lb. rump-steak*, 3 *sheep's kidneys*, *a few mushrooms, pepper, salt, stock, a good suet crust*.

Mode.—Line a buttered basin with the crust, put in a layer of the steak cut small rolled in flour and pepper and salt, next one of the kidneys treated in the same manner, then the larks cleansed and prepared, the oysters, the mushrooms, and fill up with the remainder of the steak and kidney. Pour in enough stock to fill the basin without its running over, then cover with the crust. Tie up and boil for 6 hours. When served, take off the pudding-cloth and pin a serviette round the basin. Have a little hot stock ready to fill up the pudding when cut.

Time, 6 hours. *Average cost*, 6s. to 6s. 6d. *Sufficient* for 6 persons. *Seasonable* in autumn.

RABBIT (CURRIED).

INGREDIENTS.—1 *rabbit*, 2 *oz. butter*, 3 *onions*, 1 *pint stock*, 1 *tablespoonful curry-powder*, 1 *tablespoonful flour*, 1 *teaspoonful mushroom powder*, *the juice of* ½ *lemon*, ½ *lb. rice*.

Mode.—Empty, skin, and wash the rabbit thoroughly, and cut it neatly into joints. Put it into a stewpan with the butter and sliced onions, and let them acquire a nice brown colour. Pour in the stock, which should be boiling; mix the curry-powder and flour smoothly with a little water, add it to the stock, with the mushroom-powder, and simmer for rather more than ½ hour; squeeze in the lemon-juice, and serve in the centre of a dish, with an edging of boiled rice. Water may be substituted for the stock, but in this case the meat and onions must be very nicely browned. A little sour apple and rasped cocoa-nut may be stewed with the curry.

Time, altogether, ¾ hour. *Average cost*, 1s. 9d. *Sufficient* for 4 persons. *Seasonable* in winter.

RABBIT PIE.

INGREDIENTS.—1 *rabbit, a few slices ham, salt and white pepper to' taste*, 2 *blades pounded mace*, ½ *teaspoonful grated nutmeg, a few forcemeat balls*, 3 *hard-boiled eggs*, ½ *pint gravy, puff crust*.

Mode.—Cut up the rabbit, remove the breastbone, and bone the legs. Put the rabbit, slices of ham, forcemeat balls, and hard eggs, by turns, in layers, and season each with pepper, salt, pounded mace, and grated nutmeg. Pour in about ½ pint water, cover with crust, and bake in a well-heated oven for about 1½ hours. Should the crust acquire too much colour, place a piece of paper over it to prevent its burning. When done, pour in at the top, through the hole in the middle of the crust, a little good gravy, which may be made of the breast and leg-bones of the rabbit and 2 or 3 shank-bones, flavoured with onion, herbs, and spices.

Time, 1½ hours. *Sufficient* for 5 or 6 persons. *Seasonable* from September to February.

Note.—The liver of the rabbit may be boiled, minced, and mixed with the forcemeat balls.

SALMI OF PARTRIDGES OR OTHER GAME.

(*Suitable also for pheasants, moor-game, &c.*)

INGREDIENTS.—3 *young partridges*, 3 *shallots, a slice lean ham*, 1 *carrot*, 3 *or* 4 *mushrooms, a bunch savoury herbs*,

2 *cloves*, 6 *whole peppers*, ¾ *pint stock*, 1 *glass sherry or madeira, a small lump of sugar.*

Mode.—After the partridges are plucked and drawn, roast or bake them to be rather underdone, and cover with paper, as they should not be browned; cut them into joints, take off the skin from the wings, legs, and breasts; put these into a stewpan, cover them up, and set by until the gravy is ready. Cut a slice of ham into small pieces, and put them, with the carrots sliced, the shallots, mushrooms, herbs, cloves, and pepper, into a stewpan; fry lightly in a little butter, pour in the stock, add the bones and trimming from the partridges, and simmer for ¼ hour. Strain the gravy, let it cool, and skim off every particle of fat; put it to the legs, wings, and breasts, add a glass of sherry or madeira, and a small lump of sugar; let all gradually warm through by the side of the fire, and when on the point of boiling, serve, and garnish the dish with croûtons. The remains of roast partridge may be dressed in this way. This recipe is equally suitable for pheasants, moor-game, &c.; but care must be taken always to skin the joints.

Time, altogether 1 hour. *Average cost*, 3s. 6d. and upwards a pair. *Sufficient*, 2 or 3 partridges for an *entrée*. *Seasonable* from the 1st of September to the beginning of February.

VENISON (HASHED).

INGREDIENTS.—*The remains of roast venison, its own gravy, thickening of butter and flour.*

Mode.—Put neat slices cut from the bones into its own gravy. Should there not be enough, stew the bones and trimmings for about an hour in a pint of good gravy, and strain. Put a little flour and butter into the stewpan, and keep stirring until brown, then add the strained gravy, and give it a boil up. Skim and strain again. When a little cool, put in the slices of venison; and when on the point of simmering, serve. Do not allow it to boil. Send red-currant jelly to table with it.

Time, altogether, 1½ hour.

Note.—If any sauce or ketchup is used, it must be added very sparingly.

WILD DUCK (HASHED).

INGREDIENTS.—*The remains of cold roast wild duck*, 1 *pint good brown gravy*, 2 *tablespoonfuls breadcrumbs*, 1 *glass claret; salt, cayenne, and mixed spices to taste;* 1 *tablespoonful of lemon or Seville orange juice.*

Mode.—Cut the remains of the duck into joints, put them into a stewpan, with all the above ingredients; let them get gradually hot, and occasionally stir the contents. When on the point of boiling, serve, and garnish the dish with sippets of toasted bread.

POULTRY AND GAME.

Roast Wild Duck.

Crême Chicken in Aspic.

Boned Capon.

Roast Gosling.

Roast Fowls.

Stuffed Larks.

Capon with Sauce.

Roast Partridges.

Roast Pigeons and Watercress.

CARVING.

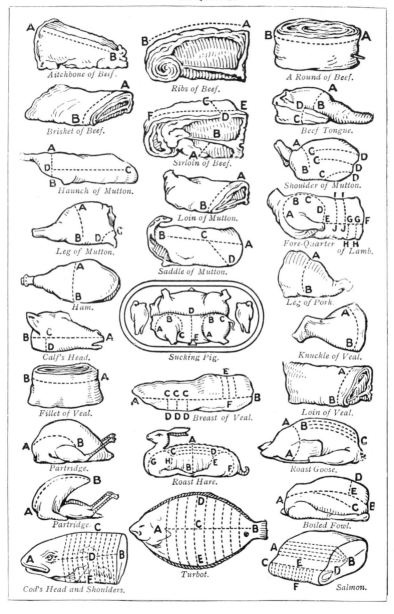

Aitchbone of Beef.

Ribs of Beef.

A Round of Beef.

Brisket of Beef.

Sirloin of Beef.

Beef Tongue.

Haunch of Mutton.

Loin of Mutton.

Shoulder of Mutton.

Leg of Mutton.

Saddle of Mutton.

Fore-Quarter of Lamb.

Ham.

Leg of Pork.

Calf's Head.

Sucking Pig.

Knuckle of Veal.

Fillet of Veal.

Breast of Veal.

Loin of Veal.

Partridge.

Roast Hare.

Roast Goose.

Partridge.

Turbot.

Boiled Fowl.

Cod's Head and Shoulders.

Salmon.

CARVING

BEEF CARVING.

AITCH-BONE OF BEEF.

A BOILED aitch-bone of beef is not a difficult joint to carve, as will be seen on reference to the accompanying engraving. By following with the knife the direction of the line from A to B, nice slices will be easily cut. It may be necessary, as in a round of beef, to cut a thick slice off the outside before commencing to serve.

BRISKET OF BEEF.

There is but little description necessary to add, to show the carving of a boiled brisket of beef, beyond the engraving. The only point to be observed is, that the joint should be cut evenly and firmly quite across the bones, so that, on its reappearance at table, it should not have a jagged and untidy look.

RIBS OF BEEF.

This dish resembles the sirloin, except that it has no fillet or undercut. The mode of carving is similar, viz., in the direction of the dotted line from A to B.

SIRLOIN OF BEEF.

The undercut, or fillet of a sirloin, is best eaten when hot; the carver should raise the joint, and cut some slices from the under side, in the direction of from A to B. The upper part of the sirloin should be cut in the direction of the line from F to E, and care should be taken to carve it evenly and in thin slices. It will be found a great assistance if the knife be first inserted just above the bone at the bottom, and run sharply along between the bone and meat, and also to divide the meat from the bone in the same way at the side of the joint. The slices will then come away more readily. Some carvers cut the upper side of the sirloin across, as shown by the line from C to D; but this is a wasteful plan. With the sirloin, very finely scraped horseradish is usually served, and a little given, when liked, to each guest. Horseradish sauce is preferable, however, for serving on the plate.

A ROUND OF BEEF.

To carve a round of beef properly, a thin-bladed and very sharp knife is necessary. Off the outside of the joint, at its top, a thick slice should first be cut, so as to leave the surface smooth; then thin and even slices should be cleverly carved in the direction of the line A to B; and with each slice of the lean a delicate morsel of the fat should be served.

BEEF TONGUE.

Passing the knife down in the direction of from A to B, a not too thin slice should be helped; and the carving of a tongue may be continued in this way until the best portions of the upper side are served. The fat can be served by turning the tongue, and cutting in the direction of from C to D.

FISH CARVING.

The few illustrations on the "Carving" plate indicate the method of carving the fish they represent. John Dory and Brill are carved as Turbot. Soles are best cut through bone and all, and served in convenient sized pieces. Whiting, Pike, Haddock, &c.,

when sufficiently large, may be carved as Salmon, or divided lengthwise along the back; when smaller they may be cut through bone and all.

MUTTON AND LAMB CARVING.

LEG OF MUTTON.

This joint is almost invariably served at table as shown in the engraving. In carving, the knife should be carried sharply down in the direction of the line from A to B, and slices taken from either side, as the guests may prefer The fat should be sought near the line C to D.

LOIN OF MUTTON.

This joint should be thoroughly well jointed by the butcher before it is cooked. The knife should be inserted at A, and after feeling your way between the bones, it should be carried sharply in the direction of the line A to B. As there are some people who prefer the outside cut, while others do not like it, the question as to their choice of this should be asked

SADDLE OF MUTTON.

This joint is usually cut in the direction of the line from A to B, quite down to the bones, in evenly-sliced pieces. A fashion, however, patronised by some, is to carve it obliquely, in the direction of the line from C to D; in that case the joint would be turned round the other way, having the thin end on the right of the carver.

SHOULDER OF MUTTON.

Draw the knife from the outer edge of the shoulder in the direction of the line from A to B, until the bone of the shoulder is reached. As many slices as can be carved in this manner should be taken, and afterwards the meat lying on either side of the blade-bone should be served, by carving in the direction of C to D and C to D. The uppermost side of the shoulder being now finished, the joint should be turned, and slices taken off its whole length.

FORE-QUARTER OF LAMB.

In the manipulation of this joint, the separation of the shoulder from the breast is the first point to be attended to; this is done by passing the knife lightly round the dotted line, as shown by the letters A, B, C, D, and E, so as to cut through the skin; and then, by raising with a little force the shoulder, into which the fork should be firmly fixed, it will come away with just a little more exercise of the knife. In dividing the shoulder and breast, the carver should take care not to cut away too much of the meat from the latter, as that would rather spoil its appearance when the shoulder is removed. The breast and shoulder being separated, it is usual to lay a small piece of butter, and sprinkle a little cayenne, lemon-juice, and salt between them; and when this is melted and incorporated with the meat and gravy, the shoulder may, as more convenient, be removed into another dish. The next operation is to separate the ribs from the brisket, by cutting through the meat on the line E to F. The joint is then ready to be served to the guests; the ribs being carved in the direction of the lines from I to J, and the brisket from G to H. The carver should ask those at the table what parts they prefer—ribs, brisket, or a piece of the shoulder.

LEG OF LAMB, LOIN OF LAMB, SADDLE OF LAMB, SHOULDER OF LAMB, are carved in the same manner as the corresponding joints of mutton.

CARVING OF PORK.

SUCKING-PIG

A sucking-pig is usually sent to table in the manner shown in the engraving. The first point to be attended to is to separate the shoulder from the carcass, by carrying the knife quickly and neatly round the circular line, as shown by the letters A, B, C; the shoulder will then easily come away. The next step is to take off the leg; and this is done by cutting round this joint in the direction shown by the figures 1, 2, 3, in the same way as the shoulder. The ribs then stand fairly open to the knife, which should be carried down in the direction of the line D to E; and two or three helpings will dispose of these. The other half of the pig is served, of course, in the same manner. Different parts of the pig are variously esteemed; some preferring the flesh of the neck others, the ribs; and others, again, the shoulders. The truth is, the whole of a sucking-pig is delicious, delicate eating; but, in carving it, the host should consult the various tastes and fancies of his guests.

HAM.

In cutting a ham the carver must be guided according as he desires to practise economy, or have, at once, fine slices out of the prime part. Under the first supposition, he will commence at the knuckle end, and cut off thin slices towards the thick part of the ham. To reach the choicer portion, the knife, which must be very sharp and thin, should be carried quite down to the bone, in the direction of the line A to B. The slices should be thin and even, and always cut down to the bone.

LEG OF PORK.

The knife should be carried sharply down to the bone, clean through the crackling, in the direction of the line A to B. Sage-and-onion and apple sauce are usually sent to table with this dish—sometimes the leg of pork is stuffed; and the guests should be asked if they will have either or both. A frequent plan, and we think a good one, is now pursued, of sending sage and onion to table separately with the joint, as it is not everybody to whom the flavour of this stuffing is agreeable.

Note.—The other dishes of pork do not call for any special remarks as to their carving or helping.

VEAL CARVING.

BREAST OF VEAL.

The breast of veal consists of two parts—the rib-bones and the gristly brisket. These two parts should first be separated by sharply passing the knife in the direction of the line A, B. When they are entirely divided, the rib-bones should be carved in the direction of the lines E to F; and the brisket can be helped by cutting pieces in the direction C to D. The carver should ask the guests whether they have a preference for the brisket or ribs; and if there be a sweetbread served with the dish, as it often is with roast breast of veal, each person should receive a piece.

CALF'S HEAD.

In the first place, inserting the knife quite down to the bone, cut slices in the direction of the line A to B; with each of these should be helped a piece of what is called the throat sweetbread, cut in the direction of from C to D. The eye, and the flesh round, are favourite morsels with many. The jawbone being removed, there will then be found some nice lean; and the palate, which is reckoned by some a tit-bit, lies under the head. On a separate dish there is always served the tongue and brains, and each guest should be asked to take some of these.

FILLET OF VEAL.

The carving of this joint is similar to that of a round of beef. Slices, not too thick, in the direction of the line A to B, are cut; and the only point to be careful about is, that the veal be *evenly* carved. Between the flap and the meat the stuffing is inserted, and a small portion of this should be served to every guest.

KNUCKLE OF VEAL.

The engraving, showing the dotted line from A to B, sufficiently indicates the direction which should be given to the knife in carving this dish. The best slices are those from the thickest part of the knuckle, that is, outside the line A to B.

LOIN OF VEAL.

When the jointing is properly performed, there is little difficulty in carrying the knife down in the direction of the line A to B. To each guest should be given a piece of the kidney and kidney-fat, which lie underneath, and are considered great delicacies.

POULTRY CARVING.

ROAST DUCK.

If the bird be a young duckling, it may be carved like a fowl. If a large bird, the better plan to pursue is to carve it like a goose.

BOILED FOWL.

In carving a boiled fowl, fix the fork firmly in the breast, let the knife be sharply passed along the line shown from A to B; then cut downwards from that line to c; and the wing, it will be found, can be easily withdrawn. Let the fork be placed inside the leg, which should be gently forced away from the body of the fowl; and the joint being thus discovered, the carver can readily cut through it, and the leg can be served. The legs and wings on either side having been taken off, the carver should draw his knife through the flesh in the direction of the line D to E; by this means the knife can be slipped underneath the merrythought, which, being lifted up and pressed backwards, will immediately come off. The collar or neck bones are the next to consider: these lie on each side of the merrythought, close under the upper part of the wings; and, in order to free these from the fowl, they must also be raised by the knife at their broad end, and turned from the body towards the breastbone, until the shorter piece of the bone breaks off. There will now be left only the breast, with the ribs. The breast can be, without difficulty, disengaged from the ribs by cutting through the latter, which will offer little impediment. The side-bones are now to be taken off; and, to do this, the lower end of the back should be turned from the carver, who should press the point of the knife through the top of the backbone, near the centre, bringing it down towards the end of the back, completely through the bone. If the knife is now turned in the opposite direction, the joint will be easily separated from the vertebræ. The backbone being now uppermost, the fork should be pressed firmly down on it, whilst at the same time the knife should be employed in raising up the lower small end of the fowl towards the fork, and thus the back will be dislocated about its middle. The wings, breast and merrythought are esteemed the prime parts of a fowl, and are usually served to the ladies of the company, to whom legs, except as a matter of paramount necessity, should not be given. If the fowl is, capon like, very large, slices may be carved from its breast in the same manner as from a turkey's.

ROAST FOWL.

A roast fowl is carved in the same manner as a boiled fowl.

ROAST GOOSE.

Evenly-cut slices, not too thick or too thin, should be carved from the breast in the direction of the line from B to c. A hole should be made in the apron, passing it round the line as indicated by the letters A, A, A. where the stuffing is placed, and some of this should be served on each plate. As many slices as can be taken from the breast being carved, the bird should be dismembered in the same manner as a boiled fowl.

PIGEON.

In carving a pigeon, divide the bird lengthwise, cutting it into two precisely equal and similar parts.

ROAST TURKEY.

The only art in carving a turkey consists in getting from the breast as many fine slices as possible. The carver should commence cutting slices close to the wing lengthwise, and then proceed upwards towards the ridge of the breast-bone; this is not the usual plan, but in practice will be found the best. The legs are not often eaten the first day, but serve, devilled, for a good breakfast dish. A boiled turkey is carved in the same manner.

GAME CARVING.

BLACKCOCK.

Begin by taking slices from the breast, lengthwise; after which the merrythought may be displaced, and the leg and wing removed, following the directions given under the head of boiled fowl, reserving the thigh, which is considered a great delicacy, for the most honoured guests, some of whom may also esteem the brains of this bird.

WILD DUCK.

Of wild fowl, the breast alone is considered by epicures worth eating, and slices are cut from this lengthwise; if necessary, the leg and wing can be taken off, following the directions described for carving boiled fowl.

ROAST HARE.

The hare, having its head to the left, as shown in the illustration, should be first served by cutting slices from each side of the backbone, in the direction of the lines from c to D. The leg should next be disengaged by cutting round the line indicated by the letters E to F. The shoulders will then be taken off by passing the knife round from G to H. The back of the hare should now be divided by cutting quite through its spine, as shown by the line A to B, taking care to feel with the point of the knife for a joint where the back may be readily penetrated. It is the usual plan not to serve any bone in helping hare; and thus the flesh should be sliced from the legs and placed alone on the plate. In large establishments it is often the case that the backbone, especially in old animals, is taken out, and then the process of carving, is, of course, considerably facilitated.

RABBITS.

In carving a boiled rabbit, let the knife be drawn on each side of the backbone, the whole length of the rabbit, dividing it into three parts. Now let the back be divided into two equal parts crosswise, and then remove the leg and shoulder.

A roast rabbit is rather differently trussed from one that is meant to be boiled; but the carving is nearly similar. The back should be divided into as many pieces as it will give, and the legs and shoulders can then be disengaged in the same manner as those of the boiled animal.

PARTRIDGES.

There are several ways of carving this most familiar game bird. The more usual and summary mode is to carry the knife sharply along the top of the breastbone of the bird and cut it quite through, thus dividing it into two precisely equal and similar parts, in the same manner as carving a pigeon. Another plan is to cut it into three pieces: viz., by serving a small wing and leg on either side from the body, by following the line A to B in the upper picture; thus making two helpings, when the breast will remain for a third plate. The most elegant manner is that of thrusting back the body from the legs, and then cutting through the breast in the direction shown by the line A to B; this plan will give 4 or more small helping.

GROUSE.

Grouse may be carved in the way first described in carving partridge.

PHEASANT.

Fixing the fork in the breast, let the carver cut slices from it; then let the legs and wings be disengaged in the same manner as described in carving boiled fowl.

SNIPE.

One of these small but delicious birds may be given, whole, to a gentleman; but, in helping a lady, it will be better to cut them quite through the centre, lengthwise, completely dividing them into equal and like portions, and put only one half on the plate.

HAUNCH OF VENISON.

An incision being made completely down to the bone, in the direction of the line A to B (shown in haunch of mutton), the gravy will then be able easily to flow; when slices, not too thick, should be cut along the haunch, as indicated by the line D to C; that end of the joint marked C having been turned towards the carver, so that he may have a more complete command over the joint.

WOODCOCK.

This bird, like a partridge, may be carved by cutting it exactly into two like portions, or made into three helpings, as described in carving partridge. This bird is served on toast which has received its dripping whilst toasting; and a piece of this toast should invariably accompany each plate.

Ptarmigan are carved as partridges and pheasants.

Quail, Plovers, and *Teal* are carved as wild duck.

VEGETABLES

COOKING VEGETABLES.

ARTICHOKES (BOILED).

INGREDIENTS. — *To each ½ gallon water*, 1 *heaped tablespoonful salt and a piece of soda size of a hazel nut; artichokes.*

Mode.—Wash the artichokes well, taking care that no insects remain, trim away the leaves at the bottom, and cut off the stems. Put them into boiling water in which salt and soda have been dissolved as above, boil quickly in an uncovered saucepan until tender; take them out, drain for a minute or two, and serve in a napkin or with a little white sauce poured over; a tureen of melted butter should accompany them. Artichokes are better for having been gathered 2 or 3 days.

Time, 20 to 25 minutes after the water boils. *Average cost*, 3d. to 6d. each. *Sufficient*, 5 or 6 for 4 persons. *Seasonable*, July to beginning of September

ARTICHOKES (FRIED).

INGREDIENTS.—5 *or* 6 *artichokes, salt and water; for the batter*, ¼ *lb. flour, a little salt, yolk of* 1 *egg, milk.*

Mode.—Trim and boil the artichokes, and rub over with lemon-juice to keep them white. When quite tender, take them and divide the bottoms, dip each piece into batter, fry in hot lard or dripping, and garnish with crisped parsley. Serve with plain melted butter.

Time, 20 minutes to boil, 5 to 7 to

fry. *Average cost, &c.,* as in preceding recipe

ARTICHOKES, JERUSALEM (BOILED).

INGREDIENTS. — *To each ½ gallon water,* 1 *heaped tablespoonful of salt; artichokes.*

Mode.—Wash and peel the artichokes, and put them in a saucepan with sufficient salted cold water to cover. Boil gently until tender; take them up, drain, and serve in a napkin, or plain. Send to table with a tureen of melted butter.

Time, about 20 minutes after the water boils. *Average cost,* 2d. to 3d. per lb. *Sufficient,* 10 for 6 persons. *Seasonable,* September to June.

Note.—The artichokes may also be mashed. Boil as above, drain, mash with fork, season with white pepper and salt, and stir up in a saucepan over the fire with a little butter.

ASPARAGUS (BOILED).

INGREDIENTS. — *To each ½ gallon water allow* 1 *heaped tablespoonful salt; asparagus.*

Mode.—Asparagus should be dressed as soon as possible after it is cut, although it may be kept for a day or two by putting the stalks into cold water. Scrape the white part of the stems, *beginning* from the *head,* and throw them into cold water; then tie them into bundles of about 20 each, keeping the heads all one way, and cut the stalks evenly, that they may all be the same length; put them into *boiling* water with the salt; keep them boiling quickly until tender, with the saucepan uncovered. Dish the asparagus upon toast, which should be dipped in the water the asparagus was cooked in, and leave the white ends outwards each way, with the points meeting in the middle. Serve with a tureen of melted butter.

Time, 15 to 18 minutes after the water boils. *Average cost,* in full season, 2s. 6d. the 100 heads. *Sufficient*—allow about 50 heads for 4 or 5 persons. *Seasonable*—may be had, forced, from January, but cheapest in May, June, and July.

ASPARAGUS (STEWED).
(German Recipe.)

INGREDIENTS.—100 *heads of asparagus,* 3 *oz. of butter,* ¼ *lb. breadcrumbs,* 2 *eggs, a little mace, salt.*

Mode.—Having scraped the asparagus, cut the heads twice across into equal portions, lay the heads aside, and boil the other parts till half done. Next, put the butter, mace, and salt into a stewpan, then all the asparagus, and simmer gently for 1½ hours. Dish the asparagus on a hot dish, and pour the sauce over.

Time, 1½ hours. *Average cost,* 3s. *Sufficient* for 8 persons. *Seasonable* from May to August.

AUBERGINES (BAKED).
(German Recipe.)

INGREDIENTS. — 4 *medium - sized aubergines, a few mushroom buttons,* 1½ *oz. of butter,* 2 *oz. of fat bacon,* 3 *or* 4 *minced shallots, a teaspoonful of olive oil, seasoning of minced parsley, salt and pepper, breadcrumbs.*

Mode.—Wash the aubergines and cut them lengthwise in two; remove some of the pulp, and add half that quantity of breadcrumbs, soaked in the stock, and half of chopped mushrooms, and the seasoning. Fry this with the butter, oil, shallots, and parsley. Fill up the halves of the aubergines with this forcemeat, smooth over and breadcrumb the tops, and bake for half an hour, then brown over.

Time, ½ an hour. *Average cost,* 1s. 4d. *Sufficient* for 6 persons. *Seasonable* in autumn.

BEANS, BROAD (BOILED).

INGREDIENTS. — *To each ½ gallon water allow* 1 *heaped tablespoonful salt; beans.*

Mode.—After shelling the beans, put them into *boiling* water, salted as above, and let them boil rapidly until tender. Drain in a colander; dish, and serve with them separately a tureen of parsley and butter. Boiled bacon is often eaten with this vegetable, but the beans should be cooked separately. It is usually served with the beans laid round, and the parsley and butter in a tureen.

Time, very young beans, 15 minutes; moderate size, 20 to 25 minutes, or longer. *Average cost,* unshelled, 6d. per peck. *Sufficient*—allow one peck for 6 or 7 persons. *Seasonable* in July and August.

Note.— Old broad beans should have their skins rubbed off after boiling and be mashed and re-heated with a little butter, pepper, and salt.

BEANS, FRENCH (BOILED).

INGREDIENTS. — *To each ½ gallon*

water allow 1 *heaped tablespoonful salt ; a* very small *piece of soda.*

Mode.—Cut off the heads and tails, and a thin strip on each side of the beans, to remove the strings. Then divide each bean into 4 or 6 pieces lengthwise in a slanting direction, and, as they are cut, put them into cold water, with a small quantity of salt dissolved in it. Have ready a saucepan of boiling water, with salt and soda as above; put in the beans, keep them boiling quickly, with the lid uncovered, and be careful they do not get smoked. When tender, which may be ascertained by their sinking to the bottom of the saucepan; take them up, pour them into a colander, and drain; dish, and stir into them a little piece of butter. When very young, beans are sometimes served whole.

Time, very young beans, 10 to 12 minutes; moderate size, 15 to 20 minutes, after the water boils. *Average cost,* 1d. to 3d. per lb.; but, when forced, very expensive. *Sufficient*—allow ½ peck for 6 or 7 persons. *Seasonable* from the middle of July to the end of September; but may be had, forced, from February to the beginning of June.

BEETROOT (BOILED).

INGREDIENTS. — *Beetroot, boiling water.*

Mode.—Wash the beets thoroughly, taking care not to break or prick the skin. Put them in sufficient boiling water to well cover, and boil until tender. If served hot, rub off the peel quickly, and cut the beet into thick slices. For salads, pickles, &c., let the root cool, then peel and cut into slices.

Time, small beetroot, 1½ to 2 hours; large, 2½ to 3 hours. *Average cost,* in full season, 2d. each. *Seasonable*—may be had at any time.

BEETROOT (PICKLED).

INGREDIENTS. — *Vinegar to cover,* 2 oz. *whole pepper,* 2 oz. *allspice to each gallon vinegar.*

Mode.—Wash carefully, taking care not to damage the skin. Put into boiling water, and simmer; when three-parts done (1½ hours), take them out and let them cool. Boil the vinegar and spice for 10 minutes, and, when cold, pour over the beets, previously cut into slices ½ inch thick. Cover with bladder, to exclude the air; in a week they will be fit for use.

Average cost, 3s. per gallon.

BROCCOLI (BOILED).

INGREDIENTS. — *To each* ½ *gallon water allow* 1 *heaped tablespoonful salt ; broccoli.*

Mode.—Strip off the outside leaves, and the inside ones cut off level with the flower; cut off the stalk close, and put the broccoli into cold salt and water, with the heads downwards. When they have remained in this for about ¾ hour, and they are *perfectly* free from insects, put them into a saucepan of *boiling* water, salted as above, and keep them boiling quickly over a brisk fire, with the saucepan uncovered. Take up with a slice the moment they are done; drain well, and serve with a tureen of melted butter, a *little* of which should be poured over the broccoli. If left in the water after it is done, it will break, its colour will be spoiled, and its crispness gone.

Time, small broccoli, 10 to 15 minutes; large one, 20 to 25 minutes. *Average cost,* 3d. each. *Sufficient,* 2 for 4 or 5 persons. *Seasonable* from October to March; plentiful in February and March.

BRUSSELS SPROUTS (BOILED).

INGREDIENTS. — *To each* ½ *gallon water allow* 1 *heaped tablespoonful salt ; a very small piece soda.*

Mode.—Clean the sprouts from insects, nicely wash them, and pick off any dead or discoloured leaves; put them into a saucepan of *boiling* water, with salt and soda; keep the pan uncovered, and let them boil quickly over a brisk fire until tender; drain, dish, and serve. Another mode of serving is when they are dished, to stir in about ½ oz. of butter, and a seasoning of pepper and salt. They must be sent to table very quickly.

Time, from 9 to 12 minutes after the water boils. *Average cost,* 2d. to 3d. per lb. *Sufficient*—allow 3 lbs. for 6 persons. *Seasonable* from November to March.

CABBAGE (BOILED).

INGREDIENTS. — *To each* ½ *gallon water allow* 1 *heaped tablespoonful salt ; a* very small *piece soda.*

Mode.—Pick off all the dead outside leaves, cut off the stalk, and cut the cabbages across twice, at the stalk end; if very large, quarter them. Wash well in cold water, place them in a colander, and drain; then put them into *plenty* of *fast-boiling* water, to which have been added salt and soda as above.

Stir the cabbages down once or twice in the water, keep the saucepan uncovered, and let them boil quickly until tender. The instant they are done, take them up in a colander, place a plate over them, let them thoroughly drain; dish, and serve.

Time, large cabbages, or savoys, ½ to ¾ hour; young summer cabbage, 10 to 12 minutes, after the water boils. *Average cost*, 1d. and 2d. each in full season. *Sufficient*, 1 large one for 4 or 5 persons. *Seasonable*, cabbages and sprouts of various kinds at any time.

CARROTS (BOILED).

INGREDIENTS. — *To each ½ gallon water allow 1 heaped tablespoonful salt; carrots.*

Mode.—Cut off the green tops, wash and scrape the carrots. If very large, cut them in halves, divide them lengthwise into four pieces, and put them into boiling water, salted as above; let them boil until tender, which may be ascertained by thrusting a fork into them; dish, and serve very hot. This vegetable is an indispensable accompaniment to boiled beef. When thus served, it is usually boiled with the beef; a few carrots are placed round the dish as a garnish, and the remainder sent to table in a vegetable-dish. Young carrots do not require nearly so much boiling, nor should they be divided. These make a nice addition to stewed veal, &c.

Time, large carrots, 1¾ to 2¼ hours; young ones, about ½ hour. *Average cost*, 3d. to 6d. per bunch. *Sufficient*, 4 large carrots for 5 or 6 persons. *Seasonable*, young carrots from April to June, old ones at any time.

CAULIFLOWER (BOILED).

INGREDIENTS. — *To each ½ gallon water allow 1 heaped tablespoonful salt.*

Mode.—Trim off the decayed outside leaves, and cut the stalk off. Open the flower a little in places, to remove the insects, which generally are found about the stalk, and let the cauliflowers lie in salt and water for an hour previous to dressing them, with their heads downwards; this will effectually destroy all the insects. Then put them into fast-boiling water, with the addition of salt as above, and let them boil briskly, keeping the saucepan uncovered. The water should be well skimmed; and when the cauliflowers are tender, take them up with a slice; drain, and place them upright in the dish. Serve with plain melted butter, a little of which may be poured over the flower.

Time, small cauliflower, 12 to 15 minutes; large one, 20 to 25 minutes, after the water boils. *Average cost*, for large cauliflowers, 4d. each. *Sufficient*—allow 1 large cauliflower for 3 persons. *Seasonable* from the beginning of June to the end of September.

CAULIFLOWER (FRIED).

INGREDIENTS.—*2 cauliflowers, 2 oz. of butter, 1 teaspoonful of olive oil, 4 tablespoonfuls of flour, ½ pint of vinegar, the whites of 2 eggs, 1 tablespoonful of salt, 1 bunch of parsley, 2 quarts of water.*

Mode.—Clean and trim the cauliflowers and boil them in salt and water. Make a batter with the butter (melted in a little hot water), the flour, oil, and salt, and mix with this the whites of the eggs well beaten. Drain the cauliflowers well; then divide them into branches and shake them well in the vinegar, seasoned highly with pepper and salt; then fry the branches in butter, taking care that they do not stick together. Pile the cauliflowers in a mound on a hot dish, garnishing with some fried or fresh parsley.

Time, ½ hour. *Average cost*, 1s. 6d. *Sufficient* for 8 persons. *Seasonable* in summer.

CAULIFLOWERS WITH CHEESE.

INGREDIENTS.—*2 small cauliflowers, grated parmesan, white sauce, breadcrumbs, cayenne, salt.*

Mode.—Cleanse and boil the cauliflowers till *almost* done, drain them, break off the branches, put a layer in a buttered pie-dish, sprinkle them with a dust of cayenne and salt, then put over some cheese. Repeat this till the dish is full, then pour over a little white sauce, cover with breadcrumbs and brown in the oven.

Time, about ¼ hour to boil the cauliflowers. *Average cost*, 8d. *Sufficient* for 4 persons. *Seasonable* in summer.

CELERY.

This vegetable is usually served with the cheese, and is then eaten in its raw state. Wash the roots free from dirt, cut off all the decayed and outside leaves, preserving as much of the stalk as possible, and carefully remove all specks or blemishes. Should the celery be large, divide it lengthwise into quarters, and place it, root downwards in a celery-glass, rather more than half-filled with water. The top leaves may be curled, by shredding them in narrow strips with the point of a clean skewer, at a distance of about 4 inches from the top.

Average cost, 2d. per head. *Sufficient*—allow 2 heads for 4 or 5 persons. *Seasonable* from October to April.

Note.—Useful for flavouring soups, sauces, &c., and makes a very nice addition to winter salad.

CELERY (FRIED).
(Italian Recipe.)

INGREDIENTS.—*6 heads of celery, 2 or 3 slices each of bacon and ham, ½ pint of stock, 2 eggs, breadcrumbs, pepper and salt.*

Mode. — Thoroughly cleanse the celery, remove the leaves and cut it into 4 inch lengths. Then put into a stewpan with the ham, bacon, stock and seasoning, and simmer for about a quarter of an hour. Let the celery cool, then take it out, dip it in egg and breadcrumbs and fry in butter. Arrange it neatly on a dish and serve with tomato sauce.

Time, altogether, ½ an hour. *Averag cost,* 2s. *Sufficient* for 7 or 8 persons *Seasonable* in autumn and winter.

CUCUMBERS (TO DRESS

INGREDIENTS.—*3 tablespoonfuls salad oil, 3 tablespoonfuls vinegar, salt and pepper to taste ; cucumber.*

Mode.—Pare the cucumber, cut it into *very thin* slices, and *commence* cutting from the *thick end ;* if commenced at the stalk, the cucumber will most likely have a bitter taste. Put the slices into a dish, sprinkle over salt and pepper, and pour over oil and vinegar in the above proportion, and turn the cucumber about. This is a favourite accompaniment to boiled salmon, is a nice addition to all descriptions of salads, and makes a pretty garnish to lobster salad.

Average cost, from 4d. to 1s. each. *Seasonable,* forced from the beginning of March to the end of June ; in full season in July, August, and September.

ENDIVE.

This beautiful vegetable makes an excellent addition to winter salad, when other salad herbs are not obtainable. It is usually placed in the centre of the dish, with slices of beetroot, hard-boiled eggs, and curled celery placed round it. Carefully wash and cleanse it free from insects, which are generally found near the heart ; remove any decayed or dead leaves, and dry it thoroughly by shaking in a cloth. This vegetable may also be served hot, stewed in cream, brown gravy, or butter ; not very highly seasoned, as that would destroy and overpower the flavour of the vegetable.

Average cost, 2d. per head. *Sufficient* —1 head for a salad for 4 persons. *Seasonable* from November to March.

HARICOT BEANS.

INGREDIENTS.—*Beans, a little piece of soda, a little butter, pepper and salt.*

Mode.—Soak the beans over night with a small piece of soda in the water. Drain them, throw away any that float, then boil them till tender in fresh water. When quite done, drain and dish them, shaking in a seasoning of pepper and salt, and a little butter.

Time, about 2 hours to boil the beans. *Average cost,* 2d. pint.

HORSERADISH.

This root, scraped, is always served with hot roast beef, and is used for garnishing many kinds of boiled fish. Let the horseradish remain in cold water for an hour ; wash it well, and, with a sharp knife, scrape it into very thin shreds, commencing from the thick end of the root. Arrange some of it lightly in a small glass dish, and the remainder use for garnishing the joint : it should be placed in tufts round the border of the dish, with 1 or 2 bunches on the meat. (*See* "Horseradish Sauce.")

Average cost, 2d. per stick.

LENTILS (BOILED).

INGREDIENTS.—*Lentils, a little butter, pepper and salt.*

Mode.—Put the lentils to soak in water over night. Strain them in the morning and boil them in fresh water till tender but not broken. Drain them and put them back in the pan with a little butter, pepper, salt, and a spoonful of lemon-juice or vinegar, and serve when hot.

Time, 30 or 40 minutes to boil the lentils. *Average cost,* 2d. a pint.

LETTUCES.

These form one of the principal ingredients for summer salads; should be nicely blanched and eaten young. They may also be stewed and sent to table in a good brown gravy, flavoured with lemon-juice. In preparing them for salad, carefully wash them free from dirt, pick off the decayed and outer leaves, and dry them thoroughly by shaking them in a cloth. Cut off the stalks, and halve or cut the lettuces into small pieces. The manner of cutting them up entirely depends on the salad for which they are intended. In France the lettuces are sometimes merely wiped with a cloth, the cooks there declaring that the act of washing them injures the pleasant crispness of the plant: in this case scrupulous attention must be paid to each leaf, and the grit thoroughly wiped away.

Average cost, when cheapest, 1d. each. *Sufficient*—allow 2 lettuces for 4 persons. *Seasonable* from March to the end of August, but may be had all the year.

MUSHROOMS (BAKED).

INGREDIENTS.—16 *to* 20 *mushroom flaps, butter, pepper to taste.*

Mode.—For this mode of cooking, the mushroom-flaps are better than the buttons. Cut off a portion of the stalk, peel the top, and wipe the mushrooms carefully with a piece of flannel and a little fine salt. Put them into a tin baking-dish, with a very small piece of butter placed on each; sprinkle a little pepper, and let them bake about 20 minutes, or longer should the mushrooms be very large. Pile the mushrooms high in the centre of a very hot dish, pour the gravy round, and send them to table quickly, with very *hot* plates.

Time, 20 minutes; large mushrooms. ½ hour. *Average cost*, from 9d. to 1s. 6d. lb. *Sufficient* for 5 or 6 persons. *Seasonable*, meadow mushrooms in September and October; cultivated mushrooms may be had at any time.

MUSHROOMS (BROILED).

(A Breakfast, Luncheon, or Supper Dish.)

INGREDIENTS.—*Mushroom-flaps, pepper and salt to taste, butter, lemon-juice.*

Mode.—Wipe the mushrooms with a piece of flannel and a little salt; cut off a portion of the stalk, and peel the tops; broil them over a clear fire, turning them once, and arrange them on a very hot dish. Put a small piece of butter on each mushroom, season with pepper and salt, and squeeze over a few drops of lemon-juice. Place the dish before the fire, and when the butter is melted, serve very hot and quickly. Moderate sized flaps are better than the buttons, which are more suitable for stews.

Time, 10 minutes for medium-sized mushrooms. *Average cost*, 9d. to 1s. 6d. lb. *Sufficient*—allow 5 or 6 mushrooms to each person. *Seasonable*, meadow mushrooms in September and October; cultivated mushrooms may be had at any time.

MUSHROOMS (STEWED).

INGREDIENTS.—1 *pint mushroom buttons*, 3 *oz. fresh butter, white pepper and salt to taste, lemon-juice*, 1 *teaspoonful flour, cream or milk*, ¼ *teaspoonful grated nutmeg.*

Mode.—Cut off the ends of the stalks, and pare neatly a pint of mushroom-buttons; put them into a basin of water, with a little lemon-juice as they are done. When all are prepared, take them from the water with the hands, to avoid the sediment, and put them into a stewpan with the fresh butter, white pepper, salt, and the juice of ½ lemon; cover the pan closely, and let the mushrooms stew gently from 20 to 25 minutes; then thicken the butter with the flour, add gradually sufficient cream; or cream and milk, to make the sauce of a proper consistency, and put in the grated nutmeg. If the mushrooms are not perfectly tender stew them for 5 minutes longer, remove every particle of butter which may be floating on the top, and serve.

Time, ½ hour. *Average cost*, from 9d. to 2s. per pint. *Sufficient* for 5 or 6 persons. *Seasonable*, meadow mushrooms in September and October.

MUSHROOMS (TO DRY).

Mode.—Wipe them clean, take away the brown part, and peel off the skin; lay them on sheets of paper to dry in a cool oven. Keep them in paper bags in a dry place. When wanted for use, put them into cold gravy, bring them gradually to simmer, and it will be found they will nearly regain their natural size.

ONIONS, SPANISH (BAKED).

INGREDIENTS.—4 *or* 5 *Spanish onions, salt, and water.*

Mode.—Put the onions, with their skins on, into a saucepan of boiling water slightly salted, and boil quickly for an hour. Take them out, wipe them thoroughly, wrap each in a separate piece of paper, and bake them in a moderate oven for 2 hours, or longer. They may be served in their skins, and eaten with a piece of cold butter and a seasoning of pepper and salt; or they may be peeled, and a good brown gravy poured over them.

They are also very nice with a little forcemeat baked in the centre of each.

Time, 1 hour to boil, 2 hours to bake. *Average cost,* 1d. lb. *Sufficient* for 5 or 6 persons. *Seasonable* from September to January.

ONIONS, SPANISH (STEWED).

INGREDIENTS.—5 *or* 6 *Spanish onions,* 1 *pint good broth or gravy.*

Mode.—Peel the onions, taking care not to cut away too much of the tops or tails, or they would then fall to pieces; put them into a stewpan capable of holding them without piling one on the top of another; add the broth or gravy, and simmer *very gently* until the onions are perfectly tender. Dish them, pour the gravy round, and serve. Or they may be stewed very gradually over a slow fire with a large piece of butter: they will produce plenty of gravy.

Time, to stew in gravy, 2 hours, or longer if very large. *Average cost,* 1d. lb. *Sufficient* for 6 or 7 persons. *Seasonable* from September to January.

Note.—Stewed Spanish onions are a favourite accompaniment to roast shoulder of mutton.

PARSLEY (FRIED).

INGREDIENTS.—*Parsley; hot fat.*

Mode.—Thoroughly cleanse and dry the parsley, put it in a frying-basket and plunge it for a minute in hot fat, lifting it out the instant it is crisp, and drain before the fire.

PARSNIPS (BOILED).

INGREDIENTS.—*Parsnips; to each* ½ *gallon water allow* 1 *heaped tablespoonful of salt.*

Mode.—Wash the parsnips, scrape thoroughly, remove any black specks, and, if very large, cut the thick part into quarters. Put them into a saucepan of boiling water salted as above, boil rapidly until tender; take them up, drain them, and serve in a vegetable dish. Parsnips are usually served with salt fish, boiled pork, or boiled beef: when sent to table with the latter, a few should be placed alternately with carrots round the dish as a garnish.

Time, large parsnips, 1 to 1½ hours; small ones, ½ to 1 hour. *Average cost,* 1d. each. *Sufficient*—allow 1 for each person. *Seasonable* from October to May.

PEAS, GREEN (BOILED).

INGREDIENTS.—*Green peas; to each* ½ *gallon water allow* 1 *small teaspoonful moist sugar,* 1 *heaped teaspoonful salt, a few sprigs of mint.*

Mode.—Green peas should be young, and not *gathered* or *shelled* long before they are dressed. Shell the peas, wash them well in cold water, and drain: then put them into a saucepan with plenty of *fast-boiling* water, to which mint, salt, and moist sugar have been added in the above proportion; boil quickly over a brisk fire, with the lid of the saucepan uncovered. When tender, pour them into a colander; put them into a hot vegetable dish, and in the centre of the peas place a piece of butter the size of a walnut.

Should the peas be very old, and difficult to boil a good colour, a very tiny piece of soda may be thrown in the water previously to putting them in; but this must be very sparingly used, as it causes the peas to have a broken appearance.

Time, young peas, 10 to 15 minutes; the large sorts, such as marrowfats, &c., 18 to 20 minutes; old peas, ½ hour. *Average cost,* when cheapest. 6d. per peck; when first in season, 1s. to 1s. 6d. per peck. *Sufficient*—allow 1 peck of unshelled peas for 4 or 5 persons. *Seasonable* from June to the end of August.

PEAS (DRIED GREEN).

INGREDIENTS. — 1 *pint of Prepared Peas, a little soda, a pinch of carbonate of soda, a tablespoonful of brown sugar, salt, a sprig of mint,* ½ *oz. of butter.*

Mode.—Soak the peas overnight in water with a little soda; cook in fresh water in a pudding dish in the oven, with the carbonate of soda, mint, salt, and sugar. Serve with butter stirred in.

Time, about ½ an hour to boil the peas. *Average cost*, 3d. *Sufficient* for 3 persons. *Seasonable* at any time.

POTATOES (BAKED).

INGREDIENTS.—*Potatoes.*

Mode.—Choose large potatoes, as much of a size as possible; wash in lukewarm water, and scrub them well, for the browned skin of a baked potato is by many persons considered the better part of it. Put them into a moderate oven and bake for 2 hours, turning them three or four times whilst they are cooking. Serve in a napkin immediately they are done. Potatoes may also be roasted before the fire in an American oven; but when thus cooked they must be done very slowly. Do not forget to send to table with them a piece of cold butter.

Time, large potatoes, in a hot oven, 1½ to 2 hours; in a cool oven, 2 to 2½ hours. *Average cost*, 3s. 6d. per bushel. *Sufficient*, allow two potatoes to each person. *Seasonable* all the year, but not good just before and whilst new potatoes are in season.

POTATOES (BOILED).

INGREDIENTS.—10 *to* 12 *potatoes; to each* ½ *gallon water allow* 1 *heaped tablespoonful salt.*

Mode.—Choose potatoes of an equal size, pare them, take out the eyes and specks, and as they are peeled throw them into cold water. Put them into a saucepan, with sufficient *cold* water to cover them, with salt in the above proportion, and let them *boil gently* until tender. Drain away the water, put the saucepan by the side of the fire, with the lid partially uncovered, to allow the steam to escape, or put a cloth over, and let the potatoes get thoroughly dry. Send them to table very hot, and with an opening in the cover of the dish, that the steam may not fall back on the potatoes.

Time, moderate-sized old potatoes; 15 to 20 minutes after the water boils; large ones, ½ hour to 35 minutes. *Average cost*, 3s. 6d. per bushel. *Sufficient* for 6 persons. *Seasonable* all the year, but not good just before and whilst new potatoes are in season.

POTATOES (Boiled in their Skins).

Potatoes if boiled in their skins require about 5 minutes more than peeled potatoes. They should be previously well washed, and, if necessary, scrubbed with a clean brush. When done, peel quickly, and serve in a hot vegetable dish, either with or without a napkin, or with the skins on, putting a small plate beside each guest.

POTATOES (FRIED).

Potatoes may be fried in several ways. Cold potatoes sliced and fried are a nice accompaniment to bacon or steak. Mashed with a little butter, seasoning, and chopped parsley, they can be fried as rissoles. Raw potatoes peeled and pared as an apple, fried in boiling lard, are the potato ribbons so usually served with game and small birds.

POTATOES (MASHED).

INGREDIENTS.—*Potatoes; to every lb. mashed potatoes allow* 1 *oz. butter*, 2 *tablespoonfuls milk, salt to taste.*

Mode.—Boil the potatoes in their skins; when done, drain, and let them get thoroughly dry by the side of the fire; then peel them, and, as they are peeled, put them into a clean saucepan, and, with a *large fork*, beat them to a light paste; add the butter, milk, and salt, and stir all the ingredients well over the fire. When thoroughly hot, dish them lightly and draw the fork backwards over the potatoes, to make the surface rough, and serve. They may be browned at the top with a salamander, or before the fire. Some cooks press the potatoes into moulds, then turn them out, and brown them in the oven: this is a pretty mode of serving, but it makes them heavy.

Time, from ½ to ¾ hour to boil the potatoes. *Average cost*, 3s. 6d. per bushel. *Sufficient*—1 lb. mashed potatoes for 3 persons.

POTATOES, NEW (BOILED).

INGREDIENTS.—*Potatoes; to each* ½ *gallon water allow* 1 *heaped tablespoonful salt; mint.*

Mode.—Get the potatoes as fresh as possible; they are never good when they have been out of the ground some time. Well wash them, rub off the skins with a coarse cloth, and put them into *boiling* water, salted in the above proportion, with a little mint. Let them boil until tender; try them with a fork, and when done pour the water away from them; let them stand by the side of the fire with the lid of the saucepan partially uncovered, and when the potatoes are thoroughly dry put them into a hot vegetable dish with a piece of butter the size of a walnut; pile the potatoes over this, and serve. If the potatoes are too old to have the skins rubbed off, boil them in their jackets; drain, peel, and serve them as above, with a piece of butter placed in the midst of them.

Time, ¼ to ½ hour, according to the size. *Average cost*, in full season, 1d. per lb. *Sufficient*—allow 3 lbs. for 5 or 6 persons. *Seasonable* in May and June, but may be had, forced, in March

POTATOES (STEAMED).

INGREDIENTS. — *Potatoes; boiling water*.

Mode.—Pare the potatoes, throw them into cold water as they are peeled, then put them into a steamer. Place the steamer over a saucepan of boiling water, and steam the potatoes from 20 to 40 minutes, according to the size and sort. When a fork goes easily through them they are done.

Time, 20 to 40 minutes. *Average cost*, 3s. 6d. per bushel. *Sufficient*—allow 2 large potatoes to each person. *Seasonable* all the year, but not so good whilst new potatoes are in season.

SALAD (RUSSIAN).

INGREDIENTS.—*Equal quantities of any cold vegetables except potatoes or parsnips, a few boned and filleted anchovies, some stoned olives, any cold fish flaked, mayonnaise sauce, aspic jelly.*

Mode.—Chop all the vegetables fine, add the fish, then the sauce, sufficient to coat all; mix well in a bowl, then turn out and arrange on a dish, garnishing with the olives and the jelly.

A prettier way of serving this salad is to use the aspic jelly for a border-mould, coating it first, then laying in small pieces of fish and a little finely-cut beetroot, then more jelly and fish till the mould is full. When turned out the salad should be piled in the centre as in illustration.

Seasonable at any time.

SALAD (SUMMER).

INGREDIENTS.—3 *lettuces*, 2 *handfuls*

mustard and cress, 10 *young radishes, a few slices cucumber, dressing.*

Mode.—Let the herbs be as fresh as possible, and, if at all stale or dead-looking, let them lie in water for an hour or two to refresh them. Wash and carefully pick them over, remove any decayed or worm-eaten leaves, and drain thoroughly by swinging them gently in a clean cloth. With a silver knife cut the lettuces into small pieces, and the radishes and cucumbers into thin slices; arrange these ingredients lightly on a dish, with the mustard and cress, and pour under, but not over the salad, dressing, and do not stir it up until it is to be eaten. Garnish with hard-boiled eggs, cut in slices; sliced cucumbers, nasturtiums, and many other things that taste will always suggest to make a pretty and elegant dish. Young spring onions, cut small, are by many persons considered an improvement to salads; but before these are added the cook should always consult the taste of her employer. Slices of cold meat or poultry added to a salad make a convenient and quickly-made summer luncheon dish; or cold fish flaked will also be found exceedingly nice mixed with it.

Average cost, 9d. for a salad for 5 or 6 persons; but more expensive when the herbs are forced. *Sufficient* for 5 or 6 persons. *Seasonable* from May to September

SALAD (WINTER).

INGREDIENTS.—*Endive, mustard and cress, boiled beetroot*, 3 *or* 4 *hard-boiled eggs, celery, dressing, oil, and vinegar.*

Mode.—Shred the celery into thin pieces, having carefully washed and cut away all worm-eaten pieces; cleanse the endive and mustard and cress, and arrange these high in the centre of a salad-bowl or dish; garnish with the hard-boiled eggs and beetroot, both of which should be cut in slices, and pour into the dish, but not over the salad. Never dress a salad long before it is required for table, as, by standing, it loses its freshness and pretty crisp and light appearance; the sauce, however, may always be prepared a few hours beforehand, and, when required for use, the herbs laid lightly over it.

Average cost, 9d. for a salad for 5 or 6 persons. *Sufficient* for 5 or 6 persons. *Seasonable* from the end of September to March.

SEA-KALE (BOILED).

INGREDIENTS—*To each ½ gallon water allow 1 heaped tablespoonful salt.*

Mode.—Well wash the kale, cut away any worm-eaten pieces, and tie it into small bunches; put it into *boiling* water, salted in the above proportion, and let it boil quickly until tender. Take it out, drain, untie the bunches, and serve with plain melted butter or white sauce, a little of which may be poured over the kale. Sea-kale may also be parboiled, and stewed in good brown gravy; it will then take ½ hour altogether.

Time, 15 minutes; when liked very thoroughly done, allow an extra 5 minutes. *Average cost,* in full season, 9d per basket. *Sufficient*—allow 12 heads for 4 or 5 persons. *Seasonable* from February to June.

SAUERKRAUT.

INGREDIENTS.—2 *lbs. of sauerkraut (it can be bought in England in small barrels),* 2 *oz. each of lard, butter, and suet, juniper berries, carraway seeds, salt.*

Mode.—Melt the lard, butter, and suet over the fire in a stewpan with a little water and salt; add the berries and seeds tied in a bag, and the sauerkraut; cover close, and boil quickly for 1½ hours. Before serving, thicken with boiled peas or grated potato.

Time, 1½ hours. *Sufficient* for 6 persons. *Seasonable* in late autumn and winter.

SPINACH (BOILED).

INGREDIENTS.—2 *pailfuls spinach,* 2 *heaped tablespoonfuls salt,* 1 *oz. butter, pepper to taste.*

Mode.—Pick the spinach carefully, and see that no stalks or weeds are left amongst it. Have ready two large pans or tubs filled with water, put the spinach into one of these, and thoroughly wash it; then, *with the hands,* take out the spinach and put it into the *other tub* of water (by this means all the grit will be left at the bottom of the tub); wash it again, and should it not be perfectly free from dirt, repeat the process. Put it into a very large saucepan, with about ½ pint of water, just sufficient to keep the spinach from burning, and the above proportion of salt. Press it down frequently with a wooden spoon, that it may be done equally; and when it has boiled for rather more than 10 minutes, or until perfectly tender, drain it in a colander, squeeze it quite dry and chop it fine. Put the spinach into a clean stewpan, with the butter and a seasoning of pepper; stir over the fire until quite hot, then put it on a hot dish, and garnish with sippets of toasted bread.

Time, 10 to 15 minutes to boil the spinach, 5 minutes to warm with the butter. *Average cost* for the above quantity, 8d. *Sufficient* for 5 or 6 persons. *Seasonable*—spring spinach from March to July; winter spinach from November to March.

Note.—Grated nutmeg, pounded mace, or lemon-juice may also be added to enrich the flavour; and poached eggs are also frequently served with spinach; they should be placed on the top of it, and it should be garnished with sippets of toasted bread.

TURNIP GREENS (BOILED).

INGREDIENTS.—*To each ½ gallon water allow 1 heaped tablespoonful salt; turnip greens.*

Mode.—Wash the greens well in two or three waters, and pick off all the decayed and dead leaves; tie them in small bunches, and put them into plenty of boiling water, salted in the above proportion. Keep them boiling quickly, with the saucepan uncovered, and when tender, pour them into a colander; drain, arrange in a vegetable dish, remove the string, and serve.

Time, 15 to 20 minutes. *Average cost,* 3d. for a dish for 3 persons. *Seasonable* in March, April, and May.

TURNIPS (BOILED).

INGREDIENTS.—*Turnips; to each ½ gallon water allow 1 heaped tablespoonful salt.*

Mode.—Pare the turnips, and, should they be very large, divide them into quarters. Put them into a saucepan of boiling water, salted in the above proportion, and let them boil gently until tender. Try them with a fork, and, when done, take them up in a colander; let them thoroughly drain, and serve. Boiled turnips are usually sent to table with boiled mutton, and are nicer when mashed than served whole.

Time, old turnips, ¾ to 1¼ hours; young ones, 18 to 20 minutes. *Average cost,* 4d. per bunch. *Sufficient*—allow a bunch of 12 turnips for 5 or 6 persons. *Seasonable*—may be had all the year; but in spring only useful for flavouring gravies, &c.

TURNIPS (MASHED).

INGREDIENTS.—10 *or* 12 *large turnips; to each ½ gallon water allow* 1 *heaped tablespoonful salt*, 1 *oz. butter, cayenne or white pepper to taste.*

Mode.—Pare the turnips, quarter them, and put them into boiling water, salted in the above proportion; boil until tender, drain them in a colander, and squeeze as dry as possible by pressing them with the back of a large plate. When quite free from water, rub the turnips with a wooden spoon through the colander, and put them into a clean saucepan; add the butter, white pepper, or cayenne, and, if necessary, a little salt. Keep stirring them over the fire until the butter is well mixed with them, and the turnips are thoroughly hot; dish, and serve. A little cream or milk, added after the turnips are pressed through the colander, is an improvement.

Time, from ½ to ¾ hour to boil the turnips; 10 minutes to warm them through. *Average cost*, 4d. per bunch. *Sufficient* for 4 or 5 persons. *Seasonable*—may be had all the year, but in spring only good for flavouring gravies.

VEGETABLE MARROW (BOILED).

INGREDIENTS.—*To each* ½ *gallon water allow* 1 *heaped tablespoonful salt ; vegetable marrow.*

Mode.—Have ready a saucepan of boiling water, salted in the above proportion, put in the marrows after peeling, and boil until quite tender; take them up with a slice, halve, and, if very large, quarter them. Dish on toast, and send to table with them a tureen of melted butter, or small pat of salt butter. Large vegetable marrows may be preserved throughout the winter by storing them in a dry place. When wanted for use, a few slices should be cut and boiled in the same manner as above; but, when once begun, the marrow must be eaten quickly, as it keeps but a short time after it is cut. Vegetable marrows are also very delicious mashed; they should be boiled, drained, and mashed smoothly with a wooden spoon. Heat them in a saucepan, add a seasoning of salt and pepper, and a small piece of butter, and garnish with a few sippets of toasted bread.

Time, young vegetable marrows, 10 to 20 minutes; old ones, ½ to ¾ hour. *Average cost*, in full season, 2d. to 3d. each. *Sufficient*—allow 1 moderate-sized marrow for 4 persons. *Seasonable* in July, August, and September; but may be preserved all the winter.

PARTRIDGES (LARDED).

ROAST PARTRIDGES.

ROAST FOWLS.

LARDED GUINEA FOWL.

ROAST PHEASANT.

BOILED CAPON WITH WHITE SAUCE.

ROAST GOSLING.

ROAST PIGEONS.

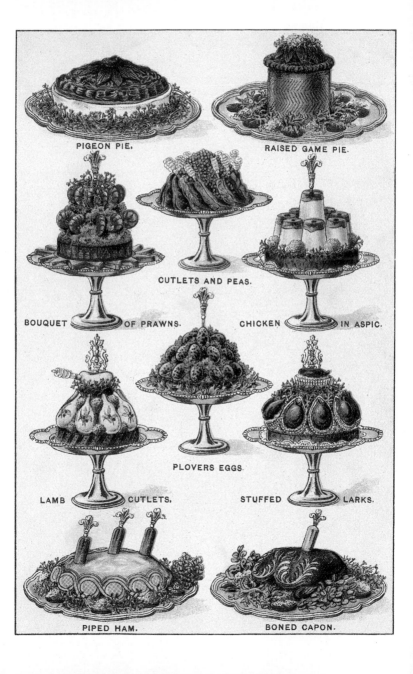

PIGEON PIE.

RAISED GAME PIE.

CUTLETS AND PEAS.

BOUQUET OF PRAWNS.

CHICKEN IN ASPIC.

PLOVERS EGGS.

LAMB CUTLETS.

STUFFED LARKS.

PIPED HAM.

BONED CAPON.

VEGETARIANISM

I⊤ would not be possible in this book to consider and treat of all the arguments in favour or disfavour of a vegetarian diet.

There are some who think it right to abstain from meat from a moral view; others, and a larger number, perhaps, because they consider a vegetarian diet a more healthy one than one in which meat is consumed.

No one will deny that the foods we are apt to eat too much of are those absent from a purely vegetarian fare, such as meat, game, fish, eggs, &c., upon which materials the culinary art seems exercised to tempt us beyond the satisfying of the appetite. It is also a fact that in England we have not made sufficient use of vegetable food, being equally ignorant of its nutritive value and the modes of preparing it in the most attractive manner.

Vegetarianism has worked an improvement in this direction, and its many restaurants in London show the fact how the taste for this diet has been on the increase of late. One very great and undeniable advantage in the teaching of this school, is the showing us how many foods we possess and how few, comparatively speaking, we have used. Also, it proves to us how much cheaper we could live by utilising all the foods at our command except meat, and abstaining from the latter. Even at a restaurant, where something must be put down for the ordinary expenses of an hotel, besides profit on the food itself, we can get a good dinner of three courses for 6d. Surely at home one should be able to have the same for about half the price.

Far be it from us to argue against the use of meat; but where an income is small the butcher's bill forms a heavy item in the expenditure, and might be lessened by an occasional vegetarian dinner.

Amongst the poorer classes in England, the variety of foods in use is lamentably few; and they are not only ignorant of the value of others mostly cheaper than the ones they are accustomed to, but also of any knowledge how they should be cooked, except in the simplest way.

Say in the country amongst labourers. They have potatoes and they boil them, milk and they drink it, with no knowledge how pleasantly they might vary their fare by turning the two, with the small addition of a little vegetables and seasoning, into a new soup. Soup without meat! they would scorn the idea of it; nor could they imagine a savoury pie (one of the nicest of the vegetarian dishes) in which it did not occur.

But to return to ourselves: there are very few houses where a good vegetarian dinner would be served; and those who, from religious scruples, abstain from meat in Lent, or who, at any time, are ordered to do so by medical authority, often have but a course of starvation while their abstinence lasts.

This need not be the case. Vegetable food, looked at from the old-fashioned standpoint, used to mean an addendum to the meat course only; now it may compose a healthy diet which will give us all we need, in its constituents of water, starch, sugar, fat, salts, and flesh-formers, and be a pleasant and varied one as well.

We have used the word vegetarian as applying to those who simply abstain from animal food; and, strictly speaking, it is not right to include under that classification those who consume eggs, cream, butter, and cheese. Still, as it is the common term, we must accept it; and as these animal foods are not open to the same objections as meat, it would be a pity to lose the nourishment they contain. They enter into our recipes, as well as in many of those in good vegetarian cookery books, and therefore all the recipes in this book that do not contain animal food may be esteemed as equally vegetarian ones as the following.

RECIPES FOR VEGETARIAN COOKERY.

SOUPS.

STOCK FOR VEGETABLE SOUPS.

INGREDIENTS.—2 oz. of haricot beans, the same of split peas, 1 carrot, 1 onion, the outside leaves of a stick of celery, a bunch of parsley and herbs, 4 cloves (stuck in the onion), a blade of mace, pepper and salt, water.

Mode.—Boil all the above vegetables and seasoning in 2 quarts of water for 3 to 4 hours, then strain. This will serve for the basis of a great many soups and sauces, just as stock from meat is used. All good cooks know that if there be no gravy at hand when required, the liquor in which any vegetables have been boiled (except potatoes) is better to make it with than water.

Time, 3 to 4 hours. Average cost, for this quantity, 3d.

COUNT RUMFORD'S SOUP.

INGREDIENTS.—¼ lb. of Scotch barley, 3 oz. of split peas, ¾ lb. of potatoes, 2 tablespoonfuls of vinegar, ¼ lb. of bread, sweet herbs, pepper, salt, 2 quarts of water.

Mode.—Boil the barley and peas in the water very slowly for 2 hours; then add the potatoes, peeled and sliced, the vinegar and the seasoning, and simmer for another hour. Put in the bread just before serving.

Time, 3 hours. Average cost, for this quantity, 4d. Sufficient for 6 persons. Seasonable at any time.

GREEN-PEA SOUP.

INGREDIENTS.—1 pint of freshly gathered peas with their shells, a small lettuce, a few sprigs of parsley and mint, ½ pint of milk, a leek, a teaspoonful of sugar, a small piece of soda, salt and pepper, 2 quarts of water.

Mode.—Put the peas, shelled, and

their shells, and the other vegetables and herbs, into the water, which should be boiling, with the soda. In about 20 minutes, when the peas are cooked, take out a few for a garnish, then pour the soup into a pan through a sieve, through which rub the rest of the vegetables, and as far as possible the shells of the peas. Boil the soup again, adding the seasoning and the milk, then put in the whole peas and serve with croûtons of fried bread.

Time, ½ an hour. *Average cost,* 8d. *Sufficient* for 4 persons. *Seasonable* at any time.

HOTCH-POTCH.

INGREDIENTS.—3 *oz. of pearl barley,* 1 *small cabbage,* 2 *carrots,* 2 *onions,* 1 *turnip, parsley and herbs,* 2 *oz. of butter, pepper and salt,* 3 *quarts of water.*

Mode.—Put the barley on the fire in the water. Scrape one of the carrots and put it aside in a little water. Chop all the rest of the vegetables very small, and when the water boils put them in with the butter and seasoning. There should be enough vegetable to make the soup thick. Boil the soup for 2 hours, then put in the scraped carrot and boil another ½ hour.

Time, 2½ hours after the water boils. *Average cost,* 6d. *Sufficient* for 8 persons. *Seasonable* in winter.

POTATO SOUP.

INGREDIENTS.—2 *lbs. of potatoes,* 1 *leek,* 1 *stick of celery,* 1½ *pints of milk,* 2 *oz. of butter,* 2 *oz. of sago or tapioca, salt and pepper,* 2 *quarts of water.*

Mode.—Cut up the vegetables, using only the white part of the leek, and put them in a lined saucepan with the butter. Let them cook for about 10 minutes but not take colour; then add the milk and water, and boil about ¾ of an hour, or till it is soft enough to rub through a fine sieve. Boil it again, adding more milk if necessary, and the sago, which should simmer, till transparent.

Time, 1¼ hours or rather more. *Average cost,* 10d. *Sufficient* for 6 persons. *Seasonable* in winter.

VEGETABLE SOUP (BROWN).

INGREDIENTS.—1 *cabbage,* 1 *turnip,* 2 *onions,* 2 *carrots,* 2 *potatoes, a little parsley, pepper, salt, a tablespoonful of oil,* 2 *quarts of water, a slice of bread.*

Mode.—Fry one of the onions, sliced, in the oil at the bottom of a large saucepan. When it is brown, add the water,

the bread toasted, the vegetables cut up small, and the seasoning. Boil 3 or 4 hours, then mash the soup through a colander, or in the saucepan, with a wooden spoon, and boil another 10 minutes. If too thick, add more water; and boil for 10 minutes; if it is thin, boil fast with the lid off the pan until thick enough. Any vegetables can be used.

Time, 4 hours. *Average cost,* 5d. *Sufficient* for 6 persons. *Seasonable* any time.

WHITE SOUP.

INGREDIENTS.—2 *lbs. weight of any white vegetables of several kinds—say onions, turnips, artichokes, potatoes and celery,* ½ *pint of milk,* 1 *dessertspoonful of cornflour,* 1 *oz. of butter, white pepper and salt,* 3 *pints of water.*

Mode.—Cut the vegetables in small pieces, and boil them in the water with the butter and the seasoning till quite soft. Rub through a colander, put back in the saucepan, and boil with the milk. Mix the cornflour smooth with a little water or milk, add it to the soup, and boil once. Serve with dice of fried bread.

Time, altogether 1 hour. *Average cost,* 6d. *Sufficient* for 4 persons. *Seasonable* at any time.

PORRIDGE.

HOMINY PORRIDGE.

INGREDIENTS. — *Hominy, water, a piece of butter.*

Mode.—Pour boiling water over the hominy at night and let it stand till morning. If it has absorbed too much water add more, and boil for not less than ½ an hour. Stir in the butter just before serving.

Time, ½ an hour.

HOMINY FRITTERS.

INGREDIENTS.—*Any remains of cold hominy porridge, a little flour, fat for frying.*

Mode.—Cut the cold porridge into slices about an inch thick, flour, and fry them in butter or oil.

Time, 5 minutes. *Average cost,* for 3 persons, 3d.

LENTIL PORRIDGE.

INGREDIENTS.—3 *oz. of lentil flour,* ¼ *oz. of butter,* 1 *pint of water, salt.*

Mode.—Put the flour and salt in a

basin with a little cold water, add the rest of the water, boiling, put it on the fire and boil 10 minutes, stirring in the butter just before serving. Half lentil and half barley or wheat flour also makes a nice porridge, resembling closely Revalenta Arabica.

Time, 10 minutes to boil the porridge.

MAIZE MEAL PORRIDGE.

INGREDIENTS.—*Indian meal, water, salt.*

Mode.—Boil a saucepan half full of water, strew in meal with one hand and stir with the other. Thicken according to taste, and boil 5 to 10 minutes. Stir in a piece of butter and serve very hot.

Time, 5 to 10 minutes.

OATMEAL OR WHEATMEAL PORRIDGE.

INGREDIENTS.—*To each pint of water allow about 4 oz. of meal, cold milk, salt or sugar.*

Mode.—Three qualities of meal are sold—fine, medium, and coarse, either can be used, but the coarse needs longer boiling. There are also several different ways of making porridge, but the usual one is that pursued with maize meal, boiling the water with salt, then strewing in the meal with one hand while stirring constantly with the other. When thick enough, and on this point opinions differ, set it by the side of the fire to simmer for half an hour. An easier way to ensure no lumps in the porridge is to pour cold water on the meal in a basin and stir it smooth before boiling; while a third way is to pour boiling water over the meal and let it soak all night, then in the morning boil until of the required thickness. Serve with cold milk, and either salt or sugar according to taste.

Time, ½ an hour to simmer the porridge.

QUAKER OATS PORRIDGE.

INGREDIENTS. — *Quaker oats, water, milk, salt or sugar.*

Mode.—Make as in preceding recipe, using oats instead of meal.

Time, ½ hour to simmer the porridge.

OATMEAL SCONES.

INGREDIENTS. — *Cold oatmeal porridge, flour, butter.*

Mode.—Knead into the cold porridge as much flour as will make a paste that can be rolled out. Roll it about ⅔ of an inch thick, cut it into three-cornered pieces, and bake on a greased griddle or in the oven. Serve hot, split open and buttered.

Time, 15 minutes.

PEA FRITTERS.

INGREDIENTS.—*Cold lentil porridge or pease brose, breadcrumbs, herbs, onions, seasoning, butter or oil for frying.*

Mode.—Mix with what remains of some cold porridge the same quantity of breadcrumbs, add a seasoning of pepper and salt, chopped onion and herbs; shape into flat cakes, flour them, and fry a nice brown.

PEASE BROSE.

INGREDIENTS. — *2 tablespoonfuls of pease meal, rather less than ½ a pint of water, 1 oz. of butter, salt.*

Mode.—Prepare and cook as directed in lentil porridge.

GRAVY AND SAUCES.

BROWN GRAVY.

INGREDIENTS.—*1 onion, ½ a carrot and a turnip, a bunch of herbs, a bayleaf, 1 oz. of butter, 1 dessertspoonful of vinegar, a lump of sugar, spice and seasoning, a dessertspoonful of sauce, 1 pint of water, 1 tablespoonful of flour.*

Mode.—Chop the vegetables and fry them in the butter till they are of a dark brown; add the flour and water and stir till it boils; then put in the herbs, vinegar, sugar, spice, and seasoning. Let it simmer by the side of the fire for an hour. Strain it and add the sauce. If it is not dark enough it can be coloured with burnt sugar or browning. Let the onions be fried with their skins, as they give a nice colour.

Time, 1 hour to simmer   *Average cost*, 4d.

SHARP SAUCE.

INGREDIENTS. — *A wineglassful of salad oil, a tablespoonful of vinegar, 3 mushrooms, a scrap of garlic, 1 tomato, 1 onion, 1 oz. of flour, sweet herbs, pepper, salt, nutmeg, ¾ pint of water.*

Mode.—Put into a saucepan the oil, tomato, onion, the mushrooms and garlic, all finely chopped. After about 10 minutes add the flour, then the water (for which a weak stock makes a good substitute), and stir till the sauce boils.

Put in the vinegar and the herbs, simmer for a few minutes, then strain and serve.

Time, about ½ hour. *Average cost*, 6d.

TOMATO SAUCE.

INGREDIENTS.—1 *lb. of tomatoes*, ½ *oz. of butter*, ½ *oz. of flour*, ½ *pint of water*, *seasoning of pepper and salt.*

Mode.— Put the tomatoes in just enough water to prevent them burning, and cook them in the oven till soft. Pass them through a sieve and warm them again, adding the seasoning. Make melted butter with the flour, water, and butter ; add the tomatoes to it and give one boil. They may be warmed again, after going through the sieve, without the melted butter, and should be served so for chops or anything at all greasy.

WHITE SAUCE FOR PUDDINGS.

INGREDIENTS.—1 *lemon*, 2 *tablespoonfuls of milk*, 1 *teaspoonful of cornflour, the same of white sugar*, ½ *pint of water.*

Mode.—Boil the lemon-rind in the water, mix the cornflour with milk to a smooth paste, and pour the boiling water on. Put it back in the saucepan with the sugar and let it boil ; add the juice of the lemon and serve. This is a very nice sauce for many different kinds of puddings, and it could be flavoured with a little wine if liked.

Time, about 15 minutes. *Average cost*, 2d. *Sufficient* for 1 pudding.

SAVOURY DISHES.

BEAN CROQUETTES.

INGREDIENTS. — *Beans previously boiled*, *breadcrumbs*, *salt*, *pepper*, *onion*, *flour*, *milk*, *oil to fry.*

Mode.—Take some cold boiled haricot beans, mash them, add enough breadcrumbs to make them stiff enough to mould, a little chopped onion and a seasoning of pepper and salt. Form into flat cakes, dip them into milk and flour, and fry in hot oil.

Croquettes of peas or lentils can be made in the same way, and the addition of a little lemon-peel or the substitution of it for the onion is thought, by some people, an improvement.

Time, about 5 minutes to fry the croquettes.

BEANS AND TOMATOES.

INGREDIENTS.—1 *oz. of flour* ½ *oz. of butter, baked or boiled haricot beans*, ½ *pint of the water in which they were cooked*, 2 *tablespoonfuls of tomato sauce.*

Mode.—Strain the water from the beans and thicken it with flour and water, add the tomato sauce and let it boil. Put in the beans, and serve as soon as they are hot.

BEANS (POTTED).

INGREDIENTS.—½ *a pint of haricot beans*, 2 *oz. of grated breadcrumbs*, 2 *oz. of butter*, 2 *oz. of strong cheese*, *grated, cayenne, pepper, salt, and nutmeg to taste.*

Mode.—Bake the beans in a slow oven, pound them smooth in a mortar, adding the other ingredients gradually. Put into pots, and run a little melted butter over them. This makes very good sandwiches between thin slices of buttered bread or toast.

Average cost, for this quantity, 5d.

BREAD CUTLETS.

INGREDIENTS.—*Slices of stale bread*, *milk, egg, seasoning of chopped parsley*, *herbs, lemon-peel, pepper and salt, a few breadcrumbs, oil for frying.*

Mode.—Cut the slices about ¾ of an inch thick, soak them in milk, but not long enough to break, and mix the seasoning together with the crumbs. Beat the egg on a plate, dip each slice in, then in the seasoning, and fry a nice brown in hot oil.

Time, about 3 minutes to fry the slices. *Average cost*, 1d. for a large slice.

CHITCHKEE CURRY.

INGREDIENTS.—*Any cold vegetables, the greater the variety the better, fresh onions, butter, curry-powder, gravy, rice.*

Mode. — Slice the onions and fry them brown in some butter, mix the curry-powder to a paste with a little gravy, and stir in, then the vegetables, chopped fine, and seasoned with pepper and salt. Simmer until thoroughly done, and serve with boiled rice.

CROQUETTES OF HOMINY.

INGREDIENTS.—1 *breakfastcupful of hominy*, 1 *quart of milk*, 1 *oz. of butter*, 2 *eggs, cayenne and salt to taste, breadcrumbs, oil for frying.*

Mode.—Soak the hominy overnight

in water, then boil it in the milk till tender. Let it cool, then add the butter, 1 egg, and the seasoning. When cold, form into balls of·equal size, egg-and-breadcrumb them, and fry in a saucepan of oil. (The oil can be used again.)

Time, 5 minutes to fry the croquettes. *Average cost,* 1s. *Sufficient* for a dish. *Seasonable* at any time.

CARROT PUDDING.

INGREDIENTS.— *Boiled carrots, half their bulk in breadcrumbs, 1 or 2 eggs, according to the quantity of carrots, butter, pepper and salt, white sauce.*

Mode.—Boil some carrots until soft, rub them through a sieve, add the crumbs and butter, with egg enough to bind the mixture, and seasoning to taste. Butter a pudding-basin, put in the pudding, and steam for an hour to an hour and a half, according to size. Serve with a savoury white sauce poured round.

This pudding can be made with other or mixed vegetables.

Time, 1 to 1½ hours. *Average cost,* for a small pudding, 6d. *Sufficient* for 4 persons. *Seasonable* when carrots are good.

BEANS (CURRIED).

INGREDIENTS. — ½ *pint of haricot beans, 1 sour apple, 1 onion, ½ a carrot, a tablespoonful of oil or butter, 1 teaspoonful each of curry-powder and flour, ½ pint of water or vegetable stock, rice.*

Mode.—Bake the beans in a slow oven with water till soft, mince the vegetables and apple, melt the oil and fry them in it for 5 minutes. Mix the flour and curry-powder with a little stock, and put in, and last of all the stock or some of the water the beans have been boiled in. Boil and thicken the sauce, add the beans, make all thoroughly hot, and serve with border of rice, boiled by recipe.

Time, 2 hours. *Average cost,* with rice, 6d. *Sufficient* for 2 or 3 persons. *Seasonable* in winter.

FORCEMEAT FRITTERS (Mrs. Brotherton's Recipe).

INGREDIENTS.—*2 oz. of breadcrumbs, 3 oz. of butter, 4 eggs, ½ pint of cream, 1 oz. of chopped parsley, ½ oz. of leeks, ¼ oz. of sweet marjoram, winter savoury and thyme mixed.*

Mode. — Rub the butter into the

breadcrumbs, add the parsley, leeks and herbs, season with pepper and salt; mix the whole with the eggs, well beaten, add the cream; fry in fritters, together with a hard-boiled egg, cut in slices, and serve with brown sauce poured over the whole, and currant jelly.

Time, 5 to 10 minutes to fry the fritters. *Average cost,* 1s. 4d. *Sufficient* for 4 persons. *Seasonable* at any time.

LENTIL RISSOLES.

INGREDIENTS.—½ *lb. of lentils, either boiled or baked, ½ oz. of butter, pepper and salt, a little parsley.*

Mode.—Cook the lentils until soft enough to mash, and add the butter and seasoning. Roll the pastry out very thin, and cut it in rounds with a cutter. Into each round put a little of the mixture, as much as it will hold to allow of the edges being wetted and pinched together. Egg - and - breadcrumb the rissoles, and fry them in oil. Serve hot with fried parsley.

Time, 5 minutes to fry the rissoles. *Average cost,* 6d.

MACARONI AND ONION FRITTERS.

INGREDIENTS.—¼ *lb. of onions, 2 oz. of macaroni, 6 oz. of breadcrumbs, 2 eggs, seasoning of pepper and salt.*

Mode.—Stew the macaroni in water, and when tender, drain and cut it in pieces; add the onions, boiled and chopped, the breadcrumbs moistened with a little water, and the eggs well beaten; season with pepper or salt, fry in butter or oil, and serve with brown gravy.

Time, 10 minutes to fry the fritters. Average cost, 4d. *Sufficient* for 3 or 4 persons. *Seasonable* at any time

MUSHROOM PUDDING.

INGREDIENTS.—¾ *lb. of flour, 4 oz. of butter, a little baking-powder, 1 pint of mushrooms picked and peeled, pepper and salt.*

Mode.—Make a crust with the flour and 3 oz. of butter, the baking-powder, add sufficient cold water. Line a greased pudding-basin with this, put in the mushrooms with the remainder of the butter and the seasoning, and finish the pudding in the same way as a meat one. Boil 1½ hours.

Time, 1½ hours to boil the pudding. *Average cost,* 1s. 3d. *Sufficient* for 4 persons. *Seasonable* in autumn.

POLENTA AND CHEESE.

INGREDIENTS.—*Cold maize meal porridge, butter, grated cheese, cayenne, salt.*

Mode. — Cut the cold polenta into squares about ½ an inch thick. Arrange a layer in a buttered baking dish or tin, cover this with grated cheese and the seasoning, then another layer of the polenta and another of cheese. Let the cheese be on the top, and on this put a few pieces of butter. Bake till brown in a quick oven and serve hot.

Time, 15 minutes to bake.

POTATO PIE.

INGREDIENTS.—*2 lbs. of potatoes, an onion, ½ stick of celery, 1 oz. of butter, 1 oz. of sago, water or milk, paste to cover the pie, seasoning.*

Mode.—Slice the potatoes and celery, fry the onion in half the butter, and fill a pie-dish with them, strewing in the sago and seasoning. Fill up with water or milk, and put on a cover of plain paste made with butter or oil. Bake in a good oven for an hour or a little more.

Time, 1 hour. *Average cost*, 10d. *Sufficient* for 4 or 5 persons. *Seasonable* at any time.

POTATO ROLLS.

INGREDIENTS. — *Potatoes, turnips, celery, onion, parsley, sweet herbs, seasoning, butter, pastry.* .

Mode.—Cut the potatoes up small, and to each pound allow a small turnip, ½ a stick of celery, a small onion, all chopped with parsley, herbs and seasoning to taste, ½ oz. of butter. Roll out the paste rather thin, and cut it in squares. On each put as much of the mixture as it will hold, then wet the edges, and fold up like a sausage roll, and bake for about ¾ of an hour.

Time, ¾ of an hour. *Average cost*, with 1 lb. of potatoes, 7d. *Sufficient* for 4 persons. *Seasonable* at any time.

POTATO SANDERS.

INGREDIENTS.—*Boiled potatoes, flour, breadcrumbs, soaked in a little water, chopped parsley and herbs, ½ an onion, soaked in boiling water, seasoning.*

Mode.—Boil the potatoes, and while hot work into them by mashing as much flower as will make a stiff paste. Roll this out and cut in squares. Squeeze the bread dry, and make a forcemeat with it and the other ingredients. Put a little into each square of potato paste and roll like a sausage roll. Bake in a good oven for 20 minutes.

Time, 20 minutes to bake the sanders. *Average cost*, for a small dish, 4d. *Seasonable* at any time.

POTATOES AND CHEESE.

INGREDIENTS.—*1 lb. of boiled potatoes, 3 oz. of grated cheese, 2 tablespoonfuls of milk, 1 oz. of butter, breadcrumbs, pepper and salt.*

Mode.—Mash the potatoes while hot, adding the milk, the cheese, and the seasoning, and half the butter. Butter a pie-dish with the remainder, strew it thickly with breadcrumbs, fill up with potato and cheese, and bake for half an hour in a good oven; turn it out and serve hot.

Time, ½ an hour. *Average cost*, 5d. *Sufficient* for 3 or 4 persons. *Seasonable* at any time.

SAVOURY RICE.

INGREDIENTS.—*½ lb. of rice, 1 onion, 3 tablespoonfuls of grated cheese, the same of tomato sauce, a tablespoonful of chopped parsley and herbs, 1 oz. of butter, cayenne and salt.*

Mode.—Boil the rice in water, and when tender and nearly dry, stir to it the other ingredients. Mix well together, and make a mound of it in a dish.

Time, ½ an hour. *Average cost*, 7d. *Sufficient* for 4 persons. *Seasonable* at any time

SPINACH PUDDING.

INGREDIENTS.—*2 lbs. of spinach, 6 oz. of veal forcemeat, 2 oz. of butter, ½ pint of Béchamel, ¼ pint of stock, a few potatoes, turnips, and carrots, 3 eggs, salt and pepper*

Mode.—Pick, clean, and wash the spinach; then chop, boil, drain, and cool it. Put it in a saucepan with the butter, sauce, and stock, and simmer for 5 minutes. When cool add the forcemeat, the yolks of the eggs, and the seasoning. Put in a mould and cook in a bain-marie. Turn out on to a dish and garnish with the cooked vegetables, cut into fanciful shapes. Serve with Spanish sauce.

Time, altogether about ¾ hour. *Average cost*, 1s. 9d. *Sufficient* for 7 or 8 persons. *Seasonable* in winter and spring.

SUCCOTASH.

INGREDIENTS.—*Lima or string beans, green corn, milk, butter, pepper and salt.*

Mode.—Shell the beans, or if string ones are used, string and cut them in small pieces. Cut the corn from the cob and let there be about a third more corn than beans. Put the beans in a saucepan of boiling water and boil 20 minutes, then drain and mix with the corn. Put them into the saucepan with enough boiling water to cover them, and a little salt, and after stewing them ½ an hour, stirring often, pour off most of the water and substitute milk. Add butter, salt, and pepper to taste, and let the whole stew 10 minutes longer. Serve very hot.

Time, 1 hour. *Seasonable* from July to October.

TOMATOES (SCALLOPED).

INGREDIENTS. — *Tomatoes, breadcrumbs, butter, a very little sugar, pepper and salt.*

Mode.—Peel and slice the tomatoes, and put them in a buttered pudding-dish in alternate layers, with a force-meat made of the other ingredients. Fill the dish, and let a layer of tomatoes come at the top, on each slice of which put a tiny piece of butter; scatter over a few breadcrumbs and bake covered with a tin, for ½ an hour, then take off the plate and brown the top with a salamander or before the fire. Finely chopped pork, green corn, and onion may be substituted for the forcemeat.

Time, ½ an hour to bake. *Seasonable* from June to October.

VEGETABLE GOOSE.

INGREDIENTS.—½ *lb. of bread, a teaspoonful of chopped parsley and sage, 1 onion, pepper and salt, 1 oz. of butter.*

Mode.—Soak the bread in water, boil the onion and chop it fine, squeeze the bread nearly dry, mash it, and mix with the other ingredients. Butter a Yorkshire-pudding dish, put the mixture in, and bake for 1 hour; serve hot.

Time, 1 hour. *Average cost*, 2½d. *Sufficient* for 2 or 3 persons. *Seasonable* at any time.

VEGETABLE PIE.

INGREDIENTS.—*A small teacupful of green peas, an onion, a carrot, a turnip, a small stick of celery, ½ oz. of tapioca, 1 oz. of butter, a teaspoonful of flour, pepper and salt, paste to cover the pie.*

Mode.—Stew all the ingredients together in a very little water until nearly cooked. Cut the vegetables into small pieces and fill a pie-dish with them. Cover this with a crust, as a meat pie, and bake until the crust is done. Any other vegetables may be used for this pie, and a few mushrooms are a great improvement to its flavour.

Time, ¾ of an hour to bake the pie. *Average cost*, 10d. *Sufficient* for 4 persons. *Seasonable* at any time.

SWEET DISHES.

GINGERBREAD PUDDING.

INGREDIENTS.—½ *lb. of flour, the same of treacle, 2 oz. of butter, a teaspoonful of baking-powder, ½ a teaspoonful of powdered ginger, 1 egg, a little salt.*

Mode.—Mix the ginger, salt, and baking-powder with the flour, rub in the butter, then mix with the treacle and the egg, well beaten. Flour a pudding cloth, put in the mixture, tie up, and boil for 1½ hours.

Time, 1½ hours to boil the pudding. *Average cost*, 6d. *Sufficient* for 3 or 4 persons. *Seasonable* at any time.

PASTRY WITHOUT BUTTER.

INGREDIENTS.—1 *lb. of flour, a teaspoonful of baking-powder, a wineglassful of salad oil, water, salt.*

Mode.—Mix the baking-powder and salt with the flour, add the oil, the water, and stir the paste to a consistency for rolling. Roll out two or three times and bake without delay.

Average cost, for this quantity, 3½d.

PLUM PUDDING (Mrs. Brotherton's Recipe).

INGREDIENTS.—1 *lb. of flour, ½ lb. of currants, ½ lb. of sultanas, ¼ lb. of sugar, 4 oz. of butter, 3 eggs, the grated rind of a lemon, a teaspoonful of baking-powder, salt.*

Mode.—Mix the powder and salt with the flour, rub in the butter, and add the currants, sultanas, and sugar, the lemon-peel finely grated, a little nutmeg, and the eggs, well beaten. Put the pudding in a buttered basin, boil or steam for 4 hours, and serve with sweet sauce.

Time, 4 hours. *Average cost*, 1s. 4d.
Sufficient for 5 or 6 persons. *Seasonable* in winter.

MINCEMEAT (Mrs. Brotherton's Recipe).

INGREDIENTS.—6 *lemons*, ½ *lb. of apples*, 1 *lb. of raisins, weighed after being stoned*, 1 *lb. of currants*, 1 *lb. of sugar*, ½ *lb. of fresh butter*, 4 *ozs. each of candied orange and citron.*

Mode.—Grate the yellow rind, cut the lemons in two, and squeeze out the juice. Boil the rinds in spring water till tender, but not soft, changing the water 4 or 5 times to take out the bitterness, and putting a large tablespoonful of salt into the water in which they are boiled. When done, drain the water from them, and take out the seeds and skins, then chop them with the raisins, in a wooden bowl. When finely chopped, add the currants, sugar, the apples, previously prepared as for sauce, the grated rind of the lemons, the juice, ½ a tablespoonful of cayenne pepper, a small teaspoonful of mace, another of powdered cinnamon, 15 drops of almond flavour, the candied orange and citron, cut in thin slices, and lastly the butter, melted, and poured in.

This mincemeat may have brandy or other spirit added to it the same as ordinary mincemeat, and it keeps it fresh longer; but, as teetotalism and vegetarianism so often go hand in hand, we have not put it amongst the ingredients.

The pastry recipe may be used for the mince pies or ordinary puff-paste.

Average cost, for this quantity, 3s. *Seasonable* at Christmas.

POTATO PUDDING.

INGREDIENTS.—½ *lb. of mashed potatoes*, 2 *oz. of butter*, 2 *eggs*, ½ *pint of milk*, ¼ *saltspoonful of salt*, 2 *oz. of sugar, the juice and rind of a small lemon, a few pounded sweet almonds.*

Mode.—Boil sufficient potatoes to make half a pound when mashed, and mash them thoroughly with a fork, add the butter, eggs, milk, lemon-juice, sugar and the almonds pounded ; mince the lemon-peel very finely and beat all the ingredients well together ; put the pudding into a buttered pie-dish and bake for rather more than ½ an hour. This pudding may be enriched by adding one more egg and another ounce of butter.

Time, ½ an hour to bake the pudding. *Average cost*, 8d. *Sufficient* for 5 or 6 persons. *Seasonable* at any time.

PRESERVED AND TINNED PROVISIONS

Such large quantities of preserved and tinned provisions are now imported into this country, that it is necessary to find space in this book to give a little advice for their proper treatment.

People differ as to the value of tinned meats, some considering that there is as much nourishment in them as in fresh meat; others, and particularly the hard-working poor, complain that they are not half so satisfying, and would rather have a few pieces of inferior fresh meat than a tin of American or Australian.

Whatever may be thought on the question of nourishment, however, there can scarcely be any doubt that the tinned meats are of the best quality, and it is a thing to be wondered at that the prejudice of many should be so against them, specially, as we have said, existing amongst the poorer class, to whom they might be considered a boon. Perhaps if there were a better general knowledge how to prepare them for eating, they would be more appreciated.

The cooking of tinned meats should be no more than just heating them through, so that when vegetables are used with them they must first be cooked.

It should be remembered that the meat has already been rather over than under-cooked. The mode of its preparation necessitates this. The tins containing the meat are placed in a bath of boiling chloride of zinc, the boiling point of which is considerably above that of water. Thus the contents of the tins are heated to the highest point, and a jet of steam or air pours from the one small hole in each. As soon as the air is exhausted and only steam remains, a drop of solder closes the tin, which in cooling

collapses. If any air remains fermentation takes place, and this may be known by the bulging of the sides of the tin

The best of all tinned provisions are undoubtedly the soups, which we have no hesitation in saying are, as a rule, far nicer than an *ordinary* plain cook would prepare.

In large establishments or families, where there is a good deal of meat cooked and a stock-pot is kept going, tinned soups should not be needed; but in small households they are invaluable in cases of emergency. They make a capital addition to pot liquor, and a single tin of good meat soup, such as mock turtle or ox-tail, added to the liquor in which a joint has been boiled, will give several quarts of cheap and good family soup. If served without the addition of any stock, a little sherry will be found an improvement, particularly to the clear soups.

Tinned fish cannot be said to be as good—or rather we should say as pleasant in flavour—as fresh, but it is very useful for sauces, mayonnaises, &c., and answers well for little dishes where a good sauce can be introduced. Amongst the best are the oysters, which most people employ for sauce now, and which scalloped are quite a dainty dish.

The best tinned salmon, freed from the moisture adhering to it, and also lobster, come in well for a mayonnaise, with a good sauce and some crisp salad; while prawns, which are always costly when bought fresh, are excellent curried.

Since the tinned provisions, have come the frozen ones. A great deal of what we should call fresh meat is frozen perfectly hard directly it is killed, and, in that state, put on board ships fitted with refrigerating chambers, where the air is kept always several degrees below freezing point. Meat and poultry travel perfectly fresh in this way, but should be cooked very soon after thawing, as they soon go bad in an ordinary temperature.

It may be interesting to some of our readers to see the menu of a dinner prepared from tinned and preserved provisions, which was decided to be a success by those who partook of it. Bread and milk may be called the only fresh provision used, for eggs (those for the sauce) and potatoes, were both stored ones.

The pastry was made from the tinned marrow, sold for the purpose; the raspberries were bottled ones, the custard was made from what is generally called egg-powder, and the compôte of fruit consisted of tinned pine, apricots, and peaches, flavoured with wine, liqueur, and sugar.

Recipes will be found below for the dishes in this menu of eight courses, and it may be said that such a dinner would cost about one third of what would have to be paid for the same in which all fresh provisions were employed. Our readers will not probably care to try the entire meal as it stands, but it may give suggestions for one or two courses that could be introduced in an ordinary dinner.

MENU.

Caviare croûtons.
Mock-turtle soup.
Salmon cutlets.   Tartare sauce.
Curried prawns.   Salmi of game.
Beef à la mode.   Green peas.   Mashed potatoes.
Raspberry tart.   Custard.   Orange jelly.
Macaroni cheese.
Compôte of fruit.

COOKING TINNED AND PRESERVED PROVISIONS.

PRAWNS (CURRIED).

INGREDIENTS.—1 *small tin or half a large one of prawns, ½ lb. of rice, 1 onion, 1 apple or a stick of rhubarb or a few gooseberries, according to the season, ½ a lemon, a dessertspoonful of curry-powder, a teaspoonful of flour, ½ pint of water, or stock if at hand, 1 oz. of butter, or the same of the fat from tinned meat.*

Mode.—Chop the onions and apple, and fry in the butter or fat. Mix the curry-powder and flour with the stock or water, put all into a saucepan and stir till it boils. Let it boil 10 minutes, then put in the prawns and heat them through. Just before sending them to table add the grated rind and the juice of the lemon.

The rice should be boiled by the following recipe, and may be served as a border to the curry, or, as generally preferred, in a separate dish.

Time, ½ hour.   *Average cost,* 1s.
Sufficient for 4 persons.   *Seasonable* at any time.

Note.—A tin of lobster or salmon may be curried in the same way.

RICE FOR CURRY.

INGREDIENTS.—*Rice, water, salt.*

Mode.—Wash the rice in several waters, then leave it in cold water to soak for ½ an hour. Strain off the water and put it in a saucepan with enough water to cover it, 2 inches above the rice, add a little salt and boil over a brisk fire. When the rice is tender take the pan off the fire, and while the rice is still boiling throw in a cupful of cold water, shake the pan, then strain the rice and let it stand back from the fire with a cloth over it for a little time before serving.

It is most important in serving a curry to have the rice well boiled. The grains should be separated and quite dry, although perfectly tender.

LOBSTER SALAD.

INGREDIENTS.—1 *tin of lobster*, 1 *large or* 2 *small lettuces, a handful of small salad, a small piece of beetroot, salad dressing.*

Mode.—Take the lobster out of the tin, drain it from all moisture and divide into neat pieces. Wash, thoroughly dry, and cut up the lettuce and small salad. Make a dressing by following recipe, mix half with the salad, pile the lobster in the centre of a dish and put the remains of the dressing over it ; put round it the salad and garnish with the beetroot in slices, or stamped with a cutter, and the white of egg left from the dressing.

Average cost, 1s. 3d., including the dressing. *Sufficient* for 6 persons. *Seasonable* at any time.

SALAD DRESSING.

INGREDIENTS.—2 *eggs,* 1 *small teaspoonful of raw mustard,* ½ *a teaspoonful of salt,* 3 *tablespoonfuls of salad oil,* 1½ *of vinegar.*

Mode.—Boil the eggs hard, and when cold rub the yolks smooth in a mortar with the mustard and salt, add slowly the oil, stirring all the while, then the vinegar, drop by drop, and stir to a cream.

LOBSTER (SCALLOPED).

INGREDIENTS.—1 *tin of lobster,* ¼ *lb. of breadcrumbs,* 1 *oz. of butter,* 1 *teaspoonful lemon-juice, cayenne, salt.*

Mode.—Butter a shallow tin, and strew over it a layer of breadcrumbs. Take out the lobster, drain away the moisture, mince it, season well with cayenne and salt and the lemon-juice ; spread over the breadcrumbs, and cover with the remainder, putting what is left of the butter in small pieces over the top. Bake in a quick oven 10 minutes, in a slow one 15, and, if necessary, brown with a salamander or before the fire before sending to table.

Time, 10 to 15 minutes. *Average cost,* 1s. *Sufficient* for 4 persons. *Seasonable* at any time.

OYSTERS (SCALLOPED).

INGREDIENTS.—1 *tin of oysters,* 1½ *oz. of butter, breadcrumbs, salt, cayenne or pepper.*

Mode.—Butter some small tins or saucers (4 or 5), line them with breadcrumbs, over which shake a little salt, divide the oysters and lay an equal quantity in each tin, season them with the cayenne, and put over each about 2 teaspoonfuls of the liquor ; cover thickly with breadcrumbs, and put small pieces of butter over the top. Bake for about 10 minutes, or cook in a Dutch oven before the fire. It is essential that they should look a nice bright brown. Serve on a napkin, with a cut lemon.

Time, 10 minutes to bake. *Average cost,* 10d. *Sufficient* for 4 persons. *Seasonable* at any time.

SALMON CUTLETS.

INGREDIENTS.—½ *tin of salmon,* 1 *egg, breadcrumbs, butter for frying, chopped parsley, seasoning of pepper or cayenne and salt.*

Mode.—Free the salmon from skin and bone, and, after mincing, pound it smooth in a mortar with seasoning of pepper or cayenne and salt. Beat the egg, form the salmon into small cutlets, dip in the egg, then in the crumbs, and fry a bright, golden brown in the butter. Place the cutlets on a piece of blotting paper before the fire, if at all greasy in appearance, and send to table on a white paper or napkin, garnish with cut lemon and parsley, with an accompaniment of tartar sauce.

Time, 5 minutes to fry the cutlets. *Average cost,* 8d. (exclusive of the sauce). *Sufficient* for 3 or 4 persons. *Seasonable* at any time.

TARTAR SAUCE.

INGREDIENTS.—*Yolks of* 4 *eggs,* 1 *teaspoonful of mustard,* ½ *teaspoonful of salt, olive oil, equal parts of tarragon and ordinary vinegar, pepper, cayenne,* 2 *shallots or* 2 *teaspoonfuls of chopped pickled onions and gherkins.*

Mode.—Break the yolks into a basin with the salt and mustard, then stir in a tablespoonful of oil, then one of the mixed vinegars alternately, stirring well until the sauce is of the right consistency. The mixing must be done very gradually, lastly add the chopped shallot or pickles.

Average cost, for this quantity, 6d. *Seasonable* at any time.

SALMON MAYONNAISE.

INGREDIENTS.—1 *tin of salmon,* 2 *lettuces, a little small salad, mayonnaise sauce,* 4 *anchovies,* 2 *eggs.*

Mode.—Free the salmon from skin and bone, drain it from moisture, and pile it in the centre of a dish. Put round it the salad when well washed and shredded, and pour over a sauce made by recipe given. Garnish with the anchovies, filleted, and slices of hard-boiled egg.

Average cost, 1s. 10d. *Sufficient* for 6 persons. *Seasonable* at any time.

BEEF À LA MODE.

INGREDIENTS.—*A* 2-*lb. tin of meat,* 4 *dessertspoonfuls of ground rice,* 1½ *pints of stock,* 2 *bay-leaves,* 6 *peppercorns,* 1 *onion,* 4 *cloves,* 2 *tablespoonfuls of mushroom ketchup, pepper, salt.*

Mode.—Take the dripping or fat from the meat and mix it to a smooth paste with the rice; add the seasoning and stock and let it boil, then simmer from 15 to 20 minutes. Skim it, then return it to the pan, and add a little browning. Cut the meat into even pieces (any very small scraps may be saved for rissoles), and warm it in the sauce. Serve very hot.

Time, 20 minutes. *Average cost,* 1s. 6d. *Sufficient* for 6 persons. *Seasonable* at any time.

BEEF COLLOPS.

INGREDIENTS.—1 *lb. of tinned beef,* 4 *oz. of butter or dripping,* 1 *onion,* ¼ *pint of stock,* 1 *lemon,* 1 *teaspoonful of mushroom ketchup or any other sauce, pepper, salt, mashed potatoes.*

Mode.—Mince the beef very fine, put the butter or dripping into a stewpan, with the onion chopped fine, till nicely browned. Add the lemon, stock, sauce and seasoning, and simmer 5 minutes, then add the meat and simmer for another 5 minutes. Make a border or wall of mashed potatoes, and pour the collops in the centre. If there is much fat on the meat, it will serve instead of the butter or dripping.

Time, 15 minutes. *Average cost* 1s. *Sufficient* for 3 or 4 persons. *Seasonable* at any time.

BEEF PIE.

INGREDIENTS.—1 *tin of roast meat,* ¼ *pint of stock,* 3 *lbs. of potatoes, a dessertspoonful of Worcester sauce or ketchup, pepper, salt, flour,* 1 *oz. of butter.*

Mode.—Cold potatoes will serve for this dish, but if none be at hand, fresh ones must be boiled. Mash them with the butter, or any fat that can be taken from the meat, and pepper and salt. Cut the meat into small pieces, lay them in a deep pie-dish dredging them with flour, put in the stock and seasoning, cover with the potatoes and bake for half an hour in a good oven.

Time, half an hour. *Average cost,* 1s. 6d. *Sufficient* for 4 or 5 persons. *Seasonable* at any time.

COLD MEAT.

INGREDIENTS.—1 *tin of meat, parsley, beetroot.*

Mode.—Tinned meat cold serves for a breakfast or luncheon dish; but the tin must be carefully opened and the meat neatly turned out, or the appearance of the dish will be spoiled. Having turned out the meat in as compact a form as possible, with some flat instrument—a paper-knife does very well—clear away all the fat or dripping that adheres to the meat, and garnish prettily with the parsley and the beetroot, cut in very thin slices or stamped out with a cutter. Serve with pickles or salad, and some nicely fried or mashed potatoes.

Another way of serving the meat without cooking it is to divide it in neat pieces, to arrange them in a circle on a dish, and to fill up the centre with salad, over which a good mayonnaise sauce should be poured. Garnish the meat with small piles of lettuce, hard-boiled egg, and slices of beef.

Average cost, 1s. 2d. for 2-lb. tin. *Seasonable* at any time.

BEEF (CURRIED).

INGREDIENTS.—*A* 2-*lb. tin of Australian beef,* 3 *oz. of butter or the dripping (if sufficient) from the meat,* 1 *onion,* 1 *apple or a stick of rhubarb,* ½ *pint of stock or any weak broth,* 1 *dessertspoonful of curry-powder, the same of flour.*

Mode.—Slice the onion and fry it in the fat or butter in a stewpan till a bright brown; add the stock, the sour apple or rhubarb, minced fine, and work in gradually and smoothly the curry-powder and flour. Keep the mixture stirred well over the fire for a few minutes, then pass it through a sieve; cut the meat into neat square pieces, dredge them with flour, and simmer them for five minutes keeping them well covered with the gravy. Serve with boiled rice.

Time, ¼ hour; 20 minutes to boil the rice. *Average cost*, 1s. 6d. *Sufficient* for 5 or 6 persons. *Seasonable* at any time.

BEEF (HARICOT).

INGREDIENTS. — 1 *pint of haricot beans*, 1 *lb. of tinned beef*, 1½ *oz. of butter*, 2 *onions*, ½ *pint of stock*, 1 *carrot*, 1 *turnip*, 1 *glass of port or sherry*, 1 *tablespoonful of Worcester sauce*, *pepper*, *salt*, *flour*, 1 *tablespoonful of ground rice*.

Mode. — Having soaked the beans over-night, drain them and put them in a saucepan with 2 quarts of water, and boil 2 hours, or more if necessary, for they must be thoroughly tender. Drain off the water, and leaving the lid of the pan slightly raised, put them to dry by the fire ; then add ½ an oz. of butter and a seasoning of pepper and salt.

In another saucepan prepare a sauce as follows :—Put an ounce of butter in the pan, and after slicing the onions fry them a nice brown ; cut up the carrot and turnip, add them and also the stock in which the ground rice has been smoothly mixed, the wine and the sauce, and simmer for half an hour.

Take the beef from the tin, cut it in pieces, dredge them in flour and simmer them in the sauce for five minutes. Make a border of the beans and put the meat and sauce in the centre.

Time, 2 hours altogether. *Average cost*, 1s. 4d. *Sufficient* for 4 persons. *Seasonable* at any time.

IRISH STEW.

INGREDIENTS.—*A* 2-*lb. tin of Australian mutton*, 4 *onions*, 3 *lbs. of potatoes*, 1½ *pints of stock or water*, *seasoning of pepper and salt*.

Mode. — Peel and slice the onions, and put them in the stock to stew till tender, adding the potatoes, peeled, and cut in half if large, and a plentiful seasoning of pepper and salt. When the potatoes are done, add the mutton cut into neat pieces, and simmer for 5 minutes. Serve in a deep dish.

Time, 1 hour altogether. *Average cost*, 1s. 8d. *Sufficient* for 6 persons. *Seasonable* at any time.

MEAT AND EGG TOAST.

INGREDIENTS. — 6 *slices of bread*, 2 *eggs*, 2 *tablespoonfuls of milk*, 2 *oz. of butter*, 1 *tablespoonful of tomato sauce*, *salt*, *pepper*, ½ *tin of meat*.

Mode. — Cut some rounds of bread and fry them in half the butter. Mince the meat finely and set aside. Put in a saucepan the remainder of the butter, the eggs, milk and seasoning ; stir over the fire, and when the eggs begin to thicken, add the meat and the sauce. Stir again over the fire till the mixture is as thick as cream, then pour it over the toast and serve very hot.

Time, 10 minutes. *Average cost*, 9d. *Sufficient* for 3 persons. *Seasonable* at any time.

MEAT AND MACARONI.

INGREDIENTS.—*A* 2-*lb. tin of meat*, ½ *lb. of macaroni*, ½ *pint of stock*, *a pinch of powdered cinnamon*, *seasoning of pepper and salt*.

Mode.—Put the macaroni into sufficient boiling water to cover it, and let it stew till tender, chop and mince the meat finely, add the seasoning and put it in the stewpan with the stock and let it get hot. Serve on a round of toast, with the macaroni as a border.

Time, 1½ hours. *Average cost*, 1s. *Sufficient* for 6 persons. *Seasonable* at any time

MEAT AND MACARONI PUDDING.

INGREDIENTS.—*Tinned meat*, *macaroni*, *a slice of bacon or ham*, *or a couple of pork sausages*.

Mode.—Put some macaroni into a saucepan in cold water, let it come to the boil, then strain off the water. Butter a basin and line it with the macaroni. Chop some meat fine with the bacon, season it, add a little bread soaked in stock ; mix all well together, fill the basin, pressing it down and covering it with buttered paper. Steam for 1½ hours, and serve with a good brown gravy poured round.

Time, 1½ hours. *Average cost*, 10d. *Sufficient* for 4 persons. *Seasonable* at any time

MEAT AND POTATO PIE.

INGREDIENTS.—2 *lbs. of tinned mutton*, 2 *lbs. of potatoes*, 1 *oz. of butter*, ½ *pint of gravy*, 4 *onions*, *pepper and salt*.

Mode.—Boil and mash the potatoes, and line a buttered pie-dish with them. Boil and slice the onions. Put a layer of slices of meat in the dish, then one of onions, seasoning both ; next a layer of potatoes. Repeat this and make the two layers of each fill the dish. Put some small pieces of butter on the top of the potatoes and bake for half an hour.

Time, ½ an hour. *Average cost*, 1s. 8d. *Sufficient* for 6 persons. *Seasonable* at any time.

MEAT CROQUETTES.

INGREDIENTS.—1 *lb. of meat, a few cold potatoes, ¼ lb. of dripping, 1 egg, some lard for frying, a little parsley, salt and pepper, breadcrumbs.*

Mode.—Chop the meat fine, then mix it thoroughly with the potatoes, mashed, the dripping and the seasoning. Form the mixture into small rolls, dip them in beaten egg, then in the crumbs, and fry them a nice brown in the boiling lard. Fry the parsley also, and use it, for a garnish. They may be served with or without gravy.

Time, 10 minutes to fry the rissoles. *Average cost*, 1s. *Sufficient* for 4 persons. *Seasonable* at any time.

MEAT SANDERS.

INGREDIENTS.—*Cold boiled potatoes, some tinned meat of any kind, or any cold meat, 2 oz. of butter, white of 1 egg, pepper, salt, flour.*

Mode.—Mash the potatoes thoroughly, adding salt with butter and flour, enough to make a paste that will roll out. Roll it out evenly and cut it into squares, about the same size as the paste for sausage rolls. Into each of them put some chopped and seasoned meat, fold over and glaze with the white of egg and bake in a quick oven till nicely browned. Serve hot.

Time, ¼ of an hour. *Average cost*, 8d. *Sufficient* for 4 persons. *Seasonable* at any time.

CORNED BEEF (MOULDED).

INGREDIENTS.—½ *tin of corned beef, ¼ lb. of suet (Atora), spice, herbs, lemon-peel, pepper and salt.*

Mode.—Mince the meat and suet fine, add the seasoning, and press it into a plain buttered mould; cover this with buttered paper and steam for 1 hour. Serve hot with a good brown gravy.

Time, 1 hour. *Average cost*, 10d. *Sufficient* for 3 persons. *Seasonable* at any time.

MUTTON AND CAPER SAUCE.

INGREDIENTS.—*A 2-lb. tin of boiled mutton, caper sauce.*

Mode.—Take off the top of the tin and put it in a saucepan of boiling water that comes to within two inches of the top of the tin. Heat the meat thoroughly, then turn it out into a dish and serve with caper sauce made by recipe given.

Time, ½ an hour. *Average cost*, 1s. 8d. *Sufficient* for 6 persons. *Seasonable* at any time.

POTATO AND MUTTON PIE.

INGREDIENTS.—*A tin of roast mutton, 2 lbs. of potatoes, 2 oz. of butter, 2 onions, a little sauce, milk, breadcrumbs, pepper and salt.*

Mode.—Turn out the mutton and remove the fat. Boil the potatoes and mash them with butter, milk, and seasoning; slice the onions and fry them in the fat from the mutton. Butter a deep pie-dish and line it with potatoes; then put in the mutton cut in slices, mixed with the onions and well seasoned and cover with a thick layer of potatoes. Put the breadcrumbs over the top, and over these again small pieces of butter, and bake in a quick oven.

Time, to bake the pie, 20 minutes. *Average cost*, 1s. 6d. *Sufficient* for 6 persons. *Seasonable* at any time.

BEEF, ROASTED (TINNED), AND GREEN PEAS.

INGREDIENTS.—*A 6-lb. tin of beef, 2 tins of peas, butter.*

Mode.—Take the meat out of the tin and remove all fat; jelly, and gravy from it, putting them into the dripping pan. Tie the meat up with wide, strong tape, and hang it before a bright, but not too fierce, roasting fire, basting continually with the fat in the pan, in which, after pouring off the fat, make a gravy, adding a little extract of meat and a thickening of flour. Warm the peas in a stewpan with some butter, and serve in a separate dish.

Time, 1 hour. *Average cost*, 4s. 6d. *Sufficient* for 10 persons. *Seasonable* at any time.

CHICKEN CROQUETTES.

INGREDIENTS.—½ *a tin of chicken, 2 slices of lean ham or tongue, ¼ tin of mushrooms, 1 oz. of cornflour, yolks of 2 eggs, 1½ oz. of butter, a little white sauce, cayenne, salt and pounded mace for seasoning, egg, breadcrumbs, and lard for frying.*

Mode.—Free the chicken from skin

and bone and mince it finely with the mushrooms and the ham. Put the butter in a saucepan, let it melt, then dredge in the flour, boil, put in the meat, seasoning, and sauce, then stir in the yolks of two eggs, well beaten. Put the mixture aside to cool, and when cold form into balls, brush them over with egg, then dip them in crumbs and fry a nice brown. Serve with white sauce.

Time, 10 minutes to fry the croquettes. *Average cost*, 2s. *Sufficient* for a good-sized dish. *Seasonable* at any time.

CURRIED RABBIT.

INGREDIENTS.—1 *tin of rabbit*, 2 *oz. of butter*, 3 *onions*, 1 *pint of stock*, 1 *sour apple*, *a tablespoonful each of curry-powder and flour, the juice of* ½ *a lemon.*

Mode.—Slice and fry the onions and apple in the butter, boil the stock and pour it boiling into the stewpan, mix the flour and curry-powder with a little of the stock and simmer for ½ an hour, add the rabbit, cut up, and warm thoroughly, then squeeze in the lemon and serve with a dish of rice, boiled as in recipe given.

Time, 35 minutes. *Average cost*, 2s. 6d. *Sufficient* for 6 persons. *Seasonable* in winter.

SALMI OF GAME.

INGREDIENTS.—1 *tin of game of any kind*, 1 *onion stuck with cloves, a few whole peppers, a strip of lemon-peel, salt, a thickening of butter and flour*, 1 *glass of port*, 1 *tablespoonful of lemon-juice*, 1 *of ketchup or sauce*, 1 *pint of stock.*

Mode.—Set aside the best parts of the game, put the smaller pieces and trimmings into a stewpan with the stock, onion, peel, pepper and salt, and simmer; stew for ¾ of an hour, then strain the gravy, thicken it with butter and flour, add the ketchup, lemon-juice, and wine, then put in the pieces of game and let them warm through. If the gravy is not brown enough, a little browning should be added.

Time, 40 minutes. *Average cost*, 2s. 9d. *Sufficient* for an *entrée. Seasonable* in autumn and winter.

FRUIT TARTS.

INGREDIENTS.—*Any kind of bottled fruit*, 1 *lb. of flour*, ¼ *lb. tinned marrow, sugar, water.*

Mode.—Fill the dish with the fruit and add sugar in proportion, put the flour in a basin and rub in the marrow with a teaspoonful of powdered white sugar (a little baking-powder may be added if liked); wet up with enough water to make a stiff paste, roll out and cover the tart in the usual way, and bake in a gentle oven. With some fruits (gooseberries, for example) there is too much juice, and a little should be left out or it will boil over and spoil the appearance of the tart.

Time, ½ an hour to bake the tart. *Average cost*, 1s. 3d. for a small tart. *Seasonable* at any time.

ORANGE JELLY.

INGREDIENTS.—1 *quart packet of table jelly*, 1 *pint of water.*

Mode.— Put the jelly into a basin and pour on the water *nearly* boiling; stir the jelly till dissolved, then run it through a jelly bag; wet a mould thoroughly, and pour in the jelly, and set in a cool place. All the table jellies are prepared in the same manner. The orange is quite sufficiently flavoured, but a glass of sherry is an improvement added to the plain calves' foot jelly. If this is put, the same quantity of water should be omitted. A little gold leaf in tiny flakes makes these jellies look very pretty, or they may be moulded with preserved cherries or grapes.

Time, jelly should always be made the day before it is required. *Average cost*, 9d. *Sufficient* for a quart mould. *Seasonable* at any time.

COMPÔTE OF FRUITS.

INGREDIENTS.—½ *tin of each, peaches, apricots, and pineapple* (*any fresh fruit may be added if liked, the greater the variety the better*), 2 *glasses of sherry*, 2 *glasses of liqueur, white sugar to taste.*

Mode.—Cut the slices of pine into dice and the half peaches and apricots in quarters, and put them in a bowl. Take the syrup from the three tins and boil it with the sugar over the fire in a lined saucepan. Set this aside to cool, and when cold pour it over the fruit; add the wine and liqueur and give all a good stir.

Time, 15 minutes to boil the syrup. *Average cost*, 3s. *Sufficient* for 8 persons. *Seasonable* at any time.

CROQUETTE POTATOES.

SPINACH AND EGGS.

ASPARAGUS.

MUSHROOMS.

FRENCH SALAD.

CAULIFLOWER.

NEW PEAS.

FRENCH BEANS.

STUFFED TOMATOES.

NEW CARROTS.

JOINTS AND VEGETABLES.

Carrots.   New Peas.

Roast Forequarter of Lamb.

Tomatoes Farcies.

Roast Beef and Horseradish.

Spinach and Eggs.   Flageolettes.

BREAKFAST AND SUPPER DISHES

EGGS.

EGGS AND BACON.

INGREDIENTS.—Bacon ; eggs.

Mode.—Cut the bacon into thin slices, trim away the rusty parts, and cut off the rind. Put it into a *cold* frying-pan, that is, do not place the pan on the fire before the bacon is in it. Turn 2 or 3 times, and dish on a hot dish. Poach the eggs, slip them on to the bacon, and serve quickly.

Time, 3 or 4 minutes. *Average cost*, 10d. to 1s. per pound for the primest parts. *Sufficient*, allow 6 eggs and 6 rashers for 3 persons.

Note.—Fried rashers of bacon, curled, serve as a pretty garnish to many dishes, and answer very well as a substitute for boiled bacon with a small dish of poultry, &c.

EGGS AND HAM.

INGREDIENTS.—*Ham ; eggs.*

Mode.—Cut the ham into slices of the same thickness in every part. Cut off the rind, and if the ham should be particularly hard and salt, soak it for about 10 minutes in hot water, and then dry it in a cloth. Put it into a cold frying-pan, set it over the fire, turn the slices 3 or 4 times whilst they are cooking. When done, place them on a dish, which should be kept hot while the eggs are being poached. Poach the eggs, slip them on to the slices of ham, and serve quickly.

Time, 7 or 8 minutes to broil the ham. *Average cost*, 10d. to 1s. per lb. for the best part.

EGGS AND TOMATOES.

INGREDIENTS.—6 *medium-sized tomatoes*, 6 *fresh eggs*, *buttered toast*, *pepper and salt.*

Mode.—Scoop out the centre of each

193

tomato and with this pulp make a well-seasoned sauce. In each of the cavities of the tomatoes break an egg carefully and season with salt and pepper. Put the tomatoes in a well-buttered tin in the oven and bake till done. Have ready some buttered toast, on which place the tomatoes, pouring the gravy round.

Time, about 10 minutes. *Average cost*, 1s. 2d. *Sufficient* for 6 persons. *Seasonable* when tomatoes are in season.

EGGS AND TOMATOES.

INGREDIENTS.—*2 good-sized tomatoes, 4 eggs, a little ham or tongue, butter, seasoning.*

Mode.—Cut the tomatoes in half and cook them in a tin with a little butter in the oven till nearly done. Take a little out of the middle of each, sprinkle in some finely chopped ham and a dash of cayenne, and break an egg into each. Cook till the eggs are set, then sprinkle over some finely chopped parsley and serve on some croûtons or small rounds of buttered toast.

Time, about 15 minutes. *Average cost*, 1s. *Sufficient* for 3 or 4 persons.

EGGS À L'ESPAGNOLE.

INGREDIENTS.—*2 Spanish onions, 4 eggs, dripping, bread, pepper, salt.*

Mode.—Fry some rounds of bread a bright brown in dripping, then fry the onions sliced, adding as they cook a sprinkling of pepper and salt. Pile the onion on the croûtons and on each place a nicely poached egg.

Time, 20 minutes. *Average cost*, 8d. *Sufficient* for 4 persons.

EGGS (ANCHOVY).

INGREDIENTS.—*4 eggs, 2 or 3 slices of bread, a little anchovy paste, cayenne, 1 oz. butter, lard or clarified dripping for frying.*

Mode.—Boil the eggs hard, shell them when cold, and cut them in half. Put the yolks in a mortar or basin with the butter, anchovy paste, and cayenne, and pound smooth. Stamp out small rounds of the bread and fry them a bright brown then set aside till cold. Fill the halves of the eggs with the yolk mixture, stand each one on a croûton, and garnish with parsley.

Time, 5 minutes to fry the croûtons. *Average cost*, 8d. *Sufficient* for 3 or 4 persons. *Seasonable* at any time.

EGGS IN AMBUSH.

INGREDIENTS.—*6 eggs, 1 lb. sausages, a little vermicelli, 1 beaten egg, pepper and cayenne, fat for frying.*

Mode.—Boil the eggs hard, and when cold shell them. Take the sausage meat out of the skins and add a little more seasoning to it if necessary. Roll each egg in the meat, covering it smoothly, then dip in egg and afterwards crushed vermicelli and fry a bright brown. When cold cut the eggs in half and lay each on a fried croûton or round of toast, arrange neatly on a dish, and garnish with parsley or cress.

Time, 10 minutes to fry. *Average cost*, 1s. 8d. *Sufficient* for 4 persons. *Seasonable* when sausages are in season.

EGGS (POACHED).

INGREDIENTS.—*Eggs, water. To every pint of water allow 1 tablespoonful vinegar.*

Mode.—Eggs for poaching should be perfectly fresh, but not quite new-laid; those that are about 36 hours old are the best. If quite new laid, the white is so milky it is almost impossible to set it; and if the egg be at all stale it is difficult to poach it nicely. Strain some boiling water into a deep, clean frying-pan, add the vinegar, break the egg into a cup, and, when the water boils, remove the pan to the side of the fire, and gently slip the egg into it. Place the pan over a gentle fire, and keep the water simmering until the white looks nicely set. Take it up gently with a slice, cut away the ragged edges, and serve on toasted bread or on slices of fried ham, or bacon, or on spinach, &c. A poached egg should not be overdone, or its appearance and taste will be quite spoiled. When the egg is slipped into the water, the white should be gathered together, or the cup should be turned over it for ½ minute. To poach an egg to perfection is rather difficult; so, for inexperienced cooks, a tin egg-poacher may be purchased, which greatly facilitates this manner of dressing eggs.

Time, 2½ to 3½ minutes, according to size. *Sufficient*, 2 eggs to each person. *Seasonable* at any time, but less plentiful in winter.

EGGS (POACHED), WITH CREAM.

INGREDIENTS.—*1 pint of water, 1 teaspoonful salt, 4 teaspoonfuls vinegar, 4 fresh eggs, ½ gill cream, salt, pepper, and pounded sugar to taste,* 1 *oz. butter.*

Mode.—Put the water, vinegar, and salt into the frying-pan, and break each egg into a separate cup, bring the water to boil, and slip the eggs gently in. Simmer from 3 to 4 minutes, and, with a slice, lift them on to a hot dish, and trim the edges. Empty the pan, put in the cream, add a seasoning to taste, bring the whole to the boiling-point, add the butter, broken into small pieces, toss the pan round till the butter is melted, pour it over the eggs and serve. It is a good plan to warm the cream with the butter, &c., before the eggs are poached, so that it may be poured over them immediately they are dished.

Time, 3 to 4 minutes to poach the eggs, 5 minutes to warm the cream. *Average cost,* for the above quantity, 10d. *Sufficient* for 2 persons.

EGGS (SCRAMBLED).

INGREDIENTS.—4 *eggs,* 1 *oz. of butter,* 4 *slices of buttered toast, pepper and salt.*

Mode.—Melt the butter in a lined saucepan, break the eggs into a basin and beat them up with a fork, then pour them into the butter and stir till set, adding seasoning of pepper and salt to taste. Have the toast ready and hot; spread on the mixture and serve quickly.

Time, 5 minutes. *Average cost,* 8d. *Sufficient* for 4 persons. *Seasonable* at any time.

EGGS (TO BOIL).

Eggs for boiling cannot be too fresh, or boiled too soon after they are laid, but rather a longer time should be allowed for boiling a new-laid egg than for one that is three or four days old if for eating hot. For boiling hard they should not be too new laid. Put the eggs into a saucepan of boiling water gently with a spoon, letting the spoon touch the bottom of the saucepan before it is withdrawn, that the egg may not fall and crack. For lightly boiled eggs, 3 minutes will be sufficient; 3¾ to 4 minutes will set the white nicely; and, if liked hard, 6 or 7 minutes will not be too long. If the eggs be unusually large, as those of black Spanish fowls, allow an extra ½ minute. Eggs for salads should be boiled from 10 minutes to ¼ hour, and placed in a basin of cold water for a few minutes; they should then be

rolled on the table with the hand, and the shell will peel off easily. Eggs may be boiled by putting them in cold water and just bringing it to the boil.

Time—to boil eggs lightly for invalids or children, 3 minutes; to boil eggs to suit the generality of tastes, 3¾ to 4 minutes; to boil eggs hard, 6 or 7 minutes; for salads, 10 to 15 minutes.

OMELETTE (PLAIN).

INGREDIENTS.—6 *eggs,* 1 *saltspoonful salt,* ½ *saltspoonful pepper,* 3 *oz. butter.*

Mode.—Break the eggs into a basin, omitting the whites of 3, and beat them up with the salt and pepper until extremely light; then add 1 oz. of butter, broken into small pieces, and stir this into the mixture. Put the other 2 oz. of butter into a frying pan, make it quite hot, and as soon as it begins to bubble, whisk the eggs, &c., very briskly for a minute or two, and pour them into the pan; stir the omelette with a spoon, one way, until the mixture thickens, and becomes firm. Then fold the edges over so that the omelette assumes an oval form, and when it is nicely brown on one side and quite firm it is done. Hold the pan before the fire for a minute or two, and brown the upper side of the omelette with a salamander or hot shovel. Serve expeditiously on a very hot dish. The flavour of this omelette may be very much enhanced by adding minced parsley, minced onions or eschallot, or grated cheese, allowing 1 tablespoonful of the former and half the quantity of the latter to the above proportion of eggs. Shrimps or oysters may also be added, the latter scalded in their liquor, and then bearded and cut into small pieces. Omelettes are sometimes sent to table with gravy, which should be thickened with arrowroot or rice flour, and served in a tureen.

Time, with 6 eggs, in a frying-pan 18 or 20 inches round, 4 to 6 minutes. *Average cost,* 11d. *Sufficient* for 4 persons.

OMELETTE (HAM).

INGREDIENTS.—6 *eggs,* 3 *oz. butter,* ½ *saltspoonful pepper,* 2 *tablespoonfuls minced ham.*

Mode.—Mince the ham fine without any fat, and fry it for 2 minutes in a little butter; then make the batter for the omelette, stir in the ham, and proceed as in preceding recipe. Do not add any salt to the batter. Serve hot and quickly, without gravy. Cooked lean bacon or tongue may be used instead of ham.

Time, 4 to 6 minutes. *Average cost*, 1s. 6d. *Sufficient* for 4 persons.

OMELETTE (KIDNEY).

INGREDIENTS.—6 *eggs*, 1 *saltspoonful salt*, ½ *teaspoonful pepper*, 2 *sheep's kidneys, or 2 tablespoonfuls minced veal kidney*, 3 *oz. butter*.

Mode.—Skin the kidneys, cut them into small dice, and toss them in a frying-pan, in 1 oz. butter, over the fire for two or three minutes. Mix the ingredients for the omelette as in recipe for plain omelette, and when the eggs are well whisked, proceed as before.

Time, 4 to 6 minutes. *Average cost*, 1s. 7d. *Sufficient* for 4 persons.

OMELETTE (SWEET).

INGREDIENTS.—6 *eggs*, 3 *oz. butter*, *a pinch of salt, some apricot jam, sifted sugar.*

Mode.—Make as a plain omelette, omitting the pepper; lay on a hot dish, spread over thinly to the jam, roll up and sift over the sugar. A little warmed apricot juice should be poured round.

Time, 4 to 6 minutes. *Average cost*, 1s. *Sufficient* for 4 persons. *Seasonable* at any time.

CHEESE.

CHEESE BISCUITS AND STRAWS.

INGREDIENTS.—2 *oz. each butter, flour, and cheese, the yolk of an egg, cayenne.*

Mode.—Pound or grate the cheese according to whether it be hard or soft, well season it with cayenne, rub it with the butter into the flour and moisten it with the egg. Roll the paste out thin and stamp into little biscuits with a tin-cutter. Bake 10 minutes in a fairly hot oven. The same paste will serve for cheese straws. It must be rolled thin, and cut in very narrow strips. These twisted and baked on a greased paper.

If the straws are cut about 4 inches long and about ½ doz. put through a little ring of paste stamped with two cutters, one smaller than the other, and baked separately from the straws, it forms a pretty way of serving. The straws should stand up as little sheaves.

Time, 10 minutes. *Average cost*, 5d. *Sufficient* for a small dish.

CHEESE (MODE OF SERVING).

At well-appointed tables it is usual to have the cheese handed by the servants when it is cut in very small squares, and placed in a triple dish, the other two leaves of which are filled respectively with tiny balls of butter and small biscuits. When it is preferred, it should be placed upon the table; if a Stilton a napkin must be pinned round it, and in the case of other cheeses the rind must be carefully pared and the portion or portions, if cut up, placed on a folded napkin in the cheese dish.

CHEESE PUDDING.

INGREDIENTS. — 4 *oz. cheese*, 2 *eggs, butter, stale bread, mustard*, 1 *pint of milk.*

Mode.—Cut some slices of thin bread-and-butter, put a layer in a buttered basin, put over some cheese grated or cut in very thin slices, and sprinkle over a dust of mustard. Fill the basin in this way, then pour in a custard of the milk and eggs and steam for ¾ hour.

Time, ¾ hour. *Average cost*, 9d. *Sufficient* for 4 or 5 persons.

CHEESE SOUFFLÉ.

INGREDIENTS.—3 *oz. cheese, a teacupful of milk*, 3 *eggs*, 2 *tablespoonfuls flour, cayenne, salt.*

Mode.—Put the butter over the fire, shake in the flour, stir smooth, add the milk and seasoning. When the mixture has boiled, let it partly cool, then stir in the yolks of the eggs, the cheese grated, and lastly the whites of the eggs well beaten. Pour in a well-buttered soufflé tin, if there is not one, a cake tin, either of which must have a strip of buttered paper put round the top to support the soufflé as it rises, and bake in a quick oven, serving immediately with a napkin pinned round the tin.

Time, about 10 minutes. *Average cost*, 6d. *Sufficient* for 3 persons.

CHEESE (MACARONI).

INGREDIENTS.—½ *lb. pipe macaroni*, 2 *oz. butter*, 6 *oz. Parmesan or Cheshire cheese, pepper and salt to taste*, 1 *pint milk*, 2 *pints water, breadcrumbs.*

Mode.—Put the milk and water into a saucepan with sufficient salt to flavour it; place on the fire, and when it boils quickly drop in the macaroni. Keep the water boiling until it is quite tender; drain the macaroni, and put it into a deep dish. Have ready the grated cheese, either Parmesan or Cheshire; sprinkle it amongst the macaroni and some of the butter cut into small pieces, reserving some of the cheese for the top layer. Season with a little pepper, and cover the top layer of cheese with fine breadcrumbs. Warm, without oiling, the remainder of the butter, and pour it gently over the breadcrumbs. Place the dish before a bright fire to brown the crumbs; turn it once or twice, that it may be equally coloured, or brown with a salamander, and serve very hot. If browned in the oven, the butter would oil and impart a disagreeable flavour to the dish. In boiling the macaroni, let it be perfectly tender but firm, and the form entirely preserved. It may be boiled in plain water, with a little salt, instead of using milk, but should then have a small piece of butter mixed with it.

Time, 1½ to 1¾ hours to boil the macaroni; 5 minutes to brown it before the fire. *Average cost*, 1s. *Sufficient* for 6 or 7 persons.

Note.—Ribbon macaroni does not require boiling so long a time.

TOASTED CHEESE, OR SCOTCH RAREBIT.

INGREDIENTS.—½ *lb. good rich cheese, 1 oz. butter, a teaspoonful made mustard, 2 tablespoonfuls milk or ale, buttered toast.*

Mode.—Melt the cheese and butter chopped finely together in a lined stewpan, add the ale or milk and stir till smooth, then pour over slices of hot buttered toast and serve quickly.

Time, about 5 minutes. *Average cost*, 10d. *Sufficient* for 3 persons.

TOASTED CHEESE, OR WELSH RAREBIT.

INGREDIENTS. — *Slices bread, butter, Cheshire or Gloucester cheese, mustard, and pepper.*

Mode. — Cut the bread into slices about ½ inch in thickness; pare off the crust, toast the bread slightly, and spread it with butter. Cut some slices from a good rich fat cheese; lay them on the toasted bread in a cheese-toaster; be careful that the cheese does not burn, and let it be equally melted. Spread

over the top a little made mustard and a seasoning of pepper, and serve very hot. The cheese may be cut into thin flakes, or toasted on one side before it is laid on the bread. It is a good plan to melt the cheese in small round silver or metal pans, and to send these pans to table, allowing one for each guest. Slices of dry or buttered toast should always accompany them, with mustard, pepper, and salt.

Time, about 5 minutes to melt the cheese. *Sufficient*—allow a slice to each person.

FISH.

FISH PIE.

INGREDIENTS.—*Remains of any cold fish, some mashed potatoes, anchovy sauce, butter, breadcrumbs, cayenne.*

Mode. — Butter a shallow pie-dish and strew over a few breadcrumbs. Flake the fish and season it with cayenne and anchovy, lay it in the pie-dish, fill up with the mashed potatoes, and over them put a few breadcrumbs, lastly some small pieces of butter. Bake for ¼ of an hour.

Time, 15 minutes. *Average cost*, exclusive of the fish, 4d. *Sufficient* for 4 persons. *Seasonable* at any time.

FISH RISSOLES.

INGREDIENTS. — *Remains of cold fish or some tinned salmon, breadcrumbs, 2 eggs, seasoning of cayenne and anchovy sauce, lard or butter for frying.*

Mode. — Flake and mince the fish finely (if tinned fish be used, let it be freed from the moisture), mix with it one-third of its proportion of breadcrumbs, moisten with a beaten egg, and season to taste. Make into balls or rolls, dip in beaten egg, then in fine dry breadcrumbs, and fry a bright golden brown. Serve with cut lemon and parsley garnish; and a very nice accompaniment is some thin brown bread-and-butter.

Time, 5 minutes to fry the rissoles. *Average cost*, exclusive of the fish, 6d. *Sufficient* for 4 persons. *Seasonable* at any time.

KEDGEREE.

INGREDIENTS. — *A little cold white fish (about ½ lb.), a teacupful boiled* rice, 2 hard-boiled eggs, 1 oz. butter, cayenne, salt.

Mode.—Flake the fish, and chop the eggs, and put with the rice and butter in a stewpan. Add seasoning to taste, make all hot, and serve quickly.

Time, 10 minutes. *Average cost,* exclusive of the fish, 4d. *Sufficient* for 2 or 3 persons.

LOBSTER CREAM.

INGREDIENTS. — 1 *lobster,* ¼ *pint of cream,* ½ *pint of milk,* 3 *eggs, a dessertspoonful of anchovy sauce, a cupful of breadcrumbs, cayenne.*

Mode.—Boil the milk and pour it over the crumbs. Mince the flesh of the lobster fine, and when the breadcrumbs are nearly cold mix it with them; then the eggs, beaten, the seasoning of cayenne, the sauce, a little salt if necessary, and lastly the cream. Butter a mould, fill with the mixture, put a buttered paper over the top and steam for 1 hour.

Average cost, 2s. 6d. *Sufficient* for 6 persons. *Seasonable* at any time.

LOBSTER PATTIES.

INGREDIENTS. — 1 *lobster, Béchamel sauce, a little anchovy, lemon-juice and cayenne, puff-paste,* 1 *egg.*

Mode.—Stamp out some rounds from the paste rolled very thin, about 3 inches in diameter, and double the number from the paste about a third of an inch thick. Stamp these again with a smaller cutter so as to leave a ring only. Lay the thin rounds on a baking sheet and over each 2 of the rings, joined by white of egg; fill up the centre with flour or bread and lay a little round on the top of each; brush over with the yolk of egg and bake a light colour. Mince the lobster very fine, add 4 tablespoonfuls of Béchamel sauce and seasoning to taste; stir the mixture over the fire for 5 minutes, then take out the flour or bread from the patty cases, fill them with the lobster and replace the tops.

Time, about 5 minutes after the cases are ready. *Average cost,* 2s. 6d. *Seasonable* at any time. *Sufficient* for 12 small patties.

SALMON MAYONNAISE.

INGREDIENTS. — *Remains of cold boiled salmon,* 2 *lettuces, a little small salad and beetroot,* 3 *hard-boiled eggs,* a very little oil and vinegar, pepper and salt, ¼ pint of mayonnaise sauce.

Mode.—Wash and thoroughly dry the lettuces and small salad, and use the outer leaves sprinkled with oil and vinegar for the foundation of the mayonnaise. On them, in a circle overlapping one another, lay the salmon in neat cutlets, well masked with the sauce. In the centre and round the salmon put the rest of the salad cut up finely, arranging it in groups of dark and light colour and garnishing with slices of the egg and beetroot.

Average cost, exclusive of the cold fish, 1s. 4d. *Seasonable* at any time. *Sufficient* for 8 persons.

MAYONNAISE SAUCE (for above).

INGREDIENTS.—*The yolks of* 2 *eggs,* 6 *tablespoonfuls of salad oil,* 4 *tablespoonfuls of vinegar,* 1 *tablespoonful of white stock,* 2 *of cream.*

Mode.—Put the yolks of the eggs into a basin with a seasoning of pepper and salt; have ready the oil and vinegar in separate vessels, and add them, using first the oil, *very gradually* to the eggs. Keep stirring the mixture with a wooden spoon, as herein lies the secret of having a nice smooth sauce. It cannot be stirred too frequently and should be made in a very cool place. When the oil and vinegar are well incorporated, add the cream and stock, stirring all the while. If no cream is used, substitute the same quantity of oil. It becomes thicker by keeping.

Average cost, for this quantity, 10d. *Sufficient* for a good-sized salad. *Seasonable* at any time.

SARDINE TOAST.

INGREDIENTS.—6 *sardines,* 6 *croûtons, seasoning of cayenne, a dessertspoonful of Worcester sauce, a teaspoonful of anchovy sauce,* 1½ *oz. of butter, lemon-juice, a little flour.*

Mode.—Bone and scale the sardines and pound them to a smooth paste in a mortar with the butter. Cut the bread for the croûtons about ½ an inch thick, cut off the crust and fry a nice brown in butter. Spread the mixture on the croûtons and put them in the oven. Make a sauce of the other ingredients, with ¼ pint boiling water, simmering it till the flour is properly cooked; then pour over the croûtons and serve very hot.

Time, about 15 minutes. *Average cost*, 1s. *Sufficient* for 4 persons. *Seasonable* at any time.

SAVOURY DISHES.

CRÉME DE LIEVRE.

INGREDIENTS.—*The remains of cold roast hare, breadcrumbs, ham, 2 or 3 eggs, seasoning, a little milk.*

Mode.—Mince the flesh of the hare finely mixing with it a small quantity of grated ham, and pound to a smooth paste. Add one-third the quantity of breadcrumbs soaked in milk and squeezed fairly dry, and a savoury seasoning, and blend all with 2 or 3 eggs according to the quantity. Well-butter a plain mould, fill it with the mixture, cover with buttered paper, and steam for 40 minutes or rather longer if the cream be a large one. Make a gravy from the bones of the hare, a little thickening and browning, and serve with the cream turned out of the mould and red-currant jelly.

Time, 40 minutes. *Average cost*, exclusive of the hare, 8d. *Seasonable* in winter.

DEVILLED TURKEY.

INGREDIENTS. — *Legs of cold turkey, made mustard, salt and cayenne*

Mode.—Score the legs, cutting lengthwise to the bone, and well press in the seasoning. Grill them over a bright, clear fire till they are crisp and brown; then serve quickly and very hot with small pieces of cold butter upon them.

Time about 7 or 8 minutes to grill. *Sufficient* for 4 persons. *Seasonable* in winter.

FOIE GRAS IN JELLY.

INGREDIENTS. —*1½ pints of aspic jelly, a few leaves of chervil and watercress, a small tin of foie gras, some fresh salad.*

Mode. — Melt the jelly and thickly coat a mould. Put in small squares of the foie gras interspersed with leaves of the cress and chervil, arranging them so that they may look nice when the jelly is turned out, then some more jelly and some more of the foie gras

and leaves till the mould is full. The jelly must each time be cool. Cut up some fresh salad and dress it, if liked, with a little oil, vinegar, pepper, and salad, or leave it plain. Turn out the mould and garnish with the salad made to look bright with sliced tomatoes or beetroot.

Average cost, 2s. 6d. *Sufficient* for a quart mould. *Seasonable* at any time.

HAM TOAST.

INGREDIENTS.—*A few slices of cold ham, 1 oz. butter, parsley, cayenne, buttered toast.*

Mode.—Melt the butter in a small saucepan, add the ham very finely mixed and a little chopped parsley. Season with cayenne, make the mixture thoroughly hot and spread over slices of buttered toast.

Time, about 5 minutes.

INDIAN VEAL COLLOPS (Indian Recipe).

INGREDIENTS.—*1½ lbs. of fillet of veal, cut as a cutlet, 1 small cupful of breadcrumbs, 1 dessertspoonful of curry-powder, 2 yolks of eggs, butter, gravy, pepper and salt.*

Mode.—Cut the veal into neat shaped pieces about 3 inches across, beat them, then dip in beaten yolk of egg, then in breadcrumbs which should cover them thickly, and curry-powder; repeat this, then fry in butter. Make a sauce with a little gravy, curry-powder, and a small piece of butter, thickened with flour; squeeze in the juice of a lemon, boil, and serve, poured round the collops.

KALLEAH YEKHUNEE (Indian Recipe).

INGREDIENTS.—*2 lbs. of lean mutton, 3 or 4 onions, ½ oz. each of ginger and cloves, 1 tablespoonful of sugar, 2 of lime-juice, a dessertspoonful of curry-powder, salt and cayenne, water.*

Mode.—Slice the meat into a stewpan with enough water to cover, and the seasoning, and stew until the meat is tender. Strain off the gravy into another saucepan, mix the sugar, lime-juice, and curry-powder together with a little water; mix this again with the gravy, pour it back to the meat, and simmer for ¼ hour.

Time, about 2 hours. *Seasonable* at any time.

TOMATOES AND BACON.

INGREDIENTS.—*4 tomatoes, 4 rashers of bacon, a little pepper, bread.*

Mode.—Warm a frying-pan over the fire, lay in it the rashers neatly trimmed. Fry, turning them several times, and set aside. Cut some rounds of bread, take off the crust, and fry in the bacon-fat. Lastly fry the tomatoes in slices, adding a seasoning of pepper and using a little more fat if necessary. Serve the rashers on the bread with the tomatoes round.

Time, about 10 minutes. *Average cost*, 10d. *Sufficient* for 4 persons.

POTTED BEEF (Cold Meat Cookery).

INGREDIENTS.—*The remains of cold roast or boiled beef, ¼ lb. butter, cayenne to taste, 2 blades pounded mace.*

Mode. — Cut the meat into small pieces and pound it well, with a little butter, in a mortar ; add cayenne and mace, reducing the latter ingredient to the finest powder, or a little anchovy sauce may be used in place of the mace.

When the ingredients are thoroughly mixed, put into glass or earthen potting-pots, and when cold pour on the top a coating of clarified butter.

Note.—If cold roast beef is used, remove all pieces of gristle and dry outside pieces.

POTTED HAM, that will keep good for some time.

INGREDIENTS.—*To 4 lbs. lean ham allow 1 lb. fat, 2 teaspoonfuls pounded mace, ½ nutmeg grated, rather more than ½ teaspoonful cayenne, clarified lard.*

Mode.—Mince the ham, fat and lean, in the above proportions, and pound it well in a mortar, seasoning it with cayenne pepper, pounded mace, and nutmeg ; put the mixture into a deep baking-dish, and bake for ½ hour. Press it well into a stone jar, fill up the jar with clarified lard, cover it closely, and paste over it a piece of thick paper. If well seasoned it will keep a long time in winter, and will be found convenient for sandwiches, &c.

Time, ½ hour.

SAVOURIES AND HORS D'ŒUVRES

The taste for savouries under their names of *appétisans* and *hors d'œuvres* is on the increase, and we find them seldom omitted from a good dinner menu. But, besides these little dishes, usually consisting of such things as caviare, stuffed olives, *devils*, which are served as preliminary or between the courses, we have many others now that form courses in themselves. Salads, not the plain, old-fashioned ones, but most elaborate dishes, very often served in jelly, composed of prawns, anchovies, olives, foie gras and other delicacies in addition to the vegetable portion, mushrooms cooked in various ways, eggs and cheese in happy combinations, all go pleasantly to vary the monotony of "sweets." Many ladies now prefer such courses to those of pastry and sweet dishes, and gentlemen, almost without exception, choose them. We give a few recipes for some of the nicest of the small savouries that can be made easily at home; also some for some sandwiches that are usually served at afternoon "at home" teas.

ANCHOVY CANAPÉS.

Ingredients.—*Slices of stale bread, eggs, anchovies, butter or clarified dripping for frying.*

Mode.—Cut the bread about one-third of an inch in thickness, stamp out small rounds from it with a cutter about the size of half-a-crown, and fry a nice bright brown in butter. Boil 1 or more eggs hard, according to quantity required, and chop yoke and white fine. Bone and fillet the anchovies (3 will be enough for 12 rounds of bread), curl a fillet on each round, fill the centre with the chopped egg, season with a few grains of cayenne and arrange neatly on a small dish, garnishing with water-cress.

Average cost, 9d. Sufficient for 6 persons.

ANCHOVY SANDWICHES.

Ingredients. — *Brown bread, fresh butter, anchovy paste, mustard and cress, cayenne.*

Mode.—Cut some thin slices of bread-and-butter; spread these thinly with anchovy paste, chop the mustard and cress and scatter over, then season with a dash of cayenne. Lay the slices together and cut into neat little sandwiches, which pile nicely, or arrange in a ring on a dish and garnish with parsley.

Average cost, 7d. Sufficient for 6 persons.

ANGELS ON HORSEBACK.

Ingredients.—1 *doz. oysters, a few very thinly cut rashers of bacon, some finely minced sweet herbs, Nepaul pepper, 12 rounds of bread fried, a little lemon-juice.*

Mode.—Trim the bacon into little squares just large enough to roll round an oyster, sprinkle over these the herbs and a little pepper. Lay in each one an oyster, squeeze over a drop or two of lemon-juice, roll them up, run them on a skewer and fry till the bacon is cooked. Have the rounds of bread nicely fried and hot, lay on each an oyster and serve quickly, garnished with cut lemon and parsley.

Time, 8 minutes to fry. *Average*

cost, 3s. *Sufficient* for 6 persons. *Seasonable* from September to March.

CAVIARE CROÛTONS.

INGREDIENTS. — *Some small fried rounds of bread, a little butter (plain or Montpellier), caviare, Nepaul pepper.*

Mode. — When the croûtons, fried a bright brown, are cold, spread them with the caviare, season lightly with the pepper, and run over in a pattern with a cone, a little butter.

Average cost, 1d. each. *Sufficient* to allow 2 or 3 for each person. *Seasonable* at any time.

CAVIARE SANDWICHES.

INGREDIENTS.—*Caviare, thin slices of brown bread-and-butter, pepper or cayenne, lemon-juice.*

Mode.—Spread half the slices with caviare, seasoned with a little pepper, squeeze over a little lemon-juice, put the slices together and cut into narrow fingers. Arrange these, two one way, then two another, and so on as pastry sandwiches, and fill in the centre with carefully picked watercress.

Average cost, 1d. each. *Sufficient* to allow 2 or 3 for each person. *Seasonable* at any time

CUCUMBER SANDWICHES.

INGREDIENTS.—*Bread, butter, cucumber, oil, vinegar, pepper.*

Mode.—Cut some thin slices of bread-and-butter, and stamp out rounds from them the size of the rounds of cucumber. Peel and slice the cucumber and lay it a little while in a dressing made of oil, vinegar, and pepper, then drain from this, and lay each round between two rounds of the bread-and-butter, and arrange in a ring on a dish, the sandwiches overlapping each other.

Average cost for a dish, 6d. *Sufficient* for 6 persons. *Seasonable* in summer.

DEVILLED BISCUITS.

INGREDIENTS. — *Some milk biscuits, butter, cayenne, salt.*

Mode.—Butter the biscuits on both sides, season them slightly with salt, well with cayenne, and put them in the oven to get thoroughly hot.

Average cost, 2d. *Sufficient* for 6 persons.

FOIE GRAS SANDWICHES.

INGREDIENTS.—*Foie gras pâté as sold in china pots, brown or white bread-and-butter, cress, a little seasoning if necessary.*

Mode.—Cut the bread and butter very thin, spread half the slices with foie gras, scatter over a little cress, lay over the other slices and stamp out in little rounds. If preferred, cut off the crusts, and then cut the sandwiches into neat little squares; serve garnished with cress.

Average cost, 1½d. each. *Sufficient* to allow 3 or 4 for each person.

LOBSTER CANAPÉS.

INGREDIENTS.—*12 croûtons fried in butter, lobster butter (see recipe), the tail of a small lobster, a few capers, oil, vinegar, and pepper.*

Mode.—Have ready some fried rounds of bread drained and cold. Cut small slices of the lobster and soak in oil and vinegar for a few minutes, spread the croûtons with lobster butter, lay on each a slice of lobster, and over that a few capers. Serve on a bed of very finely cut, light green endive or lettuce.

Average cost, 9d. *Sufficient* for 4 persons.

OYSTER DARIOLES.

INGREDIENTS.—*1 doz. oysters, 2 eggs, 2 oz. of flour, 1 oz of butter, ½ pint of milk, nutmeg, salt, cayenne, lemon-juice.*

Mode.—Beard the oysters and scald them in their liquor, strain and cut in 3 or 4 pieces. Put the flour and butter in a saucepan, add the oyster liquor, then the milk, and stir till boiling. Beat the eggs well and add with the seasoning, and lastly the oysters. Butter some small moulds, pour in the mixture, and steam gently for 20 minutes.

Time, 20 minutes to steam. *Average cost*, 2s. *Sufficient* for 4 persons. *Seasonable* from September to March.

OYSTER SANDWICHES.

INGREDIENTS.—*½ doz. large oysters, thin brown bread-and-butter, lemon-juice, cayenne.*

Mode.—Pound the oysters in a mortar with the lemon-juice and cayenne, lay them between the slices of bread-and-butter, and cut into small sandwiches.

Average cost, 1s. *Sufficient* for 2 or 3 persons. *Seasonable* from September to March.

OLIVES (STUFFED).

INGREDIENTS. — 12 *large Spanish olives, forcemeat made from sardines or anchovies, 12 fried croûtons, lobster butter, 12 capers, a little lemon-juice.*

Mode.—Free the anchovies or sardines from scales and bone, and pound them in a mortar with a few drops of lemon-juice and a seasoning of cayenne. Stone the olives and fill them with the forcemeat, putting a caper on the top of each ; butter the croûtons and stand on each an olive. Serve garnished with sprigs of parsley and a little aspic jelly, if at hand.

Average cost, 9d. *Sufficient* for 4 or 5 persons. *Seasonable* at any time.

SARDINE SAVOURIES.

INGREDIENTS.—*Slices of bread, 6 sardines,* 1 *teaspoonful of anchovy sauce,* 1 *teaspoonful of Worcester sauce,* 1½ *oz. of butter, a dessertspoonful of flour, cayenne, lemon-juice, and water.*

Mode.—Fry the stamped-out rounds of bread, bone the sardines, pound them in a mortar with the butter, and spread over the croûtons. Mix the other ingredients with rather less than half a pint of boiling water ; simmer till the flour is cooked, then pour over the sardines.

Time, ¼ of an hour. *Average cost,* 1s. *Sufficient* for 6 persons. *Seasonable* at any time.

SAVOURY CANAPÉS.

INGREDIENTS. — 1 *or* 2 *sardines,* 3 *anchovies,* 6 *oysters, a few shrimps, a small head of celery,* 1 *shallot, cress, tarragon,* 1 *hard - boiled egg, Montpellier butter, lobster coral, aspic jelly mayonnaise sauce.*

Mode.—Bone and shred the fish, cut the celery very fine, pound the shallots and mix with the cress in the sauce. Fill small brioche cases with the mixture and run a little butter round the edges. Garnish with some lobster coral, the egg, chopped fine, put on the top of each, and the aspic jelly, roughed with a fork, laid round the canapés. Except in large establishments, such a variety of materials would not be likely to be at hand at once ; but then canapés can very easily be made with only one or two kinds of fish ; in which case the quantities of each must be increased. Also the butter and coral garnish could be dispensed with.

Average cost, 2s. *Sufficient* for 6 persons. *Seasonable* from September to March.

ASPIC JELLY FOR SAVOURIES.

INGREDIENTS.—1½ *oz. of gelatine,* 1 *tablespoonful of Lemco or other extract of meat, whites of* 2 *eggs,* 2 *shallots,* 1 *carrot,* 1 *turnip,* 1 *onion, the rind of* 1 *lemon,* 8 *teaspoonfuls of vinegar,* 1 *glass of sherry, celery seed, bay-leaves, cloves, water.*

Mode.—Mix the extract with two quarts of water and simmer with the vegetables and the cloves, stuck in the onion, the celery seed and bay-leaves, till the stock is well flavoured. Add the lemon-rind, cut thin, the sherry and the vinegar ; swell the gelatine in water, then add it to the stock with the whites of eggs and stir till it is dissolved ; let it boil up, then remove the pan to the side of the fire and let it simmer for half an hour. Strain through a jelly-bag till clear.

This jelly may be set to cool in a plain basin or soup-plate, and when it is required it should be cut in thin slices and again in diamonds ; or it looks pretty for a garnish roughed with a fork.

Average cost, 2s.

LOBSTER BUTTER.

INGREDIENTS. — *Lobster coral, fresh butter, salt, cayenne.*

Mode.—Rub down the coral smooth in a mortar, adding butter till it is of creamy consistency and of deep red colour. Add cayenne to taste and a little salt, and if wanted to keep for some time make the seasoning stronger than if for present use ; put into pots and tie over.

Seasonable at any time.

MONTPELLIER BUTTER FOR SAVOURY DISHES.

INGREDIENTS. — *Watercress, fresh butter, pepper and salt.*

Mode.—Pull the leaves, which must be very green and fresh, from the stalks and chop them finely. Dry them in a cloth, then mince again and knead them up with butter till it is of a bright green colour, seasoning with pepper and salt.

Parsley butter may be made in the same way, and will be found a nice accompaniment to cold fish such as soles, turbot, or salmon. It should be served in tiny balls or rolls.

Seasonable at any time.

PASTRY AND PUDDINGS

PUFF PASTRY.

INGREDIENTS.—1 *lb. flour*, 1 *lb. butter, a few drops of lemon-juice*, 1 *egg, water.*

Mode.—Squeeze all the water out of the butter ; put the flour—which should be the best, and thoroughly dry—on a board or slab, and make a hollow in the centre of the heap ; into this put a small piece of butter, the yolk of the egg, a small pinch of salt, the lemon-juice, and enough water to make into a smooth paste. Work all well together and shape into a square piece. Roll this out lengthways and lay on it the butter, pressed into a square, flat cake, and fold the paste well over it. If the weather be hot, set the paste aside for about 10 minutes, then roll out again lengthways, fold in three, and again set aside for a quarter of an hour. Repeat this process twice, and the paste will be ready.

It will be found impossible to make good puff paste unless the kitchen and larder are cool, or without ice, in very hot weather.

It is a good plan to start the pastry-making early in the day, and it does not matter how long it is made before it is used.

Time, not less than 1 hour. *Average cost*, 1s. 3d. for this quantity. *Sufficient* for 2 or 3 tarts.

MEDIUM PUFF PASTE.

INGREDIENTS.—*To every lb. of flour allow* 8 *oz. butter and* 3 *oz. lard, not quite* ½ *pint water.*

Mode.—This paste may be made by the directions in the preceding recipe, only using less butter and substituting lard for a portion of it. It should be rolled three times, and may have the butter and lard put on in little pieces at each rolling, the first with butter, the second with lard, and the third with butter.

Average cost, 7d. per lb.

COMMON PASTE, for Family Pies.

INGREDIENTS.—1¼ *lbs. flour*, ½ *lb. butter, rather more than* ½ *pint water.*

Mode.—Rub the butter lightly into the flour, mix it to a smooth paste with the water, and roll it out two or three times. This paste may be converted into an excellent short crust for sweet tarts, by adding to the flour, after the

butter is rubbed in, 2 tablespoonfuls of fine-sifted sugar.

Average cost, 5d. per lb.

VERY GOOD SHORT CRUST FOR FRUIT TARTS.

INGREDIENTS.—*To every lb. flour allow* ¾ *lb. butter*, 1 *tablespoonful sifted sugar*, ⅓ *pint water.*

Mode.—Rub the butter into the flour, after having ascertained that the latter is perfectly dry, add the sugar, and mix the whole into a stiff paste with about ⅓ pint water. Roll it over two or three times, folding the paste over each time.

Average cost, 8d. per lb.

ANOTHER GOOD SHORT CRUST.

INGREDIENTS.—*To every lb. flour allow* 8 *oz. butter, the yolks of* 2 *eggs*, 2 *oz sifted sugar, about* ¼ *pint milk.*

Mode.—Rub the butter into the flour, add the sugar, and mix the whole as lightly as possible to a smooth paste, with the yolks of eggs well beaten, and the milk. The proportion of the latter ingredient must be judged by the size of the eggs ; if these are large, so much will not be required, and more if the eggs are smaller.

Average cost, 8d. per lb.

COMMON SHORT CRUST.

INGREDIENTS.—*To every lb. flour allow* 2 *oz. sifted sugar*, 3 *oz. butter, about* ½ *pint boiling milk.*

Mode.—Crumble the butter into the flour as finely as possible, add the sugar, and work the whole up to a smooth paste with the boiling milk. Roll it out thin, and bake in a moderately hot oven.

Average cost, 4d. per lb.

BUTTER CRUST, for Boiled Puddings.

INGREDIENTS.—*To every lb. flour allow* 6 *oz. butter*, ½ *pint water.*

Mode.—With a knife, work the flour to a smooth paste with ½ pint of water ; roll the crust out rather thin, place the butter over it in small pieces, dredge lightly over it some flour, and fold the paste over ; repeat the rolling once more, and the crust will be ready.

Average cost, 5d. per lb.

SUET CRUST, for Pies or Puddings.

INGREDIENTS.—*To every lb. flour allow* 5 *or* 6 *oz. beef suet*, ½ *pint water.*

Mode.—Free the suet from skin and

shreds, chop it extremely fine, and rub it well into the flour; work the whole to a smooth paste with the above proportion of water, and roll it out. This crust is quite rich enough for ordinary purposes, but when a better one is desired, use from ½ to ¾ lb. of suet to every lb. of flour. Some cooks, for rich crusts, pound the suet in a mortar, with a small quantity of butter. It should then be laid on the paste in small pieces, the same as for puff crust, and will be found exceedingly nice for hot tarts. 5 oz. of suet to every lb. of flour will make a very good crust; and even ¼ lb. will answer very well for children, or where the crust is wanted very plain.

Average cost, 4d. per lb.

DRIPPING CRUST, for Kitchen Puddings Pies, &c.

INGREDIENTS.—*To every lb. flour allow 6 oz. clarified beef dripping, ½ pint water.*

Mode.—Weigh the dripping, and to every lb. of flour allow the above proportion. With a knife, work the flour into a smooth paste with the water, rolling it out three times, each time placing on the crust 2 oz. of the dripping, broken into small pieces. If this paste is lightly made, if good dripping is used, and *not too much* of it, it will be found very nice, and by the addition of two tablespoonfuls of fine moist sugar, it may be converted into a common short crust for fruit pies.

Average cost, 4d. per lb.

BAKED APPLE DUMPLINGS (a Plain Family Dish).

INGREDIENTS.—6 *apples, ¾ lb. of short, dripping, or suet crust, sugar to taste.*

Mode.—Pare and take out the cores of the apples without dividing them, and make ½ lb. of crust by recipe; roll the apples in the crust, previously sweetening them by filling up the holes left by the cores with sugar, and taking care to join the paste nicely. When formed into round balls, put them on a tin, and bake them for about ½ hour, or longer; arrange them pyramidically on a dish, and sift over them some pounded white sugar. These may be made richer by using one of the puff pastes.

Time, ½ to ¾ hour, or longer. *Average cost,* 1½d. each. *Sufficient* for 4 persons. *Seasonable* from August to March, but flavourless after the end of January.

BOILED APPLE DUMPLINGS.

INGREDIENTS.—6 *apples, ¾ lb. of suet crust, sugar to taste.*

Mode.—Pare and take out the cores of the apples without dividing them, sweeten, and roll each apple in a piece of crust, made by recipe given; be particular that the paste is nicely joined. Put the dumplings into floured cloths, tie them securely, and put them into boiling water. Keep them boiling from ½ hour to ¾ hour, remove the cloths, and send them hot and quickly to table.

Time, ¾ to 1 hour, or longer should the dumplings be very large. *Average cost,* 1½d. each. *Sufficient* for 4 persons. *Seasonable* from August to March, but flavourless after the end of January.

BAKED APPLE PUDDING.

INGREDIENTS.—*Five moderate-sized apples, 2 tablespoonfuls finely chopped suet, 3 eggs, 3 tablespoonfuls flour, 1 pint milk, a little grated nutmeg.*

Mode.—Mix the flour to a smooth batter with the milk, add the eggs, which should be well whisked, and put this batter into a well-buttered pie-dish. Wipe, but do not pare, the apples, cut them in halves, and take out the cores; lay them in the batter, rind uppermost, shake the suet on the top, over a little nutmeg; bake in a moderate oven for an hour, and cover, when served, with sifted loaf sugar. This pudding is also very good with the apples pared, sliced, and mixed with the batter.

Time, 1 hour. *Average cost,* 10d. *Sufficient* for 5 or 6 persons.

BOILED APPLE PUDDING.

INGREDIENTS.—*Suet crust, apples, sugar to taste, 1 small teaspoonful finely minced lemon-peel, 2 tablespoonfuls lemon-juice.*

Mode.—Make a crust by recipe, using, for a moderate-sized pudding, from ¾ to 1 lb. of flour, with the other ingredients in proportion. Butter a basin, line it with some of the paste; pare, core, and cut the apples into slices, and fill the basin with these; add the sugar, the lemon-peel, and juice, and cover with crust; pinch the edges together, flour the cloth, place it over the pudding, tie it securely, and put it into plenty of fast-boiling water. Let it boil from 1½ to 2½ hours, according to the size; then turn it out of the basin, and send it to table. Apple puddings boiled in a cloth, *without* a basin, must be served without the least delay, as the crust so soon becomes heavy. Apple pudding is a very convenient dish to have when the dinner-hour is rather uncertain, as it does not spoil by being boiled an extra hour, if it is kept well covered with the water, and not allowed to stop boiling.

Time, from 1½ to 2½ hours, according to the size of the pudding and the quantity of the apples. *Average cost*, 10d. *Sufficient*, made with 1 lb. of flour, for 7 or 8 persons. *Seasonable* from August to March; but the apples become flavourless and scarce after the end of January.

APPLE SNOWBALLS.

INGREDIENTS.—2 *teacupfuls of rice, apples, moist sugar, cloves.*

Mode.—Boil the rice in milk until three-parts done, then strain it off, and pare and core the apples without dividing them. Put a small quantity of sugar and a clove into each apple, put the rice round them, and tie each ball separately in a cloth. Boil until the apples are tender, then take them up, remove the cloths, and serve.

Time, ½ hour to boil the rice separately; ½ hour to 1 hour with the apple. *Seasonable* from August to March.

APPLE TART.

INGREDIENTS.—*Puff-paste, apples ; to every lb. of unpared apples allow 2 oz. moist sugar, ½ teaspoonful of finely minced lemon-peel, 1 tablespoonful lemon-juice.*

Mode.—Make ½ lb. puff-paste by either of the recipes given, place a border of it round the edge of a pie-dish, and fill it with apples, pared, cored, and cut into slices ; sweeten, add the lemon-peel and juice, and 2 or 3 tablespoonfuls of water ; cover with crust, cut it evenly round close to the edge of the pie-dish, and bake it in a hot oven from ½ to ¾ hour, or rather longer if large. When three-parts done, take it out of the oven, put the white of an egg on a plate, and, with the blade of a knife, whisk it to a froth ; brush the pie over with this, then sprinkle upon it some sifted sugar, and then a few drops of water. Put the pie back into the oven, and finish baking, and be careful that it does not catch, as it is very liable to do after the crust is iced. If made with a plain crust, the icing may be omitted.

Time, ½ hour before the crust is iced, 10 to 15 minutes afterwards. *Sufficient* —allow 2 lbs. of apples for a tart for 6 persons. *Seasonable* from August to March; but the apples become flavourless after January.

Note.—Many things are suggested for the flavouring of apple pie ; some say 2 or 3 tablespoonfuls of beer, others the same quantity of sherry, which very much improves the taste; whilst the old-fashioned addition of a few cloves, or a few slices of quince, is, by many persons, preferred to anything else.

APPLE TART (German Recipe).

INGREDIENTS.—10 *apples of fair size, ½ lb. of flour, ¼ lb. of butter, ¼ pint of milk, 1 egg, 3 dessertspoonfuls of castor sugar, ½ oz. of yeast, cinnamon.*

Mode.—Put the flour into a basin, make a hole in the middle, put in all but about ½ oz. of the butter, a little sugar, the milk lukewarm and the yeast, and allow the mixture to rise slowly. Afterwards roll out thin, and lay on a buttered tin, spreading over a little melted butter, powdered sugar, and cinnamon ; then lay over this the apples, peeled, cored, and each cut into 8 pieces. Bake in a quick oven.

Time, 1¼ hours. *Average cost*, 10d. *Sufficient* for 4 persons. *Seasonable* from August to March.

Note.—Tarts of other fresh fruits are made in the same way.

CREAMED APPLE TART.

INGREDIENTS.—*Puff crust, apples ; to every lb. of pared and cored apples allow 2 oz. moist sugar, ½ teaspoonful minced lemon-peel, 1 tablespoonful lemon-juice, ½ pint boiled custard.*

Mode.—Make an apple tart by preceding recipe, omitting the icing. When baked, cut out the middle of the crust, leaving a border all round the dish. Fill up with boiled custard, and grate a little nutmeg over the top. This tart is usually eaten cold.

Time, ½ to ¾ hour. *Average cost*, 1s. *Sufficient*, made with 2 lbs. apples, for 5 or 6 persons. *Seasonable* from August to March.

BAKED OR BOILED ARROWROOT PUDDING.

INGREDIENTS.—2 *tablespoonfuls of arrowroot, 1½ pints milk, 1 oz. butter, the rind of ½ lemon, 2 heaped tablespoonfuls moist sugar, a little grated nutmeg.*

Mode.—Mix the arrowroot, with cold

milk, into a smooth batter, moderately thick; put the remainder of the milk into a stewpan with the lemon-peel, and let it infuse for about ½ hour; when it boils, strain it gently to the batter, stirring all the time to keep it smooth; then add the butter; beat this well in until thoroughly mixed, and sweeten with moist sugar. Put the mixture into a pie-dish, round which has been placed a border of paste, grate a little nutmeg over the top, and bake from 1 to 1½ hours in a moderate oven, or boil it the same length of time in a well-buttered basin. To enrich this pudding, stir to the other ingredients, just before it is put in the oven, 3 well-whisked eggs, and add a tablespoonful of brandy. For a nursery pudding, the latter ingredients will be found quite superfluous, as also the paste round the edge of the dish.

Time, 1 to 1½ hours, baked or boiled. *Average cost*, 7d. *Sufficient* for 5 or 6 persons.

AUNT NELLY'S PUDDING.

INGREDIENTS. — ½ lb. flour, ½ lb. treacle, ½ lb. suet, the rind and juice of 1 lemon, a few strips candied lemon-peel, 3 tablespoonfuls milk, 2 eggs.

Mode.—Chop the suet finely; mix with it the flour, treacle, lemon-peel minced, and candied lemon-peel; add the milk, lemon-juice, and 2 well-beaten eggs; beat the pudding well, put it into a buttered basin, tie with a cloth, and boil from 3½ to 4 hours.

Time, 3½ to 4 hours. *Average cost*, 1s. *Sufficient* for 5 or 6 persons. *Seasonable* at any time, but more suitable for a winter pudding.

BACHELOR'S PUDDING.

INGREDIENTS.—4 oz. grated bread, 4 oz. currants, 4 oz. apples, 2 oz. sugar, 2 or 3 eggs, a few drops essence of lemon, a little grated nutmeg.

Mode.—Pare, core, and mince the apples very fine, sufficient, when minced, to make 4 oz.; add the currants (well washed), the grated bread, and sugar; whisk the eggs, beat these up with the remaining ingredients, thoroughly mix, put the pudding into a buttered basin, tie down with a cloth, and boil for 3 hours.

Time, 3 hours. *Average cost*, 6d. *Sufficient* for 4 or 5 persons. *Seasonable* from August to March.

BARONESS'S PUDDING (Author's Recipe).

INGREDIENTS.—¾ lb. suet, ¾ lb. raisins weighed after being stoned, ¾ lb. flour, ½ pint milk, ¼ saltspoonful salt.

Mode.—Chop the suet fine, stone the raisins, cut them in halves, and mix these ingredients with the salt and flour; moisten with milk, stir the mixture well, and tie the pudding in a floured cloth, previously wrung out in boiling water. Put the pudding into a saucepan of boiling water, and let it boil 4½ hours. Serve with plain sifted sugar.

Time, 4½ hours. *Average cost*, 1s. 1d. *Sufficient* for 7 or 8 persons. *Seasonable* in winter, when fresh fruit is not obtainable.

Note.—This pudding is highly recommended. The recipe was kindly given to the Author's family by a lady who bore the title here prefixed to it. The time of boiling should never be *less* than that mentioned.

BAKED BATTER PUDDING.

INGREDIENTS.—1½ pints milk, 4 tablespoonfuls flour, 2 oz. butter, 4 eggs, a little salt.

Mode.—Mix the flour with a small quantity of cold milk; make the remainder hot, and pour it on to the flour, keeping the mixture well stirred; add the butter, eggs, and salt; beat the whole well, and put the pudding into a buttered pie-dish; bake for ¾ hour, and serve with sweet sauce, wine sauce, or stewed fruit. Baked in small cups, this makes very pretty little puddings.

Time, ¾ hour. *Average cost*, 8d. *Sufficient* for 5 or 6 persons.

BAKED BATTER PUDDING, with Dried or Fresh Fruit.

INGREDIENTS.—1½ pints milk, 4 tablespoonfuls flour, 3 eggs, 2 oz. finely shredded suet, ¼ lb. currants, a pinch of salt.

Mode.—Mix the milk, flour, and eggs to a smooth batter; add a little salt, the suet, and the currants, which should be well washed, picked, and dried; put the mixture into a buttered pie-dish, and bake in a moderate oven for 1½ hours. When fresh fruits are in season, this pudding is exceedingly nice with damsons, plums, red currants, gooseberries, or apples; when made with these, the pudding must be thickly sprinkled over with sifted sugar. Boiled batter pudding, with fruit, is made in the same manner, by putting the fruit into a buttered basin, and filling it up with batter in the above proportion, but omitting the suet. Send quickly to table, and cover plentifully with sifted sugar.

Time, baked batter pudding, with fruit, 1¼ to 1½ hours; boiled ditto, 1½ to 1¾ hours. Smaller puddings will be done enough in ¾ or 1 hour. *Average cost*, 9d. *Sufficient* for 7 or 8 persons. *Seasonable* at any time, with dried fruits.

BOILED BATTER PUDDING.

INGREDIENTS.—3 *eggs*, 1 *oz. butter*, 1 *pint milk*, 3 *tablespoonfuls flour*, *a little salt*.

Mode.—Put the flour into a basin, and add sufficient milk to moisten, carefully rub down the lumps with a spoon, pour in the remainder of the milk and stir in the butter, previously melted; keep beating the mixture, add the eggs and a pinch of salt, and when the batter is quite smooth, put it into a well-buttered basin, tie down very tightly, and put it into boiling water; move the basin about for a few minutes after it is put into the water, to prevent the flour setting in any part, and boil for 1¼ hours. This pudding may also be boiled in a floured cloth that has been wetted in hot water; it will then take a few minutes less than when boiled in a basin. Send very quickly to table, and serve with sweet sauce, wine sauce, stewed fruit, or jam of any kind.

Time, 1¼ hours in a basin, 1 hour in a cloth. *Average cost*, 7d. *Sufficient* for 5 or 6 persons.

BAKED BREAD PUDDING.

INGREDIENTS.—½ *lb. grated bread*, 1 *pint milk*, 3 *eggs*, 2 *oz. butter*, 4 *oz. moist sugar*, 2 *oz. candied peel*, 6 *bitter almonds*, 1 *tablespoonful brandy.*

Mode.—Put the milk into a stewpan, with the bitter almonds; let it infuse for ¼ hour; bring it to the boiling point; strain it on to the breadcrumbs, and let these remain till cold; then add the eggs, which should be well whisked, the butter, sugar, and brandy, and beat the pudding well until all the ingredients are thoroughly mixed; line the bottom of a pie-dish with the candied peel sliced thin, put in the mixture, and bake for nearly ¾ hour.

Time, nearly ¾ hour. *Average cost*, 1s. *Sufficient* for 5 or 6 persons.

Note.—A few currants beaten in with the mixture may be substituted for the candied peel.

BAKED BREAD-AND-BUTTER PUDDING.

INGREDIENTS.—9 *thin slices bread-and-butter*, 1½ *pints milk*, 3 *eggs*, *sugar to taste*, ¾ *lb. currants*, *flavouring of vanilla*, *grated lemon-peel or nutmeg.*

Mode.—Cut 9 slices of bread-and-butter, not very thick, and put them into a pie-dish, with currants between each layer and on the top. Sweeten and flavour the milk, either by infusing a little lemon-peel in it, or by adding a few drops of essence of vanilla; well whisk the eggs, and stir these to the milk. *Strain* this over the bread and butter, and bake in a moderate oven for 1 hour, or rather longer. This pudding may be very much enriched by adding cream, candied peel, or more eggs than stated above. It should be sent to table in the pie-dish, and is better for being made about 2 hours before it is baked.

Time, 1 hour, or rather longer. *Average cost*, 9d. *Sufficient* for 6 or 7 persons.

BOILED BREAD PUDDING.

INGREDIENTS.—1½ *pints milk*, ¾ *pint breadcrumbs*, *sugar to taste*, 3 *eggs*, 1 *oz. butter*, 3 *oz. currants*, ¼ *teaspoonful grated nutmeg.*

Mode.—Make the milk boiling, and pour it on the breadcrumbs; let these remain till cold; then add the other ingredients, taking care that the eggs are well beaten, and the currants well washed, picked, and dried. Beat the pudding well, and put it into a buttered basin; tie it down tightly with a cloth, plunge it into boiling water, and boil for 1¼ hours; turn it out of the basin, and serve with sifted sugar. Any odd pieces or scraps of bread answer for this pudding; but they should be soaked overnight, and, when used, should have the water well squeezed from them.

Time, 1¾ hours. *Average cost*, 9d. *Sufficient* for 6 or 7 persons.

VERY PLAIN BREAD PUDDING.

INGREDIENTS.—*Odd pieces of crust or crumb of bread; to every quart allow* ½ *teaspoonful salt*, 1 *teaspoonful grated nutmeg*, 3 *oz. moist sugar*, ½ *lb. currants*, 1½ *oz. butter.*

Mode.—Break the bread into small pieces, and pour on them as much boiling water as will soak them well. Let these stand till the water is cool; then press it out, and thoroughly mash the bread with a fork. Measure this pulp, and to every quart stir in salt, nutmeg, sugar, and currants in the above proportion; mix all well together, and put into a well buttered pie-dish. Smooth the surface with the back of a spoon, and place the butter in small pieces over the top; bake in a moderate oven for 1½ hours, and serve very hot. Boiling milk may be substituted for the boiling water.

Time, 1½ hours. *Average cost* for large pudding, 6d., exclusive of the bread. *Sufficient* for 7 or 8 persons.

A PLAIN CABINET OR BOILED BREAD-AND-BUTTER PUDDING.

INGREDIENTS.—3 *oz. raisins, a few thin slices bread-and-butter, 3 eggs, 1 pint milk, sugar to taste, ¼ nutmeg.*

Mode.—Butter a pudding-basin, and line the inside with a layer of raisins previously stoned; then nearly fill the basin with slices of bread-and-butter with the crust cut off, and in another basin beat the eggs; add to them the milk, sugar, and grated nutmeg; mix all well together, and pour the whole on to the bread-and-butter. Let it stand ½ hour; then tie a floured cloth over it; boil for 1 hour, turn out, and serve with sweet sauce. The basin must be quite full before the cloth is tied over.

Time, 1 hour. *Average cost*, 9d. *Sufficient* for 5 or 6 persons. *Seasonable* at any time.

CANARY PUDDING.

INGREDIENTS.—*The weight of 3 eggs in sugar and butter, the weight of 2 eggs in flour, the rind of 1 small lemon, 3 eggs.*

Mode.—Melt the butter, but do not allow it to oil; add the sugar and finely minced lemon-peel, gradually dredge in the flour; keep the mixture well stirred; whisk the eggs; add these to the pudding; beat all the ingredients until thoroughly blended, and put them into a buttered mould or basin; boil for 2 hours, and serve with sweet sauce.

Time, 2 hours. *Average cost*, 1s. *Sufficient* for 4 or 5 persons.

BAKED OR BOILED CARROT PUDDING.

INGREDIENTS.—½ *lb. breadcrumbs, 4 oz. suet, ¼ lb. stoned raisins, ¾ lb. carrot, ¼ lb. currants, 3 oz. sugar, 3 eggs, milk, ¼ nutmeg.*

Mode.—Boil the carrots until tender enough to mash to a pulp, add the

remaining ingredients, and moisten with sufficient milk to make the pudding of the consistency of thick batter. If to be boiled, put the mixture into a buttered basin, tie it down with a cloth, and boil for 2½ hours; if to be baked, put it into a pie-dish, and bake for nearly an hour; turn it out of the dish, strew sifted sugar over it, and serve.

Time, 2½ hours to boil; 1 hour to bake. *Average cost*, 1s. *Sufficient* for 5 or 6 persons. *Seasonable* from September to March.

CHEESE PUDDING.

INGREDIENTS.—¼ *lb. Cheddar cheese cut into thin slices; 1 oz. butter; 2 eggs well beaten.*

Mode.—Put the cheese and butter into a saucepan, and stir over the fire till all is melted. Remove the saucepan, add the eggs. Mix all together, put into a shallow tin, and brown before the fire.

Time, 10 minutes. *Average cost*, 5d.

CHERRY TART.

INGREDIENTS.—1½ *lbs. cherries, 2 small tablespoonfuls moist sugar, ½ lb. short crust.*

Mode.—Pick the stalks from the cherries, put them with the sugar into a *deep* pie-dish, just capable of holding them, with a small cup placed upside down in the midst. Make a short crust with ½ lb. of flour, by either of the recipes given; lay a border round the edge of the dish; put on the cover, and ornament the edges; bake in a brisk oven from ½ hour to 40 minutes; strew finely sifted sugar over, and serve hot or cold. Make two or three tarts at one time, as the trimmings from one tart answer for lining the edges of the dish for another, and so much paste is not required as when they are made singly. Unless meant for family use, never make fruit pies in very *large* dishes; select them, however, as *deep* as possible.

Time, ½ hour to 40 minutes. *Average cost*, in full season, 1s. *Sufficient* for 5 or 6 persons. *Seasonable* in June, July, and August.

Note.—A few currants added to the cherries will be found to impart a nice piquant taste to them.

A PLAIN CHRISTMAS PUDDING FOR CHILDREN.

INGREDIENTS.—1 *lb. flour, 1 lb. breadcrumbs, ¾ lb. stoned raisins, ¾ lb. cur-*

rants, ½ lb. suet, 3 or 4 eggs, milk, 2 oz. candied peel, 1 teaspoonful powdered allspice, ½ saltspoonful salt.

Mode.—Let the suet be finely chopped, the raisins stoned, and the currants well washed, picked, and dried. Mix these with the other dry ingredients, and stir well together; beat and strain the eggs to the pudding, stir these in, and add just sufficient milk to make it mix properly. Tie it up in a well floured cloth, put it into boiling water, and boil for at least 5 hours. Serve with a sprig of holly placed in the middle of the pudding, and a little pounded sugar sprinkled over it.

Time, 5 hours. *Average cost*, 1s. 9d. *Sufficient* for 9 or 10 children. *Seasonable* at Christmas.

ROYAL COBURG PUDDING.

INGREDIENTS.—1 pint new milk, 6 oz. flour, 6 oz. sugar, 6 oz. butter, 6 oz. currants, 6 eggs; a little brandy, and nutmeg to taste.

Mode.—Mix the flour to a smooth batter with the milk, add the remaining ingredients *gradually*, and when well mixed put it into four basins or moulds half full; bake ¾ hour; turn the puddings out on a dish, and serve with wine sauce.

Time, ¾ hour. *Average cost*, 1s. 10d. *Sufficient* for 7 or 8 persons.

CRACKER PUDDING.

INGREDIENTS.—A breakfastcupful of cracker in crumbs, ½ lb. of suet, 2 tablespoonfuls of sugar, 3 eggs, 3 cups of milk, a little salt.

Mode.—While preparing the other ingredients, soak the crumbs in milk. Chop the suet very fine, beat the eggs, adding the sugar, mix the egg and sugar with the cracker, then the suet, with a pinch of salt, and work to a smooth paste. Butter a pudding-dish, pour in the mixture, and bake for ¾ of an hour. A fruit sauce is a nice accompaniment to this dish.

Time, ¾ of an hour. *Average cost*, 8d. *Seasonable* at any time.

CURRANT DUMPLINGS.

INGREDIENTS.—1 lb. flour, 6 oz. suet, ½ lb. currants, rather more than ½ pint water.

Mode.—Chop the suet fine, mix it with the flour, and add the currants (washed, picked, and dried); mix the whole to a limp paste with the water or milk; divide it into 7 or 8 dumplings; tie them in cloths and boil for 1¼ hours. If boiled without a cloth they should be dropped into boiling water, and be moved about at first, to prevent them from sticking to the bottom. Serve with a cut lemon, cold butter, and sifted sugar.

Time, in a cloth, 1¼ hours; without, ¾ hour. *Average cost*, 8d. *Sufficient* for 6 or 7 persons.

BOILED CURRANT PUDDING (Plain and Economical).

INGREDIENTS.—1 lb. flour, ½ lb. suet, ½ lb. currants, milk.

Mode. — Wash, pick, and dry the currants; chop the suet fine; mix all the ingredients together; make the pudding into a stiff batter with the milk; tie it up in a floured cloth, put it into boiling water, and boil for 3½ hours; serve with a cut lemon, cold butter, and sifted sugar.

Time, 3½ hours. *Average cost*, 10d. *Sufficient* for 7 or 8 persons. *Seasonable* at any time.

BLACK OR RED-CURRANT PUDDING.

INGREDIENTS. — 1 quart of red or black currants, measured with the stalks, ½ lb. moist sugar, suet crust, or butter crust.

Mode.—Make, with ¾ lb. flour, either a suet crust or butter crust (the former is usually made); butter a basin, and line it with part of the crust; put in the currants stripped from the stalks, and sprinkle the sugar over them; put the cover of the pudding on; make the edges very secure; tie it down with a floured cloth, put it into boiling water, and boil from 2½ to 3 hours. Boiled without a basin, allow ½ hour less. We have given rather a large proportion of sugar; but fruit puddings are much more juicy and palatable when *well sweetened* before they are boiled. A few raspberries added to red-currant pudding are a very nice addition; about ½ pint would be sufficient for the above quantity of fruit. Fruit puddings are very delicious if, when they are turned out of the basin, the crust is browned with a salamander, or put into a very hot oven for a few minutes to colour it; this makes it crisp on the surface.

Time, 2½ to 3 hours; without a basin, 2 to 2½ hours. *Average cost*, in full season, 10d. *Sufficient* for 6 or 7 per sons. *Seasonable* in June, July, and August.

RED CURRANT AND RASPBERRY TART.

INGREDIENTS.—1½ *pints picked currants, ½ pint raspberries, 4 heaped tablespoonfuls of moist sugar, ½ lb. short crust.*

Mode.—Strip the currants from the stalks, and put them into a deep pie-dish, with a small cup placed in the midst, bottom upwards; add the raspberries and sugar; place a border of paste round the edge of the dish, cover with crust, ornament the edges, and bake from ½ to ¾ hour; strew some sifted sugar over before being sent to table. This tart is generally served cold.

Time, ½ to ¾ hour. *Average cost*, 1s. 2d. *Sufficient* for 5 or 6 persons. *Seasonable* in June, July, and August

BAKED CUSTARD PUDDING.

INGREDIENTS.—1½ *pints milk, the rind of ¼ lemon, ¼ lb. moist sugar, 4 eggs.*

Mode.—Put the milk into a saucepan with the sugar and lemon-rind, and let this infuse for about ½ hour, or until the milk is well flavoured; whisk the eggs, yolks and whites; pour the milk to them, stirring all the while; then have ready a pie-dish, lined at the edge with paste ready baked; strain the custard into the dish, grate a little nutmeg over the top, and bake in a *very slow* oven for about ½ hour, or rather longer. The flavour of this pudding may be varied by substituting bitter almonds for the lemon-rind; and it may be very much enriched by using half cream and half milk, and doubling the quantity of eggs.

Time, ½ to ¾ hour. *Average cost*, 8d. *Sufficient* for 5 or 6 persons.

Note.—This pudding is usually served cold with fruit tarts.

DAMSON PUDDING.

INGREDIENTS.—1½ *pints damsons, ¼ lb. moist sugar, ¾ lb. suet crust.*

Mode.—Make a suet crust with ¾ lb. of flour by recipe given; line a buttered pudding-basin with a portion; fill the basin with the damsons, sweeten them, and put on the lid; pinch the edges of the crust together; tie over a floured cloth, put the pudding into boiling water, and boil from 2¼ to 3 hours.

Time, 2¼ to 3 hours. *Average cost*, 8d. *Sufficient* for 6 or 7 persons. *Seasonable* in September and October.

DELHI PUDDINGS.

INGREDIENTS.—4 *large apples, a little grated nutmeg, 1 teaspoonful minced lemon-peel, 2 large tablespoonfuls sugar, 6 oz. currants, ¾ lb. suet crust.*

Mode.—Pare, core, and cut the apples into slices; put them into a saucepan, with the nutmeg, lemon-peel, and sugar; stir them over the fire until soft; roll the crust out thin, spread the apples over the paste, sprinkle over the currants, roll the pudding up, closing the ends properly, tie it in a floured cloth, and boil for 2 hours.

Time, 2 hours. *Average cost*, 1s. *Sufficient* for 5 or 6 persons. *Seasonable* from August to March.

EMPRESS PUDDING.

INGREDIENTS.—½ *lb. rice, 2 oz. butter, 3 eggs, jam, sufficient milk to soften the rice.*

Mode.—Boil the rice in the milk until very soft; then add the butter; boil it again for a few minutes, and set it by to cool. Well beat the eggs, stir these in, and line a dish with puff-paste; put over this a layer of rice, then a thin layer of jam, then another layer of rice, until the dish is full; and bake in a moderate oven for ¾ hour. This pudding may be eaten hot or cold; if cold, pour a boiled custard over it.

Time, ¾ hour. *Average cost*, 1s. *Sufficient* for 6 or 7 persons.

FOLKESTONE PUDDING-PIES.

INGREDIENTS.—1 *pint milk, 3 oz. ground rice, 3 oz. butter, ¼ lb. sugar, flavouring of lemon-peel or bay-leaf, 6 eggs, puff-paste, currants.*

Mode.—Infuse 2 laurel or bay-leaves, or the rind of ½ lemon, in the milk, and when it is well flavoured strain it, and add the rice; boil these for ¼ hour, stirring all the time; then take them off the fire, stir in the butter, sugar, and eggs, the latter to be well beaten; when nearly cold line some patty-pans with puff-paste, fill with the custard, strew over each a few currants, and bake from 20 to 25 minutes in a moderate oven.

Time, 20 to 25 minutes. *Average*

cost, 1s. 6d. *Sufficient* to fill a dozen patty-pans.

FRUIT TURNOVERS (suitable for Picnics).

INGREDIENTS.—*Puff-paste, any kind of fruit, sugar to taste.*

Mode.—Make some puff-paste by recipe; roll it out to the thickness of about ¼ inch, and cut it out in circular pieces; pile the fruit on half of the paste, sprinkle over some sugar, wet the edges, and turn the paste over. Press the edges together, ornament them, and brush the turnovers with the white of an egg; sprinkle over sifted sugar, and bake on tins, in a brisk oven, for about 20 minutes. Instead of putting the fruit in raw, it may be boiled down with a little sugar, and then inclosed in the crust; or jam, of any kind, may be substituted for fresh fruit.

Time, 20 minutes. *Average cost*, 1s. *Sufficient*—½ lb. of puff-paste will make 8 turnovers.

GINGER PUDDING.

INGREDIENTS.—½ *lb. flour*, ¼ *lb. suet*, ¼ *lb. moist sugar*, 2 *large teaspoonfuls grated ginger.*

Mode.—Shred the suet very fine, mix it with the flour, sugar, and ginger; stir well together; butter a basin, and put the mixture in *dry;* tie a cloth over, and boil for three hours.

Time, 3 hours. *Average cost*, 4d. *Sufficient* for 5 or 6 persons.

GOLDEN PUDDING.

INGREDIENTS. — ¼ *lb. breadcrumbs*, ¼ *lb. suet*, ¼ *lb. marmalade*, ¼ *lb. sugar*, 4 *eggs.*

Mode.—Put the breadcrumbs into a basin; mix them with the suet (finely minced), the marmalade, and the sugar; stir these ingredients well together, beat the eggs to a froth, moisten the pudding with these, and when well mixed, put it into a mould or buttered basin; tie down with a floured cloth, and boil for 2 hours. When turned out strew a little fine-sifted sugar over the top, and serve.

Time, 2 hours. *Average cost*, 8d. *Sufficient* for 5 or 6 persons.

Note.—The mould may be ornamented with stoned raisins, arranged in any fanciful pattern, before the mixture is poured in. For a plainer pudding, double the quantity of breadcrumbs, and if the eggs do not moisten it sufficiently, use a little milk.

BAKED GOOSEBERRY PUDDING.

INGREDIENTS.—*Gooseberries*, 3 *eggs*, 1½ *oz. butter*, ½ *pint breadcrumbs, sugar to taste.*

Mode.—Put the gooseberries into a jar, previously cutting off the tops and tails; place this jar in boiling water, and let it boil until the gooseberries are soft enough to pulp; then beat them through a coarse sieve, and to every pint of pulp add 3 well-whisked eggs, 1½ oz. of butter, ½ pint of breadcrumbs, and sugar to taste; beat the mixture well, lay a border of puff-paste round the edge of a pie-dish, put in the pudding, bake for about 40 minutes, strew sifted sugar over, and serve.

Time, about 40 minutes. *Average cost*, with a quart of fruit, 10d. *Sufficient* for 4 or 5 persons. *Seasonable* from May to July.

BOILED GOOSEBERRY PUDDING.

INGREDIENTS.—¾ *lb. suet crust*, 1½ *pints green gooseberries*, ¼ *lb. moist sugar.*

Mode.—Line a pudding-basin with suet crust, rolled to about ½ inch in thickness, cut off the tops and tails of the gooseberries; fill the basin with the fruit, put in the sugar, and cover with crust. Pinch the edges of the pudding together, tie over it a floured cloth, put it into boiling water, and boil from 2½ to 3 hours; turn it out of the basin, and serve with cream or custard.

Time, 2½ to 3 hours. *Average cost* 10d. *Sufficient* for 6 or 7 persons. *Seasonable* from May to July.

GOOSEBERRY TART.

INGREDIENTS.—1½ *pints gooseberries*, ½ *lb. short crust*, ¼ *lb. moist sugar.*

Mode.—With a pair of scissors cut off the tops and tails of the gooseberries; put them into a deep pie-dish, pile the fruit high in the centre, and put in the sugar; line the edge of the dish with a short crust, put on the cover, and ornament the edges of the tart; bake in a good oven for about ¾ hour, and before being sent to table, strew over it some fine-sifted sugar. A jug of cream, or a dish of boiled or baked custard, should accompany this dish.

Time, ¾ hour. *Average cost*, 7d. *Sufficient* for 5 or 6 persons. *Seasonable* from May to July.

HALF-PAY PUDDING.

INGREDIENTS.—¼ *lb. suet*, ¼ *lb. currants*, ¼ *lb. raisins*, ¼ *lb. flour*, ¼ *lb.*

breadcrumbs, 2 tablespoonfuls treacle, ½ pint milk.

Mode.—Chop the suet fine; mix with it the currants (nicely washed and dried), the raisins (stoned), the flour, breadcrumbs, and treacle; moisten with the milk, beat up the ingredients until thoroughly mixed, put them into a buttered basin, and boil the pudding for 3½ hours.

Time, 3½ hours. *Average cost*, 8d. *Sufficient* for 5 or 6 persons.

HUCKLEBERRY PUDDING (American Recipe).

INGREDIENTS.—*A pint of huckleberries* (or *whortleberries, as we call them*), 2 *eggs, a pint of milk, a saltspoonful of salt,* ¼ *teaspoonful of soda,* ½ *teaspoonful of cream of tartar, enough flour to make a thick batter.*

Mode.—Mix the cream of tartar with the flour, and dissolve the soda in hot water, then make into a thick batter with the other ingredients. Pick and mash the berries, dredge them with flour, and stir into the batter. Pour the mixture into a buttered mould, and boil 1 hour. Serve with some very sweet sauce.

Time, 1 hour. *Average cost*, 7d. *Sufficient* for 4 persons.

ITALIAN PUDDING (Italian Recipe).

INGREDIENTS. — ¼ *lb. of any plain sweet biscuits,* 6 *macaroons,* 2 *oz. of candied peel,* 1 *oz. of sultanas,* 1 *oz. of pistachio nuts,* 8 *eggs,* ½ *pint of cream, a small glass of liqueur or rum.*

Mode. — Pound the biscuits and macaroons, chop the peel, sultanas, and nuts fine, and mix with 3 whole eggs, the whites of the rest, the cream and liqueur. Put the mixture in a mould, buttered and lined with paper, and cook in a bain - marie for about 1 hour. Punch or sweet sauce may be served with this pudding.

Time, 1 hour. *Average cost*, 2s. 2d. *Sufficient* for 6 persons. *Seasonable* at any time.

BAKED LEMON PUDDING.

INGREDIENTS.—*The yolks of 4 eggs,* 4 *oz. pounded sugar,* 1 *lemon,* ¼ *lb. butter, puff-crust.*

Mode.—Beat the eggs to a froth; mix with them the sugar and warmed butter; stir these ingredients well together, putting in the grated rind and strained juice of the lemon. Line a shallow dish with puff-paste; put in the mixture, and bake in a moderate oven for 40 minutes; turn the pudding out of the dish, strew over it sifted sugar, and serve.

Time, 40 minutes. *Average cost*, 10d., exclusive of crust. *Sufficient* for 5 or 6 persons.

BAKED LEMON PUDDING (Richer).

INGREDIENTS.—*10 oz. breadcrumbs,* 2 *pints milk,* 2 *oz. butter,* 1 *lemon,* ¼ *lb. pounded sugar,* 4 *eggs,* 1 *tablespoonful brandy.*

Mode.—Bring the milk to the boiling point, stir in the butter, and pour these hot over the breadcrumbs; add the sugar and very finely-minced lemon-peel; beat the eggs, and stir these in, with the brandy, to the other ingredients; put a rim of paste round the dish, and bake for ¾ hour.

Time, ¾ hour. *Average cost*, 1s. 3d. *Sufficient* for 6 or 7 persons.

BOILED LEMON PUDDING.

INGREDIENTS.—½ *lb. chopped suet,* ¾ *lb. breadcrumbs,* 2 *small lemons,* 6 *oz. moist sugar,* ¼ *lb. flour,* 2 *eggs, milk.*

Mode.—Mix the suet, breadcrumbs, sugar, and flour well together, adding the lemon-peel, finely minced, and the juice (strained). Moisten with the eggs and sufficient milk to make the pudding of the consistency of thick batter; put it into a well-buttered mould, and boil for 3½ hours; turn it out, strew sifted sugar over, and serve with or without wine sauce.

Time, 3½ hours. *Average cost*, 10d. *Sufficient* for 7 or 8 persons.

Note.—This pudding may also be baked; it will take about 2 hours.

PLAIN LEMON PUDDING.

INGREDIENTS.—¾ *lb. flour,* 6 *oz. lard,* or ¼ *lb. dripping, the juice of* 1 *large lemon,* 1 *teaspoonful flour, sugar.*

Mode.—Make the flour and lard into a smooth paste, and roll it out to the thickness of about ½ inch. Squeeze the lemon-juice, strain it into a cup, stir the teaspoonful of flour into it, and as much moist sugar as will make it into a stiff and thick paste; spread this mixture over the paste, roll it up, secure the ends, and tie the pudding in a floured cloth. Boil for 2 hours.

Time, 2 hours. *Average cost*, 6d. *Sufficient* for 5 or 6 persons.

MANCHESTER PUDDING (to eat cold).

INGREDIENTS.—3 oz. *grated bread,* ½ *pint milk, a strip lemon-peel, 4 eggs,* 2 *oz. butter, sugar to taste, puff-paste, jam,* 3 *tablespoonfuls brandy.*

Mode.—Flavour the milk with lemon-peel, by infusing it in the milk for ½ hour; strain it on to the breadcrumbs, and boil it for 2 or 3 minutes; add the eggs (leaving out the whites of 2), the butter, sugar, and brandy; stir all these well together; cover a pie-dish with puff-paste, and at the bottom put a thick layer of any kind of jam; pour the above mixture, cold, on the jam, and bake the pudding for an hour. Serve cold, with a little sifted sugar sprinkled over.

Time, 1 hour. *Average cost,* 1s. 4d. *Sufficient* for 5 or 6 persons.

MILITARY PUDDING.

INGREDIENTS.—½ *lb. suet,* ¾ *lb. bread-crumbs,* ½ *lb. moist sugar, the rind and juice of* 1 *large lemon.*

Mode.—Chop the suet fine, mix it with the breadcrumbs and sugar, and mince the lemon-rind and strain the juice; stir these into the other ingredients, mix well, put the mixture into small buttered cups, and bake for rather more than ½ hour; turn them out on the dish, and serve with lemon-sauce. The above ingredients may be made into small balls, and boiled for about ½ hour.

Time, rather more than ½ hour. *Average cost,* 7d. *Sufficient* to fill 6 or 7 moderate-sized cups.

MINCEMEAT.

INGREDIENTS.—1 *lb. raisins,* 1½ *lbs. currants,* ½ *lb. raw lean beef,* 1 *lb. beef suet,* 2 *lbs. moist sugar,* 3 *oz. citron,* 6 *oz. candied lemon-peel,* 3 *oz. candied orange-peel,* 1 *small nutmeg,* 1 *lb. apples, the rind and juice of* 1 *lemon,* ¼ *pint brandy. Mixed spice may be added to taste.*

Mode.—Stone and *cut* the raisins once or twice across, but do not chop them; wash, dry, and pick the currants free from stalks and grit, and mince the beef and chop the suet very fine; slice the citron and candied peel, grate the nutmeg, and pare, core, and mince the apples; mince the lemon-peel, strain the juice. Mix these ingredients well together, adding the brandy when the other things are well blended; press the whole into a jar, carefully exclude the

air, and the mincemeat will be ready for use in a fortnight. Many persons prefer this mincemeat without the beef.

Average cost for this quantity, 4s. *Seasonable*—make this about the beginning of December.

MINCE PIES.

INGREDIENTS.—*Good puff-paste (by recipe), mincemeat.*

Mode.—Make some good puff-paste by either of the above recipes; roll it out to the thickness of about ¼ inch, and line some good-sized patty-pans with it; fill them with mincemeat, cover with the paste, and cut it off all round close to the edge of the tin; put the pies into a brisk oven to draw the paste up and bake for 25 minutes, or longer; brush them over with the white of an egg, beaten with the blade of a knife to a stiff froth; sprinkle over pounded sugar, and put them into the oven for a minute or two, to dry the egg; dish the pies on a white d'oyley, and serve hot. They may be merely sprinkled with pounded sugar, instead of being glazed. To re-warm them, put the pies on the patty-pans, and let them remain in the oven for 10 minutes or ¼ hour, and they will be almost as good as if freshly made.

Time, 25 to 30 minutes; 10 minutes to re-warm them. *Average cost,* 3d. each. *Sufficient,* ½ lb. of paste for 6 pies. *Seasonable* at Christmas time.

NUDELN (German Recipe).

INGREDIENTS.—*Flour, milk,* 2 *oz. of butter,* 4 *eggs, grated rusk.*

Mode.—With the eggs and a small cup of milk, mix sufficient flour to make a paste; knead this on a board, constantly dredging with flour, until it is a stiff dough. Cut into four pieces, roll out as thin as *possible* and throw over a pole to dry. After half an hour again divide in four, lay the pieces one over the other, roll them up, and cut into strips, a quarter of an inch wide, then shake them apart. The *nudeln* is then ready for use, but it will keep some weeks. When wanted boil till tender, in plenty of boiling water, with salt in it, turn into a drainer and pour boiling water over. Serve with sauce made with milk, salt and fresh butter, and cover with grated rusk.

Time, boil till tender. *Average cost,* 10d. *Sufficient* for 8 or 10 persons. *Seasonable* at any time.

PARADISE PUDDING.

INGREDIENTS.—3 *eggs*, 3 *apples*, ¼ *lb. breadcrumbs*, 3 oz. *sugar*, 3 oz. *currants*, *salt and grated nutmeg to taste, the rind of ½ lemon, ½ wineglassful brandy.*

Mode.—Pare, core, and mince the apples into small pieces, and mix them with the other dry ingredients; beat up the eggs, moisten the mixture with these, and beat it well; stir in the brandy, and put the pudding into a buttered mould; tie it down with a cloth, boil for 1½ hours, and serve with sweet sauce.

Time, 1½ hours. *Average cost*, 1s. *Sufficient* for 4 or 5 persons.

PASTRY SANDWICHES.

INGREDIENTS.—*Puff-paste, jam of any kind, the white of an egg, sifted sugar.*

Mode.—Roll the paste out thin; put half of it on a baking-sheet or tin, and spread equally over it apricot, greengage, or other preserve. Lay over this preserve another thin paste; press the edges together all round; and mark the paste in lines with a knife on the surface, to show where to cut it when baked. Bake from 20 minutes to ½ hour; and, a short time before being done, take the pastry out of the oven, brush it over with the white of an egg, sift over it pounded sugar, and put it back in the oven to colour. When cold, cut it into strips; pile these on a dish pyramidically, and serve. These strips, cut about 2 inches long, piled in circular rows, and a plateful of flavoured whipped cream poured in the middle, make a very pretty dish.

Time, 20 minutes to ½ hour. *Average cost*, with ½ lb. of paste, 9d. *Sufficient*, ½ lb. of paste will make 2 dishes of sandwiches.

PEASE PUDDING.

INGREDIENTS.—1½ *pints split peas*, 2 *oz. butter, pepper and salt to taste.*

Mode.—Put the peas to soak overnight, in rain-water, and float off any that are worm-eaten or discoloured. Tie them loosely in a clean cloth, leaving a little room for them to swell, and put them on to boil in cold rain-water, allowing 2½ hours after the water has simmered up. When the peas are tender, take them up and drain; rub them through a colander with a wooden spoon; add the butter, pepper, and salt; beat all well together for a few minutes, until the ingredients are well incorporated; then tie them tightly in a

floured cloth; boil the pudding for another hour, turn it on to the dish, and serve very hot. This pudding should always be sent to table with boiled leg of pork, and is an exceedingly nice accompaniment to boiled beef.

Time, 2½ hours to boil the peas, tied loosely in the cloth; 1 hour for the pudding. *Average cost*, 6d. *Sufficient* for 7 or 8 persons. *Seasonable* from September to March.

PLUM-PUDDING OF FRESH FRUIT.

INGREDIENTS.—¾ *lb. suet crust*, 1½ *pints of Orleans or any other kind of plum*, ¼ *lb. moist sugar.*

Mode.—Line a pudding-basin with suet crust rolled out to the thickness of about ½ inch; fill the basin with the fruit, put in the sugar, and cover with crust. Fold the edges over, and pinch them together, to prevent the juice escaping. Tie over a floured cloth, put the pudding into boiling water, and boil from 2 to 2½ hours. Turn it out of the basin, and serve quickly.

Time, 2 to 2½ hours. *Average cost*, 10d. *Sufficient* for 6 or 7 persons. *Seasonable*, with various kinds of plums, from the beginning of August to the beginning of October.

BAKED PLUM-PUDDING.

INGREDIENTS.—2 *lbs. flour*, 1 *lb. currants*, 1 *lb. raisins*, 1 *lb. suet*; 2 *eggs*, 1 *pint milk, a few slices candied peel.*

Mode.—Chop the suet fine; mix with it the flour, currants, stoned raisins, and candied peel; moisten with the eggs, well-beaten, and add sufficient milk to make the pudding of the consistency of very thick batter. Put it into a buttered dish, and bake in a good oven from 2¼ to 2½ hours; turn it out, strew sifted sugar over, and serve. For a very plain pudding, use only half the quantity of fruit, omit the eggs, and substitute milk or water for them.

Time, large pudding, 2¼ to 2½ hours; half the size, 1½ hours. *Average cost*, 2s. 4d. *Sufficient* for 9 or 10 persons. *Seasonable* in winter.

CHRISTMAS PLUM PUDDING
(Very Good).

INGREDIENTS.—1½ *lbs. raisins*, ½ *lb. currants*, ½ *lb. mixed peel*, ¾ *lb. breadcrumbs*, ¾ *lb. suet*, 8 *eggs*, 1 *wineglassful brandy.*

Mode.—Stone and cut the raisins in

halves, but do not chop them; wash, pick and dry the currants, and mince the suet fine; cut the candied peel into thin slices, and grate down the bread into fine crumbs. When all these dry ingredients are prepared, mix them well together; then moisten the mixture with the eggs, which should be well beaten, and the brandy; stir well, that everything may be very thoroughly blended; and *press* the pudding into a buttered mould; tie it down tightly with a floured cloth, and boil for 5 or 6 hours. It may be boiled in a cloth without a mould, and will require the same time allowed for cooking. As Christmas puddings are usually made a few days before they are required for table, when the pudding is taken out of the pot, hang it up immediately, and put a plate or saucer underneath to catch the water that may drain from it. The day it is to be eaten, plunge it into boiling water, and keep it boiling for at least 2 hours; then turn it out of the mould, and serve with brandy-sauce. On Christmas Day a sprig of holly is usually placed in the middle of the pudding, and about a wineglassful of brandy poured round it, which, at the moment of serving, is lighted, and the pudding thus brought to table encircled in flame.

Time, 5 or 6 hours the first time of boiling; 2 hours the day it is to be served. *Average cost,* 3s. *Sufficient* for a quart mould, for 7 or 8 persons. *Seasonable* on the 25th of December, and on various festive occasions till March.

AN EXCELLENT PLUM-PUDDING
(Made without Eggs).

INGREDIENTS. — ½ *lb. flour,* 6 *oz. raisins,* 6 *oz. currants,* ¼ *lb. chopped suet,* ¼ *lb. brown sugar,* ¼ *lb. mashed carrot,* ¼ *lb. mashed potatoes,* 1 *table-spoonful treacle,* 1 *oz. candied lemon-peel,* 1 *oz. candied citron.*

Mode.—Mix the flour, currants, suet, and sugar well together; stir the mashed carrot and potato into the other ingredients; add the treacle and lemon-peel; but put no liquid in the mixture, or it will be spoiled. Tie it loosely in a cloth, or, if put in a basin, do not quite fill it, as the pudding should have room to swell; and boil it for 4 hours. Serve with brandy-sauce. This pudding is better for being mixed over-night.

Time, 4 hours. *Average cost,* 1s. 6d. *Sufficient* for 6 or 7 persons. *Seasonable* in winter.

POTATO PASTY.

INGREDIENTS.—1½ *lbs. rump-steak or mutton cutlets, pepper and salt to taste,* 1½ *pints weak broth or gravy,* 1 *oz. butter, mashed potatoes.*

Mode.—Place the meat, cut in small pieces, at the bottom of the pan; season with pepper and salt, and add the gravy and butter broken into small pieces. Put on the perforated plate with its valve-pipe screwed on, and fill up the whole space to the top of the tube with nicely mashed potatoes mixed with a little milk, and finish the surface of them in any ornamental manner. If carefully baked, the potatoes will be covered with a delicate brown crust, retaining all the savoury steam rising from the meat. Send it to table as it comes from the oven, with a napkin folded round it.

Time, 40 to 60 minutes. *Average cost,* 2s. 3d. *Sufficient* for 4 or 5 persons.

PUMPKIN PIE (Australian Recipe).

INGREDIENTS.—*Pumpkin,* 6 *eggs,* 3 *pints of milk, flavouring of mace, nutmeg, or lemon, as preferred.*

Mode.—Pare the pumpkin, take out the seeds, and stew till soft. Press through a sieve, and to each quart of the pulp allow the ingredients named above. Mix first with the pulp the sugar, then the yolks and whites of the eggs, beaten separately, and the flavouring, and beat all together. Line the rim of a buttered dish with puff paste, pour in the mixture, and bake in a rather quick oven.

Time, ¾ of an hour to bake the pie. *Seasonable* in summer.

QUICKLY MADE PUDDING.

INGREDIENTS.—½ *lb. butter,* ½ *lb. sifted sugar,* ¼ *lb. flour,* 1 *pint milk,* 5 *eggs, a little grated lemon-rind.*

Mode.—Make the milk hot; stir in the butter, and let it cool; then stir in the sugar, flour, and eggs (well whisked), and omit the whites of 2; flavour with a little grated lemon-rind, and beat the mixture well. Butter some small cups, rather more than half fill them; bake from 20 minutes to ½ hour, and serve with fruit, custard, or wine sauce, a little of which may be poured over them.

Time, 20 minutes to ½ hour. *Average cost,* 1s. *Sufficient* for 6 puddings.

BAKED RAISIN PUDDING (Plain and Economical).

INGREDIENTS.—1 *lb. flour*, ¾ *lb. stoned raisins*, ½ *lb. suet, a pinch of salt*, 1 *oz. sugar, a little grated nutmeg, milk.*

Mode.—Chop the suet finely; stone the raisins and cut them in halves; mix with the suet, add the salt, sugar, and grated nutmeg, and moisten the whole with sufficient milk to make it of the consistency of thick batter. Put the pudding into a buttered pie-dish, and bake for 1½ hours, or rather longer. Turn it out of the dish; strew sifted sugar over, and serve. This is a very plain recipe, and suitable where there is a family of children. It can be improved by the addition of candied peel, and rather a larger proportion of suet; a few eggs would also make the pudding richer.

Time, 1½ hours. *Average cost*, 10d. *Sufficient* for 7 or 8 persons. *Seasonable* in winter.

BOILED RAISIN PUDDING (Plain and Economical).

INGREDIENTS.—1 *lb. flour*, ½ *lb. stoned raisins*, ½ *lb. chopped suet*, ½ *saltspoonful of salt, milk.*

Mode.—Stone the raisins and chop the suet fine, mix them with the flour, add the salt, and when these dry ingredients are thoroughly mixed, moisten with sufficient milk to make it into rather a stiff paste. Tie it up in a floured cloth, put it into boiling water, and boil for 4 hours; serve with sifted sugar. This pudding may also be made in a long shape, the same as rolled jam-pudding, and will then require only 2½ hours' boiling.

Time, made round, 4 hours; in a long shape, 2½ hours. *Average cost*, 8d. *Sufficient* for 8 or 9 persons. *Seasonable* in winter.

BOILED RHUBARB PUDDING.

INGREDIENTS.—4 *or* 5 *sticks fine rhubarb*, ¼ *lb. moist sugar*, ¾ *lb. suet crust.*

Mode.—Make a suet crust with ¾ lb. of flour in accordance with recipe, and line a buttered basin with it. Wash and wipe the rhubarb, and, if old, string it, that is to say pare off the outside skin. Cut it into inch lengths, fill the basin with it, put in the sugar, and cover with crust. Pinch the edges together, tie over a floured cloth, put it into boiling water, and boil for 2 to 2½ hours. Turn it out of the basin, and

serve with a jug of cream and sifted sugar.

Time, 2 to 2½ hours. *Average cost*, 8d. *Sufficient* for 5 or 6 persons. *Seasonable* in spring.

RHUBARB TART.

INGREDIENTS.—½ *lb. puff-crust, about* 5 *sticks large rhubarb*, ¼ *lb. moist sugar.*

Mode.—Make a puff-crust by recipe; line the edges of a deep pie-dish with it, and wash, wipe, and cut the rhubarb into pieces about 1 inch long. If old and tough, string it, that is to say pare off the outside skin. Pile the fruit high in the dish, as it shrinks in the cooking; put in the sugar, cover with crust, ornament the edges, and bake the tart in a well-heated oven from ½ to ¾ hour. If wanted very nice, brush it over with the white of an egg beaten to a stiff froth, then sprinkle on it some sifted sugar, and put it in the oven just to set the glaze: this should be done when the tart is nearly baked. A small quantity of lemon-juice, and a little of the peel minced, improve the flavour.

Time, ½ to ¾ hour. *Average cost*, 10d. *Sufficient* for 4 or 5 persons. *Seasonable* in spring.

BAKED RICE PUDDING.

INGREDIENTS. — 1 *small teacupful rice*, 2 *eggs*, 1 *pint milk*, 2 *oz. fresh butter*, ¼ *lb. currants*, 2 *tablespoonfuls brandy, nutmeg*, ¼ *lb. sugar, the rind of* ½ *lemon.*

Mode.—Put the lemon-rind and milk into a stewpan, and let it infuse till the milk is well flavoured with the lemon; boil the rice until tender in water, with a very small quantity of salt, and thoroughly drain. Beat the eggs, stir them in the milk, which should be strained, the butter, brandy, currants, and remaining ingredients; add the rice, and mix. Line the edges of the dish with puff-paste, put in the pudding, and bake for about ¾ hour in a slow oven. Slices of candied peel may be added, or sultana raisins substituted for currants.

Time, ¾ hour. *Average cost*, 1s. *Sufficient* for 5 or 6 persons. *Seasonable*—suitable for a winter pudding.

BAKED RICE PUDDING (Plain and Economical; a nice Pudding for Children).

INGREDIENTS.—1 *teacupful rice*, 2 *tablespoonfuls moist sugar*, 1 *quart milk*, ½ *oz. butter or* 2 *small tablespoon-*

fuls of chopped suet, ½ teaspoonful grated nutmeg.

Mode.—Wash the rice, put it into a pie-dish with the sugar, pour in the milk, and stir well together; add the butter cut into very small pieces, or, instead of this, the above proportion of finely minced suet; grate a little nutmeg over the top, and bake the pudding, in a *moderate* oven, from 1½ to 2 hours. The · pudding must be very slowly baked, to give plenty of time for the rice to swell, and be very thoroughly done.

Time, 1½ to 2 hours. *Average cost*, 7d. *Sufficient* for 5 or 6 children.

PLAIN BOILED RICE PUDDING.

INGREDIENTS.—½ lb. rice.

Mode.—Wash the rice, tie it in a pudding-cloth, allowing room to swell, and put it into a saucepan of cold water; boil gently for 2 hours, and if, after a time, the cloth seems tied too loosely, tighten it. Serve with melted butter, or cold butter and sugar, or stewed fruit, jam, or marmalade.

Time, 2 hours after the water boils. *Average cost*, 2d. *Sufficient* for 4 or 5 persons.

BOILED RICE PUDDING.

INGREDIENTS.—¼ lb. rice, 1½ pints new milk, 2 oz. butter, 4 eggs, ⅓ saltspoonful salt, 4 large tablespoonfuls moist sugar, flavouring to taste.

Mode.—Stew the rice gently in the new milk, and, when it is tender, pour it into a basin; stir in the butter, and let it stand to cool; then beat the eggs, add these to the rice with the sugar, salt, and flavouring, such as nutmeg, powdered cinnamon, grated lemon-peel, essence of bitter almonds, or vanilla. When all is well stirred, put the pudding into a buttered basin, tie it down with a cloth, plunge it into boiling water, and boil for 1¼ hours.

Time, 1¼ hours. *Average cost*, 10d. *Sufficient* for 5 or 6 persons.

RICE PUDDING (with Dried or Fresh Fruit; a nice dish for the Nursery).

INGREDIENTS.—½ lb. rice, 1 pint any kind of fresh fruit that may be preferred, or ½ lb. raisins or currants.

Mode.—Wash the rice, tie it in a cloth, allowing room for it to swell, and put it into a saucepan of cold water; let it boil for an hour, then take it up, untie the cloth, stir in the fruit, and tie it up again tolerably tight, and put

it into the water for the remainder of the time. Boil for another hour, or rather longer, and serve with sweet sauce if made with dried fruit; and, with plain sifted sugar and a little cream or milk, if made with fresh fruit.

Time, 1 hour to boil the rice without the fruit; 1 hour, or longer, afterwards. *Average cost*, 5d. *Sufficient* for 6 or 7 children.

Note.—This pudding is very good made with apples, pared, cored, and sliced thin.

BAKED OR BOILED GROUND RICE PUDDING.

INGREDIENTS.—2 pints milk, 6 tablespoonfuls ground rice, sugar to taste, 3 eggs, flavouring of lemon-rind, nutmeg, bitter almonds, or bay-leaf.

Mode.—Put 1½ pints of the milk into a stewpan, with the flavouring, bring to the boiling-point, and with the other ½ pint of milk mix the ground rice to a smooth batter; strain the boiling milk to this, and stir over the fire until the mixture is tolerably thick; then pour it into a basin, and when nearly or quite cold sweeten it to taste, and add the eggs, previously well beaten, with a little salt. Put the pudding into a well-buttered basin, tie it down with a cloth, plunge it into boiling water, and boil for 1½ hours. For a baked pudding proceed in the same manner, using only half the ground rice, with the same quantity of the other ingredients: an hour will bake the pudding in a moderate oven. Stewed fruit, or preserves, or marmalade, may be served with either the boiled or baked pudding. The eggs may be omitted for a plain baked pudding.

Time, 1½ hours to boil, 1 hour to bake. *Average cost*, 9d. *Sufficient* for 5 or 6 persons.

MINIATURE RICE PUDDING.

INGREDIENTS.—¼ lb. rice, 1½ pints milk, 2 oz. fresh butter, 4 eggs, sugar to taste; flavouring of lemon-peel, bitter almonds, or vanilla; a few strips candied peel.

Mode.—Let the rice swell in 1 pint of the milk over a slow fire, putting with it a strip of lemon peel; stir to it the butter and the other ½ pint of milk, and let the mixture cool. Then add the eggs, well-beaten, and a few drops of essence of almonds or essence of vanilla; butter well with small cups or moulds, line them with a few pieces of candied peel, sliced thin, fill them three-parts full, and bake for about 40 minutes; turn them out of the cups on to a white d'oyley, and serve with sweet sauce. Stewed fruit or preserve may be served with these puddings, omitting the flavouring and candied peel.

Time, 40 minutes. *Average cost*, 1s. 2d. *Sufficient* for 6 puddings.

ROLY-POLY JAM PUDDING.

INGREDIENTS.—¾ *lb. of suet-crust*, ¾ *lb. of any kind of jam.*

Mode.—Make a suet crust by recipe, and roll it out to the thickness of about ½ inch. Spread the jam equally over it, leaving a small margin where the paste joins. Roll it up, fasten the ends, and tie it in a floured cloth; put the pudding into boiling water, and boil for 2 hours. Mincemeat or marmalade may be substituted for the jam.

Time, 2 hours. *Average cost*, 7d. *Sufficient* for 5 or 6 persons. *Seasonable*—suitable for winter puddings when fresh fruit is not obtainable.

SAGO PUDDING (BAKED).

INGREDIENTS.—1½ *pints milk*, 3 *tablespoonfuls sago, rind of ½ lemon*, 3 *oz. sugar*, 3 *eggs*, 1½ *oz. butter, grated nutmeg, puff-paste.*

Mode.—Put the milk and lemon-rind into a stewpan by the fire until the milk is flavoured. Strain; mix with it the sago and sugar and simmer for 15 minutes. Let the mixture cool a little, and stir to it the eggs, well beaten, and the butter. Line the edges of a pie-dish with puff-paste, pour in the pudding; grate a little nutmeg over, and bake for ¾ hour or 1 hour.

Time, ¾ to 1 hour, or more if the oven is very slow. *Average cost*, 1s. *Sufficient* for 5 or 6 persons.

SAGO PUDDING (BOILED).

Ingredients and Mode as preceding recipe, allow 2 extra spoonfuls of sago, and boil in buttered basin from 1¼ to 1¾ hours.

SUET PUDDING (to serve with Roast Meat).

INGREDIENTS.—1 *lb. flour*, 6 *oz. finely chopped suet*, ½ *saltspoonful salt*, ½ *pint milk or water.*

Mode.—Chop the suet very fine, and mix it well with the flour; add the salt and pepper, and make the whole into a smooth paste with the milk or water. Tie the pudding in a floured cloth, or put it into a buttered basin, and boil

from 2½ to 3 hours. To enrich it, substitute 3 beaten eggs for some of the milk or water, and increase the suet.

Time, 2½ to 3 hours. *Average cost*, 6d. *Sufficient* for 5 or 6 persons.

Note.—When there is a joint roasting or baking, this pudding may be boiled in a long shape, and cut into slices a few minutes before dinner is served; these slices should be laid in the dripping-pan for a minute or two, and then browned before the fire. Where there is a large family of children it is a most economical plan to serve up the pudding before the meat, as, in this case, the consumption of the latter article will be much smaller than it otherwise would be.

SEMOLINA PUDDING (BAKED).

INGREDIENTS.—3 *oz. semolina*, 1½ *pints milk*, ¼ *lb. sugar*, 12 *bitter almonds*, 3 *oz. butter*, 4 *eggs.*

Mode.—Flavour the milk by infusing the bitter almonds in it for ½ hour by the side of the fire; strain and mix it with the semolina, sugar, and butter. Stir over the fire for a few minutes, then take them off and mix in the eggs, well beaten. Line a buttered pie-dish with puff-paste, put in the pudding, and bake in a rather slow oven, 40 or 50 minutes. Serve either plain, or with custard sauce or stewed fruit, a little of which may be poured over the pudding.

Time, 40 to 50 minutes. *Average cost*, 1s. *Sufficient* for 5 or 6 persons.

TAPIOCA PUDDING (BAKED).

INGREDIENTS.—3 *oz. tapioca*, 1 *quart milk*, 2 *oz. butter*, ¼ *lb. sugar*, 4 *eggs, flavouring of vanilla, grated lemon-rind, or bitter almonds.*

Mode.—Wash the tapioca and stew it gently in the milk for ¼ of an hour, occasionally stirring it; then let it cool a little, and mix with the butter, sugar, and eggs, well beaten; flavour with about 12 drops of either essence of almonds or vanilla. Butter a pie-dish, line the edges with puff-paste; put in the pudding, and bake, in a moderate oven, for an hour.

Time, 1 hour. *Average cost*, 1s. *Sufficient* for 5 or 6 persons.

TAPIOCA PUDDING (BOILED).

Ingredients, &c., as in preceding recipe, allowing a little more tapioca, and 1½ hours to boil.

ROLLED TREACLE PUDDING.

INGREDIENTS.—1 *lb. suet crust*, ¼ *lb. treacle*, ½ *teaspoonful grated ginger.*

Mode.—Make with 1 lb. of flour a

suet crust by recipe given ; roll it out to the thickness of ½ inch, and spread the treacle equally over it, leaving a small margin where the paste joins ; close the ends, tie the pudding in a floured cloth, plunge it into boiling water, and boil for 2 hours. This pudding is economical, and a favourite one with children ; it is, of course, only suitable for a nursery, or very plain family dinner. Made with a lard, instead of a suet, crust, it would be very nice baked, and would be sufficiently done in from 1½ to 2 hours.

Time, boiled pudding, 2 hours ; baked pudding, 1½ to 2 hours. *Average cost*, 7d. *Sufficient* for 5 or 6 persons.

YEAST DUMPLINGS.

INGREDIENTS.—½ *quartern dough, boiling water.*

Mode.—Make a light dough as for bread, using, to mix it, milk, instead of water ; divide it into 7 or 8 dumplings ; plunge them into boiling water, and boil them for 20 minutes. Serve the instant they are taken up ; and in eating them do not touch them with a knife, but tear them apart with two forks. They may be eaten with meat, gravy, or cold butter and sugar. If not convenient to make the dough, a little from the baker's answers as well, only it must be placed for a few minutes near the fire, in a basin, with a cloth over it ; let it rise again before it is made into dumplings.

Time, 20 minutes. *Average cost,* 2¼d. *Sufficient* for 5 or 6 persons.

YORKSHIRE PUDDING (to serve with hot Roast Beef).

INGREDIENTS.—1½ *pints milk, 6 large tablespoonfuls flour, 3 eggs, 1 salt-spoonful salt.*

Mode.—Put the flour into a basin with the salt, and stir gradually to this enough milk to make into a stiff batter. When perfectly smooth, add the remainder of the milk and the eggs, well beaten. Beat the mixture for a few minutes, and pour it into a shallow tin, previously well rubbed with beef dripping. Put the pudding into the oven, and bake for an hour ; then, for another ½ hour place it under the meat, to catch a little of the gravy. Cut the pudding into small square pieces, put them on a hot dish, and serve. If the meat is baked, the pudding may at once be placed under it, resting the former on a small three-cornered stand.

Time, 1½ hours. *Average cost,* 7d. *Sufficient* for 5 or 6 persons.

BREAD, BUNS. CAKES, ETC.

In ancient times bread was a very different kind of food to what it is now. The Assyrians, Egyptians, and Greeks used to make it with oil and spices, more like a cake than a loaf, for leavened bread was then a thing unknown. The art of making it was discovered by the following accident:— The slave of an Archon at Athens had left some wheaten dough in an earthen pan, and forgotten it till he found it some days afterwards turning sour. His first impulse was to throw it away, but his master appearing at the moment he hastily mixed it with some fresh dough at which he was then working. The bread thus produced by the introduction of the fermented dough was found delicious by the Archon and his friends, and the slave was summoned to tell the secret. This secret spread all over Athens, and, everybody wanting leavened bread, some persons set themselves to make it, and then the trade (before unknown) of a baker began. In a very short time bread-making became quite an art with the Athenians, and theirs was quoted all over Greece as the best bread to be had.

Bread has now become an article of food of the first necessity, and properly so, for it contains in itself all the necessary classes of food—gluten, fibrin, fat, phosphates, starch, and sugar. The finest and most wholesome bread is that made from wheaten flour; next to this comes rye bread, then that made with barley, rice, maize, oats, potatoes, &c.

Here in England it is not regularly the custom to bake at home, except when living far from towns and bakers; but it seems a pity that we should be so dependent upon the honesty of these tradesmen for the " staff of life," when it is so easy to have our own bread made of the best flour and yeast, free from adulteration, at a smaller cost than if we bought it.

Some people argue against home baking on the ground that flour can be adulterated as well as bread, and this is quite true; but the adulteration can be far more easily detected in the flour than the bread.

Good flour is dry, and does not lose more than 12 per cent. in weight when heated in the oven. It should be white with a yellowish tinge, adherent, so that a handful squeezed together keeps its shape, and it should, above all, make a good loaf of bread. If, with care and good yeast, the flour will not do this, it cannot be as pure as it should be, and it is always best to test it before buying a large quantity.

Yeast for making bread is of various kinds. In the East Indies, "toddy" (a liquor which flows from the wounded cocoanut trees, and in the West Indies, "dunder," the refuse of the distillation of rum) is used; but here we have, as a rule, brewer's yeast, or the dried yeast imported from France and Germany. It may not be known to every one that yeast is a living plant, but such is the fact. Under a microscope the plants can easily be seen, and put into flour and water they grow and multiply, producing more yeast plants like themselves. This for cooks is a thing to be remembered, because, given a little good yeast, it is easy to increase the quantity; another fact being that if brewer's yeast, as often happens, is bitter, it will soon grow some new yeast that is not.

Baking powder is often used in the place of yeast, but whereas this makes a nice loaf to vary other kinds of bread, it is not so good for a large quantity for every-day consumption. There are many patent breads, that are manufactured by machinery and are too well known to need description here; and one of the best fancy breads is Messrs. W. Hill & Sons' "German Bread."

For home-made bread the utensils required are simple, and the trouble less than those who have yet hesitated to undertake the task would imagine. It is necessary to have a trough or pan of a size suitable for the quantity of bread to be made, deep enough to allow for the dough to be mixed without spilling the flour, and to rise without running over the pan. Besides this there should be a sieve for straining the yeast and a large, strong spoon. If there is a good place to keep the bread, three bakings a week should be sufficient in an ordinary family (in many country places it is not unusual to have only two), for home-made bread does not so soon get stale as that made by the bakers. The best way of keeping bread fresh is to put it in a covered earthen pan, raised a little from the ground so that a current of air can pass underneath; if kept till rather stale, it can be freshened by being warmed through in a gentle oven.

Very plain cakes and buns for children can be made from the bread dough with the addition of a little sugar, currants or raisins, and dripping; and, while on the subject of baking, we may here give a few hints respecting the oven for both bread and cakes. For bread, the oven should be quick and the heat so regulated as to penetrate the dough without hardening the outside. The drawback to many ovens in ordinary ranges is that the heat is often nearly all at one side, thus necessitating the constant opening of the door to turn the loaves; and this has not at all a good effect upon the bread. Some ovens, however, are so constructed that the heat circulates, and baking is comparatively easy. In any case, bring the oven to the right heat *before* putting in the bread, instead of relying upon its getting hot enough, and perhaps too hot, afterwards. For cakes, the heat of the oven is of great importance. If a cake is put in one not sufficiently hot it is certain to become heavy, when trouble in making it is lost and good materials spoiled. It is well, therefore, to think of the oven before the cake, and see that it will be safe to *cook* it before you decide to make it. Ovens for both cakes and pastry must be hot to start with.

To ascertain whether bread and cakes are sufficiently done, the best plan is to thrust a sharp knife into them; and if it comes out all sticky it is certain they are not sufficiently cooked.

When the oven is very hot and the tops of the cakes are taking too much colour, put over clean sheets of white paper.

We have spoken of materials for bread, and it may not be out of place to say a word here about the ingredients for cakes and buns, though our recipes for the former appear in the body of the book.

It is a fact that a little carelessness in the preparation of the materials often ruins the cakes.

Currants, after being well washed, should be thoroughly dried and freed from grit and stones.

Good butter should be used for cakes. If this is too expensive, it is better to use clarified dripping than butter that is in the faintest degree rancid.

Eggs should also be perfectly good, although they need not be new laid. They should be broken one by one into a cup in case one might be bad, in which case, if put into the same basin, all would be spoiled.

For sponge cakes it is necessary to beat the yolks and whites separately; for other cakes it is advisable, as it makes them lighter Flour should be dry and of the best quality. The difference in price between the best flour and an inferior kind is not worth reckoning in the matter of a cake.

Soda should be thoroughly mixed with the water or milk used for a cake, for nothing can be more disagreeable than to *taste* it. Baking powder should be mixed with the flour before adding other ingredients. Cakes or buns should be put into the oven directly they are ready.

HOME-MADE BREAD.

INGREDIENTS.—1 *quartern of flour*, 2 *tablespoonfuls of yeast*, 1½ *tablespoonfuls of salt*, 1½ *pints of warm water*.

Mode.—Mix the salt with the flour in a pan, and make a hole in the middle. Mix the yeast with ½ pint of water very smoothly, pour into the flour and mix with it, in the centre, till a thin batter is obtained. Take some flour from the sides and sprinkle thickly over, and set near the fire for an hour to rise, with a cloth thrown over the top of the pan. It will be known when it has risen sufficiently by the yeast rising and breaking through the flour, and the bubbles rising to the surface; but an hour is a fair average time to allow. Now pour in the remainder of the water, and stir into it as much of the flour as you can with a wooden spoon. Next the dough must be kneaded, and to do this the flour should be gradually worked in from the sides of the pan, and kneaded with the knuckles of both hands. This must be done thoroughly, till there is no flour or lumps remaining and the dough does not stick to the hands. Cover again with a cloth and leave to rise a second time, and in about ¾ of an hour it should have swollen sufficiently to show cracks on the surface, when it is ready for baking. Now turn it on to a pasteboard or table and make up into loaves, which put into the oven with as little delay as possible. It may be baked in mould tins or flat ones, but in any case it is as well to make a few incisions at the tops of the loaves, as they will rise sooner if this be done. When done the bread should be removed from the tins, and laid on one side or upside down, to allow the steam to escape.

Time, to rise 1 hour first time, ¾ hour second; to bake 1¼ to 1½ hours. *Suffient* for 2 or 3 loaves.

BROWN BREAD.

Mix three parts of wholemeal flour with four parts of household, and make as directed for home-made bread. Brown bread, however, should not be so stiff as white bread, and does not require so much kneading.

HOME-MADE BREAD FOR LARGE FAMILY.

INGREDIENTS.—1 *peck of flour*, 3 *lbs. of potatoes*, ½ *pint of brewer's yeast*, 2 *oz. of salt*.

Mode.—Peel and boil the potatoes and make them perfectly smooth while warm, strain through a colander and add to it the yeast, which should have been put in water overnight to take off any bitterness.

Put the flour in a large pan and hollow it out in the centre, and having stirred the potatoes and yeast well together pour them in, mix with sufficient flour to make a light batter, shake over some flour and, covering the pan, place it near the fire for about an hour. Next add the water lukewarm, with the salt, and make up into a light dough. Set this again in a warm place for about 2 hours, then make up the dough into loaves, which bake in a good oven.

Time, 1½ hours to bake.

BAKING-POWDER BREAD.

INGREDIENTS. — 4 *lbs. of flour*, 3 *dessertspoonfuls of baking-powder*, 2 *teaspoonfuls of salt*, 1 *quart of milk*.

Mode.— Mix the powder and salt thoroughly with the flour, add the milk and, with as much expedition as possible, work into a light dough. Bake in a well-heated oven.

Time, 1 hour.

RICE BREAD.

INGREDIENTS.—2 *lbs of wheat flour*, ½ *lb. of rice*, 3 *dessertspoonfuls of yeast*, 1 *teaspoonful of salt*.

Mode.—Soak the rice in hot water till tender, pour off the water and add the rice to the flour. Mix in with the yeast salt and sufficient warm water to make a smooth dough. Let this rise by the fire, form it into loaves and bake

Apricot Fritters.

Apple Tart.

Rice Pudding.

Mince Pies.

Vanilla Cream.

Meringue Cake.

Genoa Cake.

Jam Pudding.

Pancakes.

Marmalade Tart.

from 1¼ to 1¾ hours, according to their size.

Time, 1¼ to 1¾ hours.

AMERICAN BREAD.

INGREDIENTS.—2 *breakfastcupfuls of Indian meal,* 1 *of flour,* 3 *eggs,* 2½ *cups of milk,* 1 *tablespoonful of butter,* 1 *oz. of white sugar,* 1 *teaspoonful of carbonate of soda,* 2 *oz. of cream of tartar,* 1 *dessertspoonful of salt.*

Mode.—Put the meal in a basin, add to it the sugar and salt, and work in the butter, melted, with the milk, the eggs, yolks and whites beaten separately, and the soda dissolved in a little hot water. Mix the cream of tartar with the flour and add last. Bake steadily, but not too fast, in a well-greased mould; turn out when done and serve at once, hot.

In cutting corn bread it must be remembered that the knife must be held perpendicularly, so as not to crush the spongy interior.

Time, ¾ of an hour. *Average cost,* 7d.

ROLLS.

INGREDIENTS.—*To every lb. of flour allow* 1 *oz. of butter,* 1 *pint of milk,* 1 *large teaspoonful of yeast, and a little salt.*

Mode.—Warm the butter in the milk and add to it the yeast and salt, mixing all well together. Put the flour in a pan and stir in the milk, &c., and let the dough rise in a warm place. Knead it well and make into rolls, and after they have again risen for a few minutes bake in a quick oven. Richer rolls may be made by doubling the quantity of butter, and adding an egg to each lb. of flour.

Time, 1 lb. of flour from 15 to 20 minutes. *Average cost,* 1d. each.

MUFFINS.

INGREDIENTS.—1 *quart of milk,* 1½ *oz. of German yeast, salt, flour.*

Mode.—Warm the milk, add to it the yeast and salt, and mix well together. Put in a pan and add enough flour to make a soft dough, cover with a cloth and put in a warm place to rise. When light and nicely risen, divide the dough into pieces and round them to a proper shape: place them in a layer of flour 2 inches thick, on a wooden tray and let them rise again. Then put them on a hot plate or stove and bake until slightly browned, turning them when they are done on one side

Time, from 20 minutes to ½ an hour to bake them. *Average cost,* to buy, 1d. each. *Seasonable* in winter.

MUFFINS (TO TOAST).

Mode.—Divide the edge of the muffin all round, about an inch deep, by pulling it open with the fingers. Toast them before a clear fire a nice light brown on both sides; not too quickly, or the muffin, being thick, will not get warmed through. When done, pull them apart, butter the outside lightly, and the inside more thickly, put the two pieces together and cut in halves.

Time, 5 minutes to toast.

CRUMPETS.

INGREDIENTS.—1 *quart of milk,* 1½ *oz. of German yeast, salt, flour.*

Mode. — Make these in the same manner as muffins, but let the mixture be much thinner—more like batter than dough. Let it rise for ½ an hour; pour into iron rings, which should be ready on a hot-plate; bake them, and when one side appears done turn them quickly on the other. Toast them before a clear fire on both sides and butter them well. Do not send them to table on the same dish as the muffins.

Time, 10 or 12 minutes to bake the crumpets. *Average cost,* ½d. each. *Sufficient,* allow 2 crumpets to each person. *Seasonable* in winter.

HOT CROSS BUNS.

INGREDIENTS.—2 *lbs. of flour,* 1 *wineglassful of yeast, about* 1 *pint of warmed milk,* 6 *oz. of butter,* ½ *teaspoonful of salt,* 1 *teaspoonful of mixed spice,* ½ *lb. of currants.*

Mode.—Mix the flour, sugar, spice, salt, and currants together; make a hole in the flour and pour in the yeast mixed with ½ pint of warm milk; make a thin batter and set to rise. When sufficiently risen add the butter melted and sufficient milk to make the whole into a soft dough; cover this with a dust of flour and set to rise again for ½ an hour. Shape the dough into buns and set on tins to rise for another ½ hour; then mark them with a cross with the back of a knife and bake in a quick oven for from 15 to 20 minutes. They may be glazed as directed in plain buns.

Time, 15 to 20 minutes to bake. *Average cost,* 1s. 4d. *Sufficient* to make 18 buns. *Seasonable* on Good Friday

LIGHT BUNS.

INGREDIENTS.—½ teaspoonful tartaric acid, ½ teaspoonful of bicarbonate of soda, 1 lb. flour, 2 oz. butter, 2 oz. loaf sugar, ¼ lb. currants or raisins ; when liked, a few caraway seeds, ½ pint cold new milk, 1 egg.

Mode.—Rub the tartaric acid, soda, and flour all together through a hair sieve ; work the butter into the flour ; add the sugar, currants, and caraway seeds. Mix all these well together ; make a hole in the middle of the flour, and pour in the milk, mixed with the egg, which should be well beaten ; mix quickly, and set the dough, with a fork, on baking-tins, and bake the buns for about 20 minutes. This mixture makes a very good cake, and if put into a tin, should be baked 1½ hours. The same quantity of flour, soda, and tartaric acid, with ½ pint of milk and a little salt, will make either bread or teacakes, if wanted quickly.

Time, 20 minutes for the buns ; if made into a cake, 1½ hours. Sufficient to make about 12 buns.

PLAIN BUNS.

INGREDIENTS.—2 lbs. of flour, ½ gill of yeast, 6 ozs. of moist sugar, about 1 pint of milk, ¼ lb. butter, salt.

Mode.—Mix a little salt and the sugar with the flour and put it in a pan, making a hole in the centre. Make a pint of milk lukewarm, mix with the yeast and pour in the centre of the flour, stirring enough in to make a thick cream. Cover the pan with a cloth and set the sponge to rise in a warm place for about 1¼ hours. Melt, but do not oil the butter ; stir it into the other ingredients with enough warm milk to make the whole into a soft dough. Make into buns and lay them on floured tins about 3 inches apart, and set them again in a warm place till they have risen to double their size ; then put them in a good brisk oven, and, just before they are done, brush them over with a little milk and put them back in the oven to brown. These will be found very nice buns for children, and they can be varied by the addition of a few caraway seeds, sultanas, or currants.

Time, 15 to 20 minutes to bake. Average cost, 1s. for this quantity. Sufficient for 18 buns.

TO MAKE GOOD PLAIN BUNS.

INGREDIENTS. — 1 lb. flour, 6 oz. good butter, ¼ lb. sugar, 1 egg, nearly ¼ pint milk, 2 small teaspoonfuls baking-powder, a few drops essence of lemon.

Mode.— Warm the butter, without oiling it ; beat it with a wooden spoon ; stir the flour in gradually with the sugar, and mix well together. Make the milk lukewarm, beat up with it the yolk of the egg and the essence of lemon, and stir these to the flour, &c. Add the baking-powder, beat the dough well about 10 minutes, divide it into 24 pieces, put them into buttered tins or cups, and bake in a brisk oven from 20 to 30 minutes.

Time, 20 to 30 minutes. Average cost, 1s. Sufficient to make 12 buns.

MADEIRA BUNS.

INGREDIENTS.—1 lb. of flour, 6 oz. of butter, 2 eggs, 6 oz. of lump sugar, 1 teaspoonful of powdered ginger, 1 dessertspoonful of caraway seeds, a little nutmeg, 1 wineglassful of sherry, salt.

Mode.—Mix the dry ingredients together, beat the eggs and butter to a cream ; then add to the flour, &c., and beat for half an hour, lastly add the wine. Bake in tins in a moderately quick oven.

Time, 50 minutes to 1 hour. Average cost, 1s. 4d. Sufficient to make 12 buns. Seasonable at any time.

VICTORIA BUNS.

INGREDIENTS.—1 egg, 1¼ oz. of ground rice, 2 oz. of caster sugar, 1½ oz. of currants, 2 oz. of butter, a little candied peel, flour.

Mode.—Whisk the egg and stir to it the sugar, beating well together. Beat the butter to a cream, stir in the ground rice, currants, peel, and as much flour as will make the mixture into a soft dough. Make into buns and put into the oven at once, or they will become heavy. The oven should be quick.

Time, about 40 minutes. Average cost, 6d. Sufficient to make 8 buns. Seasonable at any time.

COMMON CAKE, suitable for sending to Children at School.

INGREDIENTS.—2 lbs. flour, 4 oz. butter or clarified dripping, ½ oz. caraway seeds, ¼ oz. allspice, ½ lb. pounded sugar, 1 lb. currants, 1 pint milk, 3 tablespoonfuls fresh yeast.

Mode.—Rub the butter lightly into the flour ; add the dry ingredients, and mix well together. Make the milk warm, but not hot; stir in the yeast, and with this liquid make the whole into a light dough; knead well, and line the cake-tins with strips of buttered paper, about 6 inches higher than the top of the tin. Put in the dough; stand it in a warm place to rise for more than an hour; then bake the cakes in a well-heated oven. If this quantity be divided in two, it will take from 1½ to 2 hours' baking.

Time, 1¾ to 2¼ hours. *Average cost*, 1s. 4d. *Sufficient* to make 2 moderate-sized cakes.

A NICE PLAIN CAKE FOR CHILDREN.

INGREDIENTS.—1 *quartern dough*, ¼ *lb. moist sugar*, ¼ *lb. butter or good beef dripping*, ¼ *pint warm milk*, ½ *grated nutmeg or* ½ *oz. caraway seeds.*

Mode.—If the dough is procured from the baker's, put it into a basin as soon as it comes in, near the fire; cover the basin with a thick cloth, and let the dough remain a little while to rise. Beat the butter to a cream, and make the milk warm; and when the dough has risen, mix with it thoroughly all the above ingredients, and knead the cake well for a few minutes. Butter some cake-tins, half fill them, and stand them in a warm place, to allow the dough to rise again. When the tins are three parts full, put the cakes into a good oven, and bake them from 1¾ to 2 hours. A few currants might be substituted for the caraway seeds.

Time, 1¾ to 2 hours. *Average cost*, 10d.

A NICE PLUM CAKE.

INGREDIENTS.—1 *lb. flour*, ¼ *lb. butter*, ½ *lb. sugar*, ½ *lb. currants*, 2 *oz. candied lemon-peel*, ½ *pint milk*, 1 *teaspoonful ammonia or carbonate of soda.*

Mode.—Put the flour into a basin with the sugar, currants, and sliced candied peel; beat the butter to a cream, and mix these ingredients together with the milk. Stir the ammonia into 2 table-spoonfuls of milk; add it to the dough and beat the whole well, until everything is thoroughly mixed. Put the dough into a buttered tin, and bake the cake from 1½ to 2 hours.

Time, 1½ to 2 hours. *Average cost*, 1s.

POUND CAKE.

INGREDIENTS.—1 *lb. butter*, 1¼ *lbs. flour*, 1 *lb. pounded loaf sugar*, 1 *lb. currants*, 9 *eggs*, 2 *oz. candied peel*, ½ *oz. citron*, ½ *oz. sweet almonds; when liked, a little pounded mace.*

Mode.—Work the butter to a cream, dredge in the flour, add the sugar, currants, candied peel, cut into neat slices, and the almonds, which should be blanched and chopped, and mix these well together; whisk the eggs, and let them be thoroughly blended with the dry ingredients. Beat the cake well for 20 minutes, and put it into a round tin, lined at the bottom and sides with a strip of white buttered paper. Bake from 1½ to 2 hours, and let the oven be well heated when the cake is put in, or the currants will all sink to the bottom. To make this preparation light, the yolks and whites of the eggs should be beaten separately, and added separately. A glass of wine is sometimes added to the mixture.

Time, 1½ to 2 hours. *Average cost*, 3s. *Sufficient*, the above quantity divided in two, will make 2 nice-sized cakes.

RICE CAKE.

INGREDIENTS.—½ *lb. ground rice*, ½ *lb. flour*, ½ *lb. loaf sugar*, 9 *eggs*, 20 *drops essence of lemon, or the rind of* 1 *lemon*, ¼ *lb. butter.*

Mode.—Separate the whites from the yolks of the eggs; whisk them well, and add to the latter the butter beaten to a cream. Stir in the flour, rice, and lemon (if the rind is used, it must be very finely minced), and beat the mixture well; then add the whites of the eggs, beat the cake again for some time, put it into a buttered mould or tin, and bake it for nearly 1½ hours. It may be flavoured with essence of almonds.

Time, 1 to 1½ hours. *Average cost*, 1s. 6d.

SAUCER-CAKE FOR TEA.

INGREDIENTS.—¼ *lb. flour*, ¼ *lb. tous-les-mois*, ¼ *lb. pounded white sugar*, ¼ *lb. butter*, 2 *eggs*, 1 *oz. candied orange or lemon-peel.*

Mode.—Mix the flour and *tous-les-mois* together; add the sugar, the candied peel, cut into thin slices, the butter, beaten to a cream, and the eggs, well whisked. Beat the mixture for 10 minutes, put it into a buttered cake-tin or mould, or a soup-plate, lined with a piece of buttered paper. Bake the cake in a moderate oven from 1 to 1¼ hours, and when cold, put it away in a covered canister. It will remain good some weeks, even if it be cut into slices.

Time, 1 to 1¼ hours. *Average cost,* 1s. 1d.

SEED CAKE.

INGREDIENTS.—½ *quartern dough,* ¼ *lb. good dripping,* 6 *oz. moist sugar,* ¼ *oz. caraway seeds,* 1 *egg.*

Mode.—If the dough is sent in from the baker's put it in a basin, covered with a cloth, and set it in a warm place to rise. Then, with a wooden spoon beat the dripping to a liquid; add it, with the other ingredients, to the dough, and beat it until everything is thoroughly mixed. Put it into a buttered tin, and bake the cake for rather more than 2 hours.

Time, rather more than 2 hours. *Average cost,* 7d.

SPONGE CAKE.

INGREDIENTS.—*The weight of 8 eggs in pounded loaf sugar, the weight of 5 in flour, the rind of* 1 *lemon,* 1 *tablespoonful brandy,* 8 *eggs.*

Mode.—Put the eggs into one side of the scales, and take the weight of 8 in pounded loaf sugar, and the weight of 5 in good *dry* flour. Separate the yolks from the whites of the eggs; beat the former, put them into a saucepan with the sugar, and let them remain over the fire until *milk-warm,* keeping them well stirred. Then put them into a basin, add the grated lemon-rind, mixed with the brandy, and stir well together, dredging in the flour gradually. Whisk the whites of the eggs to a stiff froth, stir to the flour, &c., beat the cake for ¼ hour, and put it into a buttered mould strewn with a little fine sifted sugar. Put the cake immediately into a quick oven and bake for 1½ hours. The flavouring may be varied by adding a few drops of essence of almonds, instead of the lemon-rind.

Time, 1½ hours. *Average cost,* 1s. 3d. *Sufficient* for 1 cake.

BREAKFAST CAKES.

INGREDIENTS.—1 *lb. of flour,* 1 *oz. of pounded sugar,* 2 *eggs,* ¾ *pint of milk,* ½ *a teaspoonful each of salt and baking-powder.*

Mode.—Mix the flour, powder, salt, and sugar well together. Beat the eggs, add the milk, and with these work the flour into a light dough. Divide into small cakes and put them in the oven immediately.

Time, 20 minutes to bake the cakes.

Average cost, 6d. *Sufficient* for 6 persons. *Seasonable* at any time.

BOSTON BREAKFAST CAKES.

INGREDIENTS.—1 *quart of milk,* 1 *oz of sugar, a teacupful of yeast,* 2 *eggs, salt, flour.*

Mode.—Mix the ingredients to form a thick batter over-night; make up into cakes and bake in tins in the morning for ½ an hour. Should the batter, as sometimes happens, turn sour, add ½ a teaspoonful of soda, dissolved in a little milk.

Time, ½ an hour to bake. *Average cost,* 9d. *Sufficient* for 8 persons. *Seasonable* at any time.

BUCKWHEAT CAKES.

INGREDIENTS.—1 *quart of buckwheat flour,* ½ *pint of Indian corn meal,* 2 *tablespoonfuls of molasses,* 4 *oz. of yeast,* 1 *teaspoonful of salt, enough water to make a thin batter.*

Mode.—Mix together the buckwheat and meal; make a hole in the centre and pour in the yeast and salt, adding enough warm water to make a thin batter. Beat well the mixture, and set to rise, covered with a cloth in a warm place. When risen high and covered with bubbles, it is fit to bake. Heat and grease a griddle, and dip out enough batter to make 3 cakes each baking. These must be browned on one side, then turned with a broad knife and the other side browned. Serve hot with molasses.

Time, about 4 hours to rise. *Seasonable* at any time.

RICE BREAD OR CAKES.

INGREDIENTS.—3 *lbs. of flour,* ¾ *lb. of rice,* 2 *tablespoonfuls of yeast, salt to taste.*

Mode.—Boil the rice in water till quite tender, then before it is cold strain off the water and add it to the flour, mix with the yeast and salt, with enough warm water to make a smooth dough. Let it stand by the fire to rise; then form into small loaves or cakes, and bake them from ¾ to 1½ hours, according to size. A nice cake is made by substituting milk for the water in which the rice is boiled, in which case there is no need to strain the rice before mixing it with the flour.

Time, ¾ to 1½ hours to bake the cakes. *Average cost* for this quantity, if made with water, 10d. *Sufficient* for six small loaves. *Seasonable* at any time.

TEA-CAKES (TO TOAST).

Cut each tea-cake into three or four slices, according to thickness, toast them both sides before a clear fire, and as each slice is done spread it with butter on both sides. When a cake is toasted, pile the slices one on the top of the other, cut them into quarters, put them on a hot plate, and send them in to table as they are wanted, as, if allowed to stand they spoil, unless kept in a muffin-plate over a basin of boiling water.

DESSERT BISCUITS, which may be Flavoured with Ground Ginger, Cinnamon, &c.

INGREDIENTS.—1 lb. flour, ½ lb. butter, ½ lb. sifted sugar, the yolks of 6 eggs, flavouring to taste.

Mode.—Put the butter into a basin; warm it, but do not allow it to oil; then, with the hand, beat it to a cream. Add the flour by degrees, then the sugar and flavouring, and moisten the whole with the yolks of the eggs, previously well beaten. When all the ingredients are thoroughly incorporated, drop the mixture from a spoon on to a buttered paper, leaving a distance between each cake, as they spread as soon as they begin to get warm. Bake in a slow oven from 12 to 18 minutes, and do not let the biscuits acquire too much colour. In making the above quantity, half may be flavoured with ground ginger, and the other half with essence of lemon, or currants. With whatever the preparation is flavoured, so are the biscuits called, and an endless variety may be made in this manner.

Time, 12 to 18 minutes, or rather longer, in a very slow oven. Average cost, 1s. 6d. Sufficient to make from 3 to 4 dozen cakes.

RAISED BISCUITS.

INGREDIENTS.—1 quart of milk, ¼ lb. of lard, a small cup of yeast, 2 tablespoonfuls of white sugar, 1 teaspoonful of soda, lard for frying, salt.

Mode.—If wanted early in the morning, the ingredients should be mixed overnight, melting the lard and warming the milk. In the morning roll out the dough and form into biscuits. Put the cakes into a baking-pan, let them rise 20 minutes, then bake them for another 20 minutes to ½ an hour.

Time, about 40 minutes. Seasonable at any time.

CRULLERS.

INGREDIENTS.—½ lb. of sugar, 1½ oz. of butter, 3 eggs, flour, 1 tablespoonful of sweet milk, 1 teaspoonful of soda, lard for frying, salt.

Mode.—Make the lard hot in a lined saucepan, and meanwhile mix the other ingredients with enough flour to make a thick dough. Roll this out, and stamp out little cakes, which drop into the hot lard, and when brown and puffed they are done.

Seasonable at any time.

RUSKS.

INGREDIENTS.—1 lb. of flour, ¼ pint of milk, 2 oz. of white sugar, 2 eggs, 1 tablespoonful of yeast, salt, 2 oz. of butter.

Mode.—Put the butter with the milk into a saucepan and shake till the former is melted. Put the flour into a basin, with the sugar and a teaspoonful of salt, and mix well together. Beat the eggs, stir them to the milk and butter, with the yeast; and, with this liquid, make the flour into a smooth dough. Cover the basin containing the dough with a cloth and set it to rise by the side of the fire; then knead and divide into 12 pieces, which bake in a quick oven for about 20 minutes. Take the rusks out of the oven when done, break them in halves and put them back again to get crisp on the other sides. When cold put them in tin canisters to keep. If wanted to eat with cheese, omit the sugar.

Time, 20 minutes to bake the rusks, 5 minutes to crisp them. Average cost, 8d. Sufficient to make 12 rusks. Seasonable at any time.

SWEET DISHES

APPLE CHARLOTTE.

INGREDIENTS.—8 *good sized apples,
sugar, some sponge finger biscuits or*
some bread-and-butter, a lemon, or a
few drops of lemon essence.

Mode.—Peel and core the apples,
and stew them till done, with enough
sugar to sweeten them, and the rind
and juice of the lemon. Thoroughly
butter a basin, put in a piece of bread-
and-butter to fit the bottom of it, and
line the sides with strips of bread-and-
butter to overlap one another, and
form a case. Or use Savoy biscuits for
the purpose of lining. Fill in with the
apple marmalade, and put a buttered
round of bread upon the top. Lay a
tin plate on the top of the basin, and
bake in a good oven about ½ hour.

Time, about ½ hour. *Average cost,*
1s. *Sufficient* for 4 persons. *Seasonable* in autumn or winter.

APPLE CUSTARD (BAKED).

INGREDIENTS.—8 *large apples, moist
sugar to taste, 1 small teacupful cold
water, the grated rind of 1 lemon, 1
pint milk, 3 eggs, 2 oz. loaf sugar.*

Mode.—Peel, cut, and core the apples;
put them into a lined saucepan, with
the cold water, and as they heat, bruise
them to a pulp; sweeten with moist
sugar, and add the grated lemon-rind.
When cold, put the fruit at the bottom
of a pie-dish, and pour over it a custard
made with the above milk, eggs, and
sugar; grate a little nutmeg over the
top, place the dish in a moderate oven,
and bake from 25 to 35 minutes.

Time, 25 to 35 minutes. *Average
cost,* 1s. 3d. *Sufficient* for 6 or 7
persons. *Seasonable* from July to
March.

APPLE GINGER (a Dessert Dish).

INGREDIENTS.—2 *lbs. any kind of
hard apples, 2 lbs. loaf sugar, 1½ pints
water, 1 oz. tincture of ginger.*

Mode.—Boil the sugar and water

into a rich syrup, adding the ginger when it boils. Pare, core, and cut the apples into pieces; dip them in cold water to preserve the colour, and boil in the syrup until transparent; do not let them break. Put the pieces of apple into jars, pour over the syrup, and exclude the air by well covering them. It will remain good some time if kept in a dry place.

Time, from 5 to 10 minutes to boil the syrup; about ½ hour to simmer the apples. *Average cost*, 1s. 2d. *Sufficient* for 7 or 8 persons. *Seasonable*—make this in September, October, or November.

APPLE JELLY OR MARMALADE (for Entremets or Dessert Dishes).

INGREDIENTS. — *Apples ; to every pound of pulp allow ¾ lb. sugar, ½ teaspoonful minced lemon-peel.*

Mode.—Peel, core, and boil the apples, with only sufficient water to prevent them from burning; beat them to a pulp, and to every pound of pulp allow the above proportion of sugar in lumps. Dip the lumps into water; put these into a saucepan, and boil till the syrup is thick, and can be well skimmed; then add this syrup to the apple pulp, with the minced lemon-peel, and stir it over a quick fire for about 20 minutes, or until the apples cease to stick to the bottom of the pan. The jelly may then be poured into moulds previously dipped in water, when it will turn out nicely. A little custard may be poured round, and it should be garnished with strips of citron, or stuck with blanched almonds. A little cochineal or carmine will improve the appearance of this jelly.

Time, from ½ to ¾ hour to reduce the apples to a pulp; 20 minutes to boil after the sugar is added. *Sufficient*— 1½ lbs. apples sufficient for a small mould. *Seasonable* from July to March, but is best in September, October, or November.

APPLE SNOW (a pretty Supper Dish).

INGREDIENTS.—*10 good-sized apples, the whites of 10 eggs, the rind of a lemon, ½ lb. pounded sugar.*

Mode.—Peel, core, and cut the apples into quarters, and put them into a saucepan with the lemon-peel and sufficient water to prevent them from burning, rather less than ½ a pint. When tender, take out the peel, beat

them to a pulp, let them cool, and stir them to the whites of the eggs, previously beaten to a strong froth. Add the sifted sugar, continue the whisking until the mixture becomes quite stiff, and either heap it on a glass dish, or serve it in small glasses. The dish may be garnished with preserved barberries, or strips of bright-coloured jelly; and a dish of custard should be served with it, or a jug of cream.

Time, from 30 to 40 minutes to stew the apples. *Average cost*, 1s. 6d. *Sufficient* to fill a moderate-sized glass dish. *Seasonable* from July to March.

APPLES AND CUSTARD (a pretty Dish for a Juvenile Supper).

INGREDIENTS.—*7 good-sized apples, the rind of ½ lemon or 4 cloves, ½ lb. sugar, ¾ pint water, ½ pint custard.*

Mode.—Pare and take out the cores of the apples, without dividing them, and, if possible, leave the stalks on; boil the sugar and water together for 10 minutes; then put in the apples with the lemon-rind or cloves, whichever flavour may be preferred, and simmer gently until tender, taking care not to let them break. Dish them neatly on a glass dish, reduce the syrup by boiling it quickly for a few minutes; let it cool a little, then pour it over the apples. Have ready quite ½ pint of custard; and pour it round, but not over, the apples when they are quite cold. A few almonds blanched may be cut into strips and stuck in the apples.

Time, from 20 to 30 minutes to stew the apples. *Average cost*, 1s. *Sufficient* to fill a large glass. *Seasonable* from July to March.

APPLES AND RICE (a Plain Dish).

INGREDIENTS.—*8 good-sized apples, 3 oz. butter, the rind of ½ lemon minced very fine, 6 oz. rice, 1½ pints milk, sugar to taste, ½ teaspoonful grated nutmeg. 6 tablespoonfuls apricot jam.*

Mode.—Peel the apples, halve them, and take out the cores; put them into a stewpan with the butter, and strew sufficient sifted sugar over to sweeten, and add the minced lemon-peel. Stew the apples very gently until tender, taking care they do not break. Boil the rice, with the milk, sugar, and nutmeg, and, when thoroughly done, dish it, piled high in the centre;

arrange the apples on it, warm the apricot jam, pour it over the whole, and serve hot.

Time, about 30 minutes to stew the apples very gently; about ¾ hour to cook the rice. *Average cost*, 1s. 6d. *Sufficient* for 5 or 6 persons. *Seasonable* from July to March.

ICED APPLES, OR APPLE HEDGEHOG.

INGREDIENTS.—*About 8 good boiling apples, ½ lb. sugar, ½ pint water, the rind of ½ lemon minced very fine, the whites of 2 eggs, 3 tablespoonfuls pounded sugar, a few sweet almonds.*

Mode.—Peel and core a dozen of the apples without dividing them, and stew them very gently in a lined saucepan with ½ lb. sugar and ½ pint water, and, when tender, lift them carefully on to a dish. Have ready the remainder of the apples, pared, cored, and cut into thin slices; put them into the syrup with the lemon-peel, and boil gently until they are reduced to a marmalade ; they must be kept stirred, to prevent them from burning. Cover the bottom of a dish with some of the marmalade and over that a layer of the stewed apples, in the insides of which, and between each, place some of the marmalade ; then place another layer of apples, and fill up the cavities with marmalade as before, forming the whole into a raised oval shape. Whip the whites of the eggs to a stiff froth, mix with them the pounded sugar, and cover the apples very smoothly all over with the icing; blanch and cut each almond into 4 or 5 strips; place these strips at equal distances over the icing, sticking up ; strew over a little rough pounded sugar, and place the dish in a very slow oven, to colour the almonds, and for the apples to get warm through. This entremet may also be served cold, and makes a pretty supper-dish.

Time, from 20 to 30 minutes to stew the apples. *Average cost*, 1s. 9d. *Sufficient* for 6 or 8 persons. *Seasonable* from July to March.

APPLES IN RED JELLY (a pretty Supper Dish).

INGREDIENTS. — *6 good-sized apples, 12 cloves, pounded sugar, 1 lemon, 2 teacupfuls water, 1 tablespoonful Swinborne's gelatine, a few drops prepared cochineal.*

Mode.—Peel the apples and take out the cores with a scoop, and put into each apple 2 cloves, and as much sifted sugar as it will hold. Place them, without touching each other, in a large pie-dish; add more white sugar, the juice of 1 lemon, and 2 teacupfuls water. Bake in the oven, with a dish over them. Look at them frequently, and, as each apple is cooked, place it in a glass dish. They must not be left in the oven after they are done, or they will break. Strain the liquor in which they have been stewing into a lined saucepan ; add to it the rind of a lemon and a tablespoonful of Swinborne's gelatine previously dissolved in cold water, and, if not sweet, a little more sugar, and 6 cloves. Boil till quite clear ; colour with a few drops of prepared cochineal, and strain the jelly through a double muslin into a jug ; let it cool a *little*, then pour it into the dish round the apples. When quite cold garnish the tops of the apples with a bright-coloured marmalade, or jelly, or the white of an egg, beaten to a strong froth, with a little sifted sugar.

Time, from 30 to 50 minutes to bake the apples. *Average cost*, 10d., with the garnishing. *Sufficient* for 4 or 5 persons. *Seasonable* from July to March.

APRICOTS AND RICE (Australian Recipe).

INGREDIENTS.—*1 breakfastcupful of rice, 1 quart of milk, 1 breakfastcupful of sugar, a small piece of butter, 3 eggs, 18 fresh ripe apricots, a little apricot jam, 1 lemon.*

Mode.—Put the rice, milk, butter and 2 tablespoonfuls of sugar in a lined saucepan, with half the rind of the lemon, and simmer gently till the milk is all absorbed and the rice tender; then add the eggs, beaten up, and boil again, stirring well till the eggs are cooked. Take out the lemon-rind, and having put a small jam-pot in the centre of a glass dish, put the rice round it and make it smoothly slope from the edge of the pot to that of the dish. Pare and stone the apricots, make a syrup of the remainder of the sugar and the lemon-juice, and when it is boiling put in the fruit, with a few of the kernels for flavouring, and boil quickly for a few minutes. Take out the pot from the rice and put the jam at the bottom of the dish, then a little of the syrup and pile the apricots carefully as shown. The kernels or some almonds may be used for a garnish.

Time to boil the apricots, 5 minutes. *Sufficient* for 6 or 8 persons.

ARROWROOT BLANC-MANGE (an inexpensive Supper Dish).

INGREDIENTS.—4 *heaped tablespoonfuls arrowroot,* 1½ *pints milk,* 8 *laurel-leaves or the rind of* ½ *lemon, sugar to taste.*

Mode.—Mix to a smooth batter the arrowroot with ½ pint of the milk; put the other pint on the fire, with laurel-leaves or lemon-peel, whichever may be preferred, and let the milk steep until well flavoured. Strain the milk and add it, boiling, to the mixed arrowroot; sweeten it with sifted sugar and let it boil, stirring all the time, till it thickens sufficiently to come from the saucepan. Grease a mould with salad oil, pour in the blanc-mange, and, when quite set, turn it out on a dish, and pour round it a compote of fruit, or garnish with jam. A tablespoonful of brandy may be stirred in just before the blanc-mange is moulded.

Time, altogether, ½ hour. *Average cost,* 6d., without the garnishing. *Sufficient* for 4 or 5 persons.

CHEAP BLANC-MANGE.

INGREDIENTS.—¼ *lb. sugar,* 1 *quart milk,* 1½ *oz. of Swinborne's isinglass or gelatine, the rind of* ½ *lemon,* 4 *bay laurel-leaves.*

Mode.—Put the ingredients into a lined saucepan and boil gently until the isinglass is dissolved, and keep stirring the mixture over the fire for about 10 minutes; take the laurel-leaves out when it is sufficiently flavoured; strain through a fine sieve into a jug, and, when nearly cold, pour into a well-oiled mould, omitting the sediment at the bottom. Turn it out carefully on a dish, and garnish with preserves, bright jelly, or a compote of fruit.

Time, altogether ½ hour. *Average cost,* 1s. *Sufficient* to fill a quart mould.

CORNFLOUR BLANC-MANGE.

INGREDIENTS.—4 *tablespoonfuls of cornflour,* 1½ *pints milk,* ½ *rind of lemon, sugar.*

Mode. — Mix the cornflour into a smooth batter with some of the milk, boil the rest and the peel; strain on to the cornflour, add the sugar and boil 8 minutes, stirring briskly. Pour into a mould and turn out when cool.

Time, 20 minutes. *Average cost,* 6d.

LEMON BLANC-MANGE.

INGREDIENTS.—1 *quart milk, the yolk of* 4 *eggs,* 3 *oz. ground rice,* 6 *oz. pounded sugar,* 1¾ *oz. fresh butter, the rind of* 1 *lemon, the juice of* 2, ¾ *oz. gelatine.*

Mode. — Make a custard with the yolks of the eggs and ½ pint of the milk, and put it into a basin; put half the remainder of the milk into a saucepan with the ground rice, fresh butter, lemon-rind, and 3 oz. of the sugar, and let these ingredients boil until the mixture is stiff, stirring continually; when done, pour it into the bowl where the custard is, mixing both well together. Put the gelatine with the rest of the milk into a saucepan, and let it stand by the side of the fire to dissolve; boil for a minute or two, stir carefully into the basin, adding 3 oz. more of pounded sugar. When cold, stir in the lemon - juice (carefully-strained) and pour the mixture into a well-oiled mould, leaving out the lemon-peel, and set the mould in a pan of cold water until wanted for table. Should the weather be very warm, rather a larger proportion of gelatine must be allowed.

Time, altogether ½ hour. *Average cost,* 1s. 6d. *Sufficient* to fill 2 small moulds.

RICE BLANC-MANGE.

INGREDIENTS.—¼ *lb. ground rice,* 3 *oz. loaf sugar,* 1 *oz. fresh butter,* 1 *quart milk, flavouring of lemon-peel, essence of almonds or vanilla, or laurel-leaves.*

Mode.—Mix the rice to a smooth batter with about ½ pint of the milk, and the remainder put into a saucepan, with the sugar, butter, and flavouring; bring the milk to the boiling point, quickly stir in the rice, and let it boil for about 10 minutes, or until it comes easily away from the saucepan, keeping it well stirred. Grease a mould with pure salad-oil; pour in the rice, and let it get perfectly set, when it should turn out quite easily; garnish it with jam, or pour round a compote of any kind of fruit. This blanc-mange is better for being made the day before it is wanted, as it then has time to become firm. If laurel-leaves are used for flavouring, steep 3 of them in the milk, and take them out before the rice is added; about 8 drops of essence of almonds, or from 12 to 16 drops of essence of vanilla, would be required to flavour the above proportion of milk.

Time, from 10 to 15 minutes to boil the rice. *Average cost*, 7d. *Sufficient* to fill a quart mould.

CALF'S FEET JELLY.

INGREDIENTS. — 1 *quart calf's feet stock,* ¼ *lb. sugar,* ½ *pint sherry,* 1 *glass brandy, the shells and whites of 5 eggs, the rind and juice of 2 lemons,* ½ *oz. isinglass.*

Mode.—Prepare the stock as directed in recipe. Put it into a saucepan cold, without clarifying, add the remaining ingredients, and stir them well together before the saucepan is placed on the fire. Then simmer the mixture gently for ¼ hour, *but do not stir it after it begins to warm.* Throw in a teacupful of cold water, boil for another 5 minutes, and keep the saucepan covered by the side of the fire for about ½ hour, but do not let it boil again. In simmering, the head or scum may be carefully removed as it rises, but it must not be stirred in the slightest degree after it is heated. The isinglass should be added when the jelly begins to boil. Wring out a jelly-bag in hot water, fasten it on to a stand or the backs of two chairs, place it near the fire with a basin underneath it, and run the jelly through it. Should it not be perfectly clear the first time, repeat the process. Soak the moulds in water, drain them for half a second, pour in the jelly, and put it in a cool place to set. If ice is at hand, surround the moulds with it, and the jelly will set sooner and be firmer when turned out. In summer it is necessary to have ice in which to put the moulds, or the cook will be, very likely, disappointed by her jellies being in too liquid a state to turn out properly, unless a great deal of isinglass is used. When wanted for table, dip the moulds in hot water for a minute, wipe the outside with a cloth, lay a dish on the top of the mould, turn it quickly over, and the jelly should slip out easily. It is sometimes served broken in square lumps, and piled high in glasses.

Earthenware moulds are preferable to those of pewter or tin, for red jellies, their colour and transparency, being often spoiled by using the latter.

To make this jelly more economically, raisin wine may be substituted for the sherry and brandy, and the stock made from cowheels.

Time, 20 minutes to simmer the jelly.

TO MAKE THE STOCK FOR JELLY, AND TO CLARIFY IT.

INGREDIENTS.—2 *calf's feet,* 6 *pints water, eggs.*

Mode.—The stock for jellies should be made the day before it is required for use, as the liquor has time to cool, and the fat can be more easily removed. Procure 2 nice calf's feet; scald them to take off the hair; slit them in two, remove the fat from between the claws, and wash the feet well in warm water; put them into a stewpan with the cold water, bring it gradually to boil, and remove every particle of scum as it rises. When well skimmed, boil very gently for 6 or 7 hours, or until the liquor is reduced rather more than half; then strain it through a sieve into a basin, and put it in a cool place to set. As the liquor is strained, measure it, to ascertain the proportion for the jelly, allowing something for the sediment and fat at the top. To clarify it, carefully remove all the fat from the top, pour over a little warm water, to wash away any that may remain, and wipe the jelly with a clean cloth; remove the jelly from the sediment, put it into a saucepan, and, supposing the quantity to be a quart, add to it 6 oz. of loaf sugar, the shells and well-whisked whites of 5 eggs, and stir these ingredients together cold; set the saucepan on the fire, but *do not stir the jelly after it begins to warm.* Let it boil about 10 minutes after it rises to a head, then throw in a teacupful of cold water; let it boil 5 minutes longer, then take the saucepan off, cover it closely, and let it remain ½ an hour near the fire. Dip the jelly-bag into hot water, wring it out quite dry, and fasten it on to a stand or the backs of two chairs, which must be placed near the fire, to prevent the jelly from setting before it has run through the bag. Place a basin underneath to receive the jelly, then pour it into the bag, and should it not be clear the first time, run it through the bag again. This stock is the foundation of all *really good* jellies, which may be varied in innumerable ways by colouring and flavouring with liqueurs, and by moulding it with fresh and preserved fruits. To ensure the jelly being firm when turned out, ½ oz. of isinglass clarified might be added to the above proportion of stock. Substitutes for calf's feet, which lessen the expense and trouble, are now nearly always used in making jellies—isinglass and gelatine being two of the principal materials employed. Swinborne's Patent Refined Isinglass and gelatines are the best known, and careful analysis has shown that their patent isinglass is vastly superior to Russian isinglass of the first quality.

Time, about 6 hours to boil the feet for the stock; to clarify it—¼ hour to boil, ½ hour to stand in the saucepan covered. *Average cost*—calf's feet may be purchased for 6d. each when veal is in full season, but more expensive when it is scarce. *Sufficient*—2 calf's feet should make 1 quart of stock. *Seasonable* from March to October, but may be had all the year.

CHOCOLATE CREAM.

INGREDIENTS.—3 *eggs*, 1½ *oz. of gelatine.* 3 *oz. of grated chocolate,* ¼ *lb. of loaf sugar,* 1 *pint of milk,* ½ *pint of cream.*

Mode.—Beat the eggs well and add to them the chocolate, the sugar pounded, and the milk; stir these together and put in a jug in a saucepan of boiling water; stir one way till the mixture begins to thicken, but do not allow it to boil; then strain through a sieve into a basin. Have the gelatine soaked in a little boiling water and add it with the cream whipped. Oil a mould, and having stirred the mixture well, pour it in and set in a cool place on ice.

Time, about 10 minutes to stir the mixture over the fire. *Average cost,* 2s. *Sufficient* for large mould. *Seasonable* at any time.

COMPOTE OF FRUIT.

INGREDIENTS. — ½ *pint of syrup* (Recipe, "To Clarify Sugar"), *any fresh fruit, about a quart, or a tin of peaches or pine,* 1 *glass of liqueur,* 2 *glasses of sherry.*

Mode.—Prepare the fruit according to its kind, by stoning or stemming, slicing such fruits as apricots or peaches, and put in a bowl. Mix the liqueur and sherry with the syrup and pour over; then set on ice.

If tinned fruit is used half the quantity of the syrup only will be needed.

Average cost, with fresh fruit, 2s. 3d. *Sufficient* for 6 persons. *Seasonable* in summer.

BOILED CUSTARDS.

INGREDIENTS.—1 *pint milk,* 3 *eggs,* 3 *oz. loaf sugar,* 3 *bay laurel-leaves, or the rind of* ½ *lemon, or a few drops essence of vanilla,* 1 *tablespoonful brandy*

Mode.—Put the milk into a lined saucepan, with the sugar, and lemon rind or other flavouring, and let the milk steep by the side of the fire until it is well flavoured. Bring it to the point of boiling, then strain it into a basin; whisk the eggs well, and when the milk has cooled a little, stir in the eggs, and strain this mixture into a jug. Place this jug in a saucepan of boiling water over the fire; keep stirring the custard *one way* until it thickens; but *on no account* allow it to reach the boiling-point. Take it off the fire, stir in the brandy, and, when this is well mixed with the custard, pour it into glasses, each rather more than three-parts full; grate a little nutmeg over the top, and the dish is ready for table. Ducks' eggs add very much to the flavour and richness of custards, and so many are not required as of the ordinary eggs, 2 ducks' eggs to the pint of milk making a delicious custard. When desired extremely rich and good, cream should be substituted for the milk, and double the quantity of eggs used, omitting the whites. The brandy should be omitted for a plain custard.

Time, ½ hour to infuse the lemon-rind, about 10 minutes to stir the custard. *Average cost,* 10d. *Sufficient* to fill 8 custard-glasses.

ISINGLASS OR GELATINE JELLY (Substitutes for Calf's Feet).

INGREDIENTS. — 3 *oz. Swinborne's isinglass or gelatine,* 2 *quarts water.*

Mode.—Put the isinglass or gelatine into a saucepan with the cold water; bring it quickly to boil, and let it boil very fast, until the liquor is reduced one-half. Carefully remove the scum as it rises, then strain it through a jelly-bag, and it will be ready for use. If not required very clear, it may be merely strained through a fine sieve, instead of being run through a bag. Rather more than ½ oz. isinglass is about the proper quantity to use for a quart of strong calf's-feet stock, and rather more than 2 oz. for the same quantity of fruit juice. The larger the mould the stiffer should be the jelly, and where there is no ice, more isinglass must be used than if the mixture were frozen. This forms a stock for all kinds of jellies, which may be flavoured in many ways.

Time, 1½ hours. *Sufficient*, with wine, syrup, fruit, &c., to fill two moderate-sized moulds.

Note.—The above, when boiled, should be perfectly clear, and may be mixed warm with wine, flavourings, fruits, &c., and then run through the bag.

TO MAKE GOOSEBERRY FOOL.

INGREDIENTS. — *Green gooseberries ; to every pint of pulp add 1 pint milk, or ½ pint cream and ½ pint milk ; sugar to taste.*

Mode.—Cut the tops and tails off the gooseberries, put them into a jar, with 2 tablespoonfuls of water and a little good moist sugar; set this jar in a saucepan of boiling water, and let it boil until the fruit is soft enough to mash. When done beat to a pulp, work through a colander, and stir to every pint the proportion of milk, or equal quantities of milk and cream. Put in plenty of sugar, or it will not be eatable; in mixing the milk and gooseberries add milk gradually. Serve in a glass dish.

Time, from ¾ to 1 hour. *Average cost*, 4d. per pint, with milk. *Sufficient*, a pint of milk and a pint of gooseberry pulp for 5 or 6 persons. *Seasonable* in May and June.

GOOSEBERRY TRIFLE.

INGREDIENTS.—*1 quart of gooseberries, sugar to taste, 1 pint of custard, a plateful whipped cream.*

Mode.—Put the gooseberries into a jar, with moist sugar to sweeten, and boil them until reduced to a pulp. Put this pulp at the bottom of a trifle-dish; pour over a pint of very good custard, and, when cold, cover with whipped cream. The cream should be whipped the day before it is wanted for table, as it will then be so much

firmer and more solid. Garnish as fancy dictates.

Time, about ¾ hour to boil the gooseberries. *Average cost*, 1s. 2d. *Sufficient* for 1 trifle. *Seasonable* in May and June.

HULLUAH (Indian Recipe).

INGREDIENTS. — *½ pint of tous les mois, 6 oz. of butter, a few almonds, pounded, and raisins stoned and chopped, some ripe cardamoms, a stick of cinnamon, a pint of water.*

Mode.—Soak the tous les mois in water, in summer for 12 and in winter for 18 hours, strain through a duster. Add the sugar, and put in a lined saucepan over the fire. As it comes to the boil add the plums, almonds, butter and flavouring, stirring all the time till it thickens. Oil a shape or some small ones, pour in the mixture, and when cold turn out.

INDIAN FRITTERS (Indian Recipe).

INGREDIENTS.—*3 tablespoonfuls flour, boiling water, the yolks of 4 eggs, the whites of 2, hot lard or clarified dripping, jam.*

Mode.—Put the flour into a basin, and pour over it sufficient *boiling* water to make it into a stiff paste, taking care to stir and beat it well, to prevent it getting lumpy. Leave it time to cool, and then break into it (*without beating them at first*) the yolks of 4 eggs and the whites of 2, and stir and beat all well together. Have ready some boiling lard or butter, drop a dessertspoonful of batter in at the time, and fry the fritters of a light brown. Serve on a dish, with a spoonful of preserve or marmalade dropped in between each fritter. This is an excellent dish for a hasty addition to dinner if a guest unexpectedly arrives; it being so easily and quickly made, and it is always a great favourite.

Time, from 5 to 8 minutes to fry the fritters. *Average cost*, exclusive of the jam, 6d. *Sufficient* for 4 or 5 persons.

INDIAN PANCAKE.

INGREDIENTS.—*1 pint of milk, 3 eggs, ½ a teacupful of rice, ¼ lb. of sugar, flavouring of cinnamon, crystallised cherries, preserved ginger, butter for frying.*

Mode.—Boil the rice in the milk and beat it to a pulp, beat the eggs well, and add with the flavouring of cinnamon, or any other if preferred. Form the paste into a flat, round cake, and fry on one side only in butter. When done, lift it on to a hot dish, and garnish with the ginger in neat pieces, and the cherries.

Time, 7 or 8 minutes to fry. *Seasonable* at any time.

INDIAN TRIFLE.

INGREDIENTS. — 1 *quart milk, the rind of ½ large lemon, sugar to taste, 5 heaped tablespoonfuls rice-flour, 1 oz. sweet almonds, ½ pint custard.*

Mode. — Boil the milk and lemon-rind together until the former is well flavoured; take out the lemon rind and stir in the rice-flour, first moistened with cold milk, and add sufficient loaf sugar to sweeten. Boil gently for 5 minutes, and keep the mixture stirred; take it off the fire, let it cool a *little*, and pour it into a glass dish. When cold, cut the rice out in the form of a star, or any other shape that may be preferred; take out the spare rice, and fill the space with boiled custard. Blanch and cut the almonds into strips, stick them over the trifle, and garnish it with pieces of jelly, or preserved fruits, or candied citron.

Time, ¼ hour to simmer the milk, 5 minutes after the rice is added. *Average cost,* 10d. *Sufficient* for 1 trifle.

JELLIES (BOTTLED), HOW TO MOULD.

Uncork the bottle place it in a saucepan of hot water until the jelly is reduced to a liquid state; ascertain whether it is sufficiently flavoured, and if not, add a little wine. Pour the jelly into moulds which have been soaked in water, let it set, and turn it out by placing the mould in hot water for a minute; then wipe the outside, put a dish on the top, and turn it over quickly. The jelly should then slip easily away from the mould, and be quite firm. It may be garnished as taste dictates.

JUNKET.

INGREDIENTS. — *A quart of milk,* 2 *teaspoonfuls of rennet, sugar, brandy (if liked), cinnamon, Devonshire cream.*

Mode. — Put about 2 dessertspoonfuls of sugar (pounded) in a dish, add a little cinnamon to flavour, and pour over ½ wineglass of brandy. Warm the milk, stir in the rennet, and pour in the dish. Stir this to the sugar and brandy, set aside in a cool place for 2 hours, then put a few spoonfuls of cream over.

Time, 2 hours. *Average cost,* 1s. 2d. *Sufficient* for 4 persons. *Seasonable* at any time.

LEMON CREAM (ECONOMICAL).

INGREDIENTS.—1 *quart milk,* 8 *bitter almonds,* 2 *oz. Swinborne's gelatine or isinglass,* 2 *large lemons,* ¾ *lb. lump sugar, the yolks of 6 eggs.*

Mode.—Put the milk into a lined saucepan with the almonds (well pounded in a mortar), the gelatine, lemon-rind, and lump sugar, and boil for about 5 minutes. Beat up the yolks of the eggs, strain the milk into a jug, add the eggs, and pour the mixture backwards and forwards until nearly cold; then stir briskly to it the lemon-juice (strained), and keep stirring until the cream is almost cold; put it into an oiled mould. The lemon-juice must not be added to the cream when it is warm, and should be well stirred after it is put in.

Time, 5 minutes to boil the milk. *Average cost,* 2s. *Sufficient* to fill two 1½ pint moulds.

LEMON SPONGE.

INGREDIENTS. — 1 *oz. gelatine,* 2 *lemons,* 2 *eggs,* 6 *to* 8 *oz. sugar, water.*

Mode. — Simmer the gelatine, the lemon-juice and rind, and the sugar in rather more than a pint of water till the gelatine is quite dissolved. Take out the lemon-rind and when nearly cold, whisk with the whites of 2 eggs, well beaten till the mixture becomes quite spongy in appearance. Put in a wet mould and turn out when cold, or in rough lumps in a glass dish.

Time altogether about 1 hour. *Average cost,* 9d. *Seasonable,* at any time.

MACARONI AND PINEAPPLE.

INGREDIENTS.—1 *pint of clear gelatine jelly,* ½ *tin of preserved pineapple,* 6 *oz. of loaf sugar,* 6 *oz. of macaroni,* ½ *pint of custard, milk.*

Mode. — Having wetted a border mould, coat it with the jelly; cut the pineapple in dice and put in, then pour in the remainder of the jelly, which would look prettier if coloured with a few drops of cochineal. Boil the macaroni in milk till quite tender, sweeten and drain it and set it aside to cool. When the jelly is firmly set turn it out and fill with the macaroni, pouring over it a good custard made by recipe for Boiled Custards.

Average cost, 2s. *Sufficient* for 6 persons. *Seasonable* at any time.

MERINGUES.

INGREDIENTS.—½ *lb. of pounded white sugar, the white of 4 eggs, 1 pint of cream, flavouring of vanilla.*

Mode.—Whisk the whites of egg to a stiff froth, then with a wooden spoon stir in the sugar quickly before the froth goes down. Have some boards thick enough to prevent the meringues from browning when baked upon them, put in the oven. Cut some strips of white paper and lay on the boards and on this drop a tablespoonful at a time of the beaten egg and sugar, dropping it in the form of the spoon with some two inches of space between; strew over a little sifted sugar and bake for ½ an hour in a moderate oven. As soon as they begin to colour take them out; take each slip of paper by the two ends and turn the meringues on to a board. Remove the soft part with a wooden spoon, put some fresh paper on the board, lay the meringues on it upside down and replace in the oven to harden. Whip the cream, slightly sweeten it, and flavour with vanilla, then fill the meringues when cold with this, putting two together so as to take the form of an egg. The meringues must be put in the oven directly they are dropped upon the board, or they will lose their shape. They can be kept in a dry place for some time and can be filled with cream when required.

Time, ½ an hour to bake. *Average cost*, 2s. *Sufficient* for a good-sized dish. *Seasonable* at any time.

NORMANDY PIPPINS (STEWED).

INGREDIENTS.—4 *lb. Normandy pippins, 1 quart water, ½ teaspoonful powdered cinnamon, ½ teaspoonful ground ginger, 1 lb. moist sugar, 1 lemon.*

Mode.—Well wash the pippins, and put them into 1 quart of water with the cinnamon and ginger, and let them stand 12 hours; then put these altogether into a stewpan, with the lemon

sliced thinly, and half the moist sugar. Boil slowly until the pippins are half done; then add the remainder of the sugar, and simmer until quite tender. Serve on glass dishes for dessert.

Time, 2 to 3 hours. *Average cost*, 1s. *Seasonable*—suitable for a winter dish.

PANCAKES (TO MAKE).

INGREDIENTS.—*Eggs, flour, milk ; to every egg allow 1 oz. flour, about 1 gill milk, ½ saltspoonful salt.*

Mode.—Whisk the eggs well in a basin, add the flour, salt, and a few drops of milk, and beat the whole to a perfectly *smooth* batter; then pour in by degrees the remainder of the milk. The batter should be of the consistency of thick cream. Place a small frying-pan on the fire to get hot; let it be delicately clean, and, when quite hot, put into it a small piece of butter, allowing about ½ oz. to each pancake. When it is melted, pour in the batter, about ¼ teacupful to a pan 12 inches in diameter, and fry it for about 5 minutes, or until it is nicely brown on one side. By only pouring in a small quantity of batter, and so making the pancakes thin, the necessity of turning them (an operation rather difficult to unskilful cooks) is obviated. When the pancake is done, sprinkle over it some pounded sugar, roll it up in the pan, take it out with a large slice, and place it on a dish before the fire. Pancakes are never good unless eaten almost immediately they come from the frying-pan. The batter may be flavoured with a little grated lemon-rind, or the pancakes may have preserve rolled in them, instead of sugar. Send sifted sugar and a cut lemon to table with them. To render the pancakes very light, the yolks and whites of the eggs should be beaten separately, and the whites added the last thing to the batter before frying.

Time, from 4 to 5 minutes for a pancake that does not require turning ; from 6 to 8 minutes for a thicker one. *Average cost*, for 3 persons, 6d. *Sufficient*—allow 3 eggs with the other ingredients in proportion for 3 persons. *Seasonable* at any time, but specially served on Shrove Tuesday.

PEARS (BAKED).

INGREDIENTS.—12 *pears, the rind of 1 lemon, 3 cloves, 10 whole allspice ; to*

SWEET DISHES

every pint of water allow ½ lb. loaf sugar.

Mode.—Pare and cut the pears into halves, or if very large, into quarters; leave the stalks on, and carefully remove the cores. Place them in a clean baking-jar, with closely-fitting lid; add the lemon-rind, cut in strips, the juice of ½ lemon, the cloves, pounded allspice, and sufficient water to cover the whole, with the sugar. Cover the jar down closely, put it into a very cool oven, and bake the pears from 5 to 6 hours. To improve the colour of the fruit, a few drops of prepared cochineal may be added.

Time, large pears, 5 to 6 hours, in a very slow oven. _Average cost_, 1d. to 2d. each. _Sufficient_ for 7 or 8 persons. _Seasonable_ from September to January.

PEARS (STEWED).

INGREDIENTS.—8 _large pears_, 5 _oz. loaf sugar_, 6 _cloves_, 6 _whole allspice_, ½ _pint water_, ¼ _pint port wine_, _a few drops prepared cochineal._

Mode.—Pare the pears, halve them, remove the cores, and leave the stalks on; put them into a _lined_ saucepan, with the other ingredients, and simmer very gently until tender, which will be in from 3 to 4 hours. They should be watched, and, when done, carefully lifted out on to a glass dish without breaking. Boil up the syrup quickly for 2 or 3 minutes; allow it to cool a little, and pour it over the pears. To improve the colour of the fruit, a few drops of prepared cochineal may be added, which rather enhances the beauty of this dish. The fruit must not be boiled fast, but only simmered, and watched that it be not too much done.

Time, 3 to 4 hours. _Average cost_, 1s. 4d. _Sufficient_ for 5 or 6 persons. _Seasonable_ from September to January.

RICE SOUFFLÉ.

INGREDIENTS. — 1 _pint of milk_, 3 _tablespoonfuls of ground rice_, 5 _eggs_, _loaf sugar to taste_, _a dessertspoonful of butter_, _vanilla flavouring_.

Mode.—Mix the rice thoroughly with some of the milk; then put it in a lined saucepan with the remainder and the butter and stir over the fire until the mixture thickens. Take the whites and yolks of the eggs separately, beat the latter and add to them the rice, the flavouring, and enough pounded sugar to sweeten, bearing in mind that the less sugar there is used the lighter will be the soufflé. Whisk the whites of the eggs to a perfectly stiff froth; mix them with the other ingredients and pour at once into a soufflé dish, which place instantly in the oven. Bake about ½ an hour, then take out and hold a salamander or hot shovel over the top; sprinkle sifted sugar over and send to table with a napkin pinned round the dish in which it has been baked.

Other soufflés can be made in the same way, and one of the nicest is that made with cheese; but the excellence of the dish depends upon the perfect whisking of the eggs, the manner of baking, and the expedition with which it is served. If the soufflé be not served _instantly_ it is taken from the oven it will sink and its appearance be spoiled.

Time, ½ an hour. _Average cost_, 10d. _Sufficient_ for 4 persons. _Seasonable_ at any time.

RICE SNOWBALLS (a pretty dish for Juvenile Suppers).

INGREDIENTS. — 6 _oz. rice_, 1 _quart milk_, _flavouring of essence of almonds_, _sugar to taste_, 1 _pint custard made by recipe_.

Mode.—Boil the rice in the milk, with sugar and a flavouring of essence of almonds, until the former is tender, adding, if necessary, a little more milk, should it dry away too much. When the rice is quite soft, put it into teacups, or _small_ round jars, and let it remain until cold; then turn the rice out on a deep glass dish; pour over a good boiled custard, and on the top of each ball place a small piece of bright-coloured preserve or jelly. Lemon-peel or vanilla may be boiled with the rice, instead of the essence of almonds; but the flavouring of the custard must correspond with that of the rice.

Time, about ¾ hour to swell the rice in the milk. _Average cost_, with the custard, 1s. 6d. _Sufficient_ for 5 or 6 children.

TIPSY CAKE.

INGREDIENTS.—_A stale sponge cake_, _rather more than a pint of custard_, ½ _bottle of sherry or orange wine_, _a wineglassful of brandy_, ½ _lb. sweet almonds_.

Mode.—Mix the wine and brandy, make a few holes in the cake with a skewer and pour the liquor over. Let the cake thoroughly soak, pouring the wine over as it runs from the cake, then stick it with the almonds, blanched and divided, and pour over the custard.

Time, 2 or 3 hours to soak the cake. *Average cost*, 3s. *Sufficient* for 6 persons.

TRIFLE.

INGREDIENTS.—6 *sponge cakes*, ¼ *lb. ratafias*, ¼ *lb. macaroons*, *apricot jam*, *a pint of custard*, ½ *pint cream*, *sherry*, *brandy*.

Mode.—Slice the sponge cakes and put them in a glass dish, with layers of jam between, and over them place the macaroons and ratafias in layers. Soak them in sherry and brandy, then pour over the custard, and, lastly, pile up the cream, whipped stiffly with a little sugar.

Time, about 2 hours to soak the cakes. *Average cost*, 3s. 6d. *Sufficient* for supper dish.

VICTORIA SANDWICHES.

INGREDIENTS.—4 *eggs; their weight in pounded sugar, butter, and flour;* ¼ *saltspoonful salt, a layer of any kind of jam or marmalade.*

Mode.—Beat the butter to a cream; dredge in the flour and pounded sugar; stir well together, and add the eggs, previously well whisked. When the mixture has been beaten about 10 minutes, butter a Yorkshire-pudding tin, pour in the batter, and bake in a moderate oven for 20 minutes. Let it cool, spread one-half of the cake with a layer of preserve, place over it the other half, press the pieces together, and then cut into finger-pieces; pile these in cross-bars on a glass dish, and serve.

Time, 20 minutes. *Average cost*, 1s. 4d. *Sufficient* for 5 or 6 persons.

CONFECTIONERY, &c.

Cornet d'Abondance.

Rout Cakes.

Patties.

Jelly.

Christmas Pudding.

Trifle.

Vanilla Cream.

Preserved Fruits.

CONFECTIONERY AND ICES

THE very highest branches of confectionery, such as modelling in paste and the more elaborate kinds of decorative pastry, are seldom attempted in private houses; partly because of the time they take, and partly because so many expensive utensils and *tools* (if we may be allowed the word in speaking of cookery) are needed in their preparation. Still there is no reason why we should not have very pretty sweets upon our tables; nor is it unusual for either mistress or daughter of a house to undertake the making of all fancy dishes where no professed cook is kept.

Young girls generally enjoy a morning in the kitchen devoted to the task of making pretty dishes; and might we suggest that their culinary education should not end with these? It is far more important to know how to boil a potato, to roast a joint, or to fry fish, than to be able to clear a jelly or decorate a cream; yet many girls will not try to learn the homely useful division of cookery. But to return to our subject. Confectionery is not sufficiently thought of in our homes. Sweets are so cheap now that no one thinks of making them in their own kitchens, not realising how much purer and more wholesome the home-made ones would be, made from the best sugar and free from the colouring matter which renders bought sweetmeats so pretty and so injurious.

As far as children are concerned, sweets of ordinary kinds are a great deal too cheap; for, in many households the little ones have too many opportunities of eating them. The idea of sugar being injurious to the teeth is an exploded one, yet a child can easily eat too many sweetmeats, and thus load its stomach till it does not enjoy more wholesome food. We all know that sugar is very cheap, yet we cannot believe that with all the preparation, that must cost both time and money, really pure sweets can be bought at the low rate at which all kinds of sugar-plums are sold. It is far better to make our own, and we trust the few recipes we give may be useful. But there is another branch of confectionery that might well be attempted at home, such as the icing and cone decoration of cakes, and the ornamenting and making of such little things as the small rout cakes or *petit fours* that we pay so much for to adorn our supper tables.

Birthday and other cakes for children are far more appreciated and liked by the little folks if a little time has not been grudged to ice and decorate them. The icing is a very simple affair, not too difficult for any amateur to accomplish; and the only things needed for the cone decoration that makes the raised patterns and names on the cakes, consist of the simplest materials—white of egg, sugar, and a piece of paper.

The white of egg must be well whipped, mixed to a paste, with the powdered white sugar, and may be coloured with a few drops of cochineal, when required to make designs upon white cakes.

This cone decoration makes a great improvement upon the appearance of cold glazed dishes, such as tongue or ham, when fresh butter, instead of icing, must be used, and this can also be coloured if liked.

Some years ago the employment of ice in the kitchen was not usual, except in the establishments of the wealthy, but now it is cheap and easily obtained; and a freezing machine is not a very expensive article to buy, while it is a most convenient thing to possess, and often in hot weather or illness invaluable.

Even where we have not a freezing machine, in most of our kitchens we need ice, and it may not be out of place here to suggest that the best way of preserving it is to wrap it well in flannel, cross two sticks over a basin or pan and lay it on these so that it may not lie in water, which quickly melts it.

For freezing, the ice is powdered and mixed with half its quantity of baysalt, or it may be put in alternate layers with the salt, in th e machine, in its outer receptacle, the inner being left for what has to be frozen. Different machines are differently managed, but the above are the simple directions for all. Instead of the ice and salt, freezing mixtures may be used, these being generally considered cheaper than the ice and snow; as, if evaporated to dryness, they can be used again and again; but they waste in the using, even with the greatest care, and most cooks prefer the better known ice and salt. Given a machine there is nothing in the way of sweets more easy to make than ices (for which we give some recipes), and it is very pleasant in summer to be able to make our own ices, particularly where fresh fruit and cream are home products.

CLOVE DROPS.

INGREDIENTS.—1 oz. of cloves, 1 lb. of finely-pounded sugar, the whites of 2 eggs, whisked to a froth, ½ pint of water.

Mode.—Pound the cloves in a mortar, then sift the powder through a hair sieve; mix with the other ingredients. Take the mixture up in a teaspoon and drop it on stiff white writing paper, bake in a very cool oven, and take them off when cool.

Ginger, cinnamon, and other flavourings may be used.

STRAWBERRY DROPS.

INGREDIENTS. — ½ lb. of finely powdered sugar, ½ pint of juice, 2 whites of eggs, whisked to a very stiff froth.

Mode.—Mix all together and drop on tins. Bake or dry in a very cool oven. Any other fruit may be used.

APPLE PASTE.

INGREDIENTS.—Equal quantities of apple pulp and sugar.

Mode. — Peel and core some ripe sound apples and put them in water till they are quite soft; then rub them through a hair sieve with a wooden spoon. Put the pulp, with an equal weight of sugar, into a preserving pan, boil for 20 minutes, then pour out on tin plates or into moulds.

This paste may be coloured with a little cochineal, and if the apples be at all tasteless a little lemon is an improvement.

APRICOT PASTE.

INGREDIENTS.—½ lb. of sugar to each lb. of pulp.

Mode. — Put the apricots, which should be ripe, into a preserving pan, with a little sugar, placing them at the side of the fire till they are reduced to a paste, then rub them through a hair-sieve, allowing ½ lb. of sugar to each 1 lb. of fruit. Put again on the fire and boil 10 minutes. Spread it on tins to dry.

ORANGE PASTE.

INGREDIENTS.—2 lbs. of sugar to each lb. of pulp.

Mode.—Squeeze the juice of 5 Seville oranges and boil the rinds till they are perfectly soft. With a thin wooden spoon scoop out the pulp, then pound the rinds in a mortar with half the juice; rub all through a sieve, then keep it on the fire till it becomes like marmalade. Empty it out then, and weigh it, allowing to each 1 lb. 2 lbs. of sugar; boil it for 10 minutes, then spread it on tin plates to dry. Cut it in any shape liked and keep in boxes. Lemon paste may be made in the same way, with the omission of the juice.

LEMON PRALINES.

INGREDIENTS.—*Lemons, sugar.*

Mode.— Pare some lemons and cut the rinds into pieces about an inch long, and very narrow. Boil some syrup till it almost comes to a caramel, put in the shreds of lemon and stir them about with a wooden spoon till cold. Put them on a sieve and shake off the loose sugar and keep dry in boxes.

BARLEY SUGAR

INGREDIENTS.—2 *lbs. of sugar,* 1 *pint of water,* 1 *egg, lemon.*

Mode.—Put the sugar (pounded) into a well-lined saucepan, with the water, and, when the former is dissolved, set it over a moderate fire, adding the white of the egg well beaten before the mixture gets warm, and stir it well together. When it boils remove the scum as it rises and keep it boiling until no more appears, and the syrup looks perfectly clear; then strain it through muslin and put it back in the saucepan. Boil it again till brittle when a little is dropped into cold water. Add for flavouring, a little essence of lemon and a little lemon-juice, and let it stand for a minute or two. Have ready a marble slab, or large dish well rubbed over with salad oil; pour the sugar on it and cut it in strips with a pair of scissors. Twist these strips, set to harden, then store in a very dry place.

EVERTON TOFFEE.

INGREDIENTS.—1 *lb. of treacle or golden syrup,* 1 *lb. of moist sugar,* ¼ *lb. of butter.*

Mode. — Have a saucepan large enough to allow of fast boiling, over a clear fire. Put in the butter, rubbing it well over the bottom of the pan; then add the treacle and sugar, stirring gently with a knife. When it has boiled about 10 minutes, drop a little off the knife into a basin of cold water, when, if sufficiently done, it will be crisp. If not brittle, boil a little

longer. Butter thoroughly or oil a large shallow tin or dish, and into this pour the toffee. When beginning to set mark it out in squares to make it easier to divide when cold.

Time, 10 to 15 minutes. *Average cost,* 9d. *Sufficient* for 2 lbs. of toffee.

ALMOND TOFFEE.

INGREDIENTS.—2 *lbs. of brown sugar,* ½ *lb. of butter,* 1 *teacupful of water,* 1 *lemon,* ½ *lb. of almonds.*

Mode.—Butter a shallow tin or dish, blanch the almonds and divide them in halves, and lay them flat side downwards on the dish. Boil the sugar, butter, water, and ½ the rind of the lemon, and when sufficiently done (trying it as in previous recipe), let it stand aside till the boiling has ceased, then stir in the juice of the lemon.

Time, about 10 minutes. *Average cost,* 1s. 4d. *Sufficient* for 2½ lbs. of toffee.

CANDIED CHESTNUTS OR WALNUTS.

INGREDIENTS. — *Nuts, lemon-juice, syrup.*

Mode. — Take off the outer skin or shell, then put the nuts into a pan of boiling water for a minute or so till the skin comes off easily; then throw them into another pan of boiling water and boil till tender. Squeeze the juice of a lemon into a basin of lukewarm water, and put the nuts, when done, into this. When cool, dry them, dip each in clarified sugar and lay on a slab to dry.

CHOCOLATE CREAMS.

INGREDIENTS.—3 *oz. of best arrowroot,* 1 *lb. of white sugar, about* ¾ *pint of water, chocolate, essence of vanilla.*

Mode.—Mix the arrowroot with the water smoothly, put into a lined saucepan, add the sugar, and boil about 10 minutes, stirring all the while, then take it off the fire and stir till it begins to cool. Flavour with the essence, and roll into little balls; melt some chocolate, roll each ball in this, and lay on a buttered slab to cool.

COCOANUT CANDY.

INGREDIENTS.—½ *lb. of grated cocoanut,* 1½ *lb. of sugar,* ¾ *pint of water.*

Mode.—Put the sugar with the water into a pipkin and let it dissolve; boil 5 minutes then strain. Put in the grated nut, set the pipkin again on the fire and stir till the candy rises; then spread on sheets of writing-paper warmed before the fire, and before the candy is quite cold, take it off the paper and cut it into squares. See that it is perfectly dry before it is put away.

MOLASSES CANDY (American Recipe).

INGREDIENTS.—1 *quart of molasses, a gill of vinegar, a cup of sugar,* 2 *oz. of butter,* 1 *teaspoonful of soda.*

Mode. — Dissolve the sugar in the vinegar, then mix with the molasses and boil, stirring often till the mixture hardens when a little is dropped in cold water. Stir in the batter with the soda, dissolved in hot water, flavour with any essence, boil up, stirring all the while, and pour into buttered tins.

Time, about ½ an hour.

ALMOND PASTE FOR CAKES, &c.

INGREDIENTS.—1 *lb. of sweet almonds,* 6 *bitter ones,* 1 *lb. of caster sugar, the white of* 2 *eggs.*

Mode. — Blanch the almonds, dry them thoroughly and pound them in a mortar, wetting them gradually with the whites of the eggs till they form a smooth paste. Put them in a small preserving pan, with the sugar, over a clear fire, or a hot-plate, and keep stirring till the paste is dry; then take it out of the pan and cool between two dishes. It can then be spread over the top of a cake, or it may be cut into small fancy shapes and ornamented with crystallised cherries, or iced and served with rout cakes for dessert.

Time, ½ an hour. *Average cost* for quantity, 1s. 6d.

ICING FOR CAKES.

INGREDIENTS.—1 *lb. of loaf sugar, whites of* 4 *eggs,* 1 *oz. of starch.*

Mode.—Beat the whites of eggs to a stiff froth, gradually sift in the sugar, powdered as fine as possible, then the starch, also finely powdered. Beat the mixture until the sugar is smooth, then, with a broad flat knife (a paper knife answers well for this purpose), spread the icing over the cakes. They should then be put in a very cool oven to dry and harden; but care must be taken that they do not colour.

If the icing be put upon the cakes directly they are taken out of the oven it will be dry and hard before the cakes are cool.

On very rich cakes, such as wedding and christening ones, it is well to put a layer of almond paste before the icing. The cakes may be ornamented with a little of the icing coloured with cochineal and squeezed out of a paper cone in a pattern over the cake. Other pretty decorations may be made with small crystallised fruit, such as cherries, leaves cut out of angelica, diamonds cut from candied peel and the like, these being put on before the icing is dry, so that they may stick.

TO CLARIFY SUGAR FOR SYRUP.

INGREDIENTS.—*To every lb. of sugar allow* ½ *pint of water and* ½ *the white of an egg.*

Mode.—Put the ingredients (the white of egg, well-beaten) into a lined saucepan, and when it is dissolved put the pan on the fire. When it boils, throw in a teacupful of water, and do not stir the sugar after this is added. Bring it to the boiling point again, then place the pan by the side of the fire for the preparation to settle. Remove all scum and the sugar will be ready for use.

Time, 20 minutes for the sugar to dissolve, 5 minutes to boil.

Note.—To make candy sugar clarify it by the above recipe, then put it over the fire and let it boil till smooth; dip the hand into cold water, and the skimmer into the sugar, touch it with the thumb and finger and instantly open them, when a fine short thread should form.

CARAMEL SUGAR.

INGREDIENTS. — 1 *lb. of loaf sugar,* ½ *pint of spring water.*

Mode.—Boil the sugar and the water together very quickly over a clear fire, skimming it very carefully as soon as it boils. Keep it boiling until the sugar is brittle when a little is dropped into cold water; then squeeze in a little lemon-juice and let it remain an instant longer on the fire; then set the pan into another of cold water and the caramel is ready for use. This preparation should be carefully watched and taken up directly it is done, but it is a very inexpensive and a very pretty decoration for sweet dishes. Any kind of pastry, a compote of fruit or a tipsy cake can have this spun sugar to ornament it, it being drawn out in long threads with a fork and laid lightly to cover but not hide the sweet.

APRICOT ICE CREAM.

INGREDIENTS.—½ *lb. of apricot jam,*

1 *pint of cream*, 1 *lemon*, 6 *bitter almonds*.

Mode. Pound the almonds to a paste, add the strained juice of the lemon, then the cream · mix thoroughly and rub through a hair sieve. Furnish the outer receptacle with layers of ice and bay-salt as directed; then put the mixture to be frozen in the inner one, letting it be well covered with the freezing mixture. Stir or shake till the ice begins to set. If it is to be served in a mould, it must now be put into one and returned to the machine; but if only in rough pieces on plates, then, when the ice begins to set, there is nothing more to do.

Time, 25 minutes. *Average cost*, 1s. 6d. *Sufficient* for 8 persons.

CHOCOLATE ICE CREAM.

INGREDIENTS.—1 *pint of new milk*, ½ *pint of cream*, 6 *oz. of chocolate*, ¼ *lb. of sugar*.

Mode. -- Scrape the chocolate and blend it thoroughly, first with the milk, then with the cream; add the sugar, strain and freeze as directed in recipe.

Time, 25 minutes. *Average cost*, 1s. 6d. *Sufficient* for 8 persons. *Seasonable* at any time.

COFFEE ICE CREAM.

INGREDIENTS.—1 *pint of milk*, ½ *pint of cream*, 1 *oz. of arrowroot*, 6 *oz. of roasted coffee berries*, ½ *lb. of sugar*.

Mode.—Put the berries in the oven for 5 minutes and at the same time boil the milk and cream together; put in the berries, pour into a jug and cover till cold. Strain the mixture, add the arrowroot and sugar, and stir over the fire in a pan of water as a custard. Freeze as directed in recipe.

Time, 25 minutes. *Average cost*, 1s. 3d. *Sufficient* for 8 persons. *Seasonable* at any time.

FRUIT ICE CREAM.

INGREDIENTS.—*Any fresh fruit, milk, and cream in the proportion of* ½ *a pint of each to a pint of fruit-juice, sugar to taste according to the fruit used.*

Mode.—Pick over some ripe fruit, as for a tart, into an earthen pan, and mash it; then, with the back of a wooden spoon, rub it through a hair-sieve. Sweeten the juice to taste with pounded white sugar; whip the cream, add it to the milk, then to the juice, and whisk all for a few minutes. Freeze as directed in recipe.

All fresh fruit creams can be made in the same manner, fresh raspberries and strawberries making the ones most generally preferred; and a little sugar scattered over them helps to extract the juice. In winter jam may be substituted for the fresh fruit, this being melted and run through a sieve before being added to the cream and milk. And if the colour is dull, then a little cochineal will make an improvement in the appearance of the ice.

Time, 25 minutes. *Average cost*, 2d. each ice. *Seasonable*, with fresh fruit, in summer.

PINEAPPLE ICE CREAM.

INGREDIENTS.—½ *lb. of tinned pineapple freed from every bit of rind*, ¾ *of a pint of milk*, ½ *pint of cream, the juice of* 1 *lemon*, 6 *oz. of sugar*.

Mode. — Cut the pine into small pieces, which bruise in a mortar to extract the juice, add the other ingredients, strain through a sieve and freeze as directed in recipe.

Time, 25 minutes. *Average cost*, 1s. 4d. *Sufficient* for 8 persons. *Seasonable* at any time.

VANILLA ICE CREAM.

INGREDIENTS.—*A vanilla bean or any other flavouring*, 1½ *pint each of milk and cream*, ½ *lb. of loaf sugar*.

Mode.—Break the bean into pieces, and boil with the milk till sufficiently flavoured; if essence be used, put with the milk cold. Add the cream and sugar, beat well together, and freeze in a mould.

Time, ½ an hour. *Seasonable* in hot weather.

CLARIFIED SUGAR FOR WATER ICES.

INGREDIENTS.—6 *lbs. of loaf sugar*, 5 *pints of water, the white of* 1 *egg*.

Mode.—Put the sugar in the water, place the pan over a gentle fire and bring to the boil; well beat the white of the egg, add it to the water, boil for 10 minutes, then strain and bottle for use.

FRUIT WATER ICES.

INGREDIENTS.—*To every pint of fruit-juice allow* 1 *pint of syrup, made by previous recipe.*

Mode. — Take any ripe fresh fruit, such as currants, raspberries, or strawberries, pull off the stalks and mash it well in an earthen pan with a wooden spoon, adding a little sugar to help extract the juice; then rub it through a sieve. Take 1 pint of syrup, or make a pint in the same way fresh, omitting the white of the egg, let it cool, add and mix this with the juice, and freeze by recipe.

Time, ½ an hour to freeze. *Average cost*, 2d. each ice. *Seasonable*, with fresh fruit, in summer.

LEMON WATER ICE.

INGREDIENTS.—1 *pint of syrup made by " Clarified Sugar " recipe, omitting the white of egg, rather more than ¼ of a pint of lemon-juice, rinds of 4 lemons.*

Mode.—Rub the sugar on the rinds of the lemons and make syrup with it, as directed; let it cool, strain the lemon-juice, and add and stir well. Freeze by recipe.

Time, ½ an hour to freeze. *Average cost*, 2d. each ice

GINGER WATER ICE.

INGREDIENTS. — 1 *quart of lemon water ice, 6 oz. of preserved ginger.*

Mode. — Pound half the ginger in a mortar and cut the others in small thin slices; add the lemon-water ice, mix well and freeze.

Time, ½ an hour to freeze. *Average cost*, 1s. 6d. *Sufficient* for 8 persons. *Seasonable* at any time.

ICES (To Mould).

Ices and iced puddings must not be frozen too hard in the first instance, or they will not fill the crevices of the mould. The moulds should be filled as full as possible, then a piece of writing paper should be put round the edges and the top and bottom cover shut over it.

Time, about 1 hour to freeze a moulded ice.

NOUGATS WITH CREAM (French Recipe).

INGREDIENTS.—1 *lb. of sweet almonds with a few bitter ones amongst them, 1 lb. of caster sugar, 1 pint of cream, some crystallised cherries.*

Mode.—Blanch, peel and dry the almonds, cut them in thin slices lengthwise, and dry them in a *very* slow oven, without allowing them to change colour. Put the sugar in a preserving-pan or a lined saucepan, and stir gently till it is melted. When a nice yellow colour, throw in gradually the almonds, warm as they come from the oven, stirring all the time; then take off the fire and complete the mixing thoroughly. Have ready a flat tin and some small patty-pans oiled thoroughly. Take the nougat a spoonful at a time on the baking-tin, flatten it as thin as possible, using a lemon for this purpose, and line a patty-pan with each spoonful, pressing it well against the sides. When cold turn out of the pans and fill with cream.

PRESERVES, PICKLES, AND STORE SAUCES

APPLE JAM.

INGREDIENTS.—6 lbs. good cooking apples (weighed after paring and coring), 5 lbs. sugar, 2 or 3 lemons according to the sweetness of the apples, a teaspoonful of ground cloves, water.

Mode.—Peel, core, and quarter the apples, and put them with the sugar, the juice of the lemons, and the cloves into a stewpan with enough water to barely cover them. Stew gently for an hour, or till the fruit is in a pulp. When cold put in pots and tie down.

Time, about 1 hour. Average cost for this quantity, 2s. 6d. Seasonable—make in autumn.

APRICOT JAM.

INGREDIENTS.—6 lbs. apricots, skinned and stoned, 4½ lbs. sugar.

Mode.—Put the halved apricots on a large dish overnight, and cover with the sugar. In the morning put in the preserving-pan with the kernels blanched and halved, and boil gently for about ¾ hour till the fruit is done.

Time, ¾ hour. Average cost, 4s. 6d. Seasonable—make in summer.

BLACKBERRY JAM.

INGREDIENTS.—6 lbs. of blackberries weighed after being picked over, 3 lbs. of sugar, the juice of 2 lemons.

Mode.—Pick over the berries, removing the stalks and any unripe ones, put them in the pan with the sugar and the juice of the lemons, and boil for about an hour, or till the fruit is done. Cool, and put into pots in the usual way.

Time, about 1 hour. Average cost for sugar, 6d. Seasonable—make in autumn.

BLACK-CURRANT JAM.

INGREDIENTS.—6 lbs. currants weighed after picking and stemming, 4½ lbs. sugar.

Mode.—After preparing the currants put them in a preserving-pan, adding the sugar gradually. Boil till the jam stiffens when a little is poured upon a plate. Skim and stir well during the boiling.

Time, about 1 hour or more after the jam boils. Average cost, 2s. 9d. Seasonable—make in summer.

CARROT JAM TO IMITATE APRICOT PRESERVE.

INGREDIENTS. — Carrots ; to every pound carrot pulp allow 1 lb. pounded *sugar, the grated rind of* 1 *lemon, the strained juice of* 2, 6 *chopped bitter almonds,* 2 *tablespoonfuls brandy.*

Mode.—Select young carrots; wash and scrape, cut them into round pieces, put them into a saucepan with water to cover, and simmer until soft; then beat them through a sieve. Weigh the pulp, and to every pound allow above ingredients. Put the pulp into a preserving-pan with the sugar, and boil for 5 minutes, stirring and skimming all the time. When cold, add the lemon-rind and juice, almonds and brandy; mix well with the jam; then put it into pots, well covered, and keep in a dry place. The brandy may be omitted, but the preserve will then not keep. With the brandy it will remain good for months.

Time, about ¾ hour to boil the carrots; 5 minutes to simmer the pulp. *Average cost,* 1s. 2d. for 1 lb. of pulp, with the other ingredients in proportion. *Sufficient* to fill 3 pots. *Seasonable* from July to December

RED-CURRANT JAM.

INGREDIENTS.—*To every pound of fruit allow* ¾ *lb. loaf sugar.*

Mode.—Let the fruit be gathered on a fine day; weigh it, and then strip the currants from the stalks; put them into a preserving-pan with the sugar, stir and boil for about ¾ hour. Carefully remove the scum as it rises. Put the jam into pots, and when cold cover with oiled papers; over these put a piece of tissue-paper brushed over on both sides with the white of an egg; press the paper round the top of the pot, and when dry the covering will be hard and air-tight. Black-currant jam should be made in the same manner.

Time, ½ to ¾ hour, reckoning from the time the jam boils all over. *Average cost* for a 1-lb pot, from 6d. to 8d. *Sufficient*—allow from 6 to 7 quarts of currants to make 12 1-lb. pots of jam *Seasonable*—make this in July.

RED-CURRANT JELLY.

INGREDIENTS. — *Red currants; to every pint of juice allow* ¾ *lb. of loaf sugar.*

Mode.—Have the fruit gathered in fine weather; pick it from the stalks, put it into a jar, and place this jar in a saucepan of boiling water over the fire, and let it simmer until the juice is

well drawn from the currants; then strain them through a jelly-bag or fine cloth, and if the jelly is wished very clear, do not squeeze them *too much*, as the skin and pulp from the fruit will be pressed through with the juice, and so make the jelly muddy. Measure the juice, and to each pint allow ¾ lb. loaf sugar; put these into a preserving-pan, set it over the fire, and keep stirring the jelly until done, carefully removing the scum as it rises, using a wooden or silver spoon, as metal or iron spoils the colour of the jelly. When it has boiled from 20 minutes to ½ hour, put a little of the jelly on a plate, and if firm when cool, it is done. Pour it into small gallipots, cover each with an oiled paper, and then with a piece of tissue paper, brushed over on both sides with the white of an egg. Label the pots, and store away in a dry place. A jam may be made with the currants if they are not squeezed too dry, by adding a few fresh raspberries, and boiling all together, with sufficient sugar to sweeten. As this preserve is not worth storing away, a smaller proportion of sugar will be found enough. It answers very well for children's puddings, or for a nursery preserve. Black-currant jelly can also be made from the above recipe.

Time, from ¾ to 1 hour to extract the juice; 20 minutes to ½ hour to boil the jelly. *Average cost,* from 8d. to 10d. per ½-lb. pot. *Sufficient*—8 quarts of fruit will make from 10 to 12 pots of jelly: *Seasonable*—make this in July.

BAKED DAMSONS FOR WINTER USE.

INGREDIENTS.—*To every pound of fruit allow* 6 *oz. pounded sugar; melted mutton suet.*

Mode.—Choose sound fruit, not too ripe, and pick off the stalks. Put the fruit into large dry stone jars, sprinkling the sugar amongst it; cover the jars with saucers, place them in a rather cool oven, and bake the fruit until it is quite tender. When cold, cover the top of the fruit with a piece of white paper cut to size; pour over this melted mutton suet about an inch thick, and cover the tops of the jars with thick brown paper, well tied down. Keep the jars in a cool, dry place, and the fruit will remain good till the following Christmas, but not much longer.

Time, from 5 to 6 hours to bake the damsons, in a very cool oven. *Seasonable* in September and October.

FRESH FRUIT, TO BOTTLE WITH SUGAR.
Very useful in Winter.

INGREDIENTS.—*Any kind of fresh fruit; to each quart bottle allow ¼ lb. of pounded sugar.*

Mode.—Let the fruit be gathered in dry weather. Pick it carefully, and drop it into *clean* and *very dry* quart glass bottles, sprinkling over it the pounded sugar. Put the corks in the bottles, and place them in a copper of cold water up to their necks, with small hay-wisps round, to prevent the bottles from knocking together. Bring the water gradually to boil, and let it simmer until the fruit in the bottles is reduced nearly one-third. Extinguish the fire, *and let the bottles remain in the water until it is perfectly cold;* then take them out, make the corks secure, and cover them with melted resin or wax.

Time, about ½ hour from the time the water commences to boil.

GREENGAGE JAM.

INGREDIENTS.—*To every pound of fruit, weighed before being stoned, allow ¾ lb. lump sugar.*

Mode.—Divide the greengages, take out the stones, and put them into a preserving-pan. Bring the fruit to a boil, add the sugar, and keep stirring it over a gentle fire until melted. Remove the scum as it rises, and just before the jam is done, boil it rapidly for 5 minutes. To ascertain when sufficiently boiled, pour a little on a plate, and if the syrup thickens and appears firm, it is done. Have ready half the kernels blanched; put them into the jam, give them one boil, and pour the preserve into pots. When cold, cover down with oiled papers, and over these, tissue-paper, brushed over on both sides with the white of an egg.

Time, ¾ hour after the sugar is added. *Average cost*, from 6d. to 8d. per 1-lb. pot. *Sufficient*, allow about 1½ pints of fruit for every 1-lb. pot of jam. *Seasonable*—make this in August or September.

MARMALADE (ORANGE).

INGREDIENTS.—*Equal quantities of Seville and sweet oranges, to every lb. pulp 1½ lbs. loaf sugar*

Mode.—Boil the oranges whole till tender, in just enough water to cover them, changing it two or three times.

Drain them, take off the rind and take out the pips, and allow sugar as directed and ½ pint of water in which the fruit was boiled to each lb. of pulp. Boil the sugar and water 20 minutes, then with the pulp another 10 minutes, and again with the peel cut fine 10 minutes. Pour into jars and when cool tie down.

Time, 2 hours. *Average cost*, 5d. per pot. *Seasonable*—make in March.

PRESERVED MELON-RIND.

INGREDIENTS.—*Water melon, syrup made from loaf sugar, lemon-juice, ginger, vine-leaves, water, alum.*

Mode.—Pare off the skins and mince the rind of the melon, cut it in pieces, and lay it in a stewpan between two layers of vine-leaves, strewn with a little powdered alum, with enough water to barely cover the upper layer of leaves. Cover the pan and let it steam, but not boil, for 2½ hours, then take out the rind and put in cold water for 3 or 4 hours. The water should be changed twice. Make some rather thick syrup, put in the rind, and simmer for about an hour; take out the rind, lay it on a large dish in the sun, and when cold repeat the process. Some hours later put the syrup again into the pan, flavouring it with the lemon and ginger, and boil till thick. Fill some jars with the rind, fill up with the syrup, and when cool tie down.

Seasonable—make this in summer.

PLUM JAM.

INGREDIENTS.—*To every pound of plums, weighed before being stoned, allow ¾ lb. loaf sugar.*

Mode.—The quantity of sugar for each pound of fruit must be regulated by the quality and size of the fruit, some plums requiring much more sugar than others. Divide the plums, take out the stones, and put them on to large dishes, with roughly-pounded sugar sprinkled over in the above proportion, and let them remain for one day; then put them into a preserving-pan, stand them by the side of the fire to simmer gently for about ½ hour, and then boil them rapidly for another 15 minutes. The scum must be carefully removed as it rises, and the jam be well stirred all the time, or it will burn at the bottom of the pan, and so spoil the colour and flavour of the preserve. Some of the stones may be cracked, and a few kernels added to the jam just before it is done. The above proportion of sugar would answer for Orleans plums; the Impératrice, Magnum-bonum, and Winesour would not require quite so much.

Time, ½ hour to simmer gently, ¼ hour to boil rapidly. *Best plums for preserving :* Violets, Mussels, Orleans, Impératrice, Magnum-bonum, and Winesour. *Seasonable* from the end of July to the beginning of October.

RASPBERRY JAM.

INGREDIENTS.—*To every pound of raspberries, allow* 1 *lb. sugar,* ¼ *pint red-currant juice.*

Mode.—Let the fruit be gathered in fine weather, and used as soon after as possible. Take off the stalks, put the raspberries into the preserving-pan, break them well with a wooden spoon, and boil for ¼ hour, keeping them well stirred. Then add the currant-juice and sugar, and boil again for ½ hour. Skim the jam well after the sugar is added, or the preserve will not be clear. The addition of the currant-juice is a very great improvement to this preserve.

Time, ¼ hour to simmer the fruit without the sugar; ½ hour after it is added. *Average cost*, from 8d. to 1s. per 1-lb. pot. *Sufficient*—allow about 1 pint of fruit to fill a 1-lb. pot. *Seasonable* in July and August.

RHUBARB JAM.

INGREDIENTS.—*To every pound of rhubarb allow* 1 *lb. of loaf sugar, the rind of* ½ *lemon.*

Mode.—Wipe the rhubarb perfectly dry, take off the string or peel and weigh it; put it into a preserving-pan with the sugar; mince the lemon-rind very finely, add it to the other ingredients, and place the preserving-pan by the side of the fire; keep stirring to prevent the rhubarb from burning; and when the sugar is well dissolved, put the pan more over the fire, and let the jam boil until it is done, taking care to keep it well skimmed and stirred with a wooden or silver spoon. Pour it into pots, and cover down with oiled and egged papers.

Time, if the rhubarb is young and tender, ¾ hour, reckoning from the time it simmers equally; old rhubarb, 1¼ to 1½ hours. *Average cost*, 5d. per 1-lb. pot. *Sufficient*—about 1 pint sliced rhubarb to fill a 1-lb. pot. *Seasonable* from February to April.

STRAWBERRY JAM.

INGREDIENTS.—12 *lbs. of fruit,* 2 *pints red-currant juice,* 14 *lbs. loaf sugar.*

Mode.—Put the currants, freed from their stalks, in a jar, and this jar into hot water, and simmer till the juice is drawn. Strain the currants and put the juice into a preserving-pan with the sugar. When the sugar is dissolved put in the strawberries, picked, and simmer for from ½ to ¾ hour, removing the scum as it rises. Be careful in stirring to avoid the jam burning, and not to break the fruit. Put into jars, and when cold cover in the usual way.

Time, from ½ to ¾ hour. *Average cost*, 7d. lb. *Seasonable*—make in June or July.

PICKLED RED CABBAGE.

INGREDIENTS.—*Red cabbages, salt and water ; to each quart of vinegar,* ½ *oz. ginger, well bruised,* 1 *oz. whole black pepper, and, when liked, a little cayenne.*

Mode.—Take off the outside decayed leaves of a nice red cabbage, cut it in quarters, remove the stalks, and cut it across in very thin slices. Lay these on a dish, strew them plentifully with salt, and cover them with another dish. Let them remain 24 hours; turn into a colander to drain, and, if necessary, wipe lightly with a clean, soft cloth. Put them in a jar; boil up the vinegar with spices in the above proportion, and, when cold, pour it over the cabbage. It will be fit for use in a week or two. Tie down with bladder, and keep in a dry place.

Seasonable in July and August; but the pickle will be much more crisp if the frost has just touched the leaves.

MIXED PICKLE (Very good).

INGREDIENTS.—*To each gallon vinegar allow* ¼ *lb. bruised ginger,* ¼ *lb. mustard,* ¼ *lb. salt,* 2 *oz. mustard-seed,* 1½ *oz. turmeric,* 1 *oz. ground black pepper,* ¼ *oz. cayenne, cauliflowers, onions, celery, sliced cucumber, gherkins, French beans, nasturtiums, capsicums.*

Mode.—Have a large jar, with a tightly fitting lid, in which put as much vinegar as is required, reserving a little to mix the various powders to a smooth paste. Put into a basin the mustard, turmeric, pepper, and cayenne; mix with vinegar, and stir until no lumps remain; add the ingredients to the vinegar, and mix well. Keep in a warm place, and thoroughly stir every morning for a month with a wooden spoon, when it will be ready for the different vegetables to be added to it. As these come into season, have them gathered on a dry day, and after wiping them with a cloth, put them into the pickle. The cauliflowers must be divided into small bunches. Put all these into the pickle raw, and at the end of the season store it away in jars, and tie over with bladder. As none of the ingredients are boiled, this pickle will not be fit to eat till 12 months have elapsed.

Seasonable—make the pickle liquor in May or June, to be ready as the season arrives for the various vegetables to be picked.

PICKLED NASTURTIUMS (a very good Substitute for Capers).

INGREDIENTS.—*To each pint of vinegar 1 oz. salt, 6 peppercorns, nasturtiums.*

Mode.—Gather the nasturtium seeds on a dry day, when they are quite young and soft, and wipe them clean with a cloth; put them in a dry glass bottle, with vinegar, salt, and pepper as above. If you cannot find enough ripe to fill a bottle, cork up what you have got until more are fit: they may be added from day to day. Bung up the bottles, and seal or resin the tops. They will be fit for use in 10 or 12 months; and the best way is to make them one season for the next.

Seasonable—look for nasturtium seeds from the end of July to the end of August.

PICKLED ONIONS (a very Simple Method, and exceedingly Good).

INGREDIENTS.—*Pickling onions; to each quart vinegar, 2 teaspoonfuls allspice, 2 teaspoonfuls whole black pepper.*

Mode.—Gather the onions when quite dry and ripe, and, with the fingers, take off the thin outside skin; then with a silver knife (steel spoils the colour of the onions) remove one more skin, when the onion will look quite clear. As fast as the onions are peeled put them into dry bottles or jars. Pour over sufficient cold vinegar to cover them, with pepper and allspice in above proportions, taking care that each jar has its share of the latter ingredients. Tie down with bladder,

and put them in a dry place, and in a fortnight they will be fit for use. This is a most simple recipe and very delicious. Onions should be eaten within 6 or 8 months after being done, as they are liable to become soft.

Seasonable from the middle of July to the end of August.

PICKLED WALNUTS (Very Good).

INGREDIENTS.—*100 walnuts, salt and water. To each quart vinegar allow 2 oz. whole black pepper, 1 oz. allspice, 1 oz. bruised ginger.*

Mode. — The walnuts should be young, and not woody. Prick them well with a fork; put them into a strong brine (4 lbs. of salt to each gallon of water), letting them remain 9 days, and changing the brine every third day; drain them off, put them on a dish, and place it in the sun until they become perfectly black, which will be in 2 or 3 days; place the walnuts into dry jars, which should not be quite filled. Boil sufficient vinegar, for 10 minutes, with spices in the above proportion, and pour it hot over the walnuts, which must be quite covered with the pickle; tie down with bladder, and keep in a dry place. They will be fit for use in a month, and will keep good 2 or 3 years.

Time, 10 minutes. . *Seasonable*—make this from the beginning to the middle of July, before the walnuts harden.

Note.—A few shallots may be boiled with the vinegar.

BENGAL RECIPE FOR MAKING MANGO CHETNEY.

INGREDIENTS.—*1½ lbs. moist sugar, ¾ lb. salt, ¼ lb. garlic, ¼ lb. onions, ¾ lb. powdered ginger, ¼ lb. dried chillies, ¾ lb. mustard-seed, ¾ lb. stoned raisins, 2 pints best vinegar, 30 large unripe sour apples.*

Mode.—The sugar must be made into syrup; the garlic, onions, and ginger finely pounded in a mortar; the mustard-seed washed in cold vinegar, and dried in the sun; the apples peeled, cored, and sliced, and boiled in a bottle and a half of vinegar. When all this is done, and the apples are quite cold, put them into a large pan, and gradually mix the rest of the ingredients, including the remaining half-bottle of vinegar. It must be well stirred until the whole is thoroughly blended, and then put into bottles for use. Tie a piece of wet bladder over the mouths of the bottles, after they are well corked.

Note.—This recipe was given by a native to an English lady, long resident in India, and who, since her return to her native country, has become quite celebrated amongst her friends for the excellence of this Eastern relish.

LEAMINGTON SAUCE (an Excellent Sauce for Flavouring Gravies, Hashes, Soups, &c.).

(Author's Recipe.)

INGREDIENTS.—*Walnuts. To each quart of walnut-juice allow* 3 *quarts vinegar,* 1 *pint Indian soy,* 1 *oz. cayenne,* 2 *oz. shallots,* ¾ *oz. garlic,* ½ *pint port wine.*

Mode.—Choose the walnuts as soon as they appear in the market; for they are more easily bruised before they become hard and shelled. Pound them well in a mortar, strew some salt over them, and let them remain thus for two or three days, occasionally stirring and moving them about. Press out the juice, and to *each quart* of walnut-liquor allow the *above* proportion of vinegar, soy, cayenne, shallots, garlic, and port wine. Pound each dry ingredient separately in a mortar, then mix them well together, and store away in small bottles. The corks should be well sealed.

Seasonable—this sauce should be made as soon as walnuts are obtainable, from the beginning to the middle of July.

MUSHROOM KETCHUP.

INGREDIENTS.—*To each peck mushrooms,* ½ *lb. salt; to each quart mushroom liquor* ¼ *oz. cayenne,* ½ *oz. allspice* ½ *oz. ginger,* 2 *blades pounded mace.*

Mode.—Choose full-grown mushroom flaps, fresh gathered in tolerably dry weather. Put a layer of them in a deep pan, sprinkle salt over them, and then another layer of mushrooms, and

so on. Let them remain for a few hours, when break them up with the hand, put them in a cool place for three days, occasionally stirring and mashing them well to extract the juice. Ascertain the quantity of liquor without straining, and allow to each quart the above proportion of spice, &c. Put all into a stone jar, cover it up closely, put it into a saucepan of boiling water, set it over the fire, and boil for 3 hours. Turn the contents of the jar into a clean stewpan, and simmer for ½ hour; pour into a jug and stand it in a cool place till next day; then pour off into another jug and strain into very dry clean bottles. Do not squeeze the mushrooms. To each pint of ketchup add a few drops of brandy. Be careful not to shake the contents, but leave all the sediment behind in the jug; cork well, and seal or resin the cork. The ketchup should be examined occasionally after it has been put by, and if it is spoiling it should be reboiled with a few peppercorns.

Seasonable—this ketchup should be made between the beginning of September and the middle of October.

Note.—The sediment may be bottled for immediate use.

MUSTARD, HOW TO MAKE.

Make the powder into a thick paste by the addition of cold water. Mix well while in this condition, taking care to break up all lumps and to work in all powder that may be adhering to the sides of the pot. Then add gradually sufficient cold water to enable the mixture to be stirred to the consistency of cream.

N.B.—After mixing allow the mustard to stand for about 10 minutes before using. Mustard should be made fresh for every meal, and should never be allowed to stand for more than a day. Warm water should never be used in the making.

BEVERAGES

THE beverages drunk in our country may be divided into three classes: those of the simplest kind, neither effervescent nor fermented, generally infusions or decoctions of various substances, such as tea and coffee; those consisting of water containing a considerable quantity of carbonic acid, such as soda-water and lemonade; those containing alcohol, such as wine or spirit. To whichever class the beverages belong, however, there is one basis, namely water; and there is nothing more important in a household than to obtain a good supply of sufficiently pure water. *Absolutely* pure water, consisting of two parts of hydrogen to one of oxygen, does not exist in nature; and when made so by distillation it is flat and distasteful.

Water as we get it is never pure; but it is absolutely essential that we free it from impurities dangerous to health, if they exist.

There is only one way to treat really *bad* water, and that is by boiling as well as filtering it, and to both of these there is the objection of rendering the water flat and unpalatable. The best way to remedy this is to use an aerating filter, by running it through very small apertures; or if only a small quantity has to be treated by pouring it from one jug to another, each method having the effect of aerating and thus freshening the water.

TEA, COFFEE, AND COCOA.

Considered now almost a necessity of life, the most popular non-alcoholic beverage in this country is tea. For more than three centuries it has been in use in England, during which time its prices have descended from £3 per lb. to 1s.; while the rate of consumption has increased from 500 lbs. to 100,000,000 lbs.

In China, as is well known, tea is indigenous, and it flourishes best in temperate regions. A great deal is sent from India, and in both countries it is very largely cultivated. The leaves are gathered at four different times of the year, and the younger they are the finer and dearer the tea. For its adulteration in this country, leaves of the sloe, whitethorn and others have been, in fact, are still used; and in the purchase of tea, therefore, it is well to see that it possesses an agreeable odour, and that the leaves be as whole as possible.

Coffee, we are told, has been cultivated in Abyssinia from time immemorial, but its introduction into this country is of comparatively recent date.

The first coffee-house in England was in London, in George Yard, Lombard Street, and was established by a Greek named Pasgua, the servant of a Turkey merchant named Daniel Edwards, and coffee was then sold at as much as £5 the pound. Soon after that a duty was laid upon it, as a beverage, of 4d. the gallon. In two centuries, coffee, before unknown, has made its way through the civilised world, and the demand for it in the British Isles is on the increase. Of all coffees, those of Arabia are most esteemed for their beautiful flavour, and from that country we obtain our favourite Mocha. After these, in quality, are reckoned the Java and Ceylon coffees, then those of Bourbon and Martinique, and after them those of Jamaica and St. Domingo.

Much of the quality of coffee depends on the roasting of it. To do this well requires great nicety, and there can be no question between the flavours of freshly roasted and ground coffee and that which has been kept some time. Raw, it can be kept for a year or more without deterioration, but it should be used very soon after roasting; while to have it in perfection it must always be freshly ground.

Cocoa, which, unlike tea and coffee, is a nourishing food as well as drink, is an article for which the demand is fast growing larger in this country. It is prepared from the seeds of a tree grown in America, Asia, and Africa. The nut is roasted and the husk removed, and the kernel, roughly ground, is sold as cocoa nibs, the only pure form. Prepared cocoa is the kernel ground with some starchy matter and sugar, which thicken the water or milk in which it is made as a beverage and render it more pleasant to taste than that made with the nibs. Chocolate is prepared from the finest cocoa beans, ground, sweetened, and flavoured, and may be considered, if of the best quality, one of the most nourishing and pleasant drinks.

MINERAL WATERS AND EFFERVESCENT DRINKS.

To meet the demand of teetotalers and those with whom stimulating beverages do not agree, the name of the non-alcoholic drinks has become legion. Many of them are extremely refreshing, with a pleasant evanescent flavour; but taken in excess, or even as everyday drinks, they are not considered so good for the health as milk, water, and home-made lemonade, &c.

Soda-water is often an invaluable beverage in sickness, and is considered as a rule better than any other mineral water for the preparation of cups and various summer drinks. This, as well as seltzer, lemonade, and others, is largely used to mix with spirits, instead of water; but connoisseurs say that only a pure mineral water, with no taste, should be used for this purpose, and that the manufactured mineral waters destroy the flavour of the spirit, having too much of their own.

WINES.

It is too seldom now the practice to make wine at home; those who want some stimulant in this form and cannot afford good wines, being content with cheap sherry or claret in preference to the good, wholesome, old-fashioned wines. Gooseberry or cowslip many laugh at the idea of; giving their friends, instead, too often some inferior sherry or cheap champagne, against which, both in flavour and quality, the home-made ones may well compare.

Of foreign wines (except how to serve them) it would be impossible to speak here. As medicine they would be prescribed by a doctor; as a luxury individual taste must guide the selection. Only one word of advice we could give to the inexperienced : not to risk having inferior wine of any kind. By inferior we do not mean a light claret or anything of the sort, which common sense would tell us need not be costly; but such things as port or champagne, which cannot be bought both cheap and good. Far better give a good glass of beer to our friends, or even one of lemonade, if we cannot afford more, than injure their digestions and our own by unsound wine. *Good* stimulants, when needed and taken with discretion, may do us good; but bad ones will be just as likely to do us harm as the inferior food which almost every one thinks it necessary to avoid.

In decanting wines great care is needed. Some throw a deposit the whole length of the bottle as they lie in their bins; these, therefore, should be brought from the cellar a day or two before they are wanted and stood upright, so that the deposit may fall and settle at the bottom of the bottle. The wine must then be carefully poured into the decanter; for if any of the sediment go with it, it will assuredly spoil its appearance, and may also affect the flavour.

Port and claret of good quality should be disturbed as little as possible, and very great care should be taken in drawing the corks. If not drawn and decanted in the cellar, they should still be kept in the same position during the process, or the crust will be shaken into the wine.

When such wines as claret or madeira are brought from a cold cellar, they should be put in a warm place for some time before they are required If needed in a hurry, the decanters can be made warm by putting them in warm water before the wine is put in, but in no case should these wines be served as cold as they would be in a good cellar.

Except for cups and summer drinks icing is seldom needed, and inexperienced persons are too apt to ice wines whose quality is fine and bouquet delicate, and thereby spoil them.

One essential in serving wines that no good housekeeper should forget is that, no matter what the quality or kind may be, its receptacles, decanters or glasses, should be above reproach, as clear and brilliant as it is possible to have them. Fortunately for those who cannot afford to have very expensive cut or engraved glass, the nicest (and in our opinion the prettiest) of all wine-glasses, namely the perfectly plain thin ones, are not so very expensive. In these you lose none of the beauty of the wine, as one may with cut glass, and they are extremely nice to drink from, while to the housewifely mind, the fact that they can be more easily *matched* than those with a pattern is a very great recommendation.

ALMOND MILK.

INGREDIENTS. — 2 oz. of Jordan almonds, ½ oz. of bitter almonds, 2 oz. of white sugar, 1 tablespoonful of orange-flower water, 1 pint of spring water.

Mode.—Blanch the almonds and pound them with the sugar in a mortar, with the orange-flower water. When the mixture gets creamy and smooth, put it in a basin, add the water and stir it up with a silver spoon. Leave it for 2 hours, then strain and keep it in a *very* cool place, as it soon turns sour. This is a very nice drink for invalids, served with an equal quantity of cold water.

Time, 2 hours. Average cost, 4d. per pint.

CHOCOLATE.

INGREDIENTS.—3 oz. of chocolate, 1½ pints of milk, the same of water.

Mode.—Make the milk and water hot, scrape the chocolate into it and stir quickly till it is dissolved; bring to the boiling point, stir well and serve directly. Chocolate looks and is very nice if done in the foreign way with a mill. The milk is made boiling, is poured over the scraped chocolate, and is then whisked with the mill till dissolved and the mixture very frothy.

Time, 10 minutes. Average cost, 6d. Sufficient for 6 persons. Seasonable at any time.

COCOA (TO MAKE).

INGREDIENTS.—3 dessertspoonfuls of prepared cocoa, ¾ of a pint of milk, ¾ of a pint of water.

Mode.—Put a teaspoonful of cocoa into each cup, add enough milk to make it into a smooth paste, boil the milk and water together and fill up the cups, stirring the while. Rock cocoa should be scraped and well-rubbed down; then put into the hot milk and boiled with it for a minute or so.

Average cost, 3d. Sufficient for 3 large cups.

COFFEE (TO MAKE).

INGREDIENTS.—3 oz. of ground coffee 1½ pints of water.

Mode.—There are many different kinds of percolators and other coffee-pots, for the making in which the instructions vary, but there are certain rules that apply to all. To have good coffee, the berries should have been lately roasted and quite freshly ground, as it should never be boiled. As a rule the ground coffee has the boiling water forced through it by hydrostatic pressure; and directly this is done (a process of about 5 or 6 minutes after the water has been made boiling) it is ready. In an ordinary coffee-pot the process is a very simple one. A small iron ring should be made to fit the top, and to this a small bag of muslin should be sewn. Fit this bag into the pot and pour boiling water in. When the pot is warmed pour this off, put the coffee in the bag; pour over the boiling water and close the lid, and when the water has filtered through it will be ready. Remove the bag before serving. Hot milk and plenty of it should always be an accompaniment to good coffee, unless it be the *café noir*, or black coffee, served with tiny glasses of brandy after dinner.

Time, about 5 to 10 minutes. *Average cost*, 3d. *Sufficient* for 4 or 5 breakfas cups.

TEA (TO MAKE).

INGREDIENTS.—1 *teaspoonful of good tea to each person.*

Mode.—Warm the teapot with hot water, then pour it away and put in the tea. On this pour about ¾ of a pint of boiling water, let it stand to draw for 5 minutes, then fill up with boiling water. It may be said there is little art in making tea, yet it is no exception to have it served weak and flavourless; this being generally caused by the water being put off the boil. It should be put over the tea the instant it boils and the teapot should be quite hot before. When green tea is used as well as black, unless it has been bought mixed, the usual proportion is 1 teaspoonful of green to 4 of the black.

Time, about 6 minutes. *Average cost*, from 1s. 6d. to 3s. per lb.

COWSLIP WINE.

INGREDIENTS.—4 *gallons of cowslip heads*, 14 *lbs. of lump sugar*, 8 *lemons*, 1 *Seville orange*, 1 *bottle of brandy*, 4 *gallons of water*, 1½ *tablespoonfuls of brewer's yeast.*

Mode.—Boil the sugar and water for ½ an hour, removing the scum as it rises. Cut the rind from the lemons and orange and squeeze the juice of 4 lemons, and on these pour the boiling syrup. When cooled to luke warm, add the cowslip flowers picked from the stalks and seeds, and the yeast. Let it ferment 3 or 4 days; then put in a cask with the brandy, let it remain for 2 months, then bottle.

Time, ½ an hour to boil the syrup, 3 or 4 days to ferment, 2 months in cask. *Average cost*, 2s. per gallon.

ELDER WINE.

INGREDIENTS.—*To every peck of elder-berries allow* 3 *gallons of water*, 3 *lbs. of sugar*, ½ *oz. of ground ginger*, 6 *dry cloves*, 1 *lb. of raisins ;* ¼ *pint of brandy to every gallon of wine ; to every* 9 *gallons* 3 *or* 4 *tablespoonfuls of fresh brewer's yeast.*

Mode.—Pick the berries from their stalks and pour upon them the water quite boiling and let them stand covered for 24 hours; then strain through a sieve, squeezing all the juice from the fruit. Measure the liquor and allow the proportion of sugar named, then boil with the other ingredients (except the yeast and brandy) for an hour, skimming all the time. Let it stand till milk warm, then put it with the yeast into a clean cask. Let it ferment for a fortnight, then add the brandy, bung up the cask, and let it stand some months before bottling the wine.

This, though now a somewhat old-fashioned beverage, is still liked by many persons, served hot with grated nutmeg and toast or dry biscuits.

Time, to stand 24 hours ; to be boiled 1 hour, to remain in the cask 3 or 4 months. *Average cost*, exclusive of the elderberries, 1s. 6d. per gallon. *Seasonable*—make this in September.

GINGER WINE.

INGREDIENTS.—12 *oz. of bruised un-bleached ginger*, 28 *lbs. of loaf sugar*, 12 *lemons*, 12 *lbs. of raisins*, 12 *gallons of spring water*, 6 *tablespoonfuls of yeast*, 1 *oz of isinglass.* 3 *pints of brandy may be added or not.*

Mode.—Chop the raisins and put them in a pan. Boil together the water, ginger, sugar and lemon-peel for ½ an hour and pour over the raisins; add the lemon-juice and the yeast; stir every day for a fortnight, then add the isinglass, strain, and put in the cask. This it will be seen is a recipe for a large quantity, but it will be easy to see the proportions to allow for a lesser one.

Average cost, without the spirit, 1s. 2d. per gallon. *Seasonable* — to make in March or September; to drink in summer or winter.

Note.—Made in March this wine will be fit to bottle in June.

ENTREES, &c.

Cutlets and Peas.

Dish Meat Pie.

Mushrooms.

Plovers' Eggs.

Lamb Cutlets.

Russian Salad.

Raised Game Pie with Jelly.

Piped Ham.

Raised Perigord Pie.

GOOSEBERRY WINE.

INGREDIENTS.—*To every* 12 *lbs. of green gooseberries allow* 2 *gallons of water and* 6 *lbs of lump sugar.*

Mode.—The fruit should be selected just before it has attained its full growth, before it shows any tendency to ripen; and bruised, decayed, or very small berries should not be used. The fruit should be prepared as for a tart, then bruised in small quantities, so that every berry may be broken without crushing the seeds, in a tub or pan. Pour the water, warm, on the fruit, squeeze and stir it with the hand until all the pulp is removed from the skins and seeds, and cover the whole closely for 24 hours; after which strain it through a coarse bag, pressing with as much force as possible to extract the whole of the juice of the fruit. A little more hot water (in the proportion of 1 quart to 10 lbs. of fruit) may be put through the husks and then strained and pressed. The juice must now be put into a tub or pan and the sugar added. Stir well till the sugar is dissolved, place the pan in a warm place closely covered, and let it ferment for a day or two. It must then be drawn off into clean casks, placed a little on one side for the scum that rises to be thrown out, and the casks kept filled with the remaining "must" that should be reserved for that purpose. When the active fermentation has ceased, the casks should be plugged upright, again filled up if necessary, the bungs be put in loosely, and after a few more days when the fermentation is not so strong (this will be known by the cessation of the hissing noise) the bungs should be driven tight and a spill-hole made. About November or December, choosing a clear fine day, the wine should be racked from its lees into clean casks rinsed out with brandy. A month later it should be examined for bottling; but if not sufficiently clear it may be fined with isinglass, which may be dissolved in some of the wine. In March or April, when the bushes are in blossom, it should be bottled to ensure its being effervescing.

Time, 1 year. *Average cost,* 2s. per gallon. *Seasonable*—make this wine the end of May or the beginning of June, before the berries ripen.

RHUBARB WINE.

INGREDIENTS.—*Rhubarb, white sugar, isinglass, lemon.*

Mode.—Gather the rhubarb in the middle of May; take off the leaves, wipe it with a wet cloth, put it in a large wooden tub and bruise it well with a mallet or rolling-pin. When reduced to a pulp weigh it, and to every 5 lbs. add 1 gallon of cold spring water; let these remain for three days, stirring 3 or 4 times each day, and on the 4th press the pulp through a hair sieve. Put the liquor into a tub and to every gallon add 3 lbs. of sugar, stirring till quite dissolved, then add to every gallon the rind of a lemon. Let the liquor remain in the tub and in from 4 to 6 days the fermentation will begin to subside and a crust will be formed, which should be skimmed off. Put the liquor in a cask, and if it still ferments, rack it off into another cask and in a fortnight stop it down with the isinglass, ½ oz. to a gallon. If the wine be not quite sweet enough add a little more sugar, taking care that the cask is full. Bottle the wine in February or March, and in the summer it should be ready to drink.

Time, 13 or 14 months. *Average cost,* 1s. 3d. per gallon. *Seasonable,* make this wine about the middle of May.

LEMON SYRUP.

INGREDIENTS.—2 *lbs. of loaf sugar,* 1 *oz. citric acid,* ½ *drachm of essence of lemon,* 2 *pints of water.*

Mode.—Boil the sugar in the water for 15 minutes, and put it in a basin to get cold. Pound the citric acid, mix the essence of lemon with it, then add to the syrup and bottle for use.

Average cost, 9d. *Sufficient,* 2 tablespoonfuls to a glass of cold water.

MEAD.

INGREDIENTS.—7 *lbs. of honey,* 2 *gallons of water,* 2 *tablespoonfuls of yeast.*

Mode.—Boil the honey and water for an hour, straining very carefully; drain the skimmings through a sieve and return to the pan. When nearly cold, stir in the yeast and put in a cask in a cool place. In a year's time, bottle; and use 3 months afterwards.

Time, 15 months. *Average cost,* 1s. 6d. per gallon. *Seasonable* at any time; useful for a summer drink.

GINGER BEER.

INGREDIENTS.—1½ *oz. of bruised ginger,* 1 *oz. of cream of tartar,* 2½ *lbs. of loaf sugar,* 2 *lemons,* 3 *gallons of water,*

2 large tablespoonfuls of fresh brewer's yeast.

Mode.—Peel the lemons, squeeze and strain the juice, and put both in a large earthen pan, with the ginger, cream of tartar, and sugar. Pour over these the water boiling, let stand till just warm, then add the yeast, which should be thick and perfectly fresh. Stir the contents of the pan well, cover it with a cloth, and leave it near the fire all night. Next day, skim off the yeast and put the liquor into another pan, pouring carefully so as to leave the sediments behind; then bottle immediately and tie the corks firmly down. In three days the beer should be ready to drink. If to be used at once, the proportion of sugar need not be so large.

Time, 4 days. *Average cost*, 1s. 2d. *Sufficient* for 4 doz. bottles. *Seasonable* in summer.

LEMONADE.

INGREDIENTS.—*The rind of 2 lemons, the juice of 4, ½ lb. of loaf sugar, 1 quart of boiling water.*

Mode.—Rub the rind of two of the lemons on some of the lumps of sugar, and put it with the remainder of the sugar in a jug, add the lemon-juice, and pour over the whole the water boiling. When the sugar is dissolved, strain through a piece of muslin. When cold the lemonade will be ready for use. For children, 3 pints of water may be used for this proportion of lemons and sugar, and for older persons it may be improved by the white of an egg beaten up and 2 glasses of sherry.

Average cost, 6d. per quart. *Seasonable* in summer.

LEMONADE (AN EASY WAY TO MAKE).

INGREDIENTS.—1 oz. of citric acid, 1 lemon, 1 lb. loaf sugar.

Mode.—Put the sugar, acid, strained juice, and peel of lemon into a large jug, and pour over a quart of boiling water. Stir occasionally till the sugar and acid are dissolved, and when cool take out the peel and bottle for use. When needed put a little in a glass and add water to taste.

Time, 1 hour. *Average cost*, 6d. *Sufficient* for 3 to 4 quarts lemonade.

LEMONADE (TO KEEP).

INGREDIENTS.—1 oz. of powdered tartaric acid, 1 drachm of essence of lemon, 6 oz. of powdered white sugar.

Mode.—Mix the ingredients together and let them dry in the sun, then put in a small bottle, or if wanted while travelling, when it is a handy thing to have, divide it into 24 parts, and wrap each in a piece of white paper as a seidlitz powder. Each powder will make a glass with water.

Time, 12 hours. *Average cost*, 5d.

RASPBERRY VINEGAR.

INGREDIENTS.—*To every 4½ pints of raspberries allow 3 pints of the best vinegar; to each pint of liquor allow 1 lb. of loaf sugar and 1 glass of brandy.*

Mode.—Pick the raspberries (which must be freshly gathered) free from stalks. Put 1½ pints of fruit into a stone jar and pour the vinegar over; let them remain 24 hours; then strain over another 1½ pints of raspberries; again stand for 24 hours, and again pour over the same quantity of fruit and stand the 24 hours. It will be seen that only 1½ pints of raspberries must be picked each day. Wet a jelly-bag with vinegar and pass the liquor through this, and to each pint put 1 lb. of powdered loaf sugar and stir together. When the sugar is dissolved, cover the jar and put it in a saucepan of boiling water on the fire. Let it boil for an hour, removing the scum as it rises. When cool, add to each pint 1 glass of brandy; bottle, and seal the corks. This makes a refreshing drink in illness or hot weather.

Time, 3 days to make, 1 hour to boil. *Average cost*, 4s. *Sufficient*—this quantity to make 2 quarts. *Seasonable*—make this in summer when the fruit is plentiful.

CHERRY BRANDY.

INGREDIENTS.—*Morella cherries, good French brandy; to every lb. of cherries allow half the quantity of loaf sugar.*

Mode.—Have ready some clean glass bottles which must be perfectly dry. Have the cherries freshly gathered, ripe and dry, and cut off nearly all the stalk of each. Put a little pounded sugar in a bottle, then some cherries, and nearly fill, strewing the sugar in between the cherries in the proportion named. Pour in the brandy till it reaches just below the corks, put the corks in and tie over with bladder; store in a dry place. A few blanched bitter almonds improve the flavour of the brandy.

Time, should be ready in 2 or 3 months. *Average cost*, about 2s. per quart bottle. *Seasonable*, make this in August and September.

Note.—When a liqueur is more desired than the brandy cherries, put them in a large jar with 6 oz. of sugar to the lb., and the third of a bottle of brandy or good gin.

CHERRY LIQUEUR.

INGREDIENTS.—1 *lb. each of Morella and black cherries*, 12 *cloves*, ¼ *oz. of cinnamon*, ½ *lb. of sugar*, 1 *quart of brandy.*

Mode.—Split the cherries and take out the stones, crack the latter, and put the cherries, stones, the cloves, bruised, the cinnamon and the sugar in a large bottle. Over these pour the brandy (which should be good). Cork tightly, let it stand for a fortnight, then strain and bottle.

Time, 14 days. *Average cost*, 5s. *Seasonable*—make in August.

CLOVE LIQUEUR.

INGREDIENTS.—4 *oz. of cloves*, 4 *oz. of coriander seed*, ⅓ *lb. of loaf sugar*, 24 *black cherries*, 1 *quart of gin.*

Mode.—Bruise the cloves and coriander seed, then infuse the whole ingredients for a month, after which time strain and bottle.

Time, 1 month. *Average cost*, 3s. 6d. *Seasonable*—make this in summer time.

NOYEAU.

INGREDIENTS.—½ *lb. of bitter almonds*, 2 *oz. of sweet*, 2 *lbs. of powdered white sugar*, 6 *lemons*, 2 *quarts of gin*, 1 *pint of new milk*, 2 *tablespoonfuls of clarified honey.*

Mode.—Blanch and pound the almonds and mix with the sugar; boil the milk, let it stand till cold; then mix all the ingredients together and let them remain for 10 days, shaking them every day. Filter through blotting-paper, bottle off in small bottles, and seal the corks.

Time, 10 days. *Average cost*, 6s. *Sufficient* for 5 pints. *Seasonable*—may be made at any time.

ORANGE LIQUEUR.

INGREDIENTS.—4 *Seville oranges*, 1 *lb. of loaf sugar, a pinch of saffron, a bottle of gin.*

Mode.—Cut the peel from the oranges very thin, and put it with the saffron in the gin. Drop each lump of sugar

into water, and, when it has absorbed all the moisture it can, put it into a spirit. Cork tightly, and store in a warm place for a month. Filter and bottle.

Time, 1 month. *Average cost*, 3s. 6d. *Seasonable*—make this in winter.

VANILLA LIQUEUR.

INGREDIENTS.—2 *sticks of vanilla*, 3 *pints of proof gin*, 1 *lb. of sugar.*

Mode.—Break the vanilla into the gin, and let it infuse for a fortnight. Boil the sugar in a quart of water to a clear syrup, pour in the spirit and vanilla, and simmer for 10 minutes. Filter and bottle.

Time, 14 days. *Average cost*, 6s. 6d.

BISHOP.

INGREDIENTS.—1 *bottle of port*, 2 *lemons*, 2 *oz. of loaf sugar*, ½ *pint of water, spice to taste, cloves.*

Mode.—Stick one of the lemons with the cloves and bake it, boil the spice in the water, mull the wine, taking off some of the spirit with a lighted paper, add the water and baked lemon, and stand the pan near the fire. Rub the sugar on the rind of the other lemon, and put it in a bowl previously warmed, squeeze in the juice, add a little spice, then pour in the hot wine.

Average cost, 3s. 6d. *Sufficient* for 6 persons. *Seasonable* in winter.

EGG FLIP.

INGREDIENTS.—5 *eggs*, 3 *oz. of sugar*, 2 *glasses of rum*, 3 *pints of ale, spice and ginger to taste.*

Mode.—Break the eggs into a jug and beat well with the sugar and spice, heat the ale and pour it on the eggs, beating well all the time, then heat altogether and add the spirit.

Average cost, 1s. 10d. *Sufficient* for 6 persons. *Seasonable* in winter.

PUNCH (COLD).

INGREDIENTS.—1 *bottle of rum*, 1 *of champagne*, 2 *glasses of curacoa or other liqueur*, ½ *lb. of pounded sugar*, 1 *large or 2 smaller lemons*, 1 *pint of water, ice.*

Mode.—Put the sugar into a bowl with the water, into which slice the lemon. When the sugar has dissolved add the spirit, liqueur and water, and, just before serving, the champagne. Ice before putting this last in, or if more convenient, break in small pieces of ice and omit ½ pint of the water.

Time, ½ an hour. *Average cost*, 7s. 6d. *Sufficient* for 12 persons. *Seasonable* in summer.

PUNCH (HOT).

INGREDIENTS.—¾ pint of rum, ¼ pint of brandy, 3 to 4 oz. of loaf sugar, according to taste, 2 lemons, a pinch of nutmeg, 1½ pints of boiling water.

Mode.—Rub the lumps of sugar on the lemons until they have absorbed the oil, then put them in the bowl, adding the lemon-juice strained, and mix. Pour over the boiling water, next add the rum, then the brandy and nutmeg, and stir well. Save, before squeezing the lemons, 3 or 4 rounds to float at the top of the bowl. Serve very hot.

Average cost, 2s. 6d. *Sufficient* for 6 persons. *Seasonable* in winter.

MULLED ALE.

INGREDIENTS.—2 pints of ale, 1 glass of rum, 2 tablespoonfuls of pounded sugar, nutmeg, cloves.

Mode.—Heat the ale with the sugar and a few cloves; make a jug hot and pour it in with grated nutmeg to taste, and the rum.

Average cost, 1s. *Sufficient* for 4 persons. *Seasonable* in winter

MULLED CLARET.

INGREDIENTS.—1 bottle of claret, ½ the quantity of water, sugar and spice to taste.

Mode.—Boil the spice (a few cloves and half a teaspoonful of mixed spice would be a fair allowance) in the water till the flavour is extracted; add the sugar and wine and bring to boiling point. The quantity we have suggested is enough flavouring for most people, and 6 oz. of sugar would make it sweet enough, but as tastes so differ on both these points we can give no rule. The wine should be heated in a mull or a lined saucepan.

Average cost, 2s. *Sufficient* for 4 persons. *Seasonable* in winter.

NEGUS.

INGREDIENTS.—1 bottle of sherry or port, 1 glass of brandy, 1 lemon, 1 quart of water, sugar and nutmeg to taste.

Mode.—Warm the wine before the fire, slice the lemon into a jug previously heated, put the wine over it and the sugar, and pour over the water boil-

ing; add a grate of nutmeg and serve very hot.

Average cost, 3s. 6d. *Sufficient* for 6 persons. *Seasonable* in winter.

CHAMPAGNE CUP.

INGREDIENTS.—1 bottle of champagne, 2 glasses of liqueur, 1 Seville orange, a few slices of cucumber, sugar, a little verbena or borage, 2 bottles of soda water.

Mode.—Cut the rind of the orange very thin into a jug, with the sugar and sliced cucumber, and pour over the champagne, set in ice for a little while, then take out the cucumber and rind. Add the liqueur and soda water, stir well, pour into a bowl, and serve with the verbena, or borage, floating on the top.

Average cost, 5s. 6d. *Sufficient* for 6 persons. *Seasonable* in summer or for a dance at any time.

CIDER CUP.

INGREDIENTS.—1 quart bottle of cider, 1 of seltzer, ½ a glass of brandy, 1 lemon, 2 tablespoonfuls of pounded sugar, a few slices of cucumber.

Mode.—Put the lemon rind, half the juice and the cucumber, with the sugar in a jug; pour over the brandy, then the cider and set in ice. When sufficiently flavoured, take out the peel and cucumber and add the seltzer. Pour into a glass jug, and add a few sprigs of borage if obtainable.

Average cost, 2s. *Sufficient* for 6 persons. *Seasonable* in summer.

CLARET CUP.

INGREDIENTS.—1 bottle of claret, 2 glasses of maraschino or other liqueur, 2 bottles of soda or seltzer, 3 tablespoonfuls of sugar, slices of fresh fruit, such as pine or peaches, borage.

Mode.—Put the sugar in a jug and pour over it the wine and liqueur and set in ice. Slice the fruit in a bowl, pour over the contents of the jug, then add the seltzer and the borage.

Average cost, 3s. 6d. *Sufficient* for 6 persons. *Seasonable* in summer.

LOVING CUP.

INGREDIENTS.—1 bottle of champagne, ½ a bottle of Madeira, 3 glasses of brandy, ¼ lb. of loaf sugar, 2 lemons, 1½ pints of water, balm and borage, nutmeg.

Mode.—Rub the peel from one lemon

with some knobs of sugar and put them in a jug with the remainder of it, and the other lemon cut in slices. Pour over the water, then the wine and brandy, and grate in a little nutmeg. Ice before putting in the cup and float the balm or borage.

Average cost, 7s. *Sufficient* for 12 to 18 persons. *Seasonable* at any time.

GIN SLING.

INGREDIENTS.—1 *wineglassful of gin*, 2 *slices of lemon*, 3 *lumps of sugar, ice*.

Mode.—Put the gin, sugar and sliced lemon into a tumbler and fill up with small pieces of ice or iced-water. Drink through a straw.

Average cost, 3d.

LEMON SQUASH.

INGREDIENTS.— 1 *lemon*, 1 *bottle of soda water, ice*.

Mode.—Slice the lemon into a soda water glass, and squeeze out some of the juice with a spoon; add 1 or 2 lumps of ice, then pour over a bottle of soda water.

Average cost, 3d.

LIME JUICE DRINK.

INGREDIENTS. — *Fresh limes, loaf sugar, a little liqueur, iced water*.

Mode.—Strain the squeezed juice of the limes, and add sugar and liqueur to taste. Put a little of this mixture in a glass and fill up with water. This, as well as champagne or any other cup, may have slices of fresh fruit, such as pine or apricot, added with advantage.

MAY DRINK.

INGREDIENTS.—1 *bottle of hock*, 3 *oz. of powdered sugar*, ½ *a lemon, a few black currant leaves, woodruff*, ½ *pint of water, ice*.

Mode.—Put the leaves, the woodruff, and the lemon rind, with the sugar, into the water and steep till it is well-flavoured; then pour in the wine and stir. Put in a glass jug, leaving the flavourings behind, but adding a few sprigs of fresh woodruff.

Average cost, 2s. *Sufficient* for 4 persons. *Seasonable* in summer.

POMEGRANATE DRINK.

INGREDIENTS.—4 *pomegranates*, ½ *lb. of powdered loaf sugar, the juice of* 2 *limes*, 1 *pint of water*.

Mode.—Put the red pips with the sugar into a basin, bruise, pour over the water, then the lime-juice, and strain twice through muslin.

MINT JULEP.

INGREDIENTS.—*The juice of an orange, and half the rind, a sprig of mint*, 1 *teaspoonful of pounded sugar, a wineglassful of gin, ice*.

Mode.—Peel the orange and squeeze the juice through a strainer into a tumbler; add the mint, the sugar and the peel and fill up with ice in small pieces, or iced water, leaving just room to add the gin.

Average cost, 4d.

SHANDY GAFF.

INGREDIENTS.—1½ *pints of good ale*, 3 *bottles of ginger beer, a wineglassful of liqueur or brandy, ice*.

Mode.—Put some lumps of ice in a jug, pour over the ale, then the liqueur, and lastly the ginger beer, and give a stir.

Average cost, 1s. *Seasonable* in summer.

SHERRY COBBLER.

INGREDIENTS.—3 *glasses of sherry*, 1 *bottle of soda water*, 1 *tablespoonful of pounded sugar*, 1 *glass of liqueur, ice*.

Mode.—Take three tumblers, put in each a glass of sherry and a third of the glass of liqueur with a lump of ice; then divide the bottle of soda water between the three. Drink through straws.

Average cost, 1s. 3d. *Sufficient* for 3 persons. *Seasonable* in summer.

INVALID COOKERY

It is only possible in a book of this size to give a limited number of recipes for invalid cookery, therefore we have chosen the best modes of preparing those most generally known. We need scarcely add not only should the various foods be most carefully prepared, but served with the greatest nicety, that they may tempt the flagging appetites of invalids.

ARROWROOT (TO MAKE).

INGREDIENTS.—2 teaspoonfuls arrowroot, a tablespoonful cold water, ½ pint boiling water.

Mode.—Mix the arrowroot smoothly in a basin with the cold water, then pour on it boiling water, stirring all the time. If mixed with hot water only, it must be put into a clean saucepan, and boiled until it thickens. Put the arrowroot into a tumbler, sweeten with lump sugar, and flavour with grated nutmeg or cinnamon, or a piece of lemon-peel, or, when allowed, 3 tablespoonfuls of port or sherry. Arrowroot made with milk, instead of water, is far nicer, but

is not so easily digested. It should be mixed in the same manner, with 3 tablespoonfuls of cold water, the boiling milk then poured on it, and well stirred. When made in this way no wine should be added.

Time, if obliged to be boiled, 2 minutes. Average cost, 2d. per pint. Sufficient to make ½ pint of arrowroot.

BARLEY GRUEL.

INGREDIENTS.—2 oz. Scotch or pearl barley, ½ pint port wine, the rind of one lemon, 1 quart and ½ pint water, sugar to taste.

Mode.—Well wash the barley, and boil it in ½ pint of water for ¼ hour; then pour this water away; put to the barley the quart of fresh boiling water, and let it boil until the liquid is reduced to half; then strain it off. Add the wine, sugar, and lemon-peel; simmer for 5 minutes, and put it away in a clean jug. Warm from time to time, as required.

Time, to be boiled until reduced to half. Average cost, 1s. 6d. Sufficient, with the wine, to make 1½ pints of gruel.

BARLEY WATER (TO MAKE).

INGREDIENTS.—2 oz. pearl barley, 2 quarts boiling water, 1 pint cold water.

Mode. — Wash the barley in cold water; put it into a saucepan with the cold water, and boil it for about ¼ hour, then strain off the water, and add the 2 quarts of fresh boiling water. Boil it until reduced one half, and strain it. It may be flavoured with lemon-peel, after being sweetened; or a small piece may be simmered with the barley. A very pleasant drink may be more quickly prepared by using Robinson's Patent Barley, following the directions given with each packet.

Time, to boil until the liquid is reduced one half. *Sufficient* to make 1 quart of barley water.

BEEF-TEA (TO MAKE).

INGREDIENTS.—1 *lb. lean gravy-beef,* 1 *quart water,* 1 *saltspoonful salt.*

Mode.—Select a nice fleshy piece of beef, without fat. Cut it into small pieces about the size of dice, and put it into a clean saucepan. Add the water *cold* to it; put it on the fire, and bring it to the boiling point; then skim it. Put in the salt when the water boils, and *simmer gently* from ½ to ¾ hour, removing any more scum should it appear on the surface. Strain through a hair-sieve, and set it by in a cool place. When wanted for use, remove every particle of fat from the top; warm up as much as may be required, adding, if necessary, a little more salt. This preparation is simple beef-tea, and is to be administered to those invalids to whom flavourings and seasonings are not allowed. When the patient is very low, use double the quantity of meat to the same proportion of water. Should the invalid be able to take the tea prepared in a more palatable manner, it is easy to make it so by following the directions in the next recipe, which is an admirable one for making savoury beef-tea. Beef-tea is always better when made the day before it is wanted, and then warmed up. It is a good plan to put the tea into a small cup or basin, and to place this basin in a saucepan of boiling water. When the tea is warm it is ready to serve.

Time, ½ to ¾ hour. *Average cost* 8d. per pint. *Sufficient*, allow 1 lb. of meat for a pint of good beef-tea.

BEEF-TEA (SAVOURY).

(*Soyer's Recipe*).

INGREDIENTS.—1 *lb. solid beef,* 1 *oz. butter,* 1 *clove,* 2 *button onions or* ½ *large one,* 1 *saltspoonful salt,* 1 *quart water.*

Mode.—Cut the beef into very small dice; put it into a stewpan with the butter, clove, onion, and salt; stir the meat round over the fire for a few minutes, until it produces a thin gravy; then add the water, and let it simmer gently ½ to ¾ hour, skimming off every particle of fat. When done strain through a sieve, and put it by in a cool place until required. If wanted quite plain, omit the vegetables, salt, and

clove; the butter cannot be objectionable, as it is taken out in skimming.

Time, ½ to ¾ hour. *Average cost,* 10d. per pint. *Sufficient,* allow 1 lb. of beef to make 1 pint of good beef-tea.

Note.—The meat left from beef-tea may be boiled a little longer, and pounded, with spices, &c., for potting. It makes a very nice breakfast dish.

Lemco is most invaluable in cases of extreme prostration. It should not be made too strong the first time of giving it, lest the "meaty" flavour should be disliked. It must be prepared with *boiling* water, or it will taste raw. Another advantage that this Extract possesses is that it can be ready at a moment's notice.

BEEF-TEA (BAKED).

INGREDIENTS.—1 *lb. fleshy beef pinto water,* ½ *saltspoonful salt.*

Mode. — Cut the beef into small square pieces, after trimming off all the fat, and put it into a baking-jar, with the water and salt; cover the jar well; place it in a warm, but not hot oven, and bake for 3 or 4 hours. Strain, and put by in a cool place until wanted. It may also be flavoured with an onion, a clove, and a few sweet herbs, &c., when the stomach is sufficiently strong to take these.

Time, 3 or 4 hours. *Average cost,* 8d. per pint. *Sufficient*, allow 1 lb. meat for 1 pint good beef-tea.

BEEF-TEA IN HASTE.

INGREDIENTS.—1 *lb. lean beef,* 1 *pint water.*

Mode.—With a sharp knife scrape the beef into *fibres;* this should be done on a board. Place the scraped meat into a delicately-clean saucepan, and pour ¼ pint boiling water over it; cover closely, and set by the side of the fire for 10 minutes; strain into a teacup, place it in a basin of ice-cold water, remove all fat from the surface, pour into a warmed cup, and put in another basin of hot water; warm again, and serve.

Time, ¼ hour. *Average cost,* 8d. per pint.

Note. — When required of greater strength, use half of the above quantity of water; or even less, when the patient is able to take a spoonful only at a time.

CALF'S FOOT (BAKED OR STEWED).

INGREDIENTS.—1 *calf's foot,* 1 *pint milk,* 1 *pint water,* 1 *blade mace, the rind of* ½ *lemon, pepper and salt to taste.*

Mode.—Well clean the foot, and either

stew or bake it in the milk and water, with the other ingredients, from 3 to 4 hours. An onion and a small quantity of celery may be added, if approved; ½ a teacupful cream, stirred in just before serving, is also a great improvement.

Time, 3 to 4 hours. *Average cost*, in full season, 6d. to 7d. each. *Sufficient* for 1 person. *Seasonable* from March to October.

CHICKEN BROTH.

INGREDIENTS.—½ *fowl, or the inferior joints of a whole one*, 1 *quart water*, 1 *blade mace*, ½ *onion, a small bunch sweet herbs, salt to taste*, 10 *peppercorns*.

Mode.—If a young fowl be used, the inferior joints may be put in the broth, and the best pieces reserved for dressing otherwise. Put the fowl into a saucepan, with all the ingredients, and simmer gently for 1½ hours, carefully skimming the broth well. When done, strain and put by into a cool place until wanted; then take all the fat off the top, warm up as much as may be required, and serve. This broth is, of course, only for those invalids whose stomachs are strong enough to digest it with a flavouring of herbs, &c. It may be made in the same manner as beef-tea, with water and salt only; but the preparation will be but tasteless and insipid. When the invalid cannot digest this chicken broth with the flavouring, we would recommend plain beef-tea.

Time, 1½ hours. *Sufficient* to make rather more than 1 pint of broth.

Note.—A stronger "chicken flavour" is obtained by previously roasting the fowl for 20 minutes before placing in the saucepan.

CUTLET (THE INVALID'S).

INGREDIENTS.—1 *nice cutlet from a loin or neck of mutton*, 2 *teacupfuls water*, 1 *very small stick celery, pepper and salt to taste*.

Mode.—Take off all the fat from the cutlet; put it into a stewpan, with the other ingredients; stew *very gently* for nearly 2 hours, and skim off every particle of fat that may rise to the surface from time to time. The celery should be cut into thin slices before it is added to the meat, and care must be taken not to use too much of it. If the water is allowed to boil fast, the cutlet will be hard.

Time, 2 hours' very gentle stewing

Average cost, 6d. or 7d. *Sufficient* for 1 person. *Seasonable* at any time.

EGG WINE.

INGREDIENTS.—1 *egg*, 1 *tablespoonful and ½ glass cold water*, 1 *glass sherry, sugar and grated nutmeg to taste*.

Mode.—Beat the egg, mixing with it a tablespoonful of cold water; make the wine and water hot, but not boiling; pour it on the egg, stirring all the time. Add sufficient lump sugar to sweeten the mixture, and a little grated nutmeg; put all into a very clean saucepan, set it on a gentle fire, and stir the contents one way until they thicken, but *do not allow them to boil*. Serve in a glass, with sippets of toasted bread, or plain, crisp biscuits. When the egg is not warmed, the mixture will be found easier of digestion, but it is not so pleasant a drink.

Sufficient for 1 person.

BARLEY GRUEL (PATENT BARLEY).

INGREDIENTS. — 1 *tablespoonful of Patent Barley (Flour), pinch of salt, a little cold water*, ½ *pint boiling water (or milk), sugar or port to taste*.

Mode.—Mix the barley well with cold water, until a smooth paste about the thickness of cream is formed; then add to this ½ pint of boiling water (or milk, which is preferable); put into an enamelled saucepan; add sugar or wine to taste; simmer for 10 minutes, stirring all the time with a silver or wooden spoon.

Time, 10 minutes. *Average cost*, 2½d., without spirits. *Sufficien* to make ½ pint.

JELLY (INVALID'S).

INGREDIENTS. — 12 *shanks mutton*, 3 *quarts water, a bunch of sweet herbs, pepper and salt to taste*, 3 *blades mace*, 1 *onion*, 1 *lb. lean beef, a crust of bread toasted brown*.

Mode.—Soak the shanks in plenty of water for some hours, and scrub them well; put them, with the beef and other ingredients, into a saucepan, with the water, and let them simmer very gently for 5 hours. Strain the broth, and, when cold, take off all the fat. It may be eaten either warmed-up or cold as a jelly.

Time, 5 hours. *Average cost*, 1s. 3d. *Sufficient* to make from 1½ to 2 pints of jelly.

LEMONADE FOR INVALIDS.

INGREDIENTS.—½ lemon, lump sugar to taste, 1 pint boiling water.

Mode.—Pare off the rind of the lemon thinly; cut the lemon into 2 or 3 thick slices, and remove as much as possible of the white outside pith, and all the pips. Put the slices of lemon, the peel, and lump sugar into a jug: pour over the boiling water; cover it closely, and in 2 hours it will be fit to drink. It should be either strained or poured off from the sediment.

Time, 2 hours. Average cost, 1d.
Sufficient to make ½ pint of lemonade.

TO MAKE MUTTON BROTH.

INGREDIENTS.—1 lb. scrag-end of neck of mutton, 1 onion, a bunch sweet herbs, ½ turnip, 3 pints water, pepper and salt to taste.

Mode.—Put the mutton into a stewpan; pour over the water cold, and add the other ingredients. When it boils, skim it very carefully, cover the pan closely, and let it simmer very gently for an hour; strain it, let it cool, take off all the fat from the surface, and warm up as much as may be required, adding, if the patient be allowed to take it, a teaspoonful of minced parsley previously scalded. Pearl barley or rice are very nice additions to mutton broth, and should be boiled as long as the other ingredients. When either of these is added, the broth must not be strained, but merely thoroughly skimmed. Plain mutton broth without seasoning is made by merely boiling the mutton, water, and salt together, straining it, letting the broth cool, skimming all the fat off, and warming up as much as is required. This preparation would be very tasteless and insipid, but likely to agree with very delicate stomachs; whereas the least addition of other ingredients would have the contrary effect.

Time, 1 hour. Average cost, 7d.
Sufficient to make from 1½ to 2 pints of broth.

Note.—Veal broth may be made in the same manner; the knuckle of a leg or shoulder is the part usually used for this purpose. It is very good with the addition of the inferior joints of a fowl, or a few shank-bones.

RICE MILK.

INGREDIENTS.—3 tablespoonfuls rice, 1 quart milk, sugar to taste; when liked, a little grated nutmeg.

Mode.—Well wash the rice, put it into a saucepan with the milk, and simmer gently until the rice is tender, stirring from time to time to prevent the milk from burning; sweeten, add a little grated nutmeg, and serve. This dish is very suitable and wholesome for children; it may be flavoured with a little lemon-peel, and a little finely-minced suet may be boiled with it, which renders it more strengthening and more wholesome. Tapioca, semolina, vermicelli, and macaroni, may all be dressed in the same manner.

Time, from ¾ to 1 hour.

SAVOURY CUSTARD.

INGREDIENTS.—½ pint good clear stock, the yolks of 2 eggs.

Mode.—Beat up the eggs and add them to the stock with a little seasoning if required (beef tea can be used if preferred in place of the stock), and pour into a small buttered basin. Steam gently for 20 minutes.

Time, 20 minutes. Average cost, 5d.

TO MAKE TOAST-AND-WATER.

INGREDIENTS. — A slice of bread, 1 quart boiling water.

Mode.—Cut a slice from a stale loaf (a piece of hard crust is better than anything else for the purpose), toast it to a nice brown on every side, but do not allow it to burn or blacken. Put it into a jug, pour the boiling water over it, cover it closely, and let it remain until cold. When strained, it will be ready for use. Toast-and-water should always be made a short time before it is required, to enable it to get cold; if drunk in a tepid or lukewarm state, it is an exceedingly disagreeable beverage. If, as is sometimes the case, this drink is wanted in a hurry, put the toasted bread into a jug, and only just cover it with the boiling water; when this is cool, cold water may be added in the proportion required, and the toast-and-water strained; it will then be ready for use, and is more expeditiously prepared than by the first method.

SERVIETTES AND WAITING AT TABLE

SERVIETTES.

THESE should be ornaments as well as articles of use at a table, and at home should be made to look pretty without being as obtrusive as they often are at hotels and restaurants. They should be, for folding, slightly stiffened, and very evenly folded in the ironing. They are usually of plain damask, but a relief is given to their whiteness against the cloth by a monogram worked in colour or by a small bouquet.

No more useful and neat shape has yet been found than the mitre which we illustrate, but we give two others which are a little more fanciful and may be liked for a change.

THE MITRE.

Fold the napkin evenly in three, then the two edges to the centre, as in Fig. 1. Fold down the two corners, as in Fig. 2, then the napkin lengthwise, from " A " to " A " which will bring the serviette into shape as in Fig. 3 ; and, bringing the two ends round towards each other, one end on either side, it will be found that there is a sort of pocket on each side in which the ends can be slipped, as in Fig 4, *e.g.*, slip the end marked " B " into the pocket " C," and repeat on other side.

THE FAN.

Commence by opening the serviette flat on the table and making a deep pleat at the sides, as shown in Fig 1. Then fold the sides together, as in Fig. 2. Now pleat from end to end as a fan is folded, as shown in Fig. 3. Lastly, pinch down the edges of these folds to make a border to the fan ; and, gathering together the lower edges, put the serviette in a glass or napkin ring.

THE SACHET.

The napkin must first be folded in three, then the upper fold must be turned down to the middle as a hem, as in Fig. 1. Fold over the napkin end to end, as in Fig. 2, with the hem inside ; fold from the outer edge over and over, repeating the same on the other side, as in Fig. 3. Tuck in the two corners shown shaded in the little diagram above Fig. 3, to leave a triangle, as shown by " A " of Fig. 4, fold this back, and put the corners under the hem, as in " B."

WAITING AT TABLE.

In this little book it would be out of place to give instructions for those who wait at table in large establishments, where butler or butlers and footmen are kept ; but, perhaps, in the majority of good middle-class houses, we may oftenest find parlour maid and housemaid fulfilling this office, and, in many cases, housemaids combine the duties of parlour maid. No matter, however, whether one or many are employed, the mode of waiting is the same.

Say we take housemaid and parlour maid ; the former takes precedence of the latter, just as a butler does of a footman. The parlour maid would hand the plates and the housemaid would follow with vegetables and sauces ; the parlour maid would also pour out the wine. Directly a plate is finished with, it should be removed ; or if there is but one servant, who has to leave the room to bring in the dishes, it must be remembered that the plates must be taken away first, and the dishes last. As the plates are removed fresh ones for the next course, if it is one to be handed, are placed to each person ; and in clearing it is usual to put the knives and forks in separate receptacles and the plates in a zinc basket. Before dessert, slips (if used), are removed, or the crumbs taken from the cloth with a scoop or brush and a tray; then dessert is set by putting plate, finger-glass, knives and forks, and glasses according to the wine to be served to each person.

Serving should always commence from the right-hand side of the master of the house, for there will be found the lady highest in rank. Let it be the aim of those who wait at table to be as attentive, as quick and as quiet as possible, and to have their dress, in every detail, the perfection of neatness and cleanliness.

MENU CARDS.

It is usual now at quiet unostentatious houses to have these ; and very much pleasanter it is to know what is to be served, at even very simple dinners.

It being so generally the custom to have the courses printed in French, we have given them in that language as well as in English, in the following menus. Very pretty cards are sold for writing the menus upon, and the china ones, which can be used again and again, are very suitable for home use. It is not considered necessary to have a menu card for every person, but it is certainly pleasanter not to share them. If there are, however, only one to each two persons, they should be placed between the plates ; while if for the home party only two or four are used, they should be placed where all can see them.

We have seen in daily use at a well-appointed table two menu cards of china, supported by china figures which held up their burdens so that every one could read their inscriptions.

Note See illustrations of serviettes facing page 272

BREAKFAST

Amongst English people as a rule, breakfast, as a meal, does not hold a sufficiently important place; and with some it means, in reality, no meal at all, unless we reckon the proverbial "cup of tea" to form one.

There are probably several reasons why people do not care for breakfast, among which, probably, the strongest is that of late hours. Another is that they sup or dine too late; while a still more powerful one might be, in many cases, that a certain amount of air and exercise was needed before a due appreciation of a good meal could be found.

All these mistakes could be easily rectified, and should be by those who value their health; for a good breakfast lays an excellent foundation for a day's work, or even pleasure, and makes us less dependent upon the punctual serving of other meals, that by business or other engagements are often unavoidably delayed.

Housekeepers should make more of breakfast. We do not mean make it heavier or more costly, but try and give more variety in the dishes. The sameness of an ordinary English breakfast is too well-known for comment, and it is no unusual thing to hear of people having eggs and bacon *every* morning. No one would think of having the same dish for dinner even *half* the week, and it seems a most extraordinary thing that there are some who can always eat the same food at their first meal. But these contented creatures are in the minority; and it is of the majority we should think who cannot eat with relish a dish that comes daily to table. Perhaps the chief thing against having many different dishes at breakfast in average houses is, that they involve a certain amount of time and trouble which it is hard to spare early in the day; so we put up with what can be had with no expenditure of imagination and the least amount of labour. We have no hesitation in saying that there would be a considerable diminution in the cost of breakfasts in small families, if bacon and eggs (not by any means a cheap dish) was only now and then given, and the scraps of meat and vegetables from the dinner or other meals were used to make the many little dishes into which they can be converted. We give some menus for different kinds of breakfasts, ranging from those suitable for a house party to the very simple every-day one of middle-class life. Wedding breakfasts are a thing of the past, but following the menu for luncheons, will be found some for afternoon receptions now so customary after a marriage. Amongst the recipes will be found some few that may fairly be termed breakfast ones, and which we trust may be useful; but it will not be out of place to precede these by a few hints about the breakfast table itself.

LAYING OF BREAKFAST TABLE.

Why more people do not give a little more decoration and care to their breakfast tables, when they grudge no time bestowed upon those used for dinner, we do not know; but it is a fact that, more often than not, there is very little time or thought expended to make the first meal of the day attractive.

In small families, it is usual for the cups, saucers, &c., whether intended for tea or coffee, or both, to occupy only one end of the table, that at which the mistress of the household sits; the chief dish being then placed opposite the master at the other end. At a breakfast, however, where there are many to be served, tea should be put at one end and coffee at the other; that is, of course, in a household where there is a second lady to assist in filling the cups, or even a young girl, who cannot too soon learn the simple task. The cups should be neatly arranged in a semi-circle with the tea or coffee-pot, milk or cream-jug and sugar in the centre; while the urn, or spirit-kettle, if one be used, should be placed just beyond so as to be handy for replenishing the tea-pot. If there are two dishes of meat, fish, &c., and the two ends of the table are occupied, these must be placed at the sides; and the bread, butter, toast, eggs, &c., should be neatly and evenly arranged in the rest of the available space. In the centre should be some foliage or floral decoration, and, where little time or money can be spared, a fern in a pretty pot can be had for a mere trifle and made to last a long time.

According to what is to be served, so must the table be laid. Cold or hot plates must be put before the dishes for which they are intended; but to each person, on the left side, must be placed a small breakfast plate; and a small knife must be given in addition to the large knife and fork. If fish be served, fish-eaters should be placed just in the same way as at dinner, and there should be a sufficiency of carvers and spoons for serving. Small cruets only should be used, and these placed at the corner or corners of the table.

The sideboard, except in a very small family, should be laid for breakfast, and serve to hold spare plates, knives, bread, &c., and where there are many dishes, the larger of the cold ones, such as a ham, a joint of beef, or a pie. Table napkins for breakfast are usually smaller than those intended for dinner use. It is not at all necessary to have them elaborately folded, and if used a second time they are simply run through a ring.

SERVING BREAKFAST.

A good housekeeper will see that she loses no points in the *serving* of the breakfast. The tea and coffee should be well made, just in time but not too soon, so that they are at their best; there should be a good supply of hot water, and the milk for the coffee should be hot. The dishes should be garnished appropriately just as for dinner, and the plates for hot dishes should be really hot. Buttered toast or muffins, if not served in regular toast dishes should be placed, covered, on the top of a basin of hot water; rolls should be hot as they come from the bakers (if not made at home) but crisped and made hot in the oven. Dry toast should not have been made long enough to be found leathery, and should always be served in a rack. Watercresses and fruit make a table look nice, besides being excellent food when partaken of early in the day, and these should be prettily arranged in suitable dishes.

MENUS FOR BREAKFASTS.

GUESTS' BREAKFAST FOR 12 PERSONS (SPRING).

Cod Cutlets.
Ham Omelette.
Cold Chicken, Cold Tongue.
Poached Eggs.
Stewed Rhubarb.
Apricot Preserve.
Tea, coffee, milk, cream.
Bread, milk rolls, toast, butter marmalade.

GUESTS' BREAKFAST FOR 12 PERSONS (SUMMER).

Cold Salmon.
Sauce Tartare.
Fried Soles.
Lamb Cutlets.
Cold Pigeon Pie.
Grilled Ham.
Boiled and Scrambled Eggs.
Watercresses.
Strawberries.
Tea, coffee, hot milk, cream.
Bread, rolls, toast, butter, marmalade, sardines, &c.

GUESTS' BREAKFAST FOR 12 PERSONS (AUTUMN).

Fillets of Turbot.
Crême de Liévre.
Cold Pheasant.
Eggs and Tomatoes.
Ham.
Mulberries, Grapes.
Tea, coffee, milk, hot and cold, cream.
Bread, breakfast cakes, toast, plain and buttered, marmalade, potted meat, butter, preserve.

GUESTS' BREAKFAST FOR 12 PERSONS (WINTER).

Rissoles of Fish.
Devilled Turkey.
Salmi of Game.
Cold Pressed Beef.
Savoury Omelette.
Boiled Eggs.
Tea, coffee, hot and cold milk, cream, sugar.
Bread, rolls, toast, dry and buttered butter, marmalade, potted meat, &c.

FAMILY BREAKFASTS FOR A WEEK IN SUMMER.

Sunday.—Tea, coffee, hot and cold milk, bread, toast, butter, cold ham, sardine toast, boiled eggs, cresses, any fruits in season.

Monday.—Cocoa, tea, hot and cold milk, bread, dry toast, butter, broiled meat (slices of any cold meat) with tomato sauce, ham omelette, marmalade.

Tuesday.—Coffee, hot milk, bread, buttered toast, butter, fish rissoles made from cold fish and potatoes, cold tongue, strawberry jam, watercress.

Wednesday.—Tea, milk, bread, toast, butter, hot buttered scones, beef croquettes, ham and egg toast, any fresh fruit.

Thursday.—Coffee, hot milk, bread, toast, butter, legs of chickens or ducks grilled or any slices of cold meat, poached eggs, watercress.

Friday.—Tea, milk, bread, rolls, butter, broiled plaice, any cold meat, fruit.

Saturday.—Cocoa, tea, hot and cold milk, bread, toast, butter, rissoles of any cold meat, sardine toast, tomatoes.

FAMILY BREAKFASTS FOR A WEEK IN WINTER.

Sunday.—Coffee, hot milk, bread, toast, butter, broiled fish (haddock or herring), eggs.

Monday.—Coffee, tea, hot and cold milk, bread, hot rolls, kidney toast, savoury omelette, marmalade.

Tuesday.—Tea, milk, porridge, bread, toast, butter, mince made from any scraps of cold meat, brawn, marmalade.

Wednesday.—Cocoa, tea, hot and cold milk, bread, muffins, butter, rissoles made from any cold fish or from tinned salmon, grilled bacon, boiled eggs.

Thursday.—Coffee, hot milk, porridge, bread, toast, butter, mutton cutlets and fried potatoes, sardines, marmalade.

Friday.—Coffee, tea, hot and cold milk, bread, toast, butter, baked fresh herrings, broiled kidneys, marmalade.

Saturday.—Cocoa, tea, hot and cold milk, bread, buttered toast, butter, salmi or hash of cold game or poultry, scrambled eggs.

The above bills of fare are simply suggestions for a family of moderate size and income, and it will be seen that in them the remains of previous days' dinners are supposed to be used for the rissoles and other little dishes. It would be easy to take away or add a dish from any of them, but it will be found that there is a fair amount of variety in the dishes chosen.

The following list of breakfasts are for a family of small means :—

ECONOMICAL BREAKFASTS FOR ONE WEEK IN SUMMER.

Sunday.—Tea, milk, dry toast, bread, butter, porridge, brawn.

Monday.—Coffee, hot milk, rolls, bread, butter, poached eggs, watercresses.

Tuesday.—Tea, milk, bread, butter, toast, fried flounders.

Wednesday.—Coffee, hot milk, porridge, buttered toast, rissoles made from cold meat (any scraps left), any fresh fruit.

Thursday.—Coffee, hot milk, bread, butter, breakfast cakes, kedgeree, marmalade.

Friday.—Tea, milk, bread, butter, dry toast, minced meat and mashed potatoes (cold meat cookery), jam.

Saturday.—Coffee, hot milk, porridge, toast, scrambled eggs, fruit.

These breakfasts are very plain ones, suitable for a small family where there are children. For them bread and milk may be added on the mornings when there is no porridge given.

The brawn is supposed to be home-made, as also the breakfast cakes.

The rissoles, the mince and the kedgeree would all be made from small scraps of meat or fish. The last-named dish is an excellent one for breakfast, besides being a very economical one.

ECONOMICAL BREAKFASTS FOR ONE WEEK IN WINTER.

Sunday.—Coffee, hot milk, bread, toast, butter, cold boiled bacon, eggs.

Monday.—Tea, milk, rolls, bread, butter, baked fresh herrings, marmalade.

Tuesday.—Coffee, hot milk, porridge, toast, butter, scrambled eggs.

Wednesday.—Cocoa, hot milk, bread, butter, rissoles made from tinned meats or any scraps.

Thursday.—Coffee, hot milk, bread, toast, minced liver and bacon.

Friday.—Tea, milk, bread, toast, butter, broiled haddock, watercresses.

Saturday.—Tea, milk, bread, butter, kidney toast.

These breakfasts are intended for autumn and winter ones, it being more difficult to plan them out then than in summer, when fish, fruit, and other provisions are more plentiful, and it is no hardship to have a cold breakfast.

LUNCHEON

UNDER the above heading come a very great variety of meals; for we have no other name for the one that comes between breakfast and dinner. It may be a crust of bread and butter or cheese, or an elaborate meal of four or five courses; it is still "luncheon." Also it may take place at any time. The lower classes lunch between 10 and 11; the upper, some three or four hours later; but in one thing both rich and poor alike agree, that it should be of all meals the most informal.

Luncheon, like all other meals, must of necessity be regulated by various circumstances, such as individual tastes, means, and size of family. In middle-class life, where there is a nursery, it generally forms the dinner for the children; and it is for that reason simple and substantial, consisting more often than not of a joint and a pudding. Also its most substantial dish is often that which serves for the kitchen dinner, the joint being brought first into the dining-room then taken out into the kitchen. This is scarcely fair to the servants, however, who get their chief meal not only late, but cold; and it could in many cases be avoided. There are so many little dishes that can be made from remnants of the day before; and a dish of cutlets, or a little fish, would not take long to prepare after the servants had dined in comfort; while, in summer, with fresh fruits and salad obtainable, it should not be thought a hardship to have a cold meal in the middle of the day. In large establishments it is usual to have a first-rate repast served for lunch, not alone for the family, but for any chance visitor. Anything and everything that is given for dinner, such as soup, fish, entrées, game, poultry, &c., may find a place at luncheon, where means and household staff admit; but it is not usual to have so many courses, nor to serve them à la Russe, and there is less formality and less service exacted than at dinner.

LAYING THE LUNCHEON TABLE.

According to the luncheon to be served so must the table be laid; but, in any case, it should be made to look pretty, and should never lack some decoration of foliage or flowers. As we have said, it is not the custom to serve anything but vegetables off the table, therefore, all cold dishes can be put on if there is room; and with these nicely garnished, and such pretty things as salads, sweets, and fruits, it is not a difficult thing to make a table look elegant without it being a grand luncheon, if only the principal rules in laying a cloth be adhered to. These are that the cloth should be perfectly clean, the knives bright and sharp, the silver well burnished, and the glass sparkling and clear. While with these as they should be a homely meal may be made attractive, when these details are neglected it is not possible to make a more elaborate one look even well.

LUNCHEON DISHES.

Luncheon dishes, as we have said, vary according to means, station, and family; but to return to the middle-class luncheon, it may be said of it that like breakfast, with the majority, there is not sufficient change day by day, and the cold joint at the former often seems as inevitable as eggs and bacon at the latter. This is a mistake. This cold joint is, in many cases, an extravagance; for between a good breakfast and dinner we can scarcely need anything so substantial in the middle of the day. A lesser quantity of the meat warmed in some way in winter will do more good; and at this season soup should be a more frequent course at our luncheon tables than it is. We say, course, but a good basin of soup might of itself well form the luncheon. Soup costs so little, and is but little trouble, yet in most houses there is not half enough made. Not only can every scrap of meat and vegetable be utilised (with a good digester or stockpot) for this purpose, but it is worth while in small families sometimes, to purchase such inexpensive things as bones or a sheep's-head. Take the latter for instance. If boiled over night, there will be a nice cheap supper for a couple of servants, and the liquor from it will give a splendid broth for next day's luncheon with only the addition of a few herbs, vegetables, and some pearl barley.

In summer, with fresh salad, cucumber, &c., at hand, very nice little mayonaises and other dishes may be made from remains of chicken, fish, &c.; and amongst our savouries are some that are suitable for a light luncheon; but we give recipes for a few dishes specially for breakfast and luncheon.

One word more on the subject of luncheons we must add ere giving our menus for them, and that is that where they are, as generally, served with but little formality and attendance, it must be impressed upon those who lay the table that everything *likely* to be wanted, that can be, must be brought in beforehand, so that no ringing for anything be necessary. On the sideboard there should be extra plates, knives, forks, &c., and it should be seen that necessary condiments are at hand, as well as that there is a sufficient supply of both bread and butter. It is then no hardship for those in the dining-room to wait upon themselves during the meal.

GUESTS' LUNCHEON.

For an informal meal where friends may drop in without previous invitation, in a large majority of cases, menus for luncheon would be superfluous. We must give whatever is " going," if we may use the term, to our guests, supplementing the cold joint, or what has been prepared for the children's dinner, with such small dishes as can be easily and quickly arranged, if it be necessary to make any addition to the meal.

For establishments, however, where luncheon is a set meal, more elaborate than many mid-day dinners, and for those who like to bid guests to this repast, we give a menu for summer, and another suitable for autumn and winter.

LUNCHEON FOR 10 PERSONS (SUMMER).

Cold salmon, tartar sauce, cucumber.
Roast chicken, potatoes, green peas.
Cold lamb, salad.
Raspberry and currant tart (cold), custard.
Maraschino jelly.
Strawberries and cream.
Bread, butter, cheese, biscuits, &c.

LUNCHEON FOR 10 PERSONS (WINTER).

Clear soup.
Fried soles, caper sauce.
Hashed turkey, cold roast beef, beet-root, mashed potatoes.
Pheasants.
Sweet omelette, stewed prunes, and rice (cold), cheese, celery.
Pears, oranges.
Bread, butter, &c.

A more troublesome luncheon to provide is one for a picnic. We do not mean one of those grand ones where the same viands as would be found at an invitation lunch in a large establishment would be served with the same state and ceremony; but a delightfully informal meal perhaps got together at a day's notice where the different members of the party each make some contribution to the feast.

Now for this kind of meal it is not only essential that we have a menu, we also need a complete list of all articles required, independent of the actual food and drink.

A good deal of judgment is needed to plan out the different portions so that each person may take an equal part in providing; and for that reason it is better first, after making out the bill of fare, to reckon up the probable cost. The following two menus may be of use, giving as they do the average cost of luncheon, as well as the quantities needed for parties of 12 persons.

PICNIC LUNCHEON FOR 12 PERSONS

	Average Cost.	
	s.	d.
Cold salmon (about 3 lbs.)	4	6
Mayonaise sauce, cucumber (1 large).........................	1	3
Quarter of lamb, mint sauce	9	0
Chickens (2).....................	5	0
Tongue	3	6
Salad, dressing	1	3
Fruit tarts (2)...................	2	0
Custard (1 qt.)...................	0	10
Jellies or creams (2)	3	0
Strawberries (2 qts.)............	2	0
Cream (1 pt.)	1	6
½ lb. of cheese, 5d., ½ lb. of butter, 9d.	1	2
2 loaves of bread	0	6
1 lb. of biscuits	0	6
	£1 16	0

SERVIETTES.

THE SACHET.

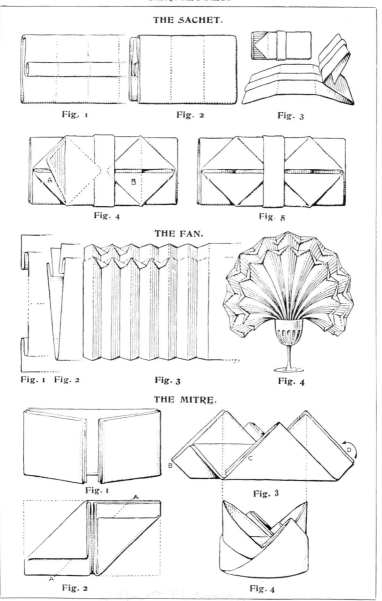

Fig. 1 Fig. 2 Fig. 3

Fig. 4 Fig. 5

THE FAN.

Fig. 1 Fig. 2 Fig. 3 Fig. 4

THE MITRE.

Fig. 1

Fig. 2 Fig. 3

Fig. 4

PICNIC LUNCHEON FOR 12 PERSONS.

Average Cost.

	s.	d.
Sardine, or other fish, sandwiches	2	0
Pigeon pie (1 large)	6	0
Cold beef (6 lbs.)	5	0
Horseradish sauce	0	4
Cucumber (1, 8d.) salad and dressing, 1s.	1	8
Fruit or jam puffs (18)	1	6
Blancmange (2 moulds)	2	0
Cheese biscuits (1 lb.)	1	0
Strawberries (2 qts.)	2	0
Cherries (2 lbs.)	1	0
3 loaves of bread, 9d., ½ lb. of butter, 9d.	1	6
	£1 4	0

These menus will be found to cost at the rate of 3s. and 2s. per head respectively; that is, reckoning the full cost of everything, and not allowing for the value of the "fragments that remain."

We have not put down in our list pepper, salt, and mustard, which will be needed; but the cost of these is almost too trifling to be mentioned. What to drink at picnics is so much a question of means and individual taste that we cannot attempt to deal with the question here, but we may say that the usual wines are champagne and claret, and that these are often served in the form of cups.

FAMILY LUNCHEONS FOR A WEEK IN SUMMER.

Monday.—Mutton cutlets and peas, cold chicken, ham, salad.—Gooseberry fool, cold milk pudding.—Bread, cheese, butter, biscuits.

Tuesday.—Mayonaise of any cold fish. —Rissoles of chicken, brawn.—Tartlets, compôte of fruit.—Bread, cheese, butter, biscuits.

Wednesday. — Cold lamb (or any other cold joint), mint sauce, patties made from any scraps of cold meat, salad.—Cake, preserves.—Bread, butter, cheese, biscuits.

Thursday.—Veal galantine, poached eggs on spinach, cucumber. — Cold fruit tart, custard pudding.—Bread, cheese, butter, biscuits.

Friday.—Fish pie or rissoles made from cold fish and potatoes.—Cold meat, beetroot.—Cake, preserves, any fresh fruits.—Bread, cheese, butter, biscuits.

Saturday.—Minced beef or any other cold meat, Russian salad.—Macaroni cheese.—Cake, fruit, bread, butter, biscuits.

Sunday. — Cold ham, salad.—Cake, preserve, strawberries and cream.— Bread, cheese, butter, biscuits.

FAMILY LUNCHEONS FOR A WEEK IN WINTER.

Monday.—Cold meat, curry of poultry, or fish, pickles, chutney.—Apple dumplings baked, any cold sweets from Sunday.—Bread, cheese, butter, biscuits.

Tuesday.—Fried filleted plaice, cold meat, winter salad, rice shape, stewed prunes.—Bread, butter, cheese, biscuits.

Wednesday.—Macaroni soup, rissoles of cold meat, or poultry, and potatoes. —Mince pies, jelly. — Bread, butter, cheese, biscuits.

Thursday. — Joint from servants' table with vegetables.—Any cold pudding.—Cake, preserve.—Bread, butter, biscuits, cheese.

Friday. — Curried cold fish, steak fried, mashed potatoes.—Tinned pine. —Custard.—Bread, butter, cheese, biscuits.

Saturday.—Pea soup, cold game or poultry, hashed meat, fried potatoes. —Tapioca pudding, preserve.—Bread, butter, cheese, biscuits.

Sunday.—Cold game pie, ham, sardines.—Cake, preserve.—Bread, butter, cheese, biscuits.

MENUS FOR WEDDING RECEPTIONS.

SUMMER.

Sandwiches.

Foié gras, cucumber, sardines, chicken and tongue, salmon-paste.

Cakes.

Wedding cake, petits fours, madeira, pound, and several kinds of fancy biscuits and small cakes.

Ices and fruit.

Beverages.

Champagne, claret, sauterne, various cups.

WINTER.

Sandwiches.

Caviare, anchovy, turkey and tongue, ham, egg and anchovy.

Cakes.

Wedding cake, sponge, madeira, macaroons, ratafias, and various biscuits.

Fruit.

Grapes, compôtes of fruit, orange salad.

Wines.

Champagne, port, sherry.

DINNER

WHATEVER differences of opinion about other meals may exist, we all agree to the fact that dinner must be our chief one.

Some do not breakfast, a larger number do not lunch, others regard supper with horror, but from peasant to duke we all *dine*; thus dinner may be, and is, called the most important of our daily needs. It has been said, with more or less of satire, that in the fact of man's being a "dining animal" lies his chief distinction from the lower ones; and however this may be, it is morally certain that those who do not look upon dinner as one of the most regular functions of our life, are few and far between.

To speak of the hours at which we partake of this meal, and the viands that should be served, might fill a volume, did we thoroughly consider and discuss the subject; here let it suffice to say that, more than they do at present, these two things should depend less upon our means and appetites than our work and the lives we lead. Were this the case fewer of us would have to suffer from what may almost be called a national complaint, that of indigestion.

We have not far to go before we can see numbers of persons who (particularly in large houses of business) are *obliged* to take their principal meal of the day in the very midst of their work, when they have not sufficient time to digest it properly before the business of the day must be resumed.

Others we see, who, without exercise of mind or body eat as much or more as those who live by the work of their brains or by manual labour.

We do not mean to assert for one moment that all natures are alike, and that exactly the same food should be consumed by two people doing exactly the same work; yet as a general rule it may be said that our needs and not our tastes should govern our meals, and of them specially our "dinner."

Variety of food is best for almost all, and it has been proved that change of diet can be as beneficial as change of air; nay, even that which we have ascribed to the latter has, in many cases, been due to the former; and in this age of cookery and cookery books it should not be difficult, even in small families and with small means, to vary the monotony of the proverbial beef and mutton of British fare.

We later give some menus suitable for dinner parties in ordinary middle-class households (these in accordance with the times, being written in French as well as English), besides some bills of fare for every-day family dinners; but we may as well precede them by a few remarks about the arrangement of the table, its decorations and its surroundings. There is acknowledged to be a great art in giving a good dinner; but a most enjoyable one need not of necessity be a grand or costly one.

Given people who enjoy meeting each other (not too large a party), a room with a pleasant temperature, a table well lighted and prettily decorated, and service sufficient; then may not a few dishes, perfectly cooked, and wine, not costly but good of its kind, afford as much enjoyment to our guests as all the luxuries of the season?

Too often it is the custom to invite just as many people as we can seat at our tables (in many cases more than our servants can wait upon), forgetting the fact that quite as important as the dinner itself is the comfort by which we are surrounded when we partake of it.

For ball suppers, wedding breakfasts, &c., the services of a caterer will be found invaluable, and, indeed, are frequently indispensable. The housewife is then relieved of all worry and anxiety, and if her resources are at all limited, the meal is generally better and more cheaply served. One of the best known catering firms in London is Messrs. W. and G. Buszard, of 197-9, Oxford Street, W., who are also famous the world over for their wedding-cakes and confectionery.

LAYING THE TABLE.

Rules that we have given for breakfast or luncheon table apply equally, if not with greater importance, to the dinner table.

It is *most* essential that the glass and silver should be bright, the knives polished, the tablecloth and serviettes above reproach; and this should not be only the case when we entertain. These should not be luxuries; they should be daily comforts, and a lot of preparation is thus saved when we give a dinner party.

According to what is to be served so must the table be set—knives, forks and spoons (with the exception of those required for dessert) according to the dishes, glasses suitable for the beverages, this applying equally to an everyday repast as to a grand dinner. If the dishes are brought to table and carved or helped there, where there is any likelihood that the cloth may be soiled by the serving of hot dishes, it is best to have a clean table-napkin laid under such ones. Water carafes or jugs and glasses, also salt-cellers, should always be put upon the table. Other condiments may be handed; but if the service does not permit of this, they must also find a place.

The *cloth*, if at all wrinkled or creased in the folding, may be damped and ironed; it should be put on perfectly even, so that the same amount should hang down at each end and at each side, and it should always be put over a baize or some thick cover and never over the mahogany itself.

The *serviettes* should be nicely folded for guests, and placed equidistant a little way from the edge of the table, with a roll or small thick piece of bread in or against them.

Knives, forks and *spoons* should be evenly arranged with the handles about half an inch from the edge of the table, and the width of a plate between knife and fork.

Glasses should be grouped according to their order just below the point of

the knife. The sideboard, spread with a white cloth, should be used for the biscuits, etc., for the cheese course, the dessert plates, knives, forks and finger-bowls; besides serving as a receptacle for spare knives, forks, glasses, plates, bread and beverages. Where there is but one servant to wait at table, it is best to bring in all such things as cold sweets, and fruit for dessert that is neither strongly perfumed nor easily spoiled by keeping in a dining-room.

In summer time, if ice be used, it should be broken ready, in small pieces, in an ice-pail, and put upon the sideboard the moment before dinner is served.

TABLE DECORATIONS.

At the present time there is quite a rage for floral decorations for the dinner table. Even at old-fashioned dinner parties, where all the dishes are put upon the table, a good deal of space is devoted to the vases and other receptacles that are used to hold the flowers; but for the dinners that are served *à la Russe*, it is absolutely necessary that the table should be covered by artistic and pretty decorations. Fashionable dinner-givers vie with each other in the quality and arrangement of their flowers as much as the dinners themselves, or the wines served; and we see new ideas for this purpose chronicled day by day. So varying is the fashion, in fact, of our tables that only a weekly journal could give any idea of the charming blends of colour, the exquisite grouping of foliage and flowers, the beauty of form of the baskets, vases, &c., in which they are arranged; or the pretty wreaths in which they are tied to lay upon the silk or damask of the dinner tables of the wealthy. One rule, however, might hold good for every decoration, and that is that it should be either high enough or low enough not to impede the view. Another might be that no strongly-scented flowers should be used; for to many people these are most objectionable. Two fashions in table decoration seem likely to continue in favour: one of these arrangements only in foliage of different kinds; another of only one colour in the flowers.

Suffice it, however, for those who neither care to nor can afford to make their decorations a fashion, to know that, do they but arrange their flowers prettily and in harmony, selecting their receptacles with due regard to the style and growth of the blossoms, they cannot very well make any error; while may we suggest to those who do not consider themselves very clever at floral arrangements, that it is easier to get a pretty and good effect out of one kind of flower, or by using one colour only, than by blending one with another. Dessert centres of plush or velvet in winter, of muslin or silk in summer, in many cases look very pretty and are decidedly useful where there is a limited supply of flowers and foliage.

For trailing over the cloth only such flowers and foliage as will stand without being in water for some time should be used, and they should be placed so as not to interfere with the diners.

We devote no other space to the subject of table decoration; so we may say here that those for supper tables should be higher and have less base than those for dinner, for the reason that there is seldom too much room for the dishes; also, the latter being often bright in colour, less is needed in the flowers.

Pretty little rustic fern-stands, in which the growing plants can be placed, form very useful decorations, and many vases require but few flowers to make them look well-filled. Roses look best in low bowls with only their own foliage, or placed singly in specimen tubes; orchids should be placed as they would be if they were growing; lilies (except water lilies) should be put in tall vases; in fact, it is the aim of good decorators now to make the flowers appear as natural as possible.

MENUS FOR TWELVE PERSONS (SPRING).

I.

English.

Spring Soup.
Stewed Trout.
Whitebait.
Chaudfroid of Chicken.
Lobster Cutlets.
Veal Olives.
Sirloin of Beef.
Potatoes.　　　Seakale.
Hors d'œuvres.
Vanilla Soufflé.
Orange Jelly.

French.

Printanière.
Truite au Vin Rouge.
Blanchailles.
Chaudfroid de Volaille.
Côtelettes de Homard.
Olives de Veau.
Aloyau.
Pommes de Terre.　Choux Marins.
Hors d'œuvres.
Soufflé de Vanille.
Gelée aux Oranges.

II

English

Asparagus Soup.
Turbot, Dutch Sauce.
Vol-au-vent of Chicken.
Veal Cutlets.
Saddle of Mutton.
Potatoes.　　　Brocoli.
Rhubarb Tart.
Macaroni and Pine-apple
Nougats with Cream.
Cheese Straws.

French.

Purée d'Asperges.
Turbot, Sauce Hollondaise.
Vol-au-Vent de Volaille.
Côtelettes de Veau.
Selle de Mouton.
Pommes de Terre.　Choufleur.
Tourte.
Macaroni aux Ananas.
Nougats.
Pailles de Parmesan.

MENUS FOR TWELVE PERSONS (SUMMER).

I.

English.

Stuffed Olives.
Crayfish Soup.
Salmon.
Whitebait.
Fricasseed Chickens.
Fried Sweetbreads.
Haunch of Venison.
Potatoes.　　French Beans.
Ducklings.
Macédoine of Fruits.
Vanilla Cream.
Ices.

French.

Olives farcus.
Potage d'Ecrevisses.
Saumon.
Blanchailles.
Fricassée de Volaille.
Ris de Veau.
Hanche de Venaison.
Pommes de Terre. Haricots Verts
Canetons.
Macédoine de Fruits.
Crème de Vanille.
Glacées.

II.

English.

Clear Soup.
Turbot, Tartare Sauce.
Lobster Cream.
Chicken Cutlets.
Quarter of Lamb.
Potatoes.   Green Peas.
Compôte of Cherries.
Strawberry Cream.
Ice Pudding.

French.

Consommé à la Royale.
Turbot, Sauce Tartare
Crème de Homard.
Côtelettes de Volaille.
Quartier d'Agneau.
Pommes de Terre.   Petits Pois.
Compôte de Cérises.
Crème aux Fraises.
Pouding Glacé.

MENUS FOR TWELVE PERSONS (AUTUMN).

I.

English.

Oysters.
Ox-tail Soup.
Fried Soles.   Red Mullet.
Mutton Cutlets and Spinach.
Hashed Game.
Saddle of Mutton.
Potatoes.   Stewed Celery.
Pheasants.
Cabinet Pudding.   Chocolate Cream.
Cheese Biscuits.

French.

Huîtres.
Potage de Queue de Bœuf.
Soles Frits.   Rougets.
Côtelettes de Mouton aux Epinards
Salmis de Gibier.
Selle de Mouton.
Pommes de Terre.   Céleri.
Faisans.
Pouding.   Crême à la Chocolat
Biscuits de Fromage.

II.

English.

Hare Soup.
Turbot, Dutch Sauce.
Smelt.
Scalloped Oysters.
Curried Rabbit.
Ribs of Beef.
Potatoes.   Brocoli.
Grouse.
Russian Salad.
Apple Tart.   Wine Jelly.

French.

Potage de Levraut.
Turbot, Sauce Hollondaise.
Eperlans.
Huîtres à la Poulette.
Lapin au Kari.
Côtes de Bœuf.
Pommes de Terre.   Choufleur.
Coqs de Bruyère.
Salad à la Russe.
Tourte aux Pommes.   Gelée au Vin.

MENUS FOR TWELVE PERSONS (WINTER)

I.

English.

Caviare.
Game Soup.
John Dory.
Curried Prawns.
Salmi of Wild Duck.
Roast Turkey.   Fillet of Beef.
Potatoes.   Brussels Sprouts.
Snipe.
Golden Jelly.
Iced Nesselrode Pudding.

French.

Caviare.
Consommé de Gibier.
Doret.
Crevettes à l'Indienne.
Salmis de Canards Sauvages.
Dindon Rôti.   Filet de Bœuf.
Pommes de Terre. Choux de Bruxelles
Bécassines.
Gelée Dorée.
Pouding à la Nesselrode Glacée.

French.

Appétisans.
Consommé à la Royale.
Truite Farcie.
Mayonnaise.
Croquettes de Volaille.
Gigot d'Agneau.
Canetons.
Pommes de Terre.   Petits Pois.
Vol-au-vent de Fruit.
Pommes à la Neige.

II.

English.

Gravy Soup.
Brill, Shrimp Sauce.
Scalloped Oysters.
Stewed Pigeons.
Sirloin of Beef.
Potatoes.   Sea Kale.
Partridges.
Salad.
Plum Pudding.   Lemon Cream.

II.

English.

Julienne Soup.
Whiting.
Curried Chicken.
Veal Rissoles.
Rump Steak, Horseradish Sauce
Chipped Potatoes.
Ptarmigans.
Lemon Cheese Cakes.
Blancmange.
Cheese Salad.

French.

Bouillon.
Barbue, Sauce aux Crevettes.
Huîtres à la Poulette.
Pigeons en Compôte.
Aloyau.
Pommes de Terre.   Choux Marins.
Perdreaux.
Salade.
Pouding.   Crème au Citron.

French.

Julienne.
Merlans.
Volaille au Kari.
Rissolettes de Veau.
Rumpsteak, Sauce Raifort.
Pommes de Terre Frits.
Ptarmigans.
Tourtelettes au Citron.
Blancmange.
Salade au Fromage.

MENU FOR EIGHT PERSONS (SPRING).

I.

English.

Appétisans.
Clear Soup.
Stuffed Trout Fried.
Fish Salad.
Croquettes of Chicken.
Leg of Lamb.
Ducklings.
New Potatoes.   Peas.
Vol-au-vent of Fruit.
Apple Snow.

MENUS FOR EIGHT PERSONS (SUMMER).

I.

English.

Soup à la Reine.
Salmon Cutlets, Tartare Sauce.
Minced Veal with Béchamel Sauce.
Leg of Mutton.
Ducks.
Potatoes.   Peas.
Foie Gras in Jelly.
Almond Pudding.
Iced Gooseberry Fool.

French.

Potage à la Reine.
Côtelettes de Saumon, Sauce Tartare.
Emincé de Veau au Béchamel.
Gigot de Mouton.
Canetons.
Pommes de Terre.   Petits Pois.
Foie Gras en Aspic.
Pouding d'Amandes.
Crême de Groseilles Glacée.

French.

Consommé de Gibier.
Filets de Turbot, Sauce Italienne.
Vol-au-vent aux Huîtres.
Champignons.
Olives Farcies.
Selle de Mouton.
Pommes de Terre. Choux de Bruxelles.
Perdreaux.
Charlotte Russe.
Crême de Valois.

II.

English.

Crayfish Soup.
Fillets of Turbot with Dutch Sauce.
Lamb Cutlets.
Hashed Chicken.
Roast Veal.
Ham.
Potatoes.   French Beans.
Raspberry and Currant Tart.
Lemon Jelly.

II.

English.

Oyster Soup.
Fried Filleted Soles.
Red Mullet.
Hashed Game.
Mutton Croquettes.
Stewed Beef, with Piquante Sauce.
Snipe.
Rice Soufflé.
Noyeau Cream.
Cheese Straws.

French.

Purée d'Ecrevisses.
Filets de Turbot, Sauce Hollondaise.
Côtelettes d'Agneau.
Salmis de Volaille.
Rouelle de Veau.
Jambon.
Pommes de Terre.   Haricot Verts.
Tourte aux Framboises.
Gelée au Citron.

French.

Potage aux Huîtres.
Filets de Soles Frits.
Rougets.
Salmis de Gibier.
Croquettes de Mouton.
Culotte de Bœuf à la Sauce Piquante.
Bécassines.
Soufflé au Riz.
Crême au Noyeau.
Pailles de Parmesan.

MENUS FOR EIGHT PERSONS (AUTUMN).

I.

English.

Game Soup.
Fillets of Turbot, Italian Sauce.
Vol-au-vent of Oysters.
Mushrooms.
Stuffed Olives.
Saddle of Mutton.
Potatoes.   Brussels Sprouts.
Partridges.
Charlotte Russe.
Valois Cream.

MENUS FOR EIGHT PERSONS (WINTER).

English.

I.

Mulligatawney Soup.
Cod's Head and Shoulders, Oyster Sauce.
Sweetbreads.
Rissolettes of Beef.
Roast Turkey.
Sausages.
Black Game.
Lemon Pudding.
Sweet Omelette.
Cheese Soufflé.

French.

Soup de l'Inde.
Cabillaud, Sauce aux Huîtres.
Ris de Veau.
Rissolettes de Bœuf.
Dindon Roti.
Saucisses.
Coqs de Bruyère.
Pouding au Citron.
Omelette aux Confitures.
Soufflé de Parmesan.

II.

English.

Mock Turtle Soup.
Turbot, Lobster Sauce.
Vol-au-vent of Oysters.
Saddle of Mutton.
Potatoes. Brussels Sprouts.
Pheasants.
Mince Pies.
Compôte of Fruit.
Angels on Horseback.

French.

Potage de Tête de Veau.
Turbot, Sauce Homard.
Vol-au-vent aux Huîtres.
Selle de Mouton.
Pommes de Terre. Choux de Bruxelles.
Faisans.
Mince Pies.
Cômpote de Fruits.
Anges en Chevaux.

FAMILY DINNERS (SPRING).

I.

Sunday.—Roast leg of lamb, mint sauce, potatoes, spinach—Gooseberry tart, custard.

Monday.—Spring soup.—Cold lamb, salad, mashed potatoes.—Baked ground rice pudding.

Tuesday. — Fried soles. — Stewed breast of veal, potatoes.—Currant dumplings.

Wednesday.—Roast chickens, ham, steak pie, potatoes, greens.—Sweet omelette.

Thursday.—Hashed chicken.—Roast leg of mutton, greens, potatoes.—Stewed prunes and rice.

Friday. — Fried whiting, melted butter.—Cold mutton, salad, mashed potatoes.—Gooseberry pudding.

Saturday.—Soup.—Haricot of cold mutton, potatoes.—Macaroni cheese.

II.

Sunday. — Julienne. — Roast veal, ham, potatoes, greens.—Amber pudding.

Monday.—Beefsteak and kidney pie, cold veal and ham, potatoes, salad.—Gooseberry tart, custard.

Tuesday.—Salmon, cucumber, Tartare sauce.—Minced veal, potatoes.—Jam tart.

Wednesday.—Vegetable soup.—Leg of lamb, mince sauce, potatoes, greens. Macaroni cheese.

Thursday. — Mayonaise of cold salmon.—Fillet of beef with vegetables. —Currant tart.

Friday.—Soup.—Cold lamb, salad, potatoes.—Exeter pudding.

Saturday. — Ribs of beef boned, rolled, and roasted, vegetables, Yorkshire pudding.—Cheese ramakins.

FAMILY DINNERS (SUMMER).

I.

Sunday.—Roast quarter of lamb, peas, potatoes.—Cold fruit tart, cream.

Monday.—Soup.—Cold lamb, tomato salad, potatoes.—Plain Charlotte Russe.

Tuesday.—Boiled mackerel, cucumber.—Stewed steak with vegetables.—Gooseberry fool, and cornflour shape.

Wednesday.—Spring soup.—Hashed lamb, veal cutlets, peas, potatoes.—Cheese salad.

Thursday. — Roast beef, summer cabbage, potatoes, Yorkshire pudding. —Cold fruit tart.

Friday.—Salmon, caper sauce.—Cold beef, salad, mashed potatoes.—Baked rice pudding.

Saturday.—Fish salad made with cold salmon.—Hashed beef, peas, potatoes.—Stewed fruit.

II.

Sunday.—Roast fillet of veal, bacon, beans, potatoes. — Raspberry and currant tart, custard.

Monday.—Lentil soup—Cold veal and bacon, salad, potatoes — Gingerbread pudding.

Tuesday.—Rissoles from cold meat. —Roast ducks, peas, potatoes.—Cherry pudding.

Wednesday.—Salmon trout.—Hashed duck, steak and tomatoes, potatoes.—Bread and marmalade pudding.

Thursday. — Roast leg of mutton, beans, potatoes.—Lemon dumplings.

Friday. — Boiled mackerel. — Cold mutton, salad, potatoes.—Fruit tart, cream.

Saturday.—Green pea soup.—Mutton collops, potatoes.—Jam pudding.

FAMILY DINNERS (AUTUMN).

I.

Sunday.—Roast goose, apple sauce, potatoes, cabbage.—Apple tart, baked custard pudding.

Monday. — Giblet soup. — Haricot mutton, potatoes.—Damson pudding.

Tuesday.—Brill and lobster sauce.—Hashed goose, potatoes.—Omelette.

Wednesday.—Fish pie.—Boiled beef, carrots, turnips, potatoes, small suet dumplings.—Cheese and tomatoes.

Thursday.—Pea soup.—Cold beef, salad, mashed potatoes.—Baked arrow-root pudding.

Friday.—Haddocks and egg sauce.—Rabbit pie, potatoes.—Celery salad.

Saturday.—Boiled mutton, caper sauce, turnips, potatoes.—Fruit.

II.

Sunday.—Roast sirloin of beef, horse-radish sauce, vegetable marrow, potatoes.—Plum tart, custard.

Monday. — Soup. — Cold beef, beet-root, mashed potatoes.—Pancakes.

Tuesday.—Fried soles.—Stewed beef and tomatoes, potatoes.—Savoury rice.

Wednesday.—Boiled rabbits and pork, onion sauce, potatoes.—Apple pudding.

Thursday.—Fillet of beef with vegetables.—Golden pudding.

Friday.—Baked fresh herrings.—Hashed beef, potatoes.—Cheese omelette.

Saturday.—Vegetable soup. — Loin of mutton boned and stuffed, greens, potatoes.—Sago pudding.

FAMILY DINNERS (WINTER).

I.

Sunday.—Roast turkey, sausages, Brussels sprouts, potatoes.—Golden pudding, mince pies.

Monday.—Oyster soup.—Beef olives.—Cold turkey, mashed potatoes.—Baked rice pudding.

Tuesday.—Fried soles, caper sauce.—Boiled beef, carrots, turnips, potatoes, small suet dumplings.—Celery salad.

Wednesday.—Soup made from liquor from beef and bones of turkey.—Croquettes of turkey, cold beef, salad, fried potatoes.—Plain plum pudding.

Thursday.—Roast mutton, greens, potatoes.—Baked batter pudding with apples.

Friday.—Cod, boiled, shrimp sauce, —Cold beef, baked potatoes, beetroot.—Jam sandwiches.

Saturday. –Mullagatawney soup.—Ragout of beef, with vegetables, potatoes.—Sago pudding and stewed prunes.

II.

Sunday. — Roast sirloin of beef, Brussels sprouts, potatoes, Yorkshire pudding.—Apple tart, custard.

Monday. — Pea soup. — Cold beef, salad, potatoes.—Baked ground rice pudding.

Tuesday.—Baked fresh herrings.—Stew of remains of cold beef, potatoes.—Treacle pudding.

Wednesday.—Boiled leg of pork, pease pudding, apple sauce, savoy or sprouts, potatoes.—Macaroni cheese.

Thursday.—Vegetable soup, made from liquor in which pork was boiled. Cold meat, pickles, mashed potatoes.—Boiled bread pudding.

Friday.—Curried pork from cold pork, fried steak, rice.—Baked apple dumplings.

Saturday.—Irish stew, made from neck of mutton.—Mince pies.—Cheese biscuits.

VEGETARIAN DINNERS.

(SUMMER.)

I.

Green Pea Soup.
Savoury Macaroni.
Vegetable Pie.
Compôte of Fruit.
Ratafia Pudding.

II.

Macaroni Soup.
Haricot Beans and Onion Sauce.
Green Peas.
Raspberry and Currant Tart.
Custard.
Celery Salad.

(WINTER.)

I.

Lentil Soup.
Forcemeat Fritters.
Potato Pie. Fried Cabbage.
Apple Tart.
Tapioca and Milk.

II.

Maize Meal Porridge.
Lentil Rissoles.
Carrot Pudding.
Macaroni and Tomatoes.
Plum Pudding.
Cheese Sandwiches.

TEA

Except in the nursery or in large homely families, the old-fashioned "tea" has ceased to exist. We are not now bidden to partake of tea-cakes, hot buttered toast, new laid eggs, and such delicacies at 5 o'clock in the afternoon; we can only then expect the ordinary "at home" tea in tiny cups with its accompanying thin bread and butter; and this in many houses which cannot lay claim to be fashionable ones.

It is so easy now to have a "reception" one day in the week at the trifling cost of a little tea and bread and butter that those who are not rich enough or hospitable enough to give good dinners or suppers to their friends, gladly take to this mild form of entertainment. Far be it from us to abuse this afternoon tea, which seems to the feminine mind almost a *necessity* where the dinner is late; but if doctors are to be believed, it is a habit we have got into that is decidedly injurious, when it sometimes happens that, calling at several places, we may consume three or four cups in one afternoon.

At the large "at homes" to which guests have formal invitations, the teas are now quite a feature, and a great variety of dainty eatables and drinkables are provided. Foie gras, cucumber, caviare, and fish sandwiches, and such things, pleasantly vary the monotony of cake and bread and butter; and for those who do not care to take either tea or coffee, there are "cups" of all kinds; while in summer, fruit and ices are almost invariably given.

"High teas" as substitutes for late dinners, are not now so frequent as they used to be, but so long as our young people care to play tennis all the evening in summer, they cannot quite go out of fashion.

A moveable feast, such as this meal may be, is a great boon to those who like to spend as much time as possible out of doors during the fine weather; and it can be a very pleasant meal even in winter as well as summer.

According to the season so are the viands for "High tea." In summer, cold fish and meats, mayonnaises, salads, fresh fruits, cream, &c., are generally the rule; and in winter, besides such cold dishes as game pie, joints, and sweets, such things as rissoles, salmis, and outlets are usually given.

Both for "At Home" and "High Tea," we give menus that we trust may be useful.

One word about "Family Teas" we must say: and we candidly confess that they are not meals to be despised. It seems to us that the tea made by the mistress of the house, and served by her in cups of reasonable size, is a far nicer beverage than that which comes from kitchen to drawing-room with greater ceremony; while the bread and butter and cake are much better eaten off a plate and at a table, than from the saucer of a tiny cup. However old-fashioned these ideas may be, family tea must be an institution in many houses, so we give some weekly menus that may offer suggestions to those who provide them, these being considered by us to be people with small or moderate establishments and means; as in all others it is almost the invariable custom to have the afternoon tea and late dinner.

MENUS FOR "AT HOME" TEA.

(SUMMER.)

Cucumber Sandwiches.
Foie Gras and Cress Sandwiches.
Anchovy and Salad Sandwiches.
Bread and Butter, White and Brown.
Rout Cakes.
Madeira Cake.
Pound Cake.
Petits Fours.
Ices, Raspberry and Cherry.
Strawberries and Cream.
Tea.   Coffee.
Claret and Champagne Cup.

(WINTER.)

Caviare Sandwiches.
Tongue Sandwiches.
Sardine Sandwiches.
Bread and Butter, White and Brown
Plum Cake.
Seed Cake.
Fancy Cakes.
Almond Cakes.
Crystallised Fruits.
Sweet Biscuits.
Tea.   Coffee.
Claret.   Sherry

MENU FOR "HIGH" TEA.

(SUMMER.)

Mayonnaise of Salmon.
Cold Dishes: Tongue.
Veal and Ham Pie.
Cucumber.   Salad.
Compôte of Fruit.
Jelly.   Cream.
Fresh Fruit.
Tea.   Coffee.   Wine.

(WINTER.)

Scalloped Oysters.
Mutton Cutlets.
Cold Pheasants.
Winter Salad.
Macaroni and Pine-apple.
Cheesecakes.
Pound Cake.
Tea.   Coffee.   Wine.

FAMILY TEAS.

Sunday. — Tea, milk, sugar, bread, cut bread and butter, strawberry jam, cake, sardines.

Monday.—Tea, &c., cut bread and butter, dry toast, hot cakes, fruit of any kind, shrimps.

Tuesday.—Tea, &c., bread, hot toast, marmalade, potted meat, watercress.

Wednesday.—Tea, &c., brown bread, teacakes, stewed fruit, boiled eggs.

Thursday.—Tea, &c., bread and butter, seed cake, any fruit in season, anchovy toast.

Friday.—Tea, &c., bread, dry toast, preserve, radishes, ham and egg toast.

Saturday.—Tea, &c., brown bread, buttered toast, honey, cake, potted fish.

MORE SIMPLE TEAS.

Sunday. — Tea, bread and butter, toast, plain cake.

Monday.—Tea, brown bread, butter, scones, shrimps.

Tuesday. — Coffee, bread, butter, toast, seed cake.

Wednesday.—Tea, bread and butter, honey, watercress.

Thursday.—Tea, bread, toast, butter, potted anchovies.

Friday.—Coffee, brown bread, butter, dry toast, jam, radishes.

Saturday. — Tea, bread, hot cakes, butter, egg toast.

SUPPER

In spite of the many objections raised against this meal, it cannot be denied that it is a very enjoyable one, coming as it does when one's work (if work we do) is over for the day; nor can we see why it should be a more injurious repast than a very late dinner.

The mistake most often made with regard to this meal is that of having it too late for the digestive organs to do their work before we go to bed. Given a supper at nine o'clock or even half-past eight, where it is the rule to retire early, there is time in summer to spend a little time out of doors, or in winter for a game of some kind, or a quiet read before we take our candles for the night.

In many families, particularly where there are young children, supper-time is the one quiet hour of the day and a meal to be enjoyed more than any that has preceded it; with the consciousness that the daily tasks are over and there is rest to follow.

The chief consideration with reference to this meal should be of what it should consist, and there are few constitutions, or rather digestions, that can stand what is generally denominated a "heavy supper." Food partaken of late in the day should not be of too solid a character, it should not be rich, and raw fruit should be avoided; but individual tastes and experience can alone determine what food agrees best and what that food should be.

With regard to supper as a general meal, it must be acknowledged it is rather a despised one. When we cannot entertain our friends in a suitable way at a dinner party, we give an "at home" and seldom think of offering them the homely kind of invitation of "come and sup with us." Yet many would accept this gladly; and at an informal meal it is so much easier for those with few servants to make their guests comfortable. Dinner in fashionable circles is at eight; why should not some of us who do not belong to them enjoy an equivalent meal at the same hour with impunity? What we have written may be almost called a plea for suppers, and we confess we think it is a pity that they are becoming things of the past.

At balls, there is seldom what used to be called a "sitting down" supper; so in our menus we give only those for serving at a buffet or table, besides those for guests and the weekly ones for the family.

With regard to children's suppers, we are probably in the minority when we suggest that the little ones should not always go supperless.

Their hour for tea is generally an early one, and after that may, and in all probability will, come active games and amusements, tending to produce appetite; and it is better then to give some very light food, such as a slice of bread and butter and a little milk, than to let them go hungry to bed.

MENUS FOR BUFFET SUPPERS.

(Summer.)

Cold Chickens (cut up)
Ham. Tongue.
Galantine of Veal.
Mayonnaise of Salmon.
Chicken Salad.
Sandwiches of Foie Gras, Anchovy, and Cucumber.
Lobster Patties.
Meringues.
Trifle.
Jellies. Creams.
Fancy Pastry.
Grapes. Pine.
Claret and Champagne Cup.
Claret. Hock. Sherry.

(WINTER.)
Game Pie.
Cold Pheasants.
Boned Turkey.
Tongue.
Lobster Salad.
Sandwiches of Caviare and Ham.
Oyster Patties.
Salad.
Maids of Honour.
Tipsy Cake.
Trifle.
Rout Cakes.
Jelly. Blancmange.
Grapes and Pears.
Cups and Wines.

MENUS FOR GUESTS' SUPPERS.

(SUMMER.)
Lobsters.
Mayonnaise of Chicken.
Cold Lamb.
Salad, Cucumber.
Mint Sauce.
Raspberry Cream.
Fruit Tart.
Custard.
Fruit. Cake.
Claret. Sherry.

(WINTER.)
Fish Rissoles.
Hashed Pheasant.
Cold Turkey.
Ham.
Salad.
Stewed Fruit.
Mince Pies.
Jelly.
Cheese Biscuits.
Claret. Sherry.

FAMILY SUPPERS FOR TWO WEEKS.

Sunday.—Cold beef, salad or beetroot, cold fruit tart, rice pudding, cheese, butter, bread, biscuits.

Monday. — Rissoles of cold meat, brawn, pickles, stewed prunes, cheese, &c.

Tuesday. — Baked fresh haddock, cold bacon or ham, cake, cheese, &c.

Wednesday. — Fish pie made from cold fish, any cold meat, salad, cake, cheese, &c.

Thursday.—Poached eggs and spinach, cold ham, bread and butter pudding, cheese, &c.

Friday.—Scalloped oysters, brawn, preserve, cheese, &c.

Saturday.—Steak or veal pie, baked potatoes, cakes, cheese, &c.

Sunday. — Cold meat, cucumber, pickles, stewed fruit, cheese, butter, bread, biscuits.

Monday.—Fried sausages and mashed potatoes, cake, cheese, butter, bread, biscuits.

Tuesday.—Cold meat of any kind, salad or tomatoes, apple cake, cheese, butter, bread, biscuits.

Wednesday. — Pie made from cold beef with dripping crust, baked potatoes, cheese, bread, butter, biscuits.

Thursday.—Kedgeree made from any cold fish, cold bread and butter pudding, cheese, butter, bread, biscuits.

Friday.—Cold ham, beetroot, cake, cheese, butter, bread, biscuits.

Saturday. — Scrambled eggs, cold meat, pickles, jam puffs, cheese, butter, bread, biscuits

WEIGHTS AND MEASURES

WEIGHTS AND MEASURES.

Avoirdupois Weight.

27½	Grains	.. =	1 Dram
16	Drams	.. =	1 Ounce
16	Ounces	.. =	1 Pound (lb.)
14	Pounds	.. =	1 Stone
28	Pounds	.. =	1 Quarter (qr.)
4	Quarters	.. =	1 Hundredweight
20	Hundredwt.	=	1 Ton

Troy.

24	Grains	= 1 Pennywt. =	24 grs.
20	Pennywts.	= 1 Ounce =	480 ,,
12	Ounces	= 1 Pound =	5760 ,,

Apothecaries'.

			Troy.
20	Grains	= 1 Scruple =	20 grs.
3	Scruples	= 1 Drachm =	60 ,,
8	Drachms	= 1 Ounce =	480 ,,
12	Ounces	= 1 Pound =	5760 ,,

Apothecaries compound their medicines by this weight, but buy and sell their drugs by avoirdupois.

Apothecaries' Fluid Measure.

60	Minims	.. =	1 Fluid Drachm
8	Drachms	.. =	1 Ounce
20	Ounces	.. =	1 Pint
8	Pints	.. =	1 Gallon

Liquid Measure.

4	Gills	.. =	1 Pint (pt.)
2	Pints	.. =	1 Quart (qt.)
4	Quarts	.. =	1 Gallon (gall.)

Dry Measure.

2	Gallons	.. =	1 Peck (pk.)
4	Pecks	.. =	1 Bushel (bush.)
3	Bushels	.. =	1 Sack
12	Sacks	.. =	1 Chaldron
8	Bushels	.. =	1 Quarter (qr.)
5	Quarters	.. =	1 Load (ld.)

Cloth.

2¼	Inches	.. =	1 Nail
4	Nails	.. =	1 Quarter
4	Quarters	.. =	1 Yard
3	Quarters	.. =	1 Flemish Ell
5	Quarters	.. =	1 English Ell
6	Quarters	.. =	1 French Ell

It will also be convenient to remember that :—

Sixty drops of any thin liquid are equal to one teaspoonful.

Two teaspoonfuls to one dessertspoonful.

Four teaspoonfuls to one tablespoonful.

Three tablespoonfuls to one wineglassful.

Four wineglassfuls to one tumblerful.

1 lb. Wheat Flour is equal to about one quart.

1 lb. 2 oz. Indian Meal to one quart.

1 lb. Butter, when soft, to one quart.

1 lb. Loaf Sugar (broken) to one quart.

1 lb. 1 oz. of White Sugar (pounded), or best moist, to one quart.

1 lb. 2 oz. Brown Sugar to the quart.

8 or 9 Hen's Eggs (ordinary size) before they are broken weigh about one pound.

TO HIS MAJESTY THE

KING

By Royal Warrants.

PEARS

TO HER MAJESTY THE

QUEEN

FOR INFANTS AND INVALIDS.

SWINBORNE'S
ISINGLASS

Is the Best.

FOR JELLIES, &c.

SWINBORNE'S
GELATINE

Is the Best.

INDEX

WARD, LOCK AND CO., LIMITED. LONDON, NEW YORK, AND MELBOURNE.